PENGUIN AFRICAN LIBRARY
Editor: Ronald Segal

Class and Colour in
South Africa 1850–1950

H. J. AND R. E. SIMONS

H. J. AND R. E. SIMONS

Class and Colour in South Africa 1850–1950

Penguin Books

Penguin Books Ltd, Harmondsworth,
Middlesex, England
Penguin Books Inc., 7110 Ambassador Road,
Baltimore, Maryland 21207, U.S.A.
Penguin Books Australia Ltd, Ringwood,
Victoria, Australia

First published 1969
Copyright © H. J. and R. E. Simons, 1969

Made and printed in Great Britain by
Hazell Watson & Viney Ltd, Aylesbury, Bucks
Set in Monotype Plantin

Contents

Contents

Foreword

Some twenty years ago, South Africa was held in high esteem as a senior member of the British Commonwealth, a bastion of western capitalism, and the most advanced economic region in Africa. Her people, black and white, could claim with some justification that their material conditions were the best in Africa. The south had the highest national income per head of population, the largest volume of trade, and the widest scope of opportunity for acquiring education or obtaining employment. Men from east and central Africa went south in search of higher wages or higher learning.

Three centuries of white settlement – phased by colonial wars, expropriations of tribal lands, slavery, forced labour and industrialism – had produced a variety of human types, an integrated multi-racial society and a way of life shared by some members of all racial groups. Colour prejudice was endemic and deeply ingrained among whites; but their policy of racial discrimination, though vicious and degrading, differed in degree rather than in kind from the discrimination practised elsewhere under colonial rule.

If racism was most bitter and intense in the south, it experienced a measure of compensation in a countervailing radicalism that stretched across the colour line in pursuit of an open-ended, non-racial social order. Nowhere else in Africa did so many whites, Asians and Coloured participate with Africans in a common struggle against class or colour oppression. A peaceful transition to parliamentary democracy without colour bars seemed plausible to some observers, as the tide of decolonization began to swell at the end of the war.

Twenty years of unbroken rule by Afrikaner nationalism have all but destroyed the hope of a peaceful revolution. South Africa remains by far the largest producer of goods and capital in Africa. Her public services – the infrastructure of political and economic organization – are still the most advanced. Her standards of public morality, law enforcement and race relations have deteriorated to such a level, however, that she is now a byword among nations for bigotry, intolerance and despotic rule. She has been turned into a police state under the control of a white oligarchy which uses fascist techniques to enforce racial totalitarianism and to suppress movements for social equality.

A wide gulf has consequently opened between the south and the rest of Africa. Millions of men and women in countries north of the Zambezi are being exhorted and trained for the tremendous task of modernizing their societies. Southern Africans, in contrast, are being forcibly regrouped – by a white bureaucracy – into tribal communities under hereditary chiefs. Thousands of Africans in the independent states occupy the highest positions in government, education, industry, commerce and finance – positions of a kind that are reserved for whites only in the south.

The balance of advantage is being tilted in favour of regions that are still considered backward by southern standards. The best that black and brown South Africans with professional qualifications can do for themselves is to escape to these countries, where their skin colour is a social asset and where they can apply their skills with dignity and in freedom. For, as long as they remain under white man's rule, they must expect to be outstripped in every field of social activity by their self-governing racial compatriots in the north.

Southern Africans have taken up arms against white supremacists to redress the balance. The freedom fighters are the vanguard of a people preparing to rise for the recovery of lost liberties and for the right to move freely on terms of equality with all men at home and abroad. Their struggle is an old one. It began 300 years ago, when the brown men of the Cape – the Nama who were called Hottentot and the Khoi who were called Bushmen – fought the white invaders with bows, arrows and spears. Bantu-speaking warriors – the Xhosa, Zulu, Sotho,

Tswana and Venda – continued the struggle, until each nation in turn was defeated and absorbed in the white man's order.

Wars of independence were succeeded by a struggle from within the industrialized society for parliamentary democracy, national liberation, or socialism. This book traces the interactions between the two main streams of resistance to white domination: the national movements of Africans, Indians and Coloured; and the class struggles of socialists and communists. Although it surveys the record of radical movements for the best part of a century, it is not a history. We prefer to think of it as an exercise in political sociology on a time scale; and we have not hesitated, therefore, to intersperse our narrative with comments and value judgements.

We find no merit in apartheid and are wholly committed, as participants and observers, to the Resistance. We have not refrained from criticizing our heroes; and freely use the advantages of hindsight in evaluating their programmes and procedures. A word of explanation is due to readers who think that this approach is unscientific, or who resent anything that seems disparaging of the early radicals.

We have no desire to muck-rake or belittle the achievements of men who, rising above the circumstances of their time and class, escaped from the stranglehold of white supremacy and suffered the penalties of opposition to an oppressive regime. We think that they must gain in stature from a frank account of the difficulties they experienced on their political pilgrimage. Our essays in political criticism of communists like Ivon Jones, Bill Andrews and Douglas Wolton, of nationalists like Dr P. K. Seme and Dr Abdurahman, of radical labour leaders like Archie Crawford and Clements Kadalie, have a wider purpose than the purely biographical.

Our view is simply this, that new generations of resisters are entitled to an honest appraisal of the past from the vantage point of the present. Many of the controversies here examined – the proper relationship between national liberation and class struggle, the choice between socialist and capitalist democracy, the concept of African (or 'black') power, the strategies of a multi-racial united front or 'non-collaboration with the Herrenvolk' –

9

are still with us and continue to produce furious debate. Our purpose is to tell a story and at the same time give resisters of today a guide to the background of these controversies.

An attempt is made in the last chapter to abstract some conclusions and project them against an analysis of the power structure. Two propositions of theoretical interest emerge from the analysis. One is that an industrialized, capitalist society can perpetuate pre-industrial social rigidities only by adopting the coercive techniques of fascist totalitarianism. The other proposition is that where class divisions tend to coincide with antagonistic national or colour groups, the class struggle merges with the movement for national liberation.

We collected the bulk of the material in South Africa over a period of about ten years, in between our professional activities and political involvement. The actual writing was done in Manchester and London. We are indebted to the University of Manchester for the generous grant of a Senior Simon Research Fellowship, which enabled us to work in the tranquillity and comfort of Broomcroft Hall; to Professor Max Gluckman and colleagues in the University's department of social anthropology and sociology, for stimulating discussions; to Miss Nancy Dick, who patiently and reliably verified quotations and sources, unearthed material inaccessible to us, and compiled the index; to Michael Harmel and Kenneth Parker for reading and criticizing the draft; and to librarians of Cape Town, Johannesburg, Manchester, London and Moscow for their courteous attention and unfailing assistance. Finally, we acknowledge a debt and pay a tribute to our colleague Lionel Forman (1928–59), whose early death deprived his country of a fine intellect and a brave fighter for freedom.

Lusaka, Zambia   RAY AND JACK SIMONS
11 September 1968

1 The Liberal Cape

Britain took the Cape by force of arms in 1806, after 150 years of Dutch rule, when the colony had a population of some 30,000 slaves, 26,000 settlers, 20,000 free Coloured, Nama and Khoi* in white employ, and an unknown number living in remote regions. Apart from the officials, gentry and shopkeepers of Cape Town, most of the settlers were farmers, who either grew crops on the coastal plains or grazed livestock on the plateau behind the mountain ranges. Racial discrimination, based on a rigid division of labour, had hardened into a set pattern. The colonists did not disdain manual labour on their own account, though they objected to working for a master. Slaves did the skilled and unskilled work in Cape Town and adjacent areas. They tailored, cobbled, built houses, cooked, traded, and made furniture, leather goods, wagons and music for their owners. They also worked on the farms, frequently with the free Coloured and Nama, the so-called Hottentots.

Townsmen and farmers had much in common, in spite of substantial cultural differences. Both were stiffnecked Calvinists, who cited scripture to justify slavery and colour-class discrimination. Both claimed for the white race an exclusive right to education, positions of public responsibility, the ownership of land and wealth. Both fornicated with slaves, Coloured and Nama, while keeping them in strict subordination. Farmers in the interior acquired, as well, the habits and outlook of pioneers and frontiersmen. They were independent and self-reliant; demanded aid from government yet resented its authority; and thought highly of physical courage, endurance, hunting skills and martial prowess. The colony resembled a feudal society in

* Other suggested generic terms are Khoi-Khoi for the 'Hottentots' and San for the 'Bushmen'.

many ways. It was divided into estates rather than classes, and strongly resisted radical reforms.

The slaves came from Holland's possessions in the East Indies, from West Africa, Madagascar and Mozambique; and belonged to a wide range of cultural and racial groups. No slave, whether Muslim, Christian or pagan, could enter into a legal marriage before 1823. Extra-marital intercourse between settlers, slaves and Nama gave rise to the Coloured, known as *kleurlinge* or *bruinmense* (brown people) in Afrikaans. The slaves never fused into a single community or acted in concert to liberate themselves while under Dutch rule. The Nama, whose cattle and sheep had grazed on land occupied by the colonists, offered some resistance in the early days of settlement. Their numbers were then greatly reduced by epidemics of smallpox and measles, and they soon succumbed to the white invaders. The Khoi, nick-named the Bushmen, were hunters and food collectors. They fought back stubbornly and with great courage, to be all but annihilated.

The colonists were quick to resent the authoritarian rule and mercantilism of the Netherlands East India Company. They complained often and bitterly of excessive taxation, restraints on trade, inefficiency and corruption in the administration. There was little effective protest. Malcontents and potential rebels could escape into the interior, where land was to be had for the taking. The first serious demand for political reform was made as late as 1779, when the current of liberalism from Europe and America combined with symptoms of the company's bank-ruptcy to produce some agitation in the western Cape. The Cape Patriots, as they called themselves after a party of that name in Holland, petitioned the company directors in Amsterdam for a written constitution, seats for burghers on the administrative council and high court, freedom to trade, and the right to flog their slaves without official restraint. Not then, nor at any other time, did the settlers propose reforms that would benefit persons of colour, whether freemen or slaves.

The frontiersmen spread rapidly over a wide area in defiance of the government's injunction to remain within a fixed boun-dary. They rode rough-shod over the prior rights of the original inhabitants to hunting, grazing and arable land. Survivors of the Nama were absorbed in the Coloured. The Khoi were hunted down and killed off like the great herds of wild animals that once roamed the plains. Bantu-speaking Africans might have shared this fate if they had not been more numerous and better equipped to meet the predatory raids of the commandos, the name given to the farmers' militia. It is significant of white attitudes that when the colonists first revolted against the government, they rose not in defence of their own liberties but to deprive Africans of land and stock.

The revolt took place in 1795 on the eastern frontier, in the district of Graaff Reinet. Honoratus Maynier, the local *landdrost* or magistrate, had prudently tried to curb the brutal treatment of Nama and Khoi by the settlers, and restrain them from prematurely launching a large-scale attack on the Xhosa in their homeland between the Sundays and Fish rivers. The first major clash between the two groups of cattle-raising agriculturists had occurred in 1779, and the Xhosa had succeeded in stopping the vanguard of the *trekboers*. The settlers gave vent to their frustration by driving Maynier away and declaring a republic. Their fellow burghers to the south, in the adjacent district of Swellendam, demanding freedom to enslave the Khoi and impose unpaid forced labour on the Nama, followed this example and elected a 'national assembly'. South Africa's first republic was born in a struggle between white settlers and an external imperial authority for the right to suppress, plunder and exploit an African people.

Holland was at this time an ally of Britain in the war against republican France. The East India Company had announced its bankruptcy. The government at Cape Town could neither bring the rebels to heel nor help them to defeat the Xhosa. Left to themselves, the colonists might have been forced to negotiate on terms favourable to the Xhosa.

The British, acting in the name of Prince William of Orange, occupied the Cape soon after the revolt in Swellendam. While most of the settlers gave their allegiance to the new regime, the malcontents of Graaff Reinet revolted twice more, first in 1799 and then in 1801, against the administration's alleged partiality to Coloured and Xhosa. British troops and Coloured riflemen were sent to quell the revolt in 1799. Farm workers, anxious to fight their white masters, joined the Coloured regiments; the rising fizzled out, and the farm workers were ordered to surrender their arms. They chose instead to join Ndhlambi's Xhosa in an attempt to drive the settlers out of the Zuurveld west of the Sundays river.

This led to a mass revolt of Coloured on the frontier and a devastating war against the Xhosa. A firm and enduring alliance between Africans and Coloured might have enabled both to free themselves from white domination. For, notes Marais, 'if the rising spread to the western Hottentots and slaves, the white man's hold on the Colony would be shaken to its foundations'.[1] The British intervened to detach the Coloured from their allies. Dundas, the acting governor, established a garrison at the site of the future Port Elizabeth, promised land to the Coloured, and assured them of better treatment on the farms. He instructed Maynier, now the resident commissioner, to register labour contracts of three months and over between farmers and servants. Though farmers objected to the labour regulation, it was amplified and extended to all parts of the colony by the Batavian administration which succeeded the British in 1803.

The extension of the Dundas regulation laid a basis for labour legislation and gave the free Coloured a modicum of legal protection. 'Under this growing rule of law,' according to Walker, 'most of the Hottentots took service, and not only ceased to be a peril to the Colony, but in due course became a reinforcement to it against the Kaffirs.'[*2] The comment neatly summarizes the divisive effects of a strategy that turned the Coloured away from their African allies and into an auxiliary of the whites. The Cape Mounted Riflemen, a predominantly Coloured regiment, played a greater part than the settlers did in subsequent wars against the Xhosa. When Ngqika, Gcaleka and Thembu struck back at Harry Smith's troops in 1850, and the Coloured in the eastern

* 'Kaffir', 'Kafir' (Arabic for infidel, unbeliever) was a name widely applied to Africans of the south-eastern Cape and Natal. It is now a dirty word and appears in this book only in quotations. The spelling follows the original in each case.

Cape rose in rebellion, some of the riflemen joined in the struggle for liberation. The regiment was reconstituted after the war into a mixed force of white and Coloured; and disbanded in 1870, on the eve of responsible government, when the whites could dispense with the service of Coloured troops. 'From that time onward the military profession was closed to Coloured men in South Africa.'[3]

Apart from some useful administrative reforms, the Batavian Republic's short interregnum of three years produced few notable changes. Slavery and serfdom were bound to disappear under the impact of Europe's expanding industrialism and bourgeois democracy. Holland would have been the emancipator if she had retained the Cape, and the battle for human rights might then have been fought out between a Dutch government and Dutch settlers. An indigenous liberalism, rooted in South African soil and embracing a section of the Afrikaner people, might have grown to maturity. Instead, it was the British who represented the age of enlightenment, and the new liberalism came to be identified in the minds of all South Africans with the policies of British imperialism. Their seizure of the Cape in 1806 led ultimately to the emancipation of slaves, the subjugation of the Africans, and a cultural dualism among the whites that developed into rival nationalisms.

Whitehall kept a tight rein on expenditure and expected the colony to pay its way. The Cape governor could, however, draw on far greater supplies of manpower, capital and armed force than the East India Company ever provided. The access of strength turned the scales in the settlers'. favour. It was the British army and not the Boer commandos that defeated the African and forced him to accept white authority. British immigrants joined Afrikaner farmers on the eastern frontier. Governor Cradock sent a large force of troops and militia to the Zuurveld in 1812. They drove 20,000 Africans back over the Fish river and built a double line of block-houses, garrisoned with troops and civilians, behind which quit-rent farms of 4,000 acres each were offered to the settlers on what had been African soil. Trained troops won a victory that had eluded the frontiersmen in more than thirty years of guerrilla warfare and cattle raids.

Slaves and the free Coloured fared scarcely better under high Tory rule. Britain outlawed the slave trade in 1807 but allowed the settlers to retain and sell or buy their human property. Caledon's proclamation of 1 November 1809 applied a strict pass law to the Coloured, made the registration of labour contracts compulsory if covering one month or more, and laid down the conditions under which an employer could withhold wages for goods supplied to his servant. Proclamations of 1812 and 1819 allowed a settler to apprentice and employ without remuneration a free Coloured child, from the age of eight to eighteen years, if it was an orphan, or destitute, or had grown up on the employer's property. The regulations might have saved the Coloured from 'utter destruction', as some observers claimed, but only by reducing them to the level of serfs, at the mercy of farmers and officials who were also farmers.

Circuit courts, having both administrative and judicial functions, were introduced in 1811. They afforded some protection against gross cruelty and neglect. Missionaries like the Dutchman Johannes van der Kemp and the Scot John Philip had no difficulty in accumulating a mass of evidence to convince Whitehall that the Coloured were being degraded by economic and social servitude. The House of Commons instructed the Cape administration to abolish legal discrimination against free persons. Bourke, the acting governor, anticipated the instruction by enacting Ordinance 50 of 1828. It repealed the offending proclamations, and so freed the Coloured from the pass system and the risk of being flogged for offences against the labour laws. The registration of service contracts continued, but their duration was limited to one year. Children could be apprenticed only with their parents' consent. The ordinance applied only to Coloured workers, yet went a long way to establishing the principle of equality before the law.

The white working class, then in its infancy, had a higher social status but a similar legal position. Workers in Britain were then, and for many years to come, liable to be imprisoned for breach of contract under the master and servant law. The colonial administration acted rigorously against defaulters of any race. The demand for punitive measures came from employers who wished to stop the desertion of workers in whom they had invested money. Immigrant artisans and labourers who received a free passage to the Cape were usually obliged to serve a given master for a specified period, or buy their release by repaying the passage money. Land and work were plentiful in the colony. Many immigrants took the opportunity to set up on their own or to change their employment in breach of their indentures. To deter them, Lord Charles Somerset's proclamation of 26 June 1818 prescribed a maximum sentence of two months' imprisonment and fine of twenty-five *rixdalers* for a defaulting servant, to which corporal punishment could be added for a second and subsequent offence.

Laws devised for indentured white immigrants, free Coloured workers and emancipated slaves were the forerunners of South Africa's master and servant laws. Emancipation itself occurred on 1 December 1834. There were then about 40,000 slaves and as many whites in the colony. Slave prices had doubled since 1807, when the importation of fresh supplies was banned. The owners were no more willing than the planters of the West Indies and America to surrender their property or to accept any limitation on their right of ownership. They objected strenuously to regulations that curbed their brutality and enforced minimum standards of care in the treatment of slaves. Bourke's Ordinance 19 of 1826, which provided for the appointment of a registrar and guardian of slaves, led to the resignation of the president and two members of Cape Town's burgher council, while owners generally agitated for a representative assembly. They wanted political rights for themselves so as to enslave others. Emancipation was forced on the colony by Britain. The social pressures that produced the Reform Act of 1832 resulted also in the Abolition of Slavery Act of 1833.

The end of formal slavery accelerated the migration of farmers into the interior and precipitated the great trek of 1836. Somerset's 1820 settlers, planted in the Zuurveld to strengthen the white man's hold on the frontier, were forbidden to keep slaves. The great majority of owners were Afrikaners, and they resented the emancipation, Ordinance 50, and the principle of equality before the law. The £1¼ million allocated by the British parliament as compensation to slave owners was, they said, less than half the market value of the slaves. Settlers denounced the colonial office for refusing to ratify D'Urban's annexation in 1835 of Xhosa territory between the Great Fish and Kei rivers. They were outraged when the government decided to sell and not make free grants of land seized from the Xhosa. Land hunger, dislike of British rule, and the rejection of racial equality in any form were the root causes of the planned exodus by whites with their Coloured servants from the colony.

The firm stand made by the Xhosa barred the way to the Transkei's rolling pastures between the sea and the great escarpment. Turning westward, the tide of white migration crossed the Orange river to invade the grasslands of the high plateau. One party of trekkers by-passed Moshoeshoe's kingdom of Lesotho and entered Natal. Here a small community of English traders, hunters and missionaries had been settled since 1824. An armed struggle for supremacy took place in the years 1837 to 1842 between Afrikaners and Zulu and between British and Afrikaners. It ended with the proclamation of Natal as a British colony in May 1843, when Napier, the Cape governor, decreed strict equality before the law of all persons in Natal, irrespective of colour, origin, language or creed. The Afrikaners then withdrew to join their fellow trekkers on the highveld. They founded republics of their own, free from British rule, on territory taken from Africans by force, and under a constitution that denied equality between white and black in either church or state.

Few settlers in the Cape accepted the humanitarian's ideal of racial equality. Emancipation opened a new stage in the relations between white and Coloured; but it did not revolutionize the society or abolish discrimination. Ordinance 1 of 1835, which was supposed to prepare the slaves for freedom, changed little more than their name. Now called apprentice-labourers, they continued to work for their former owners, without wages and on the same terms of food, clothing, lodging and medical care. Penalties harsher in some respects than those prescribed by the slave laws could be imposed under the ordinance. It provided for police settlements, houses of correction and penal gangs. Apprentices could be sentenced to hard labour, for periods ranging from one week to six months, and a whipping of fifteen, thirty or thirty-nine stripes, for different classes of offences. These included desertion, indolence, carelessness, negligence, damage to a master's property, drunkenness, brawling, insolence, unlawful conspiracy to disobey, persistent disobedience, and combined resistance against a master.

This was harsher by far than Somerset's proclamation of 1818 or Bourke's Ordinance 50, and was consequently more to the liking of employers. They had no taste for the free labour market that developed after 1 December 1838, when the apprenticeship system came to an end. Many ex-slaves left their masters for the towns, or went to farm on their own in remote areas, or settled on government land. The migration, coupled with epidemics of smallpox and measles in 1839–40, caused a shortage of labour on farms. The mean cash wage of agricultural workers in the western Cape rose from ten to fifteen shillings a month in the forties, and the customary wine ration was also increased.[4] Farmers complained of drunkenness, desertion and vagrancy among their Coloured servants, and agitated for restraints on movement and a disciplinary code. The Colonial Office had previously disallowed a vagrancy law adopted in 1834 by the settler members of the legislative council. This yielded to the pressure by passing the Masters and Servants Ordinance of 1841, based partly on a British order-in-council promulgated in 1838 for the West Indies.

The ordinance repealed Ordinance 50 of 1828, re-enacted the disciplinary code prescribed for apprenticed ex-slaves, and reduced the scale of penalties to fourteen days' imprisonment for a first offence and/or a fine of not more than a month's wages. Employers were given a firmer hold over their servants by provisions that extended the statutory limitation on oral contracts from one month to one year and on written contracts from one to three years. A contract could be terminated on a month's notice given by either party, and the notice became void if the servant failed to leave his service on the specified date. A servant was entitled to two months' wages and other contractual benefits during sickness. It was made an offence to 'coerce' servants into joining a 'club or association', but the ordinance conceded a right to combine for collective bargaining.

Ordinance 1 of 1841 was the first labour law to include workers of all races. The word 'servant' as defined included any person 'employed for hire, wages, or other remuneration to perform any handicraft or other bodily labour in agriculture or manufactures, or in domestic services'. Artisans, craftsmen, machine operators and labourers were equally affected. It was a unique case of class legislation without any trace of racial discrimination. The legislative council made it generally applicable so as to meet anticipated objections in Whitehall. A law applying only to Coloured, explained Napier, would perpetuate their status 'as an inferior and distinct people'.[5] There was an additional reason. Criminal sanctions were then commonly attached to labour contracts in Europe. The colonial administration saw no reason to exempt white workers. Belonging to the master race, they were less prone than their darker-skinned fellows to prosecution for breach of contract or disciplinary offences. The absence of a colour bar in the Cape's labour legislation had, however, a marked liberalizing effect on industrial relations in the colony.

Cape liberalism stood for racial tolerance. It was not a general characteristic of the white population. British immigrants rapidly absorbed the racial prejudices of the older white inhabitants, or acquired their own, as in Natal, where English-speaking settlers were dominant after 1850. They disfranchised Africans in 1865 and developed under British rule a white supremacy state no more tolerant of African and Asian claims to equality than were the Afrikaner republics. Liberalism took root in the western Cape because of the region's peculiar history, relative tranquillity, racial composition and cultural cleavages. British radical and humanitarian movements reached their peak in the first half of the century during the colony's formative years. It was deeply influenced, through the Colonial Office, the British clergy and missionaries, by the agitation that produced the Reform Act and the Abolition of Slavery Act. The movement ebbed in the latter half of the century, by which time the Cape had laid the foundations of equality before the law. It was sustained both by pressure of a large, partially assimilated Coloured population and by antagonisms between English- and Afrikaans-speaking whites.

Both groups of colonists were represented in the agitation during the second quarter of the century for representative government. A legislative council of five officials and six nominated settlers was formed in 1834, only to whet the appetite for self-rule. The council fell into disrepute and nearly collapsed in 1849, when Lord Grey proposed to land convicts from the *Neptune* at the Cape. His decision caused great resentment, the more so since a draft constitution was then before the privy council. A country-wide Anti-Convict Association declared a boycott of government institutions and of private firms identified with Grey's action. Demonstrations and mass meetings disrupted business and caused a minor recession. Sir Harry Smith, the governor, refused to let the convicts land; and the *Neptune* eventually sailed with its cargo of prisoners to Australia. The propertied classes of Cape Town and the eastern Cape, alarmed at the upheaval, formed themselves into a party of moderates and rallied round the government. British liberals and Afrikaner settlers used the occasion to press the demand for a new constitution.[6]

The Colonial Office had countered early requests of this kind with two objections. No colony where people were enslaved was fit for self-rule, while the rise of Dutch and British parties would nullify one of the main benefits of representative government: the cultivation of common loyalties and national cohesion. Officials at the Cape and prominent liberals like John Philip and John Fairbairn, editor of the *South African Commercial Advertiser*, reiterated the objections after emancipation. The Coloured lacked property and political experience. A settlers' parliament would pass oppressive laws depriving them forever of political power before they had learned to exercise their rights. On the other hand, British colonists, though the most wealthy, active and intelligent class, were a minority, and would not willingly submit to a Dutch majority inferior in all respects other than its numerical strength. The anti-convict agitation revealed a widespread hostility to the British government, and when the Colonial Office decided that a representative parliament could not be avoided, its chief concern was to keep power out of the hands of the anti-British faction.

Africans claims could be ignored. Though many thousands of Xhosa peasants, farm workers, prisoners of war and convicts, employed on roads and public works, inhabited the colony, the war on the eastern frontier was then at its height, and the great mass of Africans still belonged to independent states. This circumstance greatly facilitated the adoption of the colour-blind franchise insisted upon by the Colonial Office. The British government was in two minds, however, about the qualifications. The higher they were made, the smaller would be the Afrikaner and Coloured vote. British merchants, backed by Harry Smith and his colonial secretary, John Montagu, wanted a high qualification which would confine the vote to occupiers of property worth £50 or more. This, it was argued, would safeguard imperial interests by offsetting the Afrikaners' numerical superiority; and property interests, by excluding the working classes. Afrikaners, on the other hand, stood for a low qualification which would strengthen their position against the British merchants and officials in command of the legislature; and they were prepared to pay the price of extending the vote to a possibly significant number of Coloured.

A third group of liberals, led by Sir Andries Stockenstrom, William Porter the attorney-general, and Fairbairn, also advocated a low qualification, but for different reasons. They wished to secure both the imperial connexion and Coloured rights, two aims which in their minds were wholly compatible. The Coloured preferred crown colony rule to a settlers' parliament. If a settlers' parliament had to come, they would use their vote to support the imperial connexion and therefore the British minority. Porter, in particular, wanted a popular franchise for genuinely liberal reasons as well. Both 'Klaas, the Hottentot' and 'his neighbour, Mynheer van Dunder, the boer', might know very little about parliamentary issues, he told the legislative council, but the best school for teaching them was the vote. They knew enough to distinguish their friends from their enemies. The Coloured, he added, had a right to protect their labour and sell it at their own price; the right to make 'the most of whatever powers of mind and body God has given them'. To those who feared that the Coloured were politically dangerous, he replied in memorable words: 'Now, for myself, I do not hesitate to say that I would rather meet the Hottentot at the hustings, voting for his representative, than meet the Hottentot in the wilds with his gun upon his shoulder.'[7]

The constitution of 1853 gave the Cape a system of representative government, a parliament of two elected houses, and a franchise open to any man who for twelve months preceding registration had occupied property worth £25 or received an aggregate wage of either £50 or £25 with board and lodging. This was Porter's 'low franchise', which the Colonial Office adopted in the hope that it would foster common loyalties and interests among all subjects without distinction of class or colour.

Class coincided so closely with colour that the constitution was colour-blind only in form. The Coloured made up the great bulk of the poor – the landless, the low-paid, and the unemployed – who were kept off the rolls. A majority of the Coloured worked on the settlers' farms; and, it was ruled, farm labourers living in cottages owned by their masters did not 'occupy' property within the meaning of the constitution. The franchise discriminated, therefore, against a colour-class. Even in later years, when Coloured voters were marginally important in a dozen or more constituencies, they never succeeded in returning any of their own people to parliament. It remained at all times a bourgeois institution of white landowners, merchants, company directors and professional men, in which the working class, white or coloured, had no representative of their own.

A parliament of masters showed small sympathy with the working man. When only two years old, it passed the Masters and Servants Act of 1856 – a law far more ruthless than its predecessors in the range of offences and the severity of the penalties prescribed for servants. Designed to enforce discipline on ex-slaves, peasants, pastoralists and a rural proletariat, it survived a century of industrialism and became the model for similar laws in white supremacy colonies throughout south, central and east Africa. The Act of 1856 remains with its offspring on the South African statute book: a grim reminder of the country's slave-owning past and a sharp instrument of racial discrimination. For though it is nominally colour-blind, the penalties are invoked only against the darker workers, some 30,000 of whom are sentenced annually for breaches of the labour code.

The offences can be grouped under three heads: breach of contract, indiscipline, and injury to property. The first group includes failure to commence work at an agreed date, unlawful absence from work, desertion and strikes. Among the disciplinary offences are disobedience, drunkenness, brawling and the use of abusive language. Finally, a servant can be jailed if he damages his master's property with malice or negligence, uses it unlawfully, loses livestock or fails to report the loss. Convicted servants were not given the option of a fine, however trivial the offence, by the original act. It authorized a sentence of one month's imprisonment for breach of contract or discipline by a first offender, and six weeks with solitary confinement and spare diet on a second conviction. A servant who damaged his master's property faced two months' imprisonment for a first offence, and three for a second, in each case with solitary confinement and spare diet. An employer who withheld wages could be sentenced to a fine of not more than £5.

Liberals like Fairbairn and Saul Solomon put up some opposition to the act. Its victims were passive. Yet the urban proletariat, if small, was well established and articulate. In 1856 the colony had some 9,000 persons engaged in commerce, and 1,500 in manufacturing. Cape Town's list of manufactories in 1859 included a total of fifty-six brickfields, limekilns, foundries, breweries, corn and snuff mills, soap, candle, fish-curing and printing establishments. The standard wage for white carpenters, masons, bricklayers, joiners and mechanics in 1859–61 was 7s. 6d. a day, and for Coloured 6s. Employers complained that immigrants recruited in England to work in the colony for 4s. a day often struck work soon after landing at Cape Town and extracted as much as 15s. from employers.[8] When regularly employed, building artisans, tailors, printers, bakers, wagon makers, and boat builders earned enough to qualify for the vote, fifteen years before Britain's second reform act of 1867. Yet there was no working-class movement in the Cape.

Labour historians have diligently scanned the local press for early evidence of such, and with meagre results.[9] Cape Town's printers formed a protection society in 1841, which soon faded away when some of the founders set up in business on their own. Workers took part in the anti-convict agitation, held mass meetings during the minor recession that followed, and descended on the governor Smith to demand work or bread. The printers made another effort in 1857 at forming a mutual benefit society, to aid sick members, widows and orphans out of a fund to which every member subscribed 8d. a week.[10] James Marriott, a radical printer, helped to promote the first labour newspaper, the *Cape Mercury and Weekly Magazine*, which ran from January to October 1859; and the first workers' cooperative, formed in the same year 'for the cheapening of the price of provisions'. Prices were scandalously high, he wrote; and the Cape was not the land of milk and honey that immigrants were led to believe. A decent mechanic, earning £1 16s. a week, had to find £2 2s. 3d. for the food, clothing and rent that cost only £1 11s. 6d. in London.[11] The *Magazine* recorded attempts by benevolent liberals to establish a Mechanics' Institute to instruct and entertain artisans.[12] It seems, however, that the first two trade unions were formed, both in Cape Town, only in 1881: a Typographical Society, and a local branch of the English Amalgamated Society of Carpenters and Joiners.

The primary purpose of a trade union is to maintain and raise wage rates by limiting competition between workmen, preventing undercutting, and applying organized pressure on employers. For trade unions to arise, there must be a body of lifelong wage earners free to sell their labour, wholly dependent on wages, without prospect of becoming independent producers, and aware of the benefits of collective bargaining. A century ago South African workers lacked one or more of these qualities. White artisans could move easily out of their class to set up as masters on their own. Many of the less skilled workers were African peasants who retained a base in their traditional communities. Habits and attitudes inculcated during the period of slavery persisted among the ex-slaves, their descendants and former masters. Racial and cultural diversities in the working population inhibited the growth of class consciousness and solidarity.

South Africa has never provided a good living for the ordinary labourer. Wages and working conditions were adjusted to the conventionally low standards of ex-slaves, the free Coloured and tribal peasants. Immigrant working men competed with the Coloured for both skilled and unskilled work. House servants, farm hands, dairymaids, gardeners and grooms who migrated to the Cape in the nineteenth century usually lost little time in looking for more remunerative and congenial employment.[13] Opportunities kept pace with immigration, even in the sluggish economy of the period before the great diamond and gold discoveries. Thomas Pringle noted in 1824 that 'to mechanics and farm labourers of steady and enterprising character, the path to independence is still open and certain'. Many of the 200 Scottish servants and mechanics who came to the Cape a few years earlier had 'already cleared little fortunes of from £500 to £2,000'; all but a few were in prosperous and improving circumstances.[14] Germans who came under contract to farmers in the sixties were also 'intent on procuring their freedom and independence'. After completing their contract period of two years' service and repaying their passage money, nearly all left the farms to become their own masters in the towns.[15]

The economic expansion that accompanied the mining of diamonds at Kimberley accentuated the instability of the immigrant white worker. Germans, according to witnesses before the parliamentary committee of 1879 on labour resources, entered the colony in order to become masters. No sooner had they learned to be useful than they bought a horse and cart, or set up as a shopkeeper, or acquired land and competed for labour. 'The objection to Europeans,' said a witness, 'is that after a time they will set up a brandy shop or something of that kind. They become independent of labour too soon.' Only Coloured men were content to labour.[16] They were paid about 15s. to 20s. a month, with food, quarters and a garden allotment, in the western districts. Africans in the eastern Cape received from 1s. to 2s. a day with rations. White employees on the farms were much better paid. They generally occupied the position of an overseer; and if steady, active and prudent, soon became masters and employers.[17]

Not every white worker climbed. The failures often embarrassed employers and the white community. Members of parliament told the committee of 1879 that farmers were hard put to isolate English labourers from Coloured on the farms: 'they must be put on an equality, and then they take black women and go back.' The Coloured, being more skilful than the greenhorns, tended to look down on them, 'and in many cases they degenerate in consequence'. A white man was said to be a degenerate if he fraternized with the Coloured. He usually took on the prejudices of the colonists and gave a racial reason for escaping from a disagreeable occupation. White navvies employed on railway construction in the sixties refused to work alongside Coloured, and abandoned their jobs for this reason when set to work on the line at Tulbagh Kloof in the western Cape. They 'spoke about the Kloof in very strong navvy language' and said they were not going to mix with the Coloured, or teach them the way to work for the same rates of pay. Though the contractors offered higher wages to skilled men if they would stay and instruct the labourers, they refused and left for New Zealand.[18]

Any indignity associated with the work of an unskilled labourer was attached to his status as a hired man and not to the work itself. The colonists never turned work into the fetish that it became on the North American frontier. Nor did they, however, develop the repugnance to manual labour that characterized the Spanish in South America. Rough and laborious work might be thought fit only for 'Hottentots, Kafirs and Coolies' when performed for hire. A white man was not degraded, however, if he felled trees, ploughed, made hay or used pick and shovel on his own account. Many settlers practised a definite craft and combined farming with the trade of a blacksmith, mason or harness-maker.[19] Traditional attitudes placed a premium on skills which, like capital, were imported, and associated with a white skin, though not regarded in the Cape as the white man's prerogative.

A white artisan would not lose caste by working side by side with the Coloured who provided the bulk of labour, both skilled and unskilled, in the building, furniture, garment and leather industries. He maintained his superior status if he earned more, occupied a leading position, and mixed with the Coloured only when at work. This social distance deterred him from combining with Coloured artisans in a trade union. A high degree of social mobility, the smallness and isolation of the white working class account, on the other hand, for the failure of white workers to form unions of their own. These factors did not apply to the Coloured. They were restrained by an entirely different set of conditions. Two centuries of colonial rule, slavery, forced labour and arrested development had fostered in them an unquestioning submission to white authority, and inhibited the growth of either a class or national consciousness.

One important exception must be noted. The independent spirit of the pastoral Nama persisted in the offspring of unions between themselves and the colonists. The 'Bastards', or Griquas as they were later called, spoke Afrikaans and shared the culture of their white forbears. This affinity did not save them from constant persecution. They were conscripted for service with the commandos, expelled from their pastures, denied the right to own land, and forced into the least accessible parts of the country. The survivors eventually took refuge towards the end of the eighteenth century in the semi-arid tract west of the Vaal and Orange rivers, in what came to be known as Griqualand West. Here they formed a semi-autonomous state under Andries Waterboer. Another distinct Griqua state took shape after 1825 under Adam Kok at Philippolis, below the confluence of the Caledon and Orange rivers, while a third Coloured-Nama settlement, culled from mission stations, was settled by the administration in 1830 along the Kat river in the eastern Cape. The three groups of pioneers were border guards, defending the frontiers of white settlement. All lost their land to the whites, and all rose in rebellion against white settler rule.

The Kat River settlers fought with troops and commandos against the Xhosa in the wars of 1834 and 1846, suffered heavily, and received no compensation. Many of them, led by Andries Botha, took up arms and joined the Xhosa in the war of 1851. Botha was convicted of treason, the rebels' land was confiscated, and the colonists soon afterwards took over the entire settlement. In Griqualand West, Waterboer concluded mutual defence treaties with the government in 1834 and 1843. His burghers marched with Harry Smith against a party of Voortrekkers in 1848. Six years later, however, Britain recognized the Orange Free State and abandoned the Griquas. Diamonds were discovered in Griqualand West in the 1860s, and this led to the annexation of the territory by Britain in 1871. Meanwhile, farmers of the Orange Free State had overrun the Griqua farms at Philippolis. Adam Kok then led his people in 1861 to a sparsely inhabited region called Nomansland on the eastern plateau slopes of the Drakensberg. Here they founded their commonwealth of Griqualand East. It, too, was engulfed by the colonists. When Gcaleka, Ngqika and Thembu clans made another desperate attempt to liberate themselves in 1877–8, the Griquas of Griqualand East and West took up arms in a rebellion that spread across the Orange to the northern border of the colony. This was the last armed struggle of a Coloured community against white supremacy in South Africa.

The Griqua were destroyed because the colonists coveted their land. In the older parts of the colony, where they were essentially the working classes, the Coloured survived because they possessed only their labour power. Cape liberalism gave them equality before the law, access to the courts, protection against lawlessness, a free labour market, and in all other respects permitted a high degree of discrimination. They were emancipated from slavery, but not from poverty, ignorance and disease. As the legal gap narrowed, the social gap between them and the colonists widened. White supremacy was entrenched by a growing inequality in educational opportunities. Mission schools were founded for the Coloured after emancipation, and government schools for the whites. 'It is quite impossible to assess the damage suffered by the Coloured People,' notes their historian, Professor Marais, 'through their children being confined to the inferior mission schools.'[20] If an assessment were made, it might be found that segregation introduced and maintained an educational gap of thirty years between whites and Coloured. A few obtained a good middle-class education. None was admitted to a post higher than that of messenger in public services or private corporations.

That Coloured workers in the western districts were conscious of their disabilities appears from a petition presented to parliament in 1871 by Titus Lergele, Jacob Haas, Frederik Pitt and fifty-six other residents of Genadendal mission station. They protested against demands raised by colonists for discriminatory penalties under the masters and servants law for farm labourers, and a speedier procedure to deal with 'hard-necked servants' who caused 'great grievances and inconveniences'.[21] The petitioners pointed out that memorialists before them had asked for relief from laws 'which injuriously affected the labouring classes'. Yet the obnoxious statutes remained in force, while others had been added which likewise bore hard on their class. The petition set out the case for reform, in particular for the option of a fine 'instead of imprisonment as a felon'. Since they were unrepresented in parliament, and since 'strong prejudices still exist in the Colony against colour, race and class', the petitioners urged the governor, as Her Majesty's representative, to guard their interests.[22]

Britain's master and servant law, equally one-sided, prescribed imprisonment for defaulting servants but not for employers. Trade unions mounted a campaign for reform and won a minor victory in 1867.[23] The agitation touched at the Cape, where Saul Solomon 'lived himself into the heart of the Imperial Parliament' by poring over political reports of 'the best English newspapers'.[24] He championed the workers' cause in the assembly against J. C. Molteno, the main author of the 1856 Masters and Servants Act and spokesman of the farmers. Responsible government came to the Cape in 1872, with Molteno as prime minister. He introduced a bill to give farmers the stiffer penalties they demanded for their servants, though Solomon was able to obtain important concessions after a long controversy. The amending act of 1873 did discriminate against servants employed on farms by exposing only them to sentences of imprisonment with hard labour, spare diet and solitary confinement. On the other hand, magistrates were given the power to impose fines, and not imprisonment alone, on all other servants; while employers were for the first time made liable to imprisonment for breaches of contract.

Responsible government, imperial expansion and industrialism followed hard on the diamond discoveries of 1867–71. British and colonial troops made war on the Hlubi in 1873, the Gcaleka and Pedi in 1877, the Ngqika, Thembu, Pondo, Griqua and Rolong in 1878, the Zulu in 1879, the Sotho in 1880, the Ndebele in 1893, and the Afrikaner republics in 1899. The Cape absorbed the Transkei and its peoples in 1879–94. Britain annexed Basutoland in 1868, Griqualand West in 1871, the South African Republic in 1877, Zululand in 1887, Matabeleland in 1894, and the Afrikaner republics in 1900. The Zulu rebellion of 1906, in which nearly 4,000 Africans were killed, marked the last stage in 250 years of armed struggle by the traditional societies against white invaders. South Africa's industrial era was baptized in blood and the subjugation of small nations. As from the beginning of the century, the liberation movement took the form of struggles between classes and national communities.

The Cape's short-lived liberalism went into a decline after the granting of responsible government. Kimberley's mine owners produced diamonds under a regime of colour bars, pass laws and closed compounds for indentured, migratory peasant workers. Cecil Rhodes, mine magnate, politician and imperialist, dominated the colony in the last quarter of the century. The formation of an Afrikaner Bond in 1879 polarized political differences among the colonists and strengthened the tendency towards overt racial discrimination. The Transkeian annexations multiplied threefold the potential African vote, then already a significant electoral factor in eastern Cape constituencies. To keep out the 'blanket Kafir' – the term applied by racists to the Transkeian farmer – Rhodes, backed by the Bond, loaded the franchise against Africans in 1887 and 1892. Parliament excluded land held under customary tenure from the franchise qualifications, raised the landed property qualification from £25 to £75, eliminated the £25 wage qualification, and added a literacy test. The effect of the changes was to strike some 30,000 Africans off the rolls and to stimulate the growth of an African political movement.

Wars, conquest and annexations provided one of the primary requisites of industrialism – an uprooted peasantry available at low cost for rough manual work. Peasant communities lost their self-sufficiency under the pressures resulting from the confiscation of their land and cattle, the imposition of taxes, the substitution of traders' merchandise for domestic products, the spread of education and Christianity. Wage earning became unavoidable for increasing numbers of men and women. Members of small agrarian societies had to acquire the discipline and skills of the industrial worker, accustom themselves to urban society, learn the laws and language of the conqueror. They learned the hard way: on the job, without formal instruction, by working under employers, supervisors and technicians who neither understood nor respected their language and customs.

The alchemy of diamonds and gold that transmuted agrarian societies into a considerable industrial state attracted thousands of artisans, clerks, farm workers, men without special skills, fortune seekers and aggressive capitalists. South Africa's white population rose from 260,000 in 1865 to 634,000 in 1891; it grew threefold in the Transvaal, from 40,000 in 1875 to 119,000 in 1890. The newcomers included men with habits and attitudes appropriate to an industrialized society. Some were staunch trade unionists and ardent socialists. They grafted their beliefs and patterns of organization on the colonial stock. White working men, set in authority over African peasants, despised them and also feared them as potential competitors. Employers, concerned mainly to maximize profits, exploited the weak bargaining position of the peasants and substituted them, when this was expedient, for the better paid whites. Immigrant journeymen joined forces with local artisans to erect their traditional defences against undercutting.

Printers, carpenters, miners, engineers, engine drivers, iron moulders, masons, plasterers, plumbers, tailors, bakers and hairdressers formed trade unions at Cape Town, Kimberley, Durban and the Witwatersrand between 1881 and 1899. The early growth of trade unionism was an easy, uneventful process in the port towns. Small employers hobnobbed with artisans in the friendly atmosphere of a colonial community, where dark men did the dirty work and all whites belonged to a racial elite. Passions ran higher in the crude mining camps of Kimberley and the Witwatersrand. Here white working men fought against great capitalist combines for rights. The struggle rarely crossed the colour line to unite workers of all races in a common front against the employing class. White workers usually chose to fight on their own, often under the banner of white supremacy. Racial discrimination, sponsored by governments, employers and white workers, divided the working class into antagonistic racial groups. As industrialism spread, the country moved ever farther away from the ideal state contemplated by Cape liberalism, in which all persons 'without distinction of class or colour should be united by one bond of loyalty and a common interest'.

2 Diamond Diggers and the New Elite

Diamonds were found in 1867–8 along the Vaal and Orange rivers in a region where some 3,000 Griquas, 1,000 Korannas and 1,000 Afrikaners lived in uneasy proximity.[1] Britain had acknowledged the Griqua claims to the territory by treaty in 1834 and 1846. Reversing her policy, she gave independence to the Transvaal voortrekkers in 1852 and to the Orange Free State in 1854, repudiated her alliances with coloured peoples north of the Orange, excepting Adam Kok, and in effect abandoned them to Afrikaner domination. Then came the discoveries. Diamonds, prophesied the Cape's colonial secretary, Richard Southey, were 'the rock on which the success of South Africa will be built'. Britain rediscovered a moral duty towards the Griquas. Wodehouse, the Cape governor, informed Kimberley, the British secretary of state, that 'as a matter of right the native tribes are fairly entitled to that tract of country in which, for the present, the diamonds appear to be chiefly found'.[2] Kimberley agreed and added that his government would be much displeased if the republics were to extend their slave-dealing activities, oppress the natives, and cause disturbances of the peace by encroaching on Griqua territory.[3]

Britain walked off with the prize, while Griquas, Korannas, Rolong and Afrikaner republics disputed the ownership of the diamond fields. Cornelius Waterboer, the Griqua leader, had trustingly appealed to Britain for protection. An arbitration court awarded the territory to his people, and Britain annexed it in 1871 under the title of Griqualand West. A payment of £90,000 was made to the Orange Free State as compensation for the loss of her title. To the Griqua went the consolation of having their name perpetuated in one of the richest portions of the earth's surface, which once they had called their own. South

Africans of all races and a random selection of immigrants took their place. The influx raised the population of the territory by June 1871 to 37,000, of whom 21,000 were Africans and Coloured.[4] None of the administering authorities, whether Griqua, Afrikaner or British, was prepared for the rush. The diggers appointed committees to enforce order, and the Orange Free State asserted a nominal authority before the annexation, but there was a dearth of even rudimentary services.

Housing, hospitals, water supplies, sanitation, power and transport had to be improvised, usually by private agencies at rising prices. Diggers, some with families, lived in wagons, tents, huts or galvanized iron sheds. Africans, who usually walked barefooted to the fields, often arrived in an emaciated state: 'weary, grimy, hungry, shy, trailing along sometimes with bleeding feet, and hanging heads, and bodies staggering with faintness.'[5] Many came from far in the interior with the sole purpose of earning £6 for a gun, the only weapon with which they could hope to protect their land and cattle against invading colonists. No one accepted responsibility for the newcomers. Their destitution rendered them unfit for hard toil, but forced them to labour twelve hours a day and more. They slept on the bare earth without shelter or in a brushwood hut, and suffered greatly from the cold. They lived on mealie-meal, with an occasional chunk of refuse meat. Water, at 2s. 6d. a bucket, was beyond their means. Many acquired a taste for Cape brandy, retailed at 3d. a tot and 10s. 6d. a gallon. There were no laws to regulate wages and working conditions, impose safety measures against accident and disease, or enforce the payment of workmen's compensation.

Farmers trekked to the fields with oxwagon, family, and a retinue of servants who were paid £3 a year, or the price of a cow, to dig for diamonds, while the patriarch, smoking his pipe, sat at the sorting table. Recent immigrants, who accounted for one-quarter of the white population on the fields, soon adopted the South African way of life. They too hired Africans to pick, shovel, break, haul and sift ground, to cut and carry firewood, to cook and wash, and to accompany their masters to market with sack or wheelbarrow. Most whites felt disinclined for manual work during the summer, observed Sir Charles Payton, who spent six months on the diggings in 1871. 'It is quite sufficient for them to sit under an awning and sort, leaving the Kafirs to perform all the other stages of work.'[6] Middle-class English gentlemen, like Cecil Rhodes and his brother, 'delighted to find themselves in a veritable Tom Tiddler's ground, where they could not only pick up gold and silver, but have it done for them by "niggers"'.[7]

Conditions were ideal for making fat profits on a thin investment. Luck, foresight, tenacity, ruthlessness and a little capital were needed for success. Most diggers probably lacked these qualities and failed to pay their way.[8] But the successful ones could amass great wealth, by production or speculation, out of a valuable mineral extracted without expensive plant and by peasants who received no protection against gross exploitation. Diamonds to an estimated value of £1½ million were taken out of the ground by 1872.[9] The labourer's share was a weekly wage of 7s. 6d. or 10s. and rations worth 6s. 6d., consisting of twenty-five pounds of mealie-meal (but whole mealies came much cheaper), an issue of coarse meat (called 'kafir' meat in the trade), a handful of coarse tobacco, and a Saturday night's tot of crude wine, spirits or brandy. Africans could not fail to note the contrast between their poverty and the value of their labour. If they missed the point, dealers in stolen gems drove it home.

Illicit diamond mining grew into a major industry. Stolen stones passed from the labourer to a 'tout', who sold them for a small part of their value to a registered claimholder or licensed dealer. Louis Cohen, a native of Liverpool who emigrated to the diggings in 1866, noted that many wealthy diggers laid the basis of their fortunes by buying stolen gems. They robbed the small man of his diamonds and claim, became big mine owners or dealers, and were then loudest in denouncing the profession that they had previously practised with such success.[10] African and Coloured labourers supplied the stolen diamonds. Few were convicted but all were suspected, not least by unsuccessful diggers. A mythology took shape. Coloured claimholders were said to be more successful than white ones, because they received stones stolen by relatives and friends.[11] Africans, it was maintained, stole at least half the output.[12] 'The partially civilized Kaffir rapidly develops into a thief.'[13] The 'raw Kaffir', fresh from the kraal, is best and most trustworthy. 'Above all things, mistrust a Kaffir who speaks English and wears trousers,' advised Payton, who had a prodigious capacity for consuming and regurgitating colonial prejudices.[14]

Prospectors from Australia and California imported notions of a 'diggers' law'. A Diamond Diggers' Protection Society, formed in 1870, issued a set of regulations. They stipulated that 'no licence to dig should be granted to a Native', prohibited persons of colour from holding claims or diamonds in their own right, and prohibited the buying of diamonds from any servant unless he had his employer's written authority to sell. The rules were given 'the force of law' by the executive council of the Orange Free State while it claimed to administer the diggings; but lost all semblance of legal validity after Britain had annexed Griqualand West.[15] Coloured and Africans could then assert the same right as any white man to take out a licence and dig on their own account. The whites protested vigorously, especially when diamond yields declined, or prices fell, or the cost of claims rose. There was always some distress among the diggers. They blamed it on the servants who stole and the dealers who bought the stones, but, above all, on African and Coloured licensed claimholders.

Rioters swept through the streets of New Rush, the site of Kimberley, in 1872; tried to lynch an Indian accused of buying diamonds; burnt the tents and canteens of suspected traffickers in stolen gems; chased and flogged African passers-by. Two of the three British commissioners appointed to administer the diggings submitted to the campaign of violence. They issued a proclamation on 23 July suspending all digging licences held by Africans and Coloured. No more licences were to be issued to persons of colour except by leave of a diggers' committee or of a board of seven *bona fide* white claimholders.[16] Barkly, the Cape governor and high commissioner of Griqualand West, ruled that such discrimination was contrary to reason and justice, and therefore *ultra vires*.[17] He disallowed the proclamation, but undertook to see how far he could meet the rioters' demands. The diggers then submitted draft rules which would bar Africans and

Coloured from obtaining licences to search for, buy, sell, or otherwise trade in diamonds. The rules also provided for written labour contracts, the expulsion of unemployed Africans from the diggings, and the confiscation of diamonds held by servants. Barkly conceded the substance of the demands in a proclamation of 10 August 1872, described as a measure to prevent the stealing of diamonds.

Barkly kept up the appearance of equality before the law by applying the proclamation to all 'servants'. But it discriminated, and was meant to discriminate, against Africans and Coloured. In the first place, no person could become a registered claim-holder unless a magistrate or justice of the peace had certified him to be of good character, fit and proper to be registered. White officials under pressure from aggressive racists could be relied upon to use their wide powers against Africans as a class. Only a few licensed Coloured diggers, operating on the outskirts of the fields, remained to give credence to the Cape's doctrine of liberalism. Secondly, the proclamation laid the basis of the 'pass' system that spread in time to the Rand mines and from there to labour districts and towns throughout South Africa. It centred on the registration of labour contracts. Servants had to produce a certificate of registration on demand, and have it endorsed on taking their discharge. To leave the diggings lawfully, a servant had to produce the endorsed certificate and take out a pass. Any person found wandering in a mining camp without a pass and unable to give a satisfactory account of himself ran the risk of summary arrest, a £5 fine and three months' hard labour or twenty-five lashes.

The object was to detect and apprehend deserting workers, who were liable under the Masters and Servants Act to fines or imprisonment. A related aim was the recovery of stolen diamonds. A policeman or employer might without warrant search a servant's room, property and person within twenty-four hours of his leaving his place of work. Diamonds in his possession belonged to his master unless the contrary was proved.

Barkly's surrender to racism failed to appease the leaders of the malcontents. They were after bigger game than a handful of Coloured prospectors and debris-sorters. Aylward, Tucker, Ling and others like them wanted power – an unreasonable and dangerous amount of power, reported Southey, now the lieutenant-governor of Griqualand West. They would use it, he warned, to deprive Her Majesty's Coloured subjects of their rights and privileges.[18] He and his secretary John Currey resisted demands for a stringent vagrancy law and an outright ban on the employment of registered servants by Coloured and Africans for mining and the sorting of debris.

More tents were burned. Discontented diggers made common cause with plotters from the Orange Free State and speculators out to buy claims cheaply. They formed the Kimberley Defence League, organized armed vigilantes, and hoisted the black flag. Carnarvon, the secretary of state, sided with the diggers and ordered the dismissal of Southey and Currey in 1875 for having failed to establish good relations with the whites of Kimberley.[19]

The Griquas rose in rebellion in 1878, and the Cape incorporated Griqualand West in 1880. The colony's Vagrancy Act of 1867, as amended by Act 23 of 1879, could then be applied on the diggings. It supplemented the pass laws by prescribing a maximum of six months' imprisonment with hard labour, spare diet and solitary confinement for any 'idle and disorderly person' – the phrase used to describe anyone who wandered abroad without lawful means of subsistence and failed to give a good and satisfactory account of himself.

Southey had fallen foul of the Colonial Office by rejecting racial discrimination and protecting migrant workers against gross neglect. In his dispatches he complained of diggers who turned sick labourers into the street instead of caring for them as the law required. At his instance the legislative council passed Ordinance 2 of 1874 to provide hospital accommodation, medical attention and sanitary services 'for the benefit of the native labourers', though at their expense. Every master was to deduct one shilling a month from his servant's wage and pay it to the registrar of servants, for a hospital and the improvement of general sanitation. The diggers objected strenuously to the levy, which came out of the worker's pocket, although the annual African death rate in Kimberley reached the alarming figure of seventy-nine per thousand in 1879 in contrast to a rate of forty for whites.[20] The levy yielded £10,000 in 1882, and a hospital was built. Nearly twenty years later, however, sick Africans, usually suffering from scurvy, were often left 'to lie in the compounds day after day in their dirty blankets and their bodies in a filthy condition'.[21]

Human beings were cheaper than diamonds, as white workers also discovered. Men died or suffered injury in accidents caused by inexperience, lack of training, inadequate safety measures and the failure to supervise machinery. Witnesses told the Diamond Mining Commission of 1881 that no proper inquest or inquiry was held after an accident.[22] The commission suggested that safety regulations be introduced, but Cecil Rhodes and some other members of the commission seemed more anxious to prevent diamond thefts than to prevent accidents. Much attention was given to whether white employees as well as Africans should be searched for stolen stones. For the small claim-holders, whose pressure had led to the elimination of Coloured diggers, were by then being eliminated in turn. A world-wide slump in diamond prices in 1875 forced many diggers out of the fields. More left as the yellow ground became exhausted. At lower levels, when digging deep into the blue ground, men found open-cast mining impossible on small claims of thirty feet square. Rockfalls, water seepage, boundary disputes, high costs and technical difficulties associated with deep-level mining hastened the process of converting independent diggers into servants of big companies.

Successful diggers and dealers, foreign merchants and investors bought and accumulated claims, formed syndicates and merged into companies. The original 3,600 claims in the four big mines at Kimberley were reduced by 1885 to 98 properties, held by 42 companies and 56 private firms or individuals. The mergers continued until each mine was worked as a unit. Big capitalists bought or squeezed out small shareholders. Small companies formed large companies which eventually merged into one great corporation, the De Beers Consolidated Mine. It controlled all the Kimberley mines and ninety per cent of the world's output of diamonds before the end of the century.[23] Laws enacted to protect small diggers now operated for the company's benefit. Men who had clamoured for protection against illicit diamond buying found that the weapons they had helped to forge were being turned against themselves.

A special court was set up in 1880 to try cases of illicit diamond buying – 'the canker worm of the community', said the judge, Sir Jacobus de Wet. The Trade in Diamonds Consolidation Act of 1882 prescribed a maximum penalty of a thousand-pound fine or fifteen years' imprisonment or both for being in unlawful possession of uncut diamonds. Only a licensed dealer was allowed to buy the uncut stones. But heavy penalties did not stop the traffic. Attempts were therefore made to stop it at the source. Regulations of 1872 and 1880, that provided for the searching of persons when they entered or left mining ground, proved ineffective. A majority of the diggers and claimholders who replied to a questionnaire circulated by the commission of 1881 favoured the compulsory searching of African workers; some wanted whites also to be searched; and some suggested the lash, life imprisonment, banishment, or a stricter pass and vagrancy law to put down illicit diamond buying. Amended regulations of 1883 required all mine workers, other than managers, to wear uniforms and to strip naked in searching houses when they left work.

White workers complained of being degraded to the 'Kafir's' level, went on strike, demonstrated and rioted in 1883. Twenty-five Africans who had joined in the turmoil were sent to jail for disorderly conduct, and the company rescinded the order to strip. A new instruction, issued in 1884, required white employees to be searched while clothed in shirt, trousers and socks, and those who refused were threatened with instant dismissal. The men called a general strike, stopped the pumps on all mines and when the 'French' company resumed work, marched on the mine to put the hauling gear out of action. The company's guards, barricaded behind sandbags, called on them to halt, opened fire, killed four demonstrators outright and fatally wounded two more. The workers held a splendid funeral, gathered at mass meetings to protest, and went back to work after the owners had agreed to subject white employees to only irregular surprise searches.[24]

Africans were searched every day at the end of their shift. Stripped naked, they jumped over bars and paraded with arms extended before guards, who scrutinized hair, nose, mouth, ears and rectum with meticulous care. It was much the same kind of search that Africans endured in Kimberley's central prison where, remarked Judge, the civil commissioner, 'many a raw native ignorant of the laws of the province experienced the first acquaintance with civilization.'[25] Rhodes and his fellow directors took the parallel a long way further when they hit on the idea of confining African miners in closed compounds for the four or six months of their contract period. This debasing form of working-class housing was firmly entrenched by 1888, the year of the great merger of all controlling companies with De Beers. The compound was an enclosure surrounded by a high corrugated iron fence and covered by wire-netting. The men lived, twenty to a room, in huts or iron cabins built against the fence. They went to work along a tunnel, bought food and clothing from the company's stores, and received free medical treatment but no wages during sickness, all within the compound. Men due for discharge were confined in detention rooms for several days, during which they wore only blankets and fingerless leather gloves padlocked to their wrists, swallowed purgatives, and were examined for stones concealed in cuts, wounds, swellings and orifices.[26]

Kimberley's shopkeepers protested loudly that they were being deprived of trade by the company's policy of converting 'a labour contract into a period of imprisonment with hard labour and a truck system of wages'.[27] To appease them, De Beers undertook to stock its shops with goods bought only in the district; and Rhodes distributed the profits, amounting to £10,000 a year, between a sanatorium, mining school and amenities for the whites of Kimberley.[28] Africans, whose trade yielded the profit, were said to benefit in other ways from their enforced confinement. It shielded them, the company claimed, from the temptation to waste their money on strong drink and bad women or to risk unpaid imprisonment by stealing diamonds, deserting service, or breaking discipline. In truth, peasants who entered an alien world, dominated by persons of a different race, language and culture, often fell prey to traders in shoddy goods, illicit liquor sellers, pimps and prostitutes. Many lives were wasted by alcoholism, venereal disease tuberculosis and crime. But free workers who inhabited the slums and shanties of industrial towns acquired the insights, maturity and hardness of will needed for survival in a harsh environment. Neither class nor national consciousness developed among the inmates of Kimberley's compound-jails.

De Beers' monopolistic structure and political influence enabled it to rationalize mining techniques and enforce strict control of workers, output, markets and prices. Working costs dropped by half in the decade after amalgamation, to 10s. a carat, while the average price of diamonds rose from 20s. to 30s. a carat. Dividends increased from 5 per cent in 1889 to 25 per cent in 1893 and 40 per cent in 1896.[29] Rhodes, Beit, Barnato and Philipson-Stow, the four life governors, took 40 per cent of the profits in excess of £1,440,000 a year – a right which they eventually sold to the company for three million pounds' worth of shares. Through the harsh exploitation of Africans – and not, as Professor Frankel suggests, by 'miraculous industry'[30] – the mine owners extracted more than £300 millions' worth of diamonds at low capital costs in seventy years. The accumulated profits helped to finance the early mining of gold on the Witwatersrand.

Rhodes seemed indifferent to the homosexual practices that the compounds of Kimberley and the Rand injected into African life. As prime minister of the Cape, he introduced the Glen Grey Act of 1894, which imposed a labour tax and introduced individual land holdings to make peasants migrate to the mines. He showed no desire to protect their families against disintegration and the moral rot caused by excessive labour migration. Unemployed white workers, displaced by his company mergers and rationalization, were given work on his Rand mines or recruited for the pioneer column that invaded Mashonaland in 1890. But there was a time when he required police protection against the threats of unemployed diggers and bankrupt traders in Kimberley.

De Beers dominated the town. Company detectives spied on

men at work and in their private lives, reported on their political activities, and set traps for suspected dealers in stolen diamonds. When white workers banded together in 1891, they called themselves the Knights of Labour, taking the American secret society of that name as their model, and declared 'perpetual war and opposition to the encroachment of monopoly and organized capital'.[31] Some Knights had taken part in an abortive attempt to 'rush' the Premier mine, later called the Wesselton, which de Beers bought in 1891 for nearly half a million pounds. They accused Rhodes of a 'breach of trust and corruption' for taking options on the property in his capacity as managing director while at the same time, as prime minister, opposing a petition to have it proclaimed an open digging.[32]

The Knights of Labour blamed De Beers, 'that great monopoly', and the 'wealthy, overestimated, disappointing politician' Rhodes for the depressed state of the working classes during the collapse of the first gold boom. 'Unity, Charity, Fidelity' were inscribed on the society's banner. The members were pledged to champion the labouring classes everywhere against monopoly capital and 'the insidious attack of cheap labour competition'. The society aimed, on the one hand, to secure direct representation of labour in parliament, and, on the other, to exclude Indian, Chinese or 'other cheap labour competition of any Inferior Race attempting to invade our shores'. Here, in brief, was the ideological platform of the future white labour movement. But the Knights themselves failed to establish a hold. The white employees of De Beers were engine drivers, banksmen,* onsetters† or supervisors. Set in authority over the African, they earned four or five times as much, and lived in company houses in an attractive suburb with clubhouse, parks and recreation grounds. The Knights could not wean them from loyalty to the company; or, according to trade unionists, break the stranglehold of the company over their lives.

'The white miners of Kenilworth, the suburb of Kimberley,' wrote J. A. Hobson in 1900, 'are absolutely under the control of De Beers Company: drawing their wages from De Beers,

---

* Overseers at brink of pit or shaft.

† Supervisors of cage at bottom of shaft; also called 'hangers-on'.

living in houses owned by De Beers, trading with shops controlled by De Beers, they are the political and economic serfs of the company; if they object to any terms imposed upon them by the company, they must quit not only their employment but their homes, and must leave Kimberley to find a means of living outside the clutches of the diamond monopoly.'[33] The experiences of militant workers in Kimberley were to verify Hobson's analysis in years to come. Conditions in the company town made a lasting impression on white workers of the Witwatersrand. Kimberley became a symbol of the fate that would overtake them if they allowed mine owners to substitute 'indentured compound labour' for a free working class. The Knights of Labour faded away. But its vision of a war on two fronts, against Monopoly Capital and Cheap Coloured Labour, guided the thinking of organized white labour for many decades to come.

There was no doubt about the preference of the owners for cheap and docile workers whose wages could be pegged for thirty years or more at an average rate of 3s. 5d. a day, while the average wage of white miners rose in a few years from 16s. 8d. to 22s. 6d. a shift. Africans paid 2s. a month in 'pass' and hospital fees, received free quarters and medical care, and spent about 1s. 2d. a day on basic foodstuffs, mostly mealies, beans, bread and meat.[34] By stinting on food and other requirements, a diligent worker who escaped sickness and injury could save at most £20 in seven months, the time taken to complete six 'tickets' of thirty shifts each. But his diet was worse and his accommodation no better than that of the hard labour convicts who also worked on the mines. The death rate among underground workers was reduced to forty per thousand by 1914 as a result of improved sanitation and medical treatment. But the Tuberculosis Commission of that year reproached the management of De Beers' Premier mine near Pretoria for its 'extravagant waste of life and health'. And the rebuke applied more or less to all mines.[35]

The diamond mines never lacked labour. They attracted men by paying piece rates and a small reward to finders of high-priced stones. Ex-miners in the eastern Cape and Basutoland sent their sons to the compounds where they would be shielded

45

from Kimberley's vices. The ten-feet high fences cut them off
also from influences that might have made them politically
conscious. The labour movement ignored the men in the compounds. Both Coloured and African nationalists were committed
to the mine owners' party and never criticized the compound
system. It was 'as near perfection as it was possible to make it',
declared Tengo Jabavu, editor of *Imvo*, when he visited Kimberley in 1906 to collect money to found the South African
Native College of Fort Hare. Officials of De Beers guided him
through the compounds and donated £2,500 to his college.[36]
But he complained that Alfred Beit left nothing in his will for
the education of the African who had 'delved for diamonds to
make Mr Beit a Magnate'.[37] The criticism applied equally to
Rhodes, J. B. Robinson, Barney Barnato and other millionaires
who made their fortunes out of the land and labour of Coloured
and African.

Financiers and mine managers were out to develop mines and
not the miner. They adopted a *laissez faire* attitude, neglected
his physical needs, made no attempt to teach him anything – the
rudiments of mining, safety measures, the alphabet, or the
elements of his new society – and used crude punishments to
enforce required standards of discipline. Compound life consequently tended to perpetuate tribal superstitions and antagonisms. Kimberley's Coloured and African residents formed mutual
benefit and improvement societies in the eighties, but the men
in the compounds never combined. Tribalism had a divisive
effect also on other large groups of peasant workers. Fifty-six
Zulu and Fengu were killed on Old Year's Day 1883 in a 'faction
fight' among railway construction workers at De Aar. The
fighting, wrote Theal, doyen of South African historians, seemed
to the men 'a not very objectionable mode of celebrating a
holiday'.[38] His jocularity typified the colonial attitude to the
new working class, as less of a threat than the Zulu impis
(regiments) who cut down 800 British soldiers and as many
African levies at Isandhlwana in 1879. Indeed, another generation passed before African workers developed an outlook and
organization to cope with the effects of industrialism. Radical
whites and educated Africans blazed the trail.

The first African writers, journalists, ministers, teachers, clerks and politicians were sons or grandsons of tribalists and products of mission schools, among whom the Rev. Tiyo Soga (1829–71) was an early and outstanding representative. His father, a councillor of Gaika, had eight wives and thirty-nine children, and was killed in the war of 1877–8 against Gcaleka and Ngqika clans. Tiyo studied at the Lovedale Missionary Institution and the Free Church seminary in Glasgow, graduated at the age of twenty-seven in theology at Glasgow university, and was admitted to the ministry of the United Presbyterian Church – the first African from the south to take a degree and become an ordained minister. He married Janet Burnside, a Scot, and returned with her in 1857 to South Africa, where he preached, raised a distinguished family, translated *The Pilgrim's Progress* into Xhosa, composed hymns and assisted in a revision of the Xhosa Bible.[39] Described in obituary notices as 'a perfect gentleman', a 'loyal subject of the Queen' and a 'noble missionary of the Cross', he died at the early age of forty-two on the eve of great changes that brought about many schisms in mission churches between white and African leaders.

The missionary was a bearer of British culture as well as a teacher of the gospel. In both capacities he actively opposed traditional institutions such as chieftainship, the ancestor cult, the practice of magic, polygyny and bridewealth, that kept tribesmen away from the church.[40] And he sided with the colonists in their armed struggle to integrate independent states in the colonial society under British rule. The loyalties of missionary-trained Africans, on the other hand, were divided between their people and the church, to which they owed their religion, education and livelihood. By the seventies, however, educated Africans, who found employment in government, commercial, legal and printing establishments, could free themselves of dependence on the missionary and become religious or political leaders in their own right. This development received a big impetus from the aggressive policy of expansion that Britain adopted after the gold and diamond discoveries.

Reversing her policy of disengagement, Britain annexed

Basutoland in 1868 and Griqualand West in 1871. Lord Carnarvon, the secretary of state for colonies in 1874–8, decided to link colonies and republics in a federation. He met with opposition and resorted to force. Britain annexed the South African Republic in 1877 and then, to appease the burghers, made war with the aid of Swazi warriors on the Pedi under Sekukuni. The war against Cetshwayo's Zulu kingdom followed in 1879. Natal and Transvaal colonists coveted the land, and Zulu power stood in the way of federation. The annexation of the Transkei began in the same year, after a long and bloody war. Basutoland was the next victim. Acting under the Peace Preservation Act of 1878, the Sprigg ministry at the Cape ordered Africans everywhere to hand in their rifles, legitimately bought and often used to assist the British against independent tribes. The Sotho refused and turned their rifles against the Cape police in 1880. The 'war of disarmament' spread to Griqualand East, while the Transvaal republicans rose in rebellion, defeated the British at Majuba, and regained independence in 1881. Attempts at confederation were abandoned, but only after arousing passions in Afrikaners and Africans that never died away.

Educated or unlettered, Christian or pagan, all Africans were subject in some degree to the 'disarmament' act, the 'cattle removal' act of 1870, the 'vagrancy' act of 1879, pass laws, prohibition of liquor, and other measures that discriminated against their race. There was great resentment and call for protest. But the hundred years of desperate struggle on the frontier had ended in defeat. The chiefs, councillors and district heads who led the people in wars of independence were dead, exiled, deposed or absorbed as minor officials in the colonial bureaucracy. The struggle for liberation would from then on be fought within the common society by men able to wield the colonist's own weapons of education, propaganda, political organization and the vote. Leadership passed to the teachers, ministers and others like them in the eastern Cape who formed the Native Teachers' Association in 1875, the Native Education Association in 1880, the South African Aborigines' Association (Imbumba Yama Afrika) in 1882, and the Native Electoral Association in 1884.[41] Though largely confined to Xhosa-speaking people, they were non-tribal in composition and reflected the growth of an African consciousness.

John Tengo Jabavu (1859–1921), a prime mover in the formation of the Native Electoral Association, became the acknowledged leader of progressive Africans in the Cape for the next thirty years. A certificated teacher and lay preacher during his teens, he was appointed editor in 1881 of the Lovedale mission journal *Isigidimi Sama Xosa* (Xhosa Express) – the forerunner of the *Christian Express* and the present *South African Outlook* – and matriculated in 1883, the second African to do so. His political career started in 1884, when he and the Association mobilized the ninety African voters in the constituency of Victoria East behind James Rose Innes, a liberal of the old school and future chief justice. Innes won the election against six other candidates with the aid of the African voters, who plumped for him, though he was an utter stranger, because 'he favoured a fair and sympathetic policy towards the Bantu people'.[42] Jabavu left the *Isigidimi* after the election to found, with financial backing from a brother of Rose Innes and other liberals, the first independent African newspaper, *Imvo Zabantsundu* (African Opinion).

Imvo made its first notable impact with a campaign against the Sprigg government's Parliamentary Registration Act of 1887, which disfranchised thousands of Africans in the eastern Cape. Rhodes, then in opposition and angling for the Afrikaner Bond's support, wanted to go the whole way. Africans, he argued, were a subject race and should have no vote at all, as in Natal. There could be no union of South Africa unless the Cape met its neighbours on the issue of African rights. Writing in *Imvo*'s editorial columns, Jabavu claimed that the bill, in addition to being 'the severest blow' yet aimed at his people, would 'establish the ascendancy of the Dutch in the colony for ever' by disfranchising the English party's 'devoted allies'. While the Afrikaner press deplored 'the impudence of the Kafir', Sprigg told the House that *Imvo* was 'libellous and seditious'. Yet Jabavu had leaned over backwards to show that he was no radical. 'We not only preach loyalty,' he wrote, 'but we preach subordination to superiors.' The 'Kafir', he maintained, was no leveller or democrat; he believed in caste and the principle that 'some are born to rule and others to be ruled'.[43]

A petition to the Queen, protest meetings, a conference and talk of a deputation to England followed the passing of the act. Many such appeals were to be made before Africans learned the futility of looking for salvation to Victoria or her successors. Rhodes drove the constitutional lesson home in 1892 by sponsoring the Franchise and Ballot Act which raised the franchise qualifications to the disadvantage of Africans, Coloured and poor whites. It was colour-class legislation and acceptable to all sides of the House including the liberals – Rose Innes, then attorney-general in Rhodes' cabinet, John X. Merriman and J. W. Sauer – who had taken the place of Porter and Solomon as champions of coloured rights. But they opposed Rhodes in 1893 when he moved the abolition of plural voting in the Cape division, where alone each elector had four votes, to forestall the candidature of H. N. Effendi, representative of the Moslem Association. Coloured voters were expected to plump for him; and parliament insisted on remaining exclusively white. W. P. Schreiner, a famous liberal in later years, who had replaced Innes as attorney-general, defended the measure. The return of a Coloured member, he argued, might precipitate constitutional changes prejudicial to Africans. Their interests, he thought, would be best secured if they were represented in parliament by white men nominated by government.[44]

Ever willing to sacrifice African interests for an alliance with Afrikaners, Rhodes was as ready to sacrifice the alliance to build an empire. He plotted against Kruger's republic and organized the coup that ended in the fiasco of Jameson's Raid in 1896. It changed the course of politics, wrote Jabavu, by substituting 'the Dutch Question for the Native Question'.[45] Liberals who condemned the raid broke with Rhodes to join forces with the Afrikaner Bond in opposition to the pro-imperialist Progressive party formed in 1897. Schreiner, the Bond's parliamentary leader, took over the premiership in 1898 and included Merriman and Sauer in his ministry. Jabavu, who had stood with Sauer on the same platform for twenty years, supported the government and came under heavy fire from the English press.

Alfred Palmer, editor and publisher of the *South African Review*, wrote in September 1899, on the eve of Britain's war against the republics, that Jabavu 'has much to answer for'. He had helped the Bond into a position where it could manufacture 'whips for dusky backs', by turning African voters against the Englishman, who gave them the best wages and fairest treatment, compared with the 'dog's life' they led under 'Boer employment'. Rhodes, and not any Bond supervisor, was their proper leader.[46] In 1897 Rhodes promised 'equal rights for every white man south of the Zambesi'. Three years later, during the war fought, so the imperial government claimed, to enfranchise all British subjects and secure the full liberty of all in South Africa, Rhodes declared a policy of equal rights for every civilized man south of the Zambesi.[47] African and Coloured national movements were to take shape a few years later in the course of an unsuccessful struggle to hold Britain to her pledge.

3 Gold Miners and Imperialist War

Barnato, Beit, Joel, Rhodes, Robinson, Rudd and Wernher used the fortunes they had made out of diamonds to buy gold-bearing rock and to finance mining operations on the Witwatersrand. They duplicated the pattern of labour organization that had served them so well at Kimberley. Fifty-three companies employed 3,400 whites and ten times as many Africans in 1892 on outcrop claims along the Reef.[1] The whites supervised and did the skilled work. African peasant workers, who were housed and fed in compounds, usually worked for three or four months at a stretch before returning to their villages. The migratory labour system tended to be inefficient and wasteful. The large turnover of workers involved high recruiting and supervisory costs. Every new batch of peasants had to learn mining techniques and undergo the painful process of adapting themselves to a strange environment. Standards of housing and diet were subordinated to the aim of extracting the greatest output at the lowest cost. Bad living and working conditions made for high morbidity and mortality rates, and discouraged men from coming to the mines. But the owners found compensating advantages in labour-intensive methods of production; and turned down proposals to settle Africans with their families in villages along the Rand.[2]

The white miner, a director of labour rather than a labourer, owed his supervisory role to the constant flow of greenhorns down the shaft. Since his job was a function of their inexperience, he was dispensable to the extent that they learned the skills of their trade. His dependence on the ignorance of the men under his supervision and his estrangement from them made him feel insecure. He feared competition, resented the African's ability to learn by doing, and with Kimberley's example in mind suspected the mine owners' intentions.

It was a fear of being swamped by fellow countrymen, however, that stimulated men from Cornwall, Lancashire and Scotland to found the Witwatersrand Mine Employees' and Mechanics' Union on 20 August 1892. Some 2,000 men and women, meeting in Johannesburg's Market Square, protested 'against the attempt of the Chamber of Mines to flood these fields with labour by means of cheap emigration'.[3] J. Seddon, the union's first secretary, warned that the Chamber meant to cut wages by bringing out miners with wives clinging round their necks. He listed other grievances: unsafe and insanitary working conditions, excessive hours, low wages. But he would not advocate a quarrel with capital. 'If any wages had to be reduced,' he appealed, 'let the wages of black labour be cut down.'

The miners rejected class solidarity with Africans but collaborated with capitalists in establishing, also on 20 August 1892, the Transvaal National Union to campaign for equal franchise rights for all white men in the Transvaal. The union became an instrument of subversion, a tool of Rhodes, Jameson and the mine owners who conspired to bring about the abortive putsch of 1896. Trade unionists had withdrawn long before then from the movement, but their initial participation revealed a conflict of loyalties and interests. Thomas, the mine union's president, wanted the men to cooperate with the owners whose interests, he said, they shared in such matters as the franchise and the customs tariff.[4] Seddon, on the other hand, urged the men to have nothing to do with the National Union as long as the owners persisted in their 'dastardly attempt to deluge the country with miners'. It was arrogance on the part of the Chamber of Mines, he urged, to ask workmen to join the National Union while trying to 'crush them down with a worse tyranny than ever the Transvaal Government proposed to put upon the country'. They should be labour unionists first and national unionists afterwards.[5]

British workmen, most of whom were temporary residents, did not feel strongly about the franchise and suspected the aims of the employers. E. B. Rose, a member of the miners' executive and at one time president of the union, contended that 'the working man was politically the equal of the richest mine-owner' as long as neither had the vote. Indeed, he claimed, workers were better off without a vote unless it was accompanied by the secret ballot. For, as they had learned at Kimberley before the Cape introduced the ballot in 1894, employers exploited the worker's vote under the open system. The National Union's leaders rejected a proposal to include a demand for secret voting in the franchise campaign, whereupon the labour delegates withdrew from the union. They decided to put their claims directly to the government and did so, added Rose, 'invariably with the happiest results'.[6]

Mine owners on the Rand, though arrogant, commanded less power than in the Cape where Rhodes, as prime minister, was able to promote legislation in which he, as managing director of De Beers and uncrowned king of Rhodesia, had a personal pecuniary interest. Such a corrupting concentration of power could not occur in the Transvaal while Kruger and his burghers controlled the state. An alliance between white worker and Afrikaner farmer was conceivable in spite of language and cultural differences. Both groups were at loggerheads with the capitalists, who exploited the one and plotted against the other. Afrikaners recognized colour-castes and not classes. The constitution of 1856 guaranteed inequality between white and black in church or state; but Jack, if white, was as good as his master.

Mine owners rejected equality of classes and races. The *Star* sneered at the 'embryonic John Burnses and Tom Manns' who, ambitious for themselves, valued notoriety and power more than the success of the workers' cause.[7] Employers showed their teeth. Andrew Hope, the miners' new president, was told to quit the union or his job at the Simmer and Jack mine. He chose to be victimized. The union decided to offer 'passive resistance' to the company's 'tyrannical conduct' by employing Hope, at his former salary, to organize the union along the Rand.[8]

The republic was destitute of industrial laws and hardly able to protect workmen against exploitation and victimization. The government disliked intervening more than was necessary in the internal affairs of mining companies, President Kruger explained to Rose and J. T. Bain, the union's president and secretary, when they asked him in 1893 to open state-owned mines for the relief of white unemployment. He would not risk the public's money in dubious enterprises or stir up more noise in Johannesburg, from where enough noise was coming already, by competing with the owners.[9] The union was more successful when it agitated against the owners' gold theft bill. Like the Cape's Illicit Diamond Buying Act, on which it was modelled, the bill would authorize espionage and the surveillance of employees by company agents. Miners lobbied the Volksraad and demonstrated through Johannesburg streets in February 1893 behind a brass band and banners, with the slogan IGB THE SHADOW OF THE IDB – REMEMBER KIMBERLEY AND IDB. The Volksraad threw the bill out; and the miners celebrated their victory with another procession, headed by Africans carrying a coffin inscribed 'In memory of G. T. Bill.'[10]

The union claimed to have easy access to the government and a unique record of successes in obtaining legislative reforms, notably when the Volksraad adopted twenty of its twenty-three suggested amendments to the draft of the republic's first mining law of 1893.[11] It introduced long-overdue safety measures and the first explicit industrial colour bar. This stipulated that no African, Asian or Coloured might prepare charges, load drill holes or set fire to fuses.[12] The Volksraad adopted the clause by fifteen votes to eight. The minority pointed out that some 'Kaffirs' were well qualified to work with dynamite. It was unreasonable to pay a white man £5 a month for work that a black could do as well for £2. Anyone with a certificate of competency should be allowed to blast. But the state mining engineer contended that the only purpose of the clause was to prevent accidents. He, for one, had no confidence in a 'Kaffir'. Members who supported him said they would not give Africans 'so much right by law'; and read into the clause a general ban on their employment in the mines.[13]

The presence of competent Coloured and African blasters, some from the diamond fields, gave the lie to the contention that a dark skin denoted an inherent inability to acquire the skills and judgement of a skilled miner. Unqualified white men, on the other hand, were as great a danger in mining as unqualified Africans. The authorities soon found that a deficiency of pigment did not guarantee ability. The new mining code of 1896 omitted the racial test and substituted a blasting certificate. It became the hallmark of a professional miner. In terms of the regulation a trained, reliable African or Coloured could assist the certificated blaster and under his direct supervision prepare charges, load drill holes and light fuses.[14] It was evidently assumed that only white men would hold a certificate. This was not a statutory rule. But the code did introduce two new colour bars.

One regulation gave white men the sole right to work as banksmen and onsetters; another reserved the job of engine driver to certificated whites.[15] The miners' union had asked the government to prohibit the employment of unqualified men on engines that hauled cages and skips along the shafts. Not only untrained whites, explained Rose, 'but Coolies and even Kaffirs also' were thus employed, 'with the inevitable result that accidents to men employed in the mines through overwinding the cages or otherwise became more frequent.'[16] But mine owners and managers objected to the colour bar. They argued for a test based on competence and not colour. Many 'Cape Boys', they said, were as competent as white men and should not be barred, especially in small mines and prospecting shafts.[17] The government made a concession to the owners in 1897 by dropping the racial qualification for banksmen and onsetters, but retained it for engine drivers.[18] This was the only statutory colour bar left on the mines at the outbreak of war. White men did most of the skilled work, but there were areas in which Coloured and Africans could rise above the labourer's level.

Colour prejudice, Anglo-Afrikaner rivalries and a shortage of skilled men formed the matrix of the labour movement. As at Kimberley, racial and national cleavages distorted class alignments. Immigrant miners, mechanics, fitters, joiners and printers formed trade unions along traditional class lines. The Witwatersrand Mine Employees' and Mechanics' Union agitated for an eight-hour day, safety measures, and compensation for injuries; celebrated May Day; and defended trade unionism against the accusation that it was prone to violence and anarchy.[19] But the most class-conscious leaders, like the Scottish fitter J. T. Bain, also appealed to racial sentiment for protection against African miners and to republican sentiment for protection against mine owners. The immigrants were torn between class interests and national loyalties. Bain, whom some historians believe to have been South Africa's greatest trade union leader,[20] became a citizen of the republic and fought against the British army. Few men of his class followed the same course. The great majority withdrew or joined the British troops. None identified himself with his African co-worker.

Africans, observed the *Star*,[21] had no value in the community except as the equivalent of so much horsepower. They were both indispensable and expendable. Accidents or disease killed, maimed or incapacitated thousands every year. Employers recruited fresh supplies of sturdy young men from villages within a radius of 500 miles. They came by foot and rail, often riding for ten days in open cattle trucks, to be sent underground the day after their arrival and without training or time to recuperate. The resulting death rate was high. It averaged sixty-nine per thousand from diseases on Rand mines in 1902–3, when the first health statistics were compiled, and ranged from 118 to 164 in groups of men from tropical regions. Pneumonia, scurvy, meningitis, enteric, and dysentery caused the death of 3,762 Africans, or eighty-two per cent of all who died from disease on mines and works of the Witwatersrand in 1903. The death rate fell to thirty-three per thousand in 1906, after Milner's administration had enforced minimum standards of diet, housing, sanitation and hospital care.[22]

The high incidence of deaths and injuries – for which no compensation was paid – bad food, poor accommodation and unpleasant work gave the mines a bad name. 'We do not like our men to go to Johannesburg, because they go there to die,' chiefs from Basutoland told Sir Godfrey Lagden, the Transvaal's first secretary of native affairs under British rule.[23] The African's only defence was to abscond or change his job for a better. Mine owners sang the praises of free enterprise, attacked Kruger's monopolistic concessions over dynamite, liquor and railways, but did not scruple to monopolize recruiting or to restrict the worker's freedom of movement and contract. Managers petitioned in 1888 for a pass system, monthly labour contracts, penalties for deserters, and the registration of all Africans in the republic. The Chamber of Mines, formed in 1889, complained in its first annual report that competition for labourers was taking 'the regrettable form of overt attempts to bribe and seduce the employees of neighbouring companies to desert their employers'. A manager had 'standing alone, scarcely any other remedy than to raise his rates of pay'.

Rhodes, Lionel Phillips, George Farrar and other members of the Chamber took drastic action. They conspired in 1895 to bring about the downfall of the republic; agitated for a labour tax, pass laws, and a ban on liquor for Africans; and undertook to reduce wages from 2s. 3d. a shift to 1s. 6d. for skilled and 1s. for 'ordinary' workers.[24] Kruger's men disarmed Jameson's filibusters with hardly a struggle; and the Industrial Commission of 1896, keeping an eye on British allegations of 'Boer slavery', refused to recommend any measure 'equivalent to forced labour'.[25] But the Volksraad gave the owners their pass law, which they then said was ineffective to an extent that made it one of the grievances to be redressed by war. To monopolize recruiting and stop crimping, the owners formed the Native Labour Supply Association in 1896 and instructed compound managers to impose uniform conditions of service. Africans were to work not less than nine hours underground and ten on the surface, with a diet of not more than two and a half pounds of mealie-meal a day and two pounds of meat a week.[26]

The attack on wages followed in 1897. The African miner's average wage had reached a peak of 63s. 6d. for thirty completed shifts in 1895. It was reduced to 48s. 7d. on a scale ranging from 1s. 2d. to 2s. 6d. a shift. Anticipating disturbances and desertions, the Chamber asked the government to draft extra police to the mines and to instruct native commissioners 'to send forward as many natives as possible to these fields'.[27] White mining employees at Randfontein were notified at about the same time that their wages would be cut by ten shillings to 20s. a week. They struck work, and were evicted by police at Kruger's command from their company-owned houses. But the men won and went back to work at the old rates. W. H. Andrews, then employed as a fitter on Porges Randfontein, took part in the strike and claimed that it made two notable gains. It prevented a reduction of wages all along the Reef and 'exploded the fallacy that Oom Paul and his government were the friends of the workers'.[28] Whether fallacious or well founded, the belief persisted among white workers for many years after the fall of the republic.

Rhodes had engineered the armed invasion and abortive rising of December 1895 in his dual capacity of prime minister and company promoter. His fellow conspirators included members of his chartered company, leading mine owners, the Bechuanaland administration, and the British high commissioner at the Cape. Chamberlain, the responsible British minister, knew of Jameson's preparations but made no attempt to arrest the raid.[29] After it had failed, the imperial government took the initiative against the republic with the full backing and active support of a majority of mine owners. Britain drafted 10,000 troops to South Africa in August 1899 and moved troops to the Cape and Natal borders. Kruger presented an ultimatum on 9 October, demanding the withdrawal of the troops. Britain rejected the ultimatum, and the republican commandos invaded Natal and the Cape to begin a war that was to last for thirty-one months.

Britain annexed the Orange Free State on 24 May 1900, occupied Johannesburg on the 31st, and annexed the South African Republic on 1 September. Republican forces continued to fight a guerrilla war with great courage and skill against an army nine times their size. The war ended in the defeat of the republics and a peace treaty signed at Vereeniging on 31 May 1902. Britain spent £250 million on the war, put 448,000 troops in the field, lost 5,774 men killed in action and 16,168 who died of wounds and disease. Her armies burnt homes, devastated farms, and confined civilians in concentration camps. Nearly 4,000 republicans were killed in battle, 20,000 died in the camps, 31,000 were taken prisoner, and 20,000 surrendered at the end of the war.[30]

Africans and Coloured also died, unrecorded and unsung, in their masters' war. They served as scouts, spies, stretcher bearers, transport drivers, labourers and camp followers, but not as soldiers. Both British and Afrikaners respected the tradition that allowed men of colour to fight with colonists against tribal impis but never against whites. Peasants lost crops, livestock and huts, as troops, burning and pillaging, swept over the farms. Commandos, living on the land, seized the cattle of tribesmen without compensation. The tribesmen retaliated when the commandos withdrew by seizing the farmers' stock. There were inter-tribal clashes and occasional attacks on isolated bands of dispirited burghers.[31] Schreiner, the Cape premier, gloomily predicted an African rising if colonial forces fought outside the border. But Africans hoped that Britain would restore their land and made no concerted attempt to free themselves from white domination.

It was a white man's war also in terms of its objectives. Britain expressed great concern for the sufferings of Africans, Coloured and Indians in the Transvaal; and professed to be fighting for their freedom and to extend the rights and liberties of the common people. The promise of their liberation seemed to many Englishmen the war's single redeeming feature. But Africans, Coloured and Indians obtained no relief either at the peace settlement or in the post-war reconstruction. Acting under martial law, the British military authorities reduced the African miner's average wage in 1900 from 45s. to 30s. per thirty completed shifts and the standard wage to 1s. or 1s. 2d. a shift.[32] Africans lost in bargaining capacity under British rule, which turned the republics into colonies, restored authority to the defeated enemy, cultivated their loyalty, and consolidated an alliance with them on the basis of white supremacy.

The republicans fought to retain their independence. They were an oppressing as well as an oppressed nation, writes the Marxist historian Endre Sik; but as 'freedom fighters' their struggle, he claims, 'belongs to one of the most glorious chapters of the history of liberation wars'.[33] A similar opinion was current at the time in the international labour movement, not least in Britain, where the Independent Labour party's vigorous anti-war campaign made it for several years 'the most unpopular Party and its adherents and leaders the most bitterly abused persons in the country'.[34] Africans, Indians and Coloured probably agreed with Britain's Fabians that the war, if wholly unjust, was wholly necessary in the interests of civilization and the empire, whose control over such mighty forces as goldfields was to be preferred to control by small communities of frontiersmen.[35]

Rosa Luxemburg, another Marxist, saw in imperialism the political manifestation of a ravenous capitalist system which existed by invading, destroying and absorbing small peasant societies. Like the Fabians, but without their faith in Britain's civilizing mission, she claimed that the war was 'historically necessary' and the inevitable result of conflict between a 'patriarchal peasant economy' and 'modern large-scale capitalist exploitation'. Republican farmers and British capitalists, she argued, had the same aims. Both wished to subdue the African, expropriate his land, and force him into the labour market. The triumph of capitalism was a foregone conclusion in her opinion, and it was futile for the republics to resist their own absorption in a modern state.[36] The Fabian-Luxemburg thesis rested on an assumption that the republicans could not or would not change their ways to meet the needs of an industrial economy. Sir Alfred Milner, the British high commissioner, Joseph Chamberlain, the secretary of state for colonies, the British press and the mine owners used a similar argument to justify their war. But it was a false and dishonest argument.

Few agrarian societies were so richly endowed or well equipped as the Transvaal for an industrial revolution. The republic attracted educated and professional men from Holland or the Cape, and was beginning to produce its own specialists. Left to itself, it would have developed an efficient administration, a network of railways and roads, and adequate supplies of water and power. Far from being intractable, the burghers expanded production to provide foodstuffs for the Rand, built railways linking it to the ports, enacted an excellent mining code, kept order over unruly, rebellious fortune-hunters, repelled an armed imperialist invasion, and held the world's greatest military power at bay for more than two years. The mining companies under republican rule produced in 1897, after barely ten years of effective development, more than three million ounces of gold valued at £10½ million and distributed £2,817,000 in dividends. Foreign capital flowed without let or hindrance into the republic;

operated in absolute security even during the war, when Kruger set his face against a scorched-earth policy; made great profits and paid in taxes only five per cent of declared profits. A war was neither inevitable nor necessary to modernize the republic.

The mine owners claimed that the dynamite monopoly, high railway rates, an abuse of liquor by labourers, and a scarcity of African workmen cost the industry £2½ million a year, which would be saved if they could bend the government to their will. The wasted costs were exaggerated and the grievances trivial. They originated in government policy, not in a backward social structure, and were neither irremediable nor so grave as to warrant the use of force. British taxpayers should have queried the wisdom of a war that saddled them with a debt a hundred times as great as the alleged annual loss; a war fought to augment the profits of shareholders or, in J. A. Hobson's memorable phrase, 'to place a small international oligarchy of mine-owners and speculators in power at Pretoria'. His first-hand study of the Transvaal just before the war persuaded him that the mine owners had provoked it to obtain a government suited to their purpose. Their 'one all-important object' was 'to secure a full, cheap, regular, submissive supply of Kaffir and white labour'. This, concisely stated, he argued, was Britain's war aim.[37]

The judgement now seems harsh and intemperate, but it gains credibility from the content of the agitation preceding the war and from the policies that followed afterwards. If motives are to be judged by consequences, the mine owners did plot to instal a government able to tap labour resources in Africa and Asia that the republic neither commanded nor wished to utilize. Britain did not, however, make war only to benefit shareholders. South African historians have shown that Chamberlain and Milner, who forced war on the republics, had in mind broad imperial interests which were being threatened by the shift in the balance of power.[38] Gold mining was changing the Transvaal into Africa's most advanced economic region. It was likely to become the centre of a vigorous Afrikaner nationalism, radiating to the south, drawing to it the loyalties of Afrikaners throughout the sub-continent, and challenging Britain's presence in all South Africa. Chamberlain and Milner decided to prevent the growth of a rival imperialism. They demanded franchise reforms that would give British subjects the upper hand in the republic, asserted the rights of a suzerain, and when these stratagems failed, provoked the war.

This is a political interpretation. It comes from scholars who reject economic determinism as being too simple and crude an explanation of political events. The interpretation serves as far as it goes, but it does not account for all the facts. The mine owners who plotted against the republic in 1895 cannot be exonerated from blame for the war of 1899. It is of the nature of capitalists to make profits and of governments to make war. Neither will readily admit to responsibility for the other. Yet economic and political motives have seldom blended so nakedly as in the capitalists and politicians who conspired in the last decade of the century to bring about the downfall of the Transvaal. The South African war of 1899–1902 stands as a classic example of imperialist aggression prompted by capitalist greed.

Britain might have atoned for her predatory aims if she had fulfilled her pledge to free Africans, Coloured and Asians from racial tyranny. Milner told a Coloured deputation in January 1901 that he could not accept their offer to take up arms against the republican forces; but promised to secure fair treatment for all persons of colour in the Transvaal. He 'thoroughly agreed that it was not race or colour, but civilization which was the test of a man's capacity for political rights'.[39] Two months later, in the first round of peace talks at Middelburg, Kitchener laid the basis for a betrayal of African rights. He told Louis Botha that if the burghers surrendered, they would be allowed to keep their rifles under licence – 'to protect them', in Botha's words, 'from natives'. Secondly, the 'Kaffir question' would be solved by not giving franchise rights to 'Kaffirs' until after the introduction of representative government.[40]

The imperial government reacted with a firm declaration of principle. Chamberlain's cable of 6 March 1901 stated: 'We cannot consent to purchase peace by leaving the coloured population in the position in which they stood before the war.' He instructed Milner to modify Kitchener's peace proposals by stipulating that the franchise, if given after the grant of representative government, 'will be so limited as to secure the just predominance of the white race, but the legal position of the Kaffirs will be similar to that which they hold in the Cape Colony'.[41] Milner watered down the guarantee by substituting 'coloured persons' for 'Kaffirs' in the text of his letter to Kitchener; but it was clearly Britain's intention at that stage to insist on a non-racial franchise.

The republicans rejected the peace terms for reasons other than the franchise. Fighting a stubborn guerrilla war, they wore the British down and sapped their will to continue a struggle that seemed pointless and wasteful after the seizure of the gold mines. On 31 May 1902 Britain agreed at Vereeniging to a peace settlement that would put Afrikaners back in power, give them £3 million to restore the ravaged farms, and keep Africans, Coloured and Indians in subjection.

It was Smuts, on behalf of the vanquished, who drafted the decisive clause in the treaty. Article 8 stipulated: 'The question of granting the franchise to natives will not be decided until after the introduction of self-government.'[42] The treaty made no mention of Coloured rights and left the issue of the 'native' franchise to be settled after the introduction of responsible government, and not of representative government as Chamberlain had insisted. By agreeing to these terms, Britain was pledged to allow a white oligarchy to decide whether or not to give the vote to the great majority of the population in the conquered territories. She had tacitly surrendered her moral responsibilities and abandoned her self-assumed role as the protector of Africans and Coloured.

Chamberlain told Generals Botha, de Wet and de la Rey in London on 5 September 1902 that there was 'no parallel in history for conditions so generous granted by a victorious belligerent to its opponents'.[43] Others since then have praised the Vereeniging treaty as a magnanimous gesture, an act of contrition, a bold bid for Anglo-Afrikaner conciliation and a stroke of genius in the best English tradition.[44] Afrikaners and Africans disputed this verdict, the former because an unjust war had deprived them of independence, the latter because an unjust peace had entrenched white supremacy.

Referring to the peace treaty, Tengo Jabavu wrote in October

1902 that, since 'the English, the Dutch and the Native elements' had a right to be in the country, 'each should be accorded by the others the common rights of citizenship'.[45] Dr Abdurahman, the outstanding Coloured spokesman in the first quarter of the century, warned that 'in the settlement after the war and in the endeavour to conciliate the two white races the material welfare of the blacks might suffer'. His people wanted to put such 'morbid' fears aside. 'Did not our Gracious King promise protection to the Natives? Are we not loyal? Is not the British Flag synonymous with justice and freedom?' So they reasoned. 'But, alas! our forebodings were only too true.'[46]

Milner concentrated after the war on restoring the mines to full working capacity and on settling British immigrants in rural areas to offset the Afrikaner's ascendancy. Republican techniques of white domination were improved and expanded for the purpose. Africans in the Transvaal, reported lieutenant governor Sir Arthur Lawley, had hoped that 'the old position of master and servant would be altered'. But his officials were making every effort 'to maintain the relative position of the races as it existed in past days'.[47] The effort included a mass of colour bar laws, many of them churned out before elected members sat in the legislative council. Peasants were forced to give up their arms and return cattle seized during the war, but they never recovered their own stock seized by British troops and republican commandos. Every adult African male was required to pay a labour tax of two pounds, with another two pounds for the second and each additional wife of a polygynist. The administration reshaped the laws on passes, labour contracts and liquor prohibition; authorized municipalities to segregate Africans in locations; hired out African convicts to mining companies; and prohibited extra-marital intercourse between a white woman and any African, Asian or Coloured.[48] Not surprisingly, some Africans wished 'to call back the days of the Republic', since they had received better treatment and wages 'when the Boers dominated'.[49]

Britain had seven years of supreme authority in which to give the African and Coloured population of the ex-republics a new deal. Military rule was succeeded soon after the end of the war by crown colony government under a lieutenant governor assisted by two councils of civil servants. A minority of un-official white members were appointed in May 1903 to the Transvaal's legislative council. Two years later it acquired a majority of elected members for whom only white men could vote because, the Colonial Office declared, Britain was bound by the treaty of 1902 to deny representation to her coloured subjects.[50] Civil servants dominated the executive council throughout this period, however, while bills discriminating against persons not of European descent had to be reserved for attention by the secretary of state. That safeguard appeared also in the Transvaal's constitution of 6 December 1906, which set up a parliament based on an exclusively white male adult suffrage. Until then the officials had power enough to do away with legal discrimination and extend to all races the 'equal laws, equal liberty' that Chamberlain had promised in 1900 for the whole of South Africa.[51] But Milner's team of college graduates and colonial officials took over the racial ideologies as well as the offices of their republican predecessors at Pretoria and Bloemfontein.

The terms of the peace treaty, Milner's racism and the colour bar constitutions alerted Africans and Coloured to the menace of unbridled white power. They protested vigorously and on a scale that signified the presence of a large, well-informed opinion against discrimination. Africans in the Orange River Colony petitioned Britain in 1902 for political rights and the removal of colour bars; and received only windy assurances of goodwill.[52] A 'monster' petition signed by 33,000 Transvaal Africans was addressed to the king in 1905. They asked that 'their interests should be safeguarded in the granting of the constitution to the New Colonies'.[53] Coloured residents of the Transvaal made similar appeals.[54] 'As matters stand there is no help for it,' wrote Jabavu, 'but for the Natives to combine with the Coloured people and make their representations to the ruling authorities in the Transvaal, but better still at Downing Street.'[55]

The African Political Organization sent Dr Abdurahman and P. J. Daniels to England in 1906 to petition the government for a non-racial franchise in the north. Jabavu regretted that Africans, 'not being properly organized', were not represented by 'a pure-blooded Native or two'; and took comfort in the thought that the deputies spoke for them as well as for the Coloured.[56] Abdurahman urged Elgin to stipulate that Britain would extend the franchise to all races if the new colonies failed to do so within a year of obtaining self-government. The Colonial Office replied to this and all other such appeals that article 8 of the peace treaty bound Britain to limit the vote to whites and to deny representation to her coloured subjects.[57] This was a legal quibble, as Abdurahman was quick to point out. Article 8 referred only to 'natives'. It did not exclude Coloured and Asians from the projected franchise or prevent Britain from enfranchising Africans under the APO's formula. These possibilities were never explored, however, nor was any attempt made to discuss a non-racial franchise on the grounds of merit. The British government, the colonial administration, white immigrants and settlers of all classes and shades of opinion assumed as a matter of course that only white men should exercise the vote in the north.

The Transvaal Municipalities Election Ordinance of 1903 set the precedent for an all-white franchise. Lionel Curtis, the town clerk of Johannesburg and one of Milner's team of graduates from New College, Oxford, prepared the draft on which the ordinance was based. His franchise, he claimed, was so liberal 'as to include almost every white British subject, male or female'.[58] But his liberalism did not extend to persons of colour. Since article 8 of the Vereeniging treaty did not refer to local government, it could be argued that Britain was free to include them in the municipal vote. Indeed, Milner wanted to extend this vote to aliens and also to coloured British subjects who could pass an education test. Curtis objected, however, to the coloured franchise, and so did the Johannesburg municipal council, which consisted wholly of nominated white members. The official majority in the legislative council could have carried the government's proposal, but the administration preferred to yield without a struggle.

Lawley saw no reason for imposing a franchise 'in opposition to the most deep-rooted sentiments of the white population'. He found it impossible to enforce 'a principle repudiated no less by the British inhabitants than by the Dutch'. His government would not grant aliens a privilege denied to coloured British subjects, and so excluded both, though a strong body of white opinion favoured the franchise for white aliens.[59] Though patently discriminatory, the ordinance was never formally presented to the Colonial Office for approval under the reservation clause. The officials in Whitehall were aware of the facts, but chose to ignore the constitutional safeguard.[60] Yet Britain had fought the war ostensibly to enfranchise her subjects who were aliens in the republic. Her refusal to extend the vote to her coloured subjects or to aliens made a mockery of her pretensions to a high standard of political morality. She tried to justify the chicanery by pleading respect for the 'people's will', and then violated democracy by ignoring the legitimate claims of the majority.

The Colonial Office turned a blind eye on measures taken to 'keep the Kaffir in his place'. It could not similarly ignore attacks on Indians. They had a doughty champion in Mohandas Gandhi, influential friends in London, and the backing of the government in India. Britain had taken up cudgels on their behalf before the war in a dispute with the republic over the terms of Law 3 of 1885. It excluded Asians from citizenship, denied them the right to reside or own land outside segregated locations, and provided for their registration. Britain eventually agreed to the principle of residential segregation on alleged sanitary grounds, but objected to an order prohibiting Indians from trading outside the segregated areas or bazaars. The dispute went to arbitration in 1895. Negotiations followed. The republic offered to compromise if the Coloured were included in the segregation law. Milner replied that he 'could not, to help one class of British subjects, give away the rights of another class'.[61] He did just that after the war, however, in order to appease a handful of British shopkeepers.

The Orange Free State had barred Asians from settling or trading in the republic. In terms of the Pretoria Convention of 1881, the Transvaal was bound to allow 'any person other than a native' to reside and trade within its borders. For this reason, and because they developed trade with farming communities,

Kruger's government did not restrict the entry of Indians or segregate them rigorously. Milner's officials did both. They introduced a vexatious system of permits and gave notice, first in April 1902 and again a year later, of their intention to enforce the law of 1885, with exemptions for educated, wealthy Indians and for those who had traded outside the bazaars before the war. Chamberlain protested that he could not justify a continuation of the republic's discrimination, but Milner endorsed his executive's action. He did this to satisfy the White League, an organization of shopkeepers and racists, and to win support for his policy of importing indentured Asian workers. Then, too, he and his officials believed in white supremacy dogmas. Lawley made this clear in his memorandum of 13 April 1904 on the need for new legislation to fetter Indian trade and immigration.[62]

He argued, and Milner agreed, that the most momentous issue of the age was probably the struggle between East and West for the temperate zone. To honour past pledges of equality would be a greater crime than to break them, if they had the effect of handing South Africa over to an Asian people. The first duty of British statesmen was to find homes for the white race. Whites would always remain supreme in the public services, professions and farming. White artisans and mechanics could be relied upon to hold their own in the skilled trades by combining. But Indian traders and small cultivators drove white men out of the retail trade and market gardening. Guided by an instinct of self-preservation, the Transvaal republic had prohibited Indians from owning land. The same instinct was moving the commercial community to protest against Indian traders.[63]

Lord Selborne, successor to Milner, also saw no way of reconciling Asian and European claims. South Africa would either remain a 'white man's country', based on a Negro proletariat, or be peopled by natives and Asians under European control. Britain had a duty when the Transvaal was a foreign state to protect her Indian subjects, even to the extent of making their grievances a cause of war. But the government would betray a trust, no less sacred, to the whites if it repealed the republic's anti-Asian law.[64]

Nearly 1,100 Indians had served in Gandhi's Ambulance Corps

with British troops against the republics. Yet Britain preferred to betray her allies. The specific reasons given for anti-Asian legislation were as flimsy and contradictory as the Lawley-Selborne ideology. Indians were said to have insanitary habits and live in squalor. So did many poor whites in the slums of Fordsburg and Vrededorp, but they were never segregated by law. Asian immigration was said to threaten white supremacy. Yet Lawley, Milner and the mine owners imported 43,000 Chinese for the mines against protests from South Africans of all races. On the other hand, Indians were accused of out-trading whites and using their 'immense wealth', as Lawley described it, to buy out the 'credulous' and 'ignorant Dutch farmer'. Summarizing white prejudices, Gandhi noted that 'the very qualities of Indians count for defects in South Africa'. They were disliked 'for their simplicity, patience, perseverance, frugality and other-worldliness'.[65]

With British supremacy firmly entrenched and closer union in the offing, a wave of reaction swept through the Cape from the north. In 1903 the East London municipality gave notice that 'Natives and Asiatics shall not be allowed or authorized to congregate, stand or walk upon any pavement' in any principal street or square. In 1904 parliament, reacting to an outbreak of bubonic plague, passed the Native Locations Act, providing for the segregation of urban Africans. The Immigration Act of 1906 closed the Cape to Asian men over sixteen years of age from abroad and severely restricted their entry from other parts of South Africa.

In the same year Natal brutally suppressed a small Zulu revolt against the £1 poll tax, executed twelve Zulu convicted of killing two members of a tax-enforcing squad, and deployed 10,000 armed whites and some 6,000 African troops against Bambatha, the chief of a small Lala tribe in Greytown. This was the last upsurge of Zulu military power. The revolt originated in the poll tax, economic distress caused by cattle and crop diseases, and above all in the alienation of over two million acres of good farmland, representing five-twelfths of the Zulu country, to white sugar planters in 1904.[66] Gandhi, thinking 'I must do my bit in the war' left the Transvaal to join the army with a small Indian stretcher-bearer corps; and was there converted to the ideal of life-long celibacy and poverty in the service of humanity.[67]

He was 'doing his bit' when the Transvaal government introduced the 'Black Ordinance' of 1906, making fingerprint-registration compulsory for all Asians of eight years or upwards. Gandhi saw 'nothing in it except hatred of Indians' and their 'absolute ruin'. A mass meeting held in Johannesburg on 11 September took an oath to resist registration. Gandhi and H. O. Ali, a Coloured Muslim, were deputed to put the Indian case before the government in Whitehall. They interviewed Lord Elgin, the secretary of state, and told him: 'Our lot is today infinitely worse than under the Boer regime.'[68] He responded by withholding assent to the 'Black Ordinance', not out of generosity to a persecuted minority, but to evade the issue until the grant of self-government to the Transvaal. This followed in a few days. The Transvaal's new constitution was promulgated on 6 December 1906. An all-white electorate went to the polls on 20 February 1907. Botha's Het Volk party took office and promptly, on 21 March, introduced a replica of the rejected ordinance. It was passed by the unanimous vote of both houses at a single sitting.

The Asiatic Law Amendment Act laid the basis of a pass system such as that applied to Africans. Every Asian male had to register himself and produce on demand a thumb-printed certificate of identity. Unregistered persons and prohibited immigrants could be deported without a right of appeal. The bill went to Elgin under the clause reserving discriminatory laws. He recorded polite disapproval and allowed the bill to stand because, he said, his government felt 'they would not be justified in offering resistance to the general will of the Colony clearly expressed by its first elected representatives'.[69] In other words, Britain had transferred power to a racial oligarchy and turned her back on the voteless majority. The Transvaal government, now responsible only to white settlers, bore down on Indians with new discriminations; used an immigration act to keep them out of the colony; and prohibited them from trading or occupying land in proclaimed goldfields.[70] Led by Gandhi the Indians began the first sustained struggle of a persecuted racial community against unjust laws.

They refused to register, picketed the permit offices, and went to jail in batches. Smuts, the responsible minister, offered to repeal the Asiatic Law Amendment Act if a majority of Indians undertook to register voluntarily. Gandhi agreed to the compromise and was released with other Satyagrahi prisoners. They did register, but the act was not repealed. Instead, Smuts took new measures to keep Indians out of the Transvaal. Certificates were burnt ceremoniously at a large gathering on 16 August 1908. At about this time Satyagrahis from Natal started crossing the border illegally to court imprisonment and deportation. Indians overcrowded the jails. Smuts hit back by deporting resisters to India, but this the courts declared to be illegal. Some of Smuts's political principles, observed Gandhi, were 'not quite immoral'; though there was room in them 'for cunning and on occasion for perversion of truth'.[71] Gandhi appealed once more to the imperial government when he led another deputation to England in 1909 to protest against the colour bar in the Act of Union. His mission met with no more success than in 1906.

Gandhi came to South Africa in 1893 to advise on a lawsuit. He delayed his departure to lead a campaign against a bill to disfranchise Natal's Indians, founded the Natal Indian Congress in 1894, and remained for twenty years, during which he worked out his technique of Satyagraha: 'non-violent struggle born of Truth and Love'. It was a technique suited to the conditions of a small voteless community, numerically weak and temperamentally disinclined to use physical force. It would become a powerful political instrument in India, but it failed in South Africa because it never acquired a mass base. Provincial barriers, cultural differences, inequalities of wealth and status, and an uneven rate of political development inhibited the growth of a broad non-racial front against white domination. Gandhi and his fellow Indians saw in the African only an innocent tribal peasant who was being corrupted by civilization. They never thought of joining with Africans and Coloured in a common struggle. The Indians fought their battles in isolation and won only moral victories.

4 White Labour Policies

Immigrant workmen of the early twentieth century were not pioneers, frontiersmen or revolutionaries. The colonial society was not so different from their own as to cause a sense of alienation. They fitted into the order of things as they found it and did what they could to better their conditions. They combined in ways familiar to them in their home countries, pressed their claims on governments and employers, and took political action to shape legislation affecting their terms of employment. The means they used varied according to the state of the labour market, the composition of the working classes, and the attitude of their masters. These factors, rather than differences in origin or outlook, accounted for the contrasting policies adopted by the labour movement in the Cape and in the northern colonies.

The Cape's distinctive features were a non-racial franchise, an old tradition of legal identity between white and Coloured, a high proportion of Coloured artisans and factory workers, and the small size of the African population in the western districts. White and Coloured working people lived in the same neighbourhood, worked on the same jobs, inter-married occasionally and cohabited more frequently, and had much the same standard of living. The elements of an integrated society existed. Labour leaders and trade unionists accepted the position, canvassed Coloured voters and organized Coloured wage earners. When George Woollends formed a socialist party in 1904, he cited instances of hospitality extended to whites by Coloured families, and demanded justice for all working men, whether Dutch, Coloured, Malay or British-born. They should rid their minds of false ideas about colour distinctions, he urged, and unite on equal terms for socialism.[1]

Not all trade unionists at the Cape were as tolerant. A small, tight society of about 150 stonemasons refused to admit any Coloured and monopolized their trade on public buildings. Robert Stuart (1870–1950), the union's secretary, came to Cape Town from his native city of Aberdeen in 1901, took part in forming the Social Democratic Federation (SDF) in 1902, and became a leading organizer of white and Coloured unions. But he never attempted to break down the colour bar in his own trade. Other early unions in the south were less successful in maintaining a colour bar. The plasterers barred 'Coloured labour' from membership in 1901 and prohibited any member from working on the same scaffold 'with a coloured man, or a Malay, under pain of a fine'. F. Z. J. Peregrino (1853–1919, b. Accra), the West African editor and publisher of the *South African Spectator*, remarked scathingly that these 'inconsiderate and unreasonable white men' wished to perpetuate race prejudice, debase the Coloured artisan, and deny him the right to work at his trade. 'The Coloured Mechanic, Malay, black or Africander should make a common cause, and Organize, Organize, Organize.'[2] Bricklayers also adopted a colour bar in 1904. The Coloured artisans then formed their own union and undercut the white man's wage of 12s. or 14s. a day. Employers hired the cheaper man, and the white workers negotiated with the Coloured for a single union of bricklayers and plasterers.

Objections to an open, non-racial union came at times from the Coloured, as in Cape Town's bespoke tailoring trade. White journeymen, most of whom were Jewish, organized a society in 1905. It tried hard but without success to enrol the large number of Muslims in the trade. Working seventy or eighty hours a week, the Muslims cut and stitched in their homes, usually in a room where the family ate and slept, and earned on an average £3 10s. a week for piece work.[3] The union won its first victory in a test case, which decided that master tailors should pay for alterations to an ill-fitting suit. This, the union said, was tangible proof of its ability to fight also the battles of the Muslims, and should gain their confidence. The union then made an agreement with one big firm for a fifty-hour working week, a minimum wage of £4 4s. for a journeyman, and £2 for a woman. Even this victory did not convince the Muslims. They adhered to their traditional work patterns and preferred to deal directly with shopkeepers and master tailors.[4]

Manufacturers of leather goods, confectionery, cigarettes and furniture had a free hand in the absence of factory or wage legislation. They employed juveniles and adults in badly ventilated shops, without proper toilet facilities or safeguards against injury. Employers giving evidence in 1906 before a select committee on a factory bill admitted to taking on boys and girls aged twelve years and upwards at a wage of 1s. 8d. to 2s. 6d. a week. Employees worked fifty-two hours a week and, where this was feasible, took work to be completed at home. African labourers were paid 3s. 6d. or 4s. a week; Coloured men might get 1s. more for the same kind of work. One tobacco firm paid girls of fourteen and sixteen years a weekly wage of 6s. 6d. to 8s. and women cutters 15s. to 35s. Another firm employing more than 300 white girls paid them an average wage of 11s. 3d. a week, and 16s. 7d. for packers. Skilled Coloured men in a food factory received an average of £3 a week, and white skilled immigrants £4 10s. or £5 a week. Wages in the leather trade ranged from £2 to £3 a week. Most of the higher-paid men were whites, but they overlapped with Coloured in all skilled and semi-skilled grades.

The two wings of the movement worked closely together in organizing May Day celebrations, soup kitchens for the unemployed, legal defence for Needham and Lewinson, two SDF members arrested in August 1906 for 'incendiary speeches', and elections. The societies of masons, printers, engineers and cigar makers hired the Federation's hall for meetings. When the cigarette makers struck work in June for higher wages, they turned the hall into a factory and set up a 'Lock Out Cooperative'. The tailors complained that a member of the SDF was cutting prices, whereupon it decided to call on him to resign if he refused to join the union. But the tailors refused to donate money to the Federation's committee on unemployment, 'as it will lead to trouble in their union to mix up unionism with politics'.[5]

Coloured and white working men had similar interests. They joined in the big unemployment demonstrations of 1906 and in the campaigns of 1906–7 for a workmen's compensation and factories act. The Labour Advance party, formed in October 1905 by the Cape Town trades council and Social Democratic Federation, urged the adoption of a forty-eight hour working week, universal, free and compulsory education, and adult suffrage for all civilized persons.[6] The party's speakers declared that there should be no distinction between white and Coloured workers. All had the same aims and should work together.[7] Labour leaders drove the point home when addressing the cosmopolitan audiences at the Stone, the Coloured people's traditional open-air forum on the slopes of Devil's Peak in the working-class area of District Six. The Coloured were sceptical. They drew attention to a 'no Coloured labour' clause in the contract for new university buildings, and blamed the unions. John Tobin, a founding member of the African Political Organization (APO), accused socialists of being rotten with colour prejudice.

They denied the charge indignantly. Wilfrid Harrison, ex-guardsman, carpenter and Cape Town's leading socialist, asserted that the trades council had nothing to do with the obnoxious clause. All unions affiliated to the council welcomed any competent Coloured tradesman. He proclaimed himself to be a red-hot socialist revolutionary, at least in economic affairs, and like all genuine socialists repudiated a colour line. Harry MacManus, an Irish socialist, found a close resemblance between disputes over colour and the feud between Protestants and Catholics in Ireland. Le Roux, speaking in Afrikaans, ridiculed the idea that South Africa could ever be a white man's country. A. Needham, leader of the short-lived Socialist Democratic party, claimed that the 'colour question' had no relevance to socialism. They might as well speak of a 'red question' for men with red hair.[8] This was the language of orthodox socialism, couched in an idiom attuned to the liberal tolerance of the western Cape.

The Cape Federation regarded itself as a branch of the London SDF, sold its paper the *Clarion*, and adopted propaganda techniques that were suited to the conditions of a multiracial society. New members were welcomed with the singing of the Red Flag; a weekly journal, the *Cape Socialist*, appeared when funds permitted; study classes were held for immigrant

Dutchmen, Italians and Jews; and speakers harangued the crowd in Afrikaans, Xhosa and English. The Russian revolution of 1905 was applauded at a public meeting, to which Olive Schreiner sent a message of solidarity and confidence: 'we are witnessing the beginning of the greatest event that has taken place in the history of humanity during the last centuries.'

The Federation gave much attention to the 'Native Question' and the 'Coloured Question', set up a 'Kaffir Propaganda Committee', and learned from Harrison that the Coloured people were beginning to consider the question of socialism and how it affected them. He suggested holding meetings at the Stone, the APO's open-air forum, but the Coloured comrades thought that this would be 'discourteous and inadvisable'. They reported 'a good deal of interest among the Malays' and proposed a concert to assist the parliamentary election fund.[9]

Staunch socialists on the Rand, in contrast, appealed to a white electorate for protection from Asian, African and Coloured competition. The divergence between the attitudes of the southern and northern wings of the movement can be explained in terms of a response to contrasting situations. It is less easy to decide how far organized white labour in the north was responsible for racial policies which it supported, developed and exploited for sectional gains. The republic's bitter racialism had infected the whole society, until discrimination seemed as natural and inevitable as differences in skin colour. In its agrarian setting, where farmers hired craftsmen and rarely competed with them, the discrimination determined status, land ownership and political power rather than the division of labour. The industrial colour bar of the mining era was a new development. It originated in the special skills of foreign-born technicians who turned their spheres of employment into a closed preserve.

The barriers were not so high or rigid at the end of the war as to keep all dark men out of skilled work. Coloured artisans, lured to the Rand by its promise of 'a golden pound a day', worked at their trades also on the mines. Africans with industrial experience could rise above the level of a labourer. Landless Afrikaners and unskilled immigrants were available for manual work at the lower end of the scale. The position was fluid and might have been shaped into the pattern of the Cape's open labour market. It was Milner's officials, acting under the Mines, Works and Machinery Ordinance of 1903, who took the decisions that led to a rigid demarcation of work along colour lines.

The ordinance itself did not discriminate or authorize a discrimination that would have brought it within the ambit of matters reserved by the constitution for the secretary of state's approval. By repealing the republican laws 11 of 1897 and 12 of 1898, the ordinance removed the sole remaining colour bar in the Transvaal's mining legislation. But Wybergh, the commissioner of mines, introduced new colour bars in regulations issued under the ordinance. These defined the posts of manager, engine driver, banksman and onsetter in such a way as to reserve them for whites.[10] Amended regulations of 1906 did the same thing for the work of a boiler attendant, lift operator, shift boss, surface foreman, mine overseer and mechanical engineer.[11] The discriminations were imposed by an all-powerful British administration, without public pressure, stated reason, or comment by trade unions, mine managements and the legislative council. As in the case of at least two other discriminatory measures – the municipal franchise ordinance and the precious stones ordinance of 1903 – Milner failed to reserve the regulations for approval in Whitehall. Was it to avoid publicity that Wybergh discriminated in an oblique, almost furtive manner by defining work categories?

When president of the Transvaal branch of the South African League, that instrument of British imperialism, Wybergh had conducted a violent and dishonest campaign against the republic in 1898–9. His political activities lost him a lucrative post in Rhodes' Consolidated Goldfields. The firm had been deeply involved in the Jameson Raid and was not disposed to allow its staff to commit it in a similar conspiracy. Milner rewarded him after the war with the key post of commissioner of mines, but forced him to resign in 1903 for having opposed the introduction of Chinese indentured workers. Elected to the legislative assembly in 1907, Wybergh told the Mining Commission that Africans should be barred by law from working on machinery, partly because they endangered lives but mainly to secure the jobs of white workmen. He suggested that the ban could be imposed without such a bill 'as would have to be reserved for the consent of the Home Government'. Simply prescribe that white men shall be employed, he advised, 'and you avoid raising the question of imposing disabilities on natives'.[12]

Immigrant engine drivers, mechanics, miners and builders took advantage of the administration's racial bias. Many of their leaders, such as Whiteside, Walker, Waterston, Haynes, Crawford and Andrews, had served with the British army against the republics. Belonging to a conquering nation and a racial elite, they adopted the ideology of a colonial society. The crop of trade unions that sprang up after the war combined class militancy with colour bars.

Engineers, engine drivers, iron moulders and carpenters were represented on a joint mechanics committee that conducted a strike in April 1902 against piece work on the Crown Reef mine. Five months later, 103 men struck work on the Village Main Reef mine where Frederic Creswell, the mine manager, and Wilfred Wybergh, commissioner of mines, were experimenting with a white labour force. Creswell substituted two white helpers at 10s. a shift each for the five Africans who usually manned a machine drill at a wage of 2s. in cash and 1s. in board and lodging. To offset the rise in labour costs, he told the machine minders to supervise three drills instead of two. They preferred less work to more white labour, however, and walked out, taking the white helpers with them.[13] In spite of the setback, labour leaders insisted that it was sound for both economic and political reasons to employ large numbers of white labourers at rates intermediate between the African's 3s. and the artisan's 20s.

The administration was at first sympathetic, since the proposal fitted in with the Milner-Chamberlain object of attracting as many British immigrants as would swamp the Afrikaner population. Wybergh gave his official backing to the experimental use of unskilled whites on five mines.[14] The railways brought out navvies from Britain in 1903 to lay a permanent track for a wage of 5s. a day and all found.[15] But the white labourers were never given a proper trial. The mine owners had political and economic objections to their employment. Milner, ever complaisant towards the Chamber, was converted to its policy of introducing indentured Asians, and set his mind on preparing the white public for a decision that would cause as great an uproar as the proposed introduction of convicts to the Cape in 1849. Creswell and Wybergh were dismissed from their posts, the British railway navvies were repatriated, and an inter-colonial customs conference, held at Bloemfontein in March 1903, was manoeuvred into supporting the Chamber's scheme.

The conference found, on no evidence other than the reluctance of Africans to work for the prevailing rate of wages, that there were not enough of them south of the Zambesi to satisfy demands for labour. Therefore, the conference recommended, Asians should be admitted under strict state control and on the firm condition of eventual repatriation.[16] Milner appointed a Labour Commission to substantiate these findings, and negotiated for the introduction of 10,000 Indians to be employed on railway works. The Indian government rightly insisted on a relaxation of the Transvaal's anti-Asian legislation.[17] Milner refused to make any concessions, withdrew his request, and threw his weight behind the Chamber's policy of importing Chinese. The majority of the Labour Commission duly reported that 'white labour cannot profitably compete with black' in 'the lower fields of manual industry'. The gold mines, they said, were short of 129,000 labourers; the shortage would rise to 325,000 by 1908; and Africa could not meet requirements.[18]

Two commissioners, Peter Whiteside and J. W. Quinn, disputed these findings. Whiteside, an Australian-born engine driver, president of the Witwatersrand Trades and Labour Council, and a nominated member of the Johannesburg town council, was a fervent racist. His associate Quinn later took a leading part in the agitation against the Chinese and for responsible government. Both men insisted that though white labourers, if given a fair trial, would supplement and even supersede Africans, mine owners wanted to perpetuate an 'inferior race' system of labour organization. They had a political bias against a big influx of white labourers, who would strengthen the working class and enable it to determine both wages and state policy. The minority report blamed the employers for the shortage of African workers, alleged that it was temporary, and urged the adoption of a fixed ratio between white and African workers. These were principles on which the labour movement would base its white labour policy in years to come.

The economic motives for the introduction of Chinese arose out of Milner's 'struggle for British supremacy'.[19] The war had devastated the Transvaal and disrupted the recruiting system of the mines. The output of gold dropped from its peak of £1,710,000 in August 1899 – under a supposedly corrupt and inefficient regime – to £823,000 in December 1902. As many Africans worked for a wage in the Transvaal as before the war, but the number employed on gold mines declined from 107,482 in 1899 to 64,577 in June 1903.[20] The decline revealed the African's good sense and the actual source of profit. For the owners had taken advantage of the war to cut his average wage from 47s. 1d. in 1898 to 26s. 8d. in 1901–2. Men of the Cape, Basutoland and Bechuanaland 'refused altogether to engage themselves at the reduced rate of pay'.[21] Natal closed its borders to recruiters. Settlers in central Africa also opposed recruiting, which would force up wages, then 3s. or 5s. a month in Nyasaland. Mozambique alone continued to forward its conscripted workers, though even here old mine hands refused to work for the lower rate.

There was no time to spare, in the view of Milner and the owners; they wanted a ready-to-hand proletariat at the lowest possible cost who would restore the mines to full working capacity without delay, satisfy shareholders, attract new capital, save Milner's reputation and the Transvaal from bankruptcy. They would not wait for taxation and land seizures to turn African peasants into work seekers. 'Is this huge industry to be a school for teaching savages to become civilized workers?' thundered Sir George Farrar when he moved in the legislative assembly on 28 December 1903 that government be asked to legislate for the introduction of Chinese. One of the men sentenced to death by the republic's high court for their role in Jameson's raid, Farrar admitted that it was a mistake to have reduced the African's wage; or to have thought, as his side did, that the war would last only six weeks. But, he added, they would make another mistake if they imported unskilled whites, for this meant labour combinations, discontent, strikes and nothing else.

He spoke for his class. Charles Rudd, one of Rhodes' partners, and other company directors agreed that a big body of enfranchised white workers 'would simply hold the Government of the country in the hollow of their hand' and 'more or less dictate, not only on the question of wages, but also on political questions'.[22] There was, too, the fear of inter-racial fraternization. Top-ranking executives and engineers told Joseph Chamberlain in Johannesburg in January 1903 that the white man would forfeit his natural supremacy and cease to be the master if he worked side by side with Africans as fellow labourers.[23] Chamberlain's views were as misinformed and intemperate as the mine owners'. Africans alone among the world's great races, he said, believed that 'the only honourable employment for a man is fighting, that labour is the work of slaves'. Slavery had been abolished in theory, but the 'Kafir' bought his wives, who worked 'to keep him in idleness'. Abdurahman replied in a biting analysis of Chamberlain's speech, which, he pointed out, contained the same arguments as those used by mine magnates in favour of forced labour. Chamberlain had not mentioned the thirty per cent reduction in the African's wage, his unhealthy working conditions, or the over-capitalized mines 'which cannot pay a dividend until the Kafir is compelled to work at a wage fixed by the mining magnates'.[24]

Africans and Coloured stood to lose most from an influx of low-paid, indentured workers; and voiced their objections at meetings in the Cape, Transvaal and even isolated Bechuanaland. Jabavu circulated a petition to the king to 'avert this evil' of importing Asiatics 'with no idea of any rights, and with morals and habits unlike those of the European races, in which your petitioners have been hitherto trained'.[25] The Chinese, he wrote after importing had begun, cost more and did less work than the African, who 'cordially detested' them.[26]

White workers on the Rand were less united on the 'Chinese question'. The trades councils of Johannesburg and Pretoria claimed that all unions 'totally' or 'largely' opposed the importation.[27] According to Milner, however, the miners were predominantly, and other artisans mostly, in favour.[28] The trades council accused mine managements of browbeating their employees into acquiescence. For this reason, or because they believed that the industry and their jobs were in danger, a significant number of miners passed resolutions and signed petitions for the immediate introduction of indentured, non-British Asians to be employed only on unskilled work.

Mine owners told the men that they had less to fear from the Chinese than from a horde of unskilled whites who, Farrar warned, would soon become skilled 'and compete with you'. He dangled the prospect of sheltered employment before a miners' audience at Boksburg in March 1903. The Chinese, he explained, would be repatriated, prohibited from trading or holding land, and excluded by law from many specified occupations.[29] The Labour Importation Ordinance of 1904 duly prohibited the employment of Chinese in fifty-five scheduled occupations, including such non-mining trades as bricklaying, carpentry, plumbing, painting, gardening and clerical work.

Among other consequences, the agitation for and against the Chinese aroused and hardened colour prejudices, precipitated the emergence of the Afrikaner Het Volk party, prepared the ground for cooperation between Afrikaner nationalism and the white labour movement, and facilitated the introduction of a code prescribing minimum standards of housing, food, medical care and sanitation for African miners.[30]

The Chinese were employed under conditions agreed by the owners, the Transvaal administration, the British and Chinese governments, after lengthy negotiations which centred mainly round the issues of wages and repatriation. Alfred Lyttleton, the secretary of state for colonies, complained that he 'really could not defend an arrangement by which the Chinese would be used to lower Kaffir wages'.[31] He was later bullied into agreeing to a guaranteed minimum wage of 1s. to 1s. 6d. a shift, compared with the African's basic rate of 1s. 6d. for surface and 2s. for underground work. Housed in compounds and working sixty hours a week, the Chinese were allowed a daily ration of 1½ lb. of rice, ¼ lb. of vegetables, and ½ lb. of meat or fish. The maximum compensation for death or total permanent disablement was fixed at £10.

Medical officers attributed the occurrence of scurvy among African miners to the deficiencies of a mealie-meal diet and recommended the addition of rice, millet, legumes, meat and fresh vegetables.[32] The Chamber, however, 'viewed the native purely as a machine, requiring a certain amount of fuel', and took as its standard the 'minimum amount of food which will give the maximum amount of work'.[33] Regulations issued in 1906 prescribed a minimum of 2 lb. of mealie-meal and ½ oz. of salt a day, supplemented by 2 lb. of bone-free meat or fish, 1 lb. of soupmeat, 1 lb. of vegetables and 1 lb. of sugar or treacle a week. Though low in vitamins, calcium, animal protein and calories, the diet was a great improvement, saved many lives, and virtually eliminated scurvy as a cause of death. The men satisfied their craving for meat and milk by buying large quantities from the concession stores. No mine ever supplied milk, butter, cheese or eggs. Yet milk was a staple diet of men from stock-breeding communities and a primary source of the food constituents in which the mine ration was most deficient.

The same kind of cheeseparing policy was applied to housing, working conditions and medical care. Huts of brick or stone, built for the Chinese and later also for Africans, were badly overcrowded, with rooms holding twenty or forty men each. The regulations prescribed a maximum air space of 200 cubic feet per inmate, though Dr Turner, the Medical Officer of Health, insisted that even 300 cubic feet were 'far too little'.[34] The Chamber replied that the adoption of his standard would cost the owners an additional £1¼ million. No eating halls, tables or chairs were provided. The men drew their rations in tin bowls and mugs and ate squatting on the cement paving of the courtyard or sitting on the bunks in their sleeping quarters. They worked twelve hours a day on the surface or eleven hours underground without food, were often kept waiting in wet clothes for as much as three hours while the skips were being used to transport rock, and walked back to the compounds in a state of exhaustion, their bodies covered with stale sweat and grime. The regulations of 1906 compelled owners to provide change houses for white and Coloured miners, but not for Africans, many of whom contracted pneumonia and chest complaints through being exposed to sudden and great changes of temperature and altitude.[35]

Most mines had no hospitals before 1906, when the health regulations obliged the owners to provide hospital accommodation for not more than two and a half per cent of the average number of Africans employed. In 1914, the Rand mines between them had only ten full-time doctors, each attending to between 82 and 265 hospital patients. There were thirty-nine part-time doctors, who had to reconcile their duty to helpless indentured Africans with the exacting demands of white miners backed by sick-benefit societies. The part-time men usually visited the hospital once a day to look at new patients and sign death certificates. Mine hospitals were managed by unqualified superintendents and untrained African nurses who were paid 2s. or 2s. 6d. a day. Patients were underfed, mechanically treated with purgatives on admission, neglected, and forced to work during convalescence. Hospital costs were low and mortality rates high. Henry Burton, the minister of native affairs, asked in 1911: 'How is it that these things have not struck the mining people years ago? Here are these fellows, lying in their beds, and dying off like a lot of rats, [yet] nobody does a thing.' The hospital services became efficient only after the government had put a stop in 1913 to recruiting in tropical regions north of 22° south latitude and compelled the mines to pay compensation for miners' phthisis.[36]

The high turnover of migrants exposed great numbers of men to the unfavourable conditions, spread the risk of pneumoconiosis and venereal diseases over a wide area, and delayed the peasant worker's adjustment to an industrialized environment. Mine owners acknowledged that 'the immense cost' of labour was 'not in the actual wages which we pay, but in the time wasted in teaching new batches'.[37] A certain way to reduce the high death rate from pneumonia was to settle the miners with their families in villages along the Reef, advised General Gorgas of Panama fame.[38] The owners preferred to offset the cost of wasted lives and skills with savings on housing, food and wages. Africans received less than a living wage, while their families kept themselves on the land. The owners contended that the migratory system was 'a fundamental factor' in the mining economy and essential to their prosperity. If the African 'has not got the reserve subsistence to go back to', said Gemmill, the secretary of the Chamber, 'we cannot afford a wage to make it possible for him to live in an urban area'.[39]

Segregation in compounds, labour migration and job reservation accentuated the racial and cultural differences between white miner and Africans. He was their 'boss', and not a fellow worker; and he tended to enforce his orders with kicks and blows. Africans 'were knocked about by irresponsible miners underground', said George Trow at a Tembuland meeting; but they would not complain for fear of being sjambokked by African mine police.[40] Jabavu, being anxious 'to secure a perennial stream of Natives to the Goldfields' and a reciprocal flow of wages to the reserves, had no time for the 'discontented troublemaker' on the mines; he attributed their unpopularity to compound managers drawn from Natal with Zulu police.[41] The correspondence columns of his paper recorded other grievances in 1907–8, when the Chinese were being repatriated. Labour agents misrepresented conditions to recruits who loafed, deserted or struck work on finding that they had been deceived. Task work was another serious grievance. Drillers were obliged to drill at least forty-two inches during a shift, for which they were paid 2s., with $\frac{1}{2}$d. for every additional inch drilled. A driller might have to spend three or four hours clearing debris blasted out by the preceding shift before he reached the place marked for a hole. If he failed to complete the norm, however, his shift boss would refuse to mark his ticket. This meant that he was not paid for the day's work or credited with a shift towards the completion of his service contract.[42]

Pneumatic drills were then taking the place of hand drilling. Originally operated by white miners with African 'helpers', the heavy, cumbersome machine was at first considered a highly specialized tool, and the operator a skilled workman. During the war, and as Cornish miners returned home or died of phthisis, Africans were employed to 'run' the machine drill for an unskilled labourer's wage. The white miner became a supervisor, responsible for one or two drills operated by an African 'helper' and his team. Creswell, as we have seen, wanted the miner to take charge of three drills operated by white labourers and so provoked a strike in 1902 at the Village Main Reef mine. In 1907 the manager of Knights Deep mine instructed each miner to supervise three drills manned by Africans. The miners' union, at that time a craft organization confined to holders of blasting certificates, accused the owners of diluting skilled labour in preparation for large-scale retrenchments of whites. The men at New Kleinfontein mine struck work on 1 May. The strike spread until more than 4,000 miners were involved.

Smuts, as minister of mines, made his first appearance as protector of the propertied class and of mine owners in particular. He called out the imperial garrison, who broke up picket lines and protected scabs. Africans and Chinese worked the mines without close supervision. Employers declared a lockout, dismissed the strikers and took on Afrikaners in their place. The strikers trickled back to work, and the union acknowledged defeat at the end of July. The executive's members and other leading strikers were victimized, the number of white miners employed was reduced by ten per cent, and the cost of breaking rock fell by twenty-five per cent.[43] Jabavu, ever partial to Afrikanerdom, applauded the entry of young 'colonials' in the industry. Their presence would establish 'a better understanding' between burghers and the mining populations, besides stopping the drain of money remitted by Cornish miners to their families.[44]

H. L. Phooko, representing the Transvaal Native Congress, drew a more significant conclusion in evidence before the Mining Commission of 1907. By keeping the mines in production during the strike, he remarked, Africans had shown a capacity to master all parts of the mining operation. They were not intellectually inferior and often performed skilled work, though the law denied them freedom of contract and held them down as unskilled.[45] The commission, too, rejected the theory that the African was a 'mere muscular machine' and no more than 'an aid to enable the White man to earn wages sufficient to keep him in contentment'. Africans, warned the commission, were not 'barred by lack of brain and industrial training from interfering with the White man's opportunities of employment'.[46] The Transvaal Indigency Commission of 1906–8 held a similar view, and refused to recommend measures to protect white workers. Africans were being trained in regular work, showed a great yearning for education, and would in time insist on higher wages and access to superior kinds of work. Protective devices such as a fixed ratio between racial groups of employees or a minimum white wage would only discourage the employment of whites, insulate them against pressures for efficiency, and so hamper them in the coming struggle for supremacy.[47]

The miners themselves were in two minds about the white labour policy. A minority preferred African helpers. White labourers, according to this school of thought, were either casual, transient workers or Afrikaners who would learn the trade and saturate the market for skilled miners.[48] Men holding this view wished to maintain their bargaining power by limiting the diffusion of skills. Africans were socially inferior, easily handled and unlikely to compete. Jimmy Coward, a leading member of the miners' union and of the Independent Labour party. and at one time mayor of Germiston, claimed that he could take 'a raw green Kaffir from the Kraal' and within a week 'make him competent for me to leave my machine with him and go away whenever I have a mind'. White men were not willing to boss other white men in the same way as they would 'kaffirs'. He for one would not do it.[49]

Most labour leaders agreed with the Cornish miner Tom Mathews, secretary of the union from 1908 to the time of his death from phthisis in 1915. He would treat Africans decently but 'not let them be free', and would rather have a white youth under him than 'a kaffir. or two kaffirs for that matter'.[50] The engineers' union, whose chief spokesman was its national organizer W. H. Andrews, set out the reasons for this preference with prodigious subtlety in a memorandum submitted to the Mining Commission.[51] The coloured races. if unchecked would rise to the top and endanger the state itself by reason of their numbers, vitality and low standards. Unfair competition by unskilled whites was therefore more natural and infinitely more desirable than competition by Africans. Since white men were citizens and voters, they were 'far more likely to look at the matter from the point of view of the general welfare of the community.' On the other hand, 'the kaffir has no interest in the country except that he gets his living here. He has no voice in the Government'.

Trade unionists who claimed privileges in the name of the capitalist state and for the general welfare of a class society had turned their backs on radical socialism. As members both of an inferior class and of a racial elite they were in an ambivalent position. It deflected them from their traditional attitudes. Experience of labour dilution convinced them that employers would substitute the cheaper coloured worker. A racial bar hardly needed justification in their eyes. It was a protective device, like restraints on the number of apprentices or on reclassification of jobs. Since the threat came from an alien and oppressed race, however, the trade unionists identified themselves with white supremacy so as to legitimate their class interests. Though Mathews, Andrews and other socialists of the time may not have been racists, they certainly excluded the African from their vision of the ideal commonwealth. Refusing to recognize him as a fellow worker and ally, they fused their craft outlook with the colour prejudices of feudalistic landowners in a struggle against both capitalists and Africans.

The time had not yet come, however, for governments to catch votes with promises of sheltered employment. More orthodox views about the value of competition prevailed, as in the report of the Indigency Commission. Trade unionists therefore found it expedient to demand protection from competition in the guise of protection against accidents. The plea that only trained and qualified persons should be employed in positions of trust seemed reasonable. Once the principle had been established, it was easy to equate a white skin with technical skills and a sense of responsibility. The owners themselves were to blame for the myth of the African's incompetence. They objected to a regulation of 1896 that obliged managers to explain to illiterate workers, 'especially persons of colour', the rules 'appertaining to their particular occupation and duty'. Formal instruction was confined to whites, first by way of apprenticeship and classes in drilling techniques, and later at evening courses conducted by the Transvaal University College. The government mining school opened at Wolhuter in 1911, admitted only white men. Africans and Coloured had to learn their trade on the job from the white miner.

Miners and mechanics who appeared before the Mining Regulations Commission of 1907–10 could claim with some plausibility that the mines would be run more efficiently and with fewer accidents if only white and preferably certificated men were employed on all engines and machinery. Dr F. E. T. Krause, the chairman, was sympathetic. As assistant attorney-general in the republic, he had clashed with one Forster, a lawyer who defended Baron von Veltheim in 1896 on a charge of murdering the magnate Woolf Joel. A series of bizarre incidents led to Krause being sentenced at the Old Bailey in 1902 to two years' imprisonment for an alleged attempt to incite the murder of Forster. Returning to Johannesburg in 1904, Krause sat on the municipal council in 1907–8, stood for Het Volk Party against Bill Andrews in the parliamentary elections of 1910, subsequently defended communists and other radicals in political trials, and spoke up strongly against the pass laws. When chairman of the commission, however, he advocated a white labour policy. South African whites and Afrikaners in particular he urged should be trained for the mining industry.

Trade unionists admitted frankly that they wanted a colour bar to raise the status of their trade and provide employment for whites. Tom Hannegan, on behalf of the engine drivers, said that they would do all they could 'to take these boilers out of the hands of coloured men'.[52] The Amalgamated Society of Engineers similarly coupled safety measures with employment opportunities. The 'growing practice of placing kaffirs and other coloured persons in charge of boilers, winches, engines and other machinery' increased the danger to life and limb; it also reduced 'the sphere of employment for European labour without which this colony cannot progress'. The union urged that 'no Kaffir or other coloured person' should be issued with a certificate of competence or allowed to take charge of machines.[53] But none of the witnesses produced evidence to show that accidents were more likely to occur when Africans operated boilers and winches.

'It is reasoning and you do not require proof,' said Bill Andrews.

Government records showed that the number of mine accidents caused by overwinding was small and unrelated to the employment of uncertificated drivers. Managers, engineers and inspectors agreed that engines not used for hauling persons could be safely entrusted to uncertificated operators. Many uneducated and even illiterate men made excellent drivers. Training, sobriety, self-reliance and nerve were the qualities of a good driver.[54] Meeting in committee to digest the evidence, the commission viewed the proposal to license drivers of all types of engines with great scepticism. Krause suspected that the real motive was 'to prevent all intelligent work on the mines from being done by natives'. The commissioners agreed among themselves that drivers of motor cars should be licensed, but not the drivers of traction and stationary engines, including those used for hauling rock.[55]

The commission criticized mine managements for employing large numbers of unskilled whites 'often entirely ignorant of mining, and whose principal and often only recommendation is their physical fitness and their suitability for rough work'. Yet when the commission reported in 1910, it submitted draft regulations that were heavy with colour bars. Some appeared in the interpretation of terms, as when the words 'white person' were inserted in the definition of banksman, onsetter, ganger and mine manager. Some took the form of an injunction to employ only whites in specified occupations, such as blasting, running elevators. driving engines, supervising boilers and other machinery; or as shift boss and mine overseer. Furthermore, only whites would be allowed to obtain the certificates of competence required, for instance, by engine drivers and boiler attendants. The draft served as a model for the colour bar regulations issued by Smuts under the Mines and Works Act of 1911. The only reason given in the Krause report for this massive and far-reaching piece of racial discrimination was the bare and unsubstantiated assertion that 'wherever the safety of life and limb is concerned only competent White persons should be employed'.[56]

The Chamber of Mines made a formal protest. It pointed out

91

that discriminatory regulations would be *ultra vires* if not authorized by the enabling statute; and suggested that 'competent' or 'reliable' be substituted for 'white person'.[57] But the mine owners never contested the regulations until after the miners had suffered the great defeat of 1922. Owners and government acquiesced for political reasons in a discrimination that was both unjust and unlawful. The African's capacity was never seriously questioned. Engineers and mine managers agreed that selected Africans, adequately trained would be as competent as the white man for any job including that of a mine manager.[58] No attempt was ever made, however, to give him systematic training for skilled work. None of the many commissions that inquired into the state of labour organization even considered the possibility of systematic training. Their only concern, when they discussed the African's role, was the degree of protection that should be given to white workers against competition.

The claim that the colour bar has a prophylactic function is not borne out by the exceptionally high incidence of accidents on the mines. More than 30,000 men died in accidents on gold mines during the first half of the century. Untold others died from septicaemia and other effects of accidental injuries, or lost limbs and sight or were otherwise disabled by accidents. The death rate from accidents on all mines in 1910 was 4·05 per 1,000 African employees and 3·36 per 1,000 whites. The rate fell to 1·56 for both groups by 1956, but the accident rate was then 58·7 per 1,000 miners, as compared with 30 in 1927, when the existing definition of accidents was first introduced. The decline in the death rate must therefore be attributed to improvements in first aid and medical treatment rather than to more effective preventive measures. For an accident is not a fortuitous, unavoidable event. It is broadly, the result of defective adaptation or inadequate control of environment. Though unintended and unforeseen it flows from a deliberate act, and can be averted by the adoption of sufficient care or by technical and material safeguards. The high and increasing incidence of accidents on mines points to deficiencies in management.

Far from saving lives the colour bar reduced standards of efficiency and safety. By keeping Africans ignorant of their trade, the owners sent up accident rates and strengthened the white worker's claim to a monopoly of preferred occupations. Competence was identified with skin colour. Yet a large number of Africans, by dint of intelligence and long service, were more skilled than their white overseer. The Chamber acknowledged in 1914 that such men were 'in many cases as good, or better, judges as to safety underground' than the partially trained white supervisors. 'The time has now arrived,' urged Abdurahman, 'when we should agitate for the repeal of those regulations which prohibit Coloured men from performing skilled work on the mines.'[59] The regulations remained to block the African's prospects of promotion blunt his initiative and deprive him of incentives to become more proficient.

Colour bars discouraged efficiency for different reasons also in the white miner He was trained but left the actual manual work to Africans. The division of functions tended to cultivate indifference in miners and managements alike to the African's safety. Fergusson, Boksburg's outspoken mining inspector, drew attention to the consequences in his report for 1910–11.[60] In England where mining was something of an hereditary occupation, a miner's son would assist his father by doing work of the kind allocated to Africans on the Rand. The English miner took great care to secure and make safe the places where a lad was set to work, and to point out dangers to him. In the gold mines, however 'the death of a native is not looked upon by the miners here as a very serious affair'. The directors were well aware that 'hundreds of men lose their lives annually through carelessness on the part of the miners and apathy on the part of the officials'; but made no effort to have matters improved. The probable explanation for their indifference lay in the old adage: 'Dead men tell no tales' For 'a live Kaffir who has been assaulted is in a position to do a great deal of harm on his return home by persuading his friends not to allow themselves to be recruited'.

Ten pounds were paid in compensation to the dependants of an adult killed in an accident and £5 to those of a young *umfaan*.* The African was cheap in death as in life and scarcely worth the cost of safety measures that might slow down production. Mine

* Xhosa for young boy, lad.

owners objected vigorously to the first statutory obligation imposed by the Native Labour Regulation Act of 1911 to compensate Africans for injuries. The benefits ranged from £1 to £20 for partial incapacity and from £30 to £50 for total permanent disablement. A man who lost a leg and became virtually unemployable received a maximum of £20, the equivalent of four months' wages, board and lodging. The higher scale was extended in 1914 to include cases of fatal injuries. Though grossly inadequate, and notably less in relation to earning power than the benefits paid to injured white miners, the statutory scales gave mine officials a powerful incentive to reduce the number of accidents.

Africans were expendable. They had a preferential claim to rough, hard and dangerous work, as in rock drilling, which exposed the operator to deadly clouds of silica dust. When the white miner became phthisis conscious, drilling ceased to be regarded as skilled and was entrusted wholly to Africans. Asked whether white apprentices could be substituted for young Africans in cyanide works and mills, Henry Hay, the manager of the Witwatersrand Deep, replied: 'You could not put white boys in the mill work, it is too dangerous; you could put them in the cyanide works, but you would have to be careful.'[61] Conventional divisions between skilled and unskilled labour often denoted the hazards of the operator's calling or his skin colour rather than the degree of skill involved. Thousands of Africans employed as drillers, trammers, packers, or in laying and firing charges, would be considered skilled in Europe and America. They were called 'boys' in South Africa and were paid one-ninth of the white miners' wage.

Discrimination spread from the mines to other trades in which the safety factor was insignificant. English-speaking immigrants asserted a prior right to all occupations. White South Africans learned from them to agitate for a white labour policy in government, municipal and railway services, in factories, bakeries and butcher shops.[62] The cry went up also in Natal, where labour leaders railed against the employment of Indians and Africans as crane drivers, riveters, mechanics and painters.[63] White supremacy claims were expanded early in the century into a demand for total segregation. J. E. Riley, president of the Johannesburg trades council and a militant member of the Operative Masons' Society, urged in 1907 that all Africans should be confined to reserved areas in the colony.[64] The trade unionists who pressed for a colour bar seldom attempted to reconcile it with their class outlook. Appealing to race prejudice, they applied their traditional, protectionist policies to what they regarded as an extreme case of unfair competition.

Africans were said to be the unwitting instrument of the capitalist class. Housed in compounds, paid less than a living wage, denied the right to strike or combine, they threatened the white man's job. Given a free hand, the capitalists would run the country with a multitude of bonded workmen for the benefit of foreign shareholders. Legal protection for the artisan was no more than a counterweight to the African's legal disabilities. 'I hold that the Kaffir should be allowed to get free,' said Tom Mathews, 'but in the interim, as he is here only as a semi-slave, I have a right to fight him and to oust him just as the Australians ousted the Chinamen and the Kanakas.' If he were to be allowed to compete with the artisan, the African should do so on an open market, as a free worker and without the mean advantage of a servile status.[65]

Labour leaders might have been acquitted of acting out of self-interest and racial arrogance if they had demanded equal rights for all workmen. Few, however, pressed for the removal of restraints imposed on the African's bargaining power by indentured labour, compounds, pass laws and the master and servant acts. Labour men even failed to protest on humanitarian grounds against the conditions that caused the death from disease and accidents of some 5,000 Africans a year on Transvaal mines between 1903 and 1920. These were the formative years of labour legislation. A firm stand made against discrimination could have done much to narrow the gap between artisans and Africans. The racists who led the labour movement missed the opportunity, as when the Transvaal parliament passed the Industrial Disputes Prevention Act of 1909. The first of its kind in South Africa, it introduced conciliation procedures in essential municipal services, mining, the building trades, engineering and metal works; and applied only to white employees and employers of more than ten white persons.

R. Goldman, the member for Newtown, said that Africans should not have the right to strike, since they could virtually paralyse the mining industry by withholding their labour. De Villiers, the attorney-general and minister of mines, agreed. Moreover, he said, Africans were 'ignorant and not competent to appoint an arbitrator'. He hoped that the day was far distant when they would be capable of combined action in a strike. It was left to Wybergh, a leading advocate of white labour policies, to defend, if sideways, the African. Who had dislocated the mining industry if not the owners themselves, by their 'indefensible and arbitrary' act in cutting wages 'to an enormous extent' before and during the war? The more they excluded Africans from industrial laws, the greater would be the incentive to employ them 'because they were being made humble slaves, not able to speak for themselves, therefore easier to be dealt with and more satisfactory to employers than white people'. That was his great reason, he explained, for wanting Africans to be covered by the act in the same way as whites. Even this appeal to self-interest failed to move Whiteside. Reid and Sampson, the Labour party members. They were prepared to include Coloured, among whom were first class mechanics. It would be a strange thing, said Sampson, if they were to remain in the shop while white men came out on strike. 'Nobody,' he added, 'intended to include the Kaffir.'[66]

The advantages of inter-racial class solidarity seemed remote and problematical. White solidarity promised real and immediate gains. The small number of artisans in key positions could wrest concessions with comparative ease at the expense of labourers. Labour leaders were able to strengthen their hand by claiming that the interests of white workers were the same as those of the entire white community. Class struggles between whites, they argued, set a bad example to Africans. W. McLarty, the member for Durban gave this as a reason in 1903 for the introduction of industrial conciliation. A strike of white bricklayers, he said, was followed by a successful strike of African tramwaymen. 'We have the Native population growing up around us, and being educated, and they are learning to strike.' He uttered the same warning in 1909, when introducing a bill to settle disputes between employers and white working men. The Natal railwaymen's strike of that year was a grim reminder, he said, of the unsettling effects of a long strike on African, Indian and other workers.[67]

Appeals to racial sentiment strengthened the case for factory legislation. What could be more persuasive than sensational disclosures of white girls working side by side with Africans and Indians in sweated food and clothing factories? This was the line taken by C. H. Haggar, the Labour member for Durban, in moving his factories bill in 1909. He spoke of 'Kaffirs moulding and kneading the dough in the trough, and the perspiration running down them into the trough'; of laundries where 'you find Coolies sleeping on the clothing sent there'.[68] His bill contained a clause prohibiting employees of different sex and different races from working in the same rooms at the same time. This, rather than the protection of workmen against excessive exploitation, would have been the most significant effect if the bill had become law. In the event, many years were to pass before parliament implemented Haggar's proposal to segregate one racial group of factory workers from another.

5 Workers and the Vote

White labour policies emerged from an all-white franchise. Having concentrated political power in the white minority, the British administration in the Transvaal connived at giving it control of industry, commerce and the skilled trades. Political power opened the door to economic privilege. Class, colour and national antagonisms offered a wide range of possibilities. Ambitious working men could appeal to class interests against employers or to racial sentiments against Africans and Asians; combine with Britishers against 'the Boer' or with Afrikaners against 'the capitalist'. Trade unionists and socialists on the Rand made a bid for political leadership soon after the war by forming the Witwatersrand Trades and Labour Council. Its foundation members were the societies of boiler makers, bricklayers, carpenters, engine drivers, engineers, iron moulders, musicians, printers, shop assistants and stonemasons.

The council's aims were modestly worded so as to disarm any suspicion of an intent to organize unions or interfere in their domestic affairs. It would link 'all branches of the working classes' together, promote the efficiency and progress of trade societies, and 'secure the return of representatives upon all governing bodies'. A parliamentary committee was elected to report on bills and motions affecting trade and labour. Delegates could be unseated for taking part in political activity 'not in conformity with the accepted policy of the Council'.[1] This was the language of a political organization, and the council was commonly referred to as the Labour party.

Patriotic members of the council worked closely with the British administration. Both the council and the miners' union backed Milner's proposal that the Transvaal should donate £30 million to the cost of the war. Chamberlain, when visiting the

Rand in January 1903, congratulated the unions on their decision. Working men in England, he said, were also paying towards the cost. They 'would feel they were rather left in the lurch by their comrades here, if they alone of all classes were to object to any contribution'.[2] Peter Whiteside, president of the trades council, and Alexander Riatt, branch president of the ASE, were rewarded with seats on Johannesburg's nominated town council, while Milner also appointed Riatt as a member of the legislative council to represent the working classes. Born in Glasgow in 1867, Riatt qualified as a mechanical engineer, emigrated to South Africa in 1890, took a prominent part in the British agitation against the republic, and fought with Bethune's mounted infantry in the war. A leading opponent of the Chinese labour policy, he was again rewarded with a seat on the legislative council after the introduction of responsible government in 1907. He resigned his seat, however, to become Inspector of White Labour three months before he died in November 1907.

The decision to import Chinese changed the political climate and opened a period of bitter class and national conflict on the Rand. More than any other factor, the 'Chinese question' spurred British working men and Afrikaner nationalists into organized political activity. Their common cause against the 'Hoggenheimers'* laid the foundations of unity in time to come. After the enactment of the Chinese labour importation ordinance Whiteside told the trades council that he would despair of his party's future in the Transvaal were it not for the active and cordial cooperation of the Dutch. They gave the worker reason to hope that he would not have to face the foreign capitalist single-handed when the Transvaal obtained self-government.[3] Whiteside's solution revealed the labour movement's racial bias. British workers looked to anti-British landowners for allies, and disdained their African and Coloured fellow workers.

The small body of white workers was unstable, poorly organized, divided and vulnerable. Some of the bigger unions, such as the societies of miners, railwaymen and plasterers, kept aloof

* A term of abuse with an anti-Semitic flavour that was used then, and would be used even more commonly in later years, to describe the mining magnates.

from the trades council because of personal rivalries or its political activities. Not having a firm base in the working class, Whiteside, Riatt and certain other leaders collaborated with business and professional men in the White League and African Labour League against the Chinese. The inter-class alliance operated also in Johannesburg's first municipal elections of December 1903, when every voter cast thirty votes to fill thirty vacancies. The trades council threw in its lot with the United Conference group and nominated five candidates on their ticket. Miners, railwaymen and plasterers backed the opposition Reform ticket, and also put up five candidates. Only two Labour men, Riatt and Shanks, were elected. The results of the 1904 elections were as disappointing. Whiteside was the only successful candidate out of ten men who stood on a Labour platform. These setbacks and much disagreement over the participation by trade unions in elections strengthened the case for a distinct Labour party.

All signs pointed towards such a possibility. A Social Democratic Federation had sprung up in Cape Town. Another SDF held a May Day demonstration on the Rand in 1904 as a counterblast to the conservative trade unions' Labour Day rally on Good Friday. The trades council invited the 'Boer Generals' to attend the rally, and received assurances of goodwill from Smuts. Whiteside visited Cape Town a few days later. He told the local trades council that only by taking part in politics could workers obtain the legislation needed to improve their condition. Foreign financiers would not be able to play ducks and drakes with a British colony, as they were doing in the Transvaal, if workers on the Rand had the Cape's advantages of a parliament and a pro-Labour newspaper like the *South African News*.[4] He was talking to the converted. Cape Town's trade unionists had already formed the nucleus of a Labour party and entered the lists in a parliamentary election.

Five Labour candidates contested seats in the Cape's general elections of 1904. Four stood in Cape Town with the backing of the Political Labour League, an offshoot of the trades council. The fifth represented the British Workmen's Political and Defence Association of Port Elizabeth. The League's constitution and programme were suited to the colony's non-racial franchise. Membership was open to wage earners of any race or colour, and the programme required equal rights for all civilized men. This was a splendid avowal of democratic principle and a unique repudiation by white labour of racial policies. The effects were negligible. The leaders missed the opportunity of proving their sincerity by nominating a Coloured or African candidate. Their representatives were white, British and, with one exception, recent immigrants. They had little money, experience or organization behind them and were easily routed by Jameson's Progressive party, which had all three qualities, and could, in addition, rely on patriotic sentiments whipped up during the war among English-speaking and Coloured working men.

The Progressives obtained a majority of one in the legislative council and of five in the assembly. Dr L. S. Jameson, Rhodes' former lieutenant and the leader of the raid on the Transvaal, became prime minister. Britain's war had completed his mission, vindicated his political villainy, and enabled him to maintain the Rhodes tradition of combining the premiership with a directorship in the colony's richest corporation. The Labour candidates Corley, Craig and Purcell attacked his association with De Beers, accused him of supporting the Chinese policy, and demanded a tax on diamonds. They denounced his party as one pledged to the capitalists, that would not therefore introduce labour measures like workmen's compensation and compulsory arbitration in industrial disputes. Corley, a carpenter and the Labour League's president, warned his audiences that workmen would gain nothing from a representative of De Beers. A month later, defeated in the elections and blacklisted by employers, he broke up home and emigrated to New Zealand.[5]

The decision to take part in elections was reached after much debate on the rival merits of political and direct action, an issue that perplexed radical socialists for many years also in the Transvaal and Natal. The federation decided on independent political action in June 1906 and advised the trades council accordingly. It then formed a Labour Representation Committee and called a meeting of delegates from all working-class bodies to 'present a united front to the enemy at the elections'. The two wings of the movement could not agree, however, and the federation decided in March 1907 to nominate Needham, Levinson and Howard for the parliamentary elections. Ridout stood for the municipal council and obtained 1,498 votes for socialism from the workmen's single vote; but his opponent got 3,000 votes from the plural suffrage of property owners.[6]

Trade unionists took a hard knock at Kimberley, where De Beers ruled with an iron rod. The leading spirit here was James Trembath, a Cornish compositor, who settled in the town after the siege of 1900 and struggled for more than ten years to organize a labour movement. An attempt was made to put up labour candidates in 1904, and when this failed Trembath and his associates formed a trades council. Seven of its nine members worked for De Beers, which summarily dismissed them in 1905 after a dispute over workmen's compensation. One of the victimized men was Walter Madeley (1873–1947), a fitter from Woolwich, who twenty years later held office in Hertzog's cabinet. The company's behaviour gave rise to much agitation, but the company never relaxed its grip on the town. Madeley and the other victims were unable to find work locally, while the council lost what influence it had over the majority of workmen. 'There are many good trade unionists who are but indifferent politicians and many good politicians who are not trade unionists,' declared Trembath. It was unfair, he added, to force any man to pay for political propaganda to which he might be wholly opposed.[7] For these reasons, a Political Labour League was formed to fight elections and conduct political campaigns.

Trembath urged working men in all centres to combine in order to put into parliament men who belonged to their class and looked after their interests. Without direct representation, he argued, they would always be mere pawns in the parliamentary game; they would receive only crumbs of labour legislation, never the loaf. Socialists in Durban held similar views and formed the Clarion Fellowship in 1903. Appealing to an all-white and almost wholly British electorate, Natal's labour movement took on a distinctly British flavour. The Fellowship was modelled on the English society of the same name, distributed its publications, contributed to Hyndman's election expenses, and helped to send E. B. Rose as South Africa's representative to the Second International congress at Amsterdam in 1905. The founders of the movement in Durban were two Scotsmen: A. L. Clark, 'the father of railway trade unionism', and Harry Norrie, a tailor from Forfarshire. Both spent their lives in preaching socialism, passed through many stages of radicalism, and never came to grips with the realities of Natal's multi-racial society.

The Fellowship sponsored a Workers' Political Union in 1905 to fight a parliamentary by-election in Durban. Their candidate, C. H. Haggar, a bearded, colourful doctor of philosophy from East Anglia, was defeated. But he won a seat in 1906 on the borough council as the nominee of the Natal Labour Representative Committee. This led to a quarrel between trade unionists and socialists over the choice of candidates that wrecked the trades council. Later in the year, however, Haggar, N. P. Palmer, D. Taylor and J. Connolly were elected on a Labour platform to the legislative assembly. Though this seemed a spectacular success, it reflected the amorphous nature of Natal's politics rather than the strength of its labour movement.

The Witwatersrand trade council's decision to form a Political Labour League followed hard on Lyttleton's promise in July 1904 of representative government for the Transvaal. The inaugural meeting took place only a year later on 31 August. Bill Andrews, the council's president, H. W. Sampson, its secretary, and Whiteside called for an end to Labour's local isolation, the formation of branches in every colony, and an all-South African campaign. The League's programme of twenty-two points made no concession, however, to the Cape's traditional policy of racial equality; and called for a union of the white races, equal rights for their languages, responsible government, white adult suffrage and single-member constituencies. Like their masters, the Labour leaders appealed for Anglo-Afrikaner unity at the expense of Africans, Coloured and Asians.

Andrews, Sampson and J. H. Brideson represented the League in Johannesburg's municipal elections of October 1905. All were defeated in a campaign marred by internal squabbles and appeals to racial prejudice. The miners' union threw its weight against Brideson, and the League sabotaged Andrews, its president. Its executive, which included Sampson and Whiteside, publicly rebuked him for allegedly repudiating his pledge to abide by caucus decisions. The Rev. C. A. Lane, who defeated him by twenty-one votes, included in his manifesto a demand for a ban on extra-marital intercourse between black and white; it was unnatural, he claimed, for the races had been differentiated by Nature and should be kept separate by law. C. H. Short, the third candidate in the ward, accused Andrews of being supported by the mine magnates of Corner House, condemned 'the tendency to mix the races', and denounced 'the preaching of the gospel of social equality of White and Black'. Andrews alone avoided such racist incitement, though he did not repudiate the League's undertaking to employ white labour where possible in municipal services.

While laying the foundations of their movement by taking part in municipal elections, Labour leaders staked a claim to representation on a higher plane by joining in the campaign for responsible government. Mine owners and big business men, with the backing of Milner and the Colonial Office, tried to keep the reins in their hands. They formed the Transvaal Progressive Association in November 1904 and advocated strong ties with Britain, Chinese labour, equal voting rights for white men, and an interim period of representative government. Abe Bailey, a leading mine director and Progressive politician, declared that he for one would not let the Boers 'win with the ballot-box what they had failed to accomplish with the Mauser'.[8]

Botha's Het Volk party, the Transvaal Responsible Government Association led by E. P. Solomon, and Labour countered with a demand for immediate self-rule. At times they seemed to interchange their traditional roles. Germiston workers heard Whiteside (who had served as a quartermaster-sergeant against the republic) denounce the Jameson raid and praise Kruger for having offered a franchise more generous than that proposed by the Lyttleton constitution.[9] A few days later, in February 1905, A. D. Wolmarans, an uncompromising member of Het Volk's head committee, told farmers at Nylstroom that they had no quarrel with Britain. Their enemy was the capitalist, who had made war on the republic and was now fighting artisans and farmers. They should stand together, stop the importation of Chinese, give employment to white men, and make the Transvaal a white man's country.[10]

When hotheaded republicans like Wolmarans and C. F. Beyers spoke of war between labour and capital, their rural audience took them to mean the old battle against foreigners, mine magnates and British imperialism. Het Volk represented landowners and not socialists. 'Capital and Labour must work hand in hand – the one could not do without the other,' was Louis Botha's message to the Pretoria branch of the ASE at their annual dinner in June 1905. He assured the engineers that his people, in their impoverished state, had drawn closer to the working man, for whom Paul Kruger always kept an open ear.[11] British workmen and Afrikaner landowners stood far apart in language, tradition and national loyalties. Many working men in the Transvaal preferred to remain under Britain's protective mantle and supported the plea of the mine owners for representative government.[12] Labour leaders who backed the demand for immediate self-government joined forces not with Afrikaners but with English-speaking merchants and professional men.

Whiteside, Wybergh, Shanks, Riatt and Creswell helped to draft the manifesto of the Responsible Government Association, signed it in the company of eighty others, and spoke on the association's platform. The Responsibles entered into an electoral pact with Het Volk after the publication in 1905 of the Lyttleton constitution, which provided for an elected majority in the legislature and an executive council dominated by British officials. Andrews and Sampson met representatives of the Responsibles in May to discuss an extension of the pact to include Labour, and reported back to the trades council, which agreed to support the pact on condition that Labour was free to press its own claims for the eight-hour working day, workmen's compensation and other reforms.[13]

The constitutional issue was settled by a change of government in Britain. Balfour's conservative ministry fell in December 1905. Campbell-Bannerman took office, went to the country in January 1906, and won an election unique in British politics for the prominence given to a wholly colonial issue – the Chinese importations. The new Liberal cabinet scrapped Lyttleton's constitution and, acting on the recommendations of the Ridgeway committee, decided to introduce quasi-responsible government in the Transvaal. It was to have a nominated upper chamber and a legislative assembly of sixty-nine white members elected by white men only. Political parties in the colony prepared for battle. Socialists and trade unionists formed the Independent Labour party in May 1906. Het Volk's executive on the Rand turned down a motion to cooperate with Labour which, it said, had socialist tendencies. The Responsibles, including Creswell and Wybergh, merged with the Reform Club, called themselves the Transvaal Nationalist Association, and renewed their electoral agreement with Het Volk. Labour held aloof and, in December 1906, formed the Labour Representation Committee. It combined trade unionists, the ILP, and small left-wing groups of Germans, Italians and Russian Jews.

Socialists, trade unionists and political opportunists painfully edged their way to united action. Some trade unionists complained that socialists dominated the LRC. A British Labour Union, making a brief appearance before the 1907 elections, denounced the 'fallacious doctrine of socialism as propounded by the Socialist Labour Parties'.[14] At the other end of the spectrum, Jock Campbell's Socialist Labour party, formed in 1902, turned its back on all elections and distributed the works of Karl Kautsky, Daniel De Leon and his fellow syndicalists.[15] Labour managed in spite of these differences to put up thirteen candidates in the Transvaal general election of February 1907. They polled 5,216 votes out of the 13,180 cast in the thirteen constituencies and won three seats. Sampson and Whiteside were returned in Johannesburg, and J. Reid in Pretoria. Het Volk won thirty-seven seats, which gave it a clear majority of five, and Botha included E. P. Solomon and H. C. Hull, two leaders of the Transvaal Nationalist Association, in his cabinet.

Het Volk did not oppose the Labour candidates. These lost to the Nationalists in three, and to the Progressives in seven, constituencies. As in Natal and the Cape, the bulk of the working-class vote went to parties representing capitalists and the middle class. They, and not Afrikaner nationalism, were Labour's chief political rivals. Sampson said as much when he reported back in October 1907 to his constituents. He was pleased that the Progressives were not in power. Labour's representatives were having an easy time under Botha's ministry. It had passed a workman's compensation act and could be relied upon to enforce laws against Asians. Labour looked forward, he added, to the elimination of Asians from the Transvaal, and would press for a law fixing ratios between whites and Africans in all industries.[16]

Sampson was a compositor from Islington, London, who came to South Africa in 1892 at the age of twenty. He spent the next five years in Cape Town, where he helped to form a trades council; and then moved, after a printers' strike, to East London, where he founded a branch of the S.A. Typographical Union. Settling in Johannesburg in 1903, he became the union's president and also secretary of the trades council. He lost three municipal elections before winning a seat in the legislative assembly; but then his parliamentary career continued without a break from 1907 to 1931. He was elected the first chairman of the S.A. Labour party at its formation in 1910. Ambitious, arrogant and racist, he was a principal architect of the white labour policy. His own union 'committed the dreadful sin' of admitting Natal Indian printers, but there was no truth whatever in the 'oft-repeated lie' that Sampson, as president, bore a special responsibility for the decision.[17] Radicals accused him of disrupting the party caucus in the Transvaal parliament by quarrelling with Whiteside and refusing to accept party discipline.[18] Partly for this reason, the ILP at its first annual conference in October 1907 repudiated the parliamentary actions of the three Labour members.[19]

The heterogeneous elements in the Labour Representation Committee could never agree on a programme. The ILP, however, was explicitly socialist. It aimed, among other things, at 'The socialization of all the means of production, distribution and exchange, to be controlled by a democratic state in the interests of the whole community.' Whiteside explained that this was a beacon light, an ideal to be worked for, though nationalization of the mines was impracticable under existing conditions.[20] Some members wished to call themselves the

Transvaal Socialistic Party, but the annual conference rejected the motion. Delegates were divided equally on another motion, which would allow members of the 'coloured races' to join the party. New alignments and cleavages developed, however, before the various factions agreed in 1909 to form the South African Labour party. It made its official debut at Durban on 10 January 1910 as the first national political party. Labour was all set for the first round of elections under the South Africa Act.

The Act had been drafted by an all-white National Convention in 1908–9. Described as a 'compromise' between Cape liberals and white supremacists of the north, it represented the fruits of partnership or, more accurately, of antagonistic co-operation between British and Afrikaner imperialists, each intending to dominate the other. The British wanted union for economic, political and military reasons. Afrikaners accepted cooperation as the price to be paid for the spread of nationalism and the maintenance of white supremacy. Africans, Coloured and Indians were the victims of closer union. The act excluded them from both houses of parliament and denied them the vote in the three northern provinces. The background to the colour bar clauses has been admirably described by the liberal historian L. M. Thompson.[21] Here it is necessary only to comment on the attitudes of the labour and liberation movements.

None of the delegates to the National Convention represented Labour, and this was a sore point with Labour leaders. They made the most of it in their opposition to union and the draft act. The strongest opposition came from Natal, where organized Labour appeared in the same camp as ultra-British jingos. Both groups preferred isolation to Afrikaner domination. Labour men had an additional grievance in action taken by the government to break a railwaymen's strike in April-May 1909. Three of the four Labour members of the legislative assembly moved that the union parliament should have only one chamber, to be elected once in three years. Haggar, to his credit, moved the deletion of the clause barring persons of colour from the house of assembly. The amendments were defeated, and three-quarters of the 14,800 Natal voters who took part in a referendum voted in favour of union.

Whiteside, Sampson and Wybergh offered mild resistance to the draft in the Transvaal legislature. Trade unionists stated their objections in resolutions passed at a labour rally in Johannesburg on Good Friday of 1909. Madeley, C. B. Mussared, a leading member of the ILP, and Tom Kirby, president of the Pretoria trade council, moved that since workers had not been represented at the National Convention, and since the draft act was undemocratic, it should be submitted to a popular referendum. Bill Andrews and the Labour councillors John Ware and Jackson moved another resolution which called on the British government to withhold its assent until the draft had been amended and approved by a referendum of the electorate. The proposed amendments would eliminate the senate, introduce a separate 'Native and Coloured Assembly' having only advisory powers, block the extension of the Cape's 'coloured franchise', and confine the vote to adult whites, subject to retention of their rights by existing Coloured voters in the Cape.

Tengo Jabavu, cautious as ever, took an intermediate position. He would give adult suffrage to white men and women, and the Cape franchise to Africans. It had worked well and needed no change. His scheme would prevent 'native predominance'.[22] He steadfastly set his face against any agitation on behalf of the Africans while the National Convention was sitting. They should put their trust in the Cape's liberal delegates and not cry out before they were hurt. The Convention was 'a judicial tribunal set up to do justice to all sections without fear, favour or prejudice'. An agitation would be premature, give his people a bad name, and strengthen the argument that they had no place in the 'body politic'.[23] When the publication of the draft act exposed the shallowness of his optimism, he pleaded that the colour bar clauses imposed an unnecessary humiliation. Africans, he insisted, had no desire to sit in parliament where they could exert no influence.[24] He repeated this assurance on the *Armadale Castle* in July 1909, when on his way to London with an African delegation to protest against the colour bar. 'We have no wish to have a Native preponderance in the country,' he said; 'it is a thing which I should object to myself.' He 'would dread putting our people in a position of absolute equality with the

Europeans, especially in the Northern colonies'. But rights already held in the Cape should not be curtailed; 'and as to the rest, some restricted form of representation might be given'.[25]

There was a streak of the Uncle Tom in Jabavu, but he was no white man's lackey. He had principles and a strategy based on an assessment of the African's relationship to competing white power groups. Long ago, he explained, when the English dominated parliament, parties divided on the 'Native Question'. One faction, led by Porter, Solomon, Molteno, Sauer and Merriman, took a liberal view and fought for the liberties of both colonists and Africans. Opposed to them were the majority of Englishmen, who followed reactionary leaders like the Upingtons, Sprigg and later Rhodes. They adopted a 'vigorous Native policy', signalized by disarmament, disfranchisement, pass laws and other 'repressive legislation under which the Natives ... have ever groaned'. Africans naturally supported the liberals. The Afrikaner Bond as naturally allied itself with the anti-African party. The Jameson raid severed the alliance. The Bond then transferred its support to the liberal, anti-imperialist group led by Sauer, Merriman and Schreiner, which Africans had always supported and which became the South African party in 1903.[26]

The English press and party insisted that Jabavu, 'an able and most influential Kaffir', had 'gone over' to the Bond or 'Strop en Dop' party,* if only by associating with Sauer and the SAP.[27] Jabavu was too astute a politician to suppose that he could refute the charge with an historical treatise. His people were hard-headed, cold logicians, he maintained, and had no desire to instal a 'Dutch' government at Table Mountain. He wished to satisfy them that he was no Bondsman and, like they, wanted a government of 'the best Englishmen who will dispense justice evenly to English, Dutch and Native people, without fear, favour or prejudice'. On the other hand, he had to show that Africans had nothing to expect from the English Progressive party, and should vote against it at the polls. He gave two reasons. By making Jameson their leader, the Progressives had shown

* The 'Lash and Liquor' party: a reference to Cape farmers who flogged their workers and supplied them with rations of cheap wine.

themselves willing to 'hand over the government of the people to the Mining Magnates', whose sole interest was 'Wealth and not the Commonwealth of South Africa'. Secondly, the Progressives hated African rights, as was evident from Jameson's letter of 20 September 1903 to the Muslim leader H. N. Effendi. It promised 'equal rights to all civilized men' and went on to insult Africans by stating that 'It is only the aboriginal natives we consider uncivilized'.[28]

Africans might have shared Jabavu's misgivings about Jameson's party, but they certainly had less confidence in political descendants of the Afrikaner Bond, whose leader, J. H. Hofmeyr, had declared that he would sooner give franchise rights to convicts in the Breakwater prison than to the coloured races.[29] African and Coloured delegates, including Dr Abdurahman, met at Queenstown in December 1907 and decided to support the Unionist party, as the Progressives were now called. Jabavu's paper printed a vicious attack on Abdurahman – 'a man of mixed race' who was 'ashamed of his skin' – and denounced the conference. It was 'not representative'. The 'so-called vote to support the ex-Prog. candidates was passed by a few ignorant people of the rank and file'.[30] Jabavu prepared a counterblast and called a Native Electoral Convention in January. It urged constituents to vote for the SAP and passed resolutions in favour of African rights in the future Union.[31] The SAP won the election, Merriman headed the new ministry, and Jabavu jubilated. 'Of the 12 newspapers published within the Eastern circuit, *Imvo* is the only one in sympathy with the SAP.'[32]

The publication of the draft constitution in February 1909 aroused bitter resentment in Africans and Coloured. Jabavu blamed Natal for insisting on the 'European descent' clauses that barred men of colour from parliament and denied them the vote in the northern provinces.[33] The Rev. W. B. Rubusana's *Izwi Labantu* accused the Cape delegates to the National Convention of conspiring to eliminate the Cape African franchise. Rubusana, Jabavu and the Rev. J. L. Dube, editor of *Ilanga Lase Natal*, convened a South African Native Convention at Bloemfontein on 24 March. It elected an executive to defend African interests, protested against the colour bar, demanded full and equal rights for all citizens without distinction of class, colour or creed, and called on Britain to fulfil her obligations under article 8 of the Vereeniging peace treaty by extending the franchise to Africans, Coloured and Indians in all colonies.[34] The convention agreed to send a delegation to England.

The APO took a similar decision in April. Its campaign for a non-racial franchise had begun in 1906, when Abdurahman, Fredericks and Daniels journeyed to England to protest against the terms of the Ridgeway constitution. The deputation's main purpose was to establish the claims of the Coloured to the franchise under article 8 of the Vereeniging treaty, but Abdurahman spoke for all the oppressed. If Britain refused to grant a non-racial franchise, he urged, there were other ways in which she could do justice to all her subjects. She could, for instance, before granting self-government to the ex-republics, repeal their discriminatory laws. They were still there, had been augmented, and were enforced with typical British rigour. Secondly, Britain should either extend the franchise to qualified persons of all races, or retain her sovereign authority over the unrepresented masses. In no circumstances should she commit them bound hand and foot to the colonists.[35]

The deputation returned empty-handed but undaunted. The campaign continued and assumed a new dimension when the APO's executive accepted an invitation to attend the joint conference of Africans and Coloured at Queenstown. About 120 delegates came together, said Abdurahman, in 'the first genuine attempt to fuse the two sections of the population into one political whole'.[36] The men of the north, he told them, would always try to foist their repressive system on the coloured races; but would have less chance of success in a federation. For a union would be bound to follow the policies of the north more closely than Cape traditions.[37] When the National Convention met to draft the Act of Union, the APO petitioned it to respect existing rights and extend them to Coloured and Africans in the north. After the publication of the draft constitution petitions were submitted to the prime ministers, the high commissioner and the secretary of state, praying for the deletion of the colour bar clauses, the extension of the franchise to all qualified persons in the Union, and the exclusion of 'native territories' from the Union except on terms satisfactory to chiefs and councillors.[38]

Their rights were being whittled away for purely material advantages, said Abdurahman in his presidential address to the eighty-nine delegates who attended the APO's seventh annual conference in the Socialist Hall, Buitenkant St, Cape Town, on 13 April 1909. The draft act was 'un-British in that it lays down a colour-line'. The Cape's leaders had betrayed their trust; the light of freedom was vanishing before the old Transvaal republic's principle of no equality between black and white in church or state. 'No class in a State can progress,' he warned, 'if its political destinies are in the hands of a ruling caste'; or if it denied human rights that were inalienable and essential to national stability.[39] The 'European descent' clauses, which barred persons of colour from parliament, were 'the foulest work that ever South African statesmen attached their names to', wrote Abdurahman in the second issue of the *A.P.O.* 'The original insult is there as fresh and bitter as when it was first deliberately hurled at us last February. It is an injustice, and cannot be tolerated by any self-respecting man.'[40]

The decision to send a deputation, accompanied by W. P. Schreiner, to put their case before the British people and parliament, aroused great enthusiasm; and 'stimulated the feeling of union among the coloured', reported the APO's Aliwal North branch. More than twenty new branches were formed, fund-raising activities were organized as far afield as Rhodesia, and the first number of the *A.P.O.* appeared on Empire Day, 24 May 1909. Every existing newspaper was there primarily to advocate the rights of property, wrote the editor; all assumed that South Africa belonged only to the few propertied whites. The press patronizingly condescended to the coloured races and regarded them as chattels: 'ever the subject race'. The *A.P.O.* would speak for the people. Time would show that a repressive policy was 'impossible, uneconomic and disastrous to all concerned'. For nothing but moral decay and national degeneracy could come out of a racial aristocracy that dominated a degraded class.

Abdurahman, Fredericks and D. J. Lenders of Kimberley

sailed for England in June. The African delegates were Jabavu, Rubusana, D. Dwanya of Middeldrift, T. Mapikela, the general secretary of the Orange River Native Congress, and J. Gerrans of Bechuanaland. The two deputations and W. P. Schreiner, their unpaid counsellor and tireless spokesman, represented the great majority of South Africans; but they travelled at their own expense and by means of funds donated by the poor. At about the same time an official colonial delegation, accompanied by the high commissioner, travelled at the state's expense to put the bill entrenching white supremacy through the imperial parliament. The official delegation was given a roaring reception in England; the unofficial representatives were snubbed and ignored by the wielders of power. Philanthropists, missionaries, Gandhi, the prime minister of New Zealand, the British Labour party and a group of Liberals in parliament protested against the colour bar. The people of Britain were bored and indifferent. They had already surrendered sovereign power to the white oligarchy in Natal and the ex-republics. The South Africa Act merely put the final seal of Britain's approval on the betrayal at Vereeniging in 1902.

Asquith, Balfour, *The Times*, *The Economist* and other pillars of the imperial establishment oozed an unctuous optimism. They agreed, on the one hand, that the settlers would abandon unification rather than agree to an abatement of racial discrimination in the act. The British public was assured, on the other, that the racists, who would forgo the advantages of union if necessary to maintain white supremacy, could be trusted to do justice to the subject races. Not everybody was as gullible. Dilke, Keir Hardie and Ramsay MacDonald foresaw that the Act of Union would establish a permanent white oligarchy. The *Manchester Guardian* warned against deluding 'ourselves with the promise that we can undo the injustice when it is committed'.[41] J. A. Hobson commented wryly on the irony of defeated Afrikaner generals imposing on Britain a constitution which made them 'the rulers of a virtually independent South Africa'. It would 'move upon an unstable axis' and remain a source of 'weakness to the group of self-governing nationalities to which it falsely claims to belong'.[42] The *Labour Leader* declared that Britain had approved of 'the union of a Boer Landed Aristocracy with an Exploiting Capitalist Plutocracy'; and damned South African trade unionists for being anti-African to a man.[43]

'Since our arrival here it has been a terribly up-hill fight,' wrote Abdurahman on 29 July. 'We are directing all our efforts and energies to the term "of European descent", but I fear all our efforts will be in vain.' The Cape's official delegates – the prime minister Merriman, Sauer, Hofmeyr, Jameson and chief justice Lord de Villiers – were 'our worst enemies'. Without the poison from them, the British public would never agree to the hateful colour bar. They were 'moving heaven and earth to retain the obnoxious words'; and 'naturally their opinions carry great weight, because the public who will suffer directly by the words "of European descent" are the Cape Colony people.'[44] Critics of the colour bar in the Commons made their main stand on an amendment to clause 26, which would enable men of colour to represent the Cape and Natal in the senate; but the amendment was defeated by 157 votes to 57, the minority consisting of 28 Labour members, 26 Liberals, and 3 Irish nationalists.[45] The bill was reported without amendment and passed the third reading without a division.

The African and Coloured deputations returned with Schreiner to South Africa in September. They tried to glean comfort from their failure. The minds of English people had been enlightened as to the colour bar, Schreiner claimed; while Abdurahman assumed 'that at a very early date an attempt would be made to erase the blot which now stained the Constitution'.[46] Abdurahman's true assessment appeared in a leading article. Britain's national fibre had deteriorated. Everyone regretted the colour bar, but no one would reject it, apart from the Labour party and advanced radicals. 'No longer must we look to our flabby friends of Great Britain.' The political destiny of Coloured and Africans lay in their own hands. They would have to rely on economic struggle. 'We are the labour market'; and South Africa's stability depended on them. By refusing to bolster up the economy, they would bring selfish white politicians to their knees, and show white workers the value of combination – their only weapon against the cursed wage system.[47]

6 National Liberation

The teachers, ministers, editors, lawyers and doctors who founded the liberation movements were constitutionalists. They defended existing rights and resisted new discriminations in a constant struggle against aggressive white supremacists. African, Coloured and Indian leaders of the early period took their inspiration from liberal and humanitarian concepts. Their vision of the ideal society embraced equality before the law; the vote; freedom of trade, labour, movement and residence; and equal opportunities of education and employment. Their natural allies in the white community before the rise of radical socialism were liberals of wealth and standing who counselled patience, acceptance of white supremacy, and respect for law and order; and who left a deep imprint on the liberation movement, most of all in the Cape. There, the non-racial franchise gave Africans and Coloured the means of enlisting the support of progressive politicians. Jabavu was one of the first to recognize the value of an organized, disciplined African electorate. His entanglement in white party politics began with the publication of *Imvo* in 1884. Twenty years later Abdurahman embarked on a similar course when he took his seat on Cape Town's municipal council.

Gandhi rose to world-wide eminence after he had left South Africa in 1914. Jabavu and Abdurahman might also have made their way into the top rank of rulers if they had lived in a less repressive society. Racial discrimination restricted them to a minor political role, but they were great men among their people. Though unwilling, and perhaps unable, to alienate themselves from the poor and oppressed, they did not escape from the compromises that are forced on leaders without power who seek to reform but never to overthrow an evil social order. Both men witnessed the decline of Cape liberalism and the spread of racial discrimination. Abdurahman saw the process more clearly and gained a deeper insight into the structure of white power. Yet, like Jabavu, he maintained his trust in white patronage long after the futility of such an attitude had been revealed. Neither took to heart Gandhi's message that a voteless and rejected people would not obtain relief from a parliament of their oppressors, but must depend on their own strength and develop their own methods of struggle.

Dr Abdul Abdurahman (1872–1940), acclaimed as South Africa's foremost Coloured leader, was a Muslim, a member of the 'Malay' community, and a grandson of manumitted slaves, Chashullah and Betsy Jamal-ud-din (corrupted to Jamalee) who bought their freedom. They kept a fruit shop in Roeland Street, Cape Town, amassed a small fortune, and sent their son Abdul Rachman to study theology at Cairo and Mecca. He returned after an absence of ten years and married Khadija Dollie, 'the prettiest Malay girl in Cape Town'.[1] Widely known as Hadjie Abdurahman, he pioneered modern education for the Muslims and refused to put up with a second-class education for his own sons. His eldest, the future Dr Abdurahman, was admitted to the S.A. College School, the oldest high school in the country, 'where, by his diligence and ability, he outdistanced his comrades in almost every branch of school work'.[2] The college then raised a colour bar, whereupon the Hadjie went to England and stayed there, while his second son qualified as a chemist, and the youngest as a doctor. He lost his wife in England, and by her side was later buried her brother, H. M. Dollie, the father of Dr O. Dollie, who also took his children to be educated in England.[3]

Having matriculated at the Cape, Abdul Abdurahman went to Glasgow, where he spent close on four years before graduating in medicine in 1893. Two years later he came home with his Scottish bride. 'He makes a great sacrifice,' wrote Peregrino, 'in returning to a country where colour, and not character, ability or standing, makes the man.'[4] In 1904, now a successful practitioner, he was elected to the town council, the first coloured person to hold this office. 'I was reluctant to enter public life because failure at the polls would have drawn ridicule upon the coloureds,' he wrote after the election; but 'it is by individuals stepping beyond the establishments of the time that a people progress.'[5] The European support he received at the polls 'does not betoken a white race degenerating, but a sign of rejuvenescence'. The British constitution was 'the admiration of the world, and one of the greatest blessings of mankind'. As leader of the APO, Abdurahman spent much of the next five years in an unsuccessful attempt to vindicate his faith in British democracy.

The elan and vigour of the African Political Organization in its early and middle years held great promise of a mass radical movement. Founded in 1902, it soon grew into what was perhaps the first national party, open to persons of all races and with branches in all the colonies. It failed to attract significant numbers of Africans and Indians, however, and remained predominantly Coloured, centred in the western Cape and concerned mainly with Coloured affairs. Abdurahman traced its origins to the political awakening brought about by Carnarvon's confederation scheme and the Anglo-Afrikaner war; but a more immediate impulse came from participation in parliamentary politics. One of the APO's first activities was to strengthen and mobilize the Coloured vote by urging qualified men to apply for registration on the electoral rolls. It made substantial gains by taking part in white party politics, but also encountered great hazards which often threatened to wreck the organization. The first of these crises occurred soon after its formation.

John Tobin, a foundation member and an advocate of 'reconciliation' between Coloured and white Afrikaners, canvassed for the SAP-Bond alliance in the general election of 1904. W. Collins, the APO's first president, favoured the Progressives, who were supported also by Peregrino and other members of the Coloured Peoples' Vigilance Committee. To avoid a split, the organization expelled both men and invited Abdurahman to take the leadership. He joined the Cape Town branch in 1904 and was elected in 1905 to the presidency, an office which he held up to the time of his death in 1940. He was 'not a Progressive or a Bondsman,' he told the annual conference in Port Elizabeth; and would never cease to agitate on behalf of their people as long as they were unjustly treated. The Coloured people were very fortunate, wrote *Imvo*, in having him as their leader. They could not have a more trustworthy guide. Whites were woefully mistaken in thinking that they could repress the Coloured and African people, 'as a policy of that kind is only calculated to unite and make the Coloured inhabitants more determined in claiming their own'.[6]

The Chinese importations, colour bars on the mines, and the transfer of ultimate power to settlers in the Transvaal and Orange River Colony stirred Abdurahman to anger. His inaugural address at the APO's annual conference in January 1906 was one long indictment of the 'cosmopolitan exploiters' whose greed for gold had given rise to the system of indentured labour. 'Chamberlain, the great Imperial wanderer, visited South Africa, sympathized with the downtrodden Magnates, saw a Native war dance at Colenso, and gave the Rand lords forced labour at 1d. an hour.' The Flag had never been in such despicable hands since the old slave days. The ex-republics under British rule were 'simply Imperial prisons for coloured people, who are but goods and chattels in the hands of the country's exploiters'.[7] The English press accused him of 'incendiary talk' and of 'stirring up the embers of race feud'. Johannesburg's municipal council refused to let him address a Coloured audience in the town hall, whereas the anti-Chinese opposition declared that he 'expressed in most outspoken language the feeling of ninety-nine per cent of the voters'.[8]

The APO's mission to England in 1906 failed to convince the British government that it was morally bound to extend the franchise to the Coloured in the north. Abdurahman then threw his weight behind the federal cause, represented in the Cape by the Progressive party. Jameson had said that federation would enable the Cape to 'hold to our Native policy until the neighbouring colonies are sufficiently educated to agree to allow equal facilities for blacks and whites to rise in the scale of humanity'.[9] The APO accordingly agreed at its annual conference in Indwe to support the Progressives in the 1908 general election.[10] Tobin, Peregrino and Jabavu backed Merriman's South African party; it won the election and argued the case for a unitary constitution. Jameson and his fellow Progressive delegates to the National

Convention switched their allegiance, assented to a unitary constitution, and accepted without protest the exclusion of persons of colour from both houses of parliament.[11] The APO's second mission to England in 1909 failed to secure the deletion of the colour bar clauses. Abdurahman had not failed, he wrote, to learn that 'the rights of unrepresented classes of citizens are always unsafe, and are never free from invasion'.[12]

The African and Coloured delegations returned smarting under the stigma of the colour bar and toured the Cape to report on their mission. At a public banquet attended by 300 notables in Queenstown in April 1910 Abdurahman and Jabavu appealed for a political union of all the coloured races. Abdurahman reminded an African audience at Indwana a few days later that he had warned against unification, the form of constitution advocated by the SAP, which had shown no sympathy with the African and Coloured peoples. Their first duty was to have a political union. 'If they achieved that their full re-enfranchisement would be rendered easier.'[13] The need for unity was a constant theme in Abdurahman's speeches at this time. Coloured South Africans, he reiterated, were sons of the soil and had as great a claim to the country as any white settler. If 'Europeans persist in their policy of repression, there will one day arise a solid mass of Black and Coloured humanity whose demands will be irresistible.'[14]

The contemplated union never took shape. African and Coloured leaders joined in protest, but the political ties between their peoples were never more than tenuous. Geographical isolation, barriers of language, custom and race, economic differences and inequalities of status restrained them from merging into a single organization. Colour consciousness tended to smother class or national consciousness in the Coloured. They displayed an acute awareness of physical traits and a sensitiveness to gradations of colour that blocked the growth of unity within the group itself. 'And so through pride,' wrote a correspondent in the *A.P.O.*, 'the Coloured people, the true sons and daughters of South Africa, are today divided, and consequently their political and industrial positions are becoming more critical day by day.' Many slightly coloured persons passed for Europeans. 'Some of them select who, and who not, to recognize in public, through being desirous of being regarded as Europeans.' They often feared that if they supported a dark-complexioned person in political life, he would expect a greeting in the street. Until 'the slightly-coloured and the pitch black confer at one table, we will only dream of what we would be, and remain the shadows that we are.'[15]

Genealogical gossip was a favourite pastime of Afrikaners and even more popular among the Coloured. They took malicious pleasure in tracing the dark-skinned ancestry of their rulers. If the 'European descent' clause meant that no ancestor was coloured, the *A.P.O.* remarked, it would bar two ministers of the crown in the Cape, one in the Transvaal, and several members of the Cape parliament, one of whom 'bears a titular distinction'.[16] Such men might at least show sympathy with their kith and kin. 'But those who try to hide the little colour that is in them are always the bitterest anti-colour advocates.'[17] When Botha formed his cabinet after the first Union elections, the paper dubbed it the regime of 'the half-white ministry'. Five of its ten members were not of pure European descent.[18] Yet the 'piebald Botha Government' would employ only poor whites, and oust even Coloured relatives of ministers from the public service. The only government billet open to the Coloured would before long be 'a portfolio in the Union ministry'.[19]

White-baiting provided an emotional relief but left the imbalance of power unchanged. The APO failed to develop suitable methods of mass struggle in spite of the example set by Gandhi's passive resistance campaign. At Abdurahman's request, Gandhi contributed an article on his struggle 'for national honour, for conscience, and for manhood' in which he claimed that his methods were 'as pure as the ideal itself. Suffering is the panacea for all evils. It purifies the sufferers.' Passive resistance, he contended, would lead to violence only if soul force were transmuted into body force; and was therefore best for 'illiterate natives'. It taught them to break their own heads and not other people's in order to redress grievances.[20] The closest that the APO came to instituting a passive resistance campaign was to urge the Coloured in Pretoria to conduct one against the municipality's decision to segregate them in townships. The Coloured residents preferred law suits to broken heads, however, and took the council to court.[21]

A P O militants often spoke of using the 'economic weapon', but this too failed to materialize, although there were sufficient numbers of Coloured working men in the western Cape to make the political strike a feasible tactic. They were poorly organized, and reluctant to follow the A P O except during elections. Abdurahman tried hard to form trade unions, partly in order to detach Coloured workers from white labour leaders, and met with little success except among the teachers. Like Jabavu, he believed that his people would never hold their own against the colonists without a modern education, and so made this his primary concern. He fought a stubborn rearguard action against the spread of segregation in schools; used his position in the town council to force the S.A. College (later the University of Cape Town) to admit Harold Cressy and other Coloured students after him; and with J. W. Jagger, a prosperous merchant, induced the school board to establish the Trafalgar High School, the first of its kind for Coloured, in 1910.[22] Many children owed their education to his private generosity. The *A.P.O.* gave much attention to educational needs, agitated for better facilities, admonished parents to send their children to school, and ventilated the grievances of the teachers.

The formation of the S.A. Teachers' League in 1912–13 marked an important stage in the emergence of an intellectual leadership among the Coloured. Cressy, Francis Brutus, F. Hendricks and Abe Desmore, among others, worked closely with the A P O, contributed to its paper, and through their own quarterly, the *Educational Journal*, instilled in teachers a sense of national pride and of duty to their people. Employed in church schools, they were badly trained, grossly discriminated against, and underpaid at salaries ranging from £5 to £12 10s. a month. 'The argument has been brought forward persistently,' wrote Brutus, 'that Coloured teachers cannot receive anything above a mere pittance in respect of salary because of the Native teachers, whose case has still to be dealt with.'[23] They had a remedy, he suggested. Let them combine with the Africans, who were then affiliated to the white-dominated Teachers' Association. The Coloured teachers, who were timid, politically backward and race conscious, continued to segregate themselves in the League.

The APO's leadership of intellectuals and small businessmen sedulously avoided mass struggles. They adopted, instead, the techniques of a parliamentary party, and concentrated on election campaigns. Coloured and African voters held the balance in a dozen or so Cape constituencies. White candidates solicited their support during elections and ignored them at other times. Some of the money spent on elections trickled into the pockets of local agents, who were often leading members of APO branches, and from them to individual voters. The alleged corruption of the Coloured electorate, often given as a reason for taking the Coloured off the common roll, grew out of the colour bar constitution. A vote without power proved to be more demoralizing than total disfranchisement. Coloured politicians tended to become appendages of white parties, which denied them membership and rewarded them with scraps of political loot. The worst evil was not bribery, however, but the failure of the leaders to develop an alternative conception of the Coloured man's role in politics.

The Coloured were *stemvee* – voting cattle – in the Afrikaner's vocabulary of contempt. They put their cross on ballot papers but never took part in the selection of candidates or in the making of policies. Since all parliamentary parties stood for white supremacy, the Coloured voter could only choose between evils. He usually chose the English party, representing the industrialists, merchants and professions, who were protected by class barriers from Coloured competition and could therefore afford to deplore the grosser forms of racial discrimination, provided always that the darker man 'kept his place'. The leading liberal R. W. Rose Innes complained bitterly when the Rev. Rubusana, newly elected to the provincial council, exercised his right to travel in a first-class compartment with bedding, blankets and pillow supplied by the railway administration.[24] While insisting on social segregation, the English middle class objected to the industrial colour bar which interfered with the employment of the lowest-priced worker. They were his natural ally on the labour market against the policy of sheltered white labour. If the APO ever had a political theory – and only glimpses of one appeared in the diatribes against racial discrimination – it was that an expanding, progressive capitalism would dissolve caste rigidities and give all men equal opportunities in a competitive society.

It was impossible to relate this perspective to Botha's party of landowners. They preferred stagnation to progress if progress would bring equality in its train. Tradition, sentiment and party interest induced them to buttress caste divisions with statutory sanctions. The Coloured had little to expect from Afrikaner Nationalists, who made a 'white South Africa' one of their planks in the 1910 general election, remarked the *A.P.O.*[25] It reported resolutions passed by congresses of farmers urging government to expel African tenants from white-owned land, indenture their families to farmers, raise the hut tax and put convicts to work on public undertakings.[26] There was something radically wrong, the journal observed, when cabinet ministers invoked the black bogy to persuade whites to keep their children at school, accept compulsory military training, and employ whites only on skilled work.[27] Hertzog's 'narrow racialism' was a menace to the Empire. He wished to extend the harsh, in-human laws of the 'mis-named Free State' to all the provinces. 'In that prison-house of South Africa – worse even than the despotism of Russia – the Coloured people cannot work without a permit.'[28]

Abdurahman told the APO's annual conference at Port Elizabeth in 1910 that in terms of the constitution each branch would decide for itself which candidate to support in the forthcoming election of the first Union parliament. The APO as an organization could not bind itself to any particular party. Subsequently, however, he advised the branches to support Jameson's Unionists against the ruling coalition under Botha. Raynard and some other members of the APO who objected that this directive violated the constitution were expelled or resigned.[29] Jabavu, as always, backed the party of Sauer, who held a portfolio in the Botha ministry; and accused Abdurahman of 'prejudicing the case of the Coloured people in the eyes of the great Party in

Power'. He was playing into the hands of the Transvaal by setting Coloured against Coloured.[30]

Botha's coalition of Afrikaner parties, which formally merged into the S.A. National party in 1911, won the election with sixty-seven seats. The Unionists, representing mine owners, industrialists, merchants and the majority of English-speaking voters, won thirty-nine seats; the Labour party, four seats, all in the Transvaal; and eleven seats went to independents. All parties fought on a platform of white supremacy, promised to protect the interests of white workers, and accused one another of 'racialism', the current term for being anti-Afrikaner or anti-British. Botha and Smuts, in common with the Labour party, called Unionists the 'capitalist party'. Unionists on the Rand asked the electorate to 'Vote British'. The Labour party replied that the capitalists who used the slogan were foreign Jews. This was not the first time that Labour had disgraced itself with anti-Semitism. Tom Mathews lost the Fordsburg municipal seat in 1908 because he called the capitalists 'Jews'.[31]

Arthur Noon polled 296 votes for Labour in Cape Town Central against the 1,695 votes cast for Jagger, the Unionist candidate. The APO had supported Noon when he contested a municipal seat in August 1909. Then, he had been 'a true friend of all workers of every class and creed and colour', who would 'voice the views of all wage earners and tenants'.[32] In 1910, however, the APO supported Jagger. They would 'like to see Mr Noon returned some day, but it will take much time and labour to convert the people of Cape Town to Socialism'.[33] This vacillation reflected the ambivalence in Abdurahman's attitude to the labour movement.

The British Labour party's opposition to the colour bar clauses in the South African Act left a deep impression. 'It is the one party,' declared the *A.P.O.*, 'in whose hands the honour of Old England can safely be trusted.' Untainted by trade, not bemused by firearms, its democracy was pure. Labour would sweep the 'wretched hucksters' out of office at the next election. The Coloured hoped for a like display of class solidarity in South Africa. 'The same result will follow here as soon as all workers, white or black, learn that they are the country, and that on labour everything rests.'[34] When the Cape railways advertised vacancies for white labourers only on construction works at Piquetberg, the paper appealed to trade unionists to join in protest. 'Too long have black and white been played off against one another. . . . It is to the Socialists that we must look for help in our fight against a class tyranny that deprives us of political freedom.'[35]

It was a class as well as a racial tyranny. The word *kleurlyn* concealed the realities of capitalist exploitation behind the myth of racial inferiority. The 'colour line' was a subterfuge used to persuade the world that the darker races were inferior and incapable of undertaking so-called white man's work.[36] All employers took part in the exploitation. The capitalists hired 'Kaffir drudges' because these worked for a scanty wage. There was no more virtue in politicians like Sauer, Merriman and Burton, who employed convicts on their farms, than in the Rand magnates, who imported Chinese.[37] Smuts might appeal for unity between white South Africans, few of whom did physical work except on the rugby field. The whole industrial and economic structure depended on the coloured races. Even Merriman, 'the greatest jabberer of the crowd', grew pumpkins by proxy with coloured workers, 'save when he can get white aristocratic convicts to slave for less pay'.[38]

Abdurahman retained his early faith in working-class unity for many years in spite of rebuffs by white trade unionists who agitated for colour bars. White workers erred, his paper argued, in looking on the Coloured as their enemy. They should declare war on indentured labour, whether for mines, farms or domestic service. Coloured workers, like the whites, sold their skills to the highest bidder. Neither could obtain their true reward without cooperation. The employer, their economic enemy, could win only by playing off one group against the other. Unless white artisans overcame their stupid prejudices, their prospects were no brighter than the Coloured's. 'Workers of all creeds and colours must stand together; must put an end to all divisions.' Unfortunately, the spirit of solidarity – the basis of all trade unionism – was 'deeper engraved in the heart of the Coloured artisan than it is in that of the white'.[39]

When Noon and Tom Maginess spoke to APO branches on Labour's racial policies, Abdurahman declared himself to be a socialist, like any public man who tried to improve the position of the lower classes. By cooperation they could bring the capitalists to their knees within forty-eight hours. He objected to strikes, as they caused more misery than they alleviated, but the strike appeared to be the only weapon available. Maginess and many of his comrades in the Cape admittedly wanted the Coloured worker to get the same pay as the white for the same work, but the Transvaal Labour party's sole aim was to prevent the Coloured from living at all. The talk about 'dragging the white man down' was childish. The Coloured wanted to uplift themselves and all men. But the white workers on the Rand were about the most selfish lot he had heard of in any part of the world, as selfish as a pack of hungry wolves.[40]

The APO's faith in working-class solidarity turned into bitter resentment as the labour movement in the north pressed its demands for racial discrimination. Addressing the annual conference at Johannesburg in 1912, Abdurahman referred to the cumulative evidence that the general body of whites regarded his people as pariahs – banned from the Dutch Reformed Church, from schools and the army; and doomed to a condition worse than slavery. The self-styled Labour party aimed at giving white men a monopoly of skilled work for all time. Yet some skilled trades in the Cape employed a vast majority of Coloured, and the process must extend to the Rand. It was simply not practicable to assign separate classes of work to men grouped according to their colour. The interests of white artisans, too, demanded the removal of colour bars and the establishment of inter-racial working-class solidarity. Labour leaders who turned white workers against the darker races were playing into the hands of the capitalist. The division of the nation into hostile camps would give rise to a solid front of Africans and Coloured. White racists were creating the conditions for a war of extermination. Conference should meet the danger by laying the foundations of a Coloured Races Union. 'To ensure peace, one must prepare for war.'[41]

The alternatives were class war or race war, and the choice

lay with the white worker. Though radicals might believe that class antagonisms would dissolve his colour prejudice, those in the APO were more realistic. They acknowledged that the Cape's socialists were sympathetic to the Coloured worker. Was it not a fact, however, that they had joined the Labour party, whose white labour doctrines had been adopted by Botha and inserted into Het Volk's manifesto? Tom Maginess admitted to the affiliation. Labour leaders had decided on it, he said, after much hesitation, and were convinced that their party would not injure the Coloured worker. It was largely because of Abdurahman's influence, he complained, that Labour in the Cape had no seat in parliament. White and Coloured workers would not fail if they stood together, as they had done on the issue of workmen's compensation.[42] These assurances carried little weight, however, when set against such displays of hostility as the circulars issued by the Transvaal federation of trade unions, calling for a boycott of builders, owners and merchants who 'sacrificed the heritage of the white people' by employing Coloured workers.[43]

There was little in Labour's parliamentary record to evoke enthusiasm in Coloured and African voters. Creswell, Sampson, Madeley, Haggar and Andrews knew that their political bread was buttered on the side of white privilege. They represented artisans, clerks and small traders on the Rand; and rarely spoke on behalf of the entire working class. Creswell made this clear early in 1911 when moving the adoption of his party's white labour policy. It was of the utmost importance, he argued, that whites should engage in every kind of social undertaking and productive enterprise.[44] As parliament unrolled its endless chain of discriminatory laws, Labour members spoke only against those elements that might injure the white working man.

The Unionists, but not Labour, opposed 'that blasphemous piece of legislation', the Dutch Reformed Church Act.[45] Introduced on the opening day of the Union parliament's first session, it excluded coloured persons from membership of the church in any province other than the Cape. Creswell criticized the Native Labour Regulation Act of 1911 for perpetuating the 'semi-slavery system' of indentured labour which narrowed the white man's sphere of employment. But he made no protest against the medieval penal code that the act inflicted on Africans.[46] He objected to the Immigrants' Restriction Act of 1911 because it left a loophole through which Asians might enter the country; and would not condemn the restraints on freedom of movement that imprisoned South African Indians in their province of domicile.[47] Even Andrews, the only genuine socialist in parliament, could be heard asking ministers to substitute white youths for Africans on the maintenance of telegraph lines in his constituency of Germiston; or complaining that Africans were being employed to knock down rivets on railway bridges. This was a white man's job, and riveters argued that they were 'making a rod for their own backs' by teaching Africans a part of their trade.[48]

It was not only for economic reasons that socialist principles gave way to electoral expediency. Labour leaders also pandered to the white man's sexual prejudices. Madeley drew attention in the House to 'brutal outrages on white women by Kaffirs', and would have the minister advise judges to inflict 'the utmost legal penalty of the death sentence on persons convicted of rape'.[49] This display of ferocity occurred during a 'Black Peril' campaign that had been sparked off by the reprieve of an African sentenced to death at Umtali in Rhodesia for the rape of a white woman. The *A.P.O.* commented sensibly that the employment of African men in white households inevitably exposed them to temptation. Labour's official paper the *Worker* replied with an outrageous attack on the '*A.P.O.*, the mouthpiece of the black, brown, snuff and butter'; and concluded that 'after a nigger has absorbed the poison into his head he will reckon that the white woman is his game'. The *A.P.O.*'s editor, 'who, we believe, has a white wife, should get 25 of the best enthusiastically administered by someone from Umtali way'.[50]

Abdurahman retorted that it was 'foul and loathsome conduct' so to drag in the family of another editor; and asserted that the Coloured were determined to make their opinions heard. The *Worker* returned to the attack with an abusive article on the *A.P.O.*'s alleged encouragement of the 'cholera' of Coloured business enterprise. The white worker would be ousted unless he woke up. His remedy was to boycott 'everything produced by the cholera' and to demand a minimum wage for all workers. South Africa, replied the *A.P.O.*, was the home of the Coloured. They would assert their right to live and work where they liked, and would not concede privilege to any white man because of his colour. The aim of the demand for a minimum wage was to oust the Coloured man from his trade. He did not fear the whites in open contest but loathed their hypocrisy.[51]

In parliament Labour members took up the cudgels on the African's behalf only when to do so would strengthen the white worker's position. They had him in mind when they urged the House to extend the principle of statutory compensation for industrial injuries and miners' phthisis to Africans and Coloured. They, too, were human, said Madeley, and had a right to be compensated.[52] Sampson gave the real reason when he told his party's annual conference in January 1912 that black labour was being preferred to white because workmen's compensation and other industrial laws made the white man more expensive.[53] As the *A.P.O.*[54] never tired of explaining, the Labour leaders wanted to price the Coloured man out of the labour market. Alerted by these warnings, he looked askance at appeals to join hands with white workers. When Clark, president of the carpenters' society, urged Coloured artisans in Natal to organize and affiliate to his federation, they told him that white carpenters and bricklayers refused to work next to Coloured journeymen. They were consequently obliged to take a lower wage in order to keep their jobs; and would be forced out of their trade if they followed his advice.[55]

Creswell outlined his party's policy of total segregation during the debate on the Natives Land Act of 1913. They were the first, he claimed, to advocate the partitioning of South Africa between the races. The reserves should be consolidated into a continuous tract 'so that the natives might have their own institutions and develop along their own lines'. Andrews criticized the draft act in so far as it aimed at the supply of 'an abundance of cheap Kafir labour'. He would not, however, exempt the Cape or any other region from the restrictive clauses. Nor did he wish to see large areas being set aside for Africans until they had learned to work the land to its fullest value.[56] None of the Labour members protested against the injustice or examined the consequences of restricting the occupancy rights of four million Africans to less than 8 per cent of the country's area, while the $1\frac{1}{4}$ million settlers had unlimited access to the remaining 92 per cent.

The act scheduled some $10\frac{1}{2}$ million morgen,* with a promise of more to come, for occupation by Africans, who would be prohibited, except in the Cape, from buying or leasing from non-Africans outside the scheduled areas, without the governor-general's express permission. This protected white landowners from competition by Africans, who were slowly buying back some of the land filched from them or their fathers. By outlawing tenancy agreements between landowners and Africans, the act would prevent some farmers from maintaining reserves of African labour while other farmers complained of labour scarcity. Finally, the restriction on landholding by Africans would force peasants to leave the overcrowded, impoverished reserves to work for mine owners and farmers. The Cape was excluded because a ban on the right to acquire land would diminish the African franchise, which had been entrenched by the South Africa Act. Territorial segregation was imposed on the Cape only after Africans had been removed from the common roll in 1936, and it was only then that parliament redeemed its promise to set more land aside for their occupation.[57]

J. W. Sauer, the minister of native affairs, piloted the Natives Land Bill through parliament. A great champion of equality in pre-Union days, he traded his principles for cabinet rank and succumbed to the racists of the north. The *A.P.O.* called on him to resign rather than betray the confidence that Africans had placed in him. His bill was 'more barbarous than anything Kruger ever introduced'; 'the most audacious act of piracy on rights of man that has been committed in South Africa'; and 'the quintessence of tyranny and falsehood'. Nothing so base had issued from a parliament that 'since the day of its foul birth, has loaded this land with loathsome rottenness in every conceivable form of colour legislation'. It was the African's duty to send a deputation to England in the faint hope that the imperial parliament might withhold its consent.[58]

* A morgen is approximately equal to two acres.

African reactions were no less immediate and vehement. 'Awakening on Friday morning, June 20th, 1913, the South African Native found himself, not actually a slave, but a pariah in the land of his birth,' wrote Sol Plaatje, the first secretary-general of the S.A. Native National Congress.[59] He toured the areas affected by what he called the 'Plague Act' and wrote a harrowing account of the plight of tenant families evicted with their livestock from farms within two months of the act's implementation. Meetings of protest, petitions and deputations failed to obtain relief. Conferences convened by the Congress in July 1913 and February 1914 decided to send a deputation to England. Botha, the prime minister, curtly rejected a petition submitted by Dube, the Congress president, on behalf of his voteless people. ' "I'll have your land, so go to England," is practically what Botha's reply means,' commented the *A.P.O.*, 'and to England we trust the Natives will go to tell Englishmen how the sons of the soil are being robbed.'[60]

Only Jabavu among the leaders adhered loyally to Sauer, defended the act and opposed the sending of a deputation. Misrepresenting the terms of the act, he told his followers that it would secure their land against alienation to whites and provide homes for landless squatters. His people rejected his special pleading. He had offended them in 1910 by backing the Botha-Smuts government and by opposing Rubusana's candidature for the provincial council seat of Tembuland. If Africans seized the first opportunity to send one of their own people to the council, Jabavu argued, they would stir up an agitation against them and endanger their franchise in the Cape.[61] Rubusana persisted, won the election with a majority of twenty-five votes, and became the first and last African provincial councillor. In 1911 Jabavu, his son Davidson, Rubusana, Chief Dalindyebo and Palmer Mgwetyana represented Africans at the Universal Races Congress in England.[62] On his return, Jabavu formed the S.A. Races Congress in opposition to the S.A. Native National Congress, later known as the African National Congress.[63] By this time, however, he had lost his people's confidence. They looked for leadership to the ANC.

Its foundations had been laid in the preceding decade by the formation of a provincial Native Congress in Natal, the Transvaal and the Orange River Colony. The Act of Union stimulated the leaders to meet the challenge of a single, central white government. The S.A. Native Convention, held at Bloemfontein in March 1909, had elected an executive 'to promote organization and to defend the interests of the Natives' against the colour bar in the draft Act of Union. Rubusana, Dube, Silas Molema of Mafeking and other members of the executive claimed to have branches in all the provinces, Basutoland and Bechuanaland.[64] In 1911 Seme announced the proposed formation of a S.A. Native Congress. There was, he observed, a general desire for progress and for a national forum. 'We are one people. Let us forget the differences between Xhosa-Fingo, Zulus and Tongas, Basutos and other Natives.' Nearly all the leaders and greater chiefs supported the movement for a congress that would give them an effective means of making their grievances known to government and South Africa at large.[65]

Pixley ka I. Seme, born in Zululand, was related by marriage to the Zulu royal house. He graduated at Columbia University, was admitted to the Bar from the Middle Temple, and practised law in Johannesburg. He did the spade work for the conference with the aid of other young lawyers. One of them, Alfred Mangena (1879–1924), was a member of Lincoln's Inn, and became the first African from South Africa to qualify and practise as an advocate. Another, R. W. Msimang, who also qualified in Britain, drafted the ANC constitution. The notice convening the conference went out in December over Seme's signature. Conference would formally establish the ANC as 'a national Society or Union for the natives of South Africa'; adopt a constitution; elect officers; take a vote of confidence in Botha, Sauer, and the 'Native Senators'; and discuss a variety of topics, including marriage and divorce, schools and churches, pass laws, 'the black peril and the white peril', and native beer, land, courts and labour. 'If there is no other reason to attend the Congress,' remarked Plaatje, 'it is at least worth a railway fare to go and hear what the "Four Native Senators" have done to deserve a vote of confidence.'[66]

Close on a hundred delegates from all parts of South Africa

and the Protectorates attended the ANC's inaugural conference at Bloemfontein on 8 January 1912. Among them were nine influential chiefs, including Maama Seiso, representing the Basutoland monarch Letsie II, and Joshua Molema, representing the Rolong paramount Montsioa. J. Mocher, president of the Free State Native Congress, took the chair. Seme and Molema moved the institution of Congress. This thereupon adopted a constitution and elected an executive with Dube as president, seven vice-presidents including Rubusana, the corresponding secretary Plaatje, a recording secretary Attorney G. D. Montsioa of Pietersburg, and two treasurers, Seme and Mapikela. Letsie II accepted the position of honorary president, but he was only one of some eight reigning monarchs who were elected to that position; others were the kings of the Lozi, Zulu, Pondo, Tembu, Rolong, Kgatla and Ngwato.[67]

The deference shown to traditional rulers and the provision made in the constitution for an upper house of chiefs have led some writers to overestimate the influence of tribal leaders on Congress. The late I. I. Potekhin, a Soviet historian of Africa, argued that they were feudal *compradores** who controlled the ANC for many years in opposition to the progressive intellectuals of the rising national bourgeoisie. It was because of the chiefs' influence, he maintained, that Congress rejected illegal mass struggle against oppressive racial laws and crawled before the authorities. In his opinion, an insoluble contradiction existed between the aim of building a nation and the aim of strengthening tribal institutions. 'An organization of feudal compradores, such as was the ANC at first, cannot be the standard-bearers of a nation.' Seme, like other right-wing leaders, Potekhin wrote, actually lowered the level of national consciousness by teaching Africans to think of themselves as junior partners of the white man who had brought peace and goodwill to Africa. 'Congress never even put the question of national independence for the Bantu or of freedom for their country from British imperialism.'[68]

Potekhin did not adequately examine the process of amalgamating scores of formerly independent and often antagonistic

*Native agents of foreign firms. The word is used here to describe tribal chiefs.

ethnic societies into a single nation. No Marxist who is familiar with the concept 'national in form, socialist in content' should be surprised to learn that tribalism will wither away only if given free play in a non-tribal environment. The teachers, lawyers, ministers, journalists, clerks and other 'intellectuals' who set the pace would have isolated themselves from the great majority of Africans if they had rejected the traditional leaders. Sol Plaatje was no tribalist, but he welcomed the participation of chiefs. Similar attempts at unity had been made before, he noted, but 'it became evident that the Natives can never effect anything unless supported by Chiefs'. For one thing, a majority of wage earners came from beyond the borders of South Africa, and would not join a movement if it was not sponsored by their chiefs.[69] This was true also of many peasant workers in South Africa, who made their living in the towns while their families, land and livestock remained a part of the traditional community.

The chiefs were neither 'feudal' nor '*compradores*'. Cast in conflicting roles, they defended their people against the colonists and also served as minor functionaries of the white bureaucracy. The dualism produced many strains and some overt resistance to authority. Most chiefs were illiterate and backward custodians of tribal values; but some were progressive, while not a few members of the new educated elite were reactionary. Both groups confronted white power in two dimensions. One was British imperialism, the dominant force until after the Anglo-Afrikaner war. The other was an authentic budding South African imperialism. For historical and tactical reasons Africans, Coloured and Indians appealed to the external power for assistance against their immediate oppressors until experience taught them that salvation would not come from Whitehall.

The educated leaders were restrained, religious, and skilled in handling whites with tact and tolerance. Always on the defensive, Congress was constrained to appease an aggressive, bigoted South African colonialism. Rubusana, on being nominated for the Tembuland seat, declared that his people acknowledged the superiority of the white race. All they asked for was equal opportunity and the open door.[70] Congress struck the same conciliatory note in its first statement of aims.[71] It would promote 'unity and mutual cooperation between the Abantu races'; maintain a central channel of communication between them and the government; strive for the educational, social, economic and political elevation of the African people; promote mutual understanding between the chiefs; encourage a spirit of loyalty to the British crown and all lawful authority; bring about better understanding between the white and black inhabitants; safeguard the interests of Africans, and obtain redress for their just grievances. Congress failed in the early period to arrive at a consistent political theory or strategy of struggle. The movement's great achievement was to develop a national consciousness through joint action and the medium of its paper *Abantu Batho* (The People).

Meeting in Johannesburg on 8 May 1912, the executive claimed that Congress held sway over all regions except the eastern Cape, where it had encountered Jabavu's resistance. The Congress leadership tended to be centred in the north partly for this reason and because it was there that Africans had no vote and were most fully absorbed in an expanding industrialism. The approved methods of struggle were to ventilate grievances at public meetings and through the press, and make representations for redress by means of resolutions and deputations. The complaints were endless: a new dog tax in areas where dogs were needed to keep down vermin; inadequate compensation for miners injured or killed at work; poor accommodation for third-class passengers on the railways; the substitution of white for African interpreters in the courts; the denial of franchise rights; the pass laws; the harassment of women in the Free State under municipal regulations. The women made history in 1913 by organizing a passive resistance movement and went to jail in large numbers rather than take out residential permits. Congress took up their case and scored one of its few victories in the struggle against discrimination.

Congress established its claim to speak for the people when it conducted a country-wide campaign against the Natives Land Act. Recalling Abdurahman's famous speech of January 1912, it declared that his prediction of a war of extermination was being fulfilled. Some fifty delegates at a special session in Johannesburg in July 1913 heard Sotho, Zulu and Xhosa interpreters read the act line by line. In August Saul Msane (Natal), J. M. Nyoking (OFS), S. M. Makgotho (Transvaal), Enoch Mamba (Transkei), Sol Plaatje (secretary), Chief Kekane (Hamanskraal) and the Rev. Twala interviewed F. S. Malan, who had taken Sauer's place after his death in July as minister of native affairs. They gave instances of hardships caused by the act and told him of their decision to appeal to Britain. Whatever steps they took, he was assured, would be within 'the four corners of the law'. Malan replied that the act had to be obeyed and doubted the success of a mission to Britain. The leaders toured the country to explain Congress policy and collect funds for a deputation.[72]

Imvo sang Sauer's praises in obituary notices and failed to point out that his Land Act embraced the hated northern principles which he had once opposed. The Congress took its campaign into the heart of Jabavu's political domain and challenged him to debate the issue in public. He refused and struck back by standing for election to the provincial council in Tembuland against Rubusana, the sitting member. This split the African vote. A. Payne, the white candidate, won the seat with 1,004 votes, against Rubusana's 852 and Jabavu's 294. 'One of the ablest, most cultured and respected Natives, the first of his race to be elected to the Provincial Council, has been unseated through the despicable action of one who has long been discredited by a vast majority of the Bantu race.'[73] The *A.P.O.*'s comment expressed the sentiments of Africans generally, including many of Jabavu's followers. The betrayal, coming on top of his support of the Land Act, put an end to his political career; and no African was ever again elected to the provincial council. Rubusana left soon after his defeat, together with Dube, Plaatje, Mapikela and Msane, to put the African case before the British government and public. They left against the express wishes of Lord Gladstone, the governor-general, and Louis Botha; and they received no sympathy from Lewis Harcourt, the secretary of state for the colonies.

He rejected the deputation's petition, which pointed out that

Africans were the original inhabitants of South Africa, and he told the Commons that a just, considered segregation would probably lead to greater happiness for all. Britain trusted the South African government and must respect its sovereign authority. Britain had never surrendered her position as protector of the natives, but would not intervene unless gross palpable injustice was proved. The deputation had come to England against the advice of Botha and Gladstone; knew that the act would not be disallowed; and should have made their case in their own parliament.

It was not, however, their parliament. Britain had excluded them to appease white power. The South African government responded only to voters and ignored the interests of a political nullity. Congress met on 1 August 1914 to hear a report on the mission and to plan the next stage in its own campaign. Dube returned a few days later. Botha, he said, had deceived the British with assurances that all Africans evicted from farms would be given land in the reserves. Abdurahman's comment was more incisive. 'The Coloured races of the Empire may be robbed, plundered and forcibly driven into slavery by whites'; but the imperial parliament would approve as long as these things were done through legislative enactment. 'The present foundation of the Empire is rotten, and cannot last.' If 'it cannot be mended, then the sooner it is ended the better'. 'The coloured races could not possibly be worse governed when left to their own resources than they were governed under British rule.'[74] Britain went to war on 4 August. Two weeks later Abdurahman declared: 'The only question we have to ask ourselves is how we can best serve the Empire.'[75]

7 Thunder on the Left

Wilfrid Harrison claimed to be Cape Town's most noted 'mob orator'. His stock answer to hecklers who interrupted his denunciations of capitalism with interjections about the 'colour question' was, 'And what about your red nose – that is coloured, isn't it?' He would go on to explain that he was there to deal, not with the pigment in a man's skin, which was a medical mystery, but with capitalism, the cause of colour prejudice and exploitation in general.[1] The evangelical socialists of Harrison's Social Democratic Federation insisted that race discrimination, like the conditions of the poor, was a 'side issue', a symptom of the tensions inherent in capitalist society. No true socialist would allow colour prejudice to divert him from his function of persuading the people to place the means of production under public ownership. Discrimination would disappear under socialism and should be ignored as being irrelevant to the labour movement.

The notion that class interest would prevail over racial antagonism seemed more credible in the western Cape than in the north. Members of the SDF certainly tried to put their theory to the test. H. MacManus quoting in his Belfast twang from William Morris and the Bible; Hunter mixing socialism with temperance; H. B. Levinson relying on economic determinism; Arthur Noon propagating Christian socialism, and Harrison, armed revolt, took their messages to racially mixed audiences in District Six, in Salt River, and at the foot of Van Riebeeck's statue in Adderley Street. Coloured leaders reciprocated their goodwill and cooperated with socialists in the early years. H. P. Gordon, a prospective Labour candidate for Woodstock in 1904, took the initiative in directing the movement into parliamentary politics, and proposed joint action with the APO in 1905. Abdurahman replied that 'Yours, or rather ours because we feel the same, is a hard life.' None of them ever expected 'that such brutalities, and injustices would be perpetrated under the protection of the British Rule or Mis-rule. There is only one thing for us to do, and that is sink our little differences and show a united front.'[2]

The united front never took shape. For all their Hyde Park oratory, the socialists failed the sovereign test of political sincerity. They appealed for Coloured votes but were no more prepared than liberal or racist parties to nominate a Coloured candidate in municipal or parliamentary elections. Abdurahman himself built a first-rate electoral machine, which kept him in the Cape Town municipal council from 1903 until his death in 1940. He did not need the white worker's vote and, when obliged to choose between white candidates, preferred men of wealth or standing who backed him against Labour or Afrikaner Nationalist opponents. Neither white nor Coloured radicals attempted to recruit members from the Cape peninsula's 5,000 Africans, who were excluded from skilled work by convention almost as effectively as in the north. Without a large following in the Coloured population, and based on a small, conservative white working class, the socialists of the Cape remained in the cocoon stage of theoretical propaganda.

Many of the Cape's more energetic socialists – the Needham brothers, Erasmus, Davidson, McKillop, Blake, Fraser, Bateman – left South Africa or moved to the Rand during the first ten years of the century. Those who remained lost their missionary zeal, wrangled over whether or not to take part in elections, became armchair critics of the right-wing leaders, or joined the Labour party and were identified with its white supremacy policies. In spite of their failings, however, the pioneer socialists of the Cape made a significant contribution. Their insistence that class, and not race, was the basic cause of conflict left an imprint on later generations, and strengthened the hand of radicals with similar views in Natal and the Transvaal.

Socialists in the Cape belonged to the inner circle of a weak labour movement. Their counterparts on the Rand had the advantage of appealing to a large, relatively well organized and occasionally militant working class, but competed with a power-ful right-wing trade union leadership. Ideological differences were therefore sharper, the conflicts within the movement more intense, than farther south. The right wing was heavily com-mitted to racial discrimination. Socialists faced the dilemma of all radicals who contested elections based on an all-white franchise. They could denounce racism and suffer an abysmal defeat; or make a bid for success by trading radical principles for votes. Left-wing politicians were tempted to compromise. They concentrated their propaganda on the class war, evaded the colour issue, and when challenged rejected white labour policies as a betrayal of the white worker's interests. The white labour policy, according to Crawford's band of militant socialists, was a 'white kaffir policy' which would reduce all workers to the African's living standards.

Archie Crawford was labour's most notable maverick until Smuts had him deported in 1914. Born in Glasgow in 1883, and a fitter by trade, he came with the troops in 1902, worked on the railways at Pretoria, and was dismissed in 1906 for agitating against retrenchments in the workshop. In the following year he unsuccessfully contested the Boksburg West parliamentary seat, but was returned as a Labour member to the Johannesburg town council. His great achievement was to found, publish and edit the *Voice of Labour*, 'A Weekly Journal of Socialism, Trade Unionism and Politics'. It appeared regularly from October 1908 to December 1912, when it died for want of funds. Its corre-spondents included active socialists throughout the country: Harrison, Noon and Davidson of Cape Town, Norrie of Durban, Greene of Pietermaritzburg, Henry Glass of Port Elizabeth. It advertised and published extracts from the works of Marx, Engels, Plekhanov, De Leon, Eugene Debs, Blatchford and Keir Hardie; and made the first systematic attempt to spread the doctrines of revolutionary socialism. The paper, wrote its editor, 'is the barometer of working-class consciousness in South Africa'; and the failure to 'reach the moderate total of 10,000 indicates the almost criminal apathy of the working class'.

As Labour councillor, active trade unionist, member of the ILP and LRC, Crawford belonged to the top leadership until it

broke with him over the issue of the Fordsburg nominations.
He attended the series of conferences held at Durban and
Johannesburg in 1908–9 to form the Labour party and draft its
constitution. Representing his newborn Socialist Society at the
conference of October 1909, together with Davidson and members of the ILP he moved that they call themselves the S.A.
Socialist Party. This was defeated after a heated debate. Mathews,
Mussared, Nettleton and other trade unionists told the conference
that their members would not join a party bearing this name.
Socialists would do more good by organizing their fellow workers
than by preaching idealism. But the ILP delegates succeeded in
obtaining a majority vote for their motion to insert in the constitution a clause calling for 'The socialisation of the means of
production, distribution and exchange to be controlled by a
democratic State in the interests of the whole community.' This
was hailed as a great victory over the right wing, as was also the
defeat of Sampson's policy of total segregation.

Their 'native policy', said Sampson, was the rock on which
the party might founder. He would grant all Coloured persons
having one white parent full political, industrial and social
rights. The white and black races were first separated by nature
and should be kept apart. It was morally wrong for one race to
suppress or exploit another. Though he approved of the white
labour policy as a means to an end, it offered no permanent solution. It could be dangerous to the white race, by leading to the
importation of low-wage Europeans under contract. Moreover,
it disregarded the interests of Africans, who had been deprived
of their land. The only natural solution was to segregate Africans
in their own territory, where they could govern themselves and
progress in ways they found most suitable. This could be done
without taking an inch of land away from white men. Representatives of all European nations holding land in South Africa
should meet to partition the country between whites and Africans. Meanwhile, Africans should be given their own elected
councils, through which they could make direct representations
to parliament.[3]

Delegates from the Cape SDF, the ILP and Socialist Society
spoke against Sampson's motion. The most effective speech

came from James Trembath, Kimberley's labour councillor and a leader in the struggle of 1908 against De Beers over its decision to withdraw the customary half-holiday on Saturdays.[4] The colour prejudice in Johannesburg, he said, was most unreasonable. He was proud that the majority of white workers in the Cape were in favour of full equality. Labour could not afford to alienate the Coloured, who had a powerful organization in the APO. The party would be put back fifty years if they antagonized the 800 Coloured voters of Kimberley. When he successfully contested a municipal by-election, he had to overcome the handicap imposed by an anti-colour resolution moved by Bill Andrews at Johannesburg's Labour Day rally in 1909. His opponents posted copies of the resolution to every African and Coloured voter in Kimberley. 'The thing is we must either have coloured men on our side or against us.' This convinced conference, but it could not be persuaded into accepting Crawford's motion that the party should recognize only two classes in society and reject any policy based on differences of colour.

The militants were highly satisfied, in spite of this setback, which was more than compensated for by the adoption of a 'socialist objective' and the rejection of Sampson's apartheid policy. His one real regret, said Crawford, was that conference had agreed to allow trade unions to join the party on the payment of a political levy. Trembath, Sampson and Mathews had strenuously opposed his motion to admit individuals only. They wanted to get at the pockets of non-party trade unionists. Socialism was dearer than life to him, yet he would not force it on anyone.[5] His scruples – which Trembath and the Witwatersrand trades council had shared in 1905 – were related, however, to the disciplinary action taken against him in December 1909. Accusing him of disloyalty, the LRC had resolved to exclude him from its meetings. Crawford's own explanation was that the members of the committee had already nominated one another for the parliamentary elections, including the constituency of Fordsburg, to which he had a prior claim.[6]

His candidature was endorsed at the inaugural conference on 26 December of the S.A. Socialist Federation which had as chairman the great industrial agitator J. T. Bain of Pretoria.

Born in Scotland, a fitter by trade, he came to South Africa in the early 1880s, helped to form the miners' union, became a Transvaal burgher, fought on the side of the republics against the British, and was sent as a prisoner of war to Ceylon. Even his backing failed to give the Federation a flying start. Natal and Cape socialists, clinging to their customary parochialism, refused to affiliate. The Federation functioned only on the Rand and in Pretoria, largely as an opposition group to the Labour party which made its official debut at Durban on 10 January as the first national political party, with Sampson as president and Haggar as the general secretary. Labour was all set for the first round of elections under the South Africa Act.

Crawford's party disdained to join in the hue and cry against the darker man; but it did not add its voice to the protest against the colour bar in the constitution. It criticized Union in terms of the class theory, as a capitalist scheme, which had brought the workers nothing, and would take from them an increasing portion of the fruits of their labour. 'The Class War still wages' declared the *Voice* in its first issue after the inauguration of Union.[7] When challenged on the colour bar, Crawford took refuge in a philosophical discourse on socialist ethics, which knew neither race, colour nor creed. He would admit qualified Coloured men to the franchise and to the socialist society.[8] He did not follow this affirmation of principle with a campaign to recruit them to his party or to have the colour bar deleted. He argued instead that the white franchise was a capitalist device to stir up hostility between workers of different races. Colour consciousness, artificially stimulated, obscured class consciousness, which was a natural thing. 'Before they will let the white worker get hold of the reins of government, they will enfranchise the natives and exploit their ignorance.'[9]

Crawford contested Fordsburg against Bill Andrews, Krause and Patrick Duncan in the general election of 1910 and polled eight votes. His team mate Jim Davidson stood in Commissioner Street against Sampson and received twenty-five. The two socialists fought on an uncompromising class war platform, called for the abolition of capitalism, and studiously refrained from making any reference in their manifesto to racial discrimination or

African claims.[10] The Labour leaders had agreed with Het Volk that the two parties would not contest the same seats. This, said the socialists, was a betrayal of socialist principles. 'No single candidate of the South African Labour Party,' they urged, 'should receive working class support.'[11] They did not rebuke Labour for betraying its principles by adopting white supremacy policies. After the election, however, the *Voice* claimed that Crawford and Davidson were the only two candidates in the Transvaal who had refused to draw the colour line, and were the first to stand for revolutionary principles. The votes they received were given 'for revolutionary Socialism and no race or colour bar'.[12]

Two other Socialist candidates, L. H. Greene in Pietermaritzburg and Arthur Noon in Cape Town, also lost heavily. The Labour party nominated eleven candidates in the Transvaal, six in Natal and two in the Cape; and won four seats, all on the Rand, where Creswell, the party leader, Sampson, Madeley and Haggar were returned. Among those defeated were Andrews, Bain, Coward, Reid, Mathews, Mussared and Wybergh who, like Creswell, joined the party only two months before the election. Tom Maginess, the Labour candidate in Woodstock, lost by the small margin of 25 votes to John Hewat, the Unionist, and James Trembath polled 584 votes for Labour in Kimberley against the Unionist's 1,121 votes. Abdurahman canvassed for the Unionists and told Trembath that he could not expect support from Coloured voters as long as his party in the Transvaal was determined to crush the Coloured out from every sphere of employment.[13] Trembath and Maginess, said Crawford, owed their defeat to the white labour policy of the trades hall in Johannesburg.[14]

Peter Whiteside found a seat in the senate by goodwill of Het Volk. 'A Ten Years fat job for Peter and the betrayal of the Workers,' noted the *Voice*. He was a Judas, the prototype of many present leaders who preached class war, such as Tom Mann, Andrews J.P., Tom Mathews and Mussared. He had not gone to the senate to represent the workers, for he had betrayed them as far back as 1907 by preventing his engine drivers and firemen from supporting the miners' strike.[15] The 'aristocrats of labour', wrote Crawford, were selling out for the sake of a few safe seats.[16] Eyebrows were raised in some other quarters at the alliance between a 'landed aristocracy' and a working-class party.[17] Yet it was not very surprising, since the two saw eye to eye on the issue of racial discrimination. Botha had taken over the white labour policy for his election manifesto. Labour's own manifesto put forward a full-blown segregation scheme. Based on Sampson's rejected policy, it called for the subsidization of white workers in mines and factories, the expulsion of Asians, and a ban on the right of Africans to buy or occupy land outside the reserves.

Crawford put on a brave face. He was not disappointed, for to have won at the age of twenty-seven would spell popularity and put an end to his life's work! 'I stand for revolutionary Socialism,' he proclaimed, and 'refuse to draw lines of race, colour, creed, or sex. I only know the class division, its cause, and the struggle which arises therefrom; a struggle which will cease when there is only one class and that the nation.'[18] He took his defeat badly, in fact, and relinquished control of his paper and press a few weeks later to commence a thirteen months' tour of the 'industrial world'. Visiting Australia, New Zealand, the United States and Britain, he reported on wages, working conditions and the movement, hobnobbed with radicals, addressed meetings and poured scorn on 'reformism' and 'trade union fakirs'. He enlisted writers for the *Voice* and with less success potential revolutionary settlers for South Africa. This Odysseus, this wanderer, wrote his admirers, is probably 'the first of our class to circumnavigate the Industrial World on behalf of Socialism'.[19]

His small band of followers, disheartened by their poor showing and at war with the Labour party, turned their backs on parliament. The working class, they argued, could not be emancipated through politics alone. Any labour movement would lapse into reformism and class collaboration if it was not founded on revolutionary industrial unionism as defined by the American syndicalist Eugene Debs: 'the unity of all the workers within one organization, subdivided in their respective departments, and organized, not to fraternize with the exploiting capitalists, but to make war on them and to everlastingly wipe out their system under which labour is robbed of what it produces and held in contempt because it submits to the robbery.'[20] South African syndicalists agreed that craft unionism catered only for the labour aristocracy and formed a bulwark of capitalism by perpetuating sectionalism. They instanced the miners' strike of 1907 – when engine drivers, under instructions from their secretary Peter Whiteside, transported scabs and ore mined by scabs – and the Natal railway strike of 1909, also lost because of craft divisions.

Industrial unions, syndicalism and the general strike were not recent discoveries. The *Voice of Labour*, which took its name from the official journal of the American Labour Union, the initiator of the IWW, was started to spread the idea of a general workers' union. It received a great if temporary impetus from Tom Mann when, at the invitation of the Witwatersrand trades council, he visited South Africa in March 1910 on his way home from Australia. The socialists, who first hailed him as their ally against reformism, soon lamented that he was a good man fallen among thieves. Andrews, Mathews, Sampson and other reformists were accused of isolating him from the left wing, whose views he shared. Placing his great abilities and marvellous eloquence at the disposal of trade union officialdom, Mann strengthened craft divisions by advocating a policy of working through existing unions rather than forming a new organization. Unlike Keir Hardie, who had appealed for equal pay and opportunities for all workers when he toured South Africa in 1907, Tom Mann made no reference to the position of the darker working man in his public speeches. He admitted at Jeppe that industrial unionism would not work as long as eighty per cent of wage earners were excluded from the unions. Yet he refrained from urging the unions to admit Africans and Coloured. He was strong where no colour problem existed, but weak in South Africa where he adapted his teachings to all-white audiences.[21]

Mann, in a letter to Dr Abdurahman, pleaded in self-defence that he could not advance any cause if he antagonized the men whom he wished to convert. Perhaps because of his complaisance, his oratory left little permanent imprint. He persuaded the trades council to sponsor an industrial workers' union by guaranteeing two months' salary to the organizer. The council lost interest, while the union itself passed into the hands of the radical socialists. T. Glynn, the new secretary and a motorman on the Johannesburg tramways, declared that the union would have to fight 'men of the type of Creswell, Sampson, Andrews & Co.' if it was to meet the need of a 'class-conscious revolutionary organization, embracing all workers regardless of craft, race or colour', and dedicated to the entire overthrow of capitalism.[22] The union, renamed the Industrial Workers of the World (S.A.), put its theory to the test in a successful one-day strike of Johannesburg tramwaymen against a brow-beating inspector. Hailed as the first triumph of working-class solidarity among whites, the strike was contrasted with the strike of bricklayers at Pretoria, which ended after seven weeks in a defeat for the men.

The tramwaymen, dizzy with success, formed themselves into a branch of the I W W and refused to recognize a municipal committee appointed to inquire into their grievances. Their leaders Glynn and Glendon were summarily dismissed in May, and this sparked off a strike famous in S.A. labour history as the one and only militant action of the industrial unionists.[23] Yet they failed hopelessly. They had no plan of campaign, left the strikers without effective leadership and relied mainly on the support of outsiders. The council set out to break the union, called in the police, banned public meetings, and ran the trams with scabs under police protection. 'The Tram employees,' complained Dunbar, 'were not defeated by the Town Council, nor by the police with their pickshafts, but by the workers who scabbed on their fellowmen.'[24] Glynn, sentenced to three months' imprisonment for inciting a strike, won his appeal against the conviction. He and Dunbar of the I W W, Back of the S P, Cameron the veteran leader of the S L P, and Councillor Lane, the man who defeated Andrews in the municipal elections of 1905, were prosecuted and acquitted on a charge of holding an unlawful meeting. Two strikers, Whittaker and Morant, were framed by police and charged with placing dynamite on the tram lines. They were also acquitted and obtained damages against the government for illegal treatment while awaiting trial.

This was one defeat that could not be attributed to craft divisions. It was therefore a splendid occasion for bewailing capitalist iniquities, working-class frailties, and the 'cowardly incompetence' of the 'Trades Hall clique'. No doubts were allowed to disturb the vision of one great industrial union. When Cape Town printers, white and Coloured, succumbed in June after a two months' strike and lockout on the issue of a closed shop, the radicals blamed not the scabs imported from Britain, but the abominations of craft trade unionism. Engineers refused to stop the machines, railwaymen hauled and workers bought scab 'matter', post office employees transmitted news, and printers in other towns set type from matrixes forwarded by rail to Cape Town master printers.[25] Andrews, back from his assignment to assist the strikers, told a Johannesburg labour meeting that the strike had done more than years of street oratory to convert people in Cape Town to socialism. The *Voice* sneered that his craftmanship had the 'usual success' attached to his efforts as a strike leader.[26]

The radicals both detested and admired Andrews. His feud with Crawford dated from their clash in the Fordsburg election; and they resented his formidable role as organizer and political leader on the opposite side of the movement. He infuriated them with his cool, logical reasoning and exposure of sentimental humbug. Unable to find fault with his honesty and socialist sincerity, they descended to mere abuse. He was 'class war Andrews J.P.', a 'political opportunist' and 'labour fakir', who preached revolution and yet took office and title under capitalism. More than anyone else, they said, he perpetuated craft divisions and hindered class solidarity. When he contested the George-town by-election in January 1912, they accused him of being at the bottom of half the discord in the movement. He was a sleek, well paid official (on £25 a month!) who sacrificed nothing for the cause, and sneered at honest, impecunious, victimized social-ist agitators. Andrews was returned to parliament with 1,046 votes, against the 726 polled by the Unionist candidate. The Rand's working class had evidently resolved on the Labour party, remarked the *Voice*, and consoled itself with the thought that this brought closer the day of disillusionment.[27]

'Political action is useless,' argued the bellicose blacksmith Andrew Dunbar, 'so long as the workers are split up in sectional unions.' Dunbar (1879–1964) came to South Africa from Scotland in 1906, joined the Natal railways, led 2,500 men out on strike in 1909 and subsequently settled on the Rand. An aggressive socialist, he vacillated in the next three years between the SALP, Socialist League, Socialist Party and IWW, of which he became the general secretary. The *Voice* defended him as unsurpassed in energy, enterprise and enthusiasm. When 'grimy and dirty, after having slaved nine hours at an anvil', he would address workers on the vices of social reformism and the merits of industrial unionism. They could not be emancipated through political action alone, he told them; for to be of use, a socialist party must be founded on the IWW's principle of direct action.[28]

He demonstrated the advantages of 'direct action' in Johannesburg's municipal election in October 1911, together with Mary Fitzgerald, the Irish beauty who partnered Crawford in his printing plant and later became his wife. A former typist in the office of the miners' union, she had recorded the death from phthisis of thirty-two executive members in a period of eight years; and was converted into a fiery socialist. She, Dunbar and Glynn came armed with pickhandles to election meetings of councillors whom they accused of banning free speech during the strike and turned them out of the hall. Labour increased its representation on the council from five to eleven members. The IWW, said Dunbar, could claim a fair amount of credit for the success.[29] Though only in its second year, it had done more fighting than all the craft unions and political parties since their inception. He would have nothing to do with either, not even with the Socialist party, and this obduracy led to his expulsion from the IWW in February 1912.[30]

The reasons given for his expulsion were intolerance, unpredictable behaviour and intemperate attacks on his comrades; but he had sinned mainly by standing out against renewed attempts to consolidate socialist groups throughout the country in a single party. This led to a long and acrimonious debate. Dunbar and Glynn argued that the state reflected economic relations. No parliamentary action could alter its basic structure. Even if Marxists controlled parliament, military and police power would still be on the side of the capitalist class. The general strike was the most powerful weapon of the workers and they could bring about a revolutionary change only by destroying the economic structure of capitalist society. Davidson and Crawford retorted that the syndicalists had made a fetish of the IWW. It was merely a means to the end, and of relative importance to other methods of achieving socialism. Dunbar's opposition, they said, was based on the fallacy that a socialist party could grow only at the expense of the IWW; whereas they were complementary. The one could not be strong while the other was weak.

Davidson was another Scottish radical who had substituted Marxism for Calvinism. He came to Cape Town in 1898 at the age of twenty-one, worked in a bank and municipal offices, joined the SDF at its inception in 1902, and became its general secretary before moving to the Rand in 1910. Marxism, he maintained, held the view that the capitalists possessed power 'as a reflex of the ideas of the masses as expressed in the State or ideological institutions'. A revolutionary should therefore concentrate on changing the mind of the masses by both political and economic activity. The masses had swung from political to direct or economic action. It was safe to predict that they would swing back to parliamentary action in the near future. Crawford agreed. The time might come when the IWW itself would enter the parliamentary field as a final, strategic move towards working-class emancipation.

Crawford returned from his world tour after attending the unity conference at Manchester on 30 September 1911 between Hyndman's SDP, Grayson's SP, the ILP, the *Clarion*, and other left-wing groups. Finding his paper at a low ebb and the radicals in disarray, he decided to follow the British example. Mrs Dora Montefiore, a former associate of Hyndman, combined wealth with revolutionary ardour and visited South Africa at Crawford's invitation. Speaking at socialist meetings, where the 'Internationale' was sung for the first time in South Africa, she argued the case for both political and industrial action. She, Mary

Fitzgerald, Harrison, Norrie and Knowles from Durban were among the delegates at a unity conference held in Johannesburg in 1912. Agreement was reached and the United Socialist party announced its formation on May Day. The draft constitution repudiated reformism, affirmed 'the class war between the revolutionary working class and the reactionary exploiting class', and called for the overthrow of capitalism. Membership would be open to any socialist 'without discrimination as to race, sex colour or creed'.[32]

Socialists in Cape Town, Durban, Pietermaritzburg, Pretoria and Johannesburg agreed to merge and turn themselves into local branches of the USP. The merger never took place. The local groups argued over constitutions and the rival merits of industrial unionism, anarchism, and parliamentary politics. Norrie carried the USP flag at a parliamentary by-election in Greyville, Durban, a constituency with a large railway vote, and lost heavily to Tommy Boydell, the Labour party candidate. Unable to gain a foothold on the electoral ladder, the socialists ran into financial difficulties. The *Voice* was losing £20 a week and often could not pay the printers, Crawford and Mrs Fitzgerald. If the paper served as a barometer of working-class consciousness, both reached their nadir at the end of 1912. There were times, mourned the editor, when socialists appeared not to want a paper to represent their interests: they certainly did not deserve one.[33] Its obituary notice made a confession: 'We stirred things at times more well than wise, and have to pay the price in limbo.'[34]

Yet conditions were never again as favourable for the growth of a radical Labour movement on the Rand. A high proportion of the white workers were immigrant; many had a background of militant trade unionism. Industrial legislation was rudimentary and gave little or no protection against victimization, unemployment, occupational diseases or accidents. Workmen were unsettled, insecure and often came into angry conflict with employers and government. Trade unionism had taken root. Nearly all the unions then in existence were affiliated to the Transvaal Federation of Trades which replaced the Witwatersrand trades council in 1911.[35] The socialists were the kith and kin of the working man, spoke his language and worked at the same trades. The identity between white workers and radical leaders was closer in the first two decades of the century than at any later period. Trade unionists, however, generally ignored or were hostile to left-wing socialism. Marxist categories that had been delimited in advanced industrial societies seemed unconvincing in a colonial-type society where colour rather than class determined status and the distribution of power.

The radicals refused to believe that racial divisions predominated. 'The antagonism is class antagonism, and not racial,' they argued. 'The dividing line is not between white and coloured, but between property-owners and the proletariat.'[36] Africans had been specially selected for repressive legislation only because they were the largest body of wage slaves. The laws were meant to control all wage slaves, and would be applied also to whites who threatened the propertied classes. White workers conscripted under the Defence Act would be used first to chain up the African, and then to chain up the white worker. Africans would revolt one day against wage slavery. If they were crushed, whites would be reduced to the same condition. Both groups faced the same problem – how to dispossess an exploiting class. The solution for both lay in a universal organization of all workers and the general strike.[37]

Inspiration as well as theory came from abroad. 'It is just lovely to be alive in these days,' exulted the IWW. 'The whole world is seething with industrial unrest.'[38] There was unrest also among white workers in South Africa, though the socialists misread its symptoms. It arose out of a struggle for recognition within the established order, and not against capitalism. The working man voted for the parties of white supremacy and their white labour policy, and not for the standard bearers of international socialism. These tried to wean him from the right-wing leadership by accusing it of pursuing a 'white kaffir policy' which would reduce him to the African's standards. Cheap labour drove out dear. A white man required at least 10s. a day, while an African might live on 2s. 6d. The capitalist would not cut his profits. If he substituted white workers for Africans, he would pay them the lower wage. It was therefore in their interest to reject the white labour policy.[39] Appeals of this kind were more likely to intensify the white man's fear of being ousted than to convince him that he could find security and win recognition by joining hands with members of a downtrodden race.

Tom Mann had pointed out that there could be no industrial unionism or general strike unless the African took part. The socialists dodged the issue, took refuge in revolutionary phrases, and never made it their business to help the darker man to organize. That, they argued, was better left to him. Their appeals for inter-racial cooperation were construed in terms of the white worker's interests. It meant, they said, no more than that the 'Chinaman or Kaffir' would not do the work of miners who came out on strike. The purpose of cooperation was to teach the coloured worker that to undercut was to scab, the punishment for which had no limit. White workers would befriend him only as long as he did not willingly contribute to their degradation.[40] Like the right-wing leaders, the radicals assumed that the African's role was to provide white men with the higher standards of living to which they laid claim.

The socialists, to their credit, condemned the cruder forms of discrimination in the movement. The Bloemfontein branch of the typographical union induced the municipal council in 1909 to insert a fair wage clause in printing contracts, together with the stipulation that 'no skilled labour must be carried out by coloured labour'. The *Voice* protested that the restriction barred the union's own Coloured members and suggested that their people in the Cape would be well advised to withhold their votes from a party intent on raising barriers against them.[41] African miners who struck work in January 1911 at the Dutoitspan, Voorspoed and Village Deep mines were driven back to work with bloodshed by the police and white miners, and then imprisoned under the master and servants laws without protest from the labour leaders. The *Voice* commented angrily on the 'white wage slaves' who had 'prostituted themselves into guardians of Capitalist plunder'; and denounced the futility of sectional strikes.[42] Yet socialists, too, were prone to colour prejudice.

Financial difficulties could not excuse the appearance in the paper of offensive advertisements such as one inserted by the tailors Ben Pickles & Co., which asked: 'Why should you wear a Suit that has been made by sweated or coloured labour?'[43] The socialists disclosed their own racial bias when they insisted that cooperation between white and African workers did not involve 'kissing a black brother or inviting him to tea'. Peregrino, the editor from Accra, who claimed to have sat with the master minds of socialism in Europe and America, agreed that 'intelligent black men' neither urged nor desired social equality. All they wanted was the open door to political manhood.[44] This might have been a common opinion at that time, but socialists should have disowned the concession to colour prejudice. By refusing to adopt the principle of equality in every sphere, they isolated themselves behind an impregnable racial barrier from the bulk of the working class.

One or two, like Greene of Pietermaritzburg, acknowledged that it was their duty to teach the 'great industrial, inarticulate mass of coloured labour' to welcome the advent of socialism and to unite under its banner. He too, however, gave priority to the interests of white workers. Socialism would keep them afloat by doing away with inter-racial competition. Capitalism, on the other hand, stirred up hostility and would drown them in a flood of coloured labour. Africans would have to secure their own emancipation; and the sooner the better.[45]

What form would their emancipation take? Unable to envisage equality, even in a socialist society, between white and black, the socialists tended to lapse into the cant of the right-wing leaders. 'Under socialism,' wrote the editor of the *Voice*, 'the native would not be driven out of his kraal in order to be exploited. He would remain there with his own kind and develop along his own lines.'[46]

It seemed evident to the socialists that white working men would form the vanguard of revolution. Capitalist tyranny would open their eyes to the futility of colour bars and provoke industrial upheavals which were bound to culminate in the general strike. The theory was plausible under the conditions of a raw industrialism. The ruling farmers, merchants and mine owners, though adept at forcing Africans to work, knew little about trade unions or class conflict and refused to take them seriously.

Organized labour, on the other hand, had not yet achieved the status and recognition to which it aspired. Exploitation and class antagonism were most acute in the gold mining industry, whose impermanence and terrible toll of life were unparalleled, wrote the contemporary pamphleteers Campbell and Munro.[47] In March 1912 Crawford predicted that a miners' strike would follow the failure of the parliamentary Labour party to carry a bill for an eight-hour day 'from bank to bank', or from the time of going below to the time of return to the surface.[48] There were other grievances, notably an alleged tendency on the part of managers to 'blacklist' militants by making unfavourable comments on their 'tickets' or work records. The tension between managements and men reached breaking point in May 1913 on the New Kleinfontein mine.

The trouble began when the manager instructed five mechanics employed underground to work until 3.30 p.m. instead of 12.30 p.m. on Saturdays. This led to a strike for trade union recognition, the eight-hour day and the reinstatement of strikers. Tom Mathews, the union secretary, J. T. Bain, Andrew Watson, George Mason and other militant members of a strike committee went from mine to mine calling the men out. Crawford, Mary Fitzgerald, George Kendall of the ASE and other syndicalists joined the struggle and tried to turn it into a general strike against capitalism. 'The mob went from mine to mine,' said Smuts in parliament, 'and no number of police could have protected every property though we had collected numbers from all parts of the country.'[49] The owners, on the other hand, were determined to break the unions. Mines were kept in production by means of Africans and white scabs. Individual strikers called on Africans to come out as well, but the police forced them to work or remain in their compounds.

Some 18,000 whites on sixty-three mines were out on strike by the end of June. Smuts drafted police, mounted riflemen and troops of the British garrison to the Rand. The strike committee summoned workers to a meeting at Benoni on Sunday, 29 June, for a display of determination. 'Therefore the Strike Committee again asks you to come, and to come armed if you can, in order to resist any unlawful force which may be used against you.'[50]

The government invoked a republican law introduced in 1894 to check the white immigrant agitation, banned all public gatherings in Benoni, and proclaimed martial law on Friday, 4 July. The Federation of Trades called a general strike on the same day. 'The response to this was a display of spontaneous loyalty and solidarity which probably is unequalled in the history of the world's industrialism.'[51] Bands of 'excited men and women waving red flags' and numbers of youths 'armed with sticks and other weapons' appeared on the streets.[52] War had been declared, wrote the editor of the Labour party's official paper the *Worker*, and had to be fought to victory. This meant bringing the public and parliament to their knees and extorting substantial legislation in the workers' interests. In principle, if not in tactics, an industrial war justified murder, arson, destruction of property and all other forms of armed struggle.[53]

Police and troops broke up a banned meeting in Market Square, Johannesburg, on Friday afternoon. Crowds of demonstrators roamed the streets, stopped the trams, and pulled the running staff off the trains. That night hooligans burnt down a wooden ticket office at the main railway station, raided the bar, set fire to the *Star* newspaper offices, looted gunsmiths' and jewellers' shops, and exchanged shots with the police. The most serious clashes took place outside the Rand Club, the haunt of mine owners and the ruling elite, on Saturday afternoon. Demonstrators assembled outside the club, rushed the entrance, and were fired on by Dragoons. At least twenty people were killed in the fighting on Saturday, including Labuschagne, a young Afrikaner miner – Labour's first martyr. A leaflet issued soon afterwards commemorated his death in language that expressed the strikers' mood:

All civilisation cries Shame! Shame! Shame! on the work of the 1st Royal Dragoons who was backed up and urged by the devil, his government, his press and his pulpit. Labuschagne was Cowardly Murdered while defending the lives of women and little innocent children.

When the Chamber of Mines' dirty work was in full swing and honest working people were being shot down by Bums in soldiers' uniform in the employ of the Capitalist, a Man stepped off the sidewalk

in Commissioner Street nearly opposite the White Kaffirs' nest—
Rand Club—he stood and tapping his breast with his hand he said:
'Don't shoot any more women and children—shoot a Man!' For
these heroic words his Manly voice and heart was silenced by a
volley of bullets. . . .
Let the noble name of Labuschagne ring in every Working Man's
home throughout the world. Cast fear and shame behind you. Labuschagne, the Hero Miner of the Rand goldfields died as a Man,
defending the lives of women and little innocent children.

Botha and Smuts rushed from Pretoria to Johannesburg on
the Saturday and negotiated a settlement on behalf of the owners
with the strike leaders, who agreed to call off the strike on
condition that all men would be reinstated without victimization, while the government undertook to inquire into their
grievances.[54] Signing the document, said Smuts, was one of the
hardest things he ever had to do. He and Botha were in no
position to bargain. 'We made peace because the Imperial forces
informed us that the mob was beyond their control.' The town
might be sacked that night and the mines permanently ruined.
The two ministers drove away through hostile crowds and made
up their minds that such a state of affairs would never recur.[55]

The strikers, too, were dissatisfied. They met in Johannesburg
on the following Sunday in response to a leaflet issued by Bain,
the secretary of the Federation. 'The Government has declared
war against the Working Class of the Transvaal by its bloody,
brutal and utterly unprovoked attack.' In spite of this rousing
call to action in defence of civil liberties, Bill Andrews and the
Federation leaders urged the men to accept the settlement.
Opposition came from the radical socialists: Crawford, Mary
Fitzgerald, Kendall and J. P. Anderson. The Federation had
been bluffed, they said. The Chamber of Mines was not a party
to the agreement, had not met the demand for collective bargaining, and was free to set up company unions – as indeed it
did a few months later.[56] The socialists correctly evaluated the
government's weakness and the strength of the men's case. They
were never again in so favourable a condition to enforce a legitimate demand for trade union recognition by means of a strike.
Though the meeting voted for Kendall's resolution to persist

until the authorities yielded, the right-wing leaders killed the strike. Nine years later, in the great revolt of 1922, it was Crawford who pressed for a peaceful settlement and Andrews who stood out for struggle to the bitter end.

Afrikaner miners, of whom some had entered the industry as strike-breakers in 1907, loyally supported the strike. The rapidity with which they 'developed a class sentiment', noted Campbell and Munro, was one of its noteworthy features. Labour leaders widened their horizon to take in the prospect of a rapprochement with Afrikaner nationalism. The *Worker* discovered that the 'Dutch temperament' had a 'remarkable leaven of what really approaches very close to Socialistic ideas'. Hertzog had much the same outlook as Labour on such matters as 'financial imperialism', the immigration of low-paid workers, racial segregation and the white labour policy. His party and the Labour party 'represent the real forces of progress in South Africa'.[57]

A glimmering of goodwill towards the African appeared at the other end of the spectrum. Correspondents to the *Strike Herald*, a Federation broadsheet, put the case for organizing African miners. They were ready for trade unionism, and many 'intelligent natives' were willing to undertake the work. A mine could be kept going after a fashion when white workers only were on strike. If the Africans joined them, production would stop, and control of the mine would pass to the Federation. Abortive African strikes had broken out on half a dozen compounds in July, and there might have been a general stoppage along the Reef if the strikes had taken place in the weekend of 'Black Saturday'.[58] Years later, communists claimed that the 1913 strike opened the eyes of militants to the potential of Africans in the labour movement. From that time, declared Ivon Jones, 'there has been a growing minority of white workers who realize that the emancipation of the white can be achieved only by solidarity with the native working masses'.[59]

George Mason, a carpenter and staunch syndicalist from Durham, England, was one of those whom the strike converted into an advocate of solidarity with Africans. They stopped the Kleinfontein mine, he claimed, by responding almost without exception to his appeals.[60] R. B. Waterston (1881–1919), a fireman who came from Australia in 1899 to fight the republics, was also said to have urged Africans at Kleinfontein to down tools. Speaking in Fanagalo, the jargon used on the mines, he advised them to *'tchella lo baas wena meningi mali; picanniny sebenza'*, meaning 'demand more pay and less work'. Whether because of such appeals or on their own initiative, Africans did stop work on a number of mines. They demanded a rise of 2s. or more a day. Police and troops drove them down the shafts with bayonets and rifle butts and the white miners scabbed.[61]

The *A.P.O.* protested against this 'brutal savagery' and insisted that Africans should have as much right as whites to withhold their labour. No whites were prosecuted for striking, while African strike leaders were sentenced to six months' hard labour. This was outrageous, said the African National Congress. A motion of sympathy for the white strikers failed to obtain a seconder at the special conference called in July to consider the Natives Land Act. Congress declared that the dispute affected only whites, dissociated itself from rumours of 'native unrest', and asked for protection of African miners in the event of a general strike. The ANC deputation to the minister of native affairs put these issues before him and complained that the convicted strike leaders were being punished for 'doing what their white overseers told them to do'. Malan, the minister, replied that the punishment was a deterrent to others; undertook to appoint H. O. Buckle, the chief magistrate of Johannesburg, to investigate the grievances of African miners; and gave assurances of protection for them in any general strike of white workers.[62]

Threats of a general strike were being made throughout the second half of 1913. Even conservatives like Creswell declared that 'they would have to adopt other means' if constitutional protests failed. Speaking at Pretoria on 20 July, he said that workers on the Rand had done more in three days to bring the government to its knees than could be accomplished in ten years of agitation. A general strike, warned the *Worker* a week later, 'now means something like a civil war'. With ' great, general and united popular movement, it would very likely be successful, and therefore justified'. George Mason told trade unionists in

Cape Town in September that they were fighting a class war in which the police and military served as 'the bribed assassins of the "Corner House"' (the large mine company building in Johannesburg). The exhortations met with a favourable response. Both wings of the movement profited from Smuts's blunders and the arrogance of the mine owners. While new members streamed into the Labour party, the Federation made great headway with a trade union drive in the main industrial centres.

The next substantial defiance of authority came, however, not from Labour but from Natal's 140,000 Indians. They rose in November against the humiliation and injustice of restricted immigration, provincial barriers, discrimination under licensing and landholding laws, and the £3 tax imposed on persons who had not renewed their indentures. Gandhi accused Smuts of having broken his pledge to repeal the tax; and called on his people to strike.[63] They came out from coal mines, sugar fields, railways, factories, shops and offices. The police clashed with armed strikers on the plantations, killed nine and wounded twenty-five Indians. Gandhi led bands of satyagrahis three times across the Transvaal border before he and his lieutenants were imprisoned. India's government and press denounced the brutality, Botha appointed a commission to inquire into the causes of the disturbance, and Gandhi, released from jail, came to an agreement with Smuts. It closed, said Gandhi, 'the passive-resistance struggle which commenced in the September of 1906', and led to the Indian Relief Act of 1914.[64] Parliament abolished the tax and recognized the validity of Indian customary marriages.

These were meagre gains, a South African sociologist has observed.[65] Though valuable as methods of political education, Gandhi's passive resistance campaigns were ineffective techniques of liberation. 'In 1913, at a time when it appeared obvious to all that the government had been brought to bay, he chose to demonstrate Indian magnanimity of heart, rather than exploit the situation for the immediate rectification of Indian rights.' The great Indian strike crippled industry in Natal and, co-inciding with the white miners' strike on the Rand, 'placed the government in a particularly precarious position'. By calling off the Indian campaign, Gandhi left the government unhampered to suppress the miners' strike. His soul force had succumbed to Smuts's physical force.

Gandhi went to India in July 1914, never to return. 'His name,' said the *A.P.O.*, 'will be handed down to posterity as one of the greatest and truest sons of India that ever came to the shores of South Africa.'[66] The entire Indian community would have followed him if Labour had had its way. The party's fifth annual conference agreed on 1 January 1914 that the presence of Indians would 'always lead to grave difficulties', and urged the government to repatriate them with adequate compensation.[67] As to Africans, the third annual conference, meeting at Bloemfontein in January 1912, adopted a full-blown segregation policy. It would isolate them in separate areas under advisory councils; rule out any extension of their franchise; prohibit them from owning or leasing land in so-called white areas; replace them by white workers in the towns; and absorb persons so displaced in sugar and cotton plantations in the reserves. Development costs would be met out of revenue from African taxation.[68] Armed with these resolutions, Creswell told parliament in the debate on the Natives Land Bill of 1913 that his party was the first to advocate the separation of the races. Left to themselves, they would naturally tend to live apart. Indentured labour and other institutions that increased the points of contact were evil and served only the propertied classes. 'It should be the aim of the country to give the natives their own parallel institutions.'[69]

The Coloured could not be disposed of so easily, even on paper, by deportation or segregation. Labour party branches in the Cape wanted their votes; trade unions wanted to organize the Coloured artisans. George Mason, returning from his organizing tour in the south, advised the Federation in September 1913 to admit those who were prepared to demand 'civilized white standards of wages'. The *Worker* agreed. 'Altruism in this respect is also the first step towards self-protection.' Trade unionism, the paper discovered, depended 'not upon boycotting, but upon organizing the coloured workers and raising them economically'.[70] The party's third, fourth and fifth annual conferences debated these issues with great solemnity and some acerbity. A report on 'Coloured Labour Policy' came before the conference at Cape Town on 1 January 1913. Delegates affirmed the policy of maintaining white standards, accused the Coloured of undermining them, and piously proclaimed the aim of uplifting those who aspired to achieve them. The white man could not afford to surrender his monopoly of the vote 'until such time as our native policy is given effect to'.[71] This, the *A.P.O.* caustically remarked, might be 'as long in coming as the Greek Kalends'.[72]

The party constitution drew no colour line; membership was 'Open to all adults of either sex who endorse the objects of the party and are accepted by the branch they desire to join.' Commenting on this clause, the committee appointed to consider the question of membership conceded that it was unjust, indefensible and even suicidal to exclude civilized Coloured. On the other hand, nothing should be done to attract them at the expense of the party's white ideal. This schizophrenic dialectic produced a monster: 'it is undesirable to admit coloured persons to membership of the party who have not given practical guarantees that they agree to the party's policy of upholding and advancing white standards.' The fourth conference, held at Pretoria on 29 December 1913, adopted the negative condition by seventy-two votes to forty-nine. Both sides wished to maintain white supremacy, and disagreed over whether this would best be served by admitting or excluding Coloured members. Would they be more, or less, dangerous as competitors on the labour market if brought into the movement? Would the party lose more white votes than the number of Coloured votes it might gain by opening its doors? Personal prejudice or sectional interest dictated the answer.

H. D. Bernberg, the party secretary and a member of the Transvaal provincial council, confessed that he was a racist who wanted to keep the party white. George Mason, who had pulled African miners out in the New Kleinfontein strike, thought that it was ridiculous to raise the 'mongrel race' to the European's level. The Coloured man, 'all right as a friend or chum', always worked at a lower rate. The miners' delegates were personally in favour of admitting the Coloured, but their union had instructed them to vote against. John Ware, the Australian-born stonemason and another provincial councillor, said that his society would not allow a Coloured apprentice; and warned conference that the open door would frighten the rising generation of Afrikaners away from the party. The Cape Town delegates, Tom Maginess and Bill Freestone, were in favour of admitting the Coloured. Arthur Barlow agreed, and argued that the same blood flowed through white and Coloured veins. S. P. Bunting saw no objection against allowing the Coloured to help them fight for white standards. Bill Andrews declared that since the Coloured undersold the white man when work was scarce, it was in his interests to raise them to his level. Harry Haynes thought that the white man would remain supreme if he admitted Coloured members and got them to fight for the higher wage.[73]

The conference of 1913–14 elected Andrews as the party's chairman for the coming year. He predicted in his inaugural address at Pretoria that other parties would make capital out of Labour's decision to admit Coloured members. Derision would turn to fear, however, when the Coloured joined the great proletarian alliance. They never did join. The negative and humiliating resolution on membership was swept aside by the dramatic episodes of 1914: the general railwaymen's strike in January, the deportation of labour leaders, the party's subsequent successes at the polls, the outbreak of world war and the split in the party. The war was the dominant issue when the party next discussed the question of membership in August 1915 at Johannesburg. John Ware, now a senator, reminded conference that he had opposed the Pretoria resolution because it was not worth the paper it was written on. Every branch had put its own interpretation on the resolution, with the result that not a single Coloured had joined outside the Cape. He moved an amendment that would make it possible for Coloured to become members of the party.[74]

Creswell deeply regretted the motion. There were, he said, more important questions before conference. Andrews, having moved to the left on the war issue, remarked that 'the working class of this country are the Native people'. If the party was genuinely Labour, and not the middle-class party it appeared to be rapidly becoming, they would admit Africans as well. Gerald Kretzchmar, an executive member of the Federation of Trades, spoke passionately against the motion. A permanent gulf would separate English and Afrikaner workers, he warned, if the party were to concede equality to the Coloured. And the party would never gain power without the Afrikaners' support. Conference rejected Ware's motion by sixty-one votes to twenty-six, and went on to discuss the main business – the party's war policy. Andrews was voted out of the chair after a furious debate; conference carried the war policy by eighty-two votes to thirty;[75] and the anti-war faction walked out, taking along three leading officers and seven members of the executive. Denuded of its militants and radical socialists, the Labour party would never again attempt to build a bridge between white and coloured working men.

8 Loyalists and Rebels

The Labour party claimed to have close on 16,000 paid-up members in 1912, and the trade unions about 12,000 members in 1914.[1] Support for both came from the few scattered industrial areas in the port towns and at Kimberley, Bloemfontein and Pretoria, but the movement's stronghold was on the Witwatersrand. The Rand retained for many decades the feverish and unstable atmosphere of a mining camp; partly, some observers thought, through the unsettling effects of a high altitude in a sub-tropical region. The main contributory factors, however, were social. Recurring booms and slumps on the 'kaffir' share market injected a strong speculative element; while the big rewards and risks of deep-level mining encouraged a reckless and aggressive spirit in the mining community. Glaring contrasts between wealthy English-speaking suburbs and the squalid slums inhabited by Africans, Afrikaners, Indians and Coloured emphasized class, national and racial cleavages. Perhaps the most important cause of underlying tension was the presence and ceaseless rotation of the 200,000 African peasant workers. Isolated in the compounds, never allowed to become full members of the community, and yet indispensable to its prosperity, they were a constant reminder of the society's intrinsic immorality and a challenge to the democratic or socialist pretensions of the white elite.

Labour leaders often forgot that the Rand was unique. They identified the small body of artisans whom they represented with the interests of all workers. Labour's principles, said Creswell in January 1913, came from the working man's 'hard necessities' and 'were calculated to promote the best human interests of all classes'. Journals sympathetic to Labour echoed these sentiments. The movement, declared the *South African Review*, took as its platform 'those interests which are common to all'. Class consciousness meant only that workers recognized their special interests and the possibility of obtaining reforms through the political channel. The class war, on the other hand, 'was created, as it is sustained, by Toryism; it is the Labour movement which the class war seeks to destroy'.[2] The government, urged the *South African Quarterly*, should distinguish between its political and economic functions, remaining neutral in the struggle for economic sovereignty. The feeling that the state was partial to the capitalists had prompted French syndicalists to urge its overthrow by means of the general strike. South Africa should meet this danger by enforcing the principle of collective bargaining through recognized trade unions.[3]

A general strike, even if confined to the Rand, threatened to disrupt the country's economic nerve centre. Smuts was determined to forestall a repetition of the July upheaval. In December 1913 the government published the texts of five bills dealing with industrial disputes.[4] Before parliament could consider them, a new round of strikes broke out. Prompted by the effects of an economic recession, retrenchment and alleged victimization, white coal miners in Natal struck work in December for 18s. a day and the reinstatement of men declared redundant. African coal miners followed with a demand for 4s. a day. The railwaymen were the next to threaten a strike against retrenchments. The union executive called on railway and harbour workers throughout the country to stop work on 8 January if the administration refused to stop retrenchment and re-employ men who had been discharged. H. J. Poutsma, the union's general secretary, urged the Federation of Trades to call a general strike in support; and appealed to the railwaymen at Pretoria 'not to resort to violence, not to do anything that civilized people as they were should not do, but just cease work'.[5]

The Federation stood solidly behind the railwaymen, said J. T. Bain. The government, he added, had called out the troops and 'were preparing to use the same damnable force against the workers'. They, in turn, 'were prepared to use all the force they had in their power'.[6] Smuts also was prepared, to the limit of his powers under the Defence Act. He mobilized the active citizen force, ordered armed guards to be stationed at railway premises, and instructed them to shoot after warning if any unauthorized entry was attempted.[7] Ten thousand troops were brought to the Rand by 10 January, and trade union leaders in different towns were arrested, among them Waterston, Glendon, Colin Wade, Poutsma and other officials of the railway union.[8]

South Africans make a practice of dramatizing their patterns of racial discrimination. While strike leaders were receiving 'courteous treatment' in the Pretoria jail, Sotho miners at Jagersfontein diamond mine suffered serious casualties in yet another of the so-called riots that resulted from the brutal suppression of African strikes. The men struck work on the 9th because a white overseer had kicked one of their comrades to death. When the manager refused to have him arrested, the strikers attempted to break out and join forces with men in other compounds. White employees were called together, cornered the strikers, fired on them, killing eleven and wounding thirty-seven. Most of the Africans then went back to work, but 250 or so who refused were marched to jail under armed escort. A judicial inquiry was held; the white witnesses disagreed over the necessity for the shooting; and none of those responsible for the massacre was prosecuted.[9]

Back on the Rand, an overwhelming majority of the Federation's affiliated unions voted in favour of a general strike, which was timed for the 13th. Smuts put his emergency plans into operation, proclaimed martial law on the 14th, and called out 70,000 armed men, 'a larger military force', he announced in parliament, 'than was mobilized by the late Republics at the beginning of the late war'.[10] Generals Beyers and de la Rey – who were to lead an armed rebellion against the state in October – rode with the commandos into the Rand. A cordon of troops, training a field gun, besieged the Johannesburg trades hall. The police arrested the Federation's entire executive, including Bain, Crawford, Andrew Watson, J. P. Anderson and Charles Mussared. They went to jail singing the 'Red Flag'. The police swooped in all the big industrial centres and arrested hundreds of strikers, trade union and Labour party leaders, among them Creswell, Boydell and Andrews.

Deprived of their leaders, bewildered by press reports of capitulation, and intimidated by threats of dismissal, the workers lost heart. The Federation's acting executive, headed by George Kendall, tried hard to rally them by issuing a series of 'manifestos' which claimed widespread support and explained the purpose of the strike. 'This is a fight for civil liberty, a fight for better conditions.' Prepare 'to suffer and endure for the biggest fight in history.' This was a war 'not against the Community, but for it. You are battling for genuine free labour – for a land of the free, a land that men can love as their own.' The last manifesto, issued on 22 January, called on 'all workers to down tools' in the struggle for liberty, wages, and trade unionism. On the same day, however, Kendall announced that the executive had 'declared the strike off – for the present'.[11]

Andrews, as chairman of the Labour party, issued a manifesto urging 'every patriotic South African' to condemn and show his abhorrence of 'the violent and provocative methods adopted by the government'.[12] His appeal met with little response. Apart from Durban's railwaymen, few workers outside the Rand and Pretoria followed the Federation's lead. Though a majority of the unions affiliated to the Cape Federation voted in favour, the executive decided against the general strike.[13] Six hundred Coloured stevedores at Cape Town's docks struck work on the 14th for an increase in pay from 4s. 6d. to 6s. a day and for an eight-hour day; but the administration broke the strike by introducing Africans from the eastern Cape to work on the ships. Some 100 African miners broke out of the Van Ryn Estate mine compound on the 17th. They were rounded up by a large force of burghers, arrested and fined £1 each. One was shot in the leg while attempting to get away. Otherwise, reported the press, 'the attitude of the natives has in all cases been most exemplary'.[14]

Smuts sealed his victory with a high-handed show of power. He decided to eliminate the 'dangerous men' and deter others of a like disposition while the country was in turmoil and before the labour movement could organize a public protest. Orders were given for the deportation of nine leaders: Bain, Crawford, Livingstone, Mason, McKerrill, Morgan, Poutsma, Waterston and Watson. They were rushed with great secrecy to Durban, placed on board the steamship *Umgeni*, and sent off to England on 30 January, the opening day of the new parliamentary session. Smuts immediately introduced the Indemnity and Undesirables Special Deportation Bill to legalize the deportations and other unlawful acts committed under martial law. He based his defence on the urgencies of public safety, law and order; but could not deny Hertzog's accusation that since his victims had broken no law, and would not have been convicted in any court, he had ordered their abduction because he had no lawful reason to imprison them.

The six Labour members rose to great heights of parliamentary strategy in a filibuster against the bill. 'This was not a conspiracy on the part of the workers,' declared Creswell; 'it was a conspiracy between the Government and their friends, the capitalistic school of Johannesburg, to run the country in their own interests.' They had conspired to grind down the working man for the benefit of the mining magnates. Andrews said that the strike was orderly passive resistance; and accused the government of deploying the state's full resources to break trade unionism. The government had made a great blunder, he added; and would yet discover that it had failed to crush the spirit of the people.[15] In England George Lansbury called for a general strike to secure the return of the deportees. Stop work, he urged, 'until both the home and the South African governments are brought to their senses. The right of combination, the right to agitate, and the right to preach revolutionary ideas must be maintained.'[16] The deported men were advised to sue the ship-owners for unlawful imprisonment on the high seas, but the action was discontinued after war had broken out.[17] Smuts retreated under pressure and allowed the deportees to return to South Africa at the government's expense.

The arrests, imprisonment and deportations humiliated and angered the labour leaders. They were in no mood to respond sympathetically to the government's proposed measures for industrial peace. One of these, the Industrial Disputes Prevention Bill, empowered employers and employees to form conciliation boards or appoint arbitrators. Strikes and lockouts would be illegal unless preceded by an unsuccessful attempt to arrive at an agreement. The bill, which reached the statute book in an amended form only in 1924, contained a major colour bar. It excluded from the definition of employees and therefore from the conciliation machinery all pass-bearing Africans, including those subject to the terms of the Native Labour Regulation Act of 1911, and all indentured Indians. The parliamentary Labour party denounced, not the colour bar, but the partial ban on strikes. Andrews said that the bill was intended to cripple the trade unions. Creswell thought that it should be left alone until it could be considered by a new parliament 'in which the industrial population would be more congenially represented'. Haggar maintained that the class war had been forced on the workers and would be waged until one class was wiped out.[18]

The government shelved the Industrial Disputes Prevention Bill and its companion, the Trade Union Bill; but Labour could not stay the passage of the far more repressive Riotous Assemblies and Criminal Law Amendment Bill. This penalized attempts to force workers to join or not to join trade unions; banned strikes in public utility services; gave magistrates, acting under ministerial authority, wide powers to prohibit meetings expected to endanger the public peace; and allowed the police in certain circumstances to arrest speakers and listeners or, in the last resort, to fire. This was the strongest attack yet made by a South African legislature on civil liberties and working-class rights; and marked a new stage in the transition from a colonial economy to an industrialized society. Techniques of colonial repression, as exemplified by the Natal Code of Native Law, were from then on supplemented by more modern and pervasive restrictions on the labour and national liberation movements.

White voters demonstrated at the polls against Smuts's brutal attacks on trade unionism and the working class. Tom Maginess won a parliamentary by-election for Labour in Liesbeek, Cape Town; Morris Kentridge won another in Durban Central, giving Labour eight members in the assembly. Walter Snow, a victimized railwayman, was returned from Liesbeek to the provincial council. Labour won two provincial council seats in Durban and one in Bloemfontein during 1914, and scored its greatest victory in the Transvaal by contesting twenty-five and winning twenty-three seats in the provincial council. The Labour councillors had a clear majority of one in the chamber, but could not obtain control of the executive, and so were unable to implement their policy. Their two notable achievements were a new municipal rating ordinance, which the central government disallowed, and a revision of the municipal franchise, which was extended to white women and modified so as to incorporate the principle of proportional representation. Under the leadership of F. A. W. Lucas, a barrister and firm adherent of Henry George's land tax theory, the Labour group tried hard to substitute economic issues for Anglo-Afrikaner rivalries in provincial politics, and never wavered in their adherence to the party's white supremacy policy.

S. P. Bunting, who won the Bezuidenhout seat, set out the case for the policy in an election manifesto of 3,000 words. Written in his involved style, and studded with capitalized phrases, it contained both an analysis of South African society and a passionate protest against class oppression. It has additional significance as marking a stage in the development of a great South African radical. Born of middle-class parents in London in 1873 and a graduate of Oxford, Bunting came as a lieutenant in the British army to South Africa in 1900, took a law degree after the war, and settled down to practise as an attorney in Johannesburg.[19] Wybergh and Creswell were his intimate friends, and he came to share their belief in the white labour policy. He helped to found and took on the secretaryship of the White Expansion Society in 1909, with Patrick Duncan as its president and Lucas as one of the committee members. He then joined the Labour party in 1910, became the secretary of the Witwatersrand district committee, and was elected to the national executive in 1912. His manifesto, therefore, represented the views of a senior if exceptional member of the party.

He managed the *Worker*, his party's paper, in 1912, and sat on its editorial board; yet his manifesto, printed in heavy type with many capitalized phrases, came far closer in spirit to the radicalism of the rival journal *Voice of Labour*. Like Crawford, he believed that South Africa's industrial upheavals formed part of a world-wide struggle between international finance and the working classes. They were striking, not for higher wages, but FOR BETTER STATUS, the RIGHT TO LIVE, a PLACE IN THE SUN. They refused to be mere servants, and this was natural in South Africa 'where every white man has tasted more or less the sweets of masterhood himself'. But the ruling class in this, THE MOST CAPITALIST-RIDDEN COUNTRY IN THE WORLD, was determined to suppress trade unions, dispense with white workers, and run the economy with white overseers, and '"cheap", unenfranchised, unorganized Kaffirs'. This 'means eventually a Kaffir's land. THE ABOMINATION OF DESOLATION'. White South Africa was in danger, and only the Labour party resisted the REAL ANARCHIC CONSPIRACY AGAINST SOCIETY.

Labour would do away with the differences between master and servant, secure equal opportunities for all, and reconstruct society on a cooperative basis – 'the only possible means to TRUE AND UNIVERSAL LIBERTY AND WELLBEING'. It would be a white man's heaven. Africans were enemies within the gate: the 'allies, or rather tools, of Capitalism against the white workers'. There followed an odd qualification: 'But this is merely a temporary obstacle, for the native workers are bound to organize soon.' An obstacle to what? And would they organize with or against the white workers? If Bunting had misgivings about the African's role, he suppressed them in deference to the party's official policy. Ignoring the effects of industrialization and the pressures that forced peasants to enter the labour market, he maintained that they were landowners, who did not need to work if left to themselves. They were better off than the whites, and earned wages as a luxury. The party's policy was to separate them territorially, repatriate Asiatics, and gradually eliminate the Coloured by preventing miscegenation.

Racial tolerance could not be expected of Labour councillors when a man of Bunting's calibre identified himself thus wholeheartedly with white supremacy. Reviewing their 'one-sidedness', the *A.P.O.* listed some of their colour bar proposals. They refused to grant supplies unless the executive undertook to build roads departmentally and with white labourers only at adequate wages; voted money for public buildings at Warmbad with a proviso that Africans employed there be dismissed; and denied the municipal franchise to the darker peoples while conferring it on 'every pimp, prostitute and illicit liquor seller in gaol'.[20] The Labour majority introduced free secondary education to white children in the province, and opposed schools for Coloured and Africans.[21] Ware, sitting on the Witwatersrand School Board, moved the adoption of a resolution that 'the teaching of trades, or the use of tools, to Coloured people and Natives will be sternly discountenanced'. Labour members of the Johannesburg town council were notoriously rigid in denying Coloured, Indians and Africans the use of the municipal trams.

A solid phalanx of parliamentary parties – South African, Unionist, Nationalist and Labour – confronted black and brown South Africans on almost every issue involving racial discrimination. Individual Unionists occasionally protested. A few Cape liberals, notably Morris Alexander, Merriman and the Schreiners, consistently skirmished for Coloured rights. Labour stood always on the side of the extreme racialists, as in the debates on the colour bar regulations issued by Smuts under the Mines and Works Act of 1911.[22] These reserved thirty-two categories of work for whites and prohibited the issue of certificates of competence in the Transvaal and Orange Free State to any person of colour. A certificate obtained by one of them in Natal or the Cape had no validity outside that province. Merriman took up the cudgels at the request of the APO and moved the deletion of the colour bar in 1914. A petition before the House, signed by 1,624 Coloured residents of the Transvaal, complained that they were prevented from earning their living by following their trades as engine drivers, carpenters, blasters, gangers, banksmen and onsetters; and prayed that the word 'white' should be replaced by the word 'competent' in the regulations.[23]

Smuts admitted in the Senate that the discrimination against the Coloured man was indefensible and would have to go, though not in the immediate present. The strongest opposition to Merriman's proposal came from the Reef's representatives, both Unionist and Labour. Creswell repeated his familiar argument in moving an amendment to the motion. It was really directed against trade unionism, he said, and aimed at setting the coloured peoples against white workmen. His party advocated equal pay for equal work, whereas the mine owners wanted to hire labour at the lowest possible rate. They would not pay Africans a shilling more, but would, if allowed, give individuals something more to take over the white miner's occupation. It was for this reason that a number of Coloured were being given work in the mines. He was against the colour bar, as it instilled a false sense of security in white men. His amendment declared that the abolition of the colour bar would increase profits at the expense of the white, African and Coloured population as long as the mining industry employed uncivilized, servile and largely imported workers, and as long as there was no legislation to guarantee miners a civilized standard of wages. Steps should be taken to change the system before the House could take note of the petition.

It was an impossible condition in the existing social order. Indeed one must doubt if the white workers really wanted a change along the lines indicated by Creswell. They aspired, in Bunting's percipient phrase, to 'a better status' and 'a place in the sun': but not, as he suggested, to an egalitarian society. Their aim was to achieve recognition as members of the master race. They would rather supervise African servants than fraternize with persons whom they, like other whites, considered to be members of an inferior race. Creswell's party and the trade unions made no attempt to organize Africans and Coloured behind a demand for equal wages and opportunities. In spite of disclaimers, white workers had the same interests as mine owners in perpetuating the migrant labour system.

The *A.P.O.* drew the inescapable conclusion. There was a time, it said, when the Coloured were free to sell their labour on an open market. Their main concern then was to defend the franchise. As doors of employment were being closed to them everywhere, the question of where to find work overshadowed all other problems. In that frame of mind, they responded favourably to Labour leaders, and hailed their vigorous campaign in the Cape. The Labour party's attitude on the colour bar and Indian Relief Bill soon convinced many of its insincerity. The party would keep the Coloured out of the mines, and the

Indian in a semi-servile condition on the sugar plantations so as to prevent him from finding employment in other occupations. This intolerable narrowness and selfishness would disenchant the Coloured. 'The continuance of the White policy of exploitation and repression of the Coloured races is gradually welding the latter into one solid mass.' None of the existing generations would be alive when black humanity learned to speak with one irresistible voice; but that time would come.[24]

The outbreak of world war delayed the event, opened old wounds, revived the conflict between British and Afrikaner, and checked the growth of an alliance between white Labour and Afrikaner nationalism. At a special session early in September 1914 parliament adopted a resolution by ninety-two to twelve votes affirming the 'whole-hearted determination' of the House to 'take all measures necessary for defending the interests of the Union and for cooperating with his Majesty's Imperial Government to maintain the security and integrity of the Empire'. No section of the population adhered more loyally to this pledge than the African, Coloured and Indian. They must endure their domestic burdens in solemn silence, declared the *A.P.O.*, and prove themselves no less worthy than the empire's other sons.[25] Abdurahman told a crowded Coloured meeting in Cape Town to forget their many grievances while the empire's very existence was at stake. Other leaders – Carelse, Veldsman, the Rev. Dr Gow, S. Reagon, Dr A. H. Gool – echoed his appeal and undertook to raise a Coloured war relief fund. 'With all its faults,' wrote Abdurahman, 'the Empire contains some attractive force which during periods like the present converts the silken thread into bonds of steel'.[26] The APO offered to raise a corps of 5,000 men for active service. Fully 13,000 volunteered within a month. Africans also asked to be allowed 'to cast a few stones at the Germans'. Dube and other ANC leaders left a special conference on the Native Land Act to offer their services to the government at Pretoria.

Coloured and Africans who professed loyalty so spontaneously and without official exhortation were probably motivated by the usual sentiments and reasons of a people at war: a sense of duty, a spirit of adventure and desire to escape from the daily round, the prospect of a job and of gaining social esteem. Then, too, a Coloured man might hope to escape in uniform from the nagging humiliation of being 'different' and inferior. By taking part in the war effort and 'doing his bit', he would merge with the 'nation' and lay up credit for the day of victory. He could claim freedom and justice, and an easing of the black man's burden, to the extent that he made sacrifices in the common cause. This is what his leaders told him. He suffered a rude rebuff. The government would recruit Coloured men to groom army mules and drive transport wagons; but fighting Germans was a white man's privilege, reserved for the active citizens' force organized under the Defence Act of 1912.

Then came the rebellion of October. Six thousand burghers of the Transvaal and Orange Free State took up arms against Botha. Beyers, having resigned his post of commandant general, Maritz and Kemp, two high-ranking officers, and the veteran general de Wet led the revolt. It was a romantic, somewhat mystical resumption of the republics' struggle for independence, a protest against the invasion of German South West, and a crusade to avenge Slachtersnek, the concentration camp martyrs and the humiliation of Vereeniging. Botha proclaimed martial law, appealed for volunteers to fight in South West, and summoned the commandos against the rebels. Maritz led his men over the border to join the Germans. The Coloured in the northwest Cape asked for arms to defend themselves. The APO repeated its offer to raise a corps, and was again refused. This was a white man's war, the government replied. It was anxious to avoid employing Coloured citizens, or others not of European descent, in a combatant capacity against whites.[27]

Yet black and brown men were fighting on both sides in Europe and Africa. Even the Union had a quota of dark-skinned soldiers. The government assured Afrikaner nationalists that 'no armed Natives or Coloured persons were employed to assist in the suppression of the rebellion'. The statement rested on the false assumption that all South African soldiers were of pure European descent. In reality, many were coloured passing as white. 'Their dark complexion, the kink in the hair, the broad flat nose – these all betray their ancestry.'[28] Some Coloured men made their way at their own expense to England, to enlist there for active service. Bewailing the refusal to lift the colour bar in South Africa, the *A.P.O.* declared that whites would rather see the empire fall than place Coloured men in the firing line.[29] Their faith in the Allied cause remained undimmed. 'Thrice we offered our services, and thrice they were refused. We cannot do more.' They could only pray that peace would bring 'true British liberty and justice'; not the liberty that enabled a disloyal crowd to pass a Natives Land Act, rob men of their franchise rights, and ban them as outcasts; but a liberty ensuring to all in the empire an equal opportunity to live in freedom.[30]

Botha announced the conquest of German South West on 10 July 1915. Abdurahman wrote that the Coloured had small reason to rejoice. He hoped that Botha would go forward in the path of duty to the king, and with a more tender conscience to the large Coloured and African population of the conquered territory. It would be a great mistake if he gave way to pressure and appointed only Afrikaners to administer them. Very few had been trained to deal tactfully and fairly with persons of colour; most of them suffered from centuries' old colour prejudice. At least the northern half of South West, which was inhabited mainly by tribal Africans, should remain a protectorate on the model of Basutoland, to be administered directly by the crown.[31] The advice was sound, as time would show; but Botha had other considerations on his mind. Fixing his eyes on the approaching elections, he wished to reconcile Afrikaners to his successful imperial venture by promising them farms and administrative posts in the conquered territory.

Thousands of Coloured and Africans served with Botha's troops as transport drivers, medical orderlies and labourers. Now that the fighting had finished in South West Africa, troops could be sent to more distant fields, where the employment of Coloured combatants would be less obvious and perhaps less offensive to racial susceptibilities. A volunteer force had already been raised for Europe. The Coloured agitated once again for the right to kill or be killed. The war, they said, was not for white people only. The great majority of South Africans were not white. No army recruited in South Africa could be truly representative unless it included a Coloured contingent. At last, in September, they were told that the government had offered and Britain had accepted the formation of a Coloured infantry corps under white commissioned officers. Abdurahman was appointed to a recruiting committee and asked his people to take their proper place in the fighting line. 'Today the Empire needs us. What nobler duty is there than to respond to the call of your King and Country?'[32]

The Labour front was less united. The party's conference of January 1913 had committed it to a watered down version of the Socialist International's Stuttgart and Basle resolutions. If war threatened, the conference agreed, workers of all countries concerned should try to prevent it by a simultaneous stoppage of work. It was an innocuous motion, said Creswell, since it would not place any country in the position of being crippled by a general strike while its adversary carried on with the backing of the workers.[33] In keeping with this resolution, the administrative council, with Andrews in the chair, appealed on 2 August 1914 to workers everywhere to organize against the war. It had been fomented by capitalist governments, was unjust, and could benefit only armament manufacturers and other enemies of the working class. The S.A. Industrial Federation, the Cape Town SDF and Durban SDP passed similar resolutions. This was a brave stand, which put South African radicals well in the vanguard of international socialism. They found little support among the party rank-and-file.

The *Worker*, then edited by Wybergh, whipped up enthusiasm for the war after Britain's entry. A leading article in the issue of 6 August argued that the German workers had failed to make an effective protest. 'And if your best friend goes mad and attacks you with deadly weapons, you have no choice but to defend yourself.' Creswell agreed. 'If you are attacked,' he said, 'you have got to fight.'[34] The government undertook on 10 August to invade German South West. Parliament met a month later to give its approval. Botha told the House that South Africa was legally and morally committed by her allegiance to the crown. Only Hertzog's Nationalists stood out for neutrality. The South African party, Unionists and Labour, including Andrews, carried a motion of loyalty to the king and support for the war by ninety-two votes to twelve on 14 September. Madeley abstained, but joined the pro-war group before long. The first troops sailed for South West Africa on the same day.

A patriotic wave swept through the party as one branch after another voted for war in defiance of the executive's policy. The industrial federation also rescinded its anti-war resolution. Creswell and Maginess left to serve in South West. The *Worker* conducted a pro-war campaign. There was resistance to the war fever only at the highest level of the party's leadership. D. Ivon Jones, Bunting, Colin Wade and P. R. Roux claimed that the party was bound by its resolution of 1913 and the Basle declaration. The administrative council under their direction passed a series of resolutions urging the international labour movement to convene peace conferences. Wade and his colleagues formed the War on War League in September, and published the *War on War Gazette*. Though censored out of existence at the end of November, it left an imprint. Branches of the League appeared along the Reef, in Durban and Cape Town, linking pacifists and radical socialists in a united front.

Who was the defender of the true faith: Creswell, fighting in a major's uniform to extend South Africa's frontiers; or Jones, the consumptive teacher from Wales, fighting for lost causes and the underlying masses? The League maintained that the Creswellites had surrendered the party's principles for the sake of parliamentary seats. Reinforced by Andrews, and in control of the party machine, the anti-war group mustered a majority of the delegates to the annual conference at East London in January 1915. Creswell was on active service and Andrews in the chair. Conference had before it John Ware's pro-war motion. James Clark, another Transvaal provincial councillor, moved that all wars under capitalism injured the working class. Conference evaded the issue in the interests of unity by adopting a 'neutrality' resolution from which only Wybergh dissented. It allowed every member to decide, according to his reason and conscience, whether to support or oppose the war.[35]

The conference put the War on War group in the saddle by re-electing Andrews, Jones and Weinstock to the posts of president, secretary, and treasurer, and giving them a majority on the executive.[36] Party members, however, responded more eagerly to the call of war than to the call of peace. The executive intensified efforts to recruit Afrikaners, who were less susceptible than the British to war fever. Bunting had earlier predicted that a pro-war stand would ruin the prospect of attracting Afrikaner workers. The party, he said, could not hold its own with Unionists and Nationalists in the 'patriotic game'.[37] To appreciate the significance of his comment, one should bear in mind the steady movement of unskilled Afrikaners into the industrial centres, and earlier attempts by the labour movement to gain their allegiance. As far back as 1908 Frank Nettleton, the secretary of the Pretoria trades council, had cooperated with officials of Het Volk in forming Arbeid Adelt, a non-political society of unskilled Afrikaners on a white labour policy platform. The party's executive decided in January 1912 to print its constitution in Afrikaans and English. The whole-hearted participation of Afrikaners in the miners' strike of 1913 alerted the movement to their potential role.

The Labour party and Hertzog's Nationalists had much in common, argued the *Worker* at great length in August. Both rebelled against the oppression and exploitation that stemmed from capitalism; both advocated racial segregation and a ban on the importation of cheap contract labour; both represented the forces of progress. Hertzogism was bound to shed its 'racial' bias against the British and develop its socialistic side, the paper predicted.[38] Nettleton, then endeavouring to organize railway and other transport workers in one union, made a special drive to recruit Afrikaner gangers, drivers and labourers. Afrikaner leaders were not prepared, however, to stand aside while their people fell into the clutches of foreign socialists and atheists. The Rev. Brandt launched a Christian Union in Johannesburg. Madeley asserted that it was Botha's brain child. The prime minister had proposed the union's formation, took a hand in drafting its rules, and promised to obtain recognition for it on the mines.[39]

Afrikaner names appeared with growing frequency from August onwards in the *Worker*'s reports of branch activities along the Reef and, more surprisingly, in Transvaal country towns. The general strike of 1914 and the subsequent deportations gave further impetus to the spread of the party's influence among Afrikaners. S. T. Pienaar and G. H. Kretzchmar, the first Afrikaners to represent Labour in a legislative chamber, were elected to the provincial council in March by English and Afrikaner voters in Denver and Vrededorp. English-speaking candidates were returned in the predominantly Afrikaner constituencies of Krugersdorp, Maraisburg and Pretoria West. Jock van Lingen polled 600 votes for the party in the platteland constituency of Heidelberg in May. Afrikaner audiences at Ficksburg, Brandfort, Edenburg and other Free State towns gave Labour speakers a sympathetic hearing. E. W. Connelly, the secretary of the Bloemfontein branch, wrote in August that if the party were to cultivate them at every opportunity, thousands of Afrikaners would soon follow the labour movement.⁴⁰

The favourable trend was checked, though not halted, by the rising of Afrikaner nationalism in the north after the Beyers-de Wet rebellion of October 1914. Colin Wade's anti-war group tried to persuade the party's administrative council to negotiate a peaceful settlement, but it would do no more than send a deputation urging de Wet to 'obey constituted authority'. The new executive, elected in January, renewed the effort to attract Afrikaners. It appointed a rural propaganda committee headed by Bunting, who co-opted half a dozen Afrikaners, and conducted an extensive campaign in country towns with the assistance of Gideon Botha, a former member of the miners' union, and Bob Waterston, the Australian-born mechanic who had been deported by Smuts in 1914. Ivon Jones reported on 6 June 1915 that though the prospect of winning country seats at the next election had to be discounted, 'a great and unexpected advance' had been made on the platteland. Afrikaners, even when linked to a racialist party, were anxious to learn about Labour principles. From all parts came a demand for Labour leaflets and literature.⁴¹

The party's efforts to establish a basis among Afrikaners received a permanent setback in the second half of 1915. Anti-German riots broke out on the Rand after the sinking of the

Lusitania. Andrews and his executive protested publicly against the mass hysteria, whereas Creswell's supporters used the occasion to whip up sentiment for the war. He returned from the front to lead the campaign, and issued a circular letter on 30 June urging party members to endorse his 'see it through' policy at the forthcoming special conference. Most of them, he claimed, approved of the decision to vote for Botha's loyalty motion. Not one of the Labour men in parliament would have been elected if they had told their voters to disregard all ties and feelings other than the 'principles of international socialism'. Like the vast majority of socialists in the belligerent countries, he refused to believe that being a socialist involved any repudiation of one's patriotic duties. The anti-war group replied in a pamphlet denouncing the war as an imperialist venture. Creswell's policy, they maintained, disregarded the sentiments of Afrikaners. It was the party's duty, not to win the next elections at all hazards, but to stand firm on the principles of peace, international goodwill and working-class solidarity.

Bunting's report of 5 August argued that an anti-war policy was politically expedient. The party had to choose between the Afrikaner vote and support for the war. Its position in country districts had been made 'frankly desperate' by the violent imperialist sentiments of prominent members. His committee could neither disclaim nor defend such jingoism before Afrikaner audiences. The party had already lost the mass of the Afrikaner vote, and would lose it for perhaps twenty years if the forthcoming conference adopted a war policy. 'At present the Party appeals to the Afrikander about as much as to the Kaffir.' Hope of a Labour majority in parliament could never be realized until the party had regained the sympathy of the country vote.

Creswell himself preferred the assumed certainty of the British working-class vote to the doubtful prospect of obtaining Afrikaner votes in rural constituencies. Harassed by the government press, he wanted to rid the party of the taint of disloyalty. The special conference, meeting in Johannesburg on 22 August, was packed by Creswellites. They carried a pro-war resolution by eighty-two votes to thirty, and so put an end to Labour's assault on the citadels of Afrikaner nationalism.

The anti-war group staged a dramatic withdrawal, taking with them the senior officers, Andrews, Clark, Jones, Weinstock, Bunting, and half the administrative council. They went on to form the International League of the South African Labour Party. As the title indicates, their intention was to remain in the party so as to preserve unity and win it back to its 'native principles' of international socialism and anti-militarism.[42] One of their first actions was to produce a weekly, the *International*. It soon had a clear field in the movement, for the *Worker*, having lost its chief contributors, ceased publication before the year was out.

The attempt to reconcile conflicting loyalties within the party was short-lived. Electoral rivalries made compromise impossible. The new leadership insisted that every party candidate for public office should pledge loyalty to the pro-war policy. Andrews and Clark resigned in order to stand for parliament against the party nominees. A final split followed. A general meeting of League members decided on 22 September 1915 to secede and form the International Socialist League (S.A.), with Andrews as chairman, Jones as secretary, and a committee that included Clark, Crisp, Weinstock, Bunting and Dunbar.

The October parliamentary elections gave the South African party 54 seats, the Unionists 39, the Nationalists 27, Labour 4 and Independents 6. Botha remained in office with the aid of the Unionists. Labour contested 44 seats on a platform of moderate social reforms and obtained 24,444 votes, nearly 10 per cent of the poll, though its share of the Transvaal votes amounted to 16 per cent. Maginess retained Liesbeek with a majority of one vote. Labour's other candidates in the Cape peninsula, Batty, Forsyth, Freestone, Haggar and Whitaker, were heavily defeated, in spite of their attempt to woo the Coloured vote with a local manifesto urging the extension of the Cape franchise to other provinces. This violated the party's constitution, said the *A.P.O.*, and the deception was too palpable to deceive anyone.[43] The paper called on Coloured electors to oppose every Labour candidate. The party's record in the Transvaal provincial council showed that it was composed of 'a greedy pack of vultures, who would keep the black man as a helot'. They were the 'avowed enemy of the Coloured man, who should spurn them with loathing and disgust'.[44]

Coloured and African unity often buckled under the strain of coping with the bribes and blandishments of white candidates, some of whom were not averse to promoting the growth of rival organizations among the electors. A section of the APO leadership hived off from the parent body in response to such pressures in 1904, 1910 and 1913. The APO did not escape internal dissensions in the 1915 elections. Its members in Paarl and Stellenbosch defied the leaders by supporting Nationalist party candidates; while Abdurahman himself broke discipline when he backed John Hewat, the Unionist candidate in Woodstock, against the decision of the APO's executive to work for the return of the independent candidate W. Mushet. Hewat won the five-cornered contest by a comfortable margin, and the APO never fully recovered from the effects of its president's refusal to abide by the majority decision.

Abdurahman was by then deeply committed to the Unionists. They had allowed him to be returned unopposed to the provincial council in 1914 and the town council in 1915. Their candidates advertised heavily in his newspaper. It significantly ceased publication shortly after the elections for want of financial support by agents and readers. When the Unionists amalgamated with the South African party in 1921, he gave the new force his full allegiance and came to be known as Smuts's man. This involvement in white party politics exposed him to attacks from right and left. Creswell, fighting a losing battle in Kimberley in 1915, accused him of being an ally of De Beers and the 'constant catspaw' of the Unionists, the 'bulwark of the Mining Houses'. Yet their policy of importing 'cheap Kaffir labour' was equally detrimental to Africans, the civilized Coloured, and the white worker. Abdurahman's reply listed the colour bars introduced or proposed by the Labour party. He was, 'however reluctantly, forced to conclude that they are the greatest political enemies of the Coloured races'.[45]

The split in the Labour party left Coloured and Africans unmoved. Like Creswell, they were patriotic and pro-war, but his party's racialism shut the door to any prospect of gaining their goodwill. He and Sampson removed doubts that might have arisen on this score after the split by reiterating their opposition to an extension of the franchise.[46] Sampson, looking for a scapegoat to bear the blame for his party's defeat, accused the Unionists and the South African party of plotting to enfranchise Coloured and Africans in the north. 'If this Parliament lasted five years,' he said, 'there would be very few white workers here to vote at the next election.'[47] Though the International Socialists, in contrast, soon began to discard their racial bias, their violent opposition to the war made them unacceptable to Coloured and African leaders. Isolated, and without a mass basis in the working class, the socialists could offer nothing besides a bitter struggle against authority. Andrews and Clark, representing the ISL in the parliamentary elections for Georgetown and Langlaagte, constituencies which they had previously won for Labour, lost their deposits by polling no more than eighty-two and fifty-eight votes respectively.

One is tempted to attribute this resounding defeat to the ISL's stand against the war. Since pro-war Labour candidates fared only little better, it is more reasonable to suppose that voters turned their backs on Labour politics for the duration. Their reaction tended to obscure the long term consequences of the cleavage. Its immediate effect was to disrupt the party organization in its stronghold on the Rand, where eight branches went over to the ISL. This initial support faded as the East African campaign gained momentum and the economy expanded. The split may have contributed to Labour's reverses in the 1915 elections. Some historians go further and suggest that it contributed to the party's destruction.[48] This verdict is too severe, however. The party's recovery in 1920 suggests that the rupture did not permanently impair its parliamentary prospects. In the final analysis, the right wing probably suffered less from the defection of the radicals than from its growing involvement with Afrikaner nationalism.

9 The New Radicals

Class conflict abated during the war. Full employment, a rise
in profits, and patriotic sentiment generated goodwill on both
sides. Government and employers discovered that trade unions
could contribute much to industrial peace and efficiency. The
union leaders responded with a policy of avoiding action that
might reduce output. Trade unionism recovered from the setback suffered after the abortive general strike of 1914 and the
resulting large-scale victimizations. The Transvaal Federation of
Trades, in a bid to repair the damage and overcome weaknesses
disclosed by the strike, changed its name to the South African
Industrial Federation and invited the affiliation of unions
throughout the country. Only the Cape Federation of Trade
Unions held aloof. Established in 1913, it proclaimed a willingness to organize and admit all workers without regard to race,
colour or creed. Some of its affiliated unions, notably in the
printing, furniture, baking and building trades, consisted mainly
of Coloured members. Bob Stuart, the Cape Federation's
secretary and a stubborn Scot, refused to play second fiddle to
the north and rejected its white labour policy. The SAIF was
the major trade union centre and developed into a powerful
organization under the leadership of another Scot, the former
radical Archie Crawford.

Deported in 1914, Crawford returned a changed man. His
metamorphosis from an extreme radical to a right-wing bureaucrat paralleled that of Bill Andrews in the opposite direction.
They interchanged their roles. Andrews, now an uncompromising revolutionary, would accuse Crawford, in more elegant
language, of the crimes against the working class of which
Crawford had accused Andrews in the earlier period. It has been
suggested that Crawford when in exile was persuaded by British

trade unionists to adopt a policy of class collaboration.[1] He was not one to be influenced easily against his basic inclinations. It is more likely that he found an outlet for his ambition in an important office of the kind to which he had aspired without success in the days of his youthful militancy. Not satisfied with building the SAIF into a big organization, he wanted the entire trade union movement to turn around him. The war gave him an opportunity to obtain by means of diplomacy and conciliation the kind of power that he had failed to achieve through bluster and appeals for mass action.

His favoured technique was to form reference boards which enabled him to negotiate on behalf of the unions affiliated to the SAIF. He and Gemmill, the secretary of the Chamber of Mines, settled nearly all white labour disputes on the mines in this way during the war years.[2] The owners showed their goodwill by collecting trade union dues under a stop order system; while the unions reciprocated in September 1916 by agreeing to freeze wage rates for the duration of the war and three months thereafter. This, said Andrews and his associates in the ISL, amounted to a vicious collaboration that stemmed from the basic error of support for the war. The unions were seeking favours from their masters, who 'packed them off as cannon fodder, this probably being the final destination of Trade Unionism by Craft and Crawfordism'.[3]

African miners received neither favours from the owners nor aid from the white workers. When whites employed at Van Ryn Deep mine came to work on 21 December 1915, they were told to return home as the entire morning shift of 2,800 Africans had struck work in protest against an unsympathetic compound manager and to redress the grievances of drillers. The latter were kept so long at 'lashing' (removing rock dislodged from the face by the previous blast) that they could not drill the minimum norm of thirty-six inches and so were given 'loafer' tickets. Unable to obtain satisfaction, a party of strikers set off along the Main Reef Road to interview officials of the Native Recruiting Corporation in Johannesburg. A posse of mounted police intercepted them and forced them back to the compound. The strike ended when the management agreed, under pressure of government officials, to assure the men that 'their legitimate grievances would be redressed'.[4] International socialists did not fail to draw the contrast between African militancy and the passivity of white workers.

Jones and Bunting, the League's leading theorists, gave two broad reasons. The Labour party, they said, had erred by making votes its main target, only to find that it could not match the jingoism of the Unionists in a khaki election.[5] More basically the workers had been corrupted by racialism. 'Slaves to a higher oligarchy, the white workers of South Africa themselves in turn batten on a lower slave class.' They compensated for their inferior class status by lording it over Africans. More intolerant than any other working class, the whites were also more parasitical. Appeals to international unity could never evoke a sincere response from a rank-and-file so situated.[6] The war was being waged in the name of freedom, and to get it they had to give it. The fact had to be faced that the freedom for which they fought was a mere name to an overwhelming army of native wage labourers who were spat on and spurned by the great majority of their white fellow workers.[7]

Vote-catching had ruined the movement, agreed Jimmy Bain, who had preceded Crawford as secretary of the SAIF. The comment appeared in an obituary on Tom Mathews, a victim of the miners' 'white scourge' in March 1915. His last words were: 'I have served the Labour movement faithfully these twenty-one years. I hope it is satisfied.' Few men had done more for the workers than Mathews, wrote Bain, and few had received less. Born at Newlyn, Cornwall, in 1867, he migrated to the United States at the age of fifteen, rose to be president of the miners' union in Montana, and was elected in 1892 to the state house of representatives as Labour's only member. He came to the Rand in 1897, took a prominent part in the miners' union, and became its general secretary in 1907. 'Strong as a lion' and 'fearless of speech', he was more of a socialist than a Labour party man, according to Bain. He helped to found the movement 'before votes were counted of so much importance; before there were places and preferment, Provincial Councils and all other soul-stifling influences of today, at work'.[8] Mathews was succeeded by another militant, the Australian-born J. Forrester Brown, a founding member of the ISL and an advocate of inter-racial working-class solidarity. He too succumbed like Mathews to what Bain described as 'the narrow-mindedness of his own class'.

Brown, Andrews and other prominent trade unionists in the ISL were unable to detach themselves wholly from the white power structure; and had no intention of following the socialists of Durban and Cape Town into the isolation of a debating society. The League made a bid for leadership by taking part in elections at every opportunity. It nominated nine candidates in the Transvaal municipal elections of October 1915. Two, Colin Wade at Germiston and J. A. Clark in Johannesburg, were elected. J. van Lingen represented the League later in the year in a provincial council by-election and came at the bottom of the poll with 138 votes. He won a municipal seat in Germiston in October 1916, while all other League candidates were defeated. This was hardly surprising, as they fought under the slogans of 'No Conscription' and 'Away with Capitalist War and Capitalist Robbery'. The League claimed that the result was all a revolutionary party could desire.[9] Some 2,000 electors in Johannesburg, Germiston and Benoni had endorsed the revolutionary call to the workers.

Colin Wade contested Troyeville, Johannesburg, at a parliamentary by-election in January 1917 and polled thirty-two votes against Creswell's 800. The League's election manifesto denounced the war as a quarrel between national groups of bosses; it had nothing to do with workers, who were propertyless and therefore without a country to defend. Creswell's white labour policy was a fraud, since Africans were there to stay at the command of their capitalist rulers. The workers' salvation lay in industrial unionism. This would enable them to capture power and lead humanity out of chaos.[10] Andrews and Bunting stood on a similar platform in the provincial council elections in June, with the added incentive of Russia's February revolution. They called on workers to emulate this example and 'claim domination of all the countries of the earth'. The final struggle for socialism had begun. If elected, the League's candidates would strive only for the downfall of capitalism and for industrial democracy.[11]

The mob broke up the League's meetings on May Day, the miners' union asked Forrester Brown not to speak on the League's platform, and both candidates lost their deposits. Bunting polled seventy-one votes in Commissioner Street, and Andrews, 'the foremost working-class name in South African politics', obtained 355 votes in Benoni.[12]

This series of defeats spread a mood of pessimism about the value of election campaigns. Like the anti-political faction among Crawford's socialists in 1910, some members of the League argued that 'vote hunting' reduced them to the level of the reactionary parties in the public's estimation. Moreover, the election of workers to office was futile unless they were backed by economic power.[13] 'Now is the time to run up the Industrial banner,' urged John Campbell. 'Now is the time to throw all academic discussions and abstractions to the winds and to rally the workers to Industrial Unity by immediate action.'[14] A joint meeting of branches on the Rand accordingly decided in October 1917 that the League would not nominate candidates for the coming municipal election.[15] De Leon's concept of industrial unionism, which would obliterate craft and colour divisions, appeared to be the proper alternative to fruitless electioneering and the dead-end campaign against the war. The organization of all workers for industrial action, declared the executive committee, was the great revolutionary fruit of an otherwise pointless agitation.[16]

Workers who rejected the League's candidates and its anti-war policy could not be expected to embark on revolutionary strikes. Like every radical party which has exhausted the possibilities of parliamentary struggle, the League was forced to recognize that only the voteless majority would respond positively to appeals for far-reaching social changes. To be taken seriously as a contestant for power, it could trim its sails to suit the electorate and compete with the Labour party in defence of white supremacy, or it could attempt to acquire a mass base among the oppressed. The decision to take the second course marks the great divide in the development of the labour movement. From this emerged a genuine radicalism, which accepted the consequent identification with Africans, Coloured and

Indians in a struggle outside the bounds of constitutional politics. The International Socialists made their greatest contribution not by protesting against the war, but in spreading the vision of a single integrated society embracing all South Africans without distinctions of class or colour.

The vision grew out of the protest. It was the failure of the mission against militarism that led to a critical appraisal of claims to racial privilege. The League, wrote Jones after the defeat in Troyeville, could not hope for a large backing among the Labour party's constituents, the small shopkeeper and artisan. It was poised like Mohammed's coffin between the two economic bases of craft workers and the propertyless proletariat, who happened to be black and were therefore disfranchised and despised. If the League was not to be Utopian, it would have to develop their consciousness as a great emancipating and emancipated class. International socialism 'is nothing if not a virile propaganda to awaken the native wage earner, and with the native his white prototype, to a consciousness of his great mission of human reclamation'.[17]

The socialists reached this point slowly and with misgivings during two and a half years of increasing isolation. They had broken away from the Labour party to fight militarism, and not the colour bar; and they could not easily rid themselves of a belief in white supremacy. One advantage of the withdrawal, they claimed, was that it gave them 'untrammelled freedom to deal, regardless of political fortunes, with the great and fascinating problem of the native'.[18] He was a problem, and not a comrade at this stage. They could not hope to free the white, they said, until they had freed the native. The possibility that the African would free himself did not then occur to them. He was not mentioned in their original statement of aims, or in their appeals for socialist unity against militarism. When the Durban SDP replied that unity would be prejudiced by adherence to a white labour policy, the League evaded the challenge. The socialists were hitting the enemy where it hurt most, and would yet find time to clarify their attitude to 'such important matters as the Coloured and Native question'.[19]

The League's first annual conference in January 1916 defined an attitude to Africans in a resolution based on Bunting's 'petition of rights'. It called for the abolition of indentured labour, compounds and pass laws in the interests of working class emancipation; and urged 'the lifting of the Native worker to the political and industrial status of the white'. Dunbar put up the familiar pseudo-radical argument that there was not a 'native question'; only a worker's problem. Colin Wade suggested that Africans were 'biologically inferior'. Conference rejected both views, and made a concession to racism by adopting a modified version of the Labour party's segregation policy. The number of Africans employed in industry should not be increased until they had been elevated to the white man's status. Meanwhile, those in employment would be assisted to free themselves from the wage system – presumably by keeping them off the labour market. This approach represented no advance on the position taken up by radicals in 1912. The League was still paternalistic, a group of missionary socialists intent on bringing enlightenment to the darker brethren for their own sake, but primarily to save the white proletariat from itself.

The League from then on gave increasing attention to African disabilities and aspirations. The Johannesburg central branch made 'native affairs' a feature of its lecture syllabus. Africans were invited to the League's public meetings. Saul Msane of the Transvaal Native Congress listened with other Africans to the Rev. Father Hill of the Community of the Resurrection when he denounced the Natives Land Act as a barefaced attempt to force peasants into the labour market. The *International* hailed this as 'the first Labour or Socialist meeting with natives in the audience'.[20] It was, indeed, a notable stage in the education of the Rand's socialists, who could not reshape their ideas until they associated with Africans on equal terms. The League provided the opportunity, but clung to the remnant of the old segregation myth. A leading article in the *International* of 17 March 1916 blamed capitalism for breaking down the 'ethnological tendency' to a 'natural social apartness of white and black'. The system compelled white workers to recognize the African 'as perforce a permanent fellow worker'. They needed his industrial cooperation to destroy capitalism. This done, the 'natural tendency' could be allowed free play. The conclusion that Africans, having made the revolution, would then tolerate apartheid was as absurd as any reached by Crawford's socialists.

The discussions revealed no more than a growing awareness of the African's role. It was marginal to the League's main aim of soliciting votes and preaching international solidarity against militarism. The socialists were inspired less by exhortations to combine with Africans than by the strike of Cape Town's tramwaymen in May 1916, or by the prosecution of Wilfrid Harrison, 'the most policed and summonsed anti-militarist in South Africa', for distributing a melodramatic protest against the horrors of war.[21] Such events were symptoms of the class struggle, whereas the extent of the African's participation seemed problematical. George Mason found it necessary to urge an audience of League members and Africans in the Johannesburg Trades Hall to rid themselves of the stale nonsense purveyed in the movement about the African's mental capacity. Any man good enough for capitalist production was doubly so for labour organization. Since white workers were bribed to keep the African down, it was a waste of time to argue against their prejudices. The League should concentrate instead on helping intelligent Africans to organize their people. This admonition evoked no more than the derisive comment that 'George was a kind of Bobby Burns who allowed his dominant sense of kinship with the Universal Human to warp his judgement as to degrees of mental capacity'.[22]

The socialists denied racial prejudice and claimed to be guided only by good intentions. All they wanted was to protect a docile and ignorant people from exploitation. Africans would be excluded from government even under socialism until they reached maturity. Mixed marriages were objectionable not on account of colour differences, but because of the immaturity of the blacks. One correspondent of the *International* would repudiate socialism if it required him to have tea with Charlie, Jim or Sixpence. The editor replied that socialism did not mean mixed marriages: 'as to the evils of this both whites and natives largely agree'. As for segregation, only the combined pressure of all workers would compel the capitalist to dispense with the best part of his working force. '*The way to healthy social segregation is through Industrial Cooperation.*' It alone would civilize the 'Kaffir wage earners' and purify the atmosphere. A labour movement that failed to organize and educate the unskilled was by that fact a movement of only a part of labour and would surely sacrifice the rest.[23]

Logic led to the further conclusion that socialism could not be attained without the African's assistance. Only he could save himself and in so doing save the white society. The argument was repeated often, with an assurance that a growing number of white workers were grasping the point. This was a delusion. Socialists applauded Msane for saying that the important thing was to educate the whites. Africans would join trade unions, which had been formed to fight them, he said, if the barriers were lifted.[24] The socialists also needed education, however. Their emotions had not yet fused with reason to produce the passionate conviction that provides the driving force behind a genuine radicalism. They condemned the colour bar because it retarded the growth of class consciousness, not because it was an evil in itself. This was the fundamental flaw in their approach. It blinded them to the nature of the African's problems, and to the quality of his resistance to race discrimination.

The League's theory belittled the importance of social divisions other than class, and the value of combinations other than industrial. Nationalism, both African and Afrikaner, was said to be the nostalgic yearning of small proprietors for a vanishing era, or a false patriotism that blunted class consciousness. Africans and Afrikaners would turn their backs on nationalism when capitalist production forced them to work for a wage. Class divisions, said Andrews, cut across the colour line. Rich natives combined with rich whites to exploit the masses. The assertion suited his theory, and not the facts. He and other socialists distrusted educated leaders like Jabavu, Abdurahman and Grendon, the editor of *Abantu Batho*, the African National Congress's newspaper. Such men expressed loyalty to Britain, support for the war, and 'old-fashioned bookish aspirations for the vote as the be-all and end-all'. Wrongly described as a 'bourgeoisie', the intellectuals, lawyers and parsons of the national liberation movement were said to lead African and Coloured workers along the false trail of collaboration with government and the capitalist class.

African leaders clung to a liberal creed as long as they hoped to find relief in the existing social order. Their faith was being undermined by racial laws and a decline in living standards. Signs of discontent appeared towards the end of 1916. B. G. Phooko, a member of *Abantu Batho*'s staff, advised his people to shun the recruiting offices of the native labour corps until action had been taken to improve the conditions of workers who were exploited under the system of colour prejudice. The paper published articles protesting at the effects of the Native Land Act and the treatment of African wage earners. Unprotected by labour unions, they undertook all unskilled drudgery, worked the hardest for the least pay, and were often housed worse than the white man's horse or dog. The Transvaal Congress was urged to make representations to the native affairs department for remedial action. Free men, who had been robbed and ousted from their land, were being reduced to further enslavement and penury. One day they would rise against their oppressors.

The socialists viewed these outbursts of militancy with mixed feelings. They welcomed the 'initial rumblings of a spontaneous, indigenous class-conscious industrial movement', yet complained that *Abantu Batho* was the mouthpiece of the government, the capitalist class, and the 'tame wing' of lawyers and parsons in Congress. The paper's 'racialism' was irrelevant to the labour movement. After all, white workers were treated essentially in the same way. The remedy was to organize not separate African unions, but one big union of all workers, irrespective of race. The 'volcanic eruption' foreshadowed by *Abantu Batho* would fail unless preceded by sound organization, and unless it involved all workers. Though whites might blaze the trail, mainly Africans would complete the process of wresting control of the productive system from the ruling class. White unions should be invited to discuss the formation of a common movement with the African National Congress.[25]

The League launched a campaign for industrial unions which would disregard craft and colour divisions, present a united front and ultimately take over the control of industry. A solidarity committee, headed by Forrester Brown and Andrew Watson, one of the nine men deported in 1914, issued a circular drawing attention to the erosion of craft privileges by the employment of women and other unskilled workers. The Building Workers' Industrial Union was formed in March 1917, partly in opposition to Crawford's federation. Carpenters and joiners at Durban, Cape Town and Krugersdorp agreed to admit Coloured and Indian tradesmen to the union, as a preventive against scabbing and undercutting. The typographical union proposed to admit Coloured and white printers' assistants who were being attracted to a benefit fund sponsored by the master printers for non-union employees.

These were meagre gains. The B W I U adopted an open constitution, yet never admitted Coloured and Africans in the north. When white printers in Durban struck work for £5 a week, they refused to combine with Indian employees, who then decided to form a union of their own. No white union ever contemplated organizing Africans. *Abantu Batho*, taking note of the facts, warned its readers against collaboration with 'any section of white labour'. The socialists retorted that there was no colour line in the working class, 'however much some hireling Labourites draw that line'. Africans had more in common with white workers who fought against capitalism than with native property owners and agents of the Chamber of Mines. In no country did artisans as a class 'descend' to organizing the unskilled. Africans would have to do this themselves. The League had no desire to ride on their backs. Its function was to provide disinterested education.[26]

Andrews, Bunting and Jones were then rethinking their approach to Labour's segregation policy. It no longer seemed feasible or expedient to resist the pressures that turned the peasant into a wage worker. He must go through the industrial mill, said Andrews, before 'anything can be done with him'. Only an 'urban, industrialized, highly organized force', acting politically and through labour unions, could remove the ruling class. Bunting thought that the Native Administration Bill of 1917 was meant to complete the work of the Native Land Act.

Peasants would have to choose between starving in the reserves or working under whites. All parties in parliament, including Labour, wished to exploit the African's labour power, but the issue was not really one of whites against blacks. Only the organized power of all workers could deliver them from the Beast. The aims of capital, as expressed in the bill, might have to be attained before that power could take shape.[27]

Africans had no intention of being reduced without a struggle to the level of a landless proletariat. The bill reaffirmed the principle of territorial segregation; contemplated the addition of eight and a half million morgen to the scheduled reserves; provided for the final elimination of labour tenants and share croppers from the 'white' areas; and placed the 'native' areas under the exclusive control of the native affairs department, with power to legislate for them by proclamation.[28] The policy behind the measure, said Dr Dube in Cape Town, 'was really one of extermination. What the natives wanted was equality of opportunity'.[29] The African National Congress met at Bloemfontein on 31 May 1917 to discuss the bill. Sol Plaatje, back from England, denounced Smuts for having said in London that Africans must on no account be armed, as this would make them a menace to civilization. Congress resolved to agitate for the defeat of the bill, condemned Smuts's speech, deplored the government's action in introducing the measure while calling on Africans to join the overseas labour corps, and reaffirmed loyalty to the king. Neither Smuts nor the government had 'any right to rob the Natives of their human rights and guarantees of liberty under the Pax Britannica'.[30]

The League protested publicly against the bill in March 1917 at a meeting held in the Johannesburg Trades Hall. It was an historic occasion as socialists demonstrated for the first time on the Rand against racial legislation that did not directly affect whites. Msane and Mbelle, speaking from the platform, hailed the display of socialist sincerity as a triumph over colour prejudice. Africans now knew that even in Johannesburg there were white men brave enough to assail in public the detested colour bar. The link between socialists and Africans might be tenuous, but it was being forged in spite of abuse from the daily press and the right wing of the labour movement. For fraternization with Africans widened the gulf caused by the split over the war. The extent of the cleavage became visible in the middle of the year, when Andrews and Bunting stood for election to the provincial council.

Workers and soldiers broke up the League's May Day rally and besieged the hall in which it held a social; manhandled Bunting, Jones and other speakers, and forced them to suspend their outdoor meetings. Bunting could not obtain a hall for his election campaign, which the League fought under the banner of anti-militarism and social revolution. I. Kuper, the Labour party's candidate in Benoni, concentrated on the League's non-racial policy, and accused Andrews of planning to extend the franchise to Africans. Andrews replied that all segregation schemes were doomed to failure. Either lift the native up to the white standard or sink down to his. He must be given the right to combine and withhold his labour. There could be freedom and justice for all only when whites dealt with him as a fellow worker and not as a chattel. Kuper then appealed in a Dutch pamphlet to his 'brother Afrikaners' to vote for the Labour party's policy: 'First white then black', and no equal rights. 'Vote for Andrews and you vote for the downfall of the workers and the blanket or Kaffir vote.' The international socialists would allow their coloured brethren to compete in trades such as those of masons, painters, cabinet makers and mechanics.[31]

The League's stand against racism was the central issue in the elections, and probably lost it many hundreds of votes. So Bunting and Andrews thought, as they grappled with the problem of removing the white worker's fears. Attempts to reserve skilled jobs for whites, argued Bunting, could only lead to their displacement. Self-interest and principle dictated the alternative. This was to ignore colour, and rope all workers, high- and low-paid alike, into the unions. Andrews singled out a central principle on which socialists could not compromise. Africans and Coloured formed an integral part of the working class and must organize either in identical or parallel unions. The former were the ideal, but the latter might have to be chosen on tactical grounds. All other issues were subsidiary, and would be settled through industrial organization. There was no need to worry about a transfer of political power, for instance. The capitalist himself would extend the vote to masses of Africans, as a bulwark against revolution, long before they became class conscious. Inter-racial marriages would decline as poor whites, Africans and Coloured moved to a higher standard of living and education.[32]

None of the predictions came true. They were based on an assumption that class antagonisms would dissolve colour prejudice. In fact, white workers entered into an alliance with capitalists, were absorbed in the racial elite, shared its privileges and also the burden of keeping the darker man in subjection. Andrews and his associates were not blind to these possibilities. 'The governing class,' wrote Jones in April 1918, 'must almost be called the governing race.' Most white workers, skilled and unskilled, identified themselves with 'their top exploiters' and refused to free the African. And, he predicted, 'white capitalists and white artisans will unite and fight like demons to keep the native proletariat "in its place".' The socialists refused to believe that the betrayal of class principles was inevitable. Indeed white workers were yet to fight their gravest battle before they would be accepted fully into the lower ranks of the ruling hierarchy. The die had not been cast by the end of the war.

10 Socialism and Nationalism

Socialists had reason to hope that their cause would triumph as opposition to the war mounted in Europe and as soldiers or sailors on both sides mutinied. Even sceptics might be silenced by the 'seeming miracle', as Bunting called it, of the Russian upheaval. It far outstripped the wildest dreams of socialists themselves, who 'never hoped for so early a fruition of their movement'. 'This is a bourgeois revolution, but arriving when the night of capitalism is far spent', wrote Jones in March 1917. 'It cannot be a mere repetition of previous revolutions. It partakes infinitely more of a victory for the proletariat, as well as for the industrial capitalist.' With surprising insight, considering South Africa's isolation, Jones recognized that Russia was heading for a revolution 'by the side of which this and all previous ones are but "shopkeepers' riots" in immensity'. The Russian 'elemental mass' was about to enter 'the International class struggle for human emancipation. The day of its coming seems immeasurably nearer by this awakening'.[1]

Enthusiasm kept pace with the spread of soviets, the councils of workmen and soldiers, in Russia. She of all countries, 'clear-sighted, audacious, unfaltering, with magnificent contempt for the bogies and fetishes that capitalism would have us dread or revere, has suited the action to the word', wrote Bunting in June. His election manifesto of that month urged South Africans 'to rise to the occasion' by 'following the bold and inspiring lead of the Russian Workers'. When the revolution moved to its climax in the seizure of power by the Bolsheviks in November the *International* declared that they had incarnated the theories of Karl Marx. 'The Word becomes Flesh in the Council of Workmen.'[2]

Two hundred socialists from the Reef, Pretoria, Durban,

Kimberley and Cape Town met in the Johannesburg Trades Hall in August to send Andrews to the proposed peace conference in Stockholm. It was a great occasion. Among the main speakers were Sigamoney, of Durban's Indian Workers' Union, and Selope Thema, secretary of the African National Congress. A number of Africans attended. Outraged by this breach of the racial taboo, the Labour party's executive, then meeting in the same building, adjourned to a near-by hotel in protest against whites and Africans sitting together in conference. Unperturbed by this protest, the socialists passed a resolution moved by Dunbar instructing their delegate to demand peace 'on the basis of the complete destruction of the capitalist system'. This was 'mere demagogy' noted Andrews at a later period. 'Dunbar and his supporters were more revolutionary than Lenin and the Bolsheviks.'[3]

Andrews sailed in August to represent the ISL, the Cape SDF, the Jewish Socialist Society in Cape Town, the S.A. Peace and Arbitration Society in Cape Town, the Indian Workers' Union in Durban, the Native Workers' Union in Johannesburg, and Kimberley Socialists. He took with him a report 'on the state of the working-class movement in South Africa, and the state of the "minority" socialist movement and its origin through cleavages on the war question'. The report also challenged Creswell's status and claims to represent the labour movement at the allied socialist conference in London. For the white working class shared to a great extent 'the illusion of all white master communities, Athenian democracies, that they represent the whole of the people and that the mass of the serfs or slaves beneath are politically non-existent'.[4]

It was an optimistic report. The League, it claimed, had survived constant persecution for its stand against war and racism, and was now the only vigorous political organization of the working classes. The Labour party might win elections, but these were no test of real power. The League's fight against racism had far greater world-wide significance and was making headway also among white workers. Ten of the thirteen members of the League's executive committee were wage earners and staunch supporters of trade unionism without colour bars. The great bulk of Africans had not yet acquired a class consciousness, but the League was breaking through the barriers by means of propaganda and trade union organization. 'It would be hard for our European comrades to realize the significance of Indian and Native delegates sitting in a working-class gathering in South Africa. The very fact of these black fellow workers voicing their class consciousness with us lifted the Conference to a high pitch of enthusiasm.' Though not representative of the great masses, they were 'the advance guard of that mass in its struggle towards articulation'. The League's propaganda and its first fruits were of 'mighty significance for the millions of the coloured proletariat in all parts of the world, and a surety that they too will unitedly tread the path of the working class International'.

One of the first fruits was the Durban Indian Workers' Industrial Union. Gordon Lee, a follower of De Leon, took the initiative in forming it along the lines of the IWW. 'Some croakers here, Socialist and Labour,' he reported, 'say we cannot organize the coolies.' Yet he recruited in less than six months an appreciable following of printing, tobacco, laundry and dock workers. The 'common Indian worker' was realizing at last that Indian capitalists were as much his enemy as any white boss. Miners, municipal workers and the 'sugar slaves' stretched out their hands for aid, and the union would soon be able to stand alone under its own elected leaders.[5] B. L. Sigomoney took over from Lee and soon became prominent in left-wing circles. He was elected the vice-chairman of a socialist conference held at Durban in October 1917 to debate the rival merits of 'pure' industrial action and parliamentary politics. In January 1918 he represented his union at the ISL's annual conference in Johannesburg. This, too, was a memorable occasion. Never before had the League included among its delegates a member of the darker races; and it rejoiced at having made great ideological progress towards non-racial labour solidarity.[6]

'Organize and educate' produced better results when applied to Africans than to whites, discovered Charles Dones, a miner and member of the League's management committee. This was said in August after he had addressed the first of a series of classes on the labour movement held in the Johannesburg Trades Hall for Africans. Asked what they wanted, they replied *'Sifuna zonke'* – everything! 'What White Union,' remarked Bunting, 'ever aimed so high or so true?'[7] From the classes emerged later in the year the Industrial Workers Union of Africa, one of the first African trade unions, described by communists in later years as 'an "all-in" Industrial trade union, with the idea of roping in the Native and other unorganized Non-European workers'.[8] In 1918, however, when Bunting and others stood trial on a charge of inciting Africans to strike, the organizers minimized the union's role and said that it was no more than 'a little body of native students of socialism'.[9] At least five of the students were police informers and detectives. One of them, Wilfrid Njobe, had become the union's secretary; another, R. Moorosi, had been elected to the committee and represented it at a meeting with the APO. When warned that spies were present, Bunting assured the members that they had nothing to fear from the police.

Police and press kept a watchful eye on the League; and F. S. Malan, the minister of mines, hurled threats at the 'agitators' who 'played with fire' by inciting Africans to strike. Undaunted, the African National Congress called on its people to support the IWA and make it strong, for it could teach employers that workers wanted higher wages. The prime minister, Louis Botha, told a deputation from the Transvaal ANC to steer clear of international socialists. S. M. Makgatho, the provincial president, replied that Congress had decided on its own to call a strike against the Native Administration Bill. The Labour right wing, joining in the red-baiting, closed the Trades Hall to the League's non-racial gatherings. Bunting showed his disapproval by resigning as honorary secretary of the hall's management committee, which then gave the League notice to vacate its offices. Crawford, more tolerant, invited Talbot Williams, a leader of the Transvaal APO and organizer of the IWA, to address the Industrial Federation's annual conference in December. The federation refused to admit Coloured delegates from the Cape. Williams then declined to speak at a 'Pure White Labour Congress'; and delivered his address instead before a large audience of Africans and Coloured in Johannesburg on 9 January 1918.

'We who have never enjoyed our just rights, either in the labour market or politically,' he said, 'have but one weapon and that is the organization of black labour, upon which the whole commercial and mining industry rests today.' This was the only way of bringing white trade unionists to their senses. Their great grievance against the black man was that he sold his labour cheaply. Yet they worked at the sewerage plant for 5s. a day, were hired as railway porters at 6s. 6d., and went on strike at the Van Ryn mine because they wanted white men to be given the jobs of Coloured waste packers at a rate of 7s. a day. Trade unionists who refused to work 'within five yards of clean respectable intelligent Coloured men at a skilled trade', willingly worked 'side by side with a raw blanketed native' so long as he was a subordinate at their beck and call. They would rather dine and wine with mine owners than combine with their darker fellow workers. Servile, afraid of competition and prejudiced, the white man was a supervisor of labour and not a genuine worker. 'The true worker, the backbone of labour in this country, is the brown and the black man, who are now organizing against this federation of rotters.'[10]

Bunting, no less optimistic, reported that 'the different races of workers of this country, whites, coloured, natives, Indians, are rapidly coming together to form one great Industrial Workers' Union of Africa.'[11] The desired unity never took shape. Even Williams found it expedient, against the advice of the socialists, to organize Africans and Coloured in separate unions under a joint executive. White workers, with few exceptions, rejected the vision of 'proletarian freedom', but not because of any servility such as Williams alleged. They were in a strong bargaining position and exploited the advantages of a growing industrialism that outstripped the supply of skilled labour. Strikes in 1917 resulted in wage increases or a shorter working week for printers in Johannesburg, tailors, bakers and hairdressers in Cape Town, and men employed on the diamond mines. Policemen who struck work in Cape Town in January 1918 were less successful, and received only a suspended sentence for refusing duty. The socialists hailed them as young Afrikaners with a great revolutionary potential; and accused Crawford of leading white workers away from an alliance with Africans into a policy of collaboration with employers.

Even the former international socialist, Forrester Brown, the secretary of the miners' union and president of the SAIF, had turned reactionary 'under the baleful influence of Crawford, the apostle of Brother Capital and Brother Labour'. The white workers backed the Chamber of Mines in its efforts to sidetrack the inevitable revolution by keeping natives in subjection and throwing sops to whites.[12] Crawford presented a list of fifteen demands to the Chamber in July 1918 on behalf of five unions. They asked, among other things, for the dismissal of seventy-four Coloured drill sharpeners, the cancellation of a wage freeze clause adopted in 1916, an increase in the mechanics' pay to £8 2s. a week, a closed shop agreement and a paid holiday on 1 May. The Chamber agreed to maintain the prevailing practice for the employment of Coloured on the mines, introduced an improved war bonus scheme, and donated £10,000 to the Federation's cooperative stores instituted by Crawford to combat the rise in prices.

Africans, who suffered most from the steep rise in prices, received neither a cost of living allowance nor an increase in wages. The slightest display of militancy on their part evoked a violent reaction. When African miners on the East Rand boycotted concession stores in February 1918, the police arrested the pickets and broke the boycott. Botha used the occasion to lecture parliament on the evils of African trade unionism and the disastrous consequences that might follow from the activities of white men who 'were going to the native kraals urging them to combine'.[13] The capitalist press was both more ferocious and less accurate. It printed extracts from Talbot Williams's address, blamed the boycott on 'ill-balanced and fanatical Socialists of the baser sort', and detected the sinister influence of the 'IWW', which was 'notoriously financed by Germany'. The socialists of the ISL denied having had anything to do with the boycott. Indeed they regarded it as a 'misguided tactic', an attack on the branch rather than the root. Their only contribution, they said, was to collaborate with the Industrial Workers Union of Africa in compiling a leaflet in Sesutu and Zulu. It was the first serious attempt to put Marx's clarion call for unity into an African language: 'Let there be no longer any talk of Basuto, Zulu or Shangaan. You are all labourers. Let Labour be your common bond. Deliver yourself from the chains of capitalism.'[14]

A few months later the socialists faced more serious charges in consequence of an African strike wave on the Rand. White mechanics employed at the municipal power station came out on strike in May for £8 2s. a week, the equivalent, they claimed, of their pre-war wage of £6. They won their demand after leaving the town in darkness for several nights. Impressed at the success of this operation, Africans working in the municipal sanitary services asked for a modest rise from 1s. 8d. to 2s. 6d. a day. But they were black and handled lavatory buckets, not electric generators. The council refused, some fifty men struck work, and all except fifteen were convicted. Another 152 men then came out, initially in protest against having to do the work of the arrested strikers. T. G. Macfie, the chief magistrate and a staunch ally of Crawford, sentenced the 152 strikers on 12 June to two months' hard labour for breach of contract. They would be compelled to do the same work as before, he told them, without pay and under armed guard. They would be shot if they tried to escape and flogged if they refused to work. The harsh threats and the contrast between this treatment and the concessions made to the white strikers infuriated the African public. The ANC launched a campaign for the prisoners' release which soon developed into a demand for a general wage increase of 1s. a day, to be enforced if necessary by a general strike on 1 July.

Socialists and ANC leaders disapproved. Makgatho warned a meeting of nearly 2,000 Africans that striking was dangerous. Even socialists, being white, would join in shooting down Africans. The League retorted that it could have no part in the 'more reactionary, middle-class and religious-cum-racial tendencies' of Congress, though 'the close coincidence of native and working-class interests' might yet force it to play a useful role.[15] T. P. Tinker, the League's secretary, told Africans that they were too badly organized to succeed in a strike which was bound to give the enemy an excuse for violence. The ISL claimed that its job was to 'agitate, educate, organize', and not to instigate strikes. Ninety per cent of the workers were 'still sunk in ignorance and servility'. Much work would have to be done before white and black workers could bring off really effective industrial action.[16]

Macfie urged the SAIF to organize a defence force to protect women and property against the expected strike. Crawford and Forrester Brown agreed and offered to raise workers' battalions. The whites, commented Bunting, assumed that it was their duty to shoot down helots at the smallest sign of discontent; 'and one of the darkest episodes in the history of South Africa Labour is the attempted enlistment of white trade unionists in the Defence Force for the avowed purpose of so shooting them down'.[17] The daily press, the Bishop of Pretoria, and the Native Recruiting Corporation took fright and joined Africans in condemning Macfie's judgement. To relieve tension the government ordered the release of the strikers, whose sentences were hurriedly suspended by the Supreme Court on 28 June. Botha interviewed an African deputation led by Saul Msane and promised to investigate their grievances.

The strike was called off, but 15,000 men employed at three mines refused to work on 1 July. Police and troops rushed to the compounds and drove the men down the shafts after serious clashes at Ferreira mine and the Robinson Deep, where they fought back with pickhandles, jumpers,* axes and iron pipes. The grievances commissioner, J. B. Moffat, chief magistrate of the Transkei, accepted Msane's diagnosis. 'The whole trouble in the compounds is due to the colour bar. A native may know his work very well, but on account of his colour he cannot obtain advancement.' If those who possessed the necessary qualifications could obtain better pay, 'it would encourage them to improve in their work and would bring about peace and satisfaction'.[18]

The police arrived at a different diagnosis. They prosecuted

---

* Iron bars with chisel edge used in mining to bore holes.

Bunting, Tinker and Hanscombe of the League, together with five Africans – D. S. Letanka, vice-president of the Transvaal Congress; L. T. Mvabaza, a director of *Abantu Batho*; and J. Ngojo, H. Kraai and A. Cetyiwe, three members of the IWA. For 'the first time in South Africa', noted T. D. M. Skota, author of the *Black Folks' Who's Who*, 'members of the European and Native races, in common cause united, were arrested and charged together because of their political activities'.[19] The accused disclaimed direct responsibility for the strikes. The League, said Bunting, preached socialism and industrial unionism, and approved of strikes only when preceded by sound trade union organization. 'If any public organization called a strike,' he added, 'it was not the ISL but the Native Congress, with which the Socialists are at arm's length.'[20] The prosecution's case collapsed after its chief witness Luke Massina, a government informer, had admitted in cross-examination to having given perjured evidence. The attorney-general declined to indict the accused before the Supreme Court.

Moffat commented caustically on the League's claim to have done no more than educate and organize Africans for industrial unionism. This was like 'teaching children to play with matches round an open barrel of gunpowder'. Socialist propaganda would make a catastrophe inevitable if reasonable grounds of complaint were not removed. Low wages were not, however, a legitimate grievance according to Moffat. The men volunteered to work on the mines for 2s. a shift. Like other people, they should buy less if prices were high. But he said the right things about the colour bar. Africans and Coloured would not be content to do rough work only for ever. To arrest their advance would antagonize them and provoke industrial disputes. The tendency for the men to settle down and become permanent miners should be encouraged, while the government ought to withdraw the colour bar in the regulations. This would free it from the odium of being a party to obstacles that prevented Africans from rising as their industry and ability entitled them. Finally, he remarked, 'So long as natives are denied the rights of citizenship as Parliamentary voters there can be no real contentment in the country.' These were wise words. They sounded the spirit of traditional Cape liberalism; and were ignored.

Some years later Andrews made this comment on the episode: 'of course, when the workers had taken their decision and were on strike the ISL did all it could in support'.[21] The support it gave was negligible. The League did not possess the means to promote strikes and riots. Its membership had changed during its short life of three years. Most of the foundation members had drifted away, leaving a bare score of former Labour party members in the branches and only two on the management committee of thirteen. The gap was filled by a handful of white South Africans and a much larger number of immigrants from Europe, many of them Jewish, whom the League attracted by its solitary defence of the Russian revolution. Though tireless propagandists for Marxism, the new radicals lacked the industrial background of the League's founders. Andrews continued to be a source of strength among white workers. There were others, like C. B. Tyler of the Building Workers' Industrial Union, who worked mainly in the white unions. Yet the League was more isolated in 1918 from the bulk of the labour movement than at any time since its formation.

It was far more isolated from the rest of the population. The League had no Coloured or African members. In spite of their insistence on the African's revolutionary role, the socialists had failed to bridge the language and social gap between themselves and the masses, or to formulate a theory acceptable to Coloured and African leaders. The binary model of standard Marxist theory did not fit South Africa's multiple structure of colour, class and cultural groups. Even Jones, a natural Marxist of high degree, failed to appreciate the dynamic qualities of an indigenous national movement. He and his associates insisted that class, not colour, marked the great divide. They refused to bear the label 'negrophile', or support the struggle of the Africans as an oppressed race. Their mission, they said, was to agitate among white workers for solidarity with blacks, and not to concern themselves with the civil disabilities of Indian storekeepers, African lawyers or Coloured middlemen.[22]

The socialists agreed that white workers, who were the vanguard of revolution, could enter the promised land only by combining with the African. Had not Marx declared that 'Labour cannot emancipate itself in the White while in the Black it is branded?' Regrettably, the white worker feared the effects of an African rising. To allay his fears and absolve themselves of blame for riots, the socialists condemned the use of violence and even strikes as instruments of social change. Strikes, though inevitable, were old-fashioned and would diminish as the working class drew nearer to the 'general strike' which would finally eliminate the capitalist's rule. Violence did not pay, especially when pursued by the black proletariat. There was a great danger of violence if Africans were left to assert themselves without organization and guidance. The business of the League was to avoid a blood bath by preaching industrial unity and providing patient instruction. This would ensure peaceful change without 'such evils as the white workers justifiably fear'.[23]

A greater danger stemmed from the tendency of the ruling class, nowhere more pronounced than in South Africa, to use violence in defence of the established order. In discussing this classic principle of revolutionary theory, the socialists acknowledged that their main reason for rejecting violence was the prospect that white workers would join in shooting Africans who revolted. What other conclusion could be drawn from Forrester Brown's offer to form workers' battalions to suppress African strikers? A member of the League and former war-on-warite, he had often urged his miners to accept Coloured workers on an equal footing and to organize African miners.[24] Now he had succumbed to the 'corrupting influence of false labour organization, of labour-fakirdom, of miseducation, of capitalist flattery and bribery, of sectional and colour pride and prejudice'.[25] In less abusive words, Brown followed the dictates of his union members who earned ten times as much as the African, bossed him around, and feared that he might one day take over their jobs. They would put up with any kind of heresy from Brown as long as they believed that he would keep the door shut against the African.

The radical who appealed to white workers could hardly avoid reflecting their sentiments. Racial prejudice was 'insane' and 'suicidal', the socialists exclaimed, yet they confirmed it by alleging that Coloured workers had taken over the building trades in Cape Town, clerical posts in Durban, and semi-skilled work on the mines. The white man, they predicted, would be driven from all fields of employment unless he joined with the African in a struggle for equal pay.[26] This was the Labour party's argument over again. It pointed, not to inter-racial solidarity, but to the white labour policy of sheltered employment behind colour bars. The League made other concessions to prejudice. It was 'not out to get the native admitted into the White Labour Unions'; or to preach equality under capitalism, for this was indeed a contradiction in terms. Equality would come only under socialism, when there would be room and plenty for all.[27]

The League tried facing both ways and so fell between the stools of white supremacy and African nationalism. The white worker preferred racial solidarity to class war, and turned a deaf ear both to prophecies of disaster and promises of working-class power. Socialists assured him that he was not called upon to love the darker man as himself. Yet no lesser degree of devotion would persuade the African that he was being exploited as a worker and not as a member of an oppressed race. He claimed dignity, higher wages, better jobs and freedom from discrimination. The socialists gave him lectures on working-class emancipation and exhorted him to practise restraint until the day of liberation. They pleaded for unity and denied equality. The concession failed to appease the whites and antagonized the leaders of national liberation who believed neither in the class theory nor in the vision of socialism.

The upsurge of nationalism in Europe made little immediate impact on the socialists. They saw in it the surface rumblings of a greater upheaval to come and equated it with Afrikaner nationalism. It was a 'petty bourgeois' movement which looked backward to the era of small property and would vanish before the wave of industrialism. This miscalculation can be traced, if only in part, to a narrow and dogmatic interpretation of the class theory. The socialists believed, with some justification, that industrial experience would detach the Afrikaner worker from the landowners and intellectuals who led the Nationalist party.

The League opened a fund to pay for leaflets in Afrikaans, and expressed sympathy with republican aspirations which tended to weaken the grip of British imperialism and could be used to help make landless Afrikaners see their true salvation in a socialist republic. But socialists could have no truck with the Nationalist party. It demanded self-determination for Afrikaners and denied it for Africans. It bandied words like *vrede* and *vryheid* about, which meant only freedom to exploit the African. If the Nationalists came to power, and Africans resisted with the methods used by the rebels of 1914, 'it would be the signal for the greatest massacre of the native workers known in the history of South Africa'.[28]

This was a fair assessment. The socialists made the mistake of applying the same kind of yardstick to African nationalism. It, too, was racialist, they said, because it attacked whites generally and 'the Boer' in particular. Congress leaders refused to see that class cut every nationality in two. They drew their people away from the workers' struggles into a 'ruthless opportunism'. Andrews addressed Congress in December 1918 and came away sceptical. 'Servility could go no further' than the conference's protestations of loyalty to the crown. Socialists applauded the Congress campaign against the pass laws in 1919, but denounced in extravagant terms the appeals made for help to Britain and the United States. African nationalists were said to play the same part as the right wing in the labour movement. They were the 'Labour Fakirs of black South Africa, black bell-wethers for the capitalist class'.[29]

Two things need to be said about the League's approach. Africans were not racialists. They wanted equality, not black supremacy. They wished to free themselves from racial oppression and not to oppress the white man. In the second place, they were not Marxists. The basic cleavage in the society, as they saw it, did not run along class lines. White workers stood on the same side as Afrikaner landowners in the racial conflict. Africans would gain more by identifying themselves with British financial, industrial and commercial interests that profited by employing the largest possible number of low-paid workers, and therefore opposed the colour bar. In more abstract terms, African and Coloured concepts of South African politics postulated an inherent antagonism between British imperialism and Afrikaner nationalism. Queen Victoria, Cape liberalism and the Unionist party symbolized the one; Hertzog represented the other. Like other colonial peoples in later years, African and Coloured leaders appealed for British intervention against their immediate oppressors. The appeals were futile, but the underlying assumption was no more erroneous than the socialist concept of a simple two-class division. Congress at least gained a better insight than the socialists did into some realities.

It was Congress, and not the International Socialist League, that protested against the transfer of South West Africa to the Union. The Congress resolution, adopted at its seventh annual conference in March 1918, asked that the conquered territory should be placed under France or America, if Britain refused for imperial reasons to annex the colony. To hand it to the Union would expose innocent natives to burgher tyranny and defeat the ideals that Africans had in view when insisting on British protection.[30] Abdurahman and Fredericks made a similar plea on behalf of the APO to the governor-general and Lord Milner, and asked them to forward a memorandum on the issue to the Versailles peace conference. The memorandum reviewed the disabilities of the coloured peoples in the Transvaal and Orange Free State, which they regarded as the 'Slave State of the British Empire'. The people of South West wanted to be controlled directly by the Imperial government, and shrank with terror from the prospect of becoming a part of the Union. The APO prayed that the peace conference would not take any irrevocable step 'that is bound to lay up for the British Empire in general, as well as for the Union of South Africa in particular, the seeds of racial unrest and endless disputes and strife'. None of the conquered territories should be handed to South Africa until it had removed the colour bar from its constitution, extended full political rights to all coloured peoples, and repealed the republican laws which still disfigured the statute book. No racial privileges or disabilities should be tolerated in the conquered territories.[31]

The League's interest in African and Afrikaner nationalism

dwindled after the war. The few hundred radical socialists on the Rand and in the port towns fixed their eyes on 'the Light from the East'. They celebrated the anniversary of the Russian revolution in November, and not the armistice. Copies of Andrews' pamphlet on the revolution and the Soviet constitution were widely circulated. Bunting drafted blue-prints for the coming revolution. The main burden would fall on the white workers, he wrote, if socialism came quickly in western Europe. Africans might form rural *pitsos* or soviets and send delegates to a national convention.[32] Even the Labour party moved to the left in preparation for a general parliamentary election. Creswell suggested a reunion with the League 'now that the war is happily at an end', and promised a revised constitution to bring the radicals into the fold. They derided the offer as 'amusing, if not impertinent'. Andrews, who had taken over the post of secretary of the League from Tinker, scoffed at 'Labour lieutenants of the capitalist class'. There could be no unity between the Labour party, which functioned within the system, and international socialists who were dedicated to its destruction.[33]

The socialists had trouble enough in keeping their own ranks united. A syndicalist faction was pressing hard for a withdrawal from all public elections. Members of the Cape SDF complained of its isolation. It had no young members and little contact with the Coloured, while Africans, who lived apart, were regarded 'as men coming from the *bundu*'.*[34] A. Z. Berman, J. Pick and M. Lopes decided to put theory into practice and formed the Industrial Socialist League in May 1918. They adopted the principles of the IWW and its programme of industrial unionism, the general strike, and no parliamentary politics. Their first attempt to organize a trade union ended in a rout, when they found the police waiting for them at the factory. Like the SDF, Berman and his associates confined their activities largely to propaganda for socialism and the Russian revolution.

Johannesburg's unrepentant syndicalist, Andrew Dunbar, repeated his performance of 1910–12 with similar results. He

* The word *bundu* is a corruption of *bundok* (Tagalog and colloquial English) meaning wild and open spaces.

fell foul of the League's leadership by conducting a vigorous campaign against parliamentary elections, craft unionism and the alleged reformist tendencies of the ISL. Bunting had described him three years earlier as an 'industrial Cincinnatus at his forge', a frequent defendant in sedition trials, and 'the most cheery of comrades, loyal of friends, reasonable of counsellors, good tempered and broadminded of collaborators, dogged and imperturbable of fighters'.[35] Andrews, however, said he was disloyal and dropped him from the League's list of public speakers. The League's annual conference in January 1919 rejected his views and defeated a motion to delete from the constitution a clause calling for participation in elections. Later in the year Dunbar and his followers formed a Johannesburg branch of the Industrial Socialist League.

The conference decided to end the League's 'splendid isolation' by cooperating with other socialist bodies, and adopted a statement of principles drafted by Jones. This asserted that Labour could not emancipate itself until it had conquered all race and colour prejudice. The League's task was to educate, agitate and organize for revolution. The socialists would go out to inspire Africans to take their place in the ranks of the world proletariat, and to educate white workers to organize and cooperate with their African fellow worker in mine, factory and workshop. Some delegates thought that more attention should be given to Afrikaners, as little could be done with 'semi-savages'; but two African delegates from the IWA indignantly repudiated the stigma of 'savagery'. Finally, conference adopted a new statement of aims. The original objective had been to spread the message of international socialism, industrial unionism, and anti-militarism. Now the League would go forward 'To establish the Socialist Commonwealth.'[36] Revolution appeared to be just round the corner at the beginning of 1919.

Jones did not attend the conference. He was being treated for tuberculosis in Pietermaritzburg's health centre. Here he wrote and distributed a pamphlet headed 'The Bolsheviks are Coming.' It explained, in English and Zulu, that Bolshevism meant 'the rule of the working class' and would soon spread everywhere. The capitalists feared that the workers of South Africa would follow the trail and also become free and independent. The working people should get ready for the world-wide Republic of Labour by combining regardless of colour, craft or creed. For 'while the black worker is oppressed, the white worker cannot be free'. Jones was turned out of the centre and prosecuted, together with L. H. Greene, Pietermaritzburg's veteran socialist, on a charge of inciting to public violence. They submitted a statement which summarized the Communist Manifesto, and declared that their policy was the reverse of mob rule and violence. Their aim was 'to avoid on the industrial field the territorial strife of the pioneer and tribal days'.[37]

The prosecution called police officers, native affairs department officials, employers and Africans to testify that the leaflet would excite, stimulate and alarm the 'native mind'. The accused had offered 'the enticing possibility of taking over the country'. The African witnesses said that the leaflet might provoke disorder and bring back the days of Tshaka. Josiah Gumede, the secretary of the Natal Native Congress and editor of *Ilange Lase Natal*, thought that the African would be made a slave if the Bolsheviks took over the government. He feared a republic and placed his faith in British military power. The magistrate held that the leaflet was libellous, treasonable, and indeed diabolical; 'while the idea that a South African Lenin might conceivably be a Bantu suggested lunacy'. He sentenced each of the accused to pay a fine of £75 and undergo four months' imprisonment. The Supreme Court upheld the appeal and set the convictions aside. The leaflet, said the judge, advocated a policy quite unlike that of armed insurrection and could have had no effect on the prosecution of the war.[38]

Gumede left soon after the trial with an ANC deputation for England in terms of a decision taken by a special conference at Johannesburg on 16 December 1918. More than one branch had suggested that Africans should be represented at the peace conference, though *Imvo* ridiculed the 'Native Nationalists' for wasting their money on a foolish project which was bound to fail, as had the deputation of 1909.[39] Meshach Pelem, president of the Bantu Union, explained that the peace conference afforded a unique opportunity which might never recur to 'represent the vexed native question to the Imperial authorities, as well as to the Christian and the civilized world'.[40] Congress deputed L. T. Mvabaza, managing director of *Abantu Batho*, Selope Thema, its editor, Sol Plaatje, Gumede and the Rev. Ngcayiya, president of the Ethiopian church, to petition the king for Freedom, Liberty, Justice and Fairplay.

They interviewed the colonial office in May and August with the usual negative results. Britain, they were told, could not intervene in the domestic affairs of a self-governing dominion. Lloyd George gave a similar answer on 7 June to Hertzog's 'freedom' deputation of eight Afrikaner nationalist delegates. These requested independence for South Africa or, if that was denied, then independence for the Free State and Transvaal. Lloyd George replied that Britain could not mediate in a dispute between sections of the South African population. 'As one of the Dominions of the British Commonwealth, the South African people control their own national destiny in the fullest sense.' Dominion self-government, retorted Hertzog, fell far short of independence. By taking part in imperial councils, for instance, South Africa necessarily assumed responsibility for imperial policies, with all their attendant problems and dangers.[41]

Africans did not control their national destiny. This was the gravamen of their complaint. Gumede spelled it out in a long letter in September on the failure of their mission. It reproached Britain for having assented to the colour bar in the South African Act, and declared that the Natives Land Act had reduced them to a condition worse than slavery. 'Why shall veiled slavery be permitted in a British Dominion, under the British Flag?' he asked. 'A section of this British dominion wants a Republic, and how will the natives fare?' They objected emphatically to the contemplated handing over of Basutoland, Swaziland, Bechuanaland, Rhodesia and German South West Africa to the Union of South Africa. Mvabaza reminded Lloyd George that 93,000 Africans had responded to Britain's call for help in South West and East Africa. They had answered the call, and expected to get some benefit from President Wilson's Fourteen Points.

Lloyd George took special note of the ten kinds of passes that

Africans were forced to carry: the identification certificate, tax receipt, travelling pass, permit to seek work, labour registration, monthly permit, resident's permit, visitor's permit, night pass and scholar's pass. If South Africa were under the direct control of the colonial office, he would examine their grievances very carefully. He recognized with gratitude their loyal services to the flag in the great struggle for freedom throughout the world. Referring to Hertzog's deputation, he thought that it interpreted the principle of self-determination in a very curious manner by claiming independence for South Africa in the name of only one-third of the white population and none of the coloured peoples. But Britain had to take the constitutional position of a self-governing dominion into account. He could do no more than communicate direct with Botha and Smuts on the subject of the grievances, which the deputation had presented with very great power and in clear and temperate language.[42]

Africans and Afrikaners returned knowing the futility of appeals for aid from abroad. Their struggle for national liberation would be fought out on South African soil. Britain's strategic and economic interests were opposed to any kind of nationalism that would weaken the alliance between Afrikaner landowners and British investors, mine owners and industrialists. Gumede absorbed the lesson. His political career took a turn to the left that led him into close association with the communists. As president of the ANC he accompanied James la Guma to Brussels in 1927 to attend the first international conference of the League against Imperialism. He travelled further, to the Soviet Union, and came away with glowing impressions of its policy of equality and national autonomy for the dark-skinned Asians in its eastern territories. The man who had once denounced Bolshevism in a trial of communists became a firm supporter of their party. The right wing of Congress ousted him from the presidency for this reason in 1930. Many other Africans underwent a similar radical change in the stormy decade that followed the war.

11 Class Struggles Resumed

The impetus given to secondary industries during the war persisted in the boom that followed. Of the 6,000 factories recorded under the 1918 Factories Act, 4,300, with a working force of 30,000 white and 74,000 other persons, were registered in 1919–20. The number employed in all manufacturing establishments topped the 180,000 mark at the end of 1920. Trade unionism made a corresponding advance. There were ninety unions with 132,000 recorded members in 1920, compared to 10,500 trade unionists in 1915. Goods were scarce and prices soared. The wholesale price index rose from 1,000 in 1914 to 2,318 in 1919 and 2,707 in 1920. The incidence of strikes rose from twelve in 1914 to forty-seven in 1919 and sixty-six in 1920, when 105,658 employees lost an aggregate of 839,415 working days through strikes. The majority took place on the Rand and in the port towns; affected a wide range of occupations, including the police and banks; and were settled quickly by voluntary arbitration. Organized labour was strong and the employing class conciliatory.

The socialists entered 1919 with great expectations. The working class of eastern and central Europe had hoisted the red flag. Symptoms of revolt appeared from Mexico to China. South Africans, too, showed signs of renewed militancy. The SAIF's conference at Durban in January passed a resolution, by thirty-two votes to fourteen, condemning allied intervention in Russia and calling on capitalist powers to stop their intrigues against the working class. The conference also voted against the admission of Coloured delegates. The Cape Federation of Labour Unions retaliated by deciding to sever all relations with unions in the north. Such incidents were treated as minor divergences from the great forward movement.

Appeals for industrial solidarity made headway. Building workers on strike in Port Elizabeth refused to resume work unless employers included Coloured artisans in the terms of settlement. Tramwaymen in Pretoria stopped work in February 1919. Andrews urged them to form a workers' council and to run the trams in defiance of the municipality. They applauded and disregarded his advice. He was more successful in Johannesburg a few days later, at a mass meeting called by the SAIF to demand a shorter working week. The meeting passed a resolution, which he moved from the floor, protesting against the arrest and imprisonment of Africans who had demonstrated in Bloemfontein for higher wages. The ice had broken, the League declared. 'For the first time in industrial history white workers have thus publicly and corporately associated themselves with the grievances of native workers.' This was 'a historic landmark in the progress of the movement not only of this country but of the world'.[1]

Cape Town's socialists experienced a fresh rash of schisms. A. F. Batty resigned as organizer of the Labour party to found the Democratic Labour party on a non-racial platform. A Constitutional Socialist League appeared in opposition to the International Socialist League. The Industrial Socialist League published a monthly 'satirical' journal, the *Bolshevik*, under the editorship of A. Z. Berman. He, Joe Pick and Manuel Lopes were arrested on the day of the paper's first appearance and charged with contravening a century-old newspaper ordinance.

The African National Congress mounted a great passive resistance campaign on the Rand at the end of March against the pass laws. Makgatho, the ANC president, gave two specific reasons for the campaign. It was meant to forestall an extension of Free State municipal regulations that obliged men and women to pay 1s. a month for residential permits. Secondly, whenever Africans struck work, they were beaten, fined or jailed because, it was said, they had broken their service contracts under the pass laws, and not because of their colour. Congress had therefore resolved to put an end to the pass system. Thousands of men threw their passes away or surrendered them to pickets so as to court arrest and force the government to attend to their grievances. More than 700 were arrested, while scores were badly injured by police and white civilians who assaulted Africans on the streets and broke up Congress meetings. 'They were driven like cattle, trampled by mounted policemen under their horses' hoofs, shot at by white volunteers,' reported Makgatho; 'and some men and women are in their graves as a result of their refusal to buy any more passes.'[2]

At this time 650 municipal engineers and tramwaymen in Johannesburg walked out in protest against a decision to retrench men in the power station. Andrews was called from the ISL office to speak at a great town hall meeting. He gave the same advice that he had given at Pretoria, now with more success. The men elected a 'board of control' headed by J. T. Bain and W. Glendon. It invaded the council chamber, turned the councillors out, and installed Bain in the mayoral chair. The local 'soviet', as it was called, administered the municipal services for several days until the council rescinded the retrenchment order and set up a joint board of councillors and employees to settle disputes. This fine demonstration of class spirit was, however, marred by a characteristic outburst of racial antagonism. While Africans defied the pass laws, a majority of the men on strike promised assistance if called upon to quell the 'native menace' and to prevent 'outrages' on white women and children.[3]

This betrayal of class solidarity infuriated Bunting, who had an additional and personal cause of complaint, since he had been assaulted by a mob of racists outside the court house where he was defending African resisters against the pass laws. As editor of the *International* he wrote bitterly about white workers who cheered Bolshevism and beat up Africans for daring to protest against passes: 'that outward and visible sign of semi-chattel slavery'. The whites, he pointed out, never condemned the daily outrages on their fellow workers, or protected them from the police, or helped them to obtain higher wages. The municipal 'soviet' was a commendable venture, perhaps the first of its kind in the empire, but it owed its success to the fatal defect of being a sectional enterprise. It was, after all, only an aristocrats' revolution. 'Where were the masses, the underdogs of Bantu race who far outnumber the whites in Municipal employ?' The 'soviet', which claimed to be in control, did not include any of the sanitary workers who had struck nearly a year ago and whose demand for a rise of 1s. a day was haughtily ignored.[4]

The article, remarked Andrews in later years, disclosed Bunting's 'deep-seated hatred of the trade union movement which remained with him to the end and was I think a serious handicap to his usefulness and to the movement which he so faithfully and unselfishly espoused'.[5] Jones, writing from the sanatorium in Maritzburg, defended the white workers. They were separated from the African by a functional gap, and not by a conflict of interests, since to supervise was not to exploit. As the only articulate section of the proletariat, they were the masters of the situation and could themselves win dictatorship for their class. The revolution would fail within twenty-four hours, however, unless both white and black workers experienced the joyousness of freedom. White workers would soon realize that the economic machine would collapse without the cooperation of the African. Facts would fall in line with theory as the working class became one, with no demarcation of colour. To ignore or sneer at either section of the workers was to be anti-proletarian in the lowest degree.[6]

The rebuke drew applause from the trade unionists, and ignored the basic issues raised by Bunting. Was the racial division of labour merely functional, or did it constitute a serious conflict of interests? Would white workers then or under socialism accept equality, perhaps at the price of reducing their standards in order to raise those of the Africans? Or would they insist on maintaining their superior status behind colour bars? Jones did not want discussions about the future to alienate the League from what he considered to be the revolutionary vanguard. The immediate task was to convert workers to socialism, combat racism, and lay the basis for solidarity. Displays of righteous indignation at their backwardness could only damage the cause. When the 'black hundreds', as the League called white hooligans, broke up its meetings on the Rand and at Cape Town, the socialists declared that this was a reaction to their growing strength. They marched triumphantly behind their own band, playing the 'Marseillaise', in the SAIF's May Day procession, and jubilated at the re-uniting of the workers' forces. While white workers marched in peace, the police broke up a meeting of 4,000 Africans who were holding their own demonstration.

The League's 1919 May Day brochure contained photographs of John Maclean, Lenin, Trotsky, Liebknecht and Luxemburg, together with the verses of the 'International' and the 'Red Flag'. The socialist rally passed resolutions acclaiming world revolution, condemning the League of Nations, and calling for unity without distinction of craft, sex or race. Andrews regretted the absence of Africans and Coloured. May Day 1920, he predicted, would see white and black demonstrating together. This seemed credible as the radical mood spread. White trade unionists joined in public protests at Johannesburg, Durban and Cape Town against proposed legislation attacking African and radical organizations. The bill, which would amend the Public Welfare and Moratorium Act, proposed making it illegal for Africans to strike or for any one to spread ill-will among Africans towards other racial groups. Crawford's SAIF and NURAHS, the railwaymen's union, backed the protests, and the bill's most objectionable features were withdrawn.

There were other promising symptoms. The railway union kept an open door, and claimed to represent African, Coloured and white wage earners of all grades. Sam Barlin of the ISL organized a clothing workers' industrial union in Johannesburg of Coloured and white tailors – though not of the African labourers. The SAIF's trade union congress at Bloemfontein in May 1919 passed resolutions demanding the withdrawal of the Riotous Assemblies Act and other repressive legislation. Another resolution called for the nationalization of the mines, under the management of boards equally representative of the state and its employees. The congress also undertook to press for a minimum wage for white workers, and proposed an inquiry into the status of African miners. The radical phrases barely concealed a design to protect white workers securely against competition by placing the mines under the control of government, more susceptible than the mine owners to political pressure. It was the policy of trade unionists confident of their political strength, and whose socialism was geared to the structure of white supremacy.

This mood of militancy inspired the government to convene a national industrial conference of workers and employers in November and December 1919. Trade unionists from the north refused to sit with Coloured representatives of the Cape Federation, which thereupon withdrew. Radical in all other respects, the workers' delegates succeeded in carrying a resolution that urged the state to nationalize industries in the people's interests and as a prophylactic against strikes. The employers' side opposed the motion, and agreed that an overhaul of the country's primitive industrial legislation was long overdue. The conference unanimously voted for a new labour code which would provide for the recognition of trade unions, industrial councils, and benefits for white workers, including a minimum wage, paid holidays, equal pay for men and women, and bigger confinement allowances.[7] It was a splendid banquet of peace and friendship between white labour and capital, which left nothing, not even crumbs, for Lazarus outside the gate.

Africans continued doggedly on their own to press for relief from discrimination and poverty. The ANC, meeting at Queenstown in May, learned that eighty-six passive resisters had been rearrested on refusing to take out passes after serving their sentences. Congress expressed sympathy with the victims, blamed their troubles on the unjust policy of denying civil rights to which Africans were entitled as British subjects, and decided to renew its request for an extension of the franchise to all sections of the population in the north.[8] At this time H. Selby Msimang (1886–), a former court interpreter from Edendale, Pietermaritzburg, and secretary to Dr Seme, was organizing workers in Bloemfontein for an increase in wages, pegged at 2s. a day throughout the war in spite of the steep rise in prices. After holding a series of meetings, he presented a demand for 4s. 6d. a day, was arrested, and then committed for trial on a charge of incitement under the Riotous Assemblies Act. He was eventually acquitted. The case led to his being brought into contact with Clements Kadalie, the founder of the Industrial and Commercial Union in Cape Town.[9]

According to Kadalie, the initiative for this venture came from A. F. Batty, founder of the Labour Democratic party and a persistently unsuccessful candidate in municipal and parliamentary elections. He asked Kadalie to join his electoral committee in the Harbours constituency; and, after losing a by-election, decided to 'consolidate the non-European vote' by setting up a permanent organization. A meeting of Coloured and African dockers agreed in January 1919 to form the ICU and, on Batty's motion, elected Kadalie to be the secretary.[10] Msimang visited Cape Town in August at Kadalie's invitation, to speak at a public meeting called to launch the union. 'They were the real workers,' he told the audience, 'yet white workers were reaping the benefit of black labour.'[11] Returning to Bloemfontein, Msimang formed a parallel separate Industrial and Commercial Workers' Union.

Abdurahman also moved into action on the industrial front in August by forming the APO Federation of Labour, the S.A. Workmen's Co-operative Union, and a Bootmakers' Union. His executive, he explained, felt that Coloured should have separate unions which would look to their own ranks for salvation against white labour aristocracy. The Cape Federation admittedly accepted Coloured workers, but they were barred from the white unions in the north and denied admission to the skilled trades. M. J. Green of the Motor Mechanics' Union in Johannesburg had recently announced that his society would 'not have anything to do with a motor car owned or driven by Asiatics or Coloured'. Abdurahman refused to distinguish between such racists and Cape Town's trade union leaders, Stuart, Evans, Thompson, or McWilliams, who organized open unions. 'The Coloured people have not yet forgotten that the White Unions of Cape Town hounded Coloured carpenters out of their workshops and kicked Coloured bricklayers off the scaffold.' White trade unionists in Cape Town were either revolutionary bolsheviks, like A. Z. Berman, or mere place seekers, like Batty, who hoped to climb into parliament on the backs of the Coloured. All of them were actuated by self-interest.[12]

The accusation might have been levelled also against Abdurahman. He denounced racial segregation yet resented class organizations that cut across the colour line. The labour movement in the western Cape was a greater threat than the bourgeois parties to his commanding role among the Coloured. Wilfrid Harrison of the SDF opposed him, and was defeated by more than 300 votes, at a municipal election in 1918. In 1919, Batty's Democratic Labour party, with the assistance of J. J. Fraitas, Dean and other Coloured tradesmen, put Hendry, one of their number, in the town council, which Abdurahman regarded as his special preserve. Harry Evans of the Cape Federation was backed by Coloured artisans when he stood against him in the provincial council elections of 1920. Abdurahman had a political motive for wanting to divide working men into racial camps.

Coloured artisans had equally strong economic reasons for combining in open unions with white printers, cabinet makers, builders, tailors or leather workers. Fraitas, Hendry, Gamiet, Gibbs, Abrahams and Petersen said as much when attending a conference called by Abdurahman. They refused to abandon the Cape Federation for his segregated organization. The non-racial body, they argued, gave them better protection and guaranteed the rate for the job. This might be so, he replied, though only in trades where the Coloured dominated and where the white man could not improve his wages without their cooperation. In other fields he persistently scabbed on them and smashed their strikes for higher wages. White labour enforced the colour bar on the mines, prevented engineering firms in Cape Town from apprenticing Coloured youth, and would remain their deadliest enemy until they 'learned to have no truck' with it at election times, and to 'organize themselves into separate unions for industrial purposes'.[13]

Port Elizabeth was the only other centre where open trade unions took root. Here, practically all masonry, bricklaying, plastering and painting were in Coloured hands, and the unions enforced full rates for them. No less racial prejudice existed there than on the Rand, reported C. B. Tyler, the BWIU organizer; but the unions had to take the Coloured in so as to protect themselves.[14] A union might, however, open its doors to Coloured artisans for the same reason, even though there were few of them. The Durban branch of the AEU admitted Coloured mechanics because, said Boydell, they were, when unorganized, at the mercy of employers and a danger to the white artisan.[15] Trade unions in the north, with few exceptions, avoided any need to combine with the Coloured simply by excluding them from skilled work. The BWIU, for instance, kept an open door in the Cape, and barred Coloured tradesmen in the Transvaal, even to the extent of blacklisting contractors and intimidating householders who employed them as bricklayers and painters.[16]

White prejudice imposed a segregated pattern on trade union-ism in the north. Coloured and Indian workers had no alternative but to take Abdurahman's advice and form separate unions of their own. They were most successful in Durban because of the spade work done by Lee and Sigamoney. Indian dockers, shop assistants, hotel employees, tobacco workers and printers' assis-tants were organized by the end of 1919.[17] Here and elsewhere, however, the unions, whether white, Coloured or Indian, ex-cluded Africans. Relegated to work classed as unskilled, they did not compete directly with workers in the higher paid cate-gories, and were therefore ignored. Trade unionists professed sympathy with the African's demand for higher pay to meet the rise in living costs, gave him no assistance and belittled his claims. 'The native,' it was said, 'is in the happier position that he has a bit of land to go back to if his pay is unattractive – the white worker hasn't.'[18]

Yet it was the high cost of living that precipitated the ICU's first and perhaps most dramatic action towards the end of 1919. A general election was pending. All sections of the labour move-ment agitated against high prices and profiteering. The Cape Federation, backed by NURAHS, the railway union, urged dock-workers to refuse to handle foodstuffs for export. The ICU and a Cape Town branch of the IWA responded by calling the men out on 17 December; and used the occasion to demand a pay rise from 4s. to 8s. 6d. a day.[19] Two to three thousand men struck work. Police and troops were summoned. They ejected the Africans from their quarters in the docks, and prosecuted many for breach of contract under the master and servant law. The government yielded to the pressure and banned the export of food except by permit. NURAHS withdrew its moral support, white railwaymen scabbed, and the strike was called off after two weeks. The dockers received their reward in August 1920, however, when the stevedoring companies agreed to a minimum wage of 8s. for labourers, 12s. 6d. for foremen, and double pay for overtime.[20]

The international socialists denounced the 'treachery' of white workers who had scabbed so shamefully on the dockers, as on Coloured van drivers in Kimberley and Indian waiters at East London.[21] Abdurahman fulminated against 'white irresponsible agitators' who deceived 'the poor native' with false promises of support. There were surely many competent Coloured and Africans, he argued, who would help the stevedores without their having to call in 'uneducated and discredited white men'. It was necessary to organize for industrial purposes, but the white man's example should not be followed in all things. Direct action, as practised in Johannesburg and Durban, was dangerous if resorted to by Coloured workers, since it 'would result in commandos using physical force against them. They must do nothing which would give Europeans any excuse for resorting to violent methods.'[22]

Direct action held no such terrors for Harry Haynes, one of the great radicals in the movement and a leader of the Durban municipal 'soviet' of January 1920. Born in Ireland in 1877, he came to South Africa with the troops in 1899, worked on the gold mines after the war, was elected to the union's executive, and chaired the Kleinfontein strike committee in 1913. That, he said, was an epoch in his life, the point at which he and many others first began to study the class war. 'It was the year in which General Smuts planted the seeds of the working-class revolution in soil watered by blood spilt in the streets of Johannesburg.'[23] He moved from the Labour party to the War-on-War League, joined the ISL, worked on the trams in Johannesburg and settled in Durban to recover from phthisis. Here he adopted a strategy, during a strike of municipal employees, which the ISL said was worthy of the old Kleinfontein revolutionaries.

Durban's municipal employees stopped work on 7 January in protest against the alleged victimization of the assistant town clerk, H. H. Kemp, a member of the municipal union and a parliamentary Labour candidate. The strikers brought all municipal services to a standstill for three days and then installed a board of control in the town hall. They won their point after a day of workers' management. The council agreed to set up a permanent conciliation board of councillors and employees.[24] It was a minor 'seizure of power' with a distinct farcical element. There was more to it than comedy, however. The municipal 'soviets' of Johannesburg and Durban became a legend in the movement. Haynes, like J. T. Bain, had the makings of a genuine revolutionary, though they would hardly have been so bold, nor would the 'revolutionary instincts' of the rank and file have outstripped their 'socialist knowledge', to quote the *International*, if they had not obtained the sympathy of the white public.[25] Their daring reflected the white worker's post-war mood of defiance. The boldness of the strategy and its success showed that he was becoming an important political force. He was on the way to winning his struggle for admission to the white elite.

Colour-conscious and self-confident whites had no ear for the appeals and warnings of the socialists. The ISL's fifth annual conference in January urged trade unions to organize Africans and demand equal pay for equal work. All would succumb to exploitation unless white and black joined hands to emancipate themselves.[26] In practice trade unionists complained incessantly of being undercut, never scrupled to widen the wage gap and obstructed the African's efforts to raise his standards. Employees at the Johannesburg power station seemed to be breaking ground in February when they decided to submit wage demands for all racial groups. A representative meeting of white municipal workers rejected the proposal, however, and deleted the claims made on behalf of Africans and Coloured.[27] A few days later eighty of the power station workers volunteered to scab, on condition that they were given armed protection, if their African co-workers came out on strike.[28]

The offer to scab was made during a strike on the mines. A large majority of the white employees balloted early in February 1920 in favour of a strike for higher wages and a shorter working week. They obtained an increase of 8s. a day with retrospective effect from 1 November 1919. African miners then organized a series of sectional strikes for a wage of between 5s. and 10s. a day, a fair deal in the concession stores, and an opportunity to do more responsible and better paid work. They complained of the steep rise in prices and pointed out that their families in the reserves, while needing more money because of a severe drought, were receiving less from their wages. The owners granted an increase of 3d. a shift as from 1 January, thereby raising the average wage to 2s. 3d. for underground and 2s. for surface workers. The industry, said the Chamber, could not bear any additional wage increases; the removal of the colour bar was impracticable; and the strikes were due to the teaching of international socialists, particularly among the Zulu who put themselves on a par with whites. Africans continued to boycott stores on the East Rand, however; the strike spread, and 71,000 men had stopped work on twenty-two mines by 25 February.[29]

The strike put 8,600 white miners out of work. They drew full pay during the stoppage and on some mines took over the African's work, including tramming and shovelling, so as to demonstrate that they could keep the mines going without him. The executive of the SAMWU recommended its members 'to continue operations on the mines as usual' and agreed on 'the strongest possible measures to combat any attempt to imperil the colour bar'. While the Transvaal African Congress protested against assaults by the police and threatened a strike of domestic and commercial workers, the ISL circulated its famous 'Don't Scab' leaflet among the whites. 'The Native workers are beginning to wake up,' it said, and it appealed for sympathy on the grounds of fair play, trade union principle, labour solidarity, and self-interest. 'Therefore, DON'T SCAB! DON'T SHOOT! Don't take a rifle against your own hammer boys.'[30]

Joe Andrews, a member of the miners' general council and vice-chairman of his branch, was victimized for having distributed copies of the leaflet. His fellow workers at the Crown mine voted for his expulsion, and the management gave this as its reason for dismissing him. O'Leary downed tools in sympathy with Andrews and was also sacked. The socialists commented gloomily on the contrast between the behaviour of the white scabs and the 'splendid example of the power of industrial solidarity' set by Africans. They had shown a capacity to combine in 'an instinctive mass revolt against their whole status and pig level of existence'.[31] The socialists regretted that 'the barriers of race, language, and, above all, police' prevented them from 'instructing the native labourers on the principles of working-class solidarity'. Yet the Africans managed well enough on their own without such instruction.

The strike was a well planned, disciplined campaign and not an 'instinctive revolt'. It showed that many thousands of men from a wide variety of regions and peasant communities could combine effectively. It was a 'new phenomenon', remarked Sir Evelyn Wallers, president of the Chamber of Mines, this first 'native strike in the true sense of the word'. The 'absolutely peaceful cessation from work' indicated that the African 'was advancing more rapidly than we had anticipated', and would not remain satisfied for very long with his position in industry.[32] There was a high degree of organization. The strikers picketed the mines and otherwise kept quietly to the compounds. Their readiness to 'put into practice White organized labour's methods of direct action is an ominous sign of the times'.[33] This display of cohesion and discipline alarmed the government. 'General surprise and consternation were felt at the way in which the strike was engineered,' reported the department of mines; the more so, because a 'concerted attempt at violence in one form or another was not seriously attempted'.[34]

Policemen and soldiers surrounded one compound after another, told each group of strikers in turn that the rest had returned to work, and drove them down the mine with rifle butts if they refused to credit the story or to resume work for any other reason. They were said to have 'rioted' if they resisted. The strikers at the Village Deep compound barricaded themselves behind logs. The troops broke through with fixed bayonets and fired, killing three and wounding forty. Police and civilians attacked a meeting of Africans in the slums of Vrededorp, killed eight and wounded eighty.[35] The quality of the alleged rioting can be gauged from the report of a trial on a charge of public violence of three strikers from the Langlaagte compound, who were accused of having threatened the compound manager.

'You try to ape the white man by going on strike,' lectured the magistrate, 'but you do not understand a strike unless it is connected with rioting.' Yet they had not actually attacked the manager or assaulted anyone. For this reason, and because they had spent five months in jail awaiting trial, they were sentenced to only one month's imprisonment.[36]

An African, according to the ethos of racists, 'apes the white man' when he develops a taste for good clothing, food or liquor; aspires to higher education, the vote and skilled work; or acquires any trait regarded as the hallmark of a superior status. He is a 'good boy' if he practises the Christian virtues of docility and resignation, is poorly educated and 'keeps his place'. There is no way, however, of supplying education and Christianity in such doses as to immunize him against the virus of ambition. The second generation of Africans educated in mission schools, mines, factories and stores were coming to the fore in the 1920s. They saw through the white man's claim to superior moral worth and intellectual capacity. Some of them had begun to challenge his monopoly of technical skills and the jobs to which such skills gave entrance.

In retrospect, the failure of the labour movement to assist the strikers, if only by protecting them against intimidation, marked an irreversible trend to cleavage along racial lines. The African working class had matured and was ripe for organization. Given assistance, the strikers might have taken a significant step towards the 'equal pay for equal work' that the white labour leaders insisted was an essential condition for the removal of the colour bar. The refusal of the leaders to support the strike displayed their insincerity. As the ISL admitted later in the year, white workers hated the African less out of fear of competition than because they aspired to membership in the ruling caste.[37] The socialists attributed much of the hostility to the influence of Afrikaner workers. This was a delusion. The bulk of British workers were as determined to 'keep the kaffir in his place'. They did not want to narrow the wage gap or to promote solidarity between themselves and the African.

The demand for a relaxation of colour bars was the strike's most significant feature. It was not a new proposal. H. L.

Phooko and S. M. Makgatho, the president and secretary of the Transvaal Native Congress, told the mining commission of 1907 that many Africans were being paid at unskilled rates for doing skilled work. With proper training they could undertake all branches of mining operations.[38] H. O. Buckle, the native grievances commissioner of 1913–14, reported to the same effect and found that the men were justified in asking for the removal of the statutory barrier.[39] E. J. Way, in his presidential address to the S.A. Institute of Engineers in July 1914, argued that 'colour' was the only difference between the races. He agreed with H. M. Taberer, director of the Native Recruiting Corporation, that the colour bar on the mines existed largely for sentimental and political reasons, discouraged efficiency among whites, and gave the African no scope or incentive whatever. A great many white supervisors on the mines were inefficient and could be readily replaced by more experienced and efficient Africans. 'The only remedy,' Way argued, 'is that white and black shall have equality of opportunity, and the better man must win in the long run.'[40]

J. B. Moffat, who inquired into the causes of African strikes on the Rand in 1918, pointed out that the Mines and Works Act of 1911 did not authorize discrimination. The colour bar regulations under the act must therefore be regarded as *ultra vires*. It was the white workers, and not the regulations, who barred the employment of Africans on skilled or semi-skilled work. 'This means that one of the principal industrial avenues along which the natives might legitimately hope for advancement is to be closed to them, and that a policy of repression is to be followed.' The government, Moffat recommended, should free itself from the odium of being a party to such discrimination, by repealing the colour bar provisions.[41] They gave white men a monopoly of as many as thirty-two occupations in which 7,057 were employed in 1920. A conventional colour bar, not prescribed by regulation, gave another 4,020 whites an exclusive claim to nineteen other occupations.[42] It was the conventional and not the statutory barrier that the mine owners wished to abolish.

They took up the cry with great urgency. The cost of mining

gold reached a peak figure of 25s. 8d. a ton of ore milled in 1920, when the mills crushed twenty-four million tons of rock. Gold prices, which soared to a record figure of 130s. a fine ounce in February, declined sharply thereafter while working costs remained constant. The owners asserted that it would soon be unprofitable to keep the low grade ore mines in production unless labour costs were drastically reduced. White miners' wages had risen by fifty per cent since 1913, and African wages by only nine per cent. A major reason for this situation was a conspiracy by the owners to freeze African wages. Operating a 'maximum average' agreement arrived at in 1912 when the Native Recruiting Corporation was formed to organize labour supplies in South Africa, Basutoland, Bechuanaland and Swaziland, the owners pegged the rate at 2s. 3d. a shift for the largest category of miners. Fines were imposed on mines where the maximum average was exceeded. The arrangement discouraged managements from introducing monetary incentives to increase output and obliged them to reduce piecework rates whenever the bulk of workers became more efficient. Because of this inelasticity, it would be hazardous to attempt savings by cutting African wages.

The owners proposed a reshuffle of work patterns to diminish the white man's role. A government commission was appointed in 1919 to consider possible economies. It included three officials of the Chamber of Mines and three labour representatives: Archie Crawford, Forrester Brown and Bower Pohl, a member of the miners' union. The testimony of witnesses before the low grade mines commission received much publicity on the Rand and influenced the attitude of workers on both sides of the colour line.

The *Labour World* conducted a vigorous campaign against the commission and the mine owners. J. H. Gow, the editor, a town councillor and former secretary of the Labour party, had won a provincial council by-election in 1918 in the mining constituency of Siemert under the banner 'Vote for Gow and a White South Africa'. His Unionist opponent received some backing from the SAIF and white trade unionists who, according to the paper, had been taken in by Crawford's conciliation policy.[43] This experience added venom to Gow's pen. He predicted that the commission's findings were a foregone conclusion: they would defend the financial gang and recommend the abolition of the colour bar. The decision, he alleged, had been taken in London, which really controlled the industry. Sir Lionel Phillips was out to break the colour bar, probably with the approval of Crawford, Brown and Pohl. The white worker 'must now get ready to fight for his very existence'. Nemesis would overtake the owners. The African miner could not be expected to remain satisfied with his wage after hearing the praises showered by magnates and experts on his potential abilities. The police would chase and Smuts might deport Andrews, Bunting and others of the ISL if they were to tell Africans what the experts had said before the commission.[44]

Andrews, Bunting and Jones communicated with the white worker, however, and not with the African. Their reflections on the evidence given before the Low Grade Mines Commission led them to a significant stage in their long odyssey through the breakers of class and colour. The Chamber of Mines, declared Jones, 'has aligned itself on the side of right and progress. The white labour movement finds itself on the side of reaction.' The mine owners, he acknowledged, clothed their capitalist depredation in negrophile philanthropy. The plea of giving the African a chance in life was a cloak for the real object of increasing dividends. Even so, the quest for cheap labour coincided with the needs of social progress, as in the movement to do away with slavery in the U.S.A. The Chamber could link all demands for the African's advance to the demand for the abolition of the colour bar. The Labour movement, in contrast, appeared as the great enemy of four million proletarians. White workers had no moral right to a monopoly of any trade. 'Let the fact be conceded that under the Capitalist system the standard of life of the white workers and the rights of the native workers are incompatible.'[45]

The socialists refused to accept the corollary that the African miner had a common interest with the mine owner against the white labour aristocracy. To assert this would cut them off from their base in what they regarded as the vanguard of revolution. They fell back instead on speculations about the future soviet society. If Africans could not rise except by ousting the white man, then so much the worse for capitalism. Equal pay for equal work would reconcile legitimate demands for keeping up living standards with the principles of justice and humanity. This was a Utopian solution under the existing order. In fighting for it, however, the workers would achieve socialism. A 'natural goodwill' born of the interdependence between white mechanic and black helper, miner and hammer boy, railwayman and cleaner, would then be 'reflected in amity on the political plane'.[46] Africans would form their own soviets and sit in the supreme soviet where colour prejudice was weakest. The common society would take the form of an 'exchange of labour services – *en masse* – between the white and native communities, the products and functions of each being indispensable to the other'.[47] The argument stopped at this point, leaving an impression that socialism, as conceived, would perpetuate segregation or at least the traditional division of labour between skilled whites and unskilled Africans.

Africans wanted immediate relief from racial discrimination and excessive exploitation. They had all to gain, as Colonel Pritchard, the director of native labour, told the commission, by acting in concert against a system that actually prohibited their advancement.[48] If allowed to do skilled work, many would settle down as permanent and professional miners with a better status and wage than the migrant worker could hope to obtain. African miners as a class would benefit from the abolition of the colour bar by obtaining improved medical services, working and living conditions, and compensation for injuries and pneumoconiosis. There could be no doubt as to the nature of the African's interests. As for the country as a whole, Pritchard warned that it was sitting on a volcano, which was bound to erupt unless men acted in a statesmanlike way by removing the colour bar, the root cause of the inefficiency alleged to be throttling the mines, and the African's most powerful lever against government and the white community. Both government and the white community discounted the danger and ignored the warning when the African miners came out on strike.

The mine owners had no intention of paying them more unless

they could take the white man's place. The strikers went back to work at the old rates of pay and, after a few months, to a longer working day. For the owners, acting on a recommendation of the Low Grade Mines Commission, revised work schedules so as to make Africans put in an hour more per shift without an increase in wages. Crawford, Brown and Pohl, who represented Labour on the commission, also agreed to 'speed up the nigger', as the *Labour World*[49] vulgarly called the decision. They shied at the real issue, and dissented from the majority's recommendation to relax the colour bar. That would have to come, said Crawford, or the men would have to accept a wage cut, if economic calamity was to be avoided. Yet he feared the trouble that would arise before they adapted themselves to either course.[50] Other sections of the movement shared his fears. The 13,000 white men working underground would not take it lying down, warned the *Labour World*. Capitalists could afford to take a liberal view. Company directors and trade union officials 'do not have to work alongside the smelly black'. The issue was one of life or death to the poor worker. 'Breaking the colour bar will be the signal for the biggest example of "direct action" that has yet been shown on these fields.'[51]

The APO interviewed government, Unionist and Labour party members in April 1920, two months after the African miners' strike. Creswell told the deputation that his party would not cut its own throat. White miners to a man opposed the removal of the colour bar. The APO had never supported the party at elections and would continue to oppose it even if the colour bar were deleted from the constitution.[52] Merriman came to the rescue with a motion in the House similar to the one he had introduced in 1914, calling for the repeal of the colour restrictions in the mining regulations. He said that the white miner was an overseer who drew £1 10s. a day for sitting on a bucket while the African did the work for 2s. a day. Creswell, as in 1914, moved that the House decline to discuss the motion until the mine owners ceased to employ indentured workers and undertook to pay a civilized wage on an equal scale for all employees irrespective of colour. The white miners threatened an industrial revolution if the colour bars were removed. The government side adjourned the debate before the House could vote on Merriman's motion.

The forecast was shrewd, as the Rand revolt of 1922 would show; and it pointed to the beginning of Crawford's downfall. An uncompromising internationalist, he had antagonized the Labour party by setting his face against its flagwagging and patriotic gestures. He widened the breach after the war by keeping the trade unions out of the party's electoral fold, initially for syndicalist reasons and later so as to bargain with its political opponents.[53] He was equally hostile to the ISL, whose leaders had spurned him in his radical youth, although he shared its views about war and industrial unionism. His grit, determination and refusal to overlook old scores were allied to a great egotism and desire for power. The Federation of Trades grew under his management into the largest, richest and most influential section of the labour movement; and he would not share its control. He defeated Andrews in 1920 in an election for the post of secretary, and converted Forrester Brown, the miners' union secretary and former ISL leader, into a loyal disciple of what the League called Crawfordism: the use of revolutionary phrases for the purposes of reaction.[54]

Described as the Gompers of South Africa, Crawford kept a tight rein on the affiliated unions and set himself up as their chief representative. His policy met with success during the boom, since employers readily made concessions to keep the industrial peace. The full weight of the federation could then be brought to bear against men who took the bit between their teeth, or against unions, like those of the ironmoulders, engineers, municipal employees and builders, that insisted on negotiating directly with employers. This craft sectionalism destroyed Crawford's scheme of welding the workers into one great industrial union. Trade union officials resented his invasion of their authority, and accused him of bungling when he failed to produce the required results. Inflation caused a rash of wildcat strikes. The Federation congress at Bloemfontein in 1919 decided to withhold support from strikes not previously sanctioned by the central executive, and so indicated that its controls were breaking down. Crawford's report to the general council in

April 1920 called for solidarity and denounced sectional strikes. What Crawford really had in mind, said Andrews, was to negotiate with employers at the expense of the workers, and not to call for a more general strike or a bigger mass movement.

Both reformers and radicals suspected Crawford's sincerity towards the working class. It was a strange metamorphosis, they said, that had turned the one-time mob orator of the town hall steps into an intimate of mine magnates and company directors. He expounded the principles of the wage fund theory instead of singing the 'Red Flag', and advised workers to accept wage cuts so as to keep the mines in production. He appeared on public platforms with Wallers and accompanied Gemmill at the state's expense to the first international labour conference at Washington in 1919. The government appointed him to the industrial advisory board and to commissions of inquiry into the cost of living, the mining industry, and unemployment. The higher he climbed, the farther he moved from his radical past. He and his Federation demanded the dismissal of Coloured drill-sharpeners in 1918, supported the mine owners' plea in 1919 for the removal of the embargo on the recruiting of Africans in tropical regions, and took part in the anti-Asian conference called by the S.A. League in 1920.

Territories north of latitude 22° south had been closed to recruiting because of the high death rate among miners from the tropics. Home-born Africans were finding more congenial and better paid work outside the mining industry. The owners wished to tap new sources of labour, and Crawford agreed. The ban should be lifted, he argued, both to give Africans freedom of movement and to stimulate the economy. That would relieve unemployment among whites. Andrews and Bunting, giving evidence before the unemployment commission, put in a copy of the Communist Manifesto and said that capitalism caused unemployment. The competition of cheap labour was 'clearly a special contributing cause'. It also resulted in acute anti-native prejudice, particularly in whites most likely to want 'kaffir jobs'. Segregation was possible only under socialism, which did away with indentured labour; and then there would be so much less reason for it, since unemployment would disappear. The proper remedy was to nationalize the means of production, introduce a system of labour exchanges, and provide for insurance against unemployment.[55]

An emphatic protest against all forms of indentured labour came from African and Coloured trade unionists meeting at Bloemfontein on 13 July in response to a resolution moved by Msimang at the annual conference of the ANC in May. White workers had only the capitalist as their foe, he told the delegates, 'but native and coloured workers have both capitalists and trade unions to fight against'. The conference decided to form one union, called the Industrial and Commercial Workers Union, of Africans, Coloured and Indians of both sexes south of the Zambezi. The fifty delegates undertook to conduct a campaign against the pass laws and the system of recruiting men under contract. This was 'detrimental to the progress of all native races' and should be abolished at an early date.[56] Msimang was appointed president, and M. Mocher the secretary of the union. Kadalie took this badly and on his return to Cape Town persuaded his organization to dissociate itself from the proceedings at Bloemfontein.

Samuel Masabalala, another delegate, returned home to Port Elizabeth and started an agitation for higher wages. He drew large crowds and in October threatened to call workers out on strike for a wage of 10s. a day. In an attempt to pacify them, the municipal council invited Dr Rubusana to visit the town and appeal for restraint. He was assaulted at the first meeting which he addressed, and this led to Masabalala's arrest. A group of workers gathered outside the police station on 23 October to demand his release and attacked with sticks and stones. A shot was fired into the air, the demonstrators fled in all directions, and while fleeing were shot at by the police and armed civilians. Twenty demonstrators and three white bystanders were killed and 126 others wounded in what Abdurahman called South Africa's 'Amritsar'. R. Sidzumo, the secretary of the local ICWU, appealed for assistance to Msimang, who came from Bloemfontein, organized a funeral procession attended by 30,000 people, met the mayor and a group of employers, and persuaded Rubusana to withdraw his complaint. Masabalala was acquitted on a charge of public violence, and Smuts, yielding to pressure, appointed a commission of three to inquire into the causes of the disturbances.

One of them was Abdurahman, the first person of colour to be appointed to such an office. The commission found that 'all the firing which took place after the mob broke away was directed against fugitives; that it was unnecessary, indiscriminate and brutal in its callousness, resulting in a terrible toll of killed and wounded without any sufficient reason or justification'.[57] In spite of this uncompromising verdict, the government denied liability and offered only *ex gratia* payments as compensation to the victims.[58] An amount of £2,857 1s. 0d. was eventually paid to the claimants. £2,327 11s. of this went to the dependants of the three whites who had been killed, and to twelve whites injured in the disturbances; £377 7s. 6d. was paid to the dependants of one Coloured killed and two Coloured injured. The dependants of two Africans killed received £75, and one African injured, £15. The cost of burying 'unclaimed' Africans amounted to £62 2s. 6d.[59]

The international socialists deplored this brutal operation of Smuts's notorious 'don't hesitate to shoot' policy. White workers who flew to arms to 'keep order' for their masters shared responsibility for the terrible racial upheaval that would come if the African was not given the right and assistance to form trade unions. His strongest weapon was to strike quietly and without demonstrations which gave the police an opportunity to shoot and stampeded the whites into the camp of the bosses.[60] The Labour party predictably approved of the police action. The public would welcome a return to methods employed in Kruger's republic, where the police periodically raided Africans for assegais and knobkerries. Aggression such as the whites had experienced at Port Elizabeth could not be tolerated. 'We must make it quite clear to the natives that we will exact measure for measure in any unprovoked violence against our people.'[61]

Port Elizabeth's workers disregarded both threats and advice and continued to press their claims with the assistance of Msimang, who remained to look after the union's affairs. In January 1921, after white municipal workers had been given a cost of living allowance, Africans and Coloured rejected an offer to increase their wages from 4s. to 4s. 6d., and took another decision to strike. Abdurahman, who was in the eastern Cape on an electioneering tour for the South African party, intervened and negotiated a settlement with the municipal council. It agreed to pay its African and Coloured employees a similar allowance, on a scale ranging upwards from 1s. a day. Masabalala took his revenge on the government by canvassing voters on behalf of the opposition Nationalist party, much to Abdurahman's disgust. After the elections, and when the Nationalists had suffered defeat, Masabalala resumed his radical role and denounced 'the unprecedented bloodthirstiness of the capitalist class'.[62]

The police blamed the bolsheviks, complained of inadequacies in the criminal law, and urged drastic action against the 'machinations of extremists'.[63] Kadalie, the first victim of the witch hunt, was served with a deportation order in November 1920, ostensibly because he was a full time secretary of the ICU and might therefore become an economic burden to the state. The socialists protested and challenged the SAIF and other white workers' organizations 'to stand by a persecuted trade union official irrespective of his colour'.[64] Relief came, however, from another quarter. Lawyers, Scottish presbyterians, Abdurahman and his Unionist party friends applied pressure and prevailed on the government to cancel the order. 'I became as free a citizen as anyone could wish,' exulted Kadalie; and he used his liberty to consolidate the ICU and canvass voters for Hertzog's Nationalist party.[65]

12 The Communist Party Formed

Labour leaders felt unhappy about their party's prospects at the end of the war. 'We have abandoned propaganda work,' Morris Kentridge complained as he contrasted their 'timid inactivity' with the British Labour party's bold record. The war-truce had lasted too long. Imperial interests were harmful to the party if they demanded neglect of national issues. 'The Labour Party have been far too silent, submissive and inert.' As the next general election approached, the party turned its battery against the government. Botha was said to have ridden into power 'practically on the backs of Labour'; yet he and Smuts had rewarded them with whips and scorpions, cast British ideals into dust, and trampled British justice underfoot. Torn by apparently irreconcilable differences, Labour was scorned and reckoned to be 'down and out'. Each section insisted on its own point of view and found the other more hateful than the common enemy. 'Even its white ideal is challenged from within. Cursed by disintegration it treads the valley of humiliation and its enemies rejoice.'[1]

The party instituted a series of unity conferences in September 1919. Creswell queried the wisdom of the 'socialization' objective, not for reasons of personal principle, but because its ambiguity put off many potential supporters. The ISL received a belated invitation to an all-in conference in November which Ivon Jones attended in a 'semi-journalistic' capacity. He reported that the conference consisted of the old rump of Labour men without socialist guts, whose dominant aim was to get into parliament. The socialists, he claimed, had moved to firmer ground, leaving the reformists to fall back on their middle-class supporters. The League disdained 'the mugwump unity of a pot-bellied Labour Party without the fire of the Social Revolution'; and decided to contest the elections under its own banner.[2] The decision, however, resulted in a major dispute within its ranks.

The issue of political versus industrial action flared again. Syndicalists asked why they should fight elections and not for the soviet republic. Dunbar and his cronies in the Industrial Socialist League heckled the ISL's speakers and pressed for the deletion of the 'political action' clause in its constitution. The critics were told that no less an authority than Lenin himself had denounced the 'infantile disorder' of anti-parliamentarism.[3] This was so; but it was a moot point whether Lenin's argument held water in South Africa, where four-fifths of the working class had no vote. Jones conceded that conditions were unfavourable for a social democratic party. The 'political action' school brushed these considerations aside and stressed the propaganda value of an election campaign. Large majorities in the League's branches and at its annual conference in January 1920 endorsed the management committee's decision to contest elections.[4]

The conference also agreed, unanimously, to 'fall in line with world revolutionary trends' by affiliating to the Communist International. Andrews forwarded the application with the League's constitution and rules. They would show, he wrote, that 'our policy is on all fours with that of the Communist Parties of Europe and elsewhere'.[5] The Comintern accepted the application and invited both the League and the SALP to send representatives to its second congress, which opened in Petrograd on 19 July. Neither could attend. The *International* published reports of the congress proceedings, resolutions and condition for admission to the CI. A long and spirited discussion followed among the League's supporters on the prospects of uniting left wing groups into one party. Preparations were made for an extraordinary conference, the convening of which was required by article 19 of the conditions for admission.

Andrews, Bunting, Barendregt and Tyler on the Rand and Hicks in Kimberley represented the ISL in the general election of March 1920. Hamstrung by the anti-parliamentarians in their ranks, they vowed that they hated electioneering and entered the fray only 'from a stern sense of duty'. Members were told not to canvass or engage in 'any other trick of vote-catching'. Their job was to distribute the election manifesto and 150,000 leaflets on bolshevism, soviet power, the colour bar, rising prices, and the Labour party's double-talk on race. The manifesto condemned the notion of reforming parliament, urged workers to reject capitalist misrule, and proclaimed all power to the soviets. Even radical voters might have found this mixture too heady a brew. The League's candidates lost their deposits. Andrews, defeated by Madeley in Benoni, topped the League's table with seventy-eight votes – 'the irreducible minimum of votes', he declared. He attributed the socialists' defeat to the timidity of petty bourgeois supporters, a reluctance to split the labour vote against Unionists, and resentment caused by the League's 'Don't Scab' leaflet.[6]

Labour's manifesto promised benefits to the poor and needy, reaffirmed the twin aims of socialism and segregation, and made no mention of class war or revolution.[7] Creswell, more attuned than the radicals to the voters' mood, fought for the imperial connexion and against high prices, rents and profits.[8] His mixture of British patriotism and economic welfare went down well on the Rand and in the port towns, but offered small comfort to Afrikaner workers, then at a crucial stage. They were wavering in their loyalty to the political generals of South African war vintage, and vacillated between national and class affiliations. Labour's cultural insularity and sheer Britishness repelled them, however, and muffed for all time its chance of winning their allegiance. 'Dutch workers as a body are not voting for Labour candidates as by all the rules of the game they should do,' complained the *Labour World* after the elections.[9] Its correspondents gave some of the reasons.

Most of the Labour party's leaders, and all those in parliament, were immigrant and unilingual. They welcomed Afrikaners in their ranks, and expected them to communicate in English, the language of the master race. Sampson, one of the big four in the movement, deplored the 'fetish' of bilingualism, and would not make it a reason for dispensing with efficient unilingual, meaning English-speaking, trade union officials.[10] One correspondent wrote that the British working man voted for a Unionist or SAP candidate in preference to a Labour candidate who was not British-born. It was for this reason that no Afrikaners sat on the Labour benches in parliament. 'We have not played the game with our Dutch brothers, and we do not encourage them to stay with us and draw others.' Afrikaners were not wanted in the party, wrote another; they were used merely as a tool to advance the cause of British nationalism.[11]

Labour never made up on the roundabouts what it lost on the swings. It alienated Afrikaners by upholding British supremacy, and Africans by upholding white supremacy. Its members kept Coloured men out of skilled work in the north and solicited their votes in the south. The party won four seats in Cape Town and one in East London in 1920, and lost all but two of its Cape seats in 1921. The APO threw its full weight against Labour on both occasions; and also against Hicks, the ISL candidate at Kimberley in 1920. 'White Labour,' declared Abdurahman, 'has been, and is today, all over South Africa, the enemy of the Coloured people.'[12] It kept them out of motor workshops, building and electrical trades, slaughter houses and skilled mining work in the Transvaal, forced them to work for a lower wage, and then used this as a pretext for barring them from trade unions. White scabs took their jobs when Coloured workers formed their own unions and struck for higher wages. The 'white peril' would squeeze them to death if they failed to consolidate their industrial and political forces.[13] The Labour party was their 'natural enemy'. They would show their contempt for it at the polls.[14]

The APO followed the Unionists into Smuts's camp. Abdurahman had attacked him in 1910 for his racialism, and now defended him as the champion of the British connexion against Hertzog's republicans. Like other white supremacy parties, Afrikaner Nationalists consistently appealed for Coloured votes, though never so blatantly as in 1920, when they were fighting hard in the Cape against an upsurge of British patriotism. The Nationalist party took the unprecedented step of putting its name to an election pamphlet addressed to 'Coloured Afrikanders',[15] who were urged to vote for the party, 'the friends of South Africa and therefore our friends too'. Abdurahman and the APO were said to be 'politically bankrupt'. They had 'achieved nothing to better our condition' because they pinned their hopes on Britain, the Unionists and Smuts. Yet Britain, once the world's greatest slave trader, showed beyond all doubt that she would never 'interfere on our behalf in the internal affairs' of South Africa. The Unionists were double-faced, and practised all the racial discrimination that they attributed to the Nationalists. As for Smuts, he had fought Indians, Labourites, the English and his own people; 'and now he wants to fight the coloured races'. The choice was this: vote British, and vote for a flood of British immigrants 'to drown us out in our own country'; or vote South African, and 'vote for our own protection'.

The Nationalist party in the western Cape worked through Coloured agents of a Nationalist-sponsored insurance company; a Coloured newspaper, the *South African Clarion*; and a Coloured political organization, the United Afrikaner League. C. Dantu, the chief superintendent of the insurance company's Coloured division, was also the head of the newspaper's publishing department and president of the UAL. The men under him included N. R. Veldsman, A. Arendse and Abe Desmore, all former or current members of the APO. They canvassed among the Coloured in one operation for insurance, newspaper subscriptions and votes.[16] Their sole purpose, complained Abdurahman, was to fight the APO during elections on a platform made up of the Nationalist party's doctrine of disloyalty to the crown and its disgraceful abandonment of sacred principles sanctified by the blood of Coloured soldiers.[17]

The colour bar, and not republicanism, was the dominant issue, declared the Rev. Z. R. Mahabane, president of the Cape Native Congress. Africans had a duty to vote only for candidates who took a pledge to work for the elimination of racial discrimination.[18] The white supremacy parties cleared the deck, however, in the general election of 10 March 1920. Labour won 21 seats, which raised it to the peak of its parliamentary career. The South African party won 42; Hertzog's Nationalists, 44; the Unionists, 25; and independents, 3 seats. Smuts, the SAP leader and premier since Botha's death in August 1919, remained uneasily in office with the backing of Unionists and independents. Labour held the balance in a House so divided, but its attachment to the British cause limited its ability to manoeuvre. The Creswellites pressed for price and profit controls, and would not vote with the Nationalist opposition to unseat Smuts. They wanted to avert a dissolution that would force them to defend their seats; and they refused to be made responsible for opening the way to an Afrikaner republic.[19]

Smuts and Hertzog resumed their pre-election unity talks, which had broken down on the republican question. The people, said Smuts, had outgrown the old racial feud between Afrikaner and English; they were sick and tired of party politics. He proposed a national all-party government. Creswell declined; and Hertzog refused to associate with such discordant elements as Labour and the Unionists. He offered instead to enter into a parliamentary pact with the South African party alone. Smuts was right in thinking that Afrikaners wanted unity. The demand came from party branches on both sides and threatened to sweep all intransigent leaders aside. They were forced to resume negotiations. More than 500 Nationalist and SAP delegates met at Bloemfontein in September 1920. Afrikaner churches blessed their deliberations in a national day of prayer, but divine providence failed the conciliators. The Nationalists demanded and Smuts refused to concede the right to agitate from within the alliance for sovereign independence and secession from the crown.[20] Power and place were at stake in addition to principle. A bilateral pact such as Hertzog proposed would have assured him of the premiership; whereas Smuts was more likely to remain prime minister in an all-party coalition. Since neither would serve under the other, the popular movement for white national unity collapsed.

The South African party played its last card, absorbed the Unionists, and became in form as well as in function the spokesman of mine owners, industrialists and the British interest. Smuts went to the country in February 1921 to defend the constitution, he said, against secession. The Labour party accused him of wishing to upset the balance of power it held and to smash it in preparation for an attack on the white working class. The election caught the Labour movement in a state of disunity. Trade unions were indifferent or hostile to the political wing.

Socialist groups fought one another more than they fought the system.[21] Representatives of the SALP and ISL met in November 1920 for unity talks. Creswell said he wanted a peaceful revolution, whereas the ISL wished to destroy the system by force and bloodshed. Andrews replied that it was the capitalist who used force on the workers, and without protest from the right wing, which had adopted a bourgeois outlook. The real gulf existed between the reformist ideas of the second international and the revolutionary tactics of the third.[22]

The fourth general election took place on 8 February 1921. The ISL advised all socialists to stay away from the polls except at Durban, where three League candidates had entered the lists. They obtained 140 votes in all, against the 2,310 votes cast for the Labour candidates. Harry Norrie, the veteran socialist and now a respectable town councillor, threw the weight of his SDP behind the Labour party. It fared badly, however, losing three seats in Natal and nine in other provinces to the SAP. Labour had failed for the second time to win the workers' support on a patriotic issue. When told that the empire was in danger they chose to vote for the jingos in the SAP-Unionist coalition. This won 79 seats, while the Nationalists won 45, Labour 9 and independents one. Smuts had gained a clear majority at the the expense of Labour, which never fully recovered. The SAP-Unionists would always outmatch it in protestations of loyalty to the crown. The Nationalist party, on the other hand, stole Creswell's clothes, made the white labour policy its own, and attracted Afrikaner workers by appealing to language, blood, and sentiment.

Africans watched developments on the white front with forebodings. The Rev. Mahabane traced the history and effects of racial discrimination in his presidential address at the annual convention of the Cape ANC in May 1920. All white party leaders, he said, from Abraham Fischer to Smuts, were determined to keep Africans and Coloured out of the parliament of white plutocrats. Yet Africans were the rightful owners of the land, and would never consent to the status of bondsmen. The whites were foreign fortune-seekers, who had seized supreme political power with Britain's aid, and used it to entrench themselves in the state, church, civil service and economy. They had renounced the Christian doctrine of universal brotherhood for the creed of 'God our Father, the White Man our Brother, the Blackman an Outcast'. The colour bar divided the two sections of the population into hostile camps, contaminated the country's moral life, and, unless checked, would end in civil strife.[23]

Mahabane, Makgatho and Rubusana were ministers of religion who combined politics with their profession. They belonged to the same social class as the Afrikaner ministers, teachers and lawyers who inspired and guided Afrikaner nationalism. Their race alone barred them from the centres of power. By rejecting white domination in terms of liberal and Christian doctrine, they were no less radical than socialists who rejected capitalist domination in Marxist terms; but they looked for relief to an electoral system in which their influence was at most marginal. Rubusana and Abdurahman contested provincial council seats in September 1920. Rubusana lost Tembuland by 200 votes; Abdurahman won Woodstock against H. A. Evans, the Labour party candidate, by 500 votes. This was the limit to which Africans and Coloured could go in their bid for direct representation.

Since parliament was closed to them, they fell back on well-tried methods of petition and deputation. Rubusana and A. K. Soga led a deputation of Transkeian councillors and chiefs to Smuts in August 1920 over the Native Affairs Act of that year. This established a native affairs commission; provided for a system of local councils in the reserves; and authorized the administration to convene conferences of chiefs, councillors and 'prominent Natives' with a view 'to the ascertainment of the sentiments of the Native population'. Smuts, who piloted the bill through parliament, said 'we must convince the Native that we are taking the right step and are setting up the proper institutions in which his legitimate desires and aspirations can be satisfied'.[24] His bill was a shoddy device to side-track the African demand for the right to sit in parliament. The ANC denounced the measure, and when it had been passed, demanded that the commission should include at least one African. Rubusana's deputation asked Smuts to delete the colour bar from the constitution and to include an African on the commission. He replied that whites were not in a mood for the one, and time was not ripe for the other.

The time was never ripe for Africans to sit on even so futile a body as the commission. Its impotence was shockingly revealed in May 1921 when it failed to avert bloodshed at Bulhoek location near Queenstown in the eastern Cape. The Israelites, a messianic sabbatarian sect, whose ritual included baptism by total immersion at midnight, the kiss of peace, and an annual passover, had made their headquarters in the location at Ntabalanga – the Mountain of the Rising Sun. They had broken away from their parent body, the Church of God and Saints of Christ, founded in America by the Negro bishop Cowdry; but retained its title and tenet – 'God grant that we may all agree to love without respect to race, colour or condition.' The members of the church gathered in April of every year at Ntabalanga on land belonging to their prophet and leader Enoch Mgijima. They erected a tabernacle and dwellings, some on the commonage because the surveyed lots were on marshy ground and unhealthy in wet weather.[25] A small religious community of 1,000 men, women and children settled in the village, living peacefully and awaiting their redeemer. They committed no crime, apart from breaking a minor by-law by refusing to demolish huts built on crown land.

The Israelites took their religion seriously, interpreted the Bible literally, and alarmed white farmers, townsmen and officials by shutting themselves up in a world of their own and refusing to work for a wage. The white public agitated for their removal. The ISL gave warning in December 1920 that capitalism was planning 'a wholesale bloody slaughter' of the Israelites, probably because of the scarcity of farm workers. The time was near when the black-and-tan would be mobilized against white workers as well.[26] The native affairs commission visited Bulhoek in April and reported that the Israelites were a law-abiding religious community and not a political movement. Many of them were religious fanatics who had disposed of all their worldly goods for the common cause and were penniless. Any attempt to remove them by force would be resisted. The government should therefore take no immediate action, other than to offer financial assistance and accommodation on crown land for the members who agreed to disperse.[27]

The government chose to disperse them by violence instead. Members of the church were summoned to give evidence in a case in which two white men were charged with culpable homicide arising from the killing of two Africans. The witnesses refused to attend court, and the police sent a mobile column of nearly 1,000 men to Queenstown. The native affairs commission, which included two well-known liberals, Dr C. T. Loram and Adv. A. W. Roberts, visited Bulhoek again, met with unyielding defiance from Mgijima and his men, and advised the government to arrest the witnesses and remove the Israelites by force. Colonel Theodore Truter, the police commissioner, led six squadrons, a machine-gun and an artillery detachment, to Ntabalanga in the early morning of Empire Day, 24 May. Presented with an ultimatum, the prophet replied that 'the time of Jehovah has now arrived'. The Lord had informed him in a vision that war would begin in 1914 'and from thence there shall be no peace on earth. . . . The whole world is going to sink in the blood. I am not the cause of it, but God is going to cause it.'[28]

If this was so, the police were God's agents. While women and children prayed in the tabernacle, their men advanced, carrying sticks, assegais and crude swords beaten out of cartwheel bands. The police, who outnumbered the Israelites by two to one, held their fire until the men were only a few yards away. The slaughter took ten minutes, and claimed 190 lives. All those killed and wounded were shot in the front. Many were horribly mutilated with abdominal wounds and shattered limbs, torn by machine-gun fire. No cry of pain or appeal for mercy came from the wounded and dying. Many who could crept away to hide in the rough and hilly country around. The Israelite women scoured the veld after nightfall to bring in their men. One woman, a former teacher, carried twelve, one at a time, on a wheelbarrow from the outer darkness. The white press said that the advance 'into the jaws of death' could hardly be called bravery: 'it was pure fanaticism'.[29] Smuts told parliament that the 'incident' would teach every part of the population 'that the law of the land will be carried out in the last resort as fearlessly against black as against white'.[30]

Colonel Truter said that the police had fired in self-defence. No action was taken against them. Enoch Mgijima and his two brothers were sentenced to six years' imprisonment; thirty other Israelites, to three years; and seventy, to eighteen months each. Professor D. D. T. Jabavu told Fort Hare students that the government had shown as much patience and forebearance as could be expected; *Imvo* accused Nationalist and Labour party agents of causing unrest among Africans for personal and political gain.[31] The African National Congress, in contrast, protested that the law which had been so brutally 'vindicated with such terrible effusion of blood' was no more than a minor local by-law. It doubted whether equally drastic action would be taken against whites in similar circumstances; and complained that Smuts had turned down an offer from the ANC executive to mediate with the Israelites. Africans wished to live in peace, but 'if you hit the dog without ceasing it will in the end turn and bite you'. Congress condemned the police pogrom and the failure to respect religious beliefs; adjourned in honour of the martyred dead; and demonstrated through Bloemfontein's township behind a band playing the Dead March.[32]

F. S. Malan, the acting prime minister, agreed that the public wanted an inquiry. Merriman denied 'undue violence' by the police, and regretted that the 'Africa for the Africans' movement had not been stamped out years ago. 'Any time in Cape Town pure Bolshevik propaganda could be heard being taught in District Six.' Why did they drag these people in? asked Waterston: the socialists had never preached that Africans should arm themselves to kill the whites.[33] The government side-tracked the demand for an inquiry by briefing the native affairs commission to report on 'disturbing influences' among Africans, their churches, and the Israelites in particular.

Five years later, when nearly all whites had forgotten the massacre, the commission gave a précis of the court proceedings without comment, and advised that there was no need for legislation to combat the ANC, Bantu Union, ICU and ICWU.

Religious and political organizations would continue to multiply. To prevent their becoming dangerous, government should adopt a permanent native policy and proper system of native administration.[34]

Down in Cape Town members of the United Communist party distributed a pamphlet headed 'MURDER! MURDER! MURDER! THE BULHOEK MASSACRE. Christians Slaughter Their Christian Brethren. Great Empire Day Celebration.' Wilfrid Harrison, the party secretary, and William Dryburgh, then in his eighties, were prosecuted for issuing the leaflet, and were sentenced under a *placaat** of 1754 forbidding the publication of offensive, rebellious and libellous lampoons. The Appeal Court held that the statute was no longer in force and quashed the convictions; but W. Dryburgh, his son David, a well-known tailor in Adderley Street, and the hairdresser H. Green were fined on a separate charge of criminal slander for having called Truter, the police commissioner, a 'brutal assassin'.[35] The Bulhoek massacre and the prosecutions made a deep impact on left-wing groups in the Cape and accelerated the movement towards unity.[36]

The ISL's annual conference in January 1920 had appealed for unity on the basis of the Communist International's twenty-one conditions of membership.[37] These had been drafted, initially by Lenin, in expectation of approaching civil wars in Europe and the collapse of the Second International. To avoid its errors and prepare for the coming struggle, the Third International would be a single, integrated world organization rather than a loose confederation of independent national parties. The immediate need was to precipitate a breach between socialists and communists; and to stimulate the formation of revolutionary parties characterized by the bolshevik attributes of 'democratic centralism' and 'iron discipline'. Every party affiliated to the Comintern must adopt the title The Communist Party of ... (Section of the Communist International), and abide by the CI's decisions. The twenty-one points set out the duties and functions of the affiliates. They were to purge themselves of

* Proclamation or ordinance.

reformists, combine illegal with legal work if necessary, agitate in the army and among the rural proletariat, win the support of trade unions, and defend the Soviet Union. Every communist party in an imperialist state was expected to give practical aid to colonial liberation movements and to demand independence for the colonial peoples.

This was a tall order for the League's three or four hundred members. The management committee remarked in December 1920 that much of the CI's thesis applied to a revolutionary situation, which was still far off in South Africa. Indeed, it might well be 'the last country in the world to adopt Communism'. Their chief task was to educate, agitate and organize, rather than to speculate idly about the techniques of revolution or the form of a proletarian dictatorship. An illegal movement, for instance, was impracticable, being 'too easily betrayed and corrupted by police spies', and also undesirable, since the campaign for the elementary rights of combination, strike action and free speech should not appear as a conspiracy. Then, too, propaganda among the troops, though necessary, was very difficult, because of their brutalized attitude to black and until recently also to white workers. As for changing their name, the socialists could call themselves the Communist Party of South Africa (Section of the Third International), even though a faction in Johannesburg and Cape Town had 'jumped' the title earlier in the year. Alternatively, the name Socialist Party would do. If they failed to attract many new elements and were substantially the ISL over again, they might as well retain their old name for the sake of its local associations.[38]

The most warmly debated issue was the instruction to unite all militant socialists. They should not strive to unite for the mere sake of uniting, wrote Bunting, or repeat ideas of Russian bolsheviks that did not apply to South Africa.[39] Lenin had advised British communists to seek affiliation to the Labour party. This could not be done in South Africa, first because the Labour party's constitution excluded any such affiliation, and secondly because Africans might turn against socialists who supported that party. In spite of such objections and the six years' feud between them, leaders of the League and Labour party had met in November 1919 to discuss the possibilities of cooperation. They agreed only that the gulf between them could not be bridged.[40] The League's management committee reported to the annual conference in January that the Labour party would not merit their support unless it purged its ranks of '"patriots" and "social-traitors", of centrists and mere reformists, of opportunists, career-seekers, political adventurers, turncoats, and rogues'. A new 'socialist' party might become the stronger, and should continue the ISL's function, which was to show up the Labour party, oppose it at elections, goad it and scold it until it had mended its ways.[41]

Unity on the left seemed almost as remote as unity with the Labour party. Harry Norrie and A. L. Clark of the SDP in Durban rejected the twenty-one points, allegedly because they required an illegal organization and disruptive work in trade unions. 'It smells of Russia in pre-war days.'[42] The Johannesburg Jewish Socialist Society (Paolei Zion) wished to retain its identity and applied on its own to the CI for affiliation.[43] The Industrial Socialist League in Cape Town made a similar application in January 1920.

To add to the confusion, Dunbar's Industrial Socialist League in Johannesburg joined with other dissidents to form the Communist League. This in turn merged in September with the Industrial Socialist League of Cape Town into the Communist Party of South Africa.[44] Its constitution affirmed the principle of mass action and no participation in parliamentary elections. The party undertook to organize workers irrespective of colour, craft or sex in communist groups and soviets to obtain control of production, seize political power, and defend their conquests by force. Every means would be used to 'remove existing prejudices between white, coloured and native workers and to bring them together in the struggle for Communism'.

This was strong meat for some members. A. Z. Berman resigned as editor of the *Bolshevik*, the party's official organ. Manuel Lopes, the secretary of the Industrial Socialist League and now of the CPSA, took his place. Representatives of the CPSA, SDF and Constitutional Socialist League[45] held a series of meetings early in 1921 to discuss unity. The driving force came largely from E. J. Brown, an old member of the International Socialist League, who had been deported from the Belgian Congo in July 1920 for having formed a white trade union which agitated against the employment of Africans as engine drivers. Lopes was persuaded into accepting the CI's thesis on the need for parliamentary action. Even if it was wrong, he said, the whole world supported it, and South African socialists must fall into step. But the CPSA and CSL split on this issue and on the principle of the dictatorship of the proletariat.[46] Finally, only the SDF would accept the twenty-one points. It established the United Communist Party of South Africa in March 1921 with individuals from the other organizations. There followed the formation of a Young Communist League in Cape Town and, on the suggestion of its secretary, S. A. Rochlin, of a YCL in Johannesburg in May 1921. Dunbar's section of the CPSA in Johannesburg adhered to the anti-parliamentary line and refused to merge in the United Communist Party.

The ISL refused to tolerate any 'whining for "local autonomy of branches"' or other attempts to water down the principle of a strictly disciplined and centralized party. 'Better remain disunited' than admit centrists, anarchists and other improper elements. As to parliamentary elections, they were not really important in South Africa, where three-fifths of the population were disfranchised. In any event, the ISL belonged to the CI and was bound by its decisions. It would have to approve of the new party's programme and constitution. A united party that jibbed at this requirement would not be worth forming.

Did the principle of unity apply also to the national liberation movement? There had been a difference of opinion on the issue in the Comintern's second congress of July 1920. Manabendra Roy, the Indian delegate, urged congress to reject 'bourgeois democratic nationalism' and give its full backing to revolutionary mass organizations under communist leadership. Lenin, who drafted the theses on the 'national and colonial question', took the broader view; but went some way to meeting Roy's objection by substituting the words 'national revolutionary' for 'bourgeois democratic'. The resolution as finally adopted declared that the CI's policy 'must be to bring into being a close alliance of all national and colonial liberation movements with Soviet Russia'. The form of the alliance would depend on the stage of development reached by the communist movement or by the revolutionary liberation movement in the colony or dependent territory. All communist parties were under an obligation to support by deed and word the revolutionary liberation movements in these countries.[47] South Africa's socialists accepted the theses. Their traditional policies and sympathies coincided more closely with Roy's attitude to middle-class nationalism.

There could be no doubt as to the nature of Afrikaner nationalism. Bourgeois to the core, it was neither democratic nor revolutionary. Even the Labour party's right wing, which flirted from time to time with Hertzog's followers, recognized their role. 'Nurtured in racio-clerical Toryism, and built upon a caste foundation, they have already proved a priceless political and economic asset to the higher command of high finance.' For their 'orgies of tearing, raging claptrap and bitter racial venom' diverted attention from economic troubles.[48] The radical socialists agreed that Afrikaner nationalism was antagonistic; and blundered by failing to distinguish between the nationalisms of an oppressor and the oppressed. Sectarianism and inadequate insights held them back from adopting Lenin's flexible approach. African nationalism, as they saw it, was a competitor, if not an enemy, and never an ally in the class struggle.

The ISL acknowledged that nationalism might for the moment be the most powerful available weapon against the social order; but it did not pursue this promising line of thought.[49] The management committee put forward instead an unmodified class analysis, as in Bunting's statement on 'The ISL and the Coloured and Native Worker' which he presented to the annual conference on 2 January 1921.[50] South Africa, he wrote, was a 'unique case' of ruling and subject races jostling together; 'an epitome of what happens on a world scale'.[51] Just as the colonies impinged on workers in Europe and competed with them, so did the African compete with white workers in South Africa. Exploitation, the loss of land, and industrialism had diversified the subject races. While allowance should be made for the differences, the message of socialism to the African must be the same as to workers everywhere. Tribal peasants and farm labourers would be 'passive beneficiaries' of socialism rather than its creators. African industrial workers, however, had a definite part to play in the revolution. They would supply, if not the theory, then the bulk of the numerical strength, courage and spirit of the revolutionary labour movement.

Socialists should support the peasants' struggle against landowners, the Native Land Act, pass laws, and for the franchise. This followed from the Comintern's approval of national liberation movements. Yet 'nationalist native organizations' in South Africa, according to the League, were instruments of the ruling class – safety valves, like the S.A. Federation of Trades. African leaders were 'less concerned with the emancipation of their fellows from wage slavery than with an unproletarian ambition to rise in the social scale; leaning also for support on the capitalist-fed power and wealth of the chiefs'. The ideal of 'Africa for Africans' was reactionary in South Africa, for here the whites had come to stay. The crucial issue was how to bring about unity between white and African workers. Capitalism prevented unity. The white workers would sink to the black man's standards unless they raised him to their own through combined struggle. By excluding the African, the labour movement doomed itself to failure and to betrayal of socialist principles. By conniving at the policy of repression, it rendered inevitable what socialism alone could prevent: a race war between white and black.

The 100 delegates who attended the January 1921 conference included representatives of the League's branches, the Paolei Zion, CPSA, Indian trade unions, and individual members of the SALP, SAIF and African unions. It was, the League claimed, the largest and most representative gathering of socialists yet held in South Africa. They decided, by forty votes to twenty-nine, that a 'Communist Party can at no time identify itself with any nationalist or other bourgeois party, and cannot support its platform'. And further, they determined, there could be no unity with persons who refused to accept the principles of the Third International. Unity would be worthwhile only if it took the form of a strongly disciplined, centralized party affiliated to the CI. A committee was set up to call a unity conference, which met in Johannesburg on Easter Sunday. Five socialist organizations sent representatives, among them Norrie from Durban and Harrison from Cape Town.[52] The chair was taken by Colin Wade, the Benoni dentist.

The conference adopted without dissent the CI's twenty-one conditions of membership, but held that article 3, relating to illegal work, did not apply to South Africa. Socialists who objected to parliamentary elections were urged to set their differences aside. The issue was unimportant, since the centre of political gravity lay outside parliament. The SDF, CP and Jewish Socialist Society in Cape Town had already joined forces in anticipation of a wider unity. Durban's Marxian Club and local ISL branch now also agreed to merge. Norrie and the SDP, however, insisted that the twenty-one points were generally unacceptable. The League replied that communist policy, being based on the 'immutable laws of human progress', would attract the best of the working class. South African communists, acting in unison with the millions who were flocking to the banners of the International in Europe, would 'bring the capitalist system, already tottering, crashing to destruction'.[53]

Nine delegates from the Rand[54] and five from Cape Town[55] met on 30 July 1921 in a 'humble upper room' in Plein Street, Cape Town, under the chairmanship of David Dryburgh, one of the four men standing trial at about this time on charges arising out of their protest against the Bulhoek massacre. The conference set up the Communist Party of South Africa (Section of the Communist International), adopted a constitution, elected an executive and vested the ISL's printing press and newspaper in the new party. With its headquarters in Johannesburg, Tyler in the chair, Bunting as treasurer and Andrews the secretary-editor, it was virtually a continuation of the League. All the delegates and members of the executive were whites.[56] Only whites spoke at the public meeting of 2,000, more than half of whom were Coloured and Africans, in the city hall on the 29th. The party's first manifesto appealed mainly to the white working man. The communists seemed as isolated from the masses as they had been in 1915. But they left no doubt about their determination to break through the racial barrier.

Their prospects were rated highly by the police commissioner in his annual report for 1921–2. South Africa, he wrote, was 'a suitable breeding-ground for the growth of the Bolshevik germ'. Cleavages between Afrikaner and English, black and white, worker and employer, and the effects of the post-war depression tended to stimulate teachings that 'anticipate the time when all will share everything equally'. The communists fostered socialist ideals, abused the authorities in vilest terms, proclaimed Lenin as the real saviour, extolled the Israelites at Bulhoek as the first South African bolsheviks, and promised a bloody revolution to exterminate capitalists, parsons, lawyers and politicians. The leaders included Englishmen, Dutchmen, Scotsmen, Irishmen and a high proportion of Russians, whose presence must be regarded with misgiving. Commercial travellers, hawkers and low-class store-keepers spread the propaganda and tainted the native population. The communists aimed to destroy parliamentary government and institute communes. This 'visionary vista of accelerated progress culminating in equality of blacks and whites' naturally appealed to the native races, who had no share in government. Repressive legislation and counter-propaganda were needed to combat this insidious doctrine and instil respect for law and order.

The party anticipated such reactions. Its manifesto predicted an offensive by the government 'as the propaganda is seen to be working among the submissive *helot races whose enlightenment and organization the ruling class dreads above all*'. The communists would demonstrate as best they could that the adherence of 'cheap docile labour' to the working-class movement was the most deadly blow that South Africa could deal to world capitalism. Their main duty was 'to establish the widest and closest possible contact with workers of *all ranks and races*! The industrial masses would provide the 'storm troops' of the approaching revolution. All workers should go forward to the overthrow of capitalism and the establishment of a commonwealth without classes, where all men as fellow workers would receive 'the comfort and culture, the honour and the power'.[57] The appeal went out to the entire working class; and ignored the large body of African, Coloured and Indian leaders who aspired to national liberation rather than working-class power.

It was reasonable to suppose that South Africans would live together in amity only after the white group had lost its mono-poly of power. But who would bring about the change? Ivon Jones, writing from Moscow, where he and Sam Barlin attended the CI's third congress, gave the answer that seemed self-evident to communists at the time. Like many after him, he found that the colour of his skin, which gave him entry into the racial elite, was something of a handicap among radicals abroad. 'Why aren't you black?' he was asked. He confessed to feeling 'quite apologetic about our colour'. South African delegations should include Africans, but it would be a mistake to exclude whites. 'The African revolution will be led by white workers.' Yet his own analysis might have led him to doubt the proposition. He claimed that an increasing minority of white workers had learned since 1913 to put their hopes of emancipation in solidarity with the African. Yet the 'general tendency' was towards collabora-tion with the masters, who had realized their need to humour the white workers as a protection against the native masses.[58]

Jones, wasting away from tuberculosis, had left South Africa in November 1920, never to return. The *International* paid him a great tribute on his departure. His 'insight kept the party clear on revolutionary policy and tactics', avoiding freakishness, right reformism and leftism. Reviewing his ten years of strenuous political work in South Africa, Jones wrote: 'if I have lived rapidly I have LIVED, for it is the Socialist movement that brought the zest into life for me.'[59] Born at Aberystwyth, Wales, in 1883, he was orphaned at an early age, contracted tuberculosis, and left for New Zealand to recover 'by roughing it rabbit catching'. He settled in the Transvaal in 1909, worked as a clerk for the Victoria Falls power company, and came out on strike, the only office worker to do so, in 1913. Employed as a book-keeper by the miners' union under Tom Mathews, he 'found out too much', according to Andrews, and was given notice. In 1914 he was elected general secretary of the Labour party and a member of the Transvaal provincial council. He resigned from the party with other War-on-Warites in September 1915 and became the first secretary-editor of the ISL, retaining the post with interludes of ill-health until he left for Russia. 'A selfless man,' wrote Andrews, and an 'incorrigible optimist', Jones had no ulterior motives: 'all he wanted was to build the movement'.[60]

He drafted a 10,000 word report on *Communism in South Africa* for the CI while he was at Nice on his way to Moscow.[61] There he sat on Comintern committees and prepared documents as a specialist on colonial rule and nationalism. The report summarized his views and the ISL's policies before he became enmeshed in the CI's official apparatus. The divisive effects of Afrikaner nationalism, British chauvinism and white racialism, he pointed out, inhibited the growth of a strong socialist movement. The Labour party's only policy for Africans was 'the wholly utopian proposal of segregation of black from white in strictly delimited areas'. In South Africa '"class-conscious" meant white class-conscious'; and consciousness of class in white workers was 'fitful and easily lost'. Liberally paid out of the African's miserable underpaid labour, they lorded it over him and developed an increasing resistance to communist ideas.

Africans were passing through a period of acute social change from primitive communism, which persisted in the segregated reserves. These were in fact no more than 'cheap breeding grounds for black labour'. Peasants came to town to earn bride wealth, pay taxes, acquire schooling, learn the use of machinery, or to escape from tribal life. They had to contend with pass laws, starvation wages, slums and the denial of civic rights. Yet, in spite of his oppression, 'the Bantu is a happy proletarian'. Aided by the ISL and the IWA, he was awakening to the consciousness of class. His strikes revealed a capacity for industrial action as a more certain means of deliverance than tribal assegais.

What factors were favourable to revolution? Jones gleaned comfort from the sharp rise in the number of Afrikaner workers. They soon became good trade unionists and loyal agitators for their class within the limits of their colour. The industrial system was gradually weaning them from the most violent forms of prejudice. Africans, too, were forming class organizations which would 'soon dominate or displace' the Native Congress.

Congress itself was a small, loose coterie of chiefs, lawyers, clergymen and other educated persons who agitated for civic equality and political rights while fearing the mass movement of their people. The government patronized Congress and subsidized its press by advertisements, but was dubious about its latent revolutionary character. For the African's national interests could not be distinguished from his class interests. They formed the basis of a 'revolutionary nationalist movement in the fullest meaning of Lenin's term'.

The prospects were favourable. At the moment, however, the communist party depended almost entirely on a few advanced spirits drawn from the thin upper level of labour aristocracy. Africans, according to Jones, were unable to supply any active militants owing to their heavy social disabilities and political backwardness. The communists were absorbed in white trade unionism, which threw the more difficult task of native emancipation into the background. The African workers' movement was therefore being neglected. It required a special department with linguists and newspapers, the large funds for which were not available. The few militants who had shouldered the heavy burden for more than five years needed reinforcements. Like Crawford ten years earlier, Jones looked for aid to the international working class. 'A few missionaries, revolutionists who need a spell of sunshine, would be very welcome.'

Jones anticipated that the fall in gold prices – the source of the 'bribe fund' – would precipitate the crisis of 1922. The mine owners had cancelled the stop order agreement of 1916 in retaliation for an outbreak of unofficial strikes. This was a sure sign that the unofficial garrison of white workers against the larger mass of Africans had become too costly. The industry could save its profits only by raising the black standard and depressing the white, 'making towards a homogeneous working class'. Jones underestimated the capacity and willingness of the ruling class to keep the white workers in a privileged position, and exaggerated the corrosive effects of industrialism on their national and racial prejudices. The chief error in his analysis was to minimize the role of African nationalism. If the educated elite could not emancipate themselves without a mass struggle, as Jones argued, they were bound to make a great contribution in the 'national revolutionary movement'. He disregarded the justice and significance of their demand for political equality, and generally failed to appreciate fully the mood of low-paid workers in town and country as reflected in the spread of the ICU.

Transvaal farmers were then combining to put down strikes on farms, expel 'native agitators', and prevent African lawyers from defending farm workers in court. The ICWU held its annual conference at Cape Town in July 1921, with a view to bringing about unity with Kadalie's ICU. Conference agreed to make 16 December – the 'Dingaan's Day' of Afrikaner nationalism – a day of national mourning for the martyrs of Port Elizabeth and Bulhoek. Selby Msimang in his presidential address told the delegates that they had to contend with two desperate forces: the government, whose greed matched Shylock's, and the white trade unions. Africans and Coloured could extend the hand of friendship or reciprocate the insolence, and in either event must be organized.[62] Kadalie boycotted the conference, and told Msimang that their organizations should maintain separate existences behind provincial barriers. Msimang replied that the split injured the workers' interests and offered to hand his branches over to Kadalie. He agreed, Msimang withdrew, and the ICWU merged into the ICU later in the year.[63]

The ICU's conference, which was held at Port Elizabeth in October, undertook to campaign against the pass laws, organize farm workers and miners, and press for the direct representation of Africans and Coloured at the international labour conference in Geneva. The ICU, and not Mr and Mrs Archie Crawford, could speak for the genuine workers of South Africa.[64] James La Guma, the delegate from the ICU branch at Luderitz, proposed and conference agreed to inquire into the grievances of people in South West Africa. La Guma took over the secretaryship of the branch in Port Elizabeth and was transferred two or three years later to Cape Town as administrative and later general secretary, while Kadalie held the post of national secretary. Born at Bloemfontein in 1894 of French and Malagasy stock, La Guma went to work at the age of eight in Cape Town, took part in working-class demonstrations in 1906, and migrated to South West Africa, where he worked on diamond diggings near Luderitz during the war, and became one of the first Coloured radicals to abandon the concepts of Cape liberalism for Marxist theory and class struggle.[65]

Many Africans were also beginning to think in radical terms, said Davidson Don Tengo Jabavu in July 1920 at a missionary conference in Durban.[66] Born in 1885, educated at Lovedale, and refused entry to Dale College, a school for whites at King William's Town, he had completed his education in England, where he matriculated, qualified as a teacher at Birmingham university, and obtained the B.A. degree of London university. Returning to South Africa in 1914, he joined the staff of the S.A. Native College at Fort Hare and helped his brother Alexander to edit *Imvo* after their father's death in 1921. Professor Jabavu, as he was generally known, listed the people's grievances: high prices and low wages; drought and crop failure; taxation without representation; the Native Land Act; pass and other segregation laws; discrimination in schools, law courts, public services, post offices and trains. It was a well-worn catalogue of old complaints; but, warned Jabavu, leaders of a new type had appeared to arouse Africans against their oppression.

Members of the Native Labour Corps came back from the war with a strong sense of grievance and a determination to unite against the whites. Bolshevism and its nihilistic doctrines enlisted the support of many Africans in the northern provinces. Educated men, who were voteless and landless helots without a future, turned to agitation, stirring up the populace to violent deeds. Their socialism was not the mild variety of a Ramsay MacDonald's. It was heady stuff: atheistic and revolutionary. Fortunately, Jabavu assured the missionaries, a cure could be found. The Young Men's Christian Association, boys' clubs, games and other such social activities would divert activities and provide the desired antidote. This was shallow reasoning, and revealed Jabavu's refusal to face up to the realities of his society. Like many leaders of the ANC, he substituted clichés about Christian ethics, white patronage or British fair play for a precise analysis of social forces.

The African National Congress had plenty of followers but no theory of social change. The communists had plenty of theory but few followers, and tended to blame Congress for their weakness. They accused Congress of being wholly opportunist, of blinding Africans to their working-class status and so staving off their real emancipation.[67] The communists failed to recognize the radical element in the ANC, which gave people a sense of national unity and purpose in their resistance to racial oppression. When Du Bois' second Pan African Congress met at Paris in September 1921, Andrews wrote that it and other racial or nationalist movements were mere ripples on the surface of a great upheaval. Africans and Negroes would yet learn to use the weapons of strikes and boycotts. Selope Thema, Dr Dube and Sol Plaatje, who represented South Africa at the congress, were of the 'usual safe kind'. The communists' role, he said, was to expose the fallacy of racial and national aspirations. The only solution lay in the overthrow of capitalism.[68]

Revolutionary exhortations did not compensate for the failure to organize the lower paid workers. The party's resources were meagre, as Jones had pleaded, yet this was not the only restraining factor. Communists repudiated colour bars and racism; but when the Johannesburg delegates reported on the inaugural conference to their branch, it hesitated to accept Africans who applied for membership and debated the issue at three successive meetings.[69] Africans were urged to form trade unions so as to win the white workers' respect. 'Let them see your organized strength,' advised Bunting, 'so that instead of shooting you down they must recognize you as worthy fellow labourers in the common cause.' It was the ICU, however, and not the Communist party, that recruited Africans and Coloured into a trade union in the early twenties. Besides being submerged in white unions and reluctant to offend them, the communists were sceptical about the possibility of turning the peasant worker, whom they called 'submissive, docile and backward', into a revolutionary. Their main function, they said, was to direct the militancy of white workers against the capitalist system, and to transform the race war into a class war.

Racial groups fought one another for jobs as unemployment

spread. Mary Fitzgerald, now Mrs Archie Crawford, the heroine of the 'pickhandle brigade' of 1911, led another charge in July 1921, but not against the 'boss class'. Her target was the Coloured proletariat. She and members of her Women's Industrial League stormed the premises of the French Club in Johannesburg, chased the Coloured waiters out, and forced the management to hire white girls in their place. While the Johannesburg town council under Labour pressure refused to issue motor drivers' licences to Coloured, the railway administration substituted whites at twice the wage for Coloured gangers. When Dr Abdurahman led an A P O deputation to protest against this treatment, the general manager of the railways, Sir William Hoy, undertook to dismiss 800 Africans and employ Coloured men in their place. The Coloured ex-servicemen in the League of Comrades agitated for jobs held by Africans in all government and municipal services. That, protested Abdurahman, was no less detestable than the selfishness of white ex-soldiers who had shortly before demanded the dismissal of Coloured workers to make room for white Comrades. 'Who is to be sacked to make room for the native ex-soldier?'[70]

Whites and Coloured competed also in politics. The Communist party fought its first election in Cape Town's ward 7, where Harrison stood for the municipal council against Abdurahman in September 1921. The A P O reacted by attacking Harrison, communism and the Soviet Union. What man in his senses, it asked, would subscribe to communism 'in our society'? Abdurahman scored an easy victory, but the Labour party candidates, Dr Forsyth and Charlie Pearce, won parliamentary by-elections in the Gardens and Liesbeek against S A P candidates who were backed by the A P O. It attributed this defeat to African and Coloured resentment of the Bulhoek massacre; and challenged the Labour party to delete from its constitution the clauses relating to 'kaffir farming' and 'segregation'.

Alfred Palmer, editor of the *South African Review*, 'a paper which never has a kind word about Coloureds or Natives',[71] won the provincial council seat in Liesbeek for the Labour party in November 1921. This was a bitter blow to the A P O, whose candidate, Matthew Fredericks, was a foundation member and its general secretary. His long and distinguished service to the community received poor recognition at the polls. He obtained only 400 votes in a constituency which had 1,100 Coloured and African electors. Most of them abstained or voted for Palmer and the Nationalist party candidate. It was humiliating, complained the A P O, to see Africans voting for white candidates who belonged to 'two violent anti-Native political parties'.[72]

Capitalism and white domination, according to the communists, rested on the four pillars of racialism, nationalism, jingoism and reformism. White workers joined with their masters in keeping the black worker subject, and were themselves divided into warring camps. British workmen wearing war medals paraded behind the Union Jack when on strike and voted for the financiers and industrialists in the S A P-Unionist coalition; Afrikaner workers joined trade unions and voted for Hertzog's Nationalist party. Coloured voters preferred Abdurahman to Harrison; Africans followed the A N C rather than the C P. Communist faith in the eventual triumph of class consciousness over false ideologies never wavered, however. These were momentary aberrations, symptoms of a vanishing order. Industrialization would free Africans and Afrikaners from their rural backwardness. Capitalism would reduce white workers to the African's standard and force them to recognize their class interests. Inter-racial solidarity would grow out of the class struggle. Armed with this theory, the communists anticipated and welcomed the great upheaval of 1922. They believed that it was the start of a revolution which would unseat the ruling class and usher in the ideal commonwealth.

13 The Rand Revolt

The mining of gold involved many hazards. A large number of men died from injuries, silicosis or kindred diseases; many more were maimed. Of the eighteen men who formed the miners' strike committee of 1907, thirteen died from phthisis and one from a mining accident before the war. The four survivors, including Tom Mathews the union's general secretary, suffered from the disease. The work underground was rough and hard. It attracted a corresponding type of white worker. Miners in the early days tended to live recklessly and extravagantly on a high rate of pay. They earned ten times as much as the African miner, who did all the labouring work under their supervision, though he often knew more than his supervisor. White miner and African worked closely together within narrow confines underground, and lived poles apart upon the surface.

The miners' union was the oldest and usually the most militant union in the Transvaal. Loosely organized and with a fluctuating membership, it was often heavily in debt.[1] Three generations of miners passed through its ranks. First came the men from Cornwall and the north of England; then a variety of nationals from Europe; and finally Afrikaners, who constituted seventy-five per cent of the miners by the mid-twenties. The socialists thought it a triumph when Afrikaner miners on the Simmer Deep struck work in 1919 against the dismissal of Krichker, a German miner, at the instance of patriotic members of The Comrades of the Great War. This was a 'truly amazing' demonstration of international working solidarity, said the ISL. Afrikaners had become 'for the first time the motive force of the movement'. They were 'learning the meaning of Industrial Democracy and the power of Labour, and the Red Flag'.[2]

The miners, if class conscious, were also colour conscious.

Left militants, like the union's general secretary Tom Mathews and his successor J. Forrester Brown, were sympathetic to the organization of Africans in the industry. The general body of members insisted on a strict colour bar. When the SAIF agreed in 1921 that its affiliates should enjoy the right to admit Coloured members, E. S. Hendrikz, the acting secretary of the miners' union, said that it had instructed him to withdraw its representatives from any conference attended by Coloured delegates.[3] The union steadfastly opposed the entry of Coloured and Africans in what it claimed to be the white worker's preserves. Mine owners and government were fully aware of this attitude. Sir Evelyn Wallers, the Chamber of Mines president, told the Moffat commission in 1918 that any attempt to substitute Africans for whites in mining work would cause a strike which would have the backing of the great bulk of white people on the Rand.[4] Smuts admitted to an APO deputation in July 1921 that the industrial colour bar had become more pronounced since Union, particularly on the railways. The government feared that any attempt to do away with it in the mining industry would precipitate an upheaval on the Rand. F. S. Malan, the minister of mines, added that the colour bar in the mining regulations was probably *ultra vires*. He, too, predicted that its elimination would involve an industrial upheaval.[5]

The mine owners nonetheless maintained a steady pressure for some relaxation of the colour bar. It was, they declared, unjustifiable on both moral and economic grounds. Africans had awakened to a sense of its injustice. They demanded responsible work consistent with their ability, experience and education. The economic reasons were dictated by the fall in gold prices from the maximum of 127s. 4d. a fine ounce in February 1920 to 97s. 7d. in December 1921. This was fifteen per cent more than the price in December 1914; but production costs had risen since then by forty-four per cent. Three mines had closed down, and twenty-one were working at a loss or at a profit of less than 2s. a ton milled before July 1919, when the buyers began to pay a premium on the 'standard' price of 85s. a fine ounce. The owners contended that these twenty-one mines would also have to be closed if the price reverted to the standard figure, unless costs were correspondingly reduced. The argument was driven home at one conference after another between the Chamber and the miners' union. The union, though prepared to consider economies in the organization of underground work, emphatically rejected any proposal to modify the colour bar.

Crawford, negotiating for the AEU, conceded in February 1921 that many mines were in a precarious condition. He proposed a wage cut of five per cent from October to prevent unemployment, provided that the owners granted an immediate rise of five per cent for three months to save the union's face. Though it had no objection, the Chamber doubted if 'responsible craftsmen' would agree. The engineers had previously voted in favour of a strike for a forty-four hour working week and a wage increase. They now agreed by a three to one majority to accept the Chamber's counter-proposal of a reduction in wages at the end of the year. Crawford was severely criticized, and the AEU broke away from his industrial federation.[6]

At the time of the engineers' dispute in February, men on twenty-three mines came out in sympathy with a strike on the Consolidated Langlaagte mine against an obnoxious shift boss. When a ballot was taken, 4,743 miners voted for the strike and 2,820 against. Their union's executive refused to sanction the strike, since the required two-thirds majority had not approved, and ordered the men back to work. A disciplinary committee appointed by the executive punished twenty-seven of the leaders. Hendrikz was fined £60. Ernie Shaw, the general treasurer, Percy Fisher, D. Taylor and J. L. Mare were each fined £50 and barred from holding office in the union for three years. H. Spendiff, J. Wordingham, W. Richardson, A. McDermid, K. J. van Coller and others were barred from office for one to five years or punished in other ways. Crawford explained that the union had taken this severe action so as to forestall punitive measures by the Chamber, which nevertheless served notice that it would cease to collect subscriptions on the union's behalf.[7]

Some of the men penalized took a prominent part in the strike of 1922. The martial law commission which inquired into the strike found that Shaw, Fisher and Wordingham were communists, but the party acknowledged only Shaw as a member.[8] A former member of the SDF, he was an industrial unionist who preferred direct action to parliamentary elections. Fisher, on the other hand, had refused to join the miners' union in 1917 until forced to do so by the management in terms of the closed shop agreement.[9] The two men led an unofficial and successful strike on the City Deep mine in November 1920 over a breach of the eight-hour working day rule. Shaw stood for election to the secretaryship of the SAIF in January following,[10] and polled 3,254 votes against Andrews' 2,309 and Crawford's 6,899. Fisher was elected secretary of the SAMWU in the same month but the executive annulled the election because of alleged irregularities. He lost the new election by a narrow margin. These struggles in the union and against Crawford's leadership strengthened Andrews in his efforts to promote a rank-and-file movement.

A right-wing faction of Hertzog's followers made an unsuccessful bid to organize a separate *mynwerkersbond*. Militants on the left, now isolated from the official leadership, also contemplated a breakaway union. The communists held that this was contrary to the Comintern's policy. Article 9 of the twenty-one points instructed them to carry on systematic work through party cells in the existing unions, which should not be antagonized, but won over to the communist cause. The militants thereupon set up a Miners' Council of Action. Fisher made the announcement at a meeting in the Johannesburg town hall on 24 July 1921. The council reported in November that it was gaining ground, and recommended the formation of a new body to coordinate the activities of militants in all trade unions. This step was taken in January 1922, when the left trade unionists met in the Trades Hall to inaugurate a Johannesburg section of the Red International of Labour Unions, with E. J. Brown as its secretary. The struggle had reached a critical stage, they declared. The working-class forces should be consolidated in a revolutionary trade union organization.[11]

'Be with the workers WHEREVER THEY ARE' – in struggle, victory or defeat, appealed the communists. 'Success has bred defeat,' said Bunting, referring to Labour's setback in the parliamentary elections; 'defeat may breed success.' When workers had been 'really oppressed, really whipped, not to say shot down', the unions would acquire a fighting spirit destined to blow the Chamber into air. 'Let it be a fight between the workers and the shirkers,' declared the ISL in March 1921. 'Forward to the assault on the citadel of capitalism.' If the Chamber took up the challenge, the fight would turn into a revolutionary struggle for the control of industry. The alternative before white working men was to be driven with the African into helotry or to advance with him to freedom.[12]

The African miner's wage had risen by only nine per cent since 1913, and the white miner's by more than fifty per cent. 'Clearly,' argued the Chamber, 'the reduction of the excessive cost of European labour is the line along which the mines are bound to look for relief.'[13] The owners opened the attack in November by giving notice of their intention to modify the 'status quo agreement' of 1918, do away with the contract system, and reorganize underground work. The only point on which owners and miners agreed was to change work patterns in such a way as to extract more labour from Africans. Leaving the compounds from 4 a.m. onwards and returning between 2 and 6 p.m., they usually spent twelve hours or more underground without food. The number of hours spent in actual work depended on the white ganger, who was required by regulations personally to inspect every working place before mining operations could commence. Miners and owners held conferences in November under Smuts's chairmanship to discuss the Chamber's proposal. The effect of their decision was to reduce the number of supervisors and add at least an hour to the time worked by African drillers in every shift.[14]

Africans were neither present at the conference nor consulted. They themselves were chiefly to blame, remarked the *International*, since they had failed to form trade unions on the Rand, where the 'bourgeois' National Congress held the field.[15] Disregarding statements to the contrary by spokesmen of Congress, the ICU and the African miners, the writer claimed that they had no desire to do skilled work. All they wanted was more pay for the work they did. The white unions were admittedly confused and mistaken in opposing the African's advance, and would obtain his backing if only they helped him to demand higher wages and better treatment. At the same time, they were 'perfectly justified in fighting to keep up the numbers and pay of holders of blasting certificates'. This unqualified approval for the oldest and most significant colour bar on the mines revealed the decision of the communists to back the white worker against the Chamber in all circumstances.

They condemned the unions, now a chief prop of capitalism, for assisting the owners to exploit Africans more intensively. Circumstances would yet force African and white miners to recognize their identity of interests, wrote the editor of the *International*.[16] Though the day for this might seem far distant, when it came it would put an end to capitalist exploitation. The changes in underground work schedules would lead to the substitution of 'cheap native labour' for the more costly white, and pave the way for a general attack on wages and working conditions.

The abolition of the colour bar, according to this hypothesis, would benefit the owners and also lay the basis for workers' unity by depriving the white worker of his privileged status. This being so, it might seem that the proper course for radicals was to back the owners on grounds of both expediency and principle. For, Jones had argued in 1919, the owners represented the forces of progress, precisely because they clamoured for 'cheap labour'.

There was, however, an opposing tactical principle. It prescribed support for workers engaged in struggle, right or wrong. The men who defended the colour bar might be Luddites, but they formed the vanguard of revolution. The communists held in effect that a strike to maintain the colour bar was reactionary in form and progressive in content. Their theory led them to suppose that the white worker would develop a class consciousness during the struggle.

A closer analysis might have persuaded them that his interests and those of the African were incompatible, or contradictory in the Marxist sense. The social basis of class consciousness was smaller in white workers than the communists supposed.

White miners were both contractors and wage earners, exploiters as well as exploited.

Shaft sinkers and developers were the direct descendants of the contractor who in early days on the goldfields had developed, stoped or trammed* for a fixed price per unit of work done. He bought his tools and stores from the company; recruited, housed and fed his African helpers. The system had given rise to a partnership between skilled immigrant miners from Cornwall or elsewhere and white South Africans, usually Afrikaners, who hired and supervised the gang of African helpers. In later years the companies took over responsibility for recruiting and paying the African, partly to stop crimping and to peg his wages at a figure acceptable to all owners. The principle of relating the white miner's earnings to the amount of work extracted from his gang persisted.[17] He was paid both a minimum daily wage for stoping and developing and an amount determined by the area of ground broken or excavated. As an official of the Krugersdorp branch of the miners' union explained, his earnings depended on 'the efficiency per boy per fathom per day'.[18] The harder the African worked, the greater was the ganger's income.

Africans were paid a flat rate of 1s. 6d. a shift for shovelling, 1s. 8d. for tramming and 1s. 9d. or 2s. for drilling. A driller who completed more than two hours of shovelling and drilled more than thirty-six inches in the same shift was paid two-thirds of a penny per inch drilled instead of the 2s. He received no pay for the day's work if he failed to complete a specified norm. His shift was then held to be incomplete and did not count against his period of service under contract. The decision lay with the ganger, before he lost his power after the war to issue the 'loafer ticket' that deprived his helper of a day's pay. Mining authorities urged that Africans also should be put on piece work so as to provide an incentive and the opportunity to earn wages related to capacity and experience. White miners wished to retain their right to issue 'loafer tickets'; and never advocated incentive schemes for their helpers. Since the supply of African labour was constantly renewed, a ganger had no material interest

* 'Develop': open a mine by sinking a shaft; 'stope': extract ore from a staircase in the seam; 'tram': load ore into the tram or skip.

in conserving the strength or promoting the well-being of the men under him. He did not regard them as fellow workers. He was their 'baas', and so they addressed him.

The changes proposed in the contract system might reduce the miner's earnings, but not the number of men employed on work reserved for whites by the mining regulations. Any displacement or retrenchment would affect other workers, to whom the 'status quo agreement' applied. It pegged the demarcation of jobs between whites and Africans by stipulating that no member of either racial group would be allowed to encroach on the other's field of employment as defined on 1 September 1918. If the owners had their way, Africans could take the place of whites in twenty-five semi-skilled occupations in which some 4,000 men were employed.[19] The owners said that not more than 2,000 would be retrenched, and then only as a temporary measure pending the return to the former level of profits. When this happened, expansion would follow, bringing with it a rise in the number of employees, including whites. On the other hand, according to the Chamber, retrenchment on an even bigger scale would be unavoidable if the desired economies were not achieved.

Labour leaders were concerned less with the hardships of 2,000 men retrenched out of a working force of 21,000 than with a racial or national ideology. The SAMWU and the SAIF declared that they were fighting 'to protect the White race', or 'to maintain a White standard of living', or 'to preserve a White South Africa'.[20] This was not a question of wages, said Sampson and Creswell, but a 'great national issue' of breaking down or maintaining the colour bar.[21] Nationalist politicians and *predikants* harped on the same theme. 'The Chamber of Mines had declared there should be a black South Africa,' the Rev. Oosthuizen told Brakpan strikers; while dominie Hattingh thought that the souls as well as the bodies of the workers would be murdered if the colour bar were abolished.[22] Though disapproving of strikes generally, said Dr A. M. Moll, the Nationalist party supported the miners' fight against the removal of the colour bar.[23] Tielman Roos was all for a white man's country, and Hertzog claimed that ninety-five per cent of the people were behind the strikers' demand for the colour bar.[24] Wages were never an issue in the strike, declared the legal defence committee formed after the strike. 'The Strike was fought throughout on the question of the Colour Bar, including the Status Quo Agreement.' It was the same vital principle of 'National life and character' as in the Chinese labour dispute or as in the American civil war. Was free European labour to be displaced by Negro slave labour?[25]

The northern states of America made war on the south to liberate the slaves and establish the rule of equality before the law. The strikers of 1922 paralleled the south, and not the north, in their attitude to African rights. 'When Mine Negro labour is free labour it will be time enough to decide what our attitude shall be towards it,' the defence committee explained; 'but that is not the present position or question. We are not even expressing any opinion about the compounded Native Labour system for unskilled work on the Mines, since we have no desire to encroach on it.'[26] The strikers protested against the 'extension of the slave labour system' and not against its existence. In reinforcing the colour bar, they perpetuated the African's economic and social inferiority. White workers, one must conclude, would rather boss indentured Africans than compete with free Africans on an open labour market.

The dispute began on the coal mines. British coal miners had taken a big wage cut after the abortive general strike in 1921. South African colliery owners said that they could not compete on the world market with British coal at its reduced price, and asked their white employees to accept a smaller wage as well. After fruitless negotiations, a deputation from the SAIF met Patrick Duncan, minister of the interior, on 28 December and agreed on arbitration. The owners refused and gave notice of their intention to reduce the standard wage of 30s. a shift by 5s. Engineering firms had previously notified their skilled employees of a wage cut from 1 January; the Victoria Falls and Transvaal Power company rejected a demand for a wage increase; and the mine owners announced that they would replace contract and piece work rates by a daily rate of pay. This amounted to a general assault on living standards, said the trade union leaders, and they made up their minds to resist.

The coal miners decided to strike work on 2 January. A meeting of trade union delegates held on 31 December approved the strike; agreed to ballot miners, engineers and electric power workers; and formed an 'augmented executive' of members of the SAIF and unaffiliated unions. The ballot paper, which was drafted by the augmented executive, urged the workers affected to vote in favour of a strike against four 'ultimatums': the 'refusal of the Coal Owners to arbitrate'; the 'Chamber of Mines' threat to substitute cheap black labour for white'; the refusal of the power company 'to continue to negotiate' for higher wages; and the 'threatened wrecking of agreement and reduction of wages' by engineering firms.[27]

Only the colliery owners could be said to have delivered an ultimatum. Although the other issues were still open to negotiation, of the 24,000 workers concerned nearly 14,000 voted for a strike and 1,336 against. The coal miners came out on 2 January, and the rest on the 10th. Joe Thompson, chairman of the SAIF and the augmented executive, opened negotiations on the same day with the Chamber. The two sides conferred from the 15th to the 27th under the chairmanship of Justice Curlewis, and failed to agree. The Chamber issued a statement on the 28th recognizing 'the utmost importance' of preserving the Rand's white population. To safeguard the whites, the owners offered to guarantee an average ratio of one white worker to 10·5 Africans, as compared with the existing 1 to 8·5 ratio, on producing gold mines for the next two years. The ratio would place a ceiling on retrenchments due to any departures from the status quo. The owners undertook further to respect the statutory colour bar and existing agreements on hours and basic wages. In return, the men would lose their cost of living allowance and two paid holidays, May Day and Dingaan's Day.

The militants attacked the negotiators. 'The side which calls for a truce, especially when the fight is barely begun, confesses defeat,' wrote Andrews, and advised: 'Hit as hard and as quickly as possible.' Harassed by the police, the Council of Action ceased to function as a group soon after the strike began. Therefore, wrote Ernest Shaw[28] in later years, 'all the elaborate "fudge" about the Council of Action being engaged in creating fighting commandos and formulating a "red revolution" is so much "moonshine".' Individual members, acting on their own initiative, worked closely with Andrews and made his office in the Trades Hall, which was also the Communist party's headquarters, the centre of their activities. 'Our opinion,' added Shaw, 'was that the strike would end as it did.' This was also the opinion of Andrews.

Cheap labour, he argued, would drive out dear. The only solution was to narrow the gap between white workers and Africans. This the capitalists tried to do by bringing the whites down in numbers and pay. Their proper answer was to insist on civilized wages for all.[29] In a private letter, which fell into police hands, he confessed that the prospects were unfavourable. The strikers, in his opinion, were fighting for a lost cause. It was impossible to keep Africans out of industrial employment for which they were capable. But white working men would listen to reason only after bitter experience had taught them the futility of colour bars.[30]

The fight was on. The duty of communists was to guide it correctly, instil a revolutionary consciousness in the strikers, and lead them to victory. None of these aims would be attained if the strike degenerated into a race war. The party must therefore stress the common interests of all workers, develop a spirit of inter-racial solidarity, and turn the strike into a crusade against capitalism. 'What to fight for?' asked Bunting, and answered: 'Wages, then, not colour. is the point to strike about and so far as this is a strike to maintain wages, it deserves the whole-hearted support of all Labour, *including the coloured and native workers themselves.*' The supporting arguments were addressed to both groups. Colour bars were 'of course unfair', yet served the interests of all workers 'to the extent' that they helped to keep up higher wages and the number of those drawing on them. The abolition of the colour bar would benefit only a small handful of Africans, and leave the great bulk in the same low-paid position as before. Security for the white man, on the other hand, lay not in retaining the colour bar but in raising the wages of Africans.[31]

The communists never deviated in principle from this line.

Their manifesto of 30 January gladly offered the party's services to the Strike Committee. Its fight, in spite of some questionable slogans, was essentially a fight against capitalist rule. For it was impossible to maintain the 'white standard' or build a 'white South Africa' under capitalism. 'Then away with it!' The means would be found in the utmost solidarity of all workers, irrespective of race or colour, 'as this strike is plainly teaching'.[32]

If that was the lesson, it made no impact on the strikers. They ignored the appeal for solidarity and continued to fight under the banner 'For a White South Africa'. In the event, communists also participated in the strike on terms dictated by the workers' 'deficient class consciousness'.[33]

Even Jones, observing events from the Comintern's headquarters in Moscow, found some merit in the colour bar. He conceded that it put the white labour movement in the false position of resisting 'the undeniable justice of the capitalist plea for native advancement'. Yet, he claimed, the barrier provided 'the best possible condition for cooperation of white with black'. Their functions were complementary. They got on 'very happily together at the place of work'. The white workers would honestly like to do justice, without 'social contamination', to Africans. The attack on the colour bar threatened to put an end to this idyllic state. Competition, he warned, would lead to the introduction of the ugly forms of race hatred prevalent in America.[34]

Hertzog argued in the same strain that whites would never do justice to the African until they had lost their fears by taking away his vote. But no Marxist should have entertained the notion that absolute white power would guarantee justice and fair play. No patriot would buy harmony and solidarity at the price of his people's subservience.

Abdurahman, for one, did not share the communists' illusions. His petition to parliament, issued during the strike, urged the removal of the colour bar for the sake of even-handed justice, peace, harmony, goodwill and respect among all sections. Africans, Coloured and Indians in all provinces should be given the right to vote and to stand for parliament.[35] Abdurahman poured scorn on the white miners. Sheltered behind the colour bar, he said, they lived on the labour of the black man, scabbed when he struck work, and forced him to put up with the miserable wage of 2s. a day. Twenty thousand white men on the mines drew wages amounting to £10½ million a year. Ten times that number of African miners received only £6½ million. The whites were parasites, bloodsuckers and drones. They had exploited the 'White South Africa' policy to such good effect that they now filled the position of mere overseers. As experience on the coal mines had shown, Africans could manage well enough without the supervision of the white parasites.[36]

The communists viewed with gloom the continued flow of coal from the collieries. Six hundred white miners sat idly on the surface while 20,000 Africans kept up production with the aid of a handful of officials. One mine claimed record outputs; the others were scarcely affected. Andrews complained that the colour bar had disappeared from the coalfields. 'It is probably too late to rectify this grave blunder now, and it is extremely likely that the ratio of whites to blacks in the coal mines has permanently been lowered.' The moral, he added, was that all men, black or white, official or wage earner, who worked during a strike were scabs. The African had never been asked to help. Given any little encouragement by recognizing his rights to better conditions, he would strike solidly. This is what the capitalists feared.[37] So, it seemed, did the strikers. They made no effort to enlist the African's backing, yet wanted him to wait idly until the strike was over. When the Chamber announced that it had sent 28,000 men back to the reserves, Benoni strikers called on the government to nationalize the mines in view of the threat to close them by repatriating Africans.[38]

Signs of a decline in morale appeared at an early stage. The Germiston strike committee stirred turbulence on 1 February by calling for a settlement and asking Smuts to intervene. Creswell pleaded for a 'reasoned adjustment and compromise'. Crawford, back from Geneva, claimed that the augmented executive, being unconstitutional, had no authority to call a strike. The communists complained of having been excluded from the 'guiding councils in the fight', and rejected any compromise. War to the knife was the only method.[39] The strikers' leaders tended to look for a political solution. Hendrikz, the miners' secretary, told demonstrators in Johannesburg on 21 January to vote for Hertzog or Creswell and not for Smuts. The augmented executive accused Smuts of backing the owners and invited negotiations with the Nationalist party. A meeting held in Johannesburg on the 29th urged workers to substitute a government pledged to support the white race. Labour and Nationalist party spokesmen appeared on the same platform in Pretoria on the 30th. Two Labour party members of parliament, Sampson and Madeley, were deputed with two Nationalists, Tielman Roos and Pretorius, to ask the governor-general to summon parliament to meet in the Transvaal. He refused.[40]

Tielman Roos, the Nationalist party leader in the Transvaal, used the occasion to gain a foothold in the labour movement and conduct a campaign against the government. He issued a pamphlet accusing Smuts of having conspired with the Chamber of Mines to make war on the workers, and advised them to settle the dispute at the next elections. Speaking at Fordsburg on 3 February, he suggested that the state should take over the mines. Only a government sympathetic to the whole of South Africa, and not to the Chamber alone, he added, could be expected to take this step. Two days later a big meeting of strikers adopted a resolution moved by Waterston, a Labour M.P. and leader of the Brakpan commando, calling on Nationalists to join with Labour in proclaiming a republic outside the empire. A delegation, which included Shaw and Fisher of the Council of Action, put the proposal before Nationalist and Labour leaders at Pretoria, and met with no encouragement. They rejected 'the treasonable proposal', commented the martial law inquiry commission.[41]

Abdurahman reacted strongly against what he thought was an unholy alliance between Labour and Nationalists – those 'antediluvian obstructionists' encrusted with 'narrow prejudice and hoary out-of-date love of serfdom'. White workers had little, the Coloured and African far less, to hope for from the Nationalist party. It was out to exploit a national disaster for party political ends.[42] Bunting also warned against Nationalist influences. The 'white South Africa slogan had become the strikers' chief motif.'

It supplied the steam and ginger, even to the extent of bringing the strike to a 'revolutionary situation'. But it was a two-edged cry. In the mouths of the farmers' champions, it meant only 'cheap and servile black labour'. Indeed, it came close to a demand for the 'black labour country' that capitalism had made of South Africa. Communism alone, he argued, could make it a 'white man's country' in the sense of securing to all the full product of their labour.[43]

The attempt by the communists to infuse a radical content into a racial slogan followed from their unqualified support for the strike. They even justified the legend 'Workers of the World, Fight and Unite for a White South Africa.' It appeared on a red banner carried on 7 February at the head of the Fordsburg commando on its daily march with cycle outriders, advance guard and band playing the 'Red Flag'.[44] 'On the face of it,' explained Bunting, 'such a motto is a grotesque travesty of the words and meaning of Marx, but the matter must not be dismissed so hastily.' Cynicism at this muddled thinking would get them nowhere. The cry to maintain the colour bar was really a fight for civilized standards. It brought into the struggle sections of the population that would not normally be on the side of a strike for wages. In spite of appearances, there was no hostility among the strikers against African workers as such, though they loomed as a frightening spectre behind the strike. What was important was that town and country had united for the first time against Big Business. The rest would follow. The workers would yet learn that the true remedy lay not in colour bars but in solidarity against the capitalist class.[45]

The leaders of the strike were more reactionary than Bunting would acknowledge. They feared a repetition of 1914, when Smuts had rushed the commandos to the Rand. To obviate the danger, and cement the alliance between 'town and country', they tried to neutralize the farmers by hoisting the race and colour flag. A pamphlet went out from the miners' union before the strike began, with an appeal to Afrikaners to stand aside rather than assist the government to defeat the strike. In the event of a defeat, 'the Kafir in future will take up the place of the white man, and then we are doomed to national annihilation'. The quotation, and much more to the same effect, came from the Nationalist party press, which never hesitated to inflame race prejudice. As 'the Kafir' got higher wages and social status, the public were told, 'many white girls, embarrassed by the removal of the colour bar, will enter into marriage with Coloured people – a danger against which the Afrikaner is always fighting'. There was no need for farmers to come to the Rand to defend it against an African rising. Hendrikz, the union secretary, gave the assurance that the miners would be able to cope with it on their own.[46]

The strike, Smuts told Africans in a special message, was no concern of theirs. 'Stay quietly in your compounds, obey orders, and you will be protected.' Any act of disobedience or disorder, he threatened, would be put down at once and by force. With this spectre before them, the strike committee agreed with the police on 10 January to help in keeping order so long as this did not encourage scabs. The police expressly encouraged the strikers to form commandos so as to have an auxiliary corps of disciplined men on hand if Africans revolted.[47] When the Putfontein commando on the East Rand raided a police station for rifles, the police took no immediate action other than to obtain their return. The commandos exercised, drilled and paraded under the direction of ex-soldiers, but their elected commandants were nearly always Afrikaner nationalists. The SAIF endorsed the decision to raise commandos to protect the interests of white workers and 'fundamentally establish this country as a white man's country'.[48] The communists also approved, for another reason. Bunting hailed the commandos as 'Red Guards of the Rand'; and praised them for enrolling in the Red Army under the Red Flag, 'which alone can ennoble war and bloodshed'.[49]

The militants urged the commandos to seize arms, commandeer food and prepare for the fight that would surely follow the anticipated proclamation of martial law. 'The issue has got to be won by force and violence,' Fisher told a meeting in Johannesburg on 4 February. Mine owners, strike leaders and Smuts began discussions on the same day and nearly reached an agreement after three days of negotiations. The Chamber repeated its offer to observe a ratio of one white to 10·5 Africans, and made a new concession. The status quo would continue on all mines except the low grade ones until such time as government and parliament had considered the findings of an impartial board. Smuts undertook to appoint the board and give effect to its findings if they proved fair and workable. The men agreed to call off the strike provided that the 'status quo agreement' remained in force on all mines pending a final settlement based on the findings, which should adequately protect the white workers' position in the industry. No agreement was reached, other than an indefinite undertaking to meet again if 'new light was thrown on the situation'. This proved to be a turning point. Relations deteriorated from then on until the strike reached the climax of an armed battle.

Thompson and Crawford issued a circular on the 7th reaffirming the SAIF's endorsement of the commandos and instructing strike committees to use them against scabs. Fisher, Shaw, Spendiff, Wordingham and McDermid, all members of the Council of Action, were arrested on charges of incitement to public violence and taken into custody on the 8th. A large meeting held in Johannesburg on the same day demanded their release and called for a general strike. The augmented executive turned the proposal down, to the great indignation of the communists. They denounced the executive's lack of courage, ideas and initiative; and attacked the leaders for negotiating with the Chamber. Their proposals amounted to 'a considerable climb down for the men', and showed 'a distinct weakening on the question of the status quo agreement'.[50] The criticism was illogical, coming from militants who maintained throughout that the strike had been called to keep up wage standards, and not to enforce the colour bar. At this stage, however, they had turned their backs on any negotiated settlement, even if it introduced a measure of flexibility that would open fields of responsible work to Africans on the mines.

As on the war issue, the communists took up a position wholly opposed to that of Africans and Coloured. The status quo, said the *A.P.O.*, deprived them of any opportunity to rise above the unskilled level. If the colour bar were removed, they would be employed according to their ability, skill and degree of education. No Coloured man in his senses would place his trust in the white Labour movement and its ally, Afrikaner Nationalism. Selby Msimang argued that the white worker demanded both a monopoly of certain trades and the exclusive right to a high rate of wages. His object was 'to put the iron heel on the neck of both mine-owner and Native'.[51] If the line was drawn as clearly as this between the two groups of protagonists, Smuts's own position was more ambiguous.

His next move placed him squarely on the side of the owners, though he continued to insist that his role was 'to form a ring for the two parties to fight it out'.[52] He told a deputation of Nationalist and Labour party leaders on the 8th that the government could not force the Chamber to settle the dispute on the strikers' terms. On the 11th he urged the men to resume work on the Chamber's terms, and promised police protection to those who complied. As the leader of a party that represented mine owners, industrialists and bankers, Smuts had to protect their interests against the pressure of the opposition, which represented landowner and white workers. Both backed the strike on the ground that it formed part of a struggle to defend the colour bar and a white South Africa.[53] Like the communists, Smuts denied that this was the issue. Unlike them, he contended that the dispute centred round the future of the mining industry.[54] While agreeing with the Chamber that the colour bar obstructed the growth of efficient and profitable enterprise, he never accepted the view that racial discrimination was unjust to Africans and Coloured. He never departed a hair's breadth from the basic postulate of white South Africans that it was their inherent and eternal destiny to dominate persons of colour.[55]

As minister of mines in 1912, Smuts had been responsible for inserting, without parliament's mandate, colour bars in the mining regulations. As leader of the opposition in 1925, he defended his action by claiming that he had done no more than perpetuate an old republican tradition.[56] At heart he might well have sympathized with the miners' fight for white supremacy. Party politics and his involvement with the mine owners and financial interests prevented him from proclaiming his sympa-

thies in public. Unable to repudiate the concept of a white South
Africa, he took refuge in silence, evasions and finally explosive
violence. The Nationalist party demanded on 1 March an inquiry
into the shooting of three strikers by policemen at Boksburg.
Smuts rejected the motion with the historic words: 'let things
develop'. As they developed to their violent and bloody end,
he abandoned even the pretence of dealing with the merits of
the dispute, and relied wholly on the 'law and order' phrase to
defend his policy.

His statement of the 11th, calling on strikers to resume work
and owners to restart the mines, provoked a sharp reaction. 'We
accept General Smuts's challenge,' proclaimed the augmented
executive, 'and we recommend all men on Strike to stand fast.'
Tensions mounted as the prospects of a settlement receded. The
first clashes between whites and Africans took place at Fordsburg on the 13th. Forty Africans were arrested. The police
began the arrests of pickets on the 14th, and took Andrews into
custody on the next day for incitement to violence. Bunting
suggested that the government was set on removing prominent
opponents of 'Crawfordism'. Although the police denied reports
of 'anti-white outbreaks', Bunting accused the ruling class, the
administration and Abdurahman of fostering anti-trade unionism among Africans. A strikers' meeting passed resolutions
demanding 'a white standard of living for the workers' and 'a
country fit for white men and women to live in'. These events
gave the cue for yet another effort in the *International* to equate
the class struggle with colour bars.

Bunting thought that even Abdurahman, though apparently
a tool of the owners, ought to want a 'white standard' for blacks
also. The strikers admittedly still believed in 'keeping the kaffir
in his place'. Yet unconsciously, even unwillingly, they were
fighting his battles, too. Communists disagreed with the platform cry that the aim of the strike was to prevent him from rising
to the white man's level. They supported the strike for opposite
reasons. Its true purpose, they said, was to put the African on a
civilized standard as against the Chamber's objective of putting
the white man on 'kraal' standards. Defence of the colour bar
meant defending wage rates, and this merited the support also

of Africans. Ideally, the struggle should be for equal wages, but it could not be postponed until the rate for the job had been secured. The immediate, partial demand for the retention of colour bars was consistent with the movement's long-range aims. The removal of the colour bar would put money into the owner's pockets and not in the African's. His leaders who agitated against it, said the *International*, were 'simply playing the game of the capitalist'. They were his 'tools, dupes, or snobs'. Their agitation was neither spontaneous nor proletarian. They did not benefit their people by fighting the white unions. Each section of the working class was weakened by fighting the other section.[57]

While they probed the striker's mind for signs of a true proletarian instinct, the communists could hardly ignore the dilemma of their own reasoning. The penalty of defeat, they said, would be large-scale victimization and the eventual elimination of the white worker. On the other hand, if he returned to work on his own terms, his privileged position would be entrenched at the African's expense. This would be a pyrrhic victory for the cause of inter-racial solidarity. The communists looked for a solution in their revolutionary vision. Capitalism, they argued, offered no hope for white or black. It degraded by causing enmity between them. Equality could be realized only after the revolution, 'when for the first time it will lose its sting'. The central task of all workers, irrespective of colour, was to destroy the whole capitalist class, irrespective of colour. They could unite on this platform. If they were to split again on the rock-bottom issue of labour exploitation, let them face it when the question arose.

The communists hoped that struggle would purify and revolution redeem the strikers' bitter racialism. Sworn opponents, they exulted, now called one another brother and comrade. 'Labour, right, centre and left, socialist, communist, nationalist, sane trade unionist and syndicalist, Sons of England, Sinn Feiner, comrades of the great war, and war-on-warites, all may be seen mixed up.'[58] It was a united front of communists and those to the right of them. No African or Coloured appeared on the platform. They could not expect to gain from a movement so constituted, in which they had no part and the avowed aim of which was to keep them in their place. 'Nothing can make our position worse,' lamented the *A.P.O.*,[59] 'except the placing in power of men of the Labour stamp.' Just that, and not revolution, was to come out of the strike. As C. F. Glass, secretary of the Communist party's Cape Town branch, pointed out at the time, the white workers were too backward, their trade unions too weak, and the party's forces too insignificant to make a revolution.[60] Without this redeeming element, the strike ran its reactionary course.

The commandos beat up men who trickled back to work. The managements armed mine guards and strike breakers. A proclamation issued on 22 February banned commando strike pickets. Andrews and the five Council of Action members were released on bail on the same day. This was a terrible blunder, thought C. J. McCann, the general secretary of the SALP at the time. When he heard of their arrest he said, 'Thank God, I hope they will have sufficient sense to keep them there.'[61] Ivan Walker, the secretary of the strike legal defence committee in 1922 and of the labour department from 1932 to 1946, came to a similar conclusion. The government, he insinuated in later years, allowed these 'so-called "prominent exponents of violent methods"' to re-enter the struggle so that their activities might provide evidence of a 'Red Terror' or 'Revolution'.[62] The Council of Action accused Crawford of having 'framed' them.[63] He retorted that they were 'professed extremists and direct actionists' – the same charge levelled against him when deported by Smuts in 1914.

The long-standing feud of the militants with Crawford might well have hardened them against any compromise likely to re-establish his authority. Re-elected secretary of the SAIF in January, he was isolated from the augmented executive, the strike committee and the delegates who negotiated with the Chamber. Andrews and his associates had condemned 'Crawfordism' – the settlement of disputes by negotiation and compromise – since he became secretary of the SAIF in 1915. The strike gave them an opportunity to vindicate their own policy of direct action. Andrews wrote on the 25th to a correspondent in Australia that there was 'a revolutionary undercurrent in the situation'. The commandos constituted a 'military formation', largely 'Dutch', well disciplined, and if armed 'it is sub rosa'. Loose and unofficial ties between the Labour and Nationalist parties could develop into an alliance for 'complete autonomy and independence for South Africa'. The commando leaders held secret meetings towards the end of February, discussed plans for a general rising, and resolved to declare a republic.[64]

The strength of the government's armed force on the Rand, including the police, mounted riflemen, special constables and civil guards, was raised by 4,500 to 7,000 men before 10 March. The police attacked the Putfontein commando on 27 February, wounding some and arresting others. Members of the commando serenaded the prisoners by singing the 'Red Flag' outside Boksburg jail. The police fired without good cause and killed three demonstrators. A two-mile long funeral procession and big meetings along the Reef condemned the killing. The strike committee distributed leaflets urging the public to keep calm and avoid violence. 'More and more clearly the class war emerges,' wrote Andrews.[65] He pointed out that white workers, who had previously applauded and even taken part in the brutal repression of Africans, were now being hoist with their own petard. White supremacy was not the issue, he insisted. The strike had taught the lesson of labour solidarity and would be won conclusively if all workers joined. 'The time is past for any truce with the enemy excepting for the purpose of getting breathing space.' Organize the African, he appealed; extend the fight, spread the strike, force the Chamber off its pedestal and compel the government, for its own safety, to offer reasonable terms of settlement.

The augmented executive also wanted a settlement. Writing on its behalf, Crawford suggested a round table conference on 4 March with the Chamber to discuss 'possible terms upon which the strike might be declared off'. But the owners were no longer interested in negotiations. Emboldened by Smuts's wholehearted backing and the success of their attempts to restart the mines, they planned to discredit the miners' unions and detach them from the industrial federation. The Chamber replied in provocative terms that the proposed conference would be futile. 'Further, the Chamber will not in future recognize the South African Industrial Federation for any purpose.' Whatever might have been its status in the past 'under different control', it no longer represented the bulk of employees in the industry. The owners saw no reason why they should discuss their business 'with representatives of slaughtermen and tramwaymen'. The Chamber would assist the workers 'to get rid of the dangerous junta which has brought them to the present pass'.[66]

This calculated arrogance exasperated the men and jolted the augmented executive into deciding to hold a second ballot. Andrews, it seems, regarded the decision as 'cowardly and humiliating', and intervened to frustrate the last attempt to arrive at a negotiated settlement.[67] He and other militants did not believe that the strike could succeed, but they were determined to break Crawford's influence and fan the flames of revolution. Andrews, Shaw, Fisher, Spendiff, Wordingham and George Mason had previously – and probably in the Fort – formed themselves into an unofficial Committee of Action. All were 'persons who advocated the prosecution of the strike with greater determination and who worked unceasingly to encourage and assist the men'.[68] They decided on the night of the 4th to take over the leadership, stop the ballot, and call a general strike. On Sunday the 5th they addressed big meetings along the Reef, 'urged the workers to demand a general strike', and advised the commando leaders (who by then were called 'generals') to bring their troops to the Trades Hall on Monday morning.[69]

Thousands of men surrounded the building, where the augmented executive was in session, and remained there all day. The Committee of Action catered for them with 'an unceasing torrent of oratory' and food 'organized on the spot' so as 'not to allow the Commandos to disperse', observed Andrews. Virtually imprisoned and either inspired or intimidated by this show of strength, the executive declared an immediate general strike and abdicated. The leadership passed into the hands of the committee: 'the implacable enemies of capitalism' who would fight at all times to bring about its downfall.[70] Even they could not, however, persuade railwaymen, printers, factory and other workers to join in the strike. It met with less response on the Rand than the general strike of 1914, and was virtually ignored in the rest of the country.

The call for a general strike was more of a gesture than a serious attempt to retrieve a desperate situation. That the appeal would fail was evident in January, when the SAIF urged unions in all towns to prepare for a general strike. The unions in Cape Town, politically the most advanced centre after Johannesburg, took no heed, and ignored requests from the local Communist party branch to demonstrate their support. They refused to send speakers to a party meeting on 1 February, 'as the struggle in the north was purely a question of the colour bar'. A. Z. Berman, Green and Glass took the line that the strike had been called to defend living standards and not the colour bar; but Abdurahman received the backing of Coloured in the audience when he heckled the speakers. The Cape Federation of Labour unions held a special meeting on 11 March to consider the letter from Johannesburg asking them to take part in the general strike. The Coloured delegates reported that there was much resentment among workers at the treatment meted out to them in the Transvaal and at the unprovoked attacks by strikers on Africans. The meeting agreed to arrange for a demonstration outside parliament, but cried off even this display of solidarity when the government refused to meet a deputation.[71]

The strikers fought on with no effective aid from the trade union, Labour and Nationalist leaders who had edged them into battle. Frustrated men, inflamed by weeks of violent propaganda and martial exercises, vented their fears and resentments on Africans and scabs – on Africans especially. Unprovoked attacks on them were reported from many parts of the Rand on the 7th, the day of the general strike. The communists blamed provocateurs and distributed a leaflet headed 'LEAVE THE KAFFIR ALONE. WHITE WORKERS, HANDS OFF THE BLACK WORKERS!' The strike committee issued a notice prepared by the police. It asserted that 'bodies of strikers are attacking Natives wantonly and without any reason or cause'. The committee instructed strikers to cease the attacks, which provoked Africans to disorder and antagonized the general public. The

Transvaal executive of the African National Congress asked the government to proclaim martial law or to supply Africans with arms for self-defence. The APO executive urged Smuts on the 9th to protect inoffensive Coloured and Africans against 'cowardly murders' by armed bands of strikers. An ICU meeting held at Cape Town on the 12th condemned the strikers because they murdered 'our poor innocent brothers and sisters'; and demanded that 'full justice' be meted out to the guilty men.[72]

The Committee of Action urged the commandos to set up a unified command to stop 'the native trouble that had broken out'.[73] Fisher chaired a meeting of commando 'generals' in the Trades Hall to discuss 'the unrest among the natives'.[74] But the generals refused to take orders from the committee or even inform it of their plans. They turned Andrews out of the Communist party offices and held a meeting on their own. 'Racial and traditional feelings had not simply disappeared, in spite of the common struggle.'[75] The generals wanted a republic and were prepared to fight for it with guerrilla warfare. The committee dissociated itself from these aims and issued a statement denying any intention to set up a rival government, or of allowing 'our industrial strike to pass out of our hands'.[76] Communists and trade union militants lost control of the commandos. They became an independent force but without a central command of their own. The struggle developed into a series of isolated skirmishes and last-ditch stands as police and troops moved in for the kill.

Smuts declared martial law on the 10th for the fourth time in ten years, rushed to the Rand and took charge of the troops. They rounded up 1,500 strikers at the show grounds and made them prisoners. Andrews, Shaw, Mason and others, though warned of an imminent raid, were trapped in the party office. The police took them and the entire strike committee to the Fort, where they remained for the rest of the strike. Bunting joined them two days later. The *International* and the *Transvaal Post*, a Nationalist newspaper, were banned. Strikers began the attack by raiding police stations for arms. Police and troops retaliated along the Rand with air support, bombs, artillery, machine guns and tanks, driving the commandos from their strongholds at Benoni, Boksburg, Brixton and Langlaagte. Fisher and Spendiff made a last stand with their commando on the 14th at Fordsburg. Heavy artillery rained shells on them and forced their surrender. Fisher and Spendiff died, either at their own hands as the police alleged, or killed by the troops after the surrender.[77] The augmented executive formally announced the end of the strike on the 16th.

Smuts returned to a hero's welcome in parliament and asked for an act of indemnity. The strike cost between 230 and 250 lives, compared with the 113 South Africans killed in the German South West campaign and the 190 Africans killed at Bulhoek. The strike defence committee found that at least 214 were killed in the five days' fighting, of whom 78 were strikers, 76 members of the government forces, and 62 'ordinary' residents. Some 30 Africans were killed by strikers or hooligans.[78] Of 4,758 persons arrested, 953 appeared before the courts, 46 on charges of murder; of these last, 18 were sentenced to death and 4 were hanged. Sixty-seven were convicted of treason or sedition and fined or sentenced to imprisonment for periods ranging from 10 years to 14 days. All those still serving sentences were released under the Strike Condonation Act of 1922 on or before 17 May 1924, immediately prior to the general election.

Andrews, Shaw, Mason and Wordingham, the surviving members of the Committee of Action, were acquitted on charges of public violence. Bunting and seven other communists were released without having been charged. The *International*, resuming publication on 26 May 1922, printed a 'roll of honour' of party members who had felt 'the weight of the iron heel in the period of White Terror'. The only ones sentenced to imprisonment were Brown, Chapman, Glazer and Goldman. They served seven, six or four months for carrying arms or breaking martial law regulations. The press published lurid accounts of 'a foul conspiracy which seized on the strike as a means to Bolshevism'.[79] Yet not a single Communist party member stood trial on a charge of treason.

The execution of H. K. Hull, D. Lewis, S. A. Long and C. C. Stassen for murders committed during the strike increased the resentment raging against Smuts. The Labour and Nationalist parties said that his refusal to reprieve Stassen, convicted of killing two Africans, was a sop to Africans and Coloured. The execution of Taffy Long in particular caused bitter resentment. A leader of the Fordsburg commando, he was said to have served on a firing party that shot an alleged police spy. Hull, Lewis and Long went to the gallows on 17 November singing the 'Red Flag'. Their funeral was turned into a great demonstration. While Labour mourned its martyred dead, Clements Kadalie and the ICU expressed their confidence in the government 'for bringing to the scaffold resolutely in accordance with our March resolutions those responsible for the outrageous and cynical murder of our people'.[80]

Abdurahman also condemned white labour's 'bloodiest crimes' on the Rand, and asked how a repetition could be avoided. The lesson to be learnt, he said, was that the government should at once remove control of the industry from dividend-mongering directors and colour-prejudiced white trade unionists. The state must obtain a fuller control of working conditions and a fair share in the output. This implied that the African's wages, opportunities of advancement and living standards should be improved. Any settlement, however satisfactory to the state, capital and white labour, would end in disaster if it did not also recognize the invaluable services he rendered to the country or his legitimate and growing aspirations.[81]

Here was an idea for a radical programme on which communists, militant trade unionists and the national liberation movement might have combined. Its great defect was the assumption that the white man's state would be any more benevolent than employers and white workers towards the African miner. But the proposal had the merit of stressing both his claims and the need to curb white power, greed and privilege.

The March rising, said the communists, was the 'most glorious event in the history of white civilization in South Africa', or, in a more restrained evaluation, 'one of the most glorious episodes in the history of the South African workers'. Its only fault was failure.[82] The party's post-mortem appeared in Bunting's pamphlet *Red Revolt*. He remained an unrepentant defender of the colour bar regulations. 'THEIR REPEAL WILL

297

NOT BENEFIT THE NATIVE WORKER, RATHER THE REVERSE,'
he emphasized; and he rebuked Africans who were 'taught'
to say otherwise. Simple trade unionists, Afrikaner republicans,
white supremacists and a small minority of class-conscious workers had joined hands behind the battle cry for the maintenance
of white standards. Andrews, in a foreword, denied allegations of
a Bolshevik or Nationalist party plot. The rising, he said, had
begun in an ordinary strike against wage cuts, to which the
Chamber had given a political character by attempting to
replace white workers with the cheaper African. The government, alarmed at the workers' solidarity and the backing they
received from farmers and the petty bourgeoisie, had decided to
suppress the movement by force.

The executive committee of the Comintern arrived at a
similar verdict. The mine owners, it said, had turned a struggle
for wages and daily bread into an armed conflict, leading to the
murder of hundreds and the imprisonment of the flower of the
proletariat. Fisher, Spendiff and other brave labour leaders who
had honestly fought for racial equality had been torn by shrap-
nel. The magnates' idea of equality was to reduce the white
worker's living standards to the black man's level. They 'brought
the black wage slaves into the field against the white exploited
workers'.[83]

South African communists could not ignore the accusation
that strikers had taken part in brutal and unprovoked attacks on
Africans. There had been, the party acknowledged, a general
fear of a rising in March. Both sides had been alarmed. Fighting
had taken place between Africans and whites all along the Reef
on the 8th. The violence had been neither provoked nor con-
doned by the leaders. They had gone out of their way to stop it,
and had sent men to warn strikers against turning the struggle
into an anti-native pogrom. The party had distributed leaflets to
this effect. Fisher and others had risked their lives to stop
hooligans, who were more 'police stooges' than strikers, from
attacking Africans.[84]

Even so, none of the men who fought under the banner 'For
a White South Africa' or who shouted 'scab' at Africans could
be held free of blame for the outbreaks of racial violence. The

virus had infected the strike at birth. The communists realized early on that it had degenerated into a struggle for the retention of colour bars, which they condemned in principle. Doubting the success of the strike, they continued to support it, and were then pushed into defending it by alleging that Africans stood to lose rather than to gain from the abolition of the bar. The argument was false and revealed the hollowness of the appeal for inter-racial solidarity. Comradeship could not develop between the beneficiaries and victims of 'baasskap'.

The white miners had made this clear in February 1920, when the executive of the SAMWU instructed its members to scab on African strikers. Communists from Johannesburg to Cape Town denounced the betrayal of class solidarity and warned that Africans would be forced into siding with the owners against the white worker.[85] He ignored the warning and fought only to retain his privileges, never to remove their disabilities. In backing him, the communists put themselves in the position of being identified with white supremacy, in spite of their persistent and vehement rejection of racial discrimination. The party's role in the revolt gave African and Coloured leaders reason to regard communists as the left wing of an exclusively white labour movement. They brought the reproach down on their own heads; and they gave substance to the accusation by failing to repudiate the main article in the banned issue of the *International* of 20 March, the day when its editor, Bill Andrews, was arrested and taken to the Fort with other members of the Committee of Action. The article appeared in Dutch and was addressed to policemen and armed civilians on the government side. 'Are you prepared to serve idiotic capitalists as their stupid underlings and accomplices in suppressing your fellow Afrikaners? It is their intention to replace us and also you with cheap black labourers.'

14 Unity on the Right

The 'kaffir' share market boomed after the strike. Discoveries of new goldfields were announced. The industry, said to have been on the verge of bankruptcy a few months earlier, attracted large amounts of capital. The total dividends paid by the gold mines rose to the record figure of £9,558,000 in 1924. Gold prices continued to fall, and reached the 'danger' point of 85s. an ounce when Britain returned to the gold standard in 1925. Working costs had then fallen by twenty-four per cent, and the wholesale price index by twenty per cent, since 1921. Stores and equipment were cheaper, but the mines effected their biggest economies by substituting the jackhammer drill for the hand drill, and by reorganizing working methods at the expense of African and white employees. The owners exploited their victory by introducing the wage cuts and retrenchments that the men had fought to prevent.

White miners lost their cost of living bonus, supervised a larger number of Africans, and took on a bigger load of responsibility after the strike. The mines employed eight Africans to every white worker in 1918-21 and nearly ten to one in 1923-6. An additional 4,000 white men would have found work on the mines if the old ratio had been maintained. A revision of underground work schedules enabled the management to extract more labour from Africans at the same rates of pay. White miners took over from men declared redundant the supervision of pipe-fitting, tracklaying, rough timbering and pack-building.[1] Changes in the contract system reduced the white miner's average wage by 10s. to 32s. 6d. a shift. Average white incomes on the mines fell by twenty-six per cent, and total wage costs by twenty-four per cent between 1920 and 1923.[2] The strikers' defence committee claimed in its impassioned pre-election report that the owners had reduced wages 'without mercy' and abolished the colour bar. If Smuts won the election, warned the committee, at least 8,000 more whites would be thrown out of employment on the mines alone.[3]

Though the colour bar clauses were not in fact abolished, Justice Krause, who had drafted the mining regulations in 1910, held in November 1923 that they were invalid. The case before him arose out of the prosecution of a mine manager, Hildick-Smith, for employing an African 'Stephen' to drive an electric locomotive. Krause pointed out that some of the colour bars were absolute and applied to machinery in all kinds of undertakings, including mills, potteries and brickfields. In 1910, as chairman of the Mining Regulations Commission, he had held the view 'that wherever the safety of life and limb is concerned only competent White persons should be employed'. In 1923, however, he refused to believe that parliament could ever have contemplated such 'unreasonable and even capricious and arbitrary' restraints on the right to employ competent coloured persons or on their right to be employed. The Mines and Works Act gave no authority to discriminate between racial groups; and the restrictions were repugnant to the common law. 'They deprived the native from enjoying the very fruits of his advancement.' Greater repugnance, said the court, could hardly be imagined.[4]

Krause's judgement confirmed what had been suspected for many years by mine owners and lawyers, and removed the 'unnecessary and artificial restrictions' of which the Chamber had complained during the strike. Qualified Africans and Coloured could now be legally employed in any capacity. Custom, white opinion and trade unions, however, as the Low Grade Mines Commission pointed out, were at least as powerful as any legal restraint.[5] Some 600 white workers lost their jobs through the scrapping of the 'status quo agreement'.[6] The anticipated substitution of Africans for white mechanics, engine drivers and miners did not take place.[7] As the communists had predicted, Africans gained nothing from the defeat of the strike, while the whites continued to be 'Slaves to the Boss but Bosses to the Slaves'.[8] Skilled wages were depressed, commented Abdurahman, without any increase in unskilled wages. It was time, he added, for Africans to organize and resort to passive resistance against 'the demands of the overseas vampires whose interest in our country is governed solely by the desire of big dividends'.[9]

The communists looked to the organization of the working class, including the Africans, for a solution. This was the plain lesson of the 1922 strike, explained Bunting, because Africans 'in increasing measure, are producing the boss's profits, enabling him in increasing measure to flout the white workers'.[10] 'Betrayed, starved and driven to desperation,' wrote Andrews in July 1922, 'those who are necessary to the boss class' had been 'hurled back to work under slave conditions.' The 'more active spirits' were thrown into the bastilles 'to rot and eat out their hearts during long terms of imprisonment'; while the remainder were 'callously and brutally thrown on the streets to starve'.[11] Loyalty to stricken comrades, hatred of Smuts, and a strategic aim dictated the party's priorities.

The Communist International had launched a campaign for a 'proletarian united front'. South African communists interpreted the slogan to mean the unity of white trade unions and opposition parties against the government. Andrews, Shaw and Dunbar appeared on platforms with Labour and Nationalist party leaders, or sat with them on committees to obtain legal defence for prisoners, a reprieve for men sentenced to death, and relief for the victimized. The united front, declared the party, was a defensive measure against unemployment and the persecution of strikers; but its ultimate aim was to replace Smuts with a people's government.[12]

Smuts not only defended the interests of British imperialism, mine owners and Abdurahman's detested 'overseas vampires'; he also articulated the spirit of a budding South African imperialism. While crushing the Rand revolt, he was engaged in attempts to extend the Union's boundaries to the Zambesi. A majority of Rhodesian settlers rejected his invitation to make their territory a fifth province and voted instead for responsible government in a British colony.

The colonial subjects of South West Africa were not given the same right to decide their national destiny. They had innocently

believed that South Africa would restore the freedom and territory taken from them by the Germans. Their new rulers were
only concerned to provide white settlers with land and labour.
The Bondelswart section of the Nama revolted in May against
the threatened deportation of their leader Abram Morris, a
hero in the liberation war of 1906 against German colonial rule.
Police and troops, aided by aeroplanes from Pretoria, bombed
and machine-gunned them into submission. The indomitable
Morris and more than sixty of his men died fighting. His world
'had taken on the cramped lineaments of slavery' under the rule
of white men who knew no rights other than their own, wrote
Freislich, the sympathetic narrator of this Nama epic. Morris could
regain freedom only if he destroyed that world by his death.[13]

An immediate cause of the rising was an increase in the dog
tax from a flat rate of 7s. 6d. an animal to £4 10s. for four on a
sliding scale. This was an iniquitous impost on hunters and
stockbreeders who found dogs indispensable and earned at most
£1 a month when working for a white farmer. It was a labour
tax, suggested Abdurahman. No money had been set aside in
the budget, he pointed out, for schools, agricultural development
or industrial training for the Nama, though £65,000 had been
voted for the education of white children belonging to the
settler community of 10,000. He recalled his warning, given at
the time of the Versailles peace settlement, that the native races
of South West could not hope for justice under Afrikaner rule.
Bloodshed marked the path of South Africa since Union, and
all the Rand's riches or the revenue from a mere dog tax could
not compensate for the loss of human life. German submarine
atrocities were scarcely worse than the bombing of little men,
one in four or five of whom was armed with a rifle. This was
misgovernment, if not murder; and the least one could expect
was that South Africa would be arraigned before the League of
Nations.[14]

No external agency could stop the spate of racialism that
followed the Rand revolt. The communists were wrong in
supposing that defeat would sharpen class consciousness, drive
out national or racial antagonism, and imprint the moral of
working class solidarity. The labour movement looked for allies

not to African fellow workers but to Afrikaner landowners, poor whites and the petty bourgeoisie. British socialists had co-operated early in the century with Afrikaner nationalists to halt the introduction of Chinese and to defeat the Progressives, the party of British supremacy and the Chamber of Mines. Then it was Andrews, as president of the Labour Representative Committee, who had negotiated an agreement with Smuts, as leader of Het Volk. The plot was the same in 1922, though some of the actors had switched their roles. Now it was Smuts who spoke for the Chamber and the British interest; Hertzog, who represented Afrikaner nationalism and a white South Africa; Creswell, who led the labour aristocracy in the fight for colour bars.

The Nationalist and Labour parties entered into an electoral pact. It was 'born in the Fort', wrote J. W. Jarvis,[15] one of the strikers' leaders. The conception took place on the bloodstained streets of Fordsburg, Boksburg and Benoni. 'Smash Smuts' must be the slogan, said Tielman Roos to Arthur Barlow, and they plotted with Sampson and Madeley to split the English vote by detaching the working man from the United-South African party jingoes.[16] Being anti-capitalist, Labour had more in common with the Nationalists than with the SAP, said Dr Malan at the party congress in October 1922. When parliament met in the following January, Creswell seconded Hertzog's motion of no confidence in the government, and the debate strengthened their resolve to form a united front. They announced in April that their parties would work together so as to avoid splitting the anti-government vote. They agreed that the major obstacles to cooperation were the Englishman's fear of an Afrikaner republic and the Afrikaner's fear of a bolshevik seizure of property.[17] Republican and socialist principles would, therefore, be put in cold storage for the pact's duration.

Hertzog gave an assurance that if he took office, no member of his party would vote to break the ties with Britain. The Nationalists, he argued with sophistry, wanted 'independence', which was not the same as 'secession'. Their programme, he pointed out, did not call for a republic; and they were bound by conference resolutions to consult the 'volk' at a general election or referendum before taking steps to secede.[18] Creswell made his contribution to the alliance at the Labour party's annual conference in January 1923. Never a lover of the socialist objective, he moved its deletion from the party programme so as to make it more palatable to Nationalist farmers and Afrikaner *predikants*. He met with unexpected opposition from Madeley and delegates from workers' constituencies in Natal and the Cape.[19] Although Creswell failed to get the necessary two-thirds majority for his motion, conference adopted a compromise amendment that postponed the socialist commonwealth to the distant future of an 'ultimate achievement'. The outcome of these manoeuvres, scoffed Henry Burton, the minister of finance, was that Labour promised not to steal the farmers' land for five years, while the Nationalists, in exchange, promised not to rob the British workman of his flag.[20]

Labour's turn to the right facilitated the penetration of the white working class by Afrikaner nationalism and speeded up the process that led to the party's extinction. Nationalists held their branch meetings on Labour party premises, while leaders of the two parties spoke from the same platform, as when Arthur Barlow and Colin Steyn 'stood hand in hand and heart to heart' in the hall of the railwaymen's union at Bloemfontein.[21] Hertzog took great pleasure, he said at Ceres, in having convinced the Labour man that the Nationalist was not a terrifying animal, but a person with whom he could work for the country's good.[22] As that conviction spread, Labour ceased to be the artisan's only spokesman.

The pact with Afrikaner nationalism alienated the British from Labour, the more so since it had lost much of its class appeal by watering down the socialist objective. On the other hand, Labour repelled Afrikaners by rejecting the ideal of a republic, and so was left only with the white supremacy drum. Creswell beat it with might and main. Labour's national aim, he told delegates in 1923 at Durban, was to strengthen the white race, stop the 'kaffir' from turning whites out of industry, and 'ransom' Natal for whites by sending Asians back to their real homelands.[23] Year after year, he reminded parliament, Labour had advocated the extension of white employment in the interests of South Africa.[24] The Nationalists made the same appeal, more powerfully and to greater effect in the Afrikaner's language and idiom.

Hertzog declared his civilized labour policy to the Assembly on 5 February 1924, when speaking to his motion on 'the problem of unemployment and increasing poverty'. White men, he said, were fighting a losing battle against 'uncivilized labour', as on the goldfields, and 'must be prevented from sinking down to the level of the native'. Asians, no doubt, had a civilization; yet it was so alien that it could be equally disastrous to the whites. The right of whites to find work was 'the first and most important consideration', and also in the interests of Africans, who would 'be plunged back into the conditions of barbarism' if the whites left South Africa. It should be laid down as a fixed rule that the public service and the railways 'were spheres of employment for our civilized labour', both white and Coloured. Industries that required government licences or permission should also be required to employ the white man wherever possible. Only by raising fences between the races would the white man lose his fears 'and do the right thing by the native'.[25]

It was one of Hertzog's stock arguments that whites would be 'fair' to Africans only after they had been disarmed and mastered by discriminatory laws. Yet, fixing his eyes on Afrikaner supremacy, he never allowed anything so quixotic as inter-racial justice to deflect him from his goal. The 'civilized labour' policy was adopted not to help the African, but to provide sheltered employment for unskilled whites. They came from rural areas to the towns, competed with Coloured and Africans for pick and shovel work at 6s. or less a day, and violated white supremacy taboos by mixing with them in the meanest residential quarters. Afrikaners for the greater part, they were ignored by craft unions and the Labour party, and tagged on behind the Nationalists, who valued their votes. The urban poor white was nonetheless a potential recruit for a radical non-racial class movement. The Nationalists recognized the threat to white solidarity. Subsidized employment on public works would isolate him from the dark-skinned labourers and give him a stake in the perpetuation of colour-class discrimination.

The ICU's third annual conference decided to launch a

counter-campaign against the white workers' policy of ousting Africans from all branches of commerce and industry, particularly the railways. Tom Mann, then in South Africa at the invitation of the AEU, opened the conference at Cape Town in January 1923. By this time the ICU claimed eighteen branches, all situated in the Cape and South West Africa, and was at the threshhold of its most productive period. Delegates complained of the low wages and shocking conditions of farm workers, who were being paid 10s. a month; of the 4s. a day paid to railway workers; and of the dockers' wage, which was 4s. 6d. except at Cape Town, where it had been raised to 8s. after the strike of 1919. The conference resolved to demand a minimum wage of 10s. for all workers; to organize the African miners, farm and industrial workers in one big union; to conduct a struggle against passes and every other form of discrimination; and to press for representation on all governing bodies.[26]

The ICU, according to its constitution, was 'a purely industrial organization aiming for the gradual introduction of political and industrial democracy'. It was strictly 'non-political', assured the *Workers' Herald*, the union's official journal, in its first issue in April 1923; though the paper belied the claim by denouncing the Third International and all its works. This drew a rebuke from the communists. They also deplored the ICU's attack on the industrial colour bar, and its advice that Africans should undercut white workers. The 'White South Africa' slogan used in 1922, explained the communists, was misleading; it meant only that the Chamber of Mines should not drive whites out of jobs by giving them to others at lower rates of pay.[27]

The ICU returned to the charge at its fourth annual conference in January 1924 at East London, on the motion of James La Guma and 'professor' J. S. Thaele. The white labour policy, it declared, injured any reasonable prospect of inter-racial working-class solidarity, violated the principles of trade unionism, and delayed the consummation of labour rule. Conference looked forward to the day when the white unions would open their doors to all workers, under 'an enlightened policy on the basis of which may be expected friendly cooperation and ultimate fusion of all labour forces into one big union'.[28]

Leading members of the miners' union came to a similar conclusion after considering the effects of the judgement in the Hildick-Smith case. The propaganda committee pointed out in a leaflet to members that they had to choose between fighting on their own or in unison with the African miners. A general meeting of white miners held at Johannesburg in September 1923 to discuss retrenchments and the abolition of the status quo, felt that the executive should undertake to organize separate branches for Africans, and make the necessary changes in the union's constitution. This was the 'peep of dawn', claimed the communists; economic facts had forced the men to realize the necessity for inter-racial solidarity. It had always been advocated by the party, on liberal and humanitarian grounds as well as in the interests of the whites. The SAMWU bid fair to prove the most militant of all, and promised the workers' revolution. Africans would no longer be tabooed as helots, and whites would lose their bourgeois leanings in an all-South Africa labour movement.[29]

The discussion marked the sunset and not the dawn of hopes for an open miners' union. The capitalist press attacked the proposal as 'the white miners' death-knell'. 'If they want to avoid uncivilized outbreaks,' retorted the communists, 'they must not impede industrial organization, but rather welcome it in the interests of their own skins.'[30] The SAMWU's executive took fright, and dissociated itself entirely from the suggested organization of Africans. White miners had always opposed the formation of unions among Africans, declared the *Mine Worker* in its first issue in November 1923; it reminded its readers that the union's delegates had refused to sit at the Durban trade union conference in 1918 if even one Coloured delegate attended. Contrary to the communists' prediction, the miners had no intention of either fighting their battles alone or alongside the African. They took the third course of supporting the Nationalist-Labour alliance, with the expectation that it would restore the statutory colour bar on the mines.

In the face of all the evidence, the communists insisted that white workers were learning the lessons of solidarity, 'however slowly and reluctantly' and would yet discover the need of common action to establish working-class control. Unemployment was bringing the clash between white and black closer. White workers naturally blamed the African for undercutting, but he was not a willing scab. There was a world-wide tendency for cheap Coloured labour to eliminate the white worker. He could resist it only by overthrowing capitalism with the aid of the subject races. The Labour party, said the communists, offered no solution other than job reservation, segregation and 'separate development'. This was symptomatic of the opportunism and reactionary trends that had developed in the party since it lost trade union backing and turned its back on the socialist objective. Labour leaders no longer spoke of class struggle, capitalist exploitation or socialism, which were the very stuff and substance of the movement. Their policy offered Africans less than did Jannie Smuts, yet failed to stop the decline in white living standards.[31]

The premises of this analysis amounted to a thorough rejection of Creswell's chauvinism and Labour's electoral pragmatism. Yet the Communist party's second congress, meeting in April 1923, decided by a two to one majority to apply for affiliation to the Labour party. The minority objected that a united front without Africans, Coloured and Indians would compromise the party's principles. This was not so, the platform argued. The united front was an old and well-tried tactic which enabled the party to overcome the difficulty of getting the approval, or even toleration, of the white labour aristocracy for joint action with Africans. The white worker would soon be forced in self-defence to agitate, educate and organize them. Did not the Labour party conference in January include Coloured delegates from the Cape?[34] Only the communists could link white and black workers in a true unity; and to succeed in their mission they had to gain the white worker's confidence.[33]

The party had by this time lost most of the trade unionists who once formed the core of the ISL. Its exploits in the Rand revolt brought in few replacements. All the leaders, if not all the members, were whites.[34] They wanted to regain lost ground and obtain a share in the spoils of the anticipated victory over Smuts. Watching events from Moscow, Jones gave this as a reason for the united front. He told Bunting, attending the fourth congress of the Comintern in November 1922, that some contraction might be worth while 'in order to secure a working-class basis'. Jones also influenced Andrews, who sat on the Comintern's executive committee during the second half of 1923. In his last letter to Andrews, written from the tuberculosis sanatorium at Yalta on 13 April 1924, shortly before he died, Jones remarked: 'We have lost the Trade unionists'; and he added, 'Our trouble is isolation ... The point is how to get a foot in again. Now it will be very hard. There may be a chance during the elections to put you up as UF candidate with the LP somewhere. The CP would be justified in a little manoeuvring to get this. The CP as an affiliated section, with members in SALP branches, would be the thing of course.'[35] These were tactical objectives within the framework of Jones's general strategy, which he began to work out soon after the revolt.

He argued that the struggle in South Africa, unlike the class conflict of Europe, took the form of a 'colonial national movement of liberation'. The appropriate standards to apply were set out in the *Theses on the National and Colonial Question*. These called for the formation of a bloc by all anti-imperialist forces. Even the reformist Labour party could not avoid being drawn into periodical revolutionary outbursts provoked by capitalist imperialism. Lopes and other alleged 'ultra-leftists' in Cape Town objected that the united front would make them 'bedfellows' of Creswell and his fellow opportunists. This was not so, replied Jones. The object was not to unite with them, but 'to get at the masses' who still followed the reformist leaders. By forcing them to accept or reject proposals for struggle, the communists would expose their true character and emerge with an increased following.[36]

This was the Comintern's approved policy. Communists everywhere hoped to recruit new members through the technique of the united front. The significant question for South African communists was different. They had to decide whether Afrikaner nationalism belonged to the 'anti-imperialist bloc', and whether a 'national liberation movement' could include supremacy parties. Jones ignored the existence of an *imperium in imperio*: a South African imperialism that kept Africans in a condition of colonial servitude while it cooperated with or opposed British imperialism. He noted that the united front was developing into a pact between Labour and Afrikaner nationalism to the exclusion of the communists. This proved, he said, either that there was no need of a CP in South Africa or that it had incorrectly applied the tactic of the united front. The Nationalist-Labour pact was an anti-imperialist union, which should follow, and not precede, true working-class unity.

Only the CP could accomplish working-class unity, Jones argued, by becoming the link between white and black workers. To do this, it must gain the confidence of the white worker. That, indeed, was the whole problem. The communists had thought that the withdrawal of trade union backing from the Labour party would enable them to break what remained. Instead, white workers remained loyal to its past record and its ties with British labour. 'We cannot liquidate the Labour Party,' he concluded, 'because the people think it is the trade union party.' Trade union control should now be restored under the slogan 'Trade unions back into the Labour Party.' This would enable the communists to cooperate in the daily struggle of the masses.

Having set out his conception of the proper relationship between communists and the Labour party, Jones turned his attention to the problem of bridging the gulf between white workers and Africans. 'We have somewhat neutralized our sound position on the native question in the past,' he argued, 'by our horror of partial demands.' He meant that the CP should modify its unqualified rejection of colour discrimination and look for 'planks of common interest' for both sections of the working class. The Labour party's old demand for the abolition of indentured labour, he suggested, was an excellent plank for the whole gamut of the united front 'from Jim Sixpence to Creswell'.[37]

Jones should have recognized the absurdity of his basic postulates. It was unthinkable that the Labour or Nationalist party would ever take part in a movement to liberate the

African. The idea of an anti-imperialist front between the two parties and African nationalism was a romantic delusion. So was the notion of a united front between them on a limited platform. Creswell's repeated condemnation of 'indentured labour' was a shabby subterfuge. It barely masked his refusal to condone any relaxation of the colour bar. Africans working in factories and on farms were not 'indentured', yet he never suggested that they should have the same status and opportunities as whites. One can only suppose that Jones's judgement was warped by his absence from South Africa, the hectic political atmosphere of the Comintern, and his own long illness, then in its final stage. The Rand revolt had raised his hopes of a revolution. He passionately longed for its realization before he died. 'This is the revolution now here,' he exulted in October 1922. Those who were with the masses in daily struggle would lead the revolution.[38]

He wrote his last recorded message to South Africa when confined to bed with fierce pains in hips and legs, unable to walk or to sleep without morphia. As his vitality ebbed, so did his confidence in the movement that had been all his life in South Africa. 'As a cold matter of fact,' he told Andrews, 'there is no room for a CP in white South Africa *except* as the watchdog of the native, as the promoter of rapprochement, watching, *within* the broader organizations, for every opportunity to switch the white movement on right lines on this question and scotching every conspiracy to rouse race hatred and strike breaking of race against race.' He referred to 'the tremendous sacrifices, the wanderings in the wilderness of the last nine years'; and hoped that Bunting 'with all his wonderful devotion and self-sacrifice of the last nine years, will not feel that his labours have been in vain'. 'We stand for Bolshevism,' he proudly affirmed, 'and in all minds Bolshevism stands for the native worker. Now we can safely review tactics, if necessary even dissolve temporarily except for a nucleus for the paper, in order to give comrades like Bunting a breathing space.' This should be used to gain admission through the trade unions to the Labour party and 'even into the electoral machine. It would be a great asset to have the govt. pay our organizing and travelling expenses.'[39]

Jones loathed racialism, of that there can be no doubt; but he never clearly understood the interactions between racial, national and class antagonisms. It was a gross miscalculation of his to assign to communists the role of Big Brother and 'protector' of Africans in a white supremacy party. He underestimated their revolutionary potential as much as he overestimated the white worker's. Blinkered by an unconscious white chauvinism, he visualized the dissolution of the Communist party and not an alliance between it and African nationalism in a genuine liberation movement. His chief error was to imagine that the road to working class power lay through the Labour party. His views carried great weight among the communists, and were largely responsible for their decision to apply for affiliation to the Labour party and to support its alliance with the Nationalists.

Every section of the movement supported the pact, except in the western Cape. Here Communist and Labour party members, competing against Abdurahman's APO for the backing of Coloured voters, hesitated to identify themselves with Hertzog's racialists. Bunting cracked the whip of party discipline. The Comintern's line of taking up 'partial demands' in a united front, he said, was a new method of propaganda and a way of 'penetrating' the masses.[40] Lopes, yielding to the pressure, swung characteristically to the opposite extreme. 'It is now definitely accepted,' he wrote in September 1923, 'that an immediate task before the CP is to assist the Nationalist and Labour parties to political power.' Their function, he explained, was to educate the workers through disillusionment, and to obstruct Smuts's imperialist designs. Communists should therefore 'support the Nationalist Party in their political activity and propaganda, even to the extent of joining that party'.[41]

Lopes never lived down his excess of zeal. Even Labour men in Cape Town objected that the pact was a dishonourable compromise between parties having nothing in common besides a personal hatred of Smuts and an ambition for office and place. Bunting chided the 'infantile sickness' of the 'Cape Labour Die-Hards'. Echoing Jones, he claimed that the pact was 'a tactic aiming at the overthrow of the orthodox colonial imperialist government', and a powerful aid, in the hands of a 'left' Labour

313

party, to the social revolution.[42] The communists tried to present the pact in a Marxist frame by suggesting that it was an alliance between industrial and agricultural workers.[43] Even the most loyal member must have doubted, however, whether Hertzog's farmers really represented the toiling masses on their farms. The party adopted cruder slogans in the hurly-burly of election campaigns. Members were told that they would accomplish a first-class revolutionary task by delivering a blow at Smuts's prestige. 'Workers, at the sacrifice of all else, BEAT SMUTS,' they cried. 'Down with Smuts and his gang, and clear the way for the Workers' Government.'[44]

All reactions were predictable. The government and its press launched a vicious attack on the communists, accused them of having engineered the Rand revolt, and tied the bolshevik tag on the Labour party, which beat a hasty retreat, withdrew from all united action with the communists, and turned down their request for affiliation. Archie Jamieson, the LP's general secretary, wrote that Labour's aims conflicted wholly with those of the communists. The CP, he argued, was affiliated to the Third International, wished to achieve the dictatorship of the proletariat by violent revolution, and unremittingly expressed a fundamental hostility to his party. Labour's constitution, he pointed out, did not allow the affiliation. The communists retorted that the differences between the parties were marginal, and not inherently contradictory. They would disappear if fully argued. The real difficulty was the 'colour problem'. Stripped of its 'irrelevant racial matter', the problem would be seen as one of uniting dear and cheap labour in a common fight. It was disgraceful of the Labour party to oppose a united front with communists while forming one with Afrikaner Nationalists.[45]

The rebuff did not turn the communists aside from an alliance in which they had no part or any trace of influence. Indeed, it was, they admitted, a new experience to vote for Nationalists or even Labour men with whom they had in common only a determination to end the blood-rule of imperialist Smuts. But it was the duty of all opposition groups, regardless of differences in aim, to defeat the government candidate, irrespective of his antagonist's merits. This was necessary for the sake of the proletarian revolution.[46] It was wrong of Hertzog to threaten the African's vote, or of Tielman Roos to advocate racial segregation, and above all, of the Labour party to exclude Africans from the movement. Without them it would remain a 'bastard' movement, impotent, false to its own principles, a tool of capitalist imperialism, and indistinguishable from Smuts and Kenya's white settlers.[47] There could hardly be a more severe indictment of the pact. Yet the party freely promised to assist, or at least not oppose, the pact's candidates, and so threw away its only prospect of influencing Labour's policies.

The better course would have been to reject all white supremacy parties and to concentrate on the long-range aim of building a third force in alliance with the national liberation movements. Conditions were then more favourable than ever before to a radical united front. The new alignments of the white political parties reflected a general state of flux which affected the whole population. Africans were also rethinking their position under the pressure of new discriminatory laws. The African National Congress was at last losing its faith in British imperialism. Meeting at Bloemfontein in May 1923, it denounced the Natives (Urban Areas) Act as a measure that reduced Africans to perpetual serfdom; demanded equal rights with other races; and appointed a deputation to put its views to Smuts. The congress met again in July to hear that Smuts had refused to modify his policy of compulsory segregation, influx controls, and the registration of labour contracts in the towns. Congress then passed a motion of no confidence in his administration and resolved to consider giving its support to a republican form of government. For Britain had consistently refused to honour its pledges to the African people, and pleaded that it had no constitutional right to intervene on their behalf in the internal affairs of a self-governing dominion.[48]

Even the APO was turning against Smuts. Squeezed between the entrenched white artisan and African labourers from the eastern Cape, the Coloured in the western districts benefited less than other groups from the growth of industry. The government failed to provide enough schools for Coloured children, discriminated against Coloured passengers and workers on the railways, enforced a strict colour bar in the public services, and neglected the Coloured unemployed. Signs of discontent became obvious in October 1922, when the Wynberg branch of the APO supported the Nationalist party candidate in a provincial council by-election. Abdurahman, deploring the decision, acknowledged that 'there was perhaps no other alternative, except run a Coloured candidate, or abstain altogether from voting'. The APO, he warned, would have to review its policy at the next general election unless Smuts made an earnest attempt to redress the people's many grievances.[49]

The constitution barred the Coloured from standing for parliament. They could only abstain or vote for a white candidate. A mass boycott of the polls might have been an effective tactical weapon, but it was never seriously considered by Abdurahman. Its immediate effect would have been to the advantage of the Nationalist-Labour combine, and that, he argued, was immeasurably worse than the Smuts regime. 'If ever there has been an unholy alliance of political parties,' he declared, 'it is the cooperation of Nationalists and Labourites.' They had nothing in common except an intense hatred of Smuts and a determination to segregate Africans completely.

Creswell had devoted his whole political life to ousting the black from the mines. Hertzog's party, on the other hand, wanted cheap and servile Africans on the farms.[50] Abdurahman was wrong in supposing that these demands were in conflict, or that Hertzog and Creswell were poles apart on economic issues. On the contrary, the exclusion of Africans from industry dovetailed with the farmers' insatiable demand for labour. This compatibility formed the economic basis of the partnership between white landowners and the labour aristocracy. Abdurahman was right in holding that the subject races would be the only losers under a Nationalist-Labour government. 'Let us pray,' he urged, 'that such a catastrophe may be averted.'

The communists shut the door on the APO by acting as the left wing of the white labour movement – the greatest enemy of the Coloured, said Abdurahman, in the industrial world. In addition to having led the Rand revolt, communists supported the Nationalist-Labour pact, and repeatedly opposed him in elections. When he defended his provincial council seat in November 1923, his opponents were Wilfrid Harrison, the CP candidate, and two Coloured: C. C. Petersen, the Labour party's nominee, and P. Hendry of the Inter-Racial League, an organization sponsored by Coloured trade unionists in opposition to the APO. Abdurahman polled nearly twice as many votes as his three rivals, two of whom, Hendry and Harrison, lost their deposits. His victory would have been far less certain if the South African party had also entered the field. It supported him instead and so retained his allegiance.

It was 'very backward' of the working class of Hanover Street, the communists complained, blindly to support Abdurahman, largely on colour grounds, in spite of his close association with the SAP: and it was 'backward' of Abdurahman to use working class support in the SAP's interests.[51] The APO hit back. It vilified the Soviet Union, abused 'bolshevik communism', and urged the government to immunize Africans against the menace by redressing their grievances and suppressing agitators like Bunting.[52] Abdurahman's presidential address of April 1923 rejected the communists' appeal for working-class solidarity. Alas, he said, 'the greatest exploiters of Coloured labour on the Rand are the white workers, and their solidarity has resulted in our being kept down at unskilled work. A position which we should not tolerate much longer.'[53]

His address included the perennial survey of injustices to the coloured races since Van Riebeeck's landing at the Cape. He called the post-war settlement and the Act of Union their 'great betrayal', which had reduced them to 'political helotage'. They would be cowards, deserving the treatment meted out to 'caitiffs and miscreants and industrial serfs' if they were to tolerate political bondage any longer. The 'one unerring method to secure redress of grievances' still open to them was industrial warfare. If organized, they 'could bring the country to a panic in twenty-four hours' by ceasing work on farms, and mines, in factories and the white man's home. He hoped that unconstitutional methods would not be found necessary; and warned Europeans in all Africa of the 'insensate folly' of repressing the African. If they persisted in this, they would 'awaken the nationality of Colour' under the banner of freedom and independence. Egypt had struck the first note. She would soon carry the flag of liberty throughout the whole of Africa. The cry of 'Africa for Africans' would then arise. 'Then, just as the past witnessed a great scramble by Europeans for land in Africa, so the future will see a great white scuttle out of Africa.'[54]

Abdurahman's words were prophetic, and gave no immediate guide to action. His audience represented at most the Coloured population of 546,000 or 7·9 per cent of all South Africans. Though the largest ethnic group in the western Cape, the Coloured formed small minorities in the northern provinces, and could not on their own bring the country to a standstill. To be a third force, independent of the white political parties and in opposition to them, the Coloured would have to come to terms with the 4,700,000 Africans, who were poorly organized for industrial action. The ICU had not won a single wage increase since the spectacular success of Cape Town's dockers in 1920. Kadalie himself was showing signs at this early stage of becoming an opportunist politician rather than a militant trade union leader. Disregarding the persistent hostility of Afrikaner nationalism to African aspirations, he followed Hertzog in the 1924 election campaign.

Their association began in 1921, when Kadalie solicited alms for the survivors of the Bulhoek massacre. Hertzog wrote back, enclosing a guinea, and promised to exert all his influence to establish 'between the white and black Africander that faith in and sympathy with one another which is so essential for the prosperity of a nation'.[55] Flattered by this sentimental platitude, Kadalie flaunted the letter to demonstrate his respectability and became Hertzog's man. The ICU's annual conference, meeting in January 1924, rebuked Creswell for having said that his pact with Hertzog would lead to a renewal of the colour bar.[56] Kadalie continued, however, to support the pact, and with this in mind attended the annual conference of the African National Congress in May.

Africans were caught between Smuts, the feeder of 'vultures at Bulhoek', who harassed them with new restrictions under the Natives (Urban Areas) Act of 1923, and the Hertzog-Creswell combine, which threatened to squeeze them even harder in a strait jacket of segregation. The National Congress had repudiated Smuts in May 1923. A year later, Kadalie and Masabalala persuaded Congress to resolve that a change of government was necessary 'in the best interests of South Africa' – as though the interests of all South Africans were identical. Armed with this resolution, the two men called on Hertzog, who snatched the opportunity to pick up African and Coloured votes in the Cape. He arranged to have copies of the resolution printed for distribution by the congress delegates; and gave Kadalie an introduction to the Nationalist party headquarters in Cape Town. Here the party press printed, free of charge, 10,000 copies of an election issue of the ICU's paper, the *Workers' Herald*.

Kadalie and Masabalala then travelled, at the Nationalist party's expense, to King William's Town, where the Cape Native Voters' Association was holding an All-African Convention. Kadalie claimed that he induced it after an all-night sitting to adopt his motion for a change of government. The convention, in fact, drew up a list of demands for submission to the different parties, and ended by supporting Smuts.[57] 'Jubilant and strengthened by these two political victories,' wrote Kadalie, he returned to Cape Town, and became 'an important figure' in the election campaign. He canvassed African and Coloured voters on behalf of the Nationalist-Labour pact candidates, and appeared on their platform. His policy was vindicated after the elections, he claimed, when Tielman Roos, the minister of justice in the Pact government, defended the ICU's right to organize African workers in Durban.[58]

Any African more politically mature than Kadalie would have refused to put his trust in an alliance between his people's most bitter enemies. They had no more intention than Smuts of allowing African miners, factory hands or farm workers to acquire skills and form trade unions on equal terms with whites. All parliamentary parties competed for votes at the expense of the voteless majority. All endorsed the discrimination introduced by the Apprenticeship Act, the Natives (Urban) Areas Act and the Industrial Conciliation Act – three statutes that did more than any other legislation to depress the African's wages, depreciate his status and isolate him from the rest of the working class. Abdurahman argued that Africans when segregated in urban locations would be well housed and sheltered from the vices of white men and women.[59] The African National Congress was closer to the mark when it said that the Urban Areas Act condemned the people to perpetual serfdom. The act was to become a major instrument of their oppression. It made them perpetual migrants without permanent roots in the towns, put them under the surveillance of a harsh bureaucracy, and exposed them to the risk of being turned out of jobs, homes and towns if they took part in trade union and political activity.

The main purpose of the Apprenticeship Act of 1922 was to open the skilled trades to white youth and keep out other races.[60] Committees set up under the act apprenticed young persons with prescribed educational standards to approved employers. Few Coloured and no Africans were apprenticed or admitted to technical colleges. The Industrial Conciliation Act of 1924 introduced a system of collective bargaining between employers and employees, gave trade unions the status and legal protection for which they had clamoured since the beginning of the century, and facilitated the settlement of disputes by negotiation through industrial councils and conciliation boards. The act did not apply to agriculture, domestic and government services. It discriminated against pass-bearing Africans and indentured Indians by excluding from the definition of 'employee' all those whose contract of service was regulated by the Native Labour Regulation Act of 1911, the provincial pass laws, and Natal's Indian labour statutes. Wage earners who were not 'employees' could neither belong to a trade union registered under the act nor sit on industrial councils and conciliation boards. Acting in conjunction with the apprenticeship committees, the industrial councils restricted entry into the skilled trades and gave white workers a preferential access to skilled and semi-skilled occupations.

Trade union militants did not in 1924 anticipate these divisive consequences. Little attention was given to the discrimination against Africans, although it delivered a fatal blow to the ideal of working class solidarity. The militants concentrated their attack on the principle of class collaboration which, they said, had been forced on the defeated workers by Smuts and the mine owners in an attempt to tame the unions and stifle rank-and-file movements against the union bureaucracy.[61] Strong national unions, they warned, did not need industrial councils, while smaller and poorly organized groups would be deprived of the strike weapon, their only means of bringing employers to heel.

This was not the prevailing opinion. The movement had taken a hard knock. The combined trade union membership fell from the peak figure of 135,000 in 1920 to 82,000 in 1923. The SAIF, which once represented 60,000 workers, was left with barely 2,000, few of whom belonged to craft unions. They had broken away from the federation to form the Associated Trade Unions of South Africa, with an affiliated membership amounting to only 25,000. The mood of pessimism that followed the debacle, noted Bunting, found expression in a 'comparative indifference to the bloody memories of last year's outrages and a widespread revival of conciliation and negotiation talk'.[62]

Trade union leaders searched eagerly for an accommodation with government and employers; vowed that they, too, wished to avoid strikes; and, like Sampson, warned that the alternative to conciliation was 'bolshevistic' mob rule.[63] The Nationalist party also joined in the chorus of praise and declared that strikes injured workers, employers and the whole community.[64] Seldom has a major industrial law, conferring wide recognition on unions under state supervision, received so cordial and unanimous a response. Smuts might have thought with his son that he had crushed the 'too-powerful' mine workers' union; 'taught the miners a salutary, if bloody lesson'; and 'put a fear of strikes into them'.[65] He was to discover that he, and not the white workers, had suffered the real defeat. They became junior partners in a racial oligarchy. He lost the elections.

A series of defeats in by-elections reduced his majority in parliament to eight. The climax came in April 1924 at Wakkerstroom in the eastern Transvaal, where the government lost what it chose to make a test election. Smuts petulantly resigned without consulting his cabinet or caucus and went to the country to save it, he said, from Moscow and a backveld republic.[66] The

321

Chamber of Mines undertook to pay its white employees a bonus adjusted to the gold premium, declared that the supply of African workers was probably the chief determinant of the industry's prosperity, and accused Nationalists and Labour of reviving the old, discredited theory that the mines could be run solely by whites.[67] The election was fought largely with banal trivialities, recriminations, charges of bad faith and personal abuse. Yet there was a new note. It was the Nationalist party's first 'Black Peril' election, and introduced voters to the twin slogans of *Segregate the Black* and *Save the Poor White*.

The Nationalist party propagandists made the most of an interpretation by Cousins, the director of census, which alleged an African population explosion; and demanded segregation. The liberal professor Edgar Brookes gave it academic backing and explained that segregationists would withdraw Africans from industry, make room for unemployed whites, and enable Africans to develop agriculture and handicrafts in their own areas. The White South Africa League gained a new lease of life and urged whites of all parties to give preference to their own people in skilled and semi-skilled jobs. Hertzog promised to end the pact after the elections, take away the Cape African's vote, ban the entry of workers from central Africa, and restore the industrial colour bar. A *Pact Bulletin* issued by the Labour party accused the government of 'blackening' mines and railways, and of proposing to enfranchise the 'kaffirs in the Transvaal and the Free State'. Tielman Roos said that the country's greatest curse was 'the Native'. *Die Burger* said it was the mine magnates. 'Without conscience, or national loyalty, driven on by fanatic worship of Mammon,' they aimed only to exploit the mines at lowest possible cost. The Labour party, with an eye on the Coloured vote, substituted 'civilized' for 'white' in its election programme, and undertook to protect the worker against 'Native migration to European centres'; against 'wages insufficient for the maintenance of civilized standards'; and against 'the inroads of Asiatic competition'.[68]

The poisonous compound of racism, nationalism and socialism blew Smuts out of office. He and three of his ministers lost their seats. The Nationalists won 63, the SAP 53, Labour 18, and independents one. Hertzog could not rule without Creswell, and offered to take him and Boydell into the cabinet. Nothing loath, they called a special conference on 29 June to obtain the party's approval. The Communist party, which had urged workers to support the pact at the polls, now urged delegates 'in the interests of the toiling masses of South Africa to VOTE AGAINST THE COALITION'. French and German socialists had suffered heavily by joining capitalist governments. Labour could never reach its goal, which was to attract workers in town and country and obtain a parliamentary majority, if it became a minority group in a coalition. Two Labour members in a cabinet of eight would be mere hostages; whereas eighteen workers' representatives would hold the balance of power in their hands if they maintained their independence. 'Workers of the World, UNITE! But not with the forces of reaction!!'[69]

This last-minute repentance had no effect on the special conference. Creswell told delegates that the party would have less influence, and would nonetheless be held responsible for policy, if it stood outside the cabinet and kept the government in power. Moreover, a cabinet without Labour members would be more likely to ride rough-shod over workers and the English community.[70] The conference gave Creswell his mandate by a two-thirds majority. He became minister of defence and labour; Boydell, the minister of public works and postal services. The communists said that the Labour party had signed its death warrant. The right wing said that the worker's struggle of 1922 had been vindicated.

The Labour party, exultant, strode still further to the right, scattering favours and drawing prominent radicals to its procession. Walter Madeley joined the cabinet; Peter Whiteside accepted a lucrative post on the railway board; and Jimmy Briggs, the party chairman, took his place in the senate. Harry Haynes, hero of the Durban 'soviet' in 1920, moved into the editorial chair of *Forward*, the party's journal.[71] Its aim, he declared in the first issue of 11 December 1924, was 'primarily to fight for democracy'. Two weeks later he agreed that Coloured and African electors were 'rather easily influenced', and publicized a resolution from the Troyeville branch calling for their removal from the common roll.

The Rand strike, Sampson told the House, had given an unmistakable mandate to protect white men against encroachments by Africans and Asians.[72] Labour took up the mandate with unflagging zeal. 'Frankly, we rejoice that natives are to be "thrown out of their jobs",' wrote the editor of *Forward*; and branches submitted colour bar resolutions to their annual conference at Kimberley in January 1925.[73] Gabriel Weinstock, proprietor of *Forward* and a foundation member of the War-on-War League, moved that only whites should be employed in the liquor trade or be allowed to handle foodstuffs meant for whites. Conference adopted an amendment moved by A. Z. Berman, delegate from the Hanover street branch in Cape Town and a former editor of the *Bolshevik*, which would bar Africans and Asians from working on licensed premises.[74] A bill to this effect was introduced in February, and Morris Kentridge listed it as one of Labour's achievements.[75]

This was more than most communists could stomach. Having never really believed that Labour would be able to implement its white supremacy policy, they were shocked into making a crucial decision about their role in the movement. An outward show of unity was still possible in commemorations of past struggles, on May Day or at Brixton cemetery, where workers gathered to pay homage to the martyrs of 1922. The big unions took the lead, while 'the rear of the procession was brought up as usual', commented *Forward*, 'by the one body that never misses any of these occasions, the communists under both the SCP and YCL banners'.[76] Communists refused, however, to trail behind the right wing as it jettisoned socialist principles to make room for the racial ideology of Afrikaner nationalism.

The alternative was to identify themselves wholly with the victims of racial oppression. A step in this direction was taken in the Young Communist League, Johannesburg, by two South Africans, E R. Roux (1904–66) and W. Kalk (1902–), probably the first white communists born in the country. Both were sons of radicals, like many other party members in later years. Willie Kalk was a cabinet maker, whose parents were social democrats from Germany. P. R. Roux, Eddie's father, was a druggist, the secretary of a Labour party branch in Johannesburg, and before that a contributor to Crawford's *Voice of Labour*. He wrote articles on socialism and debated dialectical materialism with Gandhi, who agreed that spiritual and material phenomena were interdependent. As regards socialism, wrote Gandhi in reply to a letter by Roux, it 'will undoubtedly become a cure for all forms of intoxication when it is accepted just as much on the spiritual plane as on the material'.[77]

Roux and Kalk argued that the YCL's main job was to preach communism to the young Natives and to bring them into the organization.[78] The proposal met with great opposition from other members, notably E. S. Sachs, a young Lithuanian who came to South Africa in 1914, joined the ISL in 1917, and entered the trade union movement in 1920 as secretary of the Reef Shop Assistants' Union. He agreed that Africans should be recruited, and insisted on establishing a separate organization for them. Roux and Kalk rejected segregation and eventually won their point by appealing to the headquarters of the Young Communist International in Berlin. The same issue cropped up again, though in a different form, at the CP's annual conference in December 1924.

The question here was whether the CP should again apply for affiliation to the Labour party. Bill Andrews and C. F. Glass, the CP organizer and business administrator, put the case for affiliation largely in terms of the Comintern's policy for Britain. Bunting, supported by delegates from Cape Town and the YCL, opposed the motion, which was defeated by a slender majority. Their main task, said Bunting, was to take the message of communism to the oppressed working class, and establish their mass basis among the Africans. By rejecting affiliation, the conference adopted Bunting's policy and so made a great turn to the left. Bunting and Roux were elected chairman and vice-chairman of the party.

Andrews retired from the post of secretary-editor in February 1925 and went back to his trade as a fitter. He had returned in February 1924 from Moscow, sharing Jones's pessimism about the movement's immediate future. The communists were to some extent beating the air, he felt, and would make no headway in isolation from the organized workers.[79] Withdrawing from the political wing, he resumed his role as trade union leader. Crawford's death in December removed his chief opponent in that field. He was elected to the S.A. council of his union, the AEU, in January. In March he became the secretary, and Glass the treasurer, of the S.A. Association of Employees' Organizations, the successor to Crawford's S.A. Industrial Federation.

Ernest Shaw, the only communist besides Andrews on the Committee of Action in the 1922 strike, joined the Labour party and was adopted by the Van Brandis branch as a provincial council candidate. Glass also defected. He resigned from the central executive in February and from the party in May because, he said, it had become a sect, isolated from the rest of the movement, and regarded with some justification as an anti-white party. All its propaganda seemed to be aimed at stirring up the blacks, for whom the leaders showed a definite bias. Glass took on the position of secretary of the Tailors' Union and joined the Labour party with the intention, his critics hinted, of wrecking it from within.[80]

Even Andrews, in spite of his great prestige and acknowledged sincerity, met with suspicion. J. George, his rival for the post of secretary of the SAAEO, and a member of the strike committee in 1922, complained that many communists had shed their red labels since the pact government. Their methods led to famine, hatred and bloodshed, and they should be removed from all executive offices in the movement. The strike of 1922, he alleged, was lost largely through the intervention of these theorists, whose 'instincts of self-preservation were so well developed that when they got the general strike, they forced their way through the nearest police cordon to attain the restful sanctuary of the Fort'. The communists had nearly shattered the Labour party during the war, wrote the editor of *Forward*, and, as in Britain, 'must be treated as political lepers'. Labour branches in Johannesburg and Natal took the hint, and sent in resolutions demanding the exclusion of avowed communists from the SALP.[81]

As the right wing struggled to establish a reputation for respectability, the communists gradually began to recognize the great change then taking place in the movement. Like radical socialists before them, they had based their policies on the Marxist hypothesis of the inevitable impoverishment of the working classes. Capitalism, they believed, would grind the white workers down to the African's level until they were forced to take common action against their exploiters. The strikes of 1907, 1913–14 and 1922 were seen as rearguard actions; milestones on the way to social revolution under the white worker's leadership.

In reality, though defeated in battle, the artisan had won the struggle for recognition within the white power structure. New industrial laws, the 'civilized' labour policy, and the Labour party's presence in the coalition government marked his absorption in the ruling elite. The position of the factory operative and unskilled white worker was still in doubt. Left-wing trade unions and Afrikaner nationalism would compete for their allegiance in the following two decades. From 1925 onwards, a wide and unbridgeable gap opened within the labour movement between the party of white supremacy and the party of the oppressed. Ceasing to be the radical wing of white labour, the communists took their place with Africans, Coloured and Indians in the fight for national liberation.

15 Fruits of Partnership

Labour's role in the pact government was to detach the British working-class vote from Smuts and his imperialist South African party. Or so the Nationalists said, when explaining to their conservative followers on the platteland why it was necessary to enter into an alliance with a pack of English socialists. 'We are brothers,' said Tielman Roos; 'the Labour Party is part of us.' Its growth was almost as important to the Nationalists as their own, he claimed, and urged every Labour sympathizer to join the party. Creswell's standing in the cabinet depended on his ability to win and retain the allegiance of white workers. To get their backing he pursued a vigorous white labour policy through a new labour department and the trade unions.[1]

Industrial relations had previously been handled by a sub-division of the mines and industries department. When Creswell started his department in July 1924, it consisted of himself and a secretary, C. W. Cousins, the race-conscious former director of census. A year later the staff had grown to 154, one of whom was Ivan Walker, who resigned the secretaryship of the typographical union to take the position of chief labour inspector. The department professed to 'watch over the social and economic welfare of the Coloured race', accepted responsibility only for 'races which subscribe to a civilized standard of life' and made its first aim the relief of unemployment among whites.

As in 1902–4, when he managed a mine on the Rand, Creswell maintained that the solution was to create employment for unskilled whites in rough manual work. He proposed to do this by insisting on a 'fair wage' clause in government and municipal contracts, which would have the effect of inducing contractors to prefer whites. Unemployed Coloured, it was argued, could find work on farms or take the place of Africans expelled from towns under the Natives (Urban Areas) Act.[2] At this early stage, then, were drawn the lines along which all governments would try to reconcile the demand for unskilled labour with the shibboleths of white supremacy.

To enlist the trade unions, Creswell called the leaders together in August 1924 to discuss unemployment and the formation of a new inter-provincial centre 'able to speak with authority for the whole of the country'. A committee was appointed to draft a constitution and to convene a conference, which met at Johannesburg in March 1925. Believing in both the stick and the carrot, Creswell put before the conference an Emergency Powers Bill which, it was claimed, would 'avoid a repetition of the ghastly blunders of 1913 and 1922'.[3] The bill provided for compulsory arbitration and prohibited sabotage, intimidation, and the employment during a dispute of 'scab' or African labour. The delegates viewed the measure with mixed feelings. There was no objection, said J. George, one of Creswell's loyal adherents, to arbitration or the removal of Africans during a widespread strike; but he objected to giving the minister dictatorial powers 'almost indistinguishable' from those exercised under martial law.[4]

The conference defeated by twenty-four votes to nine a resolution moved by Glass repudiating the bill, and decided that it should be referred to a parliamentary select committee. Dealing with the main item on the agenda, Creswell urged delegates to avoid splits that enabled employers to pursue the old divide-and-rule policy; and promised to accept a strong trade union congress as the official mouthpiece of the movement. Much depended on the person chosen to guide the destinies of the new organization. 'The hour has struck and we trust the right man will be chosen.'[5]

To Creswell's dismay, the conference chose Bill Andrews in preference to George as the general secretary of the S.A. Association of Employees' Organizations, the title under which the new federation was launched. Equipped with a research and statistical division, it was designed by the right wing to make a clean break with the movement's militant past and become a respectable body, advising the government on labour relations and securing representation on public and international institutions.[6] Andrews's election spoilt this image, and gave the opposition a handle. 'Communists capture Trade Union Congress,' the daily press cried. It accused Andrews, Glass and others of pretending to leave the party in order to penetrate the unions for the furtherance of their pernicious schemes.

Miners, engine drivers, printers, bank officials, and municipal employees, among others, refused to join the Association. They were put off by the red-baiting, or objected to the non-racial constitution that admitted unions with Coloured and Indian members. This was a sensational departure from the Transvaal's tradition, a triumph for both the communists and the Cape's open door policy. To become truly national, the Association wished to merge with the Cape Federation of Labour Unions, which would not join a colour bar organization. Another reason for the Association's tolerance was the improved status of Coloured and Indian workers under the Industrial Conciliation Act. After twenty-five years of pressure by Abdurahman and the APO, they had obtained at least formal equality with whites in the system of collective bargaining. A practical basis for solidarity now existed, and Johannesburg's furniture workers recognized it by forming a union without a colour bar at a meeting convened in May 1925 by the SAAEO.

Andrews used his influence to promote inter-racial solidarity, but his main endeavour was to overcome the hostility of the unaffiliated unions. The second annual conference held in April 1926 changed its name to the S.A. Trade Union Congress and altered the basis of representation so as to give the big unions a dominant voice in the organization. Andrews set out the benefits of affiliation in prosaic trade union terms. The TUC's influence, he argued, would increase in proportion to its representative character. Like any individual union, Congress 'is not a body distinct and above the workers but *is* the worker himself in his corporate capacity acting with his fellows for the common good'.[7]

White trade unionism tolerated attacks on capitalism and not on colour bars. By taking the top executive post in the movement, Andrews became enmeshed in its white labour policies, though he never surrendered his socialist principles or reverted to his un-Marxist concepts of pre-war days. In 1907 he identified the state with the white workers, and argued that the African's vitality and low standards threatened not only their existence but 'the very State itself'.[8] In 1925, he sat on the Economic and Wage Commission and used the opportunity to lecture the public on the nature of the state. Quoting Frederick Engels, he defined it as 'an organ of class domination, the organ of oppression of one class by another'; and 'the product of society at a certain stage of its development'. State and society were not synonymous terms. When threatened in the slightest degree, the dominant class used the state's coercive apparatus to defend its interests. South Africa 'cannot even pretend to be a democratic State, but is frankly an oligarchy allowing only a small minority of its adult males to have a voice in the selection of their rulers.'[9]

'The one thing that the present Government is ruthlessly and savagely opposed to,' wrote Andrews in 1926, 'is any attempt by the native worker to assert himself as a man and a citizen.' Drastic laws prevented Africans from encroaching on the white man's preserves. The Labour party supported the policy because it depended wholly on the Nationalists for its share of ministerial portfolios and for many of its seats in parliament. White trade unions gave their backing because they saw no other way of protecting themselves from the ever-advancing African, whose cheapness endeared him to the employing class. Moreover, many trade union leaders, having adopted the class collaboration theory, denied that the interests of employers and employed were essentially antagonistic. These leaders attributed industrial friction to misunderstandings on both sides, and claimed that these could readily be removed by round-table conferences or by using the elaborate system of arbitration courts, wage boards and industrial councils.[10]

The labour movement, predicted Andrews, would never become a dominant factor in public affairs unless it opened its ranks, both political and industrial, to the great mass of workers. He did not, however, repeat the familiar radical contention that capitalism would inevitably break down the white worker's defences and force him to shed his racial prejudices. For it was evident that the unions had achieved the formal recognition under industrial laws for which they had struggled since the turn of the century. Favoured by an economic boom and the labour department's active policy of promoting industrial 'home-rule' under 'cooperative control',[11] the unions were recovering from the decline that had set in after 1922.

The Industrial Conciliation Act imposed on both employees' and employers' organizations a duty to register within three months of their formation.[12] Registration conferred corporate status, enabled a union to sue or be sued collectively, protected it and its members from claims for damages resulting from lawful action taken during a dispute, and enabled it to take part in statutory conciliation procedures. These were substantial incentives, and met with a ready response. The number of registered unions rose from 46 in 1924 to 113 in 1930, and their membership from 38,800 to 75,500. An additional 33 unregistered unions, with a combined membership of 43,000, were recorded in 1930. Workers of all racial groups felt the stimulus, and its effects were particularly noticeable on Indians and Coloured.[13]

The act encouraged the formation of permanent industrial councils, of which there were forty-three on 30 June 1931. A majority were registered for a particular province or district, and represented the skilled trades, like printing, engineering, building, motor works, tailoring, cabinet-making, hairdressing, clothing and baking. Only registered unions and employers' organizations could constitute a council. It consisted in equal numbers of representatives of both sides and a chairman appointed from among them or from outside the council. They had the power to specify minimum wage rates and other conditions of employment by agreement which, if published with ministerial approval, became binding on all employers and employees in the industry and area affected. Underpayment of wages or any other breach of an agreement might expose both parties to the risk of a fine or imprisonment. The councils relied mainly on a corps of salaried industrial agents, to inspect employers' premises and records, detect evasions and report delinquents.

Industrial councils were charged with the duty of settling disputes and preventing strikes. No strike or lockout was lawful in a field covered by an agreement while it remained in force, or until the council had considered the issue. If negotiations broke down, a majority of the council members could refer the dispute to an arbitrator, whose award was binding on the parties. In the absence of a council, the minister, at the request of a representative number of employees or employers, could appoint a conciliation board, which in effect was an ad hoc industrial council. A strike or lockout was illegal unless the minister refused to appoint a board, or unless one was appointed and failed to agree, or, if an agreement had been reached, unless it expired. Small unions, unorganized groups of workers and those employed in essential services, where strikes were prohibited, tended to use the conciliation board procedure; and it was resorted to also on the mines in preference to an industrial council. Of the 89 conciliation boards appointed in 1924–35, 32 were in municipal services, 28 in mining, and 11 in manufacturing.[14]

Left-wing critics complained that the unions were losing their independence and spirit of militancy. Collective bargaining, compulsory negotiation procedures, and the statutory ban on strikes in essential services were said to stifle or retard the growth of class consciousness. Even the industrial registrar deplored the workers' 'regrettable apathy', which he attributed to a feeling that members of registered unions were 'secure and unassailable', and could safely allow government agencies to negotiate on their behalf.[15] Indicative of the new mood, and also of the economic boom, the number of strikes declined sharply from a total of 205, involving 175,664 workmen, in 1916–22, to 44, involving 16,540, in 1923–9. The critics said that militant and well-organized unions would gain more by direct action than by conciliation. On the available evidence, however, it seemed that the privileged section, which included the upper stratum of Coloured and Indian employees, preferred negotiated settlements, if necessary at the expense of African co-workers or the general body of consumers.

Leaders of a new type took the place of the rugged, class-conscious radicals who had built the first unions. Between four and five hundred trade unionists sat on industrial councils, conciliation boards, apprenticeship committees or other public bodies; attended conferences in Johannesburg, Durban, Port Elizabeth and Cape Town; and formed part of a large bureaucracy. Some officials administered large establishments, were well paid, associated with employers' and government representatives in offices and hotels, and often depended on employers to collect membership dues under stop orders. The bureaucrats kept a firm grip on the union by manipulating constitutions and meetings, induced employers to enforce closed shop agreements, and threatened militant members or potential rivals with expulsion from the union and eventual dismissal from the trade.

The pattern was set by the printing and newspaper industry one of the first to enforce an industrial council agreement. It charged the employers with a duty of 'maintaining the discipline of the S.A. Typographical Union', provided for a joint board to sit in judgement on defaulting union members, and gave those expelled a right of appeal to the industrial council.[16] Though employers seldom acted quite so blatantly as custodians of trade union solidarity, the closed shop agreements, which denied employment in the trade to non-union workers other than Africans, applied in the Transvaal clothing, baking and tailoring trades, as well as in the printing industry. Trade union officials were given special facilities under some agreements, as in the clothing industry, to organize the workers and collect subscriptions; or employers undertook, as in biscuit factories, hotels and bakeries, to collect the union dues under a stop order agreement.

Common interests multiplied across the table in boardrooms of industrial councils. Both sides could collaborate in underselling a rival producer in another province, or protect themselves against competition from underpaying employers and undercutting workers, or enter into agreements at the expense of consumers or the lower paid worker. Africans who shared fringe benefits such as a shorter working week or paid public holidays lost more than they gained because undercutting, their chief bargaining weapon, was made illegal.

There were compensating advantages for Coloured and Indians. As 'employees' under the Industrial Conciliation Act, they could belong to registered unions and be represented on the councils. Those who gained admission to the skilled trades also benefited from the principle of the rate for the job. The effect was to stimulate a moderate growth of 'non-racial' unions, largely in the Cape and Natal. Yet what seemed at the time to foreshadow a breaking down of racial barriers turned out to be a major setback for the national liberation movement. The relatively large and important group of Coloured artisans, and to a lesser extent that of the Indian, were drawn away from the struggle against colour bars into the orbit of the white labour aristocracy. As this process matured, the vision of unity between Coloured and African workingmen, to which Abdurahman had steadfastly adhered in earlier years, receded.

Drafting errors in the Industrial Conciliation Act left loopholes through which African women generally and many African men in the Cape and Free State fell within the definition of employee.[17] Except in Cape Town, few of those qualified to do so formed or joined registered unions. Excluded from the statutory bargaining procedures, the great majority were at the mercy of employers and trade unions. Some employers took advantage of the legal confusion to dismiss employees and substitute 'pass-bearing' Africans at lower rates of pay.[18] Some industrial councils made concessions to the best paid employees at the expense of the poorest and least organized, or introduced colour bars, as when the council for the Transvaal clothing industry stipulated in 1925 that no Africans were to be employed in machining, cutting or tailoring.[19]

Racial discrimination depressed the African's standards and forced him to undercut. The unions approved of the discrimination and objected strenuously to the undercutting. The new Industrial Conciliation Act of 1936 authorized the minister to apply the terms of a wage-fixing instrument to workers other than employees.[20] More Africans were eventually brought within the scope of wage agreements than all other racial groups combined. A few, who worked at the same jobs as whites, benefited; the rest usually lost out, either because the union deliberately sacrificed them to obtain concessions for its members, or because employers refused to bargain and stipulated their own rates for occupations in which Africans were employed.[21]

Smuts's Industrial Conciliation Act had the effect of extending the pattern of labour organization on the mines to manufacturing industries. Artisans, like miners, obtained a permanent stake in the white power structure, while employers offset the cost of sheltered employment by paying Africans less than a living wage. The system tended to perpetuate the wide gap between skilled and unskilled wages that had developed in the colonial economy, and therefore prejudiced unskilled workers of all races. Given the ability to keep the voteless African and Indian in subjection, the ruling class could ignore their resentment. Unskilled whites, in contrast, were voters and a potential threat to white solidarity, since they might discover a common interest with Africans despite differences of status, race and culture. The poor white was for these reasons as much a political as a social problem. Governments attempted to solve it by absorbing the unskilled white worker in the privileged sector of the economy.

South Africa's dependence on domestic sources of skilled workers had become acute during the war, when immigration virtually ceased. Juvenile advisory boards were formed from 1915 onwards to encourage the systematic training of white youngsters in the industrial arts. The boards were given statutory recognition and wider powers by the Juvenile Act of 1921 and the Apprenticeship Act of 1922, with the primary aim of enabling young whites to acquire skills and hold their own in competition with low-paid adult workers.[22] Apprenticeship committees, consisting of equal numbers of employees and employers, determined the conditions of apprenticeship in particular trades, and authorized approved employers to apprentice youngsters with prescribed educational and age qualifications.

The printers, engineers, builders and railwaymen had established apprenticeship committees by the end of 1924. They consisted of whites only, and adopted white labour policies. Africans, Coloured and Indians were excluded by racially biased employers and trade unionists, the qualifications laid down for apprenticeship, and the inadequacy of facilities for technical education. The system also put obstacles in the way of many white youngsters, especially those with a rural background, who had neither the required standard of education for apprenticeship, nor the necessary amount of influence with employers and trade unionists. Moreover, as Creswell pointed out: 'All South African Europeans were not fit to be supervisors.' A large number were 'fit only for manual work'.[23]

Neither the Apprenticeship nor the Industrial Conciliation Acts contained an explicit colour bar. Men and women of any race could be employed on any class of work, provided that they were paid at the rates laid down by industrial councils and conciliation boards. Since underpayment was illegal, employers had no incentive to employ Africans on skilled work for which whites or Coloured were available. The market was wide open to inter-racial competition only for less skilled work. To give whites a measure of protection in this field, Creswell proposed to introduce minimum wage standards under the Wage Act of 1925.

Its forerunner, the Regulation of Wages, Apprentices and Improvers Act of 1918, applied to women and juveniles in specified industries, notably the 'sweated' trades, such as catering, tobacco, sweet and box-making. Local trade boards were appointed to fix minimum wages and regulate working conditions, with a view to keeping white women off the streets and encouraging white youths to serve an apprenticeship. Parliament decided against wage differentiation on racial grounds, however, since it might prejudice the employment of whites or lead to an increase of production costs.[24]

Similar problems arose in the administration of the Wage Act. It provided for the appointment of a single national board, able to recommend minimum wages and conditions for all or any groups of workers in an industry or range of occupations. The board could at first differentiate according to sex, age or race, and was limited in principle to recommending not less than a wage suitable to 'civilized habits of life'.[25] If it was found that employers could not afford to pay a 'civilized' wage, the board needed special ministerial authority to recommend a lower rate. This was 'the most interesting and certainly most South African provision in the whole Act', remarked one observer;[26] and the clause disclosed the primary aim of pricing Africans, Indians and Coloured out of occupations considered suitable for whites.

The act, said Creswell in the House, would 'open up greater

areas of industry for every man demanding the civilized standards of Europeans'. Boydell, the minister for posts and telegraphs, was more explicit. Nowhere was the bill more necessary, he claimed, than in Natal, where whites were being ousted from one trade after another by the 'unfair competition' of Indians who were efficient and cheap. Employers would be forced to pay them the same wages as whites.[27] This was the intention; but the wage board soon discovered that higher wage rates might put employers as well as African or Asian workers out of business. In all investigations relating to 'unskilled labourers', the board invariably reported that it could not recommend a civilized wage.[28] In effect, unskilled whites could not be fitted into the wide gap between conventional white and African rates of pay.

Wage determinations tended to maintain the gap, though Lucas, chairman of the board from 1926 to 1935, undertook to 'raise the lowest so that they conform to the highest and best standard of civilization'. The board, he claimed, was concerned only with the 'value of the job', and had neither the will nor the means to substitute white for coloured employees.[29] However, the board could not in practice ignore the racial factor, for this, rather than skill or merit, determined the spread of wages. The value of the job was made the touchstone only when it benefited whites.[30] Industrial councils and wage boards disregarded progress by individual Africans in terms of education, skill or experience, and polarized wages in manufacturing industries. Wages in the higher range fluctuated round £5 or £6 a week, and the labourer's wage between £1 1s. and £1 5s. The ratio of five or four to one persisted with few significant variations for the next thirty years. In 1956 whites employed in private manufacturing received an average income in salaries and wages of £67 10s. a month, and Africans an average of £12 10s.

Unskilled whites might be fifteen per cent more productive than the African, as the Railways claimed on insufficient evidence; yet they were paid at least twice as much, and their employment sent labour costs up by twenty per cent.[31] As industrialists were no more willing than mine owners to sacrifice profits in order to rescue whites from poverty, it was left to government to find jobs for them at the taxpayers' expense. Hertzog's circular letter of 31 October 1924 instructed all departments to substitute 'civilized' for 'uncivilized' labour where practicable.[32] An uncivilized person was one 'whose aim is restricted to the bare requirements of the necessities of life as understood among barbarous and undeveloped peoples', recorded the circular, while civilized meant a standard of living 'generally recognized as tolerable from the usual European standpoint'. The public works department considered that a wage of 8s. a day was enough to elevate a 'kafir job' to the level of civilized labour.

Though carefully worded to avoid criticism at the ILO in Geneva, the definitions were generally understood to distinguish all whites from all other persons. An APO deputation told C. W. Malan, the minister of railways, in April 1926 that Coloured dockers for whom work had been found by dismissing Africans should receive a civilized wage. He replied that the Coloured, being less civilized than whites, could not expect equal pay.[33] Ten years later, when a member of the Cape Coloured Commission, Abdurahman again argued that the aim of the civilized labour policy was to give whites preference over Africans, and not to drive the Coloured out of their jobs.[34] Government officials were less discerning and sacrificed Coloured, Indian and African employees to find jobs for 1,400 whites in 1925–6 at an extra cost of £162,000. The policy flourished most on the railways, in spite of their statutory duty to operate on business lines, and was extended also to provincial and municipal councils, while employers in the private sector were lured into collaboration with the bait of government contracts and protective tariffs.[35]

An upward swing in the economy between 1925 and 1930 did more than all the subsidized labour schemes to provide work for unskilled whites; yet they learned to look for jobs and security to government and the white supremacy parties. Labour leaders claimed the credit for the fall in unemployment, and urged more vigorous action to prevent Asiatics, Coloured and Africans from competing against wage earners who formed ninety per cent of the electorate in Transvaal urban constituencies.[36] 'Conciliation Boards, Economic Commissions, Wage Boards,' said W. D. Dey, chairman of the central areas branch of the miners' union, were 'the same tripe as Jan Smuts used to dish up by the pound, the only difference being the present crowd are slinging it out by the yard'. He persuaded his members at Jeppe to form an opposition union under the name of the Transvaal White Miners' Association, and urged them to redress the wrongs of 1913, 1914 and 1922.[37] A deputation from the SAMWU and SAAEO asked the Chamber of Mines to set a maximum ratio of four Africans to one white on all new mines and to limit the employment of foreign Africans to mines earning less than six per cent on issued capital.[38]

The Chamber wanted 'a black South Africa', warned *Forward*, and the pact government stood in the way.[39] To fulfil its electoral pledges, said Hertzog, the government introduced a bill in 1925 to restore the colour bar on the mines, and appointed a commission to provide the justification. It reported that 'throughout the mines natives are being set to do work that for its efficient carrying out requires on the part of its performers a regard for safety, a sense of responsibility and a capacity to exercise control over others, with which not even the most exceptional among their numbers are endowed'.[40] The statement was patently absurd, and belied by thirty years of mining experience. Health, safety and competence were irrelevant, however, to the main aim of placating white miners and teaching the owners to keep their profit-making within the confines of white supremacy. Self-preservation was the first law of nature, said Beyers, the minister of mines; 'we must deal with the preservation of the white race'.[41]

Smuts opposed the bill with evident discomfort. Having issued the original colour bar regulations of 1912 without a mandate from parliament, he could not consistently object to their being legalized. There was a basic difference, he argued. His regulations, to which he had consented with great reluctance, merely confirmed long-standing practice in the Transvaal and OFS, whereas the bill would extend racial discrimination to regions and communities where it was unknown. He pleaded for 'honest, plain dealing and justice between man and man' as the proper basis of racial relations; and drew the inevitable retort that he opposed the bill only to please mine owners intent on substituting cheap labour for dear.[42]

Protests came from the owners, the ICU, the APO, and the

Transkeian general council, which asked to be heard at the bar of the House and, when this was refused, preferred not to waste its time by appearing before a select committee that had already adopted the bill in principle. Trade unions with Coloured members – among them the engineers, woodworkers, printers, builders, railwaymen, and members of the Cape federation – objected that the bill was too blatantly discriminatory. Less drastic methods, they argued, should be used to protect white standards against the effects of cheap labour. The mining unions and those with a colour bar constitution enthusiastically supported the bill, and reiterated their demand for a maximum ratio of four Africans to one white worker.[43]

Beyers declared that he had never been unsympathetic to Africans and would deal with them as his children. Hertzog agreed to spare their feelings by discriminating against them in substance and not in name.[44] This was done by authorizing the executive to limit the issue of certificates of competence to whites and South Africa-born Coloured. The assembly passed the bill, while the senate, where Smuts had a majority, threw it out, in 'total disregard', mourned *Forward*, for the future European civilization of South Africa.[45] Both houses passed the 'colour bar act', as it was generally known, in 1926, thereby validating for the first time a racial discrimination that had operated on the mines since 1903. The effect of the regulations was to prohibit the employment, in either the Transvaal or the Orange Free State, of Africans and Asians in occupations for which a certificate was prescribed. These included the positions of mine manager, overseer, surveyor, engineer, assayer, blaster, driver of a winding engine, boiler attendant and lampman.[46]

The Mines and Works (Amendment) Act of 1926 differed in one notable respect from the 1912 regulations. It bracketed Coloured with whites in a position of privilege. For, explained Hertzog at Smithfield, OFS, in November 1925, there was no question of segregating the Coloured, who spoke the Afrikaner's language, shared his outlook and stood closer to him than to Africans.[47] Strategic as well as sentimental reasons dictated a policy of identity with the Coloured community in economic and political life. It would be very foolish, Hertzog told parliament

341

in 1929, 'to drive the Coloured people to the enemies of the Europeans – and that will happen if we repel him – to allow him eventually to come to rest in the arms of the native'.[48]

Speaking at Smithfield, Hertzog outlined a comprehensive segregation programme, which he later incorporated in four bills.[49] One proposed to enfranchise Coloured men in all provinces and gradually integrate them in the white political structure. The other bills would isolate Africans behind territorial and political barriers. It was necessary, said Hertzog, to redeem the pledge given in 1913 that more land would be added to the reserves. This would enable Africans to live in splendid isolation, conduct their affairs under local rural councils, and emerge only to work for whites. The Cape African franchise would disappear, that being the main purpose of the project. Instead, chiefs and handpicked notables would elect seven white men to represent them in the assembly, as well as a 'general native council' with power to legislate for Africans only on matters specified by parliament.

A great debate followed. Afrikaner nationalists, Labour men and some liberals sang Hertzog's praises. He was 'an honest upright South African' who relied on Christian principles of equity and the expert advice of authorities on the 'native problem', eulogized Professor Edgar Brookes, one of the experts. Hertzogism, he maintained, would ensure that 'White civilization gets a fair chance to develop itself without iniquitous interference on every occasion when it takes a step forward'.[50] In less elegant language, though with an equally sinister allusion to the 'anti-civilization' forces at work, *Forward* approved of any measures that would reduce the weight of the African and Coloured vote in the Cape, where all parties had to 'play up' to it in order to win seats. 'It is for this reason that even leading society ladies of Cape Town on polling day wear the most bewitching smiles to persuade the native and coloured voters to vote for "the master"'.[51]

Coloured and Africans refused with impressive unanimity to sacrifice the Cape franchise in return for concessions to either section of the population. 'We do not want to sell the Natives' rights,' assured Abdurahman, 'or to be bribed by the Government to leave the Native in the lurch.'[52] James Ngojo, president of the Cape ANC, warned that Hertzog wanted to divide the people in order to rule. His aim was 'first to disfranchise the native and after that the coloured man'.[53] Africans, said Kadalie, did not begrudge the giving of rights to the Coloured, and strongly resented the gross injustice of differentiating between them and a full-blooded race. Hertzog's policy would set the whole African population ablaze, and was 'the biggest political crime since the days of absolute monarchy'.[54]

SEGREGATION OPPOSED BY AFRICAN PROLETARIAT, reported the *Workers' Herald*: and it quoted H. D. Tyamzashe, the ICU's Transvaal provincial secretary; A. M. Jabavu, its senior vice-president and editor of *Imvo*; and R. V. Selope Thema, a former general secretary of the ANC. They agreed that segregation would be justifiable only if complete and coupled with the right of self-determination. In demanding territorial separation, whites had forfeited their right to direct the African's destinies. Let him therefore have his own state and parliament, 'which would not be under the control of the Union Government, but should form part of the British Commonwealth of Nations'.[55]

The ANC called on 'Kings, Chiefs and leaders' to defend the people's rights, and summoned a national convention, which met at Bloemfontein on 1 January 1926: the biggest and most representative gathering yet, some said, with delegates from as far afield as South West Africa and Rhodesia. They expressed a keen sense of national pride; refused to kowtow, as Mahabane would have them do, by congratulating Hertzog on his 'courage'; and applauded James Gumede when he chided them for speaking in the white man's tongue. 'We have been conquered,' he told them, 'but I do not admit that we are slaves.' Men spoke of a 'native problem', said Kadalie, whereas their problems came from white arrogance, robbery and greed. After sitting all day and night, congress reaffirmed its 'bill of rights'; rejected segregation in any form; agreed to boycott 'native conferences' called by government under the Native Affairs Act; and decided to campaign for the removal of the colour bar from the constitution.[56]

In December, at the height of the campaign, the ICU's national council banned communists from official positions and dismissed

La Guma, Gomas and Khaile. This action, predicted the party's annual conference on 1 January, would split the ICU and betray the people into the government's hands. The rank-and-file should demand the unconditional reinstatement of the dismissed officials, purge the ICU of its corrupt and bureaucratic elements, and demand an immediate campaign against the enslaving pass laws and Hertzog bills. Bunting told the delegates, among whom were Africans, Indians and Coloured, that no government had done more than the Nationalist-Labour pact to incite racial hatred. The conference denounced the bills as 'an aggravated measure of colonial oppression' which would 'enslave, impoverish and proletarianize' Africans, and consequently 'undermine the standards of the white workers also'. It called on all African organizations to promote a general strike in protest, 'which white labour organizations, if only in their own interests, should support'.[57]

The ICU's annual conference at Durban in April proposed a national day of prayer, and met with no greater response than the call for a general strike.[58] Unable to discover effective methods of struggle, the liberation movement confined its protests to meetings and resolutions. The ANC called chiefs and councillors together at Bloemfontein in April. They too rejected the bills and demanded a constitution without colour bars, full civic rights for all races, and unfettered freedom to buy land.[59] The climax of the campaign was the first 'Non-European Convention' to be held. It met at Kimberley in June, and was attended by more than a hundred delegates representing the ANC, APO, Indian Congress, Native Voters' Association, the Bantu Union, religious and welfare societies from all parts of southern Africa. They elected Abdurahman to the chair and resolved 'to take steps to combat any policy of differentiation on the grounds of colour or race'. The conference condemned Hertzog's bills, the colour bar act, the civilized labour policy and the native administration bill. On a motion by Sol Plaatje and I. J. Joshua, the APO delegate from Kimberley, it was agreed that 'the interests of South Africa as a whole can best be served by closer cooperation among the Non-European sections of South Africa and also between the non-Europeans and the Europeans'.[60]

Unity was as hard to achieve, however, as militant action. There were too many warring groups and sectional interests among the dispossessed. Indian delegates at the convention did not speak, for fear that their participation might mar the prospect of persuading the government to modify its anti-Asian bills. A group of Coloured in the Cape revived the Afrikaner National Bond and boycotted the convention because, they said, Coloured rights, standards of living, economic status and political aspirations were very different from the African's. The Bond placed implicit trust in Hertzog's honesty and assurance that the Coloured stood next to the whites.[61] Even the chiefs, at one time a pillar of the ANC, were being detached from the liberation movement by the government's promises of official recognition, as well as by sanctions contained in a severe disciplinary code introduced under the Native Administration Act of 1927.

This act was a major instrument of Hertzog's segregation scheme. Apart from creating a separate system of courts to administer African law, it extended to other provinces Natal's repressive techniques of colonial rule and turned chiefs into petty officials of the native affairs department.[62] Hertzog and Smuts agreed that it had been a great mistake and evil on the part of previous administrations to neglect tribal law, undermine the authority of chiefs, and deprive them of the power to restrain their young men.[63] This recantation marked a significant change of attitude. In the nineteenth century white settlers had feared tribal institutions and regarded them as an obstacle to economic development. Now tribalism was to be reinvigorated; made into a bulwark against radical leaders and the thrust of African nationalism.

African leaders protested that they had outgrown tribalism. 'I am a civilized man,' said Professor Jabavu, and he refused to be ruled by a chief. A. W. G. Champion, the ICU secretary in Natal, predicted that tribalism and rule by chiefs would soon be things of the past. The government should recognize the inevitable and make the best of the Africans' new civilization. Parliament ignored the objections, and welcomed the bill with a degree of enthusiasm that Hertzog found almost embarrassing. The enthusiasm centred mainly round section 29, which created the crime of 'acting with intent to promote any feeling of hostility between Natives and Europeans'. This stirred both sides of the House. They denounced bolshevism, socialism and militant trade unionism; demanded repressive action against Andrews, Glass, Kadalie and Keable Mote; and urged the minister to provide for the deportation of persons convicted under the section.

The bill's most objectionable feature, said Andrews in June 1927, was the clause allowing the police to search private premises without a warrant. As for the hostility clause, it had no bearing on him or those who shared his politics. All they did was to argue that workers of every race had the same interests and should receive the same rates of pay.[64] The police soon showed that they equated the class struggle with racial conflict. To demand equality, or to protest against discrimination, was tantamount in their opinion to creating hostility against the master race. The Native Administration Act was gazetted in September 1927. Four communist and five ICU leaders were charged under the hostility section during the next six months. The first victims were three communist officials of the ANC branch in Cape Town – Stanley Silwana, John Gomas, and Bransby Ndobe – who spent three months in jail for having protested against the shooting of an African by a white policeman at Paarl. A. Brown, another Cape Town party member, was fined £25 for suggesting, during the flag controversy, that King George, General Smuts and General Hertzog might as well be put six feet underground for all the good they did to the people, which statement, the Supreme Court ruled, was less than incitement to hostility within the meaning of the act.[65]

Kadalie returned from a tour of western Europe soon after the promulgation of the act. It was being used, he complained, to ban ICU meetings and to prevent the organization's officials from moving about the countryside. 'The real motive of the Act is clearly the suppression of the growing movement among the natives to secure a living wage.' The consequences might be disastrous to all. 'None knows better than we do how fatal is the narrow spirit of nationalism.' But who could blame the African for hating his oppressor? Denied all legitimate expression for his hopes and fears, maddened and humiliated by injustice, he would come to believe that the attainment of his liberty was synonymous with the crushing of white civilization.[66]

Smuts's party, conforming to the Box and Cox tradition in racial politics, took on the role of reactionary extremism. Opposition members harassed the government with lurid accounts of ICU agents inciting farm hands to demand a minimum of 8s. a day, and accused Madeley, the minister for posts and telegraphs, of setting the veld alight by declaring in public that no African could live decently on less. Africans everywhere, and particularly in Natal and the OFS, believed that the government approved of this opinion, complained Major Richards; while J. S. Marwick alleged that both Madeley and Boydell 'were definitely in favour of native trade unions and of revolutionary increases in the prevailing scale of native wages'. Quoting from the *Workers' Herald*, Sir Thomas Watt supposed that Africans wanted 'to pull down their white masters'; and he complained that all this was going on without any intervention by the government.[67]

Madeley's incautious statement was symptomatic of a conflict in the Labour party that affected its relations with the Nationalists. The partners had much in common, besides their ruthless determination to suppress Africans and Asians. Labour's socialist background was less objectionable to Afrikaners than the capitalist press liked to believe. They expected government to provide farmers with land and labour, assist them when crops failed, and protect them against Africans and aliens. Since his capital went into land, and not into mines and factories, the Afrikaner had no material reason to resent the growth of state enterprise. The more it spread, the greater was the opportunity for a bureaucracy to manipulate labour and trade in his interests. Labour claimed that the state steel works at Pretoria and the state diamond diggings at Alexander Bay were products of a 'revolutionary and even socialist policy'.[68] Such projects appealed no less to Afrikaner nationalists, and might easily have been initiated by them without Labour's assistance.

Both parties claimed the credit for state socialism and white racialism, but it was the Nationalists who made the bigger impact on the electorate. The Labour party recognized this, and found an additional reason for resentment in the Nationalists' ethnocentric strivings for Afrikaner unity. When achieved, this would reduce the British to a secondary role in the political hierarchy, and free the Nationalists of their dependence on Labour in parliament. A group of Labour dissidents took exception in 1925 to Hertzog's policy of sheltering infant industries behind tariff walls which, they said, would injure Britain's export trade.[89] Madeley, who led the attack, was rewarded with a seat in the cabinet where, it was hoped, his radical bent would be straightened out in administering posts and telegraphs. Barlow then complained that the promotion should have come to him, and other place-seekers in the party's national executive threatened at the annual conference in January 1926 to dissolve the pact unless the Nationalists conceded parity of posts in the cabinet.[70]

'The year that has passed has been one of the most trying in the history of the SALP,' said Briggs in his presidential address at the next annual conference.[71] Times yet more trying lay ahead. Party loyalties were severely strained in the bitter controversy over the flag, which ended with the enactment of the Union Nationality and Flag Act of 1927. Party branches accused Creswell of having sacrificed principles in order to maintain the pact, and the national council fell foul of the parliamentary caucus.[72] The dissension started a new round of self-criticism, and a re-examination of the party's racial policies. There was no unity in the movement, wrote Haynes; the white trade unions had lost their militancy since the pact, and were mere societies for raising poor salaries for harassed officials.[73] Ever since Wybergh and Sampson had drafted the ridiculous 'segregation' policy, the party had failed to give a lead on 'the burning question' of race and colour, complained J. W. Jarvis. He blamed its troubles on the 'petit-bourgeois' psychology of the white worker, who was being bribed and kept contented out of the big margin of profits extracted from the labour of the African and Coloured.

The quarrel came to a head at the annual conference in 1928. Creswell refused to sit on the national council or accept its dictates in parliament. He and nine other members of the caucus broke away, held their own conference in Bloemfontein, set up an 'emergency executive', and claimed the legitimacy of succession. The national council declared that it was defending democratic control against caucus dictatorship and expelled the ten parliamentarians with a number of their leading supporters.[75] Madeley led the national council's eight adherents in parliament, the party's branches were divided between the two factions, and members resigned or fought one another with words and fists at branch or public meetings. The quarrel put an end to negotiations, then at an advanced stage, for direct trade union representation on the council. The crisis 'only holds the movement up to ridicule', wrote Stuart of the Cape Federation. It would be unwise for the unions to 'butt in' while the party was 'in a state of chaos'.[76] Labour had forfeited its last opportunity to secure the formal allegiance of the trade union movement.

The split, said the communists, was over ministerial jobs and resulted from the opportunism of Labour leaders who collaborated with capitalists against the African.[77] Old radicals made their contribution to the diagnosis. Dunbar, writing under the pen-name Cincinnatus, claimed that the Labour party was being forced to choose between the socialist objective and white labour policies. 'It assumed the role of the superior and governing race towards the dumb millions of the exploited natives,' threw them into the arms of the capitalist party, and made Afrikaner workers feel that a vote for the Nationalists was a vote for Labour. A genuine socialist party would attract both groups. If Labour feared to adopt this policy, it was bound to disappear, and a true workers' party would take its place.[78] James Trembath blamed their troubles on the virtual abandonment of their socialist objective. The remedy, he urged, was to discontinue the pact and persuade the unions to become once again an integral part of the SALP.[79]

The party, unrepentant, ignored the advice and clung to its old habits. 'To further alleviate unemployment,' resolved the Transvaal division's annual conference in October 1928, 'the S.A. Railways or any government or municipal undertakings be approached to replace the kaffir drivers of vehicles by unskilled white men.' When told that the Supreme Court had disallowed an ordinance prohibiting African and Asian drivers from transporting persons not of their own race, the delegates decided to ask the government to enforce the substitution by act of parliament.[80] Colour prejudice was a two-edged weapon, however, as the national council discovered in November, shortly before a by-election in Turffontein. Madeley was forced out of the cabinet on the 3rd, ostensibly for having met Kadalie and other ICU members in defiance of Hertzog's wishes. Labour's candidate, D. E. Becker, was beaten because, complained *Forward*, Creswell appealed to colour prejudice, 'that last resort of a scoundrel' with the slogan 'Madeley and Kadalie'.[81]

Madeley's followers claimed that he had fallen in defence of collective bargaining by valiantly attempting to open that safety valve, the ICU, 'at present the only medium through which natives can present their grievances'.[82] Yet it was difficult to detect significant differences, other than of temperament, between the rival leaders. Creswell was a martinet, resentful of criticism, aloof and frigid at party conferences. His hauteur repelled the rank-and-file, much as they admired his passionate desire to raise the unskilled white to a standard where he could compete 'with the increasing pressure of the black hordes who are threatening his very existence'.[83] Madeley, who claimed to be of working-class stock and class conscious, would sit down to lunch with the white driver of a government car, whereas Creswell found such equality distasteful. Yet both men found it possible to cooperate with a capitalist party in a policy of ruthless racial discrimination. Though choosing to break from the pact on the issue of the ICU, Madeley was as much a racist as Creswell.*

They both sacrificed party to personal ambition and refused to heal a breach that they knew would ruin their prospects in the coming general election. The national council's conference in January 1929 gloried in its 'complete freedom from all political

* In the unlikely event of any South African here called a racist objecting to the label, we offer this definition: A racist is one who asserts a causal biological relation between physical types, intelligence and behaviour; and who discriminates against persons because of their skin colour, nose shape or hair form.

alliances', yet humbly declared its willingness to bargain for seats with the Nationalists.[84] The Nationalists rejected the offer and renewed the alliance with Creswell's group, which contested twenty seats in a crusade for 'white civilization' and won five. Both Creswell and Boydell were defeated. The national council put up as many candidates, under the banner of 'Vote Labour to make South Africa a country for white men to live in', and won three seats.[85] The party never recovered from the blow or from the effects of the pact, which proved to be indeed no less disastrous than the communists had predicted in 1924.

Smuts speculated holistically in January 1929 about the prospects of federating all British states in southern Africa. This, retorted Hertzog in a 'Black Manifesto' of unadulterated racial venom, amounted to an appeal for a great 'kaffir state'. He, on the other hand, promised to keep South Africa white by segregating Africans in the manner projected by his bills. For, he warned, unless they were removed from the common rolls, the Cape franchise would be 'the cause of the greatest tragedy in the history of South Africa'.[86] Smuts dodged the issue of the African franchise and lost the election.[87] The SAP polled 47 per cent of the votes cast and won 61 seats. The Nationalists polled 41 per cent and won 78 seats. This gave them a clear majority in the assembly, but Hertzog generously took Creswell and Sampson into the cabinet and consoled Boydell with a government senatorship.

The dividing line, said D. F. Malan, the Cape Nationalist leader, would be so drawn as to separate Africans from Coloured, who would receive much the same political rights as whites in all provinces.[88] These were false promises, said Abdurahman, and he reminded the Coloured that the government had talked of equality while sacrificing them in order to capture the poor white vote.[89] G. R. Olivier, the general secretary of the Afrikaner National Bond, urged the Coloured to vote for Hertzog, who intended to raise them above the African's level. They, who had been treated on a footing of equality with the 'blanket native' before 1925, were now being recognized as a 'definite national entity', and could look forward to becoming 'partners in the civilization and culture of the European'.[90]

D. G. Wolton, the communist candidate, polled ninety-three votes and lost his deposit in the Cape Flats, a constituency with a large Coloured and African electorate. Bunting, who represented the party in Tembuland, fought a brave campaign against police intimidation, arrests, prosecutions and threats of violence by white racists; received 289 votes and saved his deposit.[91] He, his wife Rebecca, and his electoral agent Gana Makabeni were convicted under section 29 of the Native Administration Act on a charge of promoting inter-racial hostility. The Supreme Court ruled that the prosecution had failed to prove an intent to create feelings of hostility, and upheld their appeal. The police thereupon withdrew fourteen similar charges brought against one or other of the three during the election campaign.

The choice of constituencies was significant. White workers, having 'drifted into a state of semi-dependency upon a paternal government', had lost their militancy and could no longer be regarded as a potential revolutionary force.[92] The communists turned their faces to the African masses who, as the ICU had shown, were ripe for industrial and political organization. In an uncompromising rejection of the Hertzog-Smuts doctrine of white supremacy, the party's seventh annual conference in January 1929 demanded the 'complete equality of races', and adopted the boldest programme yet advanced by any party for the removal of discriminatory laws and practices.[93] Adhering to its basic principle, the conference urged workers and peasants of all races to combine in a militant revolutionary struggle for the overthrow of capitalism and imperialist rule.

The formula was not new; but the party broke fresh ground by attaching it to the aim of a workers' and peasants' republic 'wholly independent of the British or any other empire'. Africans should have the right of self-determination, meaning their 'complete liberation from imperialist as well as bourgeois and feudal or semi-feudal rule and oppression, whether British or South African'. Power would be vested in the working class and 'all the toiling masses, whether native or otherwise'. The programme, based on the theses adopted by the CI in 1920 for the colonies, marked a major change in the policy and strategy of the Communist party.

16 The Industrial and Commercial Union

'We have nothing; and can only tell each other sad stories of our slavery. We have waited long for a liberator, but we do not know where to find him.' This was Josiah Tshangana Gumede speaking at the Congress against Colonial Oppression and Imperialism, held at the Palais Egmont in Brussels in February 1927. 'I am happy to say,' he added, 'that there are Communists also in South Africa. I myself am not one, but it is my experience that the Communist Party is the only party that stands behind us and from which we can expect something.'[1]

Gumede represented the ANC, of which he was the president; James la Guma was the Communist party's delegate; and Daniel Colraine, a boilermaker from Johannesburg, spoke for the TUC and the 'minority movement' in the white trade unions. Bill Andrews sent a message of goodwill on behalf of the South African labour movement. The three delegates submitted a resolution in the name 'of all workers and oppressed peoples of South Africa, irrespective of race, colour or creed'. It called on them to unite for the right of self-determination, the overthrow of capitalist and imperialist domination, and the removal of restrictions on freedom of organization. 'We are waiting and longing for the liberation that must come,' repeated Gumede. 'Let this not be the last congress.'[2]

Clements Kadalie, the man from Nyasaland, in whom thousands of Africans saw their liberator, denounced the conference and turned down an offer of £100 towards the cost of sending an ICU representative to Brussels. No *bona fide* trade union, he declared, would associate with a body set up and financed by Moscow for the avowed aim of stirring up class hatred and promoting revolution.[3] Yet some of Kadalie's socialist friends from Britain – Fenner Brockway, George Lansbury and Ellen

Wilkinson – attended the conference, together with many respected leaders of national liberation movements, including Madame Sun Yat-sen, Jawaharlal Nehru, Mohamed Hatta, Lamine Senghor and Hadj-Ahmed Messali. It was not the origin or composition of the League against Imperialism that deterred Kadalie, but his sudden decision to abandon the role of radical leader.

He had often said that Lenin's victory made of Russia a heaven on earth, and that he would not rest until South Africa took the same course. His May Day message to ICU branches in 1926 urged them to hail the 'victorious republic of the Russian workers' and to join with all trade unions for 'the overthrow of capitalism and the establishment of a workers' commonwealth'. Kadalie spoke in the same strain at a rally held in October to protest against his arrest for defying Natal's pass laws. His national council, he hoped, would take up the challenge and awaken in the people the kind of spirit that had moved the Russians in November 1917.[4] Yet the council took a sharp turn to the right when it met in December 1926 at Port Elizabeth.

The meeting was called, wrote Kadalie years later, to settle 'the struggle for ascendancy' between the communists and those like James Gumbs, the West Indian-born president of the ICU, who resented the CP because it was dominated by whites.[5] If there was a plot to unseat the communists, it took them by surprise. The council spent most of its time discussing whether to send a delegate to Brussels and whether La Guma should be given leave to go there as the CP's representative. Kadalie used the occasion to make an intemperate attack on the communists. They served two masters, he said; were puppets of the whites in the party, and sought to capture the union. Their main concern, he alleged, was to make propaganda and not to improve the workers' conditions.

The council resolved by six votes to five that 'No officer of the ICU shall be a member of the Communist Party.' Three party members on the council – La Guma; E. J. Khaile, the financial secretary; and John Gomas, the provincial secretary in the western Cape – refused to resign from either organization and were summarily expelled.[6] They had given more attention to political propaganda than to improving the economic conditions of the workers, explained Kadalie. 'No bribe will seduce us,' he vowed, into departing from the strictly constitutional path of peaceful methods and moral suasion. By functioning as an orthodox trade union, and without the 'artificial assistance of the Communists', the ICU hoped to overcome racial prejudice, win recognition from the 'genuine European Labour element', and reach its goal of 'equitable treatment for the sweated workers'.[7]

The expelled members served only one master: 'the down-trodden workers of Africa', replied the Communist party. It urged members to intensify their work among Africans, and to discourage any tendency to break away from the ICU. The union's branches at Port Elizabeth, Cape Town, Vereeniging and Johannesburg demanded the reinstatement of the expelled officials. Kadalie overwhelmed his critics by insisting that La Guma and his associates owed their primary allegiance to a 'white man's party'. The ICU's annual conference at Durban in April 1927 decided to 'demonstrate the international solidarity of labour' on May Day, 'the symbol of class struggle'; prohibited its members from identifying themselves in any way with the Communist party; and refused to allow S. M. Pettersen, a white party member from Durban, to take his seat as a delegate of the non-racial Seamen's Union. 'Racial antagonism is the chief stock-in-trade of the official element of the ICU,' reported the *Worker*. 'It did not seem possible to them that the interests of black, white and yellow slaves were identical as against the slave masters of all colours.'[8]

The ease of the operation suggests that Kadalie had no reason to fear a take-over by the communists, who denied any such intention and reproached themselves for having failed to anticipate and resist the expulsions from within the ICU. To avoid offending it, they had refrained from organizing trade unions on their own account or from conducting study classes while trying to persuade it to undertake this work.[9] The dual membership of the few communists who held key positions in the ICU was normal in the labour and national movement. All party members were expected to join a trade union; and no union, except the ICU, ever banned them or excluded them from office. Kadalie himself worked closely with white racists and liberals, and could hardly have been sincere in objecting to the party's non-racial membership. His argument that whites dominated the CP might have convinced his followers, but it concealed the true motives behind his reactionary policy.

The motives were suspect, said the communists at their annual conference in January 1927. 'Much more lies behind the recent splitting tactics of Kadalie & Co., than a sudden swing towards the camp of reformism.' Though the expelled members had been victimized for taking Kadalie's teaching to heart, financial and other business reasons undoubtedly entered into the action. Three years later, after Kadalie's downfall, the communists accused him of having opposed their attempt to reorganize the union in industrial sections, introduce democratic controls of funds and elections, and pursue an active strike policy. When he had insisted on retaining dictatorial powers and on appointing officials himself, the communists on the national council had threatened to expose 'the disgraceful misappropriation and squandering of funds' by officials great and small, of whom Kadalie was 'the arch pilferer'. In addition, an influential group of Europeans in England and South Africa, representing the British labour movement and the 'yellow Amsterdam International', had promised him support and recognition on condition that he expelled the communists and adopted a moderate policy.[10] Having done this, he declared that 'strikes were wicked, useless and obsolete'.[11]

Financial irregularities, autocratic rule, and inefficiency were probably by-products of a failure to adapt organizational methods to the demands made by a large and rapidly growing membership. Estimates based on enrolment figures or sheer guesswork credited the union with 30,000 members in 1925; 40,000 in 1926; from 80,000 to 120,000 in 1927; and 70,000 in 1928; but the number in financial compliance with the rules was usually less than half the reputed membership. Kadalie told the Economic and Wage Commission in September 1925 that about half the members were in financial standing: La Guma's figure for 1926 was 28,000; Bunting estimated 30,000 in 1927; and Ballinger 12,500 in February 1929.[12] Exaggerations apart, there was no doubt that large numbers joined the union in all provinces between 1924 and 1928. As Skota pointed out, 'It required experienced and strict business acumen to manage, properly, the ever-growing funds of this organization, but this, however, was sorely lacking.'[13]

Scores of untrained officials were employed to enrol members, collect their subscriptions of 6d. or 3d. a week, organize them into branches, and attend to their complaints. The most spectacular advances were made in Natal, soon the union's financial mainstay under the dynamic leadership of its provincial secretary, A. G. W. Champion. Born at Tugela in 1893, Champion worked as a mine clerk in Johannesburg after serving in the police force, organized his fellow clerks into a union, and joined the ICU in 1925. Starting from scratch, he built in less than two years a powerful organization with a paid staff of fifty-eight secretaries, organizers and clerks: all 'preaching the Gospel of the I.C.U. and the emancipation of the African Worker in all parts of Natal'.[14] Many of his staff were former teachers who found the ICU more remunerative; and who, said Kadalie, were not 'well equipped or trained for elementary trade union work'.[15]

Ignorance of bookkeeping and trade union procedures often blurred the distinction between social and private property. Dishonesty or irresponsible behaviour on the part of branch secretaries, organizers and the national council itself had brought the union into disrepute, said Kadalie at the third annual conference in 1923. 'People said the educated Native cannot be trusted; he is either a thief or a drunkard; look at the affairs of the I.C.U.'[16] These were teething troubles, unavoidable in a trades union with many members drawn from scores of occupations in town and country. White unions which experienced similar difficulties in their infancy, had the advantage of possessing a significant measure of political power. The ICU, in contrast, fought a constant battle against hostile employers and an oppressive administration that never scrupled to use pass laws and other instruments of colonial domination against the union's organizers. Since only the most resolute could stand up to the intimidation and hazards, the pressure reacted on the internal organization, blocked all attempts to achieve efficiency, and finally deflected Kadalie himself from his radical course.

He quarrelled with the communists partly because they criticized both his policy and conduct of the union's affairs. He wrote in his autobiography that the Cape Town 'Coloured' members of the national council opposed his decision to move the head office to Johannesburg. They plotted secession and, to boycott him, transferred all the union's funds to the bank account of the Cape Town branch. Having exposed their manoeuvre to the council when it met in April 1927, he was obliged to intervene, at La Guma's request, to save its members from being prosecuted for theft and fraud.[17] None of this rings true or has ever been confirmed. The union had a credit balance of only £23 7s. 6d. in its current account and £25 6s. 5d. in reserve at the end of 1925. C. H. Haggar, the veteran Labour party leader who audited the books, complimented La Guma and Khaile on having kept them 'well and carefully'. The accounts, he noted, were presented 'with a good deal of skill and consideration'.[18] The amounts involved were too small to be a bargaining counter in a dispute between the officials; the transfer of funds, if it occurred in the circumstances alleged, would not have been fraudulent; and the integrity of both La Guma and Khaile was never in doubt. Kadalie himself paid tribute to their efficiency, and stated that the national council greatly regretted their departure from the ICU.[19] C. F. Glass, the ex-communist, became the union's bookkeeper after the expulsions.

La Guma's organizational report of 6 March 1926 enumerated many of the shortcomings mentioned in Kadalie's presidential address to the annual conference in 1923.[20] The union was losing at least £500 a year through the inefficient, dishonest and irregular behaviour of officials. Inefficiency would have to be tolerated until the union could afford to employ suitably qualified secretaries; but 'strong and severe methods' must be adopted to eliminate corruption, indiscipline and unconstitutional action – 'otherwise we become party to the exploitation of the masses'. The national secretary, Kadalie, was also at fault. He set a bad example by ignoring constitutional procedures, notably in drawing heavily on the union's funds 'to bolster up an unauthorized speculation of the Johannesburg Branch in acquiring the Workers Hall, before having obtained the sanction or approval of the Board of Arbitration'. The 'greatest danger of all', La Guma reported, was 'a dictatorship in embryo'. It was 'contrary to the democratic principles upon which the organization is founded' and should be prevented.

Kadalie might have seen in these strictures a threat to his leadership; and had an additional reason for wanting to expel the communists. 'The big employers of labour throughout the country, and, probably, the Government, suspected me of communistic tendencies,' he wrote, 'while the communists themselves looked upon me as bourgeois.'[21] It was a familiar story. To be black, and a trade union leader to boot, exposed a man to many hazards; to be a red in addition made life nearly intolerable. The expulsions brought instant relief, claimed Kadalie. The public announcement of 'its policy against Communist dictatorship, won for the ICU immeasurable support from liberal European public opinion'.[22] One of the liberals put the case more emphatically:

Without international recognition, without legal protection within the country, suspected by the white Labour Party, hampered by legal restrictions, threatened by a Sedition Bill which on the least hint of extremism might lead to a disbanding of the whole organization by an apprehensive Government, the black Trade Unionists, far from profiting by their association with the Communist Party, were imperilled by it.[23]

The party's explanation was more succinct: Kadalie had 'sold out to the bourgeoisie' in 'an endeavour to placate the South African Government and prepare the way for affiliation to the IFTU'.[24]

The decision to affiliate followed a resolution of the ICU's annual conference in April 1926 to join the British TUC as a means of 'bringing the case of the African workers before the League of Nations and public opinion throughout Europe'. The TUC suggested as an alternative that the union should apply for affiliation to the International Federation of Trade Unions, the so-called Amsterdam International. Kadalie agreed, the more readily because he was advised to do so by a group of socialists and liberals in Britain and South Africa. A 'factor behind the scenes', which led him to adopt 'a middle course', was the advice and help given him by 'certain European women'. Among them were the novelist Mrs Ethelreda Lewis, Miss Margaret Hodgson (later Mrs Ballinger), Miss Mabel Palmer of Durban, and his chief sponsor, Miss Winifred Holtby, then lecturing in South Africa.[25]

She returned to England in July 1926 and busied herself on behalf of the ICU, persuaded the Independent Labour party and trade unions to regard it sympathetically, and collected about 200 books for its library. Kadalie reported in November that informal committees might be set up in England to assist the union, and 'a number of well-known names in the Socialist ranks' were planning to secure its affiliation to the International Federation of Trade Unions.[26] The ICU's anti-communist policy strengthened its claims to assistance from the ILP and the British trade unions. When protesting against the Native Administration Act in September 1927, Winifred Holtby denied that the union had preached hostility against the white settlers. On the contrary, it 'constantly sought the cooperation of white men', and expelled all communists when some of them 'attempted to inaugurate a policy of direct action'.[27] Lord Oliver, the Labour peer, was more explicit. He deprecated 'the running of a Native "Communist" Party in South Africa', and wished to see 'the I.C.U. relieved of its Communist propagandists'. When strong enough, it should 'run genuine Labour Socialist candidates of its own'.[28]

His 'middle of the road' policy, writes Kadalie, was a great success. Instead of 'heading towards its doom as foreshadowed by the Communists', the ICU grew from strength to strength. By July 1927, six months after the expulsions, it claimed 30,000 new members, ten new branches in the Transvaal and seven in the Free State, an improved financial condition, and a vigorous campaign against Hertzog's bills. It was pressing for recognition by the government and had gained support for the first time from the labour movement. Kadalie hoped that his work in Europe and the union's new prosperity would open the eyes of white workers to the folly of standing aloof. They might yet realize that the only hope for South Africa lay in the united efforts of both black and white.[29]

Constitutionalism proved to be no more effective, however, than inflammatory speeches. The application of the ICU for registration under the Industrial Conciliation Act was rejected, as it might have foreseen, since the act was so drafted as to exclude Africans from collective bargaining procedures. The registrar objected that its 'pass-bearing' members were not employees as defined, and that, being employed in 'almost every conceivable occupation', they did not constitute a statutory trade union.[30] Attempts to group the members according to occupation, with a view to forming a federation of trade unions, were abandoned after the expulsions and subsequent splits in the organization. It remained a broad undifferentiated body of mainly unskilled workers, not unlike the industrial union favoured by the early syndicalists, and without the cohesion and discipline needed to make it an effective political force.

Kadalie's bid for recognition had a more sympathetic hearing in the Amsterdam International, which accepted the ICU's application for membership in January 1927. This strengthened the union's claim to representation at the international labour conference in Geneva, and the government was asked to nominate Kadalie as the workers' delegate. It naturally refused, and as the white trade unions could not agree on a representative, there was no official workers' delegate from South Africa at Geneva in June. Kadalie went there as an unofficial delegate, 'the only black man at that great assembly', he writes, and 'the first African ambassador' to attend an ILO conference. He made a great impression, in spite of much obstruction by South Africa's government and employers' representatives, and alerted the organization to the needs of African workers throughout the continent. Harold Grimshaw, head of the ILO's colonial section, wrote to Fenner Brockway that Kadalie's visit aroused 'widespread interest' and 'secured a personal success'. He had prepared the way for a favourable reception of African delegates at future conferences.

After leaving Geneva, Kadalie went on a lecture tour of

England and Scotland under the ILP's auspices; attended a congress of the IFTU in Paris, where he was 'again the central figure of attraction'; visited Holland and Germany – but not Russia, though all arrangements were made for him to go there, because 'time was so limited'. Besides, he 'was suspected by the Union Government and part of the European public of having some connexion with Moscow'. He found time, however, to spend another two months in England, revisit Paris and Berlin, tour Austria, and revise the ICU's constitution with the aid of Grimshaw and Arthur Creech-Jones. In spite of all this goodwill and publicity, the British TUC would not let him attend its annual conference as a fraternal delegate, for fear of offending white trade unionists in South Africa. No matter; he had fulfilled his mission to present the ICU case before the bar of the international labour movement, and to expose the racial prejudices of white South Africa. While many leaders of the national liberation movement had done as much in England, he was the first African to represent his people in the socialist and trade union movement of western Europe.

He returned to South Africa in November after an absence of five months, like Moses coming down from Mount Sinai with new commandments for the children of Israel. As far back as August, when in Holland, he received news that the ICU's affairs were chaotic and needed his personal attention. Africans were flocking to the union from previously untapped fields in Natal, the northern Free State, the eastern and northern Transvaal. It was almost an evangelical movement, sometimes accompanied by mass conversions as when a Transvaal chief led his whole tribe into the union. The farmers were incensed; they demanded a 'sedition' law, refused to keep labour tenants who belonged to the ICU, burnt their huts, turned them away and confiscated their stock if they did not leave quickly enough. Contributions to the union dropped markedly in Natal. The pressure, the growth, and the spirit of militancy abroad were straining the ICU's resources and producing a crisis of leadership.[32]

'Leaders who fail to lead when the struggle is on are of no use to the workers,' declared the Communist party; and it accused the union officials of failing to organize or to support mass action. When farm workers in Natal, who were threatened with eviction for belonging to the union, suggested a strike, the officials sidetracked them with unrealistic proposals to buy land for the evicted tenants. Coal miners in Natal, many of whom were union members, struck work in June 1927. The officials denied responsibility and even declared that the strike was illegal. Dockworkers at the Point in Durban, the union's main centre, came out on strike twice within a short period, and received no help or guidance from the ICU. When men employed at Kazerne, the railway depot in Johannesburg, called a strike for higher wages, they were advised by H. D. Tyamzashe, a senior union official, to resume work pending a discussion of their grievances. They refused and were dismissed, their place being taken by peasants recruited for the mines.[33]

The duty of a real trade union was to avert and not to 'look for' or 'manufacture' strikes, wrote Tyamzashe in reply to criticisms by Eddie Roux. Born in Kimberley in 1880, the son of a minister of the Scottish Free Church, and a compositor-journalist, Henry Tyamzashe edited the *Workers' Herald* and served as Kadalie's chief public relations officer. His observations on the union's policy were therefore authoritative. 'I am glad to say,' he added, 'that owing to the broad outlook of the ICU administrators the strike weapon has only been used on three occasions by the ICU:' the first, and only successful, operation at the Cape Town docks in November 1919; at Maythams, Johannesburg, in 1927, for a breakfast hour break; and at Onderstepoort, Pretoria, in 1928, when seventy-one strikers were fined and dismissed from employment.[34] Many other strikes were initiated or led by branch committees; but the paid officials invariably intervened only to persuade the men to return to work pending negotiations, and never succeeded in obtaining any significant improvement in wages or working conditions.

The leaders never rose to the challenge of the workers' militancy. A glaring example of failure occurred on the diamond diggings at Lichtenburg, Transvaal, in June 1928, when claim holders arbitrarily and without giving notice reduced wages from 18s. and 20s. a week to 12s. Some 30,000 Africans struck work, picketed, and pulled strikebreakers out of the claims. The diggers formed commandos, urged the government to send aeroplanes, and received police reinforcements from Pretoria and Johannesburg. Government officials persuaded the diggers to offer the men 15s. a week, at which point Kadalie and his lieutenants pledged their support. They would induce the strikers to accept the 15s. and return to work while the union negotiated a final settlement. Similarly at Bellville, Cape, when quarry workers went on strike for a rise from 3s. 6d. to 5s. a day, with free quarters and free tools, the local branch of the union was left to handle the dispute without aid from the head office.[35]

The ICU acquired a reputation as an extreme radical, even revolutionary force, by virtue of its messianic role and, in the eyes of some members, almost supernatural qualities. Its 'red ticket' membership card, wrote the communist Laurie Greene, probably the ICU's only white member in Natal, was said to keep employers, police and Hertzog himself at bay, to win cases in court, and to give the possessor equal treatment with whites, even to the extent of £1 a day.[36] Kadalie rightly claimed that 'the advent of the ICU was like a beacon of light on the horizon'. There was a great desire for emancipation, and the union promised the way. The ICU 'spread from Cape Town like a veld fire over South Africa' and as far north as Nyasaland, where a member was sentenced to three years' imprisonment for possessing a copy of the *Workers' Herald*. The union 'demonstrated to the world the powers of the African workers once they were properly organized'.[37] This was so. It accomplished in the industrial field what the ANC had achieved in the political. Kadalie aroused the people to an awareness of their economic bondage, awakened a determination to escape from poverty and the stranglehold of colour bars, and fostered trade unionism. He also let the fire burn out behind him as he took his message farther to the north. He and his lieutenants shrank from turning the power they had generated into a weapon against the oppressor.

Walter Citrine, Creech-Jones, Winifred Holtby and other of

his British socialist friends were largely to blame for this futility. They impressed on him the importance of strict adherence to constitutional forms, avoiding direct action, communism, or 'politics'; and they encouraged visions of a great bureaucratic organization, with officials trained in England, separate departments for research, parliamentary and legal affairs, and specialists in every branch of industry. These plans and the constitution drafted for him in England would have taxed the resources of a powerful union with a large, regular income and an established place in the social order. The ICU had none of these qualities and could never acquire them as long as African unions were ignored or harassed by employers, police and government. Morris Alexander told parliament in 1928 that there was a significant resemblance between the turbulent phase of white trade unionism and the ICU's reputation for mass agitation and political propaganda. He moved that Africans be allowed to develop their unions freely and 'upon lines as are enjoyed by other workers'; and failed to find a seconder in a House that included eighteen Labour members.[38]

Kadalie was happier when addressing a mass audience than when pleading for small concessions from employers inferior to him in will-power and intelligence. He missed his cue by trying to become a respectable trade union bureaucrat. On his return from Europe, he declared that he would transform the ICU into a 'true trade union', cooperate with the white unions, and repudiate any African who was anti-white. None of these aims could be realized under the prevailing conditions; and attempts at reform along these lines probably marred his prospects of settling disputes and restoring unity within the organization. A special congress, held at Kimberley in December 1927, adopted his new constitution, 'based on the model of the best modern trade unions in England', and agreed, after some dissension, to accept a trade union adviser from England. Conference also debated the crisis in the Natal section of the ICU and rejected Champion's motion to impose a special levy of £1 on every member for the purchase of land. Durban alone had 56,000 members, said Kadalie, and the money could be raised if every member in Natal donated only 1s. All branch offices in

Natal were overstaffed, and he urged them to dismiss the redundant clerks.[39]

'Our Kadalie was full of English ideas,' complained Champion. 'After spreading a gigantic spirit of mistrust against the white-man and his Government he came back from overseas with a sudden revolutionized mind. He wanted a European private secretary, white girls as shorthand typists. All that was strange to us who knew his teachings so well.' The question was debated the whole of one night at Kimberley, 'where through the voices of two lady delegates, one from Capetown and another from Boksburg, he was told that he went away a black man and came back a white man'.[40] Champion was not an impartial witness; but these accusations were repeated often and with effect in the bitter wrangling that went on throughout 1928.

The trouble started in Natal, while Champion was acting national secretary during Kadalie's absence. Samuel Dunn, a member of the famous Zulu clan founded by the Englishman John Dunn in Tshaka's reign, took over the provincial secretary-ship in Natal. A powerful speaker and efficient organizer, he vied with Champion for leadership among the Zulu and like him was a bad bookkeeper. Champion had him prosecuted on a charge of theft by conversion of £865 belonging to the union, and he was sentenced to twelve months' imprisonment.[41] George Lenono, a member of the Durban branch executive, then issued a pamphlet alleging that Champion, too, was at fault. He sued Lenono for libel and lost his case. Tatham, the presiding judge, made severe criticisms of the way in which the union's affairs were administered, including Champion's practice of paying monies received by the organization into his personal bank account. These matters were discussed at length by delegates to the union's eighth annual conference at Bloemfontein in April 1928. It was the largest ever held, though many of those present were said to have come from inactive branches in anticipation of a struggle between Kadalie and Champion. The conference decided against Champion and agreed to suspend him from office pending an investigation.

Champion's followers rallied round him in an atmosphere charged with racial animosity. The Royal Agricultural Society of Natal met in February and agreed on vigilance societies, a rigid combing out of ICU members, and a ban on African meetings without magisterial approval. The ban was introduced by proclamation 252 of 1928, issued under the Native Administration Act, which prohibited any meeting, except for religious or domestic purposes, of more than ten Africans in any reserve throughout Natal, the Transvaal and Orange Free State, without the permission of a chief and magistrate. On top of all this, a number of town councils in Natal decided to introduce municipal beer halls and prohibit the domestic brewing of the African's national beverage. Incensed at this attack on their customs and an important source of family income, men and women called for a boycott of the beer halls.

Africans in Greytown, one of the places affected, gave vent to their anger in March by breaking tombstones in a white graveyard. This set off an outbreak of violence. 'Some white hooligans,' reported Champion's paper, 'have gone so far as to organize "Anti-ICU Leagues" which in practice must be anti-black.'[42] The mobs invaded ICU premises at Greytown and Krantzkop, damaged buildings, looted and burnt property of branch officials. Twenty whites were reprimanded on a charge of resisting the police, and fined £2 each for burning and damaging the effects of the ICU. There was no proof, said the magistrate, that the union was behind the desecration.[43]

This outrage, said the Communist party, was 'a definite link in the chain of ruling class policy'. Leading farmers' organizations cultivated racial hostility in order to camouflage the class struggle. A call should go out for working class solidarity to smash the disruptive policy of all racialists.[44] Champion sounded the same tocsin. 'The cause of all this misunderstanding is a starving worker of Africa.' Five-sixths of the population starved, 'while the sixth has so much that there are men who are drunk with their bank balances'. The day would come when workers would cry from one camp. 'There shall be no Trade Union Congress of Bill Andrews, neither Cape Labour Federation of Bob Stewart nor ICU of Comrade Kadalie, but there will be a camp of the starving workers vs. the big baas.'[45]

The movement splintered instead. Kadalie was called to Durban

to explain why he had 'dismissed' Champion and encountered a 'well organized, quasi military mob' that rushed him
into the ICU hall at 2 a.m. to face a crowd 1,000 strong. 'When
I rose to speak I realized that death was certainly hanging over
my head in those small hours.' The only person to offer protection was a white policeman, who escorted him out of Durban.
When Kadalie returned to Johannesburg, he learned that Champion had hastily seceded and formed a rival organization, the
ICU *Yase Natal*. 'This episode,' writes Kadalie sadly, 'would
appear to be the turning-point in the history of the ICU.'[46] He
begged Champion to return to the fold, and assured him that
the suspension was a temporary measure 'to pacify the discontented members in the other provinces'; but the breach was
final.[47] Recriminations followed. Champion was accused of
playing 'the big boss' behind Kadalie's back. 'He became so
conceited and confident about his own abilities that he allowed
the Durban Branch funds to become inextricably mixed up with
his own private funds.'[48]

The ICU stood virtually alone in its hour of need, rejected also
by the Catholics, who formed a rival Catholic African Union and
threatened to refuse the sacrament to members of the ICU.
Kadalie replied that the ICU allowed full freedom of conscience
in religion. If, he added, Catholics claimed that their union could
serve African interests without being involved in politics or
clashing with employers and government, they were asking
people to believe the 'impossible, ridiculous and untrue'.[49] His
liberal adviser, the anti-communist Mrs Ethelreda Lewis,
rallied to his defence. She disapproved of the ICU's demand for
8s. a day. That idea never came from a black man, she said,
and must have been put into the heads of the leaders. Not,
presumably, by communists, however, since she claimed that
the union had been cleansed of the elements of violence these past
eighteen months. It had changed its original aims and should
be treated fairly in the spirit of Geneva.[50]

Kadalie had broken with the communists, quarrelled with the
ANC, and repudiated strikes, all in vain. The white trade unions
denied him the recognition that he needed to set the seal of
constitutionalism on the ICU. Their colour prejudices stood in

the way of unity, said Andrews in August 1926, when talking to a crowded meeting of ICU members. Most of the white unions still stood halfway between a white-collar and a working-class policy. It was for this reason that the TUC turned down the ICU's offer of joint action in response to Cook's appeal for an embargo on coal exports during the general strike of British miners. The TUC executive, though in favour, 'thought they could not carry their membership with them'.[51] Kadalie encountered a similar resistance when he applied in December 1927 for affiliation to the TUC on the basis of 100,000 members. This was an exaggerated figure and a tactical error. 'We were all scared that he would swamp us' recorded Ben Weinbren, a communist member of the TUC executive, 'so we rejected the application'.[52]

It was examined at length by Andrews and Stuart in a memorandum submitted on 28 December to a coordinating committee of the TUC and Cape Federation of Labour Unions; and on 15 January to a meeting of trade union executives. All but two of the sixty delegates approved the memorandum and rejected the application.[53] Kadalie immediately communicated the refusal to the British TUC, LP, ILP and IFTU. The whites had made hardly any progress in their ideology, he complained, whereas the ICU sincerely rejected racial animosity and desired cooperation.[54]

Andrews drafted the memorandum. It acknowledged that the application was important to all workers and 'should not hastily either be turned down or adopted'. Africans, who were paid far less than whites in South Africa, Europe and America for identical kinds of work, had learned from the whites and had built an important industrial organization. Their political status was inferior to that of a citizen, they were at the mercy of every constable or petty official, and were excluded from collective bargaining. They therefore looked for self-expression to industrial organization and for recognition to the white worker – their 'big brother so to speak'. Haunted by the fear of competition, the white worker demanded protection 'even sometimes at the price of gross injustice to those weaker than himself'. 'Self-preservation is the first law of nature.' The policy had failed, however, to prevent Africans from encroaching on 'these privileged positions' in mining and manufacturing. A section of workers took the long view that repression and segregation could succeed only in part and for a time. They recognized that sooner or later the movement 'must include all genuine labour industrial organizations, irrespective of craft, colour or creed. The question is when and how?'[55]

'Not in our time.' This was the substance of the Andrews-Stuart memorandum. Having conceded Kadalie's case in principle, the authors rejected it on grounds of expediency. If the ICU were to affiliate with 100,000 members, it might outvote all other unions. If its voting strength were reduced to the more realistic figure of 5,000, some big white unions might secede or continue to keep aloof from the TUC. In that event, the white unions would suffer while the ICU 'would again be as they were, isolated'. Therefore, nothing more could be offered than periodic consultations; and even this gesture seemed to require justification in terms of white interests. For, wrote Andrews and Stuart, 'the native masses will find friends in the enemy's camp' and be used 'to drag us down as nearly to their level as is possible', unless the white unions associated with their unions and gave them 'the benefit of their experience and superior knowledge'.

The two most powerful leaders in the movement, and also the most radical, rejected inter-racial solidarity at a crucial stage, when Africans were demonstrating their capacity for large-scale industrial organization. As secretary-editor of the ISL and CP, Andrews in particular had worked for nearly fifteen years to bring about unity. When the test came, he withdrew, and made his stand on the issue of white labour solidarity. It was a difficult decision. Of the seventy-eight registered unions in the country, only twenty-two had affiliated to the TUC. Its annual income from fees and donations amounted to a mere £600; and Andrews's salary was £25 a month. He wanted to strengthen the organization; and yet, wrote Bunting at the time, exposed himself to much opposition from both officials and members of white unions by associating with the ICU in protests against the Native Administration Bill.[56]

Some of the delegates at a conference of affiliated unions in September 1927 criticized his stewardship. T. Brown, the ASW secretary, probably spoke for many present when he urged Andrews to be discreet in public discussions of the labour question. 'We have got to drop the Kaffir business,' he said; 'the organization of the native will come about, but the white trade unionists were not ready for this propaganda. We want to keep ourselves as pure as possible from the native and attend to the European.'[57]

Andrews had reason to suppose that his executive would reject Kadalie's application. In spite of this, his proper course was to recommend acceptance and mobilize progressive opinion for a policy of opening the door to workers of all races. He would have had the support of communists in the movement, at least eight of whom attended the conference in September; and might have convinced African workers that a strong body of white trade unionists stood with them in their struggle for recognition. In yielding to white power without a protest, Andrews and Stuart isolated the ICU at a time when it desperately needed the backing of organized labour.

'We have no intention of allowing the TUC to patronize us as inferiors,' retorted Kadalie. 'We will have full and equal status or nothing.' His spirited statement tore the Andrews-Stuart argument to pieces. They admitted that the white labour policy was unjust, yet recommended in effect that it should be maintained. They claimed to lead the white workers, yet succumbed to their blind anti-native prejudice. They professed faith in democratic rule, yet feared that the ICU might outvote the minority. They paid lip service to the idea of working class solidarity, but relied on racial antagonisms to keep their own ranks united. The ICU had offered friendship in all sincerity and suffered a rebuff. Condemned by the international labour movement as a 'narrow racialist body, devoid of any true working class spirit', the TUC would sink into the forgotten. The ICU, wrote Kadalie to the Natal Indian TUC, was more than ever determined to build the strongest trade union movement in Africa. He asked Indian workers, who had shown very little sympathy towards the ICU, to recognize that they had a common enemy in 'imperial capitalism'.[58]

Close on 10,000 Indians were employed in secondary industries

371

in 1929–30, all but 700 of them in Natal, the home of eighty per cent of South African Indians. Unskilled men who migrated from sugar plantations and farms to the town and competed with Africans, had the advantage of being able to use the statutory system of collective bargaining. This gave an impetus to trade unionism, which had declined after the pioneering efforts of Sigamoney and Lee in 1917–18. By 1928, unions had been formed for Indians in the printing, furniture, garment, leather, tobacco, liquor and catering trades.[59] Indian employers and workers had a common interest in negotiating wages lower than the rates acceptable to whites, and therefore wished to secure representation on industrial councils and conciliation boards. V. S. Sastri, the agent-general for India, recognized the pitfalls in the policy of equal pay for equal work when applied to a minority group with inferior political status and educational standards. He was largely instrumental in the decision of the Natal Indian Congress, a body of employers and property holders, to take an active part in promoting trade unions and the formation of the Natal Indian TUC in 1928.[60]

The Indians ignored Kadalie's appeal and concentrated on 'securing the benefits', as the Indian Congress put it, 'of the Industrial Conciliation Act, Wage and Apprenticeship Acts for the Indian people'. They succeeded in persuading some white unions and the TUC itself to relax the colour bar; though the white labour movement remained hostile to the African's claims. Andrews acknowledged this when replying to a questionnaire prepared for the second British Commonwealth Labour Conference held at London in July 1928. Attempts to perpetuate a caste system were 'unwise, unworkable and certain to lead to disastrous consequences', he wrote. Since industrial segregation was impossible, political segregation must fail. Yet the movement's policy was to press for the substitution where possible of whites for Africans. The unions might not support, but would probably not try to stop, the disfranchisement of Africans in the Cape. If a referendum were taken, white workers generally would approve of further restrictions on 'the liberty of the non-Europeans'.[61]

Later in the year Andrews and Bob Stuart represented the

workers' side at the Geneva ILO conference. It was indeed 'a strange turn of fortune', as Cope remarks, that brought Andrews to 'the thieves' kitchen' and 'assembly of Labour and Socialist prostitutes', as he and his fellow communists had described the conference when first Crawford and then Kadalie went to Geneva.[62] From there he went with R. McLean, president of the Durban Tramwaymen's Union, to the Commonwealth Labour Conference where, writes Cope, the British delegates 'adopted an essentially imperialist attitude'.[63] Some, like Lord Olivier, denounced South Africa's white labour policies. Andrews replied that his own views did not differ greatly from Olivier's. He was there, however, to express the opinions of his organization. Africans were encroaching on the white man's sphere and accepting lower wages, in spite of colour bar legislation. He did not say this policy was wrong; yet would insist that all sections were ruled by self-interest. McLean added that they did not intend to allow coloured people to reduce the white man's living standards.[64]

The British ILP and Walter Citrine demonstrated their sympathies by sending William Ballinger, a Glasgow-born member of the Motherwell trades council, to advise the ICU. Kadalie looked with great hopes to his coming: he 'would tremendously help the ICU to save its ship from sinking'. 'An African is a shrewd observer of human beings,' claimed Kadalie over-confidently; and he confessed to being 'somewhat disappointed' when he met his adviser.[65] The ship sank, in spite of Ballinger's attempts at rescue. More splits took place, even before he arrived. C. D. Modiakgotla and A. P. J. Maduna, the OFS provincial secretary who had moved the expulsions of communists in 1926, formed a 'Clean Administration Group' and agitated for Kadalie's own expulsion. He was said to be 'autocratic, Czarlike and despotic'. He had disregarded the decisions or authority of the congress and national council, appropriated ICU money to his personal use, monopolized the union's motor car for his private purposes, and addressed a Communist party meeting in defiance of official policy.[66]

Ballinger's mission was to shape the ICU after the model of a standard British trade union. He soon found that white supremacists objected to an African union of any kind. The immigration authorities would give him only a three months' residential permit and treated him like a criminal although, he told a reception committee at Ferreirastown, Johannesburg, in July 1928, he was actually a very respectable Scot, who had served for several years on Motherwell's parish council. No white trade unionists attended the gathering, whereas Kadalie's liberal friends from the S.A. Institute of Race Relations and the Joint Council of Europeans and Natives came in full force. Ballinger hoped that the ICU would have an opportunity to assist in making the country's laws, and emphasized that a strike should be the last effort of any trade union, for it was a gesture of despair, as they had found in the 'Old Country'. 'If any rash action is taken it will throw back the whole of your course for many years,' he told an audience at Marabastad, Pretoria. They should reorganize the ICU quietly on the lines followed by European trade unionists, and avoid the errors of their leaders who had made rash promises and wasted the union's resources.[67]

The attacks undermined confidence in Kadalie and the ICU, yet failed to appease its enemies. Sampson, the minister of posts and public works, speaking at a banquet held to celebrate his twenty-fifth year as president of the printers' union, refused to acknowledge the legitimacy of the ICU. He repudiated an organization 'of boys on the mines, kitchen boys, store boys, pastoralists, and all types of natives drawn higgledy-piggledy into a union for the glorification of one or two leaders'.[68] Champion, on the other hand, taxed Kadalie with having ignored the wishes of many prominent officials of the ICU. They had objected to the presence of Ballinger, 'a private agent of an unnamed organization' whose salary was being paid 'by mysterious people', perhaps not in Moscow but certainly in the ILP.[69] As charges were met with counter-charges, the ICU's finances deteriorated, a deficit grew to £1,500, the union's furniture was seized for a debt of £100, and Mrs Ethelreda Lewis appealed to the ILP in England for funds to pay Ballinger.[70]

Disintegration set in. Some branches in the Transvaal and western Cape broke away in October. At about the same time Maduna of the 'Clean Administration Group' joined Champion's union and accused Ballinger of having usurped Kadalie's place as 'dictator and autocratic ruler'. Kadalie tried to restore his prestige by making fiery speeches, which brought him into conflict with his advisers and liberal friends in the Joint Councils of Europeans and Natives. They accused him of having vilified Hertzog in a speech at Lichtenburg and to his great humiliation, he complained, forced him to apologize in public. The final break came in January 1929 when he was either ousted from the leadership, according to his version, or given twelve months' leave of absence on half pay. He then resigned from what he used to say was himself incarnate: I, Kadalie, am the ICU. The union's main weakness, Ballinger told Africans in Cape Town, was to have set up a sort of chieftainship and embark on strikes. They should ask employers for a living wage; and to do this they needed education, both literary and political.[71]

'I asked for an adviser,' retorted Kadalie, 'and received a dictator.' Ballinger was the ICU's secretary, president and national council all in one. It was essential for the union to be both political and industrial, and therefore it should free itself from the Joint Councils of Europeans and Natives, which had brought about his resignation. Africans would get their freedom by fighting, and not by begging, Kadalie told an audience of more than 1,000 in Johannesburg. 'Prepare yourselves to go to gaol, prepare yourselves to be hung if you want freedom.' They must stop work on the mines, railways and docks 'if the government insists on dragging the native question into the elections'.[72] He had canvassed votes in 1924 for Hertzog's party, yet it 'grossly violated' the promises it made to the people. 'We were fooled, but never again.'[33] These were the opinions also of James Gumede, the ANC president. Speaking on the same platform as Kadalie, he urged the people to raise their voice 'so that we fill all the gaols'. They must demand liberation, the franchise and seats in parliament; oppose Hertzog's imperialism; and secure a republic representing all nationalities irrespective of colour.

This was the language of the League against Imperialism, which Kadalie had denounced in 1927 as a tool of Moscow. Having fallen out with the liberals, he now moved to the left and recalled to mind his 'other European friends': the communists C. F. Glass, Bill Andrews 'who recognized no colour bar', Sidney Bunting and Edward Roux, who often addressed ICU meetings 'before the dangers and implications of Communism were generally understood'.[74] Kadalie formed a new union, the Independent ICU, in April 1929. He applied to the League for affiliation and £200 to enable him to 'build a huge militant trade union' which would 'fight capitalism to the bitter end'.[75] The League turned down both requests, and the communists lectured him on the corrupting effects of bad company. There was no real difference between Kadalie and Ballinger; both were autocratic bureaucrats fighting for supremacy, while the rank-and-file were being bled for their support. Joint Councils, the 'Joneses, Pims, Ballingers and Brookeses', and their 'Native Damnation Societies' were but instruments for retarding the African's emancipation. 'Only by a revolutionary policy based upon organized strength and relying on direct action can this be obtained.'[76]

Communists had earned the right to speak with some authority. Years of systematic work along the lines proposed in 1926 by La Guma for the ICU were bearing fruit, especially on the Rand. Kalk, Sachs, Fanny Klenerman (Mrs Glass) and B. Weinbren, among other party members, had organized unions of furniture, garment, sweet, laundry, catering and distributive workers. A parallel movement was making headway among Africans. 'We are having big successes in our work up here,' wrote Wolton from Johannesburg in February 1928. Unions had been formed of Africans in the laundry, tailoring, engineering and baking trades. 'Membership of these Unions is leaping up and our comrades are holding key positions.' Party branches were making steady progress, and the party school had eighty regular students. 'On every day of the week our Hall is crowded with Party members, potential members and close sympathizers.'[77] The school had been started in 1925 in the slums of Ferreirastown under the supervision of T. W. Thibedi, a communist from the ISL days. Among the pupils were leading ICU and party organizers: Stanley Silwana, Thomas Mbeki, Tantsi, Johannes Nkosi, Gana Makabeni and Moses Kotane.

Five African unions with a combined membership of about 10,000 drawn from furniture and clothing factories, bakeries, laundries and garages formed the S.A. Federation of Non-European Trade Unions early in 1928. With Weinbren, Kotane and La Guma as president, vice-president and general secretary, the Federation made no attempt to conceal its political sympathies. It affiliated to the Red International of Labour Unions in 1929, and was promptly accused of being a disruptive organization led by foreign agitators and financed by Moscow gold.[78] The stated aims were modest, however, and specified only a forty-eight hour working week and 'equal pay for equal work'.[79] There was no reference to the colour bar or demand for equality of opportunity. For, Roux argued in Moscow at the sixth world congress of the Communist International in August 1928, it was sounder to stress the unity of all workers against capitalism than to expose 'the parasitical nature of the white workers'.[80]

Roux, for one, thought that the new unions should press for affiliation to the TUC, the spokesman of the labour aristocracy which 'shares to a certain extent in the profits of the bourgeoisie'. The RILU's fourth congress, meeting in 1928, agreed that the amalgamation of all unions into a single centre 'should be urged as the fundamental task of the revolutionary wing of the trade union movement in South Africa'. Only a united front of white and coloured workers against capital would put an end to inter-racial hostility. To support its contention, the congress maintained that the condition of white workers had steadily deteriorated since 1922, 'in consequence of the attraction of ever larger numbers of cheap *skilled* coloured workers to the mining enterprises'.[81] In fact, however, the labour aristocracy was then more firmly than ever entrenched behind statutory colour bars. African trade union leaders had every reason to reject the futility of knocking at a door which had been firmly bolted against the ICU.

The formation of a separate Federation of Non-European Trade Unions mirrored the white workers' racial exclusiveness, and represented a significant departure from the communist ideal of inter-racial solidarity. The aim of the Federation, it declared on 2 September 1928, was to promote a united front of all 'non-European' organizations, for equality 'in every sphere of industrial, economic and political activity', as a step towards non-racial unions. 'The white worker if not absolutely incorrigible,' wrote La Guma, 'must inevitably be forced to acknowledge the incorrectness of his myopic policy of aloofness.' South Africa was in a stage of transition to a modern industrial country, using techniques of mass production and drawing on the large reserves of semi-skilled and unskilled workers. The white man would be isolated on the labour market if he did not cooperate with the black. The African would not allow himself to be used as a 'catspaw' to pull strike 'chestnuts' out of the fire for the white worker, as in the strike of Germiston clothing workers in May.[82]

Africans and Coloured had come out in sympathy with a strike of whites against victimization. White garment workers in Johannesburg failed to reciprocate two weeks later during a strike of 200 Africans for a similar reason. Seventy-five of the strikers were fined £1 each for being absent from work; Makabeni and five other leaders were charged with incitement under the Riotous Assemblies Act.[83] A more serious betrayal of solidarity occurred in the Johannesburg furniture industry towards the end of 1929. The white and African unions had signed a mutual defence pact, which the Africans loyally observed during a strike of white workers in October. 'This was a distinctly historic event,' declared the Federation; it would 'go far towards the shattering and ultimate abolition of the colour bar'. In November, however, when 200 African and Coloured mattress makers struck work to enforce a wage determination, and 160 of the Africans were prosecuted, the whites dishonoured the agreement, scabbed, and made no contribution to the strike fund. Embittered by the betrayal, the Africans gave no assistance when the whites repeated their strike, to remain out for ten weeks and fail to win their demands.[84]

A real 'break through' was claimed in the laundry trade when Weinbren, the organizer, persuaded the white union to form a joint committee with the African union on condition that each retained its identity. Employers reacted by urging the whites to resign. 'Are you going to let niggers assist you in demands for more wages?' asked one. 'You'll only raise theirs and lower your own.' The Federation continued to progress, reported Weinbren at the second annual conference in September 1929. Five new unions, representing dairy, meat, canvas, transport and engineering workers, had been added during the past year.[85] The membership was predominantly African, with a sprinkling of Coloured and Indians. The law, police, employers and racial privilege made unity between white workers and Africans almost impossible.

The obstacles to the association of whites with Coloured and Indian were less formidable. As members of the privileged 'employee' class, they could all make their voices heard on industrial councils and conciliation boards. In August 1928 the industrial registrar reported that he had received applications for registration from the Durban Hotel Employees' Union, which was predominantly Indian, and from the Witwatersrand Coloured Mine Workers' Union. The registration of parallel racial unions in a single industry or occupation, he pointed out, might lead to dual and conflicting wage agreements. As a safeguard, he suggested the adoption of a guiding principle: 'Wherever the formation of one union embracing all races in a given industry can be brought about, it should be encouraged. If this form of organization cannot be attained in certain trades, parallel unions might be registered.' The TUC replied in October that while all its affiliates recognized and approved the right of 'the Non-European worker' to organize industrially, they disagreed about their relations with Coloured and Indian workers.[86]

The Coloured MWU was formed in 1911, before Smuts's colour bar regulations restricted a wide range of mining occupations to whites. The amendment of 1926 to the Mines and Works Act removed the statutory barriers against Coloured as distinct from Africans and Asians, yet few Coloured were employed in occupations for which certificates of competence were required. The union claimed a potential membership of 2,000 Coloured mine workers employed on the Reef as timbermen, waste packers, pipe fitters, track layers, lashers and trammers, winch drivers, pump attendants, and transport drivers – occupations which were also catered for by the white miners' union.[87] Since the union's constitution contained a 'Europeans only' member-ship clause, the Coloured insisted that they were legally entitled to register their union. They were told that the SAMWU would delete the word 'European' if they accepted the principle of equal pay. But, said the Coloured, 'to ask us to demand the same rate of wages as a white man is to ask us to remain per-manently unemployed, because the employers would always give preference to the white man if he had to pay the same wage to both'.[88]

Nine out of ten mine workers on the Rand, claimed the Rev. R. B. Hattingh, belonged to the Nationalist party, and only one-third to the union.[89] To keep its end up, the union launched a bitter racialist attack on the new regulations. The government, wrote Harry Day the secretary, 'had no right to rob us of our status as white men and compel us to compete with Cape boys'. Since employers maximized profits by taking on cheap labour, 'all that will be left on the mines will be a few white bosses and cheap coloured labourers'.[90] While so protesting, the union did remove the colour bar from its constitution. This, declared George Brown, one of the Transvaal Labour members of parlia-ment and president of the Boilermakers' Union, was the finest step so far taken towards open trade unionism.[91] In fact, the SAMWU never admitted Coloured as members. The sole purpose of the constitutional amendment was to block the registration of the Coloured union.

A fraternal embrace could be as deadly as isolation. Natal Indians made the discovery after being admitted to the S.A. Typographical Society early in 1929. White printers on strike in Durban had been kept out for six weeks because the Indians remained at work, said Albert Downes, the general secretary, and he urged an open door policy. At Cape Town, he claimed, 'the number of coloured people employed in the printing indus-try had decreased since they had been admitted to member-ship'.[92] The Durban printers, reported *Forward*, wanted to eliminate Indians from the industry. About 250 of them refused to be eliminated; therefore they had to be absorbed.[93] This would deprive them of the right to undercut, their only defence against the colour bar. 'As a matter of fair play,' pleaded Sastri,

Indians who submitted to the rule of equal pay for equal labour should be allowed to acquire the technical training that would fit them to survive in open competition.[94] Twenty-five years later, Tom Rutherford, the general secretary of the union and president of the SATUC, reported that 'one could count the number of skilled Indian printers in Natal on the fingers of your one hand. They have been almost eliminated. That happened because we took them into the Union.'[95]

Varying proportions of self-interest, racial prejudice and socialist ethics produced divergent practices on the Witwatersrand. Several unions of factory workers – garment, leather, furniture, canvas – found it expedient to admit Coloured and Indians. Some national unions, notably the printers and building workers, excluded them in the Transvaal and OFS but admitted them in Natal and the Cape. When able to monopolize their trade by means of apprenticeship restrictions or political influence, white workers enforced a colour bar, as in the unions of engineers, engine drivers, reduction workers, carpenters and tramwaymen. Life itself was full of inconsistencies, remarked Andrews. 'The relationship between man and man, to say nothing of woman, is complex and full of unsolved problems.' This was a poor excuse, however, and the TUC was forced to take a stand against racial unions. It finally agreed, after a conference held in January 1929 with representatives of the labour department and Indian unions, Sastri, the Rev. Sigamoney and Ballinger, to urge the adoption of an open door policy. Trade unions should enrol all employees 'irrespective of race or colour'; or, when this was not acceptable, establish parallel branches for each racial group within a single union.[96]

Much of the pressure came from the Cape Federation of Labour Unions, whose secretary Robert Stuart was stubbornly independent and unwilling to play second fiddle to Andrews. Their personal rivalries were closely bound up, however, with a long standing disagreement between the two centres over the Coloured worker's position. Formed in 1913 to forestall an invasion by the Transvaal unions, and affiliated at one time to the RILU, the Federation was in one respect the more radical body, even though Stuart firmly rejected 'party politics' in trade unions.

It was committed by its constitution 'to strive for equality of status, rights and treatment of all workers regardless of colour or race'; and it therefore objected, Stuart said, to losing its separate identity in a unitary organization under the Transvaal's leadership. Charles Playfair, the Federation's chairman, maintained in 1927 that 'the greatest obstacle to unity was the colour differences as between the Cape and the Transvaal'.[97] Three years later Stuart pointed out that the Federation had 'consistently endeavoured to organize labour without regard to race', whereas the north opposed 'the entrance of non-Europeans into industry, or into the unions, no matter whether such a person be of mixed parentage or purely native'. This difference, he claimed, was the root cause of the Federation's preference for provincial autonomy within a federal constitution.[98]

The Federation's attitude to African unions was more ambiguous than Stuart would acknowledge. He and Playfair thought that the ICU might be political or racial rather than a genuine trade union, and gave this as a reason for supporting the TUC's decision to refuse Kadalie's application to affiliate.[99] The ICU went on its way in isolation from the rest of the movement. In January 1930 at East London the union's annual conference decided to ask for a rise from 3s. to 6s. 6d. for railway and harbour workers. This led to a successful strike, which developed into a general stoppage of work by Africans and, claimed Kadalie, 'paralysed the whole industrial and commercial system of East London'.[100] He and eight other leaders were then arrested. They stood trial on 116 counts of incitement to public violence, and were acquitted, except for Kadalie who was fined £25 on one count. Back in Johannesburg, he was banned by Oswald Pirow, the minister for justice, from attending or speaking at public meetings on the Witwatersrand. He thereupon made his home and headquarters in East London, where he used such influence as was left him to discourage any form of mass action against the regime.

The remnants of Kadalie's union in the Cape peninsula had meanwhile grouped themselves into the Industrial and Commercial Workers' Federation, an association of African and Coloured unions, instead of, like the ICU, one of individuals. It affiliated to the Cape Federation in June 1930 on the basis of an agreed voting strength, so limited as not to swamp the unions of skilled Coloured and whites. In spite of all that had been said about the 'reactionary' policies of the Cape Federation, declared *Umsebenzi*, the Communist party weekly, it was 'definitely ahead of the TUC in actual practice'. Stuart might be a 'bosses man' but he had the courage to invite all Cape unions, regardless of race or status, to the all-in conference held at Cape Town in October. The TUC passed pious resolutions condemning racial discrimination, and limited its invitations to registered unions, to the exclusion of the FNETU and the factions of the ICU. Real working-class unity, the communists urged, could be achieved only by smashing the trade union colour bar and organizing the masses of unskilled workers.[101]

Stuart turned the conference into a novel display of inter-racial solidarity. Of the eighty-six Cape delegates present, forty-two were Coloured or African. All the thirty-four delegates from national or Transvaal unions were white, except John Gomas, the communist tailor from Cape Town, who was included in the garment workers' delegation. The conference was far from being 'all-in', since there were no representatives from Natal, the OFS, or the great mass of Africans in the north. James Shuba, the communist secretary of the Cape laundry workers' union, lodged a protest on behalf of the Federation of Non-European Trade Unions. He attributed its exclusion to the 'chauvinist and reformist outlook of the white trade union', urged an abandonment of 'capitalist conciliation' for 'militant class struggle', and warned that the world economic crisis would result in an attack on the living standards of all workers. Conference should 'once and for all break sharply with the policy of resolutionism, conciliation, race superiority' and the cowardly policy of 'white South Africa'.[102]

It was a new experience for white supremacists from the north to sit in the same hall, debate and drink tea with persons of colour on an equal footing. No more effective means could have been found to convince them that the old distinction between a white elite of artisans and hordes of peasant workers was breaking down under the impact of a rapid industrialism. Workers of all races, employed in factories and services, were being organized. Their unions had begun to change the balance of forces in the movement. Don't disparage the new unions by calling them 'mushrooms', advised Cousins, the secretary of labour and chairman of the conference. 'It should be remembered that Industry had changed, and was still changing its methods, and the workers' organizations would have to adjust themselves to new conditions.'[103]

The Cape delegates argued at length against racial divisions. Harry Evans of the bakers' union crystallized their views in a motion urging the TUC to ballot its members on the principle of 'equal opportunities and equal remuneration'. The formation of a national centre, he suggested, should be made dependent on the removal of colour bars in the Transvaal. TUC spokesmen sidestepped the challenge and asked delegates to 'cut out questions of colour'. It became evident that there would be no unity on a basis of racial discrimination. The conference finally agreed to establish a S.A. Trades and Labour Council which would admit 'all *bona fide* trades and labour unions' and 'promote the interests of all organized workers'. It was a momentous decision. Trade unions in the north had for the first time agreed to admit African unions to their fellowship. The election of Shuba and two Coloured delegates to a national council of eighteen members strengthened the optimists' faith in the new venture.

Some communists were sceptical. It was a great mistake, argued Solly Sachs, to suppose that any good could come out of the conference, or from a spurious unity based on white patronage of down-trodden blacks. Leaders 'corrupted with reformism, racial chauvinism and capitalist conciliation' would never put up a fight against wage cuts. 'Let us get busy building a real trade union movement,' he urged. The CP, while agreeing with criticisms of the reformist leaders, thought that the conference should be credited with two accomplishments. It had set up a national centre without colour bars; and it had protested against oppressive legislation. These small gains represented the first 'class-war breach in the anti-Native front of white imperialism'. 'Militant trade unionists, black and white, must now concentrate on the task of building up strong unions among the unorganized and securing their affiliation to the SATLC.'[104]

Afrikaner workers, threatened Pirow, would boycott the TLC if it persisted in championing the African's cause.[105] Deterred by the warning, the miners' union refused to affiliate. Andrews replied that only by cooperating could workers resist 'the incessant pressure from the employing class to reduce them to, or even below, the bare subsistence level'. All sections had fundamental interests in common, and should not allow racial or geographical differences to keep them apart.[106] J. H. Botha, an Afrikaner economist writing his doctoral thesis in Holland at about the same time, held a similar opinion. 'The economic factors that give rise to class consciousness and solidarity among workers,' he declared, 'are apparently too strong for the traditional divisions along lines of colour. The spirit of equal treatment and cooperation has taken a strong hold on the working classes.'[107] His assessment was to receive some confirmation in the next two decades. During this period Afrikaner nationalists attempted to penetrate the trade unions, suppress the communists, and isolate Afrikaner workers from the movement towards inter-racial class solidarity.

17 Black Republic

South Africa's liberation, wrote Bunting in 1928, involved three major freedoms: formal and actual independence from British imperialism; the emancipation of Africans from white domination; and freedom for workers and peasants of all races from bourgeois rule. 'In political form, it is a struggle for a S. African Workers' and Peasants' Republic, as contrasted with the present regime of white rule over black and capitalist rule over worker.' White workers, *bywoners** and poor whites had nothing to fear from 'native rule'. To get freedom for themselves, they must get it for others. 'Experience has shown that white labour unsupported by black is powerless against the ruling class.' As in the Soviet Union, national minorities would have absolute equality under a workers' government. The correct watchword was: 'not "destroy the whites" or "white civilization", but "DESTROY THE REGIME OF WHITE DOMINATION AND EXPLOITATION, DESTROY THE RULE OF RACE OVER RACE".' In its place should come a workers' and peasants' government, 'PREDOMINANTLY NATIVE IN CHARACTER, BASED ON EQUALITY AND ON THE PREPONDERANCE OF THE NATIVES' CLAIM TO THE COUNTRY'.[1]

This was a bolder and more imaginative programme than any yet projected for the overthrow of white supremacy. Sanctioned by centuries of colonial war, slavery and forced labour; by brute force and the concentration of power in the oligarchy; by education, propaganda, Christianity and the entire range of approved institutions – white power seemed so formidable and inevitable that the most radical leaders of the liberation movement hesitated to present a direct challenge to it. They fought a defensive battle to preserve old rights or resist new assaults;

*White share-croppers.

they pleaded for acceptance as equals within the existing order, and never envisaged its destruction. The ANC's constitution, based on a draft prepared in 1919 by a committee under R. W. Msimang, stipulated no higher aim than 'to advocate by just means for the removal of the "Colour Bar" in political, education and industrial fields and for equitable representation of Natives in Parliament'.[2] It needed courage to demand 'equal rights for all civilized men', as the Congress stipulated in 1923.[3] Not then, however, nor for many years to come, did it claim universal suffrage and majority rule.

The ICU leaned towards socialism until Kadalie succumbed to the liberals. A preamble to its constitution of 1925 declared that the interests of employers and workers were irreconcilable, and affirmed the aim of striving, 'along with all other organized workers throughout the world', for a socialist society based on the principle 'from each man according to his ability, to every man according to his needs'. Kadalie never applied the formula to South African conditions or defined his concept of the African's role in a classless society. Radical socialists and communists, on the other hand, discussed these questions at length. Working-class unity, they argued, would lead to socialism; and it, in turn, to complete equality. White workers, it was assumed, would provide the main revolutionary force, and from this seemed to follow the further assumption that they would occupy the commanding heights in the new society.

Faith in the white workers' revolutionary potential had weakened since 1929. Labour leaders sensed the change and made another onslaught on the party's socialist objective. It was a mere relic, wrote Harry Haynes in November 1928, 'a sentimental memorial to the dead-and-gone working men and women who thought British – and could think no other'.[4] The old Labour party, he argued a year later, 'went "phut" through a hypocritical lip-service to white Socialism, while being in essence the political expression of the white working class'.[5] South Africa, reported the party's national organizing committee in January 1930, was 'an undeveloped continent garrisoned by a handful of white people striving to live a civilized life, superimposed upon a proletariat of black people, gradually

387

evolving from barbarism'. Socialism would not be practical politics for many years. The retention of the objective in the constitution identified the party with international concepts, cramped its actions, and alienated many potential supporters.[6]

Coalition with the Nationalists, said the committee, had justified itself and should continue.

> The Nationalists have learned that Labour men are not the violent red revolutionaries they have been painted; that a man can be a good Labourite and remain a patriotic South African. The Labour Party, on their part, have realized that Nationalists as such are not reactionaries, nor lacking in social ideals; that they are, in fact, a liberal minded, peace-loving, humanitarian and fundamentally democratic party.

The Nationalists would retain their ideal of sovereign independence, and Labour its industrial ideals. The party's constitution must be brought into line with the sentiments and beliefs of Afrikaners, now a majority of the working class. The committee accordingly proposed, and the party's annual conference adopted in 1930, a revised version of the socialist objective. It called for the common ownership of the means of production and added the rider: 'due regard being had to the presence of an overwhelming native population and the necessity of maintaining and improving the standards of life.'[7]

The Communist party's policy in 1926 was limited to a demand for the rejection of Hertzog's segregation bills, the abolition of pass laws and other racial legislation, an extension of the Cape franchise to other provinces, and the right of Africans to elect representatives to 'native councils'.[8] The party had begun to break out of its isolation from the Africans. Increasing numbers were joining the party, reported Jimmy Shields, the young Scottish communist who had come to South Africa in 1925 in search of health. They should be drawn into the administration, he told the fifth annual conference in January 1927. The conference agreed, and made history by electing Makabeni, Khaile and Thibedi to the central committee.[9] It decided to train 'cadres of class conscious native workers' and to form branches in African areas.[10] The concept of African power was so far removed from current ideologies and apparent realities, however, that even veteran communists doubted whether it was sound.

Only a person who combined a firm adherence to Marxist theory with a passionate belief in national liberation could conceive the prospect of African rule as a necessary first stage to the achievement of a classless society. Such a man was James La Guma, the expelled general secretary of the ICU and secretary of the ANC branch in Cape Town. Though he left few documentary records of his political growth, his son Alex, author and revolutionary leader, has given some insight into the father's thoughts at this period. It is evident that the great turning point was Brussels, where La Guma attended the conference of the League against Imperialism in February 1927. Here he 'had the opportunity to discuss questions pertaining to the national struggle in his own country with many leaders of the colonial countries'.[11]

The conference adopted the South African delegation's resolution on 'The right of self-determination through the complete overthrow of capitalism and imperial domination.' A general resolution on the 'Negro question' asserted in effect the principle of Africa for Africans: their full freedom, equality with all other races, and the right to govern Africa.[12] The programme was evidently drawn up for colonies in which white settlers and administrators formed an expatriate outpost of a distant imperial metropolis. What did the policy mean for South Africa, where settlers and Africans constituted a single society; or, in more abstract terms, where the imperial-colonial syndrome occurred within the confines of a highly integrated and independent political entity? Did 'self-determination' mean that Africans claimed the right to 'secede' from the multi-national state? Or did it mean the right to expel the whites? And what was to be the position of other oppressed minorities, Indians and Coloured? There were evident difficulties attached to the formula, apart from the basic issue whether African 'tribes' or linguistic groups actually constituted a single 'nation'.

La Guma found an answer in Moscow. He went there after addressing meetings in Germany, and discussed South Africa with members of ECCI (the executive committee of the CI) and especially with Bukharin – 'a genial man, unshaven and mous-tached like many others, clad in a collarless shirt, trousers held up by an old necktie, and wearing scuffed slippers'.[13] What took place is not known precisely. According to Roux, then studying botany at Cambridge, 'It was agreed that the struggle in this country was primarily an anti-imperialist one.' After explaining the reasons for this conclusion, he proceeds to set out the corollary. 'It was clear therefore that the main task of the revolution in South Africa was to overthrow the rule of the British and Boer imperialists, to set up a democratic independent Native republic (which would give the white workers and other non-exploiting whites certain "minority rights") as a stage towards the final overthrow of capitalism in South Africa.'[14] La Guma subsequently referred to these decisions as the 'ECCI resolutions on South Africa'.

The resolutions reflected a growing awareness of the common elements in the struggles of Africans against colonial rule and of American Negroes for equality. The Anglo-American secre-tariat of the CI included a Negro Sub-Committee in which Americans were prominent. They urged the CI to give special attention to the problems of Negroes and Africans, and to their role in the world revolutionary movement. La Guma's arrival in Moscow coincided with a new urgency in the Comintern's approach to the 'colonial question'.

Let us try to reconstruct the discussions in Moscow. The three South African delegates at Brussels – an African, soon to be president of the ANC; a white trade unionist, one of the skilled 'aristocrats of labour'; and a Coloured politician, the only com-munist among them – had decided, voluntarily and without intimidation, that their country should have the 'right of self-determination'. This could not mean the secession of Africans from the existing state, since they claimed prior rights to the whole territory. Nor could it mean the expulsion of any minority group, for whites, Coloured and Indians were also 'indigenous' and had no imperial homeland. Self-determination could there-fore mean only secession from the British crown and the conse-quent formation of an independent republic. Secondly the Brussels conference had adopted the general principle of African self-rule. Its application to South Africa would mean manhood or adult suffrage, one man one vote, and the prospect of majority African rule. The concept of 'a democratic independent Native republic' was certainly inherent in the Brussels resolutions, and involved no more than parliamentary reform of the kind introduced into western Europe in the second half of the nineteenth century.

Back in South Africa, La Guma and his fellow delegates were in duty bound to establish a branch of the League. Colraine, who had been elected to its national council, spoke bravely in Brussels of the bright prospects in South Africa and his devotion to the cause. 'I am determined,' he vowed, 'to do all in my power to further the aims of the organization.'[15] His militancy soon ebbed away in Johannesburg's hostile atmosphere. The Communist party's executive met Gumede and Andrews to discuss ways of implementing the Brussels resolutions. 'A certain attack of cold feet is evident on the part of both,' reported Bunting. 'Colraine has certainly relapsed into a sulky inactivity.' He complained of receiving only £75 of the £150 promised for his trip, and accused the TUC and others of using the balance for the fares of his co-delegates. There was 'very bad blood' between him and Andrews, who 'made this an excuse for joining with the reactionaries in the TUC'. They would have nothing to do with the Brussels decisions.[16]

Gumede also refused to take the lead in calling a conference. The ANC's total funds amounted to 1s. 7d., he said, and he would first have to rebuild Congress. It had been 'more or less lethargic' for some years, wrote Bunting in September, and the ICU was eclipsing it in many regions. Moreover, its 'strong reactionary elements, including some paid agents of the Chamber of Mines, etc.' strongly opposed any 'anti-imperialist programme' and preferred 'to believe that Downing Street will redress the grievances suffered at the hands of the Union Government'.[17] Bunting concluded that the South African branch of the League could not be formed at the present; 'and it will once more devolve on the Communists to carry on the propaganda alone'.[18]

At about this time the party, being refused offices in the TUC's new premises in Kerk Street, Johannesburg, returned to the working-class quarters of Ferreirastown. These were symptoms, wrote Bunting, of the decline in the ambitions and militancy of the white trade unionists. They seemed to have finally decided '*to stand on a petty bourgeois, conciliationist, and anti-native platform*'. Many old radical stalwarts had drifted away from the party, fondly believing that they would 'do more good' in the movement if released from the inconveniences of party ties. Like renegades elsewhere, however, they had turned into anti-communists. Though regrettable, the party's geographical isolation from the white unions might 'assist that constant review of our bearings' which was so necessary. For, alone in South Africa, the party 'was pioneering the anti-capitalist and anti-imperialist movement on almost uncharted seas amid a multitude of conflicting currents and, in addition, an increasing threat of enemy guns'.[19] In this uncertain enterprise, he tended to rely on old and tested doctrines of struggle in spite of a turn to the left in the ANC.

'The only friends of oppressed people are the Communists,' Gumede told an audience in Cape Town on his return from Europe. 'Division amongst our ranks is helping to maintain the present despairing conditions,' he warned, and urged the ICU to cooperate and reinstate the expelled communists. It was not the white man as such, he said in Johannesburg, 'but the capitalist class which grinds the faces of white and black the world over'. This 'was the universal truth to which my eyes were opened'. The ANC would 'stand for our people as Hertzog stood for his, and in this fight we need the services of the ICU also'.[20]

His report on the Brussels conference was well received at the ANC's annual meeting in June 1927. Of all political parties, he repeated, the Communist party was the only one that honestly and sincerely fought for the emancipation of the oppressed. Congress paid him the tribute of electing him to the post of president-general for a term of three years. E. J. Khaile, a member of the CP's central executive and one of the communists expelled from the ICU, became the general secretary. The new leadership undertook to overhaul the structure of Congress, changing it from a loose type of organization limited to sporadic propaganda campaigns into a mass organization based on individual members grouped into branches. To draw together the industrial and political wings of the movement, the conference decided to set up a separate department, called the African Labour Congress, which would be directed by H. S. Msimang and provide for the needs of workers in town and country.[21]

Prospects were favourable for a united front against capitalism, declared the *South African Worker*, then edited by James Shields. If the ANC was to become a real fighting force, it would have to reject compromises with 'any set of capitalist and imperialist robbers'. He urged the Congress executive to repudiate a resolution of the Cape ANC affirming faith in the Union Jack – that 'symbol of British imperialism' – in the great flag controversy. The ANC's policy should be one of 'fighting militancy' against capitalism.[22] This was expecting too much, however. Congress was not a socialist party, nor would it abandon its traditional policy of looking to the British for support against Afrikaner imperialism. Gumede had to take note of the strong conservative element in his ranks, and of the growing opposition to his association with the communists.

Comrade Gumede and Comrade Khaile, wrote S. M. Bennet Ncwana, a notorious political huckster, were not the sort of leaders likely to bring order 'out of a miserable state of chaos'. The 'effeminate leaders of the defunct African National Congress deliberately betrayed the confidence of the Bantu Chiefs and their people in embracing, without mandate from the provincial congress, the communist platform'.[23] When Mahabane appealed at the ICU's special conference in January 1928 for cooperation with the ANC, Champion objected that the Congress looked for aid to Russia and placed at the head of its affairs former ICU officials who had been expelled for their communist doctrines.[24]

Bunting came to the conclusion that the setting for a successful revolution was not yet present because of 'the extreme backwardness and widespread apathy of the native masses'. They certainly constituted a majority, 'but they are such an easy prey to rogues and charlatans that they will make a mess of it'.

The party's central executive, he told La Guma, would probably disapprove of 'those instructions re a Negro S.A. Republic, which seem to have originated in suggestions raised during your visit', and which were 'drawn up by people with insufficient knowledge of S.A. African affairs'. La Guma had then accepted an invitation to attend the October revolution celebrations in Moscow. Bunting thought he should stand down in favour of some one 'more closely in touch with the C.E.' (Central Executive). It would be an advantage for someone to go who 'could produce an effect, on his return, in fresh circles – e.g. pure Bantu circles, or again among whites, who still have a good deal more to say than natives on the question of war or peace'.[25]

Did this mean that the whites were more powerful, or more aware of the issues, or merely more vocal? On this occasion, at least, Bunting ignored their political backwardness and fierce rejection of radical change. He also underrated the political sense of Africans and their capacity to influence the course of events. His emotional reaction indicated that, as in 1922, he tended to equate workers' power with white power, and refused to credit the possibility of majority African rule.

Organizational and financial difficulties might have contributed to his pessimism. The party's printing press 'has eaten itself up', he informed La Guma, especially since Weinstock took away the *Forward*. The *Worker* was living on £500 borrowed from Rostron and nearly £900 from Bunting himself, 'so that my little fortune is nearly gone'. It had been decided to sell the plant and suspend publication of the *Worker*. 'Such are the difficulties of the only really anti-imperialist publication in S. Africa,' he told Gibarti, secretary of the League against Imperialism.[26] Dependent on the financial backing of white sympathizers, the party leadership might well have been apprehensive about a policy likely to alienate all but the staunchest radicals.

La Guma went to Moscow after all, and so did Gumede. They took part in the October celebrations, attended a Friends of Russia convention, and visited some of the southern and eastern republics of the USSR. While in Moscow, La Guma submitted a statement on the 'South African Situation'. The resolution on South Africa 'submitted by the ECCI', he reported, 'has not received the approval of the Central Executive of the Party' for reasons which were 'abundantly refuted by everyday facts'. It was wrong to suppose that 'the movement depends to a large extent, if not solely upon the European worker'. He obtained his privileges and concessions at the expense of Africans, with whom he refused to cooperate. Bunting's arguments drove 'the non-European comrades to the conclusion that the Central Executive of the South African Party considers the mass movement of the natives should be held up until such time as the White worker is ready to extend his favour'. A section of the party disagreed. Members of the Cape Town branch, including the whites with one exception, were for the ECCI resolutions.[27]

The party's annual conference, held at the end of 1927, viewed the Comintern's resolutions on South Africa with mixed feelings; and decided that the central executive should discuss them with La Guma and Gumede on their return from the Soviet Union before reporting to the ECCI. Meanwhile, Bunting put forward his own views in a fourteen-page document.[28] The 'native republic' slogan, he supposed, was based on Lenin's famous thesis on the colonies adopted in 1920 – a copy of which was unfortunately not available to the party in South Africa! Bunting criticized the slogan, and in doing so challenged the thesis itself.

National liberation movements, he argued, 'usually become a prey to imperialist and capitalist corruption'. This had happened also in South Africa, where the party contended with rival nationalisms, which could not be reconciled. An African movement for secession from Britain 'would probably only accelerate the fusion, in opposition to it, of the Dutch and British imperialists'. The party had 'coquetted' with Afrikaner nationalism in 1920–22 and helped it into power in 1924, 'if only to accelerate the disillusionment of Nationalist and Labourite workers'. The pact government was now the 'worst enemy of the party and of the S.A. proletariat'.

On the other hand, the party's support of the ANC and ICU 'has also led nowhere'. There was no movement among Africans for secession from British rule, which they generally preferred to Dutch rule 'as whips to scorpions'. A crusade for emancipation from empire would fail unless it gained impetus from united anti-imperialist movements in the rest of Africa. It was white overlordship that Africans resented. A 'campaign in favour of killing off, "driving into the sea", or otherwise completely eliminating practically all the whites would be very popular if it were given the chance'. Their elimination seemed to be implied in the 'native republic' slogan, as in Garvey's 'Africa for the Africans'. This was not a popular demand, partly because of repressive action taken by the white bourgeoisie, partly because the elimination was 'probably too formidable to contemplate'. Africans had long since come to regard white participation, if not leadership, as inevitable and a disagreeable necessity, 'and so in fact it is, under any system of society'.

The slogan was unjust, as well as inappropriate, according to Bunting. For it was 'directed not against the imperialists as such but against the whites as such, against large numbers of workers and peasants because they are white'. Objectively considered, they belonged to the anti-capitalist front, and many would support it but for their colour prejudice. If they were to participate in a workers' state, it could hardly be called a 'native republic'. If they were segregated in a ghetto, even with safeguards for minority rights, the existing injustice would be reversed, with whites taking the place of blacks as helots. A future 'native republic' could not, however, afford to dispense with the technical assistance and cooperation of sympathetic whites.

Their cooperation was also immediately useful because of their advantages and the low average political understanding of Africans. It was a case of uneven development due to historical circumstances, and could not be ignored. The party itself had a large majority of African members, yet white members of average experience had to undertake many tasks for which competent and reliable African members were not yet available. This unevenness was reflected in the difference of opinion in the party over the 'native republic' policy. There was more violent colour prejudice in the north than in the Cape, where the general standard of Africans was much higher. Accustomed to 'a higher average type of native' than in the Transvaal, the party members in the Cape 'form a higher estimate of the natives' capacity to dispense with white aid'. No one could predict how 'an un-armed native proletariat unaided' could defeat the capitalist class; 'but at least to win the support of their white fellow workers seems imperative'. The goal must be: All power to the soviets of workers and peasants – black and white.

A slogan that implied a direct transition to socialism was the more revolutionary in class terms. 'The future holds no inter-mediate stage,' declared the *Worker* in May 1928; 'the class struggle ever assumes a more open and undisguised form.' Disillusioned by the Labour party's squabbles and impotence, hundreds of its former supporters would turn to the com-munists, for they alone represented the interests of the entire working class.[29] On the other hand, the 'native republic' policy would establish 'black power' under majority rule, and was therefore the more revolutionary in racial terms. The contro-versy centred round the issue of 'working class power' as against 'African nationalist power'. South Africans had to choose between class war and race war. That was the essence of Bunting's appeal. There could be no doubt where he stood. One of the few surviving communists from the days of white labour militancy, he clung stubbornly to the Communist Manifesto's classic tenets.

On a point of fact, he argued that white workers were poten-tially more revolutionary than an African bourgeoisie which barely existed. The 'only effective bourgeoisie in South Africa is white'.[30] His main objection to the 'native republic' slogan was that it would neutralize the party's long struggle for unity, alienate white workers 'not altogether without justification', and drive them 'into a white united Fascist front against us and the blacks'. A race war would cloud the issue and destroy 'the tender plant of class solidarity that has just appeared above the ground'. To avert such a war, it was necessary to stress the common interests of all workers, accustom the whites 'to a prospect of black power', and make it clear that 'in our Republic blacks will not predominate *as* black, nor will whites be in a minority *as* whites; and that the future "black supremacy" will not in the least resemble the present "white supremacy"'.

La Guma, back from Moscow, challenged the view that white workers were politically more advanced.[31] They were 'saturated with an imperialist ideology', fully aware that their privileges were obtained at the African's expense, and 'therefore not prepared to assist in realizing the socialist objective in this country' – at least not until they were forced to do so. They must be educated to understand that their future 'lies in unity with the non-european masses against the exploitation of the large farmers and industrialists'. The new policy, he declared optimistically, 'would provide the necessary stimulant to the mental processes of the white "Socialist" and must ultimately produce that momentum that will drag the reluctant section of the working class of this country towards the realization of a WORKERS AND PEASANTS REPUBLIC'.

On the other hand, wrote La Guma, 'the attitude of the non-european masses is becoming sharper with the instalment after instalment of oppressive and discriminatory laws and threats of further oppression'. For this reason, and because of acute land hunger, heavy taxation, forced labour migration and political deprivation, a national consciousness was developing rapidly. The new slogan would appeal and give expression to aspirations that contained revolutionary possibilities. Citing Lenin as his authority, he argued that a national struggle for independence from imperial rule, even though led by merchants and middle-class intellectuals, would promote the working-class revolution. 'To be revolutionary, a national movement in conditions of an Imperialist yoke need not necessarily be composed of proletarian elements, or have a revolutionary or republican programme or a democratic base.' As in Egypt, a struggle for independence was 'objectively revolutionary' in spite of its bourgeois origin and antagonism to socialism, because it weakened imperialism.

Bunting thought that the road to socialism lay through working-class unity under white leadership. La Guma wanted to reverse the sequence. First establish African majority rule, he argued, and unity, leading to socialism, would follow. The party should therefore concentrate on strengthening the movement for national liberation, and at the same time retain its separate identity and role as a socialist party. Communists should 'build up a mass party based upon the non-european masses', unite landless whites and natives behind an energetic agrarian policy, give expression to the demands of African workers, and dispel their illusion that the British acted as intermediaries between them and their Afrikaner oppressors. The 'native republic' slogan would act as a political catalyst, dissolving traditional subservience to whites among Africans and racial arrogance towards Africans among whites.

The issues were thrashed out with much heat during 1928. 'All members are arming themselves with a battery of weapons for, and against the thesis,' wrote Wolton in February; and he advised La Guma to come to Johannesburg, 'adequately prepared for a battle of logic and a good deal of nonsense'.[32] Douglas Wolton, the party's newly elected secretary-editor, was a comparative newcomer to the movement. Born in England, he emigrated to Cape Town in 1921, worked on a daily newspaper, set out on a Cape to Cairo journey by foot in 1923, and got no farther than Northern Rhodesia, where he contracted malaria. On his way back he met Schack, a former social democrat from Russia, who had settled in the Cape and joined the party. Through Schack he met the local communists, including his future wife Molly Selikowitz (1906–47), A. Z. Berman's cousin, who came to South Africa from Lithuania in 1919.[33]

The Woltons ranged themselves on La Guma's side, while a majority of members on the central executive rejected his thesis. They found ample reason for confidence in their ability to give a lead on their own and without entanglements. 'At last the masses of South Africa are turning to the CP for help from their terrible conditions,' declared the *Worker*, then edited by Wolton. The answer to the 'smooth-tongued leaders', the 'money-grabbing clique' in the ICU, and 'the intellectual section' who collaborated with joint councils and 'imperialist exploiters', was the party's 'mushroom-like growth', especially in the country districts.[34] Even Basutoland had a large and active branch composed wholly of Africans. A meeting held at Vereeniging's 'location', in spite of a ban imposed by the superintendent, attracted 2,000 Africans. Several hundred, among them sixty-three women, joined the party. Its branch at Potchefstroom, the

399

ideological centre of Afrikaner Calvinism and birthplace of the Broederbond, claimed to have 700 members after only six weeks' activity. Four delegates from the branch attended a meeting of the central executive to study its methods of work, and Gana Makabeni opened a party school at Vereeniging.[35]

Equally satisfactory progress was being made on the industrial front. As the ICU split into warring camps, African workers looked to communists for aid in organizing trade unions. More than 150 delegates from half a dozen unions met in the Inchcape Hall, Johannesburg, in March 1928 to form the Non-European Federation of Trade Unions, with Ben Weinbren, a member of the party's central executive, as chairman, and La Guma as general secretary. Andrews and Tyler, both party members, told the delegates that they should not organize in opposition to the ANC or TUC, and should work closely with the ICU. This refused to cooperate, however, and accused the party of being led by white racists. The Federation claimed to have sponsored the first joint strike of Africans and whites, when clothing workers in Germiston came out in protest against the victimization of trade union members. Their action was hailed as a significant sign that economic pressures were driving the whites 'towards the ultimate unity of the entire forces of the working class movement'. Even more promising was the decision of African and white laundry workers' unions in Johannesburg to affiliate under a joint committee. Here were the seeds of 'an ultimate powerful organization recognizing and embracing all sections of the working class'.[36]

White racists attacked ICU offices in Natal and communist speakers in the Transvaal. The police also took action. They arrested African strikers for breaking service contracts, harassed party members under the pass laws, and prosecuted leaders for inciting to hostility against whites. Kadalie, prosecuted in April 1928, was the ninth victim of the infamous clause. He was followed by Sam Malkinson, a white party member in Bloemfontein, and by Mrs M. N. Bhola, organizer of the women's section of the ANC, and the first woman to stand trial on the 'hostility' charge. Few of the cases resulted in a conviction. Thibedi was acquitted at Potchefstroom when the magistrate found that the party was a legal organization, and fully entitled to agitate against the pass laws. Malkinson, charged with having distributed a pamphlet, 'What is the Communist Party?' at a convention of chiefs called by the ANC, was also found not guilty after the crown's chief witness Matebe testified that the conditions described in the pamphlet were well known to him. He had suffered under them all his life, he said, and reported that the pamphlet called on Africans to unite with white workers against the master class, white and black.[37]

The police succeeded, however, in securing a conviction against three party members at Cape Town: John Gomas, the vice-president of the Cape ANC, Bransby Ndobe, its organizer, and Stanley Silwana, a member of the executive. They were sentenced to three months' imprisonment as a result of protesting against the killing of an African and the wounding of another by a white policeman at Paarl. The three accused conducted their own appeal in the Supreme Court. Gomas made a fiery speech, attacking the Native Administration Act and the trial court. Justice Twentyman Jones cut him short and dismissed the appeal, saying that the sentence erred if at all on the side of leniency. Writing from Cape Town's Roeland Street jail, where he was in solitary confinement, Gomas appealed for books. 'I was hoping to make a complete study of Lenin's Materialism and Empirio-Criticism, but as all books are confiscated by the Prison I do not like to lose such a valuable copy.' He and his comrades found that 'in prison our wits become exceptionally sensitive'. Their thoughts were 'alive and every minute of the waking day we are reviewing in our minds the intolerable conditions which are the lot of our people'. Imprisonment had increased their bitterness; but 'the feeling of revulsion which is continually with each one of us stabilizes and strengthens our determination to work for the freedom of all oppressed'.[38]

Of all parties, said Gumede on his return from the Soviet Union in January 1928, the communists alone 'stood by us and protested when we have been shot down'. He was determined to do all in his power to emancipate his people and 'win national independence for all in South Africa, black, white or blue; a free republic for all races'. He told an ANC rally in the Inchcape

Hall of what he had witnessed in the U.S.S.R. 'I have seen the new world to come, where it has already begun. I have been to the new Jerusalem.' He had brought with him a key which with their help would unlock the door to freedom. 'Others are persuaded to be Communists. The Bantu has been a Communist from time immemorial. We are disorganized, that's all.' Gumede became the chairman and Wolton the secretary of a free speech movement, sponsored by the ANC, APO, CP, TUC and African unions. The ICU refused to take part. While Kadalie had rejected the call for unity, declared Gumede, the ANC would 'pursue its course of uniting the South African natives to help themselves'.[39]

It was a turning point in the African's history, said the communists. Gumede's conversion was 'a manifestation of the revolutionizing of the oppressed masses'.[40] He told them about the Soviet Union's policy towards national minorities, of how it helped non-literate pastoralists to freedom and equality, of its laws that made overt racialism a crime. 'Such contrasts with their own lives electrified his Bantu audiences,' wrote Wolton, 'and contributed enormously towards stimulating the new hopes which were sweeping through the Bantu peoples.'[41] Addressing a convention of the ANC's 'upper house' of chiefs in April 1928, Gumede said, 'We are nothing but slaves.' Sitting on the platform were Bunting and Wolton, the local police commissioner and Bloemfontein's white notables. Africans were grateful for the white man's civilization, said Gumede, but the colour bar retarded their progress. Open the door and let us be represented in parliament by our own colour, he appealed. Class laws were an abuse of the power held by whites, who ruled only in their own interests.[42]

Some of the chiefs objected to the president's association with the communists. Quoting Bennet Ncwana's articles, Joseph Moshesh of Matatiele said it was the most dangerous party in the world. 'What happened to the Czar and his family?' he asked. 'The Czar was of royal blood, the same as you, chiefs, and where is he now?' He called on the convention to record its disapproval of fraternization with the communists. Gumede replied that they 'were nearest to the natives, for they worked for the salvation of the oppressed'. The issue had been raised to cause a division in their ranks. Moshesh withdrew his motion on receiving an assurance that there was no connexion between the ANC and the CP, but the chiefs were not satisfied.

When he left for Moscow to attend the October celebrations, Gumede told them, he thought that people were not safe in Russia. What he saw there surprised him. They were happy and prosperous under a workers' government, after having slain the Czar, all task-masters and the drones 'who lived upon the sweat of the brows of other peoples'. A member of the audience asked: 'Do you intend to kill our chiefs?' Gumede replied that the Russians revolted because their rulers dealt with them in an arbitrary way. The new Russia, he concluded, was destined to lead mankind to a happier life. For in Russia there were neither rich nor poor; all were equal, and all shared everything that they produced. Thereupon T. M. Mapikela, a successful building contractor who had gone with the deputations of 1909 and 1914 to England, warned the chiefs that they were being dragged by hook and by crook into the hands of the Communist party, which aimed to overthrow the rulers be they white or black.[43]

The chiefs ended their session by suggesting a meeting with the ICU, then also in conference at Bloemfontein, to discuss co-operation. The two executives met and agreed on a resolution moved by Kadalie and Selope Thema. It asserted that co-operation between the ANC and ICU on matters of national policy, such as the Hertzog bills and the pass laws, was essential for progress. 'But,' continued the resolution, 'in pursuing these objects, the ANC hereby repudiates its association with the S.A. Communist Party, which of late has openly identified itself with the Congress.' He had insisted on the repudiation, boasted Kadalie, and claimed that Gumede agreed 'after some hedging'.[44] Bunting maintained that the talks had been 'stage-managed' in order 'to set on record a joint disclaimer of association with the Communists in the interests, so far as the chiefs at least were concerned, of "rulers, black and white"'; and he doubted whether the resolution had actually been adopted. 'The inference that Mr Gumede was forced to publicly repudiate the Communists is not supported by the facts.'[45]

Whether provisional or final, the resolution was a serious set-back to the party's campaign for united action with African nationalism. Would the ANC repeat the ICU's betrayal of 1926? The Cape Town branch of the ANC urged its national executive to 'explore every avenue towards the closest cooperation with the Communist Party'. Of all political parties, it alone 'unreservedly advocates freedom and equality for the non-European peoples'. It knew no colour discrimination in its ranks and correctly reflected the workers' aspirations.[46] No such repudiation came from Gumede. It seemed as though the conservative wing of Congress had forced him to retreat from the bold stand he had taken on his return from Moscow. His apparent defection must have weighed on Bunting's mind as he and his wife set off in June for Moscow to represent the party at the sixth congress of the Communist International.

Edward Roux, the third South African delegate, then working on his doctoral thesis in botany at Cambridge, travelled with them from London. Fifteen years later he wrote about the journey and the great controversy over the 'native republic' slogan. It had come 'like a bolt from the blue' to the great majority of members. 'Almost all the white communists were indignant,' and so were African members 'who had been trained in the old tradition'. They saw in the policy a revival of Marcus Garvey's cry, 'Africa for the Africans', and thought that it was the exact opposite of the party's steadfast appeal for international unity. 'We did not want to put the black man on top and the white man underneath. We wanted them to be equal.'[47]

This argument ignored La Guma's strong point, that equality could be achieved only when Africans were powerful enough to win respect from the whites. Roux never really examined the merits of the proposed policy. He says that he and Bunting were 'negrophilists'. They should therefore have welcomed the notion of African rule in all parts of Africa. Yet one is left in doubt whether they objected to the slogan in principle or only because they thought it premature and inexpedient. In either event, the policy should not have come as a shock. The guiding lines had been laid down as far back as 1920 by the Comintern's thesis on the national and colonial question. South African communists had evidently failed to study the relevant texts or to grasp their implications for the movement. Alternatively, they felt that the thesis did not apply to South Africa because there was no 'native bourgeoisie'. The chiefs and intellectuals who dominated the ANC were conservative and unreliable, while the party had demonstrated its ability to attract Africans in large numbers by militant struggle against both class exploitation and racial oppression.

Roux's main objection, however, was that the slogan had been 'forced' on the party by the Communist International in the interests of the Soviet Union.[48] It then 'regarded British capitalism as the main enemy' and attempted to weaken the empire by organizing liberation movements in the colonies. A contributory factor was the growth of a Comintern bureaucracy anxious to concentrate authority in its hands and impose uniform policies on affiliated parties. This indictment had unpleasant repercussions which Roux must have regretted. It dovetailed neatly with anti-communist sentiment and was seized on by government spokesmen and historians in South Africa to support allegations of 'domination by Moscow'.[49] Yet Roux never substantiated what appear to have been only his personal impressions. When recording them in 1943-4, he had not been a party member for at least five years and was distinctly hostile to the Soviet Union. His 'main attack', wrote Andrews in a review at that time, 'seems to be directed against the Communist International and its failure to recognize the value of his advice and opinions on the future of the African people'.[50]

The 'native republic' policy undoubtedly met with the Comintern's approval and coincided with the Soviet Union's opposition to imperialism. Approval does not mean coercion, however. Though exercising great moral authority, the CI could not compel obedience from the South African party, which had a strong tradition of internal democracy. Roux's accusation of interference from Moscow does not stand up to scrutiny for this and other reasons. As Bunting himself acknowledged, La Guma, as well as the Comintern, initiated the policy, and the policy had the support of some members in Cape Town and Johannesburg. Both sides appealed to the Comintern, as Roux himself had done in 1924 during a dispute in the Y C L over the question of African membership.

The South African party blundered by appointing three white representatives, all opponents of the new line. They seemed to present a 'white front' and aroused a suspicion at the Comintern congress of being racial chauvinists. The accusation has been repeated recently by the historian Endre Sik. 'The party leadership headed by the opportunist Bunting' and 'consisting mainly of Europeans,' he states, 'was far from devoid of the remnants of racial chauvinism.' They did not understand and they belittled the significance of African racial oppression. At the same time, they adopted a sectarian trade union policy which 'deepened the gulf between the movements of European and African labour'. For good measure he adds: 'The Communist Party, as such, in the years 1924 to 1928 displayed very feeble activity.'[51]

Apart from the reference to the dominant role of whites in the leadership, none of these statements is even faintly true. The party had been transformed since its 'turn to the masses' in 1925. It had 200 African members in 1927 and 1,600 in 1928, out of a total membership of 1,750. Twenty African and Coloured and ten white delegates, representing in all nearly 3,000 members, attended the seventh annual conference in January 1929. This advance reflected much dogged work in the face of rabid racialism and police repression. The charge of communist sectarianism in the trade unions or of indifference to national oppression has as little basis as the assertion that men like Bunting and Roux were 'opportunists' and 'racial chauvinists'. They were Marxist missionaries, who sacrificed careers and comfort to an unpopular cause and identified themselves wholly with an oppressed people. If they erred in opposing the 'native republic' policy, they acted in good faith and according to a long-standing interpretation of the class theory in relation to African nationalism.

More than any other party anywhere, declared Bunting at the sixth congress in August, the South African C P had 'as the very centre of its activities, fairly and squarely fought, conquered and killed the Dragon of Chauvinism'. This was true; though he set off on the wrong foot by saying that South Africa was 'a white man's country'. Dunne, the United States delegate, Bennett of the Anglo-American committee, and Bukharin himself saw in the phrase a 'survival of race prejudice'. Bunting hastened to explain that it merely described a factual situation. South Africa was a 'colony of settlement' with a large and permanent white population. But the damage had been done. His long and involved attack on the 'independent native republic' policy fell on deaf ears, the more so because he criticized the Comintern leadership. It had neglected to establish adequate communications with affiliated parties; and it drew an invidious distinction between the 'proletariat' of industrialized countries and the colonial 'masses'. Was not that distinction, he asked, 'exactly the way our "aristocracy of labour" treats the black workers?'[52]

A majority of the party in South Africa, said Bunting, opposed the 'independent native republic' slogan for practical reasons, in addition to serious theoretical objections. In the first place, South Africa had no 'native bourgeoisie' as was contemplated in the draft resolution, and 'certainly no movement for a native republic'. The ANC 'which the resolution wants us to boost up' was moribund. It demanded equality, not self-determination, and looked to Britain for a redress of grievances. The party gave it much attention and joined with it in a united front whenever it showed signs of life. The 'CP is itself the actual or potential leader of the native national movement'. African workers and some peasants preferred the party to 'purely native bodies' which had let them down and had fallen into the hands of the bourgeoisie. 'Put in another way, the class struggle is here practically coincident and simultaneous with the national struggle.' They had the same objects, forces, and methods of struggle. The class aspect was not less fundamental; and might even supersede the national aspect.[53]

Another important reason for rejecting the draft resolution, said Bunting, was the presence of a white exploited working and peasant class with a spirited, revolutionary tradition. The resolution urged a united front of white workers, African workers, and the national liberation movement; but the class struggles of the whites did not coincide with the national struggles of Africans. On the contrary, white workers tended to forget the class struggle and to side with their own bourgeoisie. 'Special tactics have to be adopted to prevent this, and to harmonize the national and the class movements' with a view to 'neutralizing and correcting white labour chauvinism'.

The CPSA, though almost exclusively centred in the African people, took up the cause of the white minority because of the need for labour solidarity. The fact was that the 'infant native movement' lived in a state bordering on illegality. It was in constant danger of being suppressed by legislation or by massacre, needed allies, and found the occasional support, even the neutrality, of the white trade unions of incalculable value. 'We say that the white workers are unquestionably going to be alienated by the present slogan and that instead of support from white labour we are thus quite likely going to get its hostility and Fascist alliance with the bourgeoisie. This in turn will also encourage the government to prosecute and the courts to convict everyone who preaches the slogan.'

Commenting on the speech fifteen years later, Roux wrote: 'it is probable that any communist or other labour radical in South Africa would today endorse every word of it.'[54] Like Bunting, he evidently failed to grasp the significance of the demand for an independent republic under African rule. It was, in the circumstances of the time, as remote or 'utopian' as the concept of a socialist republic under working-class rule. The shift in emphasis reflected the related changes in the party and the society at large: the absorption of the labour aristocracy in the white elite; the 'proletarianization' of Africans after fifty years of industrialism; the transformation of the party from an all-white to an overwhelmingly African membership. As prospects of unity between workers of all races receded, Africans revealed a great capacity and will for militant struggle. The value of the 'independent native republic' slogan was that it jolted the party into awareness of its new role, and inspired in Africans a determination to reject the unquestioned assumption of perpetual white domination.

The Communist party's proper role, advised the editor of *Forward*, was to educate 'the white working class to a realization of the actual economic position of the workers, irrespective of race or colour'. Africans, as a class, would remain unfitted to participate in government for many years to come. Both they and whites bitterly resented white communists who tried to lead Africans to equality 'by active participation in Socialist propaganda and agitation among natives'. When Bunting, back from Moscow, explained the new policy to an audience in the Inchcape Hall, *Forward* noted that his speech 'would certainly satisfy sensation-mongers. Such publicity has been given to his declaration of a Black Republic that every newspaper-doped South African who possesses a firearm is sleeping with it under his pillow'. There was, however, 'a vast difference between communism according to St Marx and the Gospel according to St Bunting. The first treats every worker as equal, irrespective of race, creed or colour. The second makes the black worker a member of the Chosen and the white worker an Amalekite. Thus does a misinterpreted gospel of economic liberation become the dogma of a new religion!'[55]

Was it 'in accord with Communist principles', asked La Guma, to sacrifice or delay the freedom of the large majority 'in the interest of a small minority of imperialistically imbued white workers?' They had refused to hear the party's message for twenty years, objected to its being taken to the African, and resisted every effort on his part 'toward a better and brighter day'. In 1922 they rose in arms on the Rand 'to perpetuate our serfdom'; now, through the Labour party, they supported anti-native legislation and the enactment of colour bars in industry. A 'ray of hope has appeared on the horizon in the shape of an objective – freedom and equality with other peoples', for which 'the enslaved black masses of South Africa would be prepared to demonstrate their manhood and desire'. The party must not now turn to them and say in effect, 'Yes, you will be allowed to march into the promised land at such time as it can be considered without wounding the susceptibilities of the "Baas".'[56]

Bunting loyally abided by the Comintern's ruling and accepted La Guma's plea for unqualified faith in majority African rule. He had misgivings. The slogan was defective, he thought, yet he would try to make the best of the new line. It might succeed after the initial outcry at it had receded. He and his wife met with a storm of alarmist newspaper reports on their return from Moscow. The police threatened to arrest them; white trade unionists reviled or ignored them. Old party members like Andrews and Tinker would have nothing to do with the Black Republic, and many African members, including the trade unionists, shared their doubts.[57]

Hertzog demanded 'white rule and black subjection', Bunting told a crowded meeting in the Inchcape Hall in November, whereas communists demanded a black republic. 'We are a party for freedom and independence.' If there was to be race domination, then Africans must rule. 'If there was going to be equality, there must be domination by the majority.' He explained the policy and its background in the pamphlet 'Imperialism and South Africa', and presented a shorter, more satisfactory version in a programme drafted for the seventh annual conference in December. Thirty delegates, of whom twenty were African and Coloured, marched with a crowd of supporters behind a band and flying banners from the party headquarters to the hall. Here they listened to reports of struggle and sacrifice in the teeth of persecution, intimidation and espionage; adopted a new constitution modelled on the British party's; spent a full day discussing the new programme; and elected an executive bureau of six whites and three Africans.[58]

Bunting, in the chair, ruled that any motion to reject or modify the programme would be out of order under the Comintern's rules. Wolton attacked the party's alleged 'chauvinistic errors', especially Bunting's, but the conference refused to be drawn into the quarrel. Wolton then announced that he wished to return to Britain. He was persuaded to remain in his post of secretary-editor until, he said, 'a non-European is ready to take my place'. The conference adopted the clause on 'self-determination of the African people' by eleven votes to four and accepted the programme on the understanding that it implied a workers' and peasants' republic, 'for practically all natives are workers and peasants'.

Real labour unity could be achieved, according to the programme, only when Africans had been liberated from subjection. Nothing less than a democratic revolution would destroy racial discrimination, abolish feudal relationships, and enable Africans to develop a national identity. A democratic society under African rule would lead to the abolition of class exploitation, socialism, and rule by workers and peasants. Racial emancipation and class emancipation coincided. The party's immediate task was therefore to remove all racial disabilities; restore lands and liberties seized by foreign conquerors; vindicate the principle of equality, independence and self-determination; and establish Africans in power with guarantees of equal rights for all minorities.

Communists had previously argued that equality could be realized only under socialism. First abolish class distinctions, they said, and colour bars would disappear. Bunting's programme reversed the sequence. The removal of racial discrimination in all its forms was now seen as a pre-condition for the building of a classless society. White workers were invited to abandon their role as a 'tinsel aristocracy', doomed to be either helpless or treacherous in the class struggle; and to support the demand for African power – the only practical road to workers' power. This was a great advance in the analysis of the relations between national and class forces in the liberation movement. The party had at last found a firm basis in Marxist theory for an un-equivocal affirmation of the African's claim to govern his country.

Bunting and Wolton took the new message to the electors of Tembuland and the Cape Flats in the parliamentary election of 1929. A manifesto drawn up by Roux gave the particulars: equal citizenship rights for all; the removal of colour bars from the constitution and the repeal of discriminatory laws; an open door to the public services and other spheres of employment; a fair distribution of land and an extension of the reserves; equal wages for equal work; the recognition of African trade unions; free primary education; and freedom of speech and assembly. The programme should have appealed to any voter who resented racial discrimination, but elections are not won by slogans alone. The party lacked a grass-roots organization such as the South

African party had built over many years. Wolton lost heavily in the Cape Flats, despite its high proportion of Coloured and African voters. Even La Guma, the author of the 'black republic' slogan, suffered an unexplained lapse. He canvassed for one of Wolton's opponents, an 'independent' Nationalist candidate, and was expelled from the party for his breach of discipline and 'political opportunism'.[59]

'The people of the Transkei are ready for a change,' reported Bunting in the midst of an epic electioneering campaign, the atmosphere of which was subtly conveyed in Laurens van der Post's novel *In a Province*. They came from far and near, eager to join in a militant movement against their conditions. Most of the whites were unspeakably ignorant and insolent. Hooligans broke up the first political demonstration held by Africans in Umtata. It was no more than a police camp. Nearly one-fifth of its voters were in police or government services. 'The shadow of the Kaffir wars is still over the land.' Nowhere else could a parliamentary candidate and his agents 'be shadowed throughout his election tour, night and day, by motor loads of detectives, pursuing them even into grocers' shops and lavatories and arresting and persecuting them' without legal justification and for nearly every election speech. Far more oppressive was the lifelong and inescapable persecution of the African residents.[60]

Bunting gave the reasons for his defeat in a series of articles. The police and courts had done all they could to disrupt his campaign. They convicted and expelled his driver for entering the Transkei, his only homeland, without a permit. They instituted more than a dozen prosecutions against him and his agent, Gana Makabeni, at the height of the campaign, and so wasted five valuable weeks. The ceaseless shadowing by the police, their interruptions at his meetings, and direct interference during canvassing frightened the electors away. Leading Africans visibly shunned him. Not a few stayed away from the polls for fear. Fewer than 400 had the pluck to vote communist. Intimidation, however, was the immediate rather than the main cause of timidity.

The people had been corrupted by white missionaries, who

taught them to be obedient, loyal servants of those set over them. Nothing was said in the schools of their national patriots and heroes, of the fighters for freedom from the oppressor. So crushed and moulded were the intellectuals, that some asked, like the Blind Boy, 'What is that thing called freedom or equal rights? We are content as we are.' Petty officials, interpreters and agricultural demonstrators formed a thin upper layer, deliberately created, and were often willing to help keep the masses down. The Bhunga or general council of headmen and elected members was not even a safety valve, and served as a 'screen for imperialist despotism'. So treacherous was it, that the council unanimously agreed to ask the government to take action against Bunting under Act 29 of 1897, which allowed the administration to imprison any person 'dangerous to the public peace' for three months without a trial.

The Transkei, declared Bunting in his election address, was 'a principal labour recruiting and breeding annexe of the Chamber of Mines'. Behind the scenes it controlled 'the organs of administration, police, courts, Bhunga, Native Affairs Department, yes, and the Union Cabinet itself, all dancing to the tune of big finance'. The economic standard of the people had been so adjusted by land laws and taxation 'as to ensure just that degree of poverty best calculated to drive the maximum number of able-bodied men from their homes to the mines'. They were allowed to retain a diminutive 'stake in the country' which relieved the employer of the need to pay them a living wage. By returning a communist, the electors would voice a mighty protest to the whole 'native policy' of past years, and demonstrate their will to wrest liberty, equality and self-government. The party called on the people to seek their freedom through agitation, political education, organization, demonstrations, strikes, boycotts, and now even the election. He, Bunting, had devoted twenty years to the movement of the working class and subject peoples. He had repeatedly suffered arrest and imprisonment for it, and could be trusted to fight and die for the cause of African freedom.

Wolton remained unconvinced. He blamed Bunting and other 'white chauvinists' in the party for the African's poor response to its call for national independence. They were 'hidden white supremacists' who concealed their chauvinism 'in a very stealthy fashion' by consistently discouraging the growth of an African leadership. In a 'benevolent paternal way' they 'tried to patronize the black man and thus ensure that in reality the white man would continue to direct affairs'. Wolton and his wife left in July for England with the intention of making their way to Moscow. Here they would explain the reasons for the party's shortcomings, and persuade the Comintern to intervene.⁶¹

Albert Nzula (1906–33) took Wolton's place as secretary-editor only six months after joining the party. This was remarkably quick promotion, even if he had crammed much into his short life. Born at Rouxville, OFS, he qualified as a teacher at Lovedale, and moved to Aliwal North where he taught, interpreted at the magistrate's court and acted as secretary of the ICU branch. He then took a teaching post in a mission school at Evaton, Transvaal, and here he joined the party in August 1928. Two months later, after reading Bishop Brown's 'Communism and Christianity' he decided that 'every right-minded person ought to be a Communist'. He could think of nothing else and wondered 'what part will be played by the Bantu in realizing for the world a Communist order'.⁶² A good speaker and writer, he soon showed a great aptitude for politics and became a fervent disciple of Wolton, according to whom he was the only African at this time able to hold his own in polemics with white 'socialists'. He exposed their 'faults and shortcomings' with passion and conviction, and inspired a group of African leaders to assert themselves against the entrenched white leadership.

The appointment of an African to the top position was one consequence of the party's 'turn to the masses' in 1927–8. It also led to a falling away of white supporters, taking with them valuable technical and financial resources. The loss was more than compensated for by an influx of Africans, among them teachers like Edwin Mofutsanyana and J. B. Marks, or workers like Moses Kotane and Johannes Nkosi. They Africanized the party; wrote articles for its paper in Tswana, Sesuthu, Zulu and Xhosa; organized its branches in country districts or concentrated on the trade unions. The proliferation of activities, coinciding with a splintering of the ICU into warring factions and the inertia of the ANC, transformed the party. It had formerly been the left wing of the labour movement. The communists now became the acknowledged leaders of the militant wing of the liberation movement.

18 White Terror

The Nationalist party took office for a second time in June 1929 on the eve of the great capitalist depression and South Africa's worst drought in sixty years. Workers, white and black, skilled and unskilled were plagued by wage cuts and unemployment. Africans suffered most in the lean years. Government agencies put them out of work to provide jobs for whites, and tightened pass law controls to keep work-seekers out of towns. The African National Congress set its face against any form of mass action; the communists turned their programme of black power into a practical campaign for relief from unemployment and police persecution. Oswald Pirow, the Nazi-minded minister of justice, and his under-secretary, J. F. J. Van Rensburg, later *kommandant-general* of the Ossewabrandwag,* launched a counter offensive against the radical opposition to white supremacy.

The first shots were fired on 17 June 1929, at Durban, when six Africans and two whites were killed and 108 persons injured in a race riot. Its immediate cause was a boycott of municipal beer halls and an attack by Africans on the halls at the Point and in Prince Edward Street near the ICU's headquarters. Determined to 'smash the nigger', white civilians followed the example set at Greytown and Weenen in 1928, beleaguered the ICU building, and hurled bottles through the windows. The men inside made a sortie from the hall and fought back, killing two whites. Africans rushed to the rescue from the Point and were driven back by police and the white mob, many of whom pursued the relieving column when it was in full fight. A band of white youths raided the deserted ICU premises on the following day, threw typewriters, stationery and files out of the window, and carted the safe away.[1]

* Oxwagon Sentinel, cp. Chapter 20, p. 483.

It was clear from his investigations, reported Justice de Waal, the government's commissioner, that Africans were not solely or even primarily to blame.[2] There would have been no disturbance or damage had the civilian mob not attacked the ICU hall. The whites were guilty of gross excesses; and he recommended clemency for the imprisoned Africans who alone had been prosecuted as a result of the affray. Describing the background, the commissioner found that the African in Durban was 'a most loyal and law-abiding citizen, hardworking and thrifty', whose chief desire was to be left alone to earn as much as he could in the shortest possible time 'and then to go back to his kraal'. The beer halls, according to the report, had given general satisfaction from 1908 until Champion, a remarkable man, upset the local population by urging total racial equality and condemning municipal beer brewing. He allowed such notorious communists as Bunting, Wolton and Pettersen to use his hall for meetings; therefore it was idle of him to profess a horror of their doctrines, which contributed to the general unrest. J. S. Marwick, the member of Illovo, objected to any exercise of clemency, and thought that the commissioner had underestimated the effects of communist agitation; Oswald Pirow assured the House that the law would take its course.[3]

The riots were the first fruits of Hertzog's election victory, declared the communists. They appealed for a united front against the threat of more repressive laws and against the mounting terror of raids in townships for pass and tax offenders. Bunting took the initiative. Acting on a suggestion made at the Comintern's sixth congress and in discussions with the British party's colonial commission, he arranged an all-in conference in August to form a broad organization with a limited objective. From this emerged the League of African Rights, the first successful coming together of working class and national radicals in the liberation movement. Gumede became the president; Doyle Modiakgotla of the ICU, the vice-president; Bunting, the chairman; N. B. Tantsi of the Transvaal ANC, the vice-chairman; Charles Baker, director of the party school, the treasurer. The committee included Thibedi, Kotane, and S. M. Kotu, the assistant secretary of the FNETU.[4]

A leadership so constituted was bound to combine militancy with a sense of what was practicable. The League planned to collect a million signatures to a petition for civic rights, and to organize anti-pass demonstrations on 'Dingaan's Day', 16 December, when Afrikaner nationalists came together every year to celebrate the defeat of Zulu impis in 1838 and to hear politicians ranting about contemporary 'black perils'. It had been decided by the ANC in 1928 to make this an occasion for counter-demonstrations, and the League hoped to enlist the Congress leaders in its endeavour. Armed with an emblem and a battle song, 'Mayibuye i Afrika' (Let Africa Return), the League girded itself for battle. The song, written by Tantsi and sung to the tune of 'Clementine', conveyed the aims:

> We, the Black Race, cry for freedom!
> Africa, our Mother Land,
> Was taken from our fathers
> When the darkness hemmed them round.

Chorus: Give it back now! Give it back now!
Give us back our Africa!
Let us break our chains – the passes,
Rightly striving to be free.

Gumede, Makabeni, Bunting, Roux and Modiakgotla stumped the country, speaking from the League's platform, and collecting signatures to the petition. It had many enemies, reported Makabeni, especially among the educated. They were corrupted by the 'coward-breeding education' of the missionaries, who lulled the people into acquiescence in the seizure of their country by its new rulers. There was sufficient support for the petition, however, to alarm conservative leaders in the ANC. Mahabane announced that the Non-European Christian Ministers Association would confer on methods of combating 'the menace of Communistic propaganda'.[5] The communists replied with renewed appeals for a united front against Pirow's bill to amend the Riotous Assemblies Act.

Smuts called for measures to suppress 'communist propaganda'. What he really wanted, commented *Forward*, was machinery to be used against working-class organizations and free speech. Communism, 'a gogga emanating from the guilty conscience of society', was not acceptable anywhere outside Russia.[6] Hertzog agreed that legislation was needed to offset the effect of the judgement handed down by the Supreme Court at Grahamstown in the appeals of the Buntings and Gana Makabeni against sentences imposed by the magistrate of Umtata during their election campaign. The court upheld the appeal on the ground that the prosecution had failed to prove an intention to provoke feelings of hostility. They had preached communism, 'a recognized political faith', and 'it was not easy to declare with any precision what exactly was meant by the expression "to promote any feeling of hostility between natives and Europeans" '.[7]

The police explained that it was almost impossible to prove intent in such cases, and Oswald Pirow promised his electors at Gezina, Pretoria, that he would legislate communism out of existence. The publication of a bill to amend the Riotous Assemblies Act disclosed the means. 'To our mind it will mean the practical illegalization of the Communist Party,' declared the communists, but its main aim was 'to prevent all opposition to impending legislation against the African masses'. The bill would give the minister dictatorial powers to prohibit meetings and to banish persons from specified areas. All workers, irrespective of colour, should defeat this 'damnable piece of legislation' against 'the whole nationalist movement'.[8]

A united front seemed to be in the making on 10 November, when ANC, ICU and CP speakers addressed a mass meeting of protest in Johannesburg against the bill. Pirow's effigy, inscribed *umbulali* (tyrant), was ceremoniously burnt. 'You may be burning your own fingers,' warned Gwabini of the ICU. He and Ballinger counselled caution. Africans were disorganized and split into factions, and could not afford to antagonize authority. Pirow was a reasonable gentleman who would certainly be favourable to any case that was good or fair. Kadalie approved of this moderate tone. He would like to return to the ICU fold, he said, provided that it adopted a fighting policy.[9]

Pirow struck back in Durban on the 14th with a melodramatic display of force. He led 700 policemen armed with machine-guns,

419

fixed bayonets and tear gas in a tax collecting raid on African compounds at 3.30 a.m. Tear gas bombs scattered African sightseers lining the streets, and there was no resistance. 8,000 were 'rounded up' and searched; 500 alleged tax defaulters were charged in six special courts, which sentenced those found guilty to pay the tax or serve a month's imprisonment. Tear gas had been used for the first time against inoffensive people who offered no resistance, protested Bill Andrews. They were heavily taxed without representation; and white workers, he added, must expect the same treatment in similar circumstances. Since the tax could have been collected by normal means, the operation was clearly intended to create a favourable atmosphere for the adoption of Pirow's bill.[10]

This 'bloody baboonery', as the communists called the highly publicized police performance, was preceded by inspired press reports of evidence – 'more sensational than the notorious Zinoviev letter' – of a revolutionary plot directed from Moscow to prepare the way for the black republic.[11] 'Keep cool; keep your heads; do not be rushed or bluffed into false moves even by your own leaders,' warned the executive bureau of the CP on the 15th. 'Once more the guns and bombs of the imperialist exploiters, Dutch or English, are turned on the masses.' The cause of the trouble was not Soviet gold but Rand gold, dug out by Africans whose race had been enslaved, whose national life was crushed, who were treated as enemies for the enrichment of a gang of foreign plunderers.[12]

White workers were reminded of the attempts made to crush them in 1913, 1914 and 1922; and were urged to renew the struggle for working class rule. Africans were told to keep their courage and self-respect, their hope and faith in national emancipation. 'Demonstrate in your masses everywhere, particularly on Dingaan's Day.' Kotane declared that it was time to renounce oppression and to strive for liberty under the communist banner. The party had only begun to gain a footing among Africans, yet the government was already scared to death.

Pirow flayed the English press for doubting the existence of a communist conspiracy. The government had definite proof, he said, that the CP, ANC, ICU, and League of African Rights were in correspondence with the Communist International. Gumede was an elected member of its general council and, like several others, a graduate of the communist school in Brussels. The International had instructed the party in writing on 22 October to 'wage the struggle against the Native Bills and all other forms of oppression not through petitions, but in a revolutionary manner'. Communists were told to call for militant demonstrations and strikes on 16 December under the slogan of 'Long Live the Native Republic'.[13]

At about this time, according to Roux, 'a telegram arrived from Moscow ordering the immediate dissolution of the League'.[14] The instruction was ill-advised. As a broad popular organization, with a limited and militant programme, the League of African Rights served a useful educational function, suited to the current level of political consciousness. Bunting pointed this out in a letter dated 29 October to the British party's colonial commission. Drawing on his Transkeian experience, he argued that the peasantry, having been crushed and degraded by alien conquerors, could scarcely be called the basic 'moving' force of revolution. Africans had no bourgeois propertied class to lead them, he contended, but at best only an intelligentsia. It tended to take the line of least resistance, to try peaceful methods and a moderate policy, 'because in the attempt to realize an immoderate one it will be immediately suppressed by force'. The party had to counteract the tendency; and it could not do so effectively by wishful thinking. In effect, he maintained that the revolutionary situation envisaged by the Comintern did not exist.

The diagnosis was confirmed by the attitude of delegates at a conference of the Non-European Ministers Association at Bloemfontein on 6 December. Sixty representatives of churches, the ANC, the League of African Rights, the Cape Native Voters Association and the ICU condemned the Durban raid. Like Hertzog's 'black peril' election manifesto, they said, it was meant to stampede whites into accepting repressive legislation. The autocratic powers contemplated in Pirow's bill would be used cruelly and create endless racial strife. There was no substance in the allegations against the ANC and the ICU. Neither was in any way affiliated to the CP or the Third International. Indeed, the bulk of the people refused to be drawn into the communist fold. The few exceptions who joined the party did so only because they despaired of obtaining relief from the government. 'The oppressive conditions under which the natives live are fertilizing the soil in which the Communist Party sows seeds of dissension.'[15]

'It was the old ANC' without Gumede's disturbing presence, reported Sam Malkinson, the party's leader at Bloemfontein. The delegates, he said, were trying 'to dam the rising spirit of the native mass'. He warned them that the government would yield only to organized force, but they preferred words to deeds.[16] The Rev. J. S. Likhing, general secretary of the African Orthodox Church, provincial president of the ANC in Griqualand West, and chairman of the convention, justified their timidity on the ground of political immaturity. The people, he complained, were hopelessly disorganized and divided by tribal and provincial dissensions. Internecine feuds, indifference and lethargy had reduced their political and industrial organizations to a condition of impotence. Even Doyle Modiakgotla, vice-president of the League of African Rights, urged the convention to be reasonable. The delegates should accept Hertzog's proposal to give Africans in the north some representation in parliament at the cost of their franchise in the Cape. They rejected his advice, insisted on demanding all rights, privileges and responsibilities of citizenship for their people, and decided to launch a campaign for the removal of colour discriminations. The first step would be to seek a round-table conference with the government.

Congress and ICU leaders had no qualms about associating with white liberals. Gumede, T. M. Skota and Selby Msimang accompanied Oliver Schreiner, Howard Pim, Edgar Brookes and W. Ballinger on a deputation to E. G. Jansen, the minister of native affairs, on 9 December. They asked him to repeal the pass laws. This was out of the question, he replied, though he would consider proposals for the relief of educated persons. They might, for instance, be given a distinguishing badge which would make any exempted African recognizable at sight.[17]

Gumede alone of top ANC leaders refused to be intimidated. The League of African Rights, he told delegates at its first annual conference on 15 December, must mobilize the people against the government's plans to burden them with yet more restrictions under the proposed Native Service Contract Bill, Pirow's amendment to the Riotous Assemblies Act, and a new Urban Areas Bill. Other organizations were quarrelling endlessly and vilifying one another, yet the League could fulfil its mission if only 'we are men and women enough with the mind to work for the liberation of the oppressed Africans'. They looked confidently to the League against Imperialism for support, and hoped that the world would 'once more wake up and speak out for the cause of freedom'.[18] On the next day, he, Kadalie, Bunting, and a small army of speakers addressed a Dingaan's Day demonstration held in Johannesburg under the auspices of the League, the ICU and the CP. The African National Congress stood aloof.

Demonstrations held in other big towns passed off without disturbance except at Potchefstroom, where about a hundred whites invaded the township and broke up an orderly gathering at which Marks and Mofutsanyana were the main speakers. 'Africa belongs to us,' declared Marks. 'You lie!' shouted a white bystander, and a revolver was fired at Mofutsanyana. The shot missed him and hit Hermanus Lethebe, a local party member, who died of his wounds. Joseph Weeks, secretary of the local school board and brother of the location superintendent, was put on trial for murder six months later and acquitted by the white jury. Eight white participants in the riot were convicted of public violence and dismissed with a caution at about the same time. 'For hooligans to shoot a Native is but to break a black bottle, and then congratulate themselves on being such good marksmen,' remarked Josie Mpama, one of the first African women to join the party. She, the Buntings and Chapman, a former chairman of the party, called a protest meeting in Potchefstroom after the trials, and had to demonstrate through the township before residents plucked up courage to attend.[19]

The party's eighth annual conference met on 29 December in a mood of grim determination. A year of 'unprecedentedly strenuous' struggle against 'an ever more ferocious oppressor' lay ahead. 'On top of Smuts's and Hertzog's whips come Pirow's scorpions.' The party's task for 1930 was to mobilize the people on a national scale for a 'native republic'. A start would be made by putting the communists' own house in order. The conference was expected to stop the wrangling of 'a few political demagogues' in the party who persisted in opposing the new policy.[20]

Weinbren, the chairman of the FNETU, and one of the main offenders, suddenly decided to settle in Cape Town. He left Johannesburg in January; an acknowledged 'staunch friend' and 'esteemed champion of the workers'. T. W. Thibedi, the general secretary of the Federation, was suspended from the party and then expelled for mismanaging trade union funds. Albert Nzula took his place, and was succeeded in turn by S. M. Kotu as secretary-editor of the party. Bunting grieved over the action taken against Thibedi, for many years the only African communist. The party had lost several other capable Africans, like La Guma, Ndobe, and Tonjeni, whom it could scarcely afford to lose, during 1929. But its cause was bound to win.[21]

Communists elsewhere shared this optimism. 'The outstanding feature of the present "unrest",' reported a correspondent in the Comintern's journal, 'is the fact that the *native workers* are heading the struggle *under the leadership of the* CP.' The petition circulated by the League of African Rights was widely supported; mass demonstrations were being held in spite of great resistance from the government. The working class, from which came the driving force in the fight against imperialism, was more united than ever. This showed 'a tremendous advance in the development of the revolutionary native movement'.[22]

Right wing leaders in the ANC rejected revolution. It would leave the African in a worse condition than his present state, argued Moses Mphahlele, a noted poet and secretary of the Transvaal Congress. He and Mapikela of Bloemfontein started a public campaign for the removal of Gumede from the presidency. Pirow had smeared him and the ANC as forming part of the communist conspiracy. This was bad for Congress, said the conservatives, and they complained bitterly of Gumede's communism, his visit to Moscow, his role in the League of African Rights, and, most of all, the ANC's affiliation to the League against Imperialism. 'I am not a Communist and I defy anyone to prove I am,' retorted Gumede, but he defended the party. Congress had worked with it in 1919 and again in 1927, accepted financial assistance from it in Johannesburg, and never had any trouble from those of its members who belonged to the ANC. The decision to affiliate to the League against Imperialism had been taken openly by the Congress leadership. As regards the League of African Rights, it was no more than the reincarnation of the old Funa Ma Lungelo – we seek our rights – movement. In any event, he was in sympathy with the communists, who alone pleaded the cause of the black proletariat.[23]

Hopes for a united front faded under the pressure of anti-communist propaganda and the Comintern's directive. It was the party, and not the League, that called the next all-in conference on 26 January in Johannesburg to consider ways and means of defeating the new batch of racial laws. Invitations were sent to all trade unions and radical organizations. The only whites present, apart from communists, were members of the Garment Workers' Union and the Jewish Workers' Club. The TUC and its affiliated unions, reported Solly Sachs, refused to attend for fear of being identified with the party. The conference adopted a strongly worded resolution, calling for demonstrations, strikes, passive resistance and refusal to pay taxes, with a view to compelling the government of feudal landlords and slave drivers to abandon their repressive legislation. This was a pious gesture, remarked Selby Msimang; the masses were not prepared to sacrifice lives without prospect of gain. The militants wanted a general strike, however, even though it might be unsuccessful or encounter the kind of resistance experienced at Durban and Potchefstroom. A large majority of the delegates agreed with Tantsi that the League of African Rights and the party should conduct the campaign.[24]

The League had to die, since the Comintern found it unworthy and the communists were unwilling to defy the decision. The party itself sent out a call for the general strike, with no more success than in the militant years of white trade unionism. This was not surprising. African unions were only just beginning to take root after the ICU's collapse, and scarcely existed outside the Rand and western Cape. The main obstacle was the law. There were many isolated African strikes – by dockers and quarrymen at Durban, brickmakers at Pretoria, laundry workers in Johannesburg and Cape Town, furniture and clothing makers on the Rand – but the police regularly arrested strikers and prosecuted them, usually with success, under the masters and servants laws. White trade unionists stood aloof, neither aiding nor protesting. The communists and national organizations protested, and never found a way to beat the law. In the circumstances and at a time of rising unemployment, even ardent syndicalists might have doubted the expediency of the general strike as a tactical weapon.

By adopting it, the party demonstrated its complete rejection of white supremacy and faith in the ultimate triumph of black power. 'This is a high time that we should all be pure, active extremists,' declared Edward Dambuza, one of a new crop of militants trained by Sam Malkinson in the Orange Free State. 'The Communist Party is the only party that fights honestly for the freedom of the black man in his birth country.'[25] Thousands more shared his opinion. The decision taken in 1926 to train African members for leadership and draw them into top ranking positions had given the party a mass basis. Johannes Nkosi (1905–30), farm labourer, kitchen 'boy' and ICU official, who joined the party in 1926, was making great headway at Durban, where he went soon after the beer hall riots to organize a branch. Durban had the first communist town councillor, the Norwegian shipowner S. M. Pettersen, who slipped on to the council in a by-election in January 1929. G. E. Daniels was doggedly building a branch in the bitterly racialist atmosphere of Pretoria. Josiah Ngedlane had launched a branch with 100 members in Ndabeni, Cape Town. Ndobe and Tonjeni, working closely with Gomas, the party branch secretary, were organizing Africans and Coloured in the western Cape into the most militant section of the ANC.

Much of the credit belonged to Dr Edward Roux, the new editor of *Umsebenzi* (Zulu-Xhosa: The Worker), as the party's paper was called from April 1930 onwards. It was published in Cape Town, where he had gone to take a job in the department of agriculture, which dismissed him after three months for his political activity. The paper soon became a powerful political force among Africans and Coloured, attracted hundreds of them on the platteland to the party, and filled a gap left by the closing down of Abdurahman's *A.P.O.* Publishing articles and letters in the major African languages, as well as in English and Afrikaans, *Umzebensi* attained a bigger circulation, covering a wider area, than either the *International* or the *Worker* ever achieved. Roux performed wonders on a budget of £7 10s. a weekly issue – £3 of which came from Bunting's private purse – for printing costs, rent, postage and the editor's salary! As he pointed out, the party could no longer rely on big donations from whites. Most of its members were poor workers and peasants; and the few remaining white members were not exactly rolling in money. Only the 'exploited and oppressed slaves of Africa,' he urged, could keep their paper alive.

While the party grew in size and influence, the ANC withdrew into a state of passive acquiescence. The one bright exception was the Western Province division, which led the struggles of farm workers from Worcester to Carnarvon and Barrydale. 'Follow the example of Ndobe, Tonjeni and other courageous leaders of the Cape,' appealed Malkinson on the eve of the ANC's annual conference at Bloemfontein in April. Smuts, Creswell, Hertzog and Pirow, the communists warned, were 'united in their desire to crush the growing slave revolt and maintain British and Afrikaner imperialism'. Only the united action of the whole national movement could save it from being altogether outlawed.[26]

Gumede made a similar appeal in the most forthright presidential address yet heard at a Congress convention. After describing the organizational and financial irregularities that he found on taking office in 1927, he examined the charges brought against him. Africans were dubbed agitators when they respectfully, constitutionally and moderately asked for the return of their rights. It was the spate of anti-African legislation that had upset the relations between them and the white population.

Speedy and drastic measures must be taken if they were to gain their liberty and keep their self-respect.

The world, he went on to say, was in a state of revolt and chaos. Chinese, Javanese and Indians were rising against their imperialist masters. At the same time, a terrible economic crisis threatened capitalism. Millions of unemployed were being added to an already chronic number. League of Nations talks, disarmament conferences and the like only served to hide the preparations for international war. 'Soviet Russia was the only real friend of all subjected races.' One of the ANC's aims should be to resist an onslaught against its true friend, whose ideal of emancipation inspired oppressed peoples everywhere.

Many of his people were under the illusion that they would obtain justice from Britain. Yet Ramsay MacDonald's government was at that moment trying to crush the oncoming Indian revolution. Africans had failed in their petitions to Britain, their supplications to the governor-general, their appeals to the South African government. Applications to the courts of law had resulted only in wasteful expenditure.

What was then to be done? They must rely on their own strength, on the strength of the oppressed colonial peoples, on the strength of revolutionary white workers. 'We have to demand our equal economic, social and political rights.' That could be expressed in no clearer way than by demanding a South African Native Republic with equal rights for all, and free from all foreign and local domination. Four-fifths of the population were on their side, but they had to be organized, particularly in the towns and on the farms. 'Let us go back from this conference, resolved to adopt the militant policy' in 'the spirit which has been exhibited by oppressed peoples all over the world'. No other policy would bring liberation.[27]

Pandemonium followed. The conservatives, led by Mahabane and Dube, urged delegates to reject the speech. How could they approach the government if it was approved? Nzula, Gomas, Ndobe, Tonjeni, Champion and other militants rallied behind Gumede in a hubbub of shouts, recriminations and points of order. Mapikela, the chairman, asked Ballinger to soothe the meeting, but his intervention provoked more confusion. On the next day, conference condemned the white barbarians who had broken up African meetings, demanded protection by the authorities, and decided to ask the government for a round table conference. If it was refused, suggested Ndobe, Congress should organize a national day of protest by means of strikes and mass demonstrations. Mapikela refused to accept his motion.[28] The conservatives had won the day. Gumede was ousted by fourteen votes to thirty-nine, and Seme became the new president with an executive that included Mahabane, Mapikela, Skota, Selope Thema, Dube and Dr A. B. Xuma. The parsons, chiefs, agents of the Chamber of Mines and other 'good boys', declared the communists, had effectively opposed any forward movement by the ANC.[29]

The conservatives and their white liberal advisers never quite understood their society or its power structure. They persisted in believing against all the evidence that liberation would come to them through reasoned argument, appeals to Christian ethics, and moderate, constitutional protest. Because of timidity, as Bunting alleged, or want of confidence in their people, they refused to mobilize them for mass struggle. Yet only by defying constituted authority – by 'pure active extremism' – could a voteless, fragmented proletariat and peasantry force it to consider their claims seriously. The main issues in parliamentary politics arose out of conflicts between British and Afrikaner interest groups. Neither side was interested in coming to terms with Africans, whose role was to supply labour at low cost for mines, farms and factories. All whites, apart from a handful of communists and liberals, were determined to maintain their supremacy through the ballot box, repressive sanctions and brute force.

White suffragettes got their way after twenty-five years of agitation when parliament extended the vote in 1930 to all white women over twenty-one. Universal adult suffrage for white men in the Cape and Natal followed in 1931.[30] Discrimination on grounds of colour was now a feature also of the Cape franchise, for the first time since 1852, and in spite of assurances given at Union and again in 1928 by Hertzog as regards the Coloured. He and Creswell argued that to impose a civilization test on any white person was tantamount to denying the civilization of whites in general. The logic was poor, and the Nationalist party's particular interests were unmistakable. It would gain most from the new laws, which doubled the size of the white electorate and halved the value of the African and Coloured vote.[31]

More votes for white supremacy went hand in hand with more repression for its opponents. The Riotous Assemblies Act of 1912 had been amended in 1914 to curb rebellious white workers. It was amended again in 1930 to curb the liberation movement. The minister was authorized to banish, ban or prohibit any person, public meeting or book, if in his opinion there was reason to suppose that they would cause hostility between whites and other people. He could punish without trial, and the courts had no power to overrule his decision. 'We are setting up a precedent which is fraught with the gravest concern,' warned Advocate Close, the member for Mowbray, on the third reading of the bill. 'Are we going to give away those rights and privileges which we have won, in the liberty of speech and the liberty of the person?'[32] The House passed the bill by fifty-nine votes to thirty-five. Heaton Nicholls and three other Natal members of the SAP voted with the government; Madeley and three members of the LP voted with the opposition.

While the bill was passing through its final stages, police detachments moved into towns and hamlets of the Hex River valley in the western Cape. White farmers had violently disrupted an ANC meeting of Coloured labourers at Rawsonville a few weeks earlier. An African was killed in a 'beer raid' at Worcester in April. Race riots threatened, and the magistrate of Worcester prohibited meetings in the township. The ANC defied the ban by holding a demonstration on May Day. 'Rather let us die under the ANC banner than live under the slavery of the European,' declared a speaker. The police struck back on Sunday next, invaded the township with fixed bayonets, and fired, killing five and wounding sixteen Africans. Armed whites took to the streets, assaulting Africans and Coloured, and searching for Ndobe and Tonjeni. They escaped after hiding for four days and returned to Cape Town, to resume their agitation against the right wing leaders of Congress.[33]

The communists saw their centre of political gravity shifting to the western Cape. Here, they believed, might be the textbook ingredients of a revolutionary situation. A 'bitterly exploited' rural proletariat, whose ancestors had been robbed of their land a hundred years ago, would form the backbone of the movement for a 'democratic Native republic'. The politically mature urban workers – dockers, railwaymen, factory hands – would provide the leadership. There was even a 'national bourgeoisie', consisting of Coloured and African parsons, doctors, landlords and shopkeepers, who needed mass support to free themselves from colour bars, yet feared the effects of a revolutionary upheaval. Abdurahman, the prototype of his class, gave 'nominal allegiance to the movement for national liberation', while insisting on the right of his daughter, Mrs Cissie Gool, to own a bungalow in the exclusive white suburb of Camps Bay.[34]

Villages and farm labourers might be moving forward, but Coloured intellectuals and artisans appeared to be standing still. As obsessed as whites with skin colour and hair form, they claimed to be 'brown people', denied any African ancestry, and rejected the vision of a *black* republic. Coloured voters continued to support white supremacy parties, in spite of a decision by a Non-European Conference, held at Cape Town in January 1930, to sponsor its own candidates for the provincial council. One African and five Coloured entered the lists in June. Two, Abdurahman and S. Dollie, fought each other in the Castle division; A. F. Pendla, solicitor's clerk and restaurant owner, scored 531 votes in Port Elizabeth North against the SAP candidate's 1,522; Samuelson lost heavily in Hottentots Holland; and Stephan Reagon of the APO, after defeating two white opponents on the Cape Flats, became the second Coloured man ever to sit in the council. The communists poured scorn on these proceedings. Freedom would be won, they claimed, not at the polls but by strikes, demonstrations and civil disobedience.[35]

Activists in the ANC took the same line and clashed with the conservative leaders. Splits developed within several Congress branches in the Transvaal, OFS and western Cape, where James Thaele, the Lesotho-born provincial president, moved sharply to the right. A graduate of an American Negro college, and 'well

versed in English, French, Latin, Greek and Hebrew,' according to Skota, he combined eloquence with political ambition.
Like Kadalie in 1926, he accused the communists of being a
'white man's party' and agitated for their expulsion from the
ANC. The militants rallied to their defence. Communists fought
for the bottom dog, declared Sam Hoho, a former ICU organizer.
It was largely because of the spirit Bunting left behind in the
Transkei that the Bhunga had taken a firm stand in defence of the
franchise.

While leaders squabbled 'like dogs over dry bones', complained A. M. Plaatjes, chairman of the ANC branch in Worcester,
Hertzog, Smuts and Pirow were carrying out the orders of the
white exploiters.[36] All public meetings were prohibited on
Sundays in the country districts of the western Cape. Ndobe
and Tonjeni (1895–1962), the 'black lion', found the injunction
more of a nuisance than a serious handicap and went on organizing farm workers in defiance of landowners and police. Pirow
then used his new powers under the Riotous Assemblies Act.
He issued notices in September and October banning Kadalie
and Charles Baker from attending public gatherings on the
Witwatersrand, banished Champion from Natal for three years,
and prohibited Ndobe and Tonjeni from entering the region
between Worcester and George. Ndobe replied in an open letter
written in Afrikaans. 'Your party at one time protested against
British Imperialism,' he told Pirow. 'Now that you have won a
measure of freedom for yourselves, you are assisting in keeping
a whole nation in oppression and slavery.'[37]

The bans and repression strengthened Thaele's hand. A
special meeting of the ANC executive held in September dismissed Ndobe from the post of provincial secretary because he
advocated the Communist party's policy; prohibited 'leaders
and propagandists with communistic doctrines' from addressing
Congress meetings; and banned the sale of *Umsebenzi* on Congress premises. The militants fought back with a view to gaining
control of the organization. Thaele defeated them by expelling
Ndobe's adherents. They therefore formed an Independent
African National Congress (Cape) and attempted to secure the
affiliation of country branches.[38] The police beheaded the

movement by deporting Ndobe to Basutoland and forcing Tonjeni to retreat to Port Elizabeth. Congress in the western Cape never fully recovered from these blows and its fratricidal quarrels.

The government blamed 'communist agitators' for the widespread unrest, which was symptomatic of growing misery in rural areas and brutal repression by the police. An 'appalling problem of Native poverty', reported the Native Economic Commission of 1930-32, was developing in the reserves, where people were faced with mass starvation.[39] Drought, declining crop yields, overpopulation and lean herds were driving peasants to the towns. The authorities tried to divert them to the farms by erecting legal barriers under the Natives (Urban Areas) Act, amended in 1930 so as further to curtail the right of men to move into the towns and, for the first time, to block the entry of women.[40]

Urban Africans were being herded into the segregated ghettos called locations. Here, isolated from the rest of the working class, they could be pinned down, supervised, patrolled, prosecuted for non-payment of rent, and raided for taxes, passes or prohibited liquor. Swooping down in the early hours of the morning, the police posses invaded without warrants houses and compounds, forced the occupants out of bed, arrested those who could not produce tax receipts, lodgers' permits or passes, cuffed and kicked the victims into the waiting pick-up vans. The constant raids and surveillance were reducing the inhabitants to a state of sullen submissiveness, from which the communists tried to rouse them by organizing campaigns against passes and tax laws. 'Whether educated or uneducated, rich or poor, we are all subject to these badges of slavery,' wrote Albert Nzula in a passionate appeal for united action. 'We are slaves as long as we think we can only beg and pray to this cruel government.'

'Freedom or Death,' cried Ngedlane in Cape Town. 'Let us go forward in the spirit of Dingaan, Makana and Moshesh to free our country from white imperialism.' The slogans rang out in towns throughout the country as the militants prepared for the great pass-burning demonstrations on Dingaan's Day. The communists invited the ANC, ICU and trade unions to take part in the preparations; and argued that the pass system was 'an inevitable accompaniment and prop of the whole system of robbery and forced labour'. When fifty delegates from towns in the Transvaal, OFS and Natal assembled at Johannesburg on 26 October, they met under the party's auspices. The rest of the liberation movement boycotted the conference.

Kadalie came out of his retreat at East London to warn people against the campaign. Don't burn your passes, he advised; don't follow the communists, who ever stir up trouble only to run away when it comes. Let them get money from Moscow to fight test cases in court, 'the only sensible way of getting rid of passes'. In any event, the government would soon abolish passes, so that it would be foolish to fill the jails for a cause already won. The burning of passes, added Keable Mote and Robert Sello of the Transvaal ICU, would be 'the same madness which brought tragedy to the Ama-Xosa' in 1856, when Nongquase told them that if they destroyed grain and cattle, their ancestors would help them to drive the white invaders into the sea. Africans might be slaves, as communists alleged, and in that case 'we say, "Where ignorance is bliss 'tis folly to be wise"'.[41]

So negative an attitude in men who for nearly ten years had headed the largest section of the liberation movement revealed a timorous immaturity and poverty of leadership. It was 'politically corrupt', declared the communists in a comment on recriminations between Kadalie, Champion and Ballinger. The crisis of leadership reflected the uncertainty and disunity of a people undergoing a transition to an industrialized society. The ANC, though more discreet than Kadalie, failed to take practical steps against the pass laws in spite of its decision in October 1928 to conduct a country-wide campaign for their abolition. Seme, Mahabane, Thema and their colleagues feared to take the plunge from angry rhetoric into militant mass activity. And so, deserted by their allies and crippled by Pirow's bans, the communists were left to conduct defiance unaided on 16 December.

It turned out to be a bonfire rather than the conflagration for which they had worked so hard. Thaele's followers broke up an anti-pass demonstration in Cape Town; 150 passes were burned in Johannesburg, 300 in Potchefstroom, 400 in Pretoria, and 3,000 in Durban. Here blood was spilt in a violent affray such as invariably terminated any large-scale campaign against racial oppression. The Durban branch of the party, which had grown into a powerful force under the able and devoted direction of Johannes Nkosi, began its Dingaan's Day demonstration on Cartwright Flats at eight o'clock in the morning. After four hours of speech making, the demonstrators prepared for a procession through the town, in defiance of a police command. A large force of policemen barred the way and, when the demonstrators bore down on them, attacked with clubs and assegais. Nkosi and three other Africans were stabbed to death and horribly mutilated by African constables.

The coroner commended the white police for their self-restraint and put the blame squarely on the African constables. They had 'used more force than was requisite'; 'the use of assegais was not necessary'; and 'they had failed to exercise reasonable restraint'. Several witnesses testified to having seen constables stab the murdered men, yet the police were strangely 'unable' to identify the killers.[42] They escaped prosecution, while twenty-six demonstrators were convicted of public violence, four being sentenced to six months' hard labour. Seven African witnesses swore that they had seen the chief constable shoot at Nkosi, who was stabbed after being taken into custody, but the court rejected the allegations.[43]

'An uncompromising fighter, he died as he lived, fearless and conscious of the great fight,' wrote Nzula in a widely circulated tribute to Nkosi. His final message in Zulu warned the workers to awake and throw off their shackles. 'Durban, that centre of British jingoism,' declared the Communist party, 'has once more been the scene of a fatal clash between the forces of the slave drivers' government and the rising tide of the African liberation movement.' The party's campaign against the hated pass laws was fully justified. Africans were prepared to make sacrifices and die in order to free their country from bitter oppression. There must be 'no crying off. We must avenge our martyred dead.' The anti-pass campaign should be extended to every location, farm, mine and factory.[44]

The party, struggling desperately in Durban to rally its forces and continue the burning of passes, was bludgeoned and broken by the police. Pirow banned all public gatherings on the Flats and drove hard against the militants. Using administrative procedures under the Urban Areas Act, magistrates declared that any African who held a party card or who worked with the party was 'idle, dissolute or disorderly' and liable to banishment for two years. Gana Makabeni, the new party organizer in Durban, was deported to his home in the Transkei. Abraham Nduweni, leader of an Independent ICU branch, who had taken it *en bloc* into the party, was deported under escort to his village near Standerton. More than 200 communists and militants were banished to their rural homes in the next few months without any semblance of charge or trial.[45] Deprived of its leaders, infiltrated by spies and informers, the Durban branch was forced to instruct its members to comply with the pass and tax laws so as to avoid deportation.[46]

Critics have said that the campaign was premature; that it should have been preceded by a long, intensive course of mass education in the techniques of passive resistance.[47] Yet Africans had protested and defied the pass laws for some fifteen years. Both the ICU and the ANC put passes at the top of their long list of grievances. It was the futility of verbal protests and appeals to government that justified the campaign. Some way had to be found of stimulating the people to throw off habits of conformity and acquiescence before they had been coerced into accepting passes as an inescapable evil. Only a widespread, violent rejection could stop the rot. The criticism should have been directed at ANC and ICU leaders who betrayed the movement at a crucial stage when a combined effort might have forced the government to retreat.

Both the ANC and the Non-European Conference, meeting at Bloemfontein in January 1931, discussed the burning of passes. It was one of the worst steps that could be taken, Seme told the ANC. They could obtain the respect of whites only by acting in a moderate way. The Rev. James Calata, Champion and Thaele urged Congress to rid itself of communists, who spread their doctrines under its auspices. The Non-European Conference appeared to be more militant. Right-wing leaders for the first time contemplated calling on people to destroy the passes. When Abdurahman suggested Dingaan's Day for the event, however, Kadalie objected that this would amount to forming a united front with the communists. Conference finally agreed to ask the government 'respectfully but strongly', to do away with the system, and, if it refused, to set aside a day in 1934 on which passes would be burnt. As though to underline its futility, the conference decided to send another grievance deputation to the British government; and again postponed the formation of a united body to coordinate African, Coloured and Indian political activities.[48]

The communists remarked derisively that the conference might as well have nominated the year 2034 for all the intention that it had of organizing an anti-pass campaign. Dissensions in the ANC were 'symptomatic of its present decay and futility'. Seme was expelling his rivals, including Thema, though both were 'good boys of conservative outlook'. Congress 'is now split into at least four sections and will soon come to rival the ICU in the multiplicity of its quarrelling groups, the opportunism of its leaders and its lack of a fighting policy'.[49] Before the year was out, however, communists, too, would suffer from the internal dissension that plagued the liberation movement in all its parts.

19 Theory and Practice

South African radicals gained a rare understanding of the inter-actions between labour and nationalist movements in a colonial type society. Those who served an apprenticeship in trade unions had no illusions about the colour prejudices of white workers. Communists were as familiar with the shortcomings of Coloured and African left-wing groups. Multi-racial from top to bottom, the party claimed to form a bridge between the two streams and aspired to unite them in a great revolutionary flood.

Communist theory and strategy were most effective when adjusted to local conditions and the existing level of political maturity. The party had to set the pace and yet not move so fast as to become isolated. It might then turn into a doctrinaire sect like the early socialists, or run the risk of being destroyed. A fine judgement of political possibilities was needed, and this the party had acquired, sometimes at the expense of internal strain. Though they might seem to move slowly and with too much caution, the Communists were by far the most revolutionary group in the country.

Critics in the international communist movement complained that the party was not revolutionary enough. It was accused of 'tailism'; of 'lagging behind the growing mass discontent'; of being 'practically isolated from the spontaneous movement of the masses'; of 'committing serious mistakes of a Right oppor-tunist character'. The indictment appeared in a ten-page memorandum from the ECCI, the executive committee of the Communist International.[1] Though dated 7 May 1930, it was made public only in December, when a first instalment appeared in *Umsebenzi*.

As in 1928, and in keeping with Lenin's thesis of 1920 on the national movement in colonies, the ECCI proposed two stages in

South Africa's revolution. The first phase would terminate in a capitalist democracy, the second in socialism. Lenin's thesis assigned a primary role to a revolutionary nationalist bourgeoisie in the first phase. The ECCI, in contrast, asserted that in South Africa the 'native bourgeoisie exists only in an embryonic form. The intellectuals (native teachers, native parsons) are mostly in the service of the European ruling class.' Therefore, concluded the ECCI, 'the only class capable of uniting the national-revolutionary fighting front is the native proletariat, supported by the most exploited masses of the white proletariat'. Communists were the vanguard of the working class. They should maintain their independence in all circumstances, for only in that way could they accomplish their mission: 'the complete carrying through of the nationalist revolutionary struggle, and, as the subsequent stage, the socialist revolution'.

A programme of action for the 'independent native republic' in its first phase should include demands for civic rights and the removal of discriminatory measures – pass and poll tax laws, restrictions on freedom of movement and residence, labour compounds and indentured labour – together with a return of land to the peasants and a united front between Africans and poor whites. All this was familiar. It had formed the political stock in trade for many years of the Communist party, the ANC, the ICU and, more recently, the League of African Rights. Since all agreed, would it not be sensible of them to combine their forces in a concerted effort behind the programme?

Definitely not, said the ECCI. The League, the ICU and the ANC were reformist organizations or 'petty bourgeois nationalist parties' which used radical slogans to entice the masses. By associating with 'reformists' like Gumede or 'low traitors' like Modiakgotla, the party made itself responsible for their waverings, abandoned its independent role, and allowed the League's programme to eclipse its own. For instance, the party had urged Africans to 'keep cool, keep your heads' during the Durban raids; and collected signatures on a petition to the 'slave-owning imperialist parliament'. These were reformist methods of struggle. The party should have organized demonstrations of protest among Africans and whites, committees of action and strikes in factories. Only in this way could it 'guarantee the hegemony of the proletariat in the nationalist revolutionary movement'.

There was no reason to suppose that white workers and Africans would come out on strike or act in unison for a political aim. The ECCI exaggerated the strength of the party's resources and at the same time underestimated the value of its ideological contribution. It was correct of communists to work with and within the ANC, to criticize backward leaders like Seme and Modiakgotla, to praise Gumede for his spirited defence of the party and the Soviet Union, and to adopt methods of struggle appropriate to the general level of political consciousness and organization. If there was to be no united action, not even with leaders of Gumede's calibre and not for a programme of immediate demands, why should the party aim at an 'independent native republic' instead of an out-and-out socialist revolution?

This was the central issue. Instead of facing it squarely, the ECCI complained that the party failed to understand its own policy. African members, 'still influenced by petty-bourgeois-peasant nationalism', insisted on a purely 'nationalist-revolutionary movement' and ignored 'the necessity for the dictatorship of the proletariat in the social revolution'. White communists, in contrast, retained remnants of racial chauvinism, denied the role of African nationalism, believed only in a 'purely proletarian struggle', and therefore neglected to put the party at the head of the growing nationalist revolution. Bunting, in particular, wanted to 'skip the bourgeois democratic stage' and proceed directly to the 'pure' proletarian revolution.

The criticisms of Bunting were supported by extracts – distorted or quoted out of context, he complained – from his letter of October 1929 to the British party. He, together with Andrews and Roux, was said to be a chauvinist because he had no confidence in the African's capacity for struggle; a reformist, because he would limit the national movement to a struggle for equal rights; and a right deviator because he allowed 'the native bourgeoisie and the intellectuals' to take the lead. These errors amounted to 'a tacit acceptance of European domination'.

Reduced to simple terms, the ECCI's complaint was that

African communists were nationalists at heart and that white communists belittled the national liberation movement. The supposed dichotomy rested on a misunderstanding of the party's structure and role. For the former, the party had a uniform body of principles and should have been judged as a single entity. African party members like Nzula, Mofutsanyana and Nkosi repeatedly advocated a class struggle and criticized the ANC's conservative leaders. Bunting, Roux, Baker and Malkinson, on the other hand, accepted the black republic policy, worked closely with militant African nationalists, and consistently agitated for the removal of colour bars. As regards the role, the party could not take over the ANC's function of developing a sense of national pride and unity. The party and the ANC were allies rather than rivals in a struggle against class exploitation and racial discrimination.

Congress represented a variety of interests and trends. It was hampered internally by tribal and regional rivalries; confused by external and contrary pressures from government agents, white liberals and radicals. Conservatives competed with militants for leadership. Unable to make any impression on a hard, implacable regime, the parsons and intellectuals who dominated Congress allowed it to drift into apathy and despair. D. S. Letanka, editor of *Abantu Batho* since 1912, reproached the leaders for thinking more of presidential 'honours' than of the welfare of their race. They had forfeited the confidence and loyalty of the people, he warned, by quarrelling among themselves. Africans no longer believed that Congress would put an end to tribalism and lead them against the white oppressors.[2]

The weaknesses reflected a general state of political immaturity which the ECCI ignored. The authors of the memorandum thought it quite evident that the opposition to Hertzog's bills was 'transforming itself into a struggle against the entire system of imperialist oppression'. To equip itself for the leadership, the party was advised to employ a core of full-time professional revolutionaries, form cells in factories and streets, organize revolutionary trade unions of workers and farm labourers, and launch a peasants' movement for the seizure of land. The party should also extend its activities to Bechuanaland, Basutoland and

Swaziland, establish close contact with the revolutionary toiling masses of Rhodesia, Kenya and Portuguese Africa, and become the ideological leader of communists in other parts of the continent. The party should aim at forming 'independent native workers' and peasants' republics as a transitory stage towards the subsequent Union of Socialist Soviet Republics of Africa'. It was an ambitious programme, and so far to the left that any communist who did not accept all of it ran the risk of being called a 'right deviationist'.

The party had earlier and without external prompting attempted to put its house in order for the sharp struggles that lay ahead. 'We have not yet built up a really centralized and disciplined organization,' reported the executive bureau. It decided to register only active members who paid their dues regularly, and to purge the ranks of those who were inactive or politically unreliable.[3]

One of the first to be expelled for unreliability was Manuel Lopes of Cape Town, a radical socialist of fourteen years' standing and a die-hard opponent of the black republic. It was, he maintained, Marcus Garvey's gospel of rabid Negro nationalism writ large in the constitution of the CP, and 'an opportunist distortion'. Any nationalist movement could only arrest the revolutionary class movement. To this Roux as editor replied that any white socialist who refused to acknowledge the right of the exploited and sjambokked Africans to complete national autonomy was a chauvinist. Nothing in the slogan of a 'native republic' should antagonize any genuine white revolutionary.[4]

Sterner measures were to follow. Wolton returned to South Africa in November 1930 at the request of the Comintern and with two resolutions from the ECCI. He and his wife had gone with a British delegation in July to the fifth congress of the RILU in Moscow. They reported on South Africa and helped to draft the directives.[5] Molly Wolton remained to attend the Lenin school while Douglas proceeded on his mission to South Africa. He took over the position of acting secretary from Bunting and persuaded Roux, who was impressed by his determination and apparent command of theory, to transfer the paper to Johannesburg.

The resolutions were circulated in December in preparation for the ninth annual conference.[6] They warned of a serious right-wing danger which caused sharp political disagreements, organizational chaos and 'intensely bitter, non-political and personal divisions in the leadership'. The right wing, according to the executive bureau, was fundamentally opposed to the policy adopted at the annual conference in 1928. In particular, the opposition had no confidence in the revolutionary capacity of the masses, failed to lead them in struggle, and for chauvinistic reasons prevented Africans from taking a full part in the leadership.

The indictment was repeated in a variety of forms throughout the year. Wolton, claiming the authority of a 'CI representative', installed himself firmly at the head. A new central committee 'was carefully elected to exclude the politically dangerous elements', notably Bunting and Malkinson. It consisted of nineteen Africans and four whites: Wolton, the general secretary, Roux, Sachs and Baker. For the first time, claimed Wolton, 'the conference was able to make a general analysis of the situation and tasks of the Party in this country in terms of Leninist theory'. The ninth congress, he claimed, 'marks a decisive turning point in the class struggle, away from the dangers of white chauvinism and opportunism, into the path of revolutionary struggle along the new line of independent leadership in the national revolution towards the dictatorship of the proletariat'.[7]

Wolton made an effort to reshape the party on the model adopted in advanced industrial countries. Branches were instructed to let inactive members lapse and to place the active ones in functional groups attached to factories, mines, labour compounds and townships. By concentrating its forces, the party would establish itself firmly in strategic areas. The scheme was a great improvement on the existing organization, in which members came together for propaganda purposes and rarely engaged in systematic, continuous political activity. But the branches had few members in factories or workshops and none on the mines, in spite of attempts made since July 1930 to form an African miners' union. The spade work yielded long-term results rather than immediate gains.

African trade unionism had declined on the Rand since the withdrawal of Thibedi and Weinbren from the FNETU. It was now revived under a new name – the African Federation of Trade Unions – and in the form of a broad militant movement. Instead of fighting for higher wages in specific occupations, it organized or took part in demonstrations of the unemployed, international labour day rallies, and pass burning campaigns. Wolton argued that no union worth its salt would restrict its activities to the economic struggle. The proper role of African unions was to take the struggle to a 'higher political level' and guarantee the supremacy of the working class in the national movement.

The argument was sound in the circumstances. A strong infusion of workers into the ANC's councils might have fired them with a sense of urgency and a militant spirit. Wolton, who had no practical experience of trade unions, forgot, however, that their primary function was to improve wages and conditions. A union that had passed this test might gain rather than lose by engaging in politics. As Kadalie had learned, on the other hand, no union would retain the confidence of its members if it neglected their economic interests. Wolton's policy therefore neither produced trade unions nor strengthened the influence of the workers on the liberation front.

Wolton's main concern was to instal the party as the commander-in-chief of the liberation forces. It should, he urged, steer clear of 'leaders who have repeatedly betrayed the struggle'. There must be a united front from below and with the rank-and-file. His approach turned out to be much the same as the old policy of appealing to the masses. Instead of a League of African Rights, the party instituted Ikaka Labasebenzi – the Workers' Shield – in January 1931. Affiliated to the International Red Aid, its function was to assist political prisoners, 'organize mass campaigns against all forms of White Terror', and 'fight against all forms of Racial oppression and Racial Chauvinism'.[8] Meetings were held, collections were taken, and some relief was given; but, wrote Wolton, 'the organization failed to stimulate any widespread support amongst the Bantu'.[9]

Workers and peasants, according to Wolton's thesis, were ripe for revolution. Only the influence of timid, reformist leaders restrained them. They would respond, he believed, to the party's call for a general strike, civil disobedience and any possible kind of resistance to governmental authority. Radical socialists before him – Crawford, Dunbar, Andrews, Bunting and Jones – had also followed the 'hard line'. They had appealed to a militant white proletariat, as he to the African working class, with equally disappointing results.

He did succeed in arousing a feeling of urgency. New forms of propaganda were adopted. Roux and Gomas pelted members of parliament with leaflets from the gallery of the House on 6 March, the 'international day of struggle against unemployment'. An unprecedented multi-racial demonstration on May Day in Johannesburg brought 2,000 Africans and 1,000 whites on to the streets. Advancing from different points the two columns converged and shouting 'We want bread,' 'Work or Wages,' swept down on the Carlton Hotel. Police fastened the doors and beat off the attack. The demonstrators moved on to the Rand Club, where they clashed with the police in hand-to-hand fights. Four whites and two Africans were arrested.[10] Issy Diamond, a revolutionary barber and leader of unemployed whites, was sentenced to twelve months' hard labour, the longest sentence yet imposed on a white communist.

The unusual display of inter-racial solidarity confirmed Wolton's belief that he had found the key to revolution. So slight a gain as the temporary coming together of four white unions with the AFTU reflected, he thought, 'the rapid radicalization of the workers'. Drawn together in common struggle, workers of all races would lead the peasants 'in the national revolution for a Native Republic towards a Workers' and Peasants' Government in defence of the Soviet Union'.[11] Similar optimistic forecasts recurred in a stream of manifestos, directives and appeals from the party, the AFTU, Ikaka Labasebenzi, and the Unemployed Workers' Union.

No amount of slogan shouting would stop the government's offensive. New curfew regulations required African women to carry night passes between 10 p.m. and 4 a.m. on the Rand and in other selected areas. Africans were being reduced to the level of a conquered people held down by an occupying army. The party appealed for country-wide strikes on 1 August against the 'vicious intensification of persecution'; but the people withheld their support. As A. Mopu, one of Durban's communists, explained after serving a five months' sentence for pass burning: 'I find the general idea of the Zulus in Durban is that it is no use joining the Party, as people are sent to jail.' He told them that unless they suffered, went to jail and died in struggle they would never be free. 'They said: "We must have arms. It is no use being killed without weapons." I am being deported!'[12]

The Durban demonstrators sweated out their sentences in prison road camps under warders who cursed and flogged on the slightest provocation. Communist prisoners were kept apart, short-rationed and thrashed when they complained. One died in jail of bronchial pneumonia after having been sjambokked and left for three days without medical care. Wolton exposed the conditions in *Umsebenzi* and was put on trial for *lèse-majesté*. His witnesses testified to having been flogged themselves, or to having seen others flogged, and he was sentenced to four months' imprisonment for defaming the warder in charge.

How many men would run the risk of being beaten, half-starved and locked up in stinking cells? Would the party lose its followers by calling for sacrifices greater than they were prepared to make? The leaders took an optimistic view of the revolutionary potential and blamed setbacks on organizational defects or the slackness and heresies of members. There was a great improvement in political clarity, reported Solly Sachs at a central committee meeting in July, though the party still lagged behind the masses. It had made no headway in the basic industries of mining and agriculture; and the AFTU was not yet able to build a broad basis round the existing unions. Taking his cue from the eleventh plenum of the Communist International, Wolton attributed the party's weakness to the 'right danger which consists of opportunism, white chauvinism and passivity'.[13] These were ominous words that heralded a major purge.

The axe had fallen in March on Sam Malkinson, the devoted and courageous party leader in Bloemfontein, one of Afrikanerdom's main strongholds. He had turned the township into a 'storm centre' of the liberation movement and attracted hundreds of recruits, including prominent members of the ICU. Pirow had acknowledged his influence by banning him from public gatherings. Wolton, however, deciding that he was a 'Buntingite', dropped him from the central committee, much to the annoyance of the Bloemfontein branch. Roux, then faithfully carrying out the line, explained that Malkinson was theoretically unsound. The branch continued to protest, whereupon the political bureau expelled him 'for factional activities'.[14] The party in Bloemfontein never fully recovered from this self-inflicted blow.

Disciplinary action was next mooted against Andrews for having appeared on the platform of the Johannesburg United May Day Committee in opposition to the party's non-racial demonstration. At the request of the political bureau, he submitted a memorandum on his work as secretary of the Trades and Labour Council. The party, he pointed out, expected its members to seek office in trade unions with a view to promoting its revolutionary programme. This being so, his position as secretary was not inconsistent with the party's principles. He had done what he could 'to present a barrier against reactionary tendencies and racial antagonisms and to encourage and assist the militant elements'. Against much opposition, the TLC had adopted a constitution without a colour bar and accepted the affiliation of unions which included Coloured, Indian and African members. If it was not proper for a communist to be an official of the council, he must necessarily object to his own union affiliating to such a body. It would then fall into the hands of conservative leaders who rejected the party's entire policy.[15]

Andrews argued in effect that a communist was bound by the rules of trade union democracy. It was his duty to put forward a progressive, militant policy. He should neither be censured nor resign his office if the rank-and-file refused to follow him. The political bureau emphatically rejected these views. It issued a statement of 1,500 words in September 1931, announcing the expulsion of Andrews, Tyler, Sachs, Bunting, Fanny Klenerman (Mrs Glass) and Weinbren. Apart from Bunting, all were prominent trade unionists. They were accused of having drifted away from the party into reformism and social democratic methods of work; of building 'a strong reactionary trade union apparatus, in full support of the class collaboration policy of the reformist Unions'; and of neglecting 'the red trade unions'. Bunting's case was different. He had erred by appealing for leniency when defending political prisoners in court; had attempted to secure Thibedi's reinstatement in the party; and had spoken on the same platform as members of the ICU and ANC at the Bantu Club.[16]

The specific charges were trivial or related to methods of work rather than disputes over policy. Inactive members could have been left to lapse without a fuss, as was the usual procedure. Wolton wanted to uncover a 'right wing danger' for reasons that appeared in the preamble. It predicted a 'new wave of struggles' against the 'Fascisation of the whole Bourgeois State apparatus'; deplored the failure of Communist parties everywhere to lead the masses; and alleged that the failure was giving rise to 'strong right wing tendencies within the parties of all countries'. So also in the South African party. Its 'right-wing elements' revealed themselves 'in unprincipled opportunistic acceptance of the line of the party in words, whilst rejecting it in deeds', in sabotage, passivity and in 'definite factional activities against the leadership'.

Wolton might have believed that only drastic surgery would preserve international communism; and that South Africa should set an example. Sachs, who was then a member of the political bureau, complained that it had never even met to discuss the expulsions. The resolution, he said, 'emanates from two individuals who are in charge of the Press, and not from any responsible party organ or committee!'[17] According to Roux, the expulsions were ordered by Wolton and Lazar Bach, a young communist from Latvia, who came to South Africa in 1929, joined the party in 1931, and was promoted to the political bureau within a few months. He, too, was a doctrinaire and insisted on a 'hard line' because it seemed to be consistent with the CI's current policy.

The expelled members were not accused of being chauvinists

or of opposing the black republic policy. As the daily press quickly noted, they had offended by not being 'red' enough. Pirow said they were dangerous revolutionaries, whereas Wolton and Bach took their standard from industrialized countries with a racially homogeneous population and a large, established working class. Like Kadalie, when he expelled communists from the ICU and imported a constitution from Britain, Wolton allowed himself to be guided by external influences with insufficient regard for local conditions. He insisted that the party should 'go it alone', without compromising entanglements or commitments to less radical organizations. His fervent faith in the revolutionary mood of African workers and peasants convinced most party members that his drastic measures were justified.

Durban's district party committee approved. The committee in Cape Town went one better by expelling its own 'right-wing elements': J. Pick, Mr and Mrs Plax, Wilfrid Harrison, J. Raynard and S. Fridman. La Guma was the next to go, although he had been reinstated to full membership only three months previously, on confessing his error in having opposed Wolton during the parliamentary election of 1929. The notice of expulsion, which was signed by his close associate John Gomas, alleged that he failed 'to control revolutionary work in the Red Trade Unions' and that he questioned the party's capacity to provide independent leadership in the trade union movement. He was, in effect, a victim of the 'go it alone' policy.[18]

La Guma and Gomas were then actively engaged in forming trade unions on a joint income of £4 10s. a month. Both assisted a group of garment workers who came out on strike against a wage cut of 10s. on a weekly wage of £3 10s. or less. Bob Stuart, secretary of the local union, declared that the strike was unofficial, whereupon La Guma appealed for financial help to the garment workers' union in Johannesburg. Bach intervened, with the result that the party in Johannesburg instructed La Guma to 'pursue an independent line' and refuse aid from any 'non-party' union. He ignored the directive, and filed a counter-complaint against Bach who, he said, was 'tactless, bureaucratic and disruptive', the 'cause of past friction and potential disruption', and 'a serious menace to the Party welfare, prestige and progress'.[19] Bach remained, while La Guma, the chief architect of the 'black republic' policy, was cast out into the political wilderness. There he remained until 1935, when he launched the National Liberation League under the slogan: 'For Equality, Land and Freedom.'

Most of those expelled withdrew from politics or became absorbed in trade union work. Andrews declared that he would continue to organize workers of all races and creeds for the dictatorship of the proletariat, resigned from the TLC in 1932 and went to England for a serious operation. Bunting alone fought hard for reinstatement. He did not hanker after the leadership, he explained in a circular letter to members.[20] All he wanted was to do his bit 'in the great war for African emancipation' and free himself from 'the persistent misrepresentation, boycott and persecution' to which he had been subjected for over a year. Because of the propaganda against him, much real party work had been '*scamped or most inefficiently conducted*'; while 'party *membership and general agitational activity have shrivelled* almost to a skeleton'. He had been banned '*by a small dictatorship without giving any notice (much less a hearing)*'. Members, he appealed, should insist on a conference where delegates could debate the issues and cancel the expulsion.

No such conference was held. The harder Bunting tried to get a hearing, the more he was attacked by the political bureau, until 'Buntingism' became as notorious a label as 'Trotskyism' in party circles. Roux has given a detailed account of the unworthy methods used to discredit his old friend and former leader, and to hound him from public life.[21] The story makes painful reading, the more so because Roux, who also sat on the bureau, actively participated in the persecution, even to the extent of informing against him on the merest hint of suspicion that he had joined with Thibedi in setting up an opposition Communist League, allegedly under Trotskyist influences. Bunting was a wolf in sheep's clothing, wrote J. B. Marks on this occasion; a man who had been expelled because of chauvinism, anti-native and anti-party activities. To this *Umsebenzi*, then still edited by Roux, added that Bunting was a rich lawyer, absentee landlord, and prominent son of a British peer who had fought firmly for imperialist domination.[22]

Roux objected to the abuse, and was consequently dropped from the political bureau, leaving it in the hands of Bach, Wolton and his wife Molly, who returned from the Lenin school in 1931. It was not until September 1935, during another round of expulsions, that Roux made his first public act of contrition and apologized for his share in the fratricidal feud. Eight years later, in his biography of Bunting, he gave reasons for his acquiescence: he agreed in the main with the Comintern's policy, did not completely share Bunting's outlook, and knew that he himself would be expelled if he protested. These are honest reasons, yet they do not justify Roux's attempt to shuffle off the ultimate responsibility on to Soviet Russia and the Comintern.[23] No amount of pressure from these quarters, and no Comintern representative in South Africa, could have forced the leaders to expel any members against their will. Roux, Bach and the Woltons acted freely, believing that what they did was in the interests of the movement.

Wolton has not explained his own attitude, although he wrote a book on South Africa which appeared in 1947, fourteen years after he had left the country. The book is negatively revealing. His description of the Communist party, its work and policies, takes up fifty lines. He makes no mention of his role in the party or of his wife's; indeed, never tells the reader that they lived in South Africa.[24] He is warm in his praise of Albert Nzula, but does not record that he was a party leader, or that he died in Moscow of pneumonia in 1933. Similarly, when referring to Kotane, Mofutsanyana, Marks and Nkosi, he describes them as trade unionists and never as party members. No word is said about the expulsions in his book.

Yet he had the backing of the ECCI, which approved the expulsions in a letter read by J. P. Sepeng, a stalwart from the Potchefstroom branch, to the central committee in December 1931.[25] The 'Right opportunist chauvinist Bunting clique', according to the ECCI, having opposed the 'whole line of the Comintern', had 'openly become chauvinist agents of Imperialism, appealing to Pirow and Hertzog against the party'. The

451

accusation, which no one in South Africa could possibly credit, was as groundless as the ECCI's assumption of an imminent revolutionary upsurge. 'The framework of the slave regime is beginning to burst under the pressure of the masses, who are seeking in the CP their guide and leader.'

The communists simply did not have the resources needed to carry out the ambitious programme suggested by the ECCI. It reproached them for failing to organize a peasants' revolt, strikes, and illegal cells in factories, mines, farms and reserves; for not having taken over the leadership of the national liberation movement; for defects of organization, which lagged far behind their political influence. The weaknesses were an index of the people's political backwardness and could not be cured by purely internal party reforms. It might be correct to argue that every struggle for elementary rights and pressing needs 'must inevitably become a revolutionary struggle'. The ECCI, however, studiously ignored the state's monopoly of armed force, the inability to discover effective forms of resistance against a merciless repression, and the decline of militancy in mass organizations.

Sol Plaatje told the Cape Native Voters Association at Aliwal North that 1931 had been a barren year for the ANC, and Selope Thema agreed. 'Since 1912 and during my nineteen years of service in the cause of Bantu freedom, I have never witnessed such inactivity and apathy on the part of our leaders as now.' He would not have them make a revolutionary demonstration on the lines of the Communist party, but the least they should do was to make the whites realize that Africans also formed part of the country's national life. The leaders, he complained, had no patriotism or pride of race. Divided by petty jealousies, they refused to sacrifice personal ambition for the greater ambition of their people.[26]

Communists traced the ANC's futility to its policy of avoiding mass struggle. The decision to conduct an anti-pass campaign in 1934 meant only 'this year, next year, sometime, never'. The party called for resistance to the Native Service Contract Act of 1932. It was an abominable measure that legalized the whipping of African lads under eighteen for offences against the master and servant laws, authorized African guardians to bind minor children to labour, and aimed at turning share croppers into labour tenants, working from ninety to 180 days a year for the farmer on the days of his choice. Churches protested, whereas the ANC's special conference in January 1933 merely objected to not having been consulted. Seme told Congress in the following April to pray that Hertzog would 'lay the foundations of a great temple of justice, peace and goodwill for all people'. The conference ended in disorder as delegates accused Seme of autocracy and unconstitutional behaviour.[27] How, asked the communists, could a president 'who licks the boots of this bloody imperialist robber so shamelessly', lead his people against oppression?[28]

Rejected by the ANC and rejecting it in turn, the communists went their way alone, purged, so they claimed, of all reformist dross. 'Instead of a white chauvinist Party of white shopkeepers, lawyers and petty bourgeois intellectuals, as under Bunting's regime,' wrote Eugene Dennis in 1932, 'we have become a Party of Native, Coloured and white proletarians, direct from the enterprises, from the points of exploitation and struggle, from the mines, docks, farms, reserves.'[29] Dennis (1904–61) was a lumberjack from Seattle, U.S.A., and the grandson of an Irish rebel who went to America with a British price on his head. He became the general secretary of the American party in 1948 and its chairman in 1959, after serving nearly five years in Atlanta penitentiary for contravening the Smith Act.[30] He represented the Comintern in South Africa for about twelve months in 1932–3 and concentrated on building the party by means of systematic, continuous activities round small local demands.

There were many shortcomings, he acknowledged, especially in the field of united front activity on a 'practical and concrete' programme; yet for the first time in its history, the party was finding a firm footing in basic industries and rural areas. Its membership had increased eightfold; recruits and cadres were being trained in party school; it had set up many cells in factories, mines and docks; a miners' union was taking shape; and a union of seamen and harbour workers flourished at Durban and Cape Town.

More progress might have been made along these lines but for the depression and the expulsion of competent trade unionists from the party. The extent of the depression was never properly gauged. Industrial census returns for 1930 and 1931 were not published, and the government employment exchanges catered only for whites in the big towns, and for Coloured at Cape Town and Kimberley. The number of registered work-seekers rose from 81,000 in 1930 to 188,000 in 1933, and the number who found jobs through the exchanges from 18,000 to 45,000. Last to be hired, first to be fired, Africans suffered most, and the exchanges were closed to them. Those without work were pushed back into the reserves, where unemployment was endemic, yet 14,000 Africans were estimated to be looking for jobs in Johannesburg alone at the beginning of 1932.[31]

The number of Africans, Coloured and Indians working in factories fell by 18 per cent and in mines by 10 per cent in 1929–32. The volume of white employment in this period declined by 2 per cent and 17 per cent. Government, the opposition and labour leaders renewed pressure on state departments, railways, provincial administrations, municipal councils and private employers to absorb the 15,000 whites who were out of work at the lowest point in the depression. Fair wage clauses, protective tariffs, subsidized wages and every other conceivable administrative device were brought to bear.

In May 1930, on the day that parliament debated amendments to the Riotous Assemblies Act, Creswell told the House: 'My business is to use every effort to get European labour employed instead of native labour.' Patriotic and intelligent employers, he believed, would go to as much trouble and expense as the government to find work for their own flesh and blood.[32] Nine months later he claimed that the civilized labour policy had been instrumental in creating employment for 22,000 men on railways, roads and municipal projects.[33] In November 1935 the number of 'civilized' labourers employed on subsidized schemes and relief works consisted of 21,760 whites and 1,957 Coloured.[34]

'You are the co-rulers of the country,' Pirow told white workers at Germiston in July 1931. It was up to them to see that 'public opinion declared it to be a disgrace to employ a native where a white man could be employed'. He quoted figures to show that the nine largest municipalities between them employed 14,726 Africans, 2,619 Coloured, 1,846 Indians and only 961 white labourers, at wages ranging from 2s. a day for Africans to 11s. 3d. for whites in Johannesburg.[35] A municipal conference held in September agreed that local councils should raise the proportion of their 'civilized' labourers to one-fifth of the unskilled labour force, provided that the government contributed half of the extra cost. A year later the railway board instructed departmental heads to retire African, Coloured and Indian employees over fifty-eight years of age; to retrench those over fifty whose health could be said to prejudice their efficiency, or who could be replaced by redundant whites; to dismiss any who refused to accept a wage cut; and generally to substitute whites where this could be done without extra cost.[36]

The old contention of radicals that white workers would be forced down to the African's economic level unless they raised him to their own seemed to be borne out by the conditions of relief workers. Living in tents without their families on 5s. a day and free rations, they were only slightly better off than the migrant peasant. The unskilled white had to learn that he was not above doing 'kaffir work', declared Afrikaner *predikants* at a government conference in July 1930. They would preach the virtues of thrift, self help and pride of race; urge the poor to live within their means; and stress the 'odium attaching to reliance for existence on the Church or State'.[37] The Carnegie commission on poor whites produced five volumes with a diagnosis that attributed rural poverty to the stubborn refusal of poor whites to be servile or to work for the low wages paid to African farm labourers. About 400,000 whites, nearly one-fifth of the white population, lived in 'dire poverty'. The commission, however, disapproved strongly of direct material assistance without an equivalent service. 'It causes loss of independence and may imbue them with a sense of inferiority, impairs their industry, weakens their sense of personal responsibility, and helps to make them dishonest.'

Trade unionists said that sermons would not create jobs and clamoured for a system of state insurance. An unemployment commission, which included W. Freestone of the Cape Federation and C. B. Tyler of the TLC, left Africans out of its survey, declared that 'no real cure for unemployment' could be found, and recommended the setting up of a permanent fund.[39] Capitalism was to blame, said the communists, and they damned the rulers for putting the burden of poverty and insecurity on Africans and Coloured. The party produced its own remedy in the shape of a bill for a bold and imaginative insurance fund, to be financed by contributions from the state and employers, a levy on income tax payers, and money transferred from the defence and native affairs votes. All unemployed persons were to receive a basic benefit of not less than £1 a week, and to administer the fund through elected local committees.[40]

Don't rely on parliament for bread and work, said the communists, as they called for mass action. Unemployed Afrikaners marched with Africans and Coloured for the first time in history, or sat with them on committees of an unemployed workers' union. The demonstrations were sporadic and confined to two or three big towns. Prejudice and inequality stood in the way. The whites were given work, while the police beat up African demonstrators and men who went from door to door in Johannesburg collecting food and money for a soup kitchen. Stephen Tefu, an AFTU organizer, was knocked unconscious and lost five teeth from a blow on the jaw when he intervened to protect the collectors, who were handcuffed and marched to the police station, and there beaten again in the presence of the sergeant in charge. Tefu and seventeen others were sentenced to seven weeks' hard labour for public violence and for holding an illegal procession.[44]

'Europeans out of work are called unemployed,' observed T. D. M. Skota's short-lived weekly, the *African Leader*, whereas 'Natives out of work are called loafers'.[42] A dole for the white man; an endorsement out of town for the black. Racists exploited the difference in status. T. B. Rutherford of the printers' union, P. Mostert the editor of *Forward*, and Gideon Botha, one of the few Afrikaners in the old ISL, formed a Workers' and Farmers' Bond in 1931 to organize the unemployed for white supremacy, a minimum wage of 10s. for white labourers, and the exclusion of Africans from prescribed occupations.[43] Botha returned to the radical camp in 1933. His temporary defection was a sign of the pressure applied to the left wing in the labour movement.

African trade unionism suffered badly on the Rand, where the AFTU was left with only two unions at the beginning of 1932. To make matters worse, it was involved in a dispute with one of them, the African Clothing Workers' Union, because of its close association with the parallel white union under Solly Sachs. About 800 Africans had been locked out during a strike of white garment workers in Johannesburg. The Communist party accused Sachs of refusing to give the Africans strike pay and urged their able secretary, Gana Makabeni, to sever his connexion with the Garment Workers' Union This he would not do, and was thereupon expelled from the party and the AFTU. He and Makue, his chairman, issued a summons against the AFTU for the return of the union's books and were denounced by the party as agents of Sachs, Bunting and the ruling class.[44]

The African Laundry Workers' Union also threatened to withdraw. Harmony was restored only after the AFTU had promised to make amends for its 'domineering tactics' and other shortcomings. These were symptoms of an 'ultra-leftism' that tended to alienate communists in many countries from less radical groups. The chief weakness of the movement, reported the ECCI at its twelfth plenum in 1932, was isolation. To overcome it, communist parties must abandon 'abstract and stereotyped' methods or work. In particular, empty phrases about revolutionary struggles should not be allowed to take the place of hard work for the satisfaction of immediate demands.

The AFTU was in danger of becoming a small sect, wrote Huiswood from Moscow in 1933.[45] Inexperience, want of initiative, and a top-heavy bureaucracy had brought it to the point of total collapse. He alleged that leaders called frivolously for strikes on any occasion, yet scarcely took part in the spontaneous strikes and revolts of Africans on the City Deep mine, the railways and docks at Durban and Port Elizabeth, or in the townships of Cradock and Middelburg. Moreover, the AFTU failed lamentably to draw African and white workers together in joint actions against employers and the reformist trade unionists.

The bulk of the organized workers remained in the fold of the TLC and Cape Federation, whose racial policies and dependence on industrial conciliation procedures strengthened the labour aristocracy, facilitated the excessive exploitation of Africans, and isolated them from white workers. Huiswood's proposed remedy was to form a strong revolutionary opposition in existing unions rather than to organize competing unions.

Crawford, Andrews and other radical trade unionists had suggested an identical policy long before the adoption of the Industrial Conciliation Act. Its effects were patently divisive and mediatory, and therefore obnoxious to the left wing. There was no reason to suppose that whites, or even Coloured and Indians, would forgo their privileged status under the act for the sake of unity with low-paid Africans. The proper course of action in the circumstances was to concentrate on organizing African unions, conduct a vigorous campaign for equal access to all types of skilled work, and intensify pressures for the full recognition of all unions under the act. This approach, which the communists rejected as being reformist, might have done more to weaken racial barriers than a sterile agitation against industrial councils and conciliation boards.

Communist organizers were bound sooner or later to use the statutory procedures as the most expedient means of raising wages and improving working conditions. For this purpose they registered the unions of white, Coloured or Indian workers, and formed parallel, unregistered unions of Africans. W. Kalk succeeded in persuading white, Coloured and African leather workers to combine in a single union in Johannesburg.[46] His spectacular break through the colour bar did not last, and the union eventually divided into racial groups. The pluralism had many disadvantages and often caused friction, as in the strikes of furniture and garment workers on the Rand; but no other practical solution was ever found. Its rejection by the Communist party in the early thirties, coming on top of the expulsions, probably delayed the growth of African trade unionism in the north. The party's militant policy and insistence on systematic work round specific demands had a more beneficial effect at Cape Town. Patient, pioneering efforts by Ray Alexander, Gomas, La Guma and J. Shuba among railway, harbour and factory workers produced a healthy crop of Coloured and African unions in later years.

In 1932 the communists stood alone on the peaks of revolutionary ardour, calling on the oppressed to follow them to freedom in a federation of independent African Republics. The course was plotted in a May Day manifesto. Overthrow British and Boer imperialism; confiscate the land, cattle and implements of landlords, companies and mission societies; divide the land among peasants and farm workers of all races; confiscate the mines, factories and all undertakings of the imperialist and capitalist robbers; forward to national independence under a workers' and peasants' government in a black republic.[47] This was a formula for the pure socialist society at one fell swoop such as Bunting had pleaded for at the sixth world congress of the CI in 1928. His expellers had expropriated his policy without regard to the great debate on the two-stage revolution.

Of immediate importance was the mounting offensive by Pirow's police against the party. Eddie Roux went to jail in February 1932 for two months' hard labour after defying an order banishing him from Durban. Defending himself, as was agreed would be done by all party members on trial, he told the court that though the order might be valid in law, it was not sanctioned by the people, who were unrepresented in parliament. There followed Wolton's sentence of four months' imprisonment for having exposed the brutal treatment of political prisoners. He refused to pay the fine and served his sentence. Peter Ramutla, a trade union organizer in Pretoria, was declared a 'vagrant' because he did not work for an employer, and went to a labour camp for twelve months. Stephen Tefu of Pretoria served two weeks for holding a public meeting. John Gomas received a sentence of three months for 'perjuring' himself by denying an allegation that he had hurled stones at scabs during a garment workers' strike. J. Mbete and E. Dhlamini of Pinetown, Durban, were sent to jail for six and three months because they distributed a party leaflet calling on people to demonstrate on Dingaan's Day and to refuse to pay their taxes. Mike Diamond was sentenced to six months, though the conviction

459

was set aside on appeal, for duplicating the leaflet in his barber's shop.

Defiant and undeterred, the communists brought down more wrath on their heads by breaching the racial taboo in a parliamentary by-election at Germiston in October 1932. The seat became vacant on the death of the sitting member, George Brown, a Glasgow born boiler-maker, who had held it for Labour since 1924. Four candidates, representing Labour, Nationalists, the SAP and Workers-Farmers Bond, contested the seat. Like all elections in the north, this was strictly for whites only, and the communists challenged the 'parliamentary farce' by putting J. B. Marks forward as their demonstrative candidate. A former teacher who had been dismissed from his post at Vredefort, OFS, for communist activities, Marks studied at the Lenin School in Moscow with Kotane and Mofutsanyana and returned to give all his time to the party.

The white candidates represented imperialist slavery, said Marks, who brought a message of struggle for full franchise rights, unemployment insurance and an end to colour bars, beer raids, poll tax and lodgers' permits. The permits were a great grievance. Apart from householders and their wives, no African over eighteen had a right to sleep in the township, not even in his parents' house, unless he held a permit from the superintendent on payment of 2s. a month. The police raided homes at any time of the night in search of unauthorized residents, who were liable to be fined, imprisoned and expelled from the location. Resist, said the communists, and many people did. Hundreds were arrested and some were charged with public violence.

The police struck back; broke up the communists' meetings; assaulted speakers; arrested Roux, Molly Wolton and Jeffrey Novene; and laid a charge of incitement to racial hostility. White hooligans took a hand and frogmarched Roux at the magistrate's court, where he had gone to propose Marks on nomination day. The campaign against the permits went on long after the election day until Turton, the location superintendent, led the police in an attack on a meeting. Shots were fired, a score of Africans were injured, and an elderly woman died of her wounds. An administrative court of inquiry into Turton's fitness for his office found in his favour, and brought to an end yet another skirmish in the endless battle against an insufferable bureaucracy.[48]

The South African party candidate won the Germiston seat with a large majority. The tide was running fast against the government. Pirow carried out his threat to hamstring the communists who, he said, had gained a footing on the mines. There was a danger that the infection would be spread throughout the country by miners returning to their villages.[49] Ignoring protests from the entire labour movement, he issued orders early in November banning Roux, Wolton, Sachs, Kalk and Diamond for twelve months from the Rand. Wolton moved to Cape Town to assist in a tramwaymen's strike; the others remained and took the minister to court. The appellate division confirmed the orders in September 1933, by which time a new government had taken office. Smuts, as minister of justice, cancelled the bans. Hitler was in power, war clouds were gathering over Europe, and the Communist International appealed for a united front against fascism and war. The South African communists' short period of isolation was drawing to a close.

20 Fascism and War

South Africa was insulated by gold from the worst shocks of the great depression. The value of minerals produced fell from £61 million in 1929 to £54 million in 1932, largely because the diamond mines went out of action. The gross output of manufacturing plants dropped in the same period from £112 to £91 million; and the value of agricultural exports, from £26 to £13 million. In 1933 the government went off the gold standard and started an inflationary boom that lifted the economy out of the trough. Exports, which had fallen from £83 million in 1930 to £69 million in 1932, rose to £95 million in 1933. Of this amount £22 million represented the estimated value of the 'gold premium' on exported bullion.

Hertzog and N. C. Havenga, the highly orthodox minister of finance, clung to the gold standard so as to demonstrate their faith in the sovereign quality both of gold and of South Africa's political status. A special session of parliament on 18 November 1931 rejected an opposition motion to follow Britain's example. The South African party, backed by mine owners, bankers, an increasing number of farmers and manufacturers, and the English press agitated for devaluation. The government relied on currency controls to stop the flight of capital, imposed dumping duties, raised taxes, subsidized farmers and cut the pay of railwaymen and public servants.

The gold reserves dwindled, the prices of primary products fell, and the budget's deficit mounted as politicians and economists wrangled. Tielman Roos, one of the chief architects of the Transvaal Nationalist party, then brought matters to a head by leaving the Appeal Court to re-enter politics. On 22 December 1932 he called for a national coalition government that would abandon the gold standard and save the country from communism. Money was leaving the country at the rate of £1,000,000 a day when the government announced on 27 December that South Africa had gone off gold.

Roos, a popular hero overnight, threatened to upset all political calculations. The Labour party's annual conference authorized Madeley to negotiate with him, while Smuts and Hertzog prepared to join forces against their common rival. Convinced that he would lose the next election, Hertzog, like Ramsay MacDonald in 1930, preferred to stay in power with the opposition's backing – only, he explained, to defend 'the interests of the country and the Volk'. He told his caucus that if the South African party won the election, Smuts would inevitably surrender Afrikanerdom and its language to the gold magnates and to British jingoes in Natal. 'This the Volk would never forgive us.'[1]

The two leaders agreed on 23 February to form a coalition after Smuts had surrendered his principles on the issue of the African vote in the Cape. He argued at first that it should not be tampered with while the coalition lasted, and finally agreed to the 'separate political representation of White and Black' and the retention of the civilized labour policy. Afrikaner nationalism and African rights had been sacrificed to the golden calf, scoffed Hertzog's critics in his own ranks.

All could now see, said the communists, that the bourgeois parties, which had conducted fierce battles for twenty years on alleged 'fundamental and principal differences', disagreed only over methods of exploitation. Afrikaner nationalism had suffered a defeat, yet it was bound to rally and split the coalition. Meanwhile, Pirow remained in the cabinet to continue his white terror against workers of all races. It was for the party to mobilize them in a united front from below against wage cuts, the civilized labour policy, and capitalist terror.[2]

The Labour party's national executive also damned coalition as the 'logical outcome' of capitalism's imminent collapse. 'Financial Kings and Exploiters have come together to safeguard the interests of the monied classes at the expense of the worker.'[3] Ever weaving new patterns of unity and discord, Labour prepared for battle at a special conference in March against the people's enemies, among whom were listed the parliamentary 'renegades' Creswell, Sampson, McMenamin, Shaw and Kentridge. Creswell and Sampson had refused to resign from the cabinet, thereby defying a decision taken in August 1931 by a 'peace conference' representing both factions in the party.[4] The other 'renegades' loyally obeyed the instruction to withdraw their support from the ministry, but defaulted in turn by hobnobbing with Smuts, whom they followed into the coalition.

Hertzog's new cabinet of six Nationalist and six South African party members took office on 31 March. Creswell and Sampson were dropped; Dr D. F. Malan, leader of the Cape Nationalists, refused office. Though objecting to coalition, he persuaded his followers to support it for the sake of unity and so as to make certain of being returned to parliament in the general election on 17 May 1933. It was a sweeping victory for the coalition, which won 138 seats; 75 went to the Nationalists, 61 to the SAP, and 2 to the Labour coalitionists Creswell and Fred Shaw. Six of the remaining twelve members in the assembly undertook to support the government. The opposition of six included followers of Roos, Natal 'home rulers', and two Labour men, Walter Madeley and R. T. MacArthur.

Besides promising an assortment of social services and economic handouts, Labour's election platform gave a preview of Verwoerdian apartheid.[5] There would be complete separation when Labour ruled, 'so that the Natives shall not be allowed to impinge upon us to our detriment and theirs'. The aim should be the gradual development of Native States under a white parliament where 'even the de-tribalized Natives would be only too delighted to reside'. As for those who remained near the European towns, it was an important part of Labour's policy so to control them 'that they will not be a menace to the Europeans'. The peaceful co-existence of powerful white and black states might well be South Africa's contribution to world socialism. Or so the Labour party said. Afrikaner workers, however, would not be lured into a party that had long ceased to exist as an independent force. From then on Labour could win parliamentary seats only as an appendage of a capitalist party.

The Communist party put up 'demonstrative' candidates – voteless Africans, Coloured, and two whites – on 'a programme of extra-Parliamentary struggles' for immediate needs: non-contributory unemployment relief; the abolition of civilized labour policies; complete equality of rights; full freedom of organization, assembly and speech; and the withdrawal of British and South African armed forces from the protectorates and South West Africa. It was an excellent recipe for genuine democracy, but the party refused to foster illusions. The demands could be guaranteed, it declared, only through national independence; public ownership of land, mines, factories and banks; and the setting up of an independent native republic under a workers' and peasants' government. Communists took part in the elections in order to inspire a determination to engage in 'strikes, demonstrations and other militant mass actions leading up to revolutionary struggle for State Power'.[6]

The message came through clearly on 30 May when Douglas Wolton, one of the party's candidates, was sentenced to three months' hard labour, and Ray Alexander to one month's suspended for two years. The charge against them was that they had incited bus and tram workers to strike in December for a rise from 1s. 6d. to 2s. an hour. The strike brought Cape Town's public transport to a standstill for ten days, and was broken by the police and the union's officials. Robert Stuart, the secretary, who gave evidence against the communists at the trial, was then defending his trade union empire against the militants in the African Federation of Trade Unions. The breach in the movement later affected the relations between the Cape Federation and the Trades and Labour Council; but it encouraged the growth of a militant trade union organization in the western Cape.

Wolton returned to England with his family after his release from prison. Gomas and Josiah Ngedlane went to Johannesburg to join Bach, Kotane and Roux on the party's political bureau. The infusion of new blood, notes Roux, led to the adoption of 'a more realistic policy' of renewed cooperation with other radical groups.[7] The change was bound to come under the impact of Germany's Third Reich, the spread of Nazi doctrines in South Africa, and the Communist International's appeal in

March 1933 for a united front. In June, while Wolton was still in prison, the party asked trade unions, the ANC, socialist groups and joint councils to combine against unemployment, police repression and fascism.

Hitler's triumph, Nazi savagery and the Nordic myth struck a responsive chord in Afrikaner racists. Much dormant hostility towards Jews and the British came to the surface. An immigration act restricting entry from eastern Europe passed through parliament in 1930 with threats and warnings.[8] An 'ever increasing anti-Jewish sentiment', reported the Jewish Board of Deputies in 1931, 'strives to minimize if not destroy the equal status of the Jew as a citizen'.[9] The Greyshirts – a National Socialist party – and other imitators of jackbooted Nazi auxiliaries appeared, chanting anti-Semitic slogans or denouncing 'foreign influences'. Hertzog, playing down the persecution of Jews, condemned an economic boycott of German goods. New cleavages and alignments developed in the race-ridden society.

The initial response to the communists' appeal for a united front was disappointing. None of the African organizations so much as acknowledged the offer of cooperation. Their 'pusillanimous policies' had landed them in chaos, complained Kotane, then the editor of *Umsebenzi*;[10] while ANC leaders alleged that the party had lost the people's confidence by a reckless militancy. 'Many of its followers,' wrote Halley G. Plaatje, the general secretary of Congress, 'have met with a bloody, untimely and wholly unnecessary death.'[11] What had Congress gained with its cap-in-hand policy? asked the communists; and Jameson G. Coka drew up a balance sheet in a series of articles on the African press, the ANC and its intellectual leaders.[12]

African nationalism, he argued, had forged ahead after the 1914–18 war when Congress abandoned whimpering resolutions for active struggle. Then came a flock of white liberals, missionaries, lawyers and professors to stem the tide. With money from America and the Chamber of Mines, they founded a tame press, social clubs, pathfinders, joint councils and the Institute of Race Relations. Liberalism and the lure of fat jobs corrupted the leaders. 'All the black reformists and charlatans, all the discarded race-betrayers and unprincipled time-servers suddenly became protagonists of sports, education and inter-racial co-operation.' The young were made sports minded and dance crazy; and Congress fell back into inactivity.

The crop of anti-African laws passed since 1920, wrote Coka, refuted the claim of the liberals that moderation led to better conditions. Racial prejudice, inflamed by cabinet ministers and public men, was ranker than a decade before. The blacks were steadily losing ground; lackeyism was enhanced; and the masses were befuddled, deceived and misled. Reactionary leaders like Dube, Thema, Seme and Jabavu had left the struggle; Kadalie, Mote and other bombastic speakers were silent. Only the communists held on, instilling race pride and class solidarity, pressing for the black republic and a workers-peasants government, which were surely enough to stir the blood of every oppressed worker and black man with a soul.

All but a few intellectuals recoiled from the concept of black power, however, and ignored appeals for common action against fascism, which might well have seemed irrelevant to the victims of South Africa's own brand of totalitarian rule. Congress leaders continued to put their faith in collaboration with white liberals and in non-violent forms of pressure. Yet another deputation went in December 1933 from the Transvaal ANC to Piet Grobler, the minister of native affairs, who defended the displacement of Africans by whites. The whites had created the towns, he said, and were entitled to preference on the labour market. He undertook, however, to make concessions under the pass laws to 'deserving natives'. New regulations issued in September 1934 accordingly gave the administration a discretionary power to issue exemption certificates, which had to be produced on demand, to an elite consisting of government employees, chiefs, teachers, ministers of religion and men certified to be of good character.

It was a minor concession and failed to detach the thin layer of educated and urbanized Africans from the general community. All lived under the same conditions in segregated locations or slums; all were liable to be raided and interrogated as local authorities redoubled their efforts to regulate the flow of work-seekers from the countryside. Johannesburg was proclaimed under the Urban Areas Act in July 1933; new regulations restricting the African's freedom of movement, residence and occupation in the city came into force; and magistrate van der Westhuisen broke all records by trying Africans for pass, liquor and kindred offences at the rate of 130 an hour. In April 1934 Dr Roux began serving a sentence of four months' hard labour for urging Africans on Dingaan's Day to defend themselves with arms if necessary against pick-up vans and police brutality. The party night school was closed during his absence.

More communists stood trial and went to prison. James Ncwangu of Pinetown served twelve months for telling Africans not to pay taxes or 'to sign themselves into slavery under the Native Service Contract Act'. Peter Ramutla, a member of the central committee and chairman of the newly formed Native Shop Assistants' Union in Johannesburg, was sentenced to five months' hard labour for promoting 'racial hostility'. The party could not keep up the pace on its own. While determined to maintain their 'clear and independent political line', the communists renewed their attempts to obtain the cooperation of nationalist and liberal organizations in an offensive against the pass laws. But the campaign came to a standstill. It lacked the essential element of a militant mass movement capable of developing effective methods of struggle. 'We have reformist Bantu leaders in this country,' noted Kotane in January 1934, 'but no reformist organizations worth speaking about. The once formidable African National Congress and ICU have disappeared.'[13]

Before the end of the year, the parties of white supremacy began a process that jerked the ANC out of its long passivity. Hertzog and Smuts merged their forces into the United South African National Party in December 1934. A section of the Nationalists, represented by Dr Malan and eighteen other members in parliament, rejected fusion and went into opposition. Imperialist die-hards under Colonel Stallard also refused to merge, and formed a Dominion party with five members in the House. Labour had four, one of them being M. J. van den Berg, who captured the mining constituency of Krugersdorp in a by-election.

The seven principles of fusion were studded with hackneyed

phrases about national unity, equality between Afrikaners and English, sovereign status within the empire, a civilized labour policy for white workers, and separate representation for Africans under white Christian trusteeship.[14] Africans were promised a square deal, said the communists, but all they would get was the 'square heel of the imperialist boot'. The alliance between British mine owners and Afrikaner landlords was a thin cover for more exploitation and another step towards a dictatorship. As for Malan's followers, some would fall a prey to Nazi demagogues. It was the Communist party's duty to obtain the support of poor farmers for its vision of a workers and peasants government.[15]

The comment showed more insight than the fulsome praises showered on Hertzog and Smuts. Their merger raised the level of racism, and isolated a hard core of Afrikaner nationalists. Fusion, wrote G. D. Scholtz, later the editor of *Die Transvaler*, 'caused a wave of bitterness, rancour and distrust to sweep over the Afrikaans people such as even the Rebellion of 1914–15 had not produced'.[16] It was after coalition, according to Hertzog, that Dr Malan and his lieutenants joined the Afrikaner Broederbond, a secret society formed in 1918 and dedicated to the aim of an independent Afrikaans government. The rise and fall of parties, declared the Bond's leaders in a letter to its members in January 1934, meant less than the resolve that Afrikanerdom should dominate and the Bond should rule South Africa.[17]

Another consequence of fusion was a weakening of the opposition in parliament to Hertzog's segregation bills. These had been before the country since 1926 and been defeated in 1927, 1929 and 1930. A joint committee was appointed to prepare a basis for the betrayal of Cape democracy. In 1930 the committee accepted and in successive years reaffirmed the principles of a bill drafted by Heaton Nicholls, one of Natal's foremost racists, which, he claimed, would secure 'for all time the dominance of the Europeans'.[18] With 118 members on his side in the assembly, Hertzog was certain of the two-thirds majority of both houses required by the constitution for the removal of Africans from the common roll. The publication of the committee's final report in May 1935 sounded the alarm for a campaign in defence of the franchise.[19]

The threat to the franchise and the growth of fascism were the main causes of radicalism in the next five years. Africans and Coloured rallied against Hertzog's Representation of Natives Bill and other segregation measures. White workers mustered their forces to contain uniformed bands of fascists and to defeat the Broederbond's attempts to capture or split trade unions. The separation of functions tended to divide the left along racial lines, but its immediate effects were invigorating. A resurgence of militancy healed old wounds, brought men who had fallen by the way back into the struggle, and laid a new basis for unity. The movement was able to tap fresh sources of manpower and money, especially in the Jewish community. Trade unions were stimulated into political action on a wider scale than at any time since 1922.

This was testimony to the skill and doggedness shown by communists in the cause of inter-racial class solidarity. Most of the whites employed in light industry such as the garment, textile, leather, furniture and tobacco trades were Afrikaners, rural in origin, relatively unskilled and badly paid. Unlike the artisan, they worked alongside Coloured, Indians and Africans at the same jobs and for similar wages. Many of the employers were Jews and a favourite butt for fascist abuse. Conditions could hardly be more suitable than these for the spread of fascism, yet it made little headway among factory workers; primarily because men like Kalk, Sachs, Tyler, Weinbren and Wolfson were able to neutralize racial prejudices by means of militant trade unionism and socialist education.

Whereas English-speaking artisans continued to control the craft unions, Afrikaners were soon elected to leading positions in the industrial unions. As chairmen, organizers, branch secretaries and committee members, Afrikaners were personally interested in defending the unions against disruptive movements. Men and women who had grown up in an atmosphere of narrow nationalism moved to catch sight of an international workers' commonwealth. The annual delegations that visited the Soviet Union between 1933 and 1938 included Afrikaners who returned with glowing accounts. It had done away with unemployment, they reported, and stood foremost in the fight for peace against

Nazi aggression. Johanna Cornelius, president of the Transvaal garment workers' union, J. Wolmarans, chairman of the textile union, H. S. Lamprechts, secretary of the leather workers' union, Gideon Botha, secretary of the FSU, J. Larkins and other Afrikaners spoke to rural audiences about the dangers of fascism and war. Claiming that the poor Afrikaner was bound to become an important revolutionary force, the Communist party began publishing an Afrikaans monthly, *Die Arbeider en Arme Boer* ('Worker and Peasant'), in January 1935.

Meeting in the same month, the Labour party's annual conference upheld a decision of the national council to boycott the Anti-Fascist League. They should have nothing to do with communists, said Duncan Burnside, an eloquent Scot who staggered between both ends of the labour spectrum. With barely 300 members, the party had no taste for any action that smacked of radicalism, and refused to join in protests against an amendment in July 1934 of the customs regulations, giving the government power to prohibit the importation of political literature. The first list of banned books, apart from 'pornography', included the *Communist Manifesto*, *Labour Defence News*, and *What Are the Machine Tractor Stations?* J. H. Hofmeyr, the minister of interior, was said to be a great liberal; yet he told a deputation that literature, even though not 'propaganda' in the strict sense, might be dangerous on account of South Africa's 'peculiar race question'.[20]

The League against Fascism and War was formed in March 1934 by trade unionists, communists, Labour party members, Friends of the Soviet Union and radical societies. A year later the Trades and Labour Council's annual conference decided not to affiliate to the League, and agreed by nineteen votes to eleven to oppose political dictatorships. A. A. Moore, secretary of the reduction workers' union, who introduced the motion, suspected that the League was really 'a jumping-off ground for another political party'. J. C. Bolton, the secretary of two Natal unions with a majority of Indian members, said that most people in South Africa were uncivilized. If they had a workers' dictatorship, it would have to put power in their hands.[21]

Bill Andrews objected vigorously. Moore's motion was

evidently meant to be an attack on the dictatorship of the working class – the only means by which workers could become masters of their own lives. The trade union movement owed its existence to men who grasped the nature of the conflict between the buyers and sellers of labour power. All social evils and injustices arose from the workers' dependence on the propertied classes. Nowhere was this condition more harmful than in South Africa, where the great majority were voteless helots. The real choice before conference was 'a Fascist State or a workers' and peasants' republic'.[22]

Capitalism everywhere, thought Andrews, was moving towards a naked dictatorship. The only opposition came from the Communist party. Though it was still weak and unimportant, with much unsatisfactory 'material', time-servers and even traitors in its ranks, its philosophy of an iron discipline and uncompromising struggle for power was the only possible policy. 'Pacifism leads nowhere. It has been, it is, and will be war to the knife until capitalism is destroyed.' In South Africa, however, 'it appears unlikely that we shall be in the vanguard. Our proletarians, the natives, are more nearly slaves than in most countries.' One could only continue to tell the truth and trust that events would provide the soil in which the seed might germinate.[23]

This would not come to pass, said the communists, so long as Africans 'submissively bear the derision and bad treatment of the white masters'. To do away with this shameful slavery, it was necessary to drive the Anglo-Boer slave drivers out of the country. Neither the tribal chiefs nor the bourgeoisie who jointly controlled the ANC could organize and lead the revolution. For the chiefs were government agents, exploiting and aiding the exploiters. As for the bourgeoisie, they longed for freedom yet feared to free the masses. Consequently, workers and peasants acting together and led by the party must take upon themselves the burden of their emancipation.[24]

Why should it be thought proper to form a united front with right-wing labour men and not with African nationalists? The question was debated hotly in the party, as it continued its solitary mission of firing revolt among Africans. This could not be done by stressing the danger of an internal fascism. Such might be new to you, Peter Ramutla told delegates at the Anti-Fascist League's annual conference in 1935, but Africans had lived in concentration camps for generations.[25] Coloured in the Cape joined the League, sat on its committees, and exchanged blows with L. T. Weichardt's Greyshirts. Only Africans who were politically acute, however, would recognize the common factor in colonial fascism and Nazi imperialism.

When the South African air force bombed the villages and herds of Impumbu, a rebellious Ovambo chief, in August 1932, the party urged members of the ANC and ICU to join in a campaign for the immediate withdrawal of all armed forces from South West Africa. 'Hands off Bechuanaland,' the communists demanded in 1933, when vice-admiral Evans, backed by marines and field guns, deposed Tshekedi Khama, acting chief of the Bamangwato, for sentencing a white man to be whipped. L. L. Leepile, the secretary of the Cape Town CP, and a native of Bechuanaland, denounced the Anglo-Boer imperialists who jailed, deposed and banished any chief who failed to extract blood money in the form of taxes from the starving peasants. The time would come, he predicted, when they would unite for a federation of native republics under a workers' and peasants' government.[26]

Britain had allowed Bechuanaland, Swaziland and Basutoland to drift into a deplorable state of poverty, disease and ignorance. Hertzog said as much and renewed the pressure for their transfer to South Africa. His real motive, the communists argued, was to enable mine owners and land speculators to lay their hands on the labour resources, mineral wealth and grazing lands of the three territories. 'We are for driving out all the Imperialist oppressors from South Africa and the Protectorates,' explained Lazar Bach; for the independence of Africans in the whole of the continent, and the right to rule themselves as they liked. It was the party's task to make them aware of their national destiny, to lead them in struggle for bread and freedom, and to bring about a voluntary association of national republics – Sotho, Tswana, Swazi, Zulu, Xhosa – in a federation of independent native republics.[27]

An indigenous South African imperialism was taking shape, and communists saw the signs before most people. The country's 'native policy' was best, said Smuts at Oxford, and should be imitated by settler governments in east and central Africa.[28] Pirow, now minister of defence, foresaw a 'rising tide of colour', a life and death struggle in which South Africa should be the rallying point for all champions of white civilization. The time might come, he warned, when whites in tropical Africa would need protection against black invaders. All Africa south of the Sudan, he said in November 1934, should have a 'common native policy'. In South West Africa, where the United party had won a general election, non-German whites agitated for incorporation as a fifth province, while the administration banned Nazi organizations and expelled their leaders.[29]

This was not being done out of any love for democracy, said the communists. South Africa was preparing to annex the mandated territory. As for Pirow's vision of the future Africa, it would be no more than a larger edition of the Union's slave system. The forces of history were not going to be dictated by so short-sighted and conceited a buffoon. Yet it was on Pirow's side that history in the shape of Mussolini came down in February 1935, when 3,000 soldiers steamed from Italy to the Ethiopian frontier.

The invasion of Ethiopia brought a deeper understanding of the links between fascism, war and colonial rule. A spirit of national pride spread through all social classes and tribal communities as Africans discovered that black people could stand up in defence of their homes against a white settlers' army. The communists' 'Hands off Ethiopia' campaign aroused great enthusiasm. Dockers at Cape Town and Durban refused to load ships with goods for Italian troops. Elation gave way to despair when Ethiopia fell, yet the communists kept their faith in the final victory. More wars were on the way, they predicted, and Ethiopians would regain their freedom by joining in the revolutionary struggle with anti-fascist Italian workers.

South Africa's own freedom was in danger, declared the former chief justice Sir James Rose Innes in a review of Hertzog's bill to take the vote from Africans in the Cape. 'There is a full-blooded Fascist flavour about the proceeding.'[30] An All African Convention, meeting at Bloemfontein in December 1935, rejected political and territorial segregation. It could 'only be justly carried out by means of the creation of separate states', and this was neither a good thing nor feasible.[31] At about the same time, 120 delegates from all parts of the country attended a conference of the League against Fascism and War, the most important united front conference held in Johannesburg for many years. Trade unionists, communists, liberals and intellectuals were making common cause in defence of civil liberties and the democratic ideal.

The communists, forming a slender bridge between the two fronts, had responded to the appeal issued by the seventh congress of the Communist International at Moscow in July-August 1935. The most important of its kind since Lenin's death, the congress criticized the schematic approach and faulty judgements of the sixth congress. Georgi Dimitroff, hero of the Reichstag fire trial, leader of the illegal Bulgarian Communist party, and the CI's new general secretary, lashed out at cut-and-dried schemes which substituted slogans such as 'the revolutionary way out' for a precise, factual analysis of class forces. Communist parties should rid themselves of sectarian tendencies, he said, and give all their energies to building a people's front.[32] The Comintern followed his lead in a series of directives. Workers, peasants, intellectuals must combine with the middle class in a broad movement to prevent war and defeat fascism.

'In South Africa too, for we are not exceptional,' confessed the CP's political bureau, 'the Party has suffered from left sectarian tendencies.' It must get rid of them without delay. The correction turned out to be a long and painful adjustment between opposing schools of thought. Kotane argued that a people's front would flourish only if all who took part shared both responsibility and power. Gomas hammered the point home. Those who were not party members, he said, joined the front for a specific purpose and not to carry through the party's entire programme. Communists should respect their opinions and not behave as though the party was in full control.[33]

The party would lose its identity if it took this course, warned

Bach, and he cited Bunting's experience with the League of African Rights. Anybody who underrated the strength and ideological influence of the African middle class, he said, acted in effect as an agent of the bourgeoisie. An unrepentant defender of the sixth world congress of the CI, Bach preferred the strategy of a united front from below. It left the party free to expose the reformist leaders and take the control in its own hands. In this way it would preserve an independent line of action in struggling for the 'independent native republic'.[34]

Old wounds reopened as the debate swung back to the black republic slogan. It was being revived, said Kotane, only to obscure the main issue of whether the party should form permanent local branches or persist in putting all its energy into sporadic campaigns. Though pledged to uproot sectarian tendencies, the centre objected to criticisms of past policy which, it said, disrupted the party. Stephen Tefu was suspended, and Jameson Coka, another sceptic who doubted the importance of an African middle class, was expelled in July 1935 for 'attempting to inaugurate a new counter-revolutionary Nationalist Political Party among Africans'. In September the Johannesburg district expelled four of Kotane's supporters and suspended a fifth for attacking the party's 'line and leadership'.[35]

Coka explained that at the time of his expulsion – 'for my "reformist activities"' – his chief problem was to get a job. 'I had been working for over eighteen months without a penny payment. Had I not discharged my duty to my race?' Born at Mfolozi, Zululand, in 1910, he attended missionary schools, taught at the early age of fifteen, and was diverted from the usual teaching-church career of an educated African by the ICU, which he joined in 1927. 'A general strike, passive, or even active resistance, demonstrations, or any militant move would, at that time, have changed the history of the Union. The masses were ready to follow the lead even to death.' Kadalie and Champion gave no lead. Coka then went to Johannesburg, studied communism, joined the party, left it and became a lay preacher. His patron, Dr Seme, helped him to find employment on a newspaper, and he began the uncertain career of a free-lance journalist.[36]

A gifted writer, Coka might have been an asset to the party if it had treated him more sympathetically than its rigorous standards allowed. Kotane, Ngedlane and Roux protested against the expulsions and were dropped from the political bureau, leaving it in the hands of Bach, Marks, Kalk and Edwin Mofutsanyana, the general secretary. Kotane, Roux and Gomas thereupon asked the Comintern to intervene. It invited the two factions to send representatives to Moscow. Kotane went to speak for the opposition. Maurice Richter, a Latt who had settled in the Orange Free State, was deputed to state the political bureau's point of view; and he was followed by Bach.[37]

The political pendulum was swinging against them, and neither returned to South Africa. The Comintern's control commission in Moscow expelled both from the party, and also Richter's brother Paul, for having shielded a follower of Leon Trotsky. There were additional charges against Bach. The son of a factory owner, he had hidden his social origins, laid a false claim to membership of the Latvian party, and engaged in 'disruptive fractional' activities in South Africa. Subsequent to this finding, the three men were put on trial, sentenced to death and executed.[38]

The party had by that time digested Dimitroff's message to such good effect that it undertook to back up any progressive movement. Rank-and-file Afrikaner republicans, discontented members of the British middle class, the Labour party, workers and poor farmers of all races were all likely recruits for the battle against imperialism. Or so thought George Hardy, a British communist who represented the Communist International in South Africa for the greater part of 1936. Like many radicals from abroad, he claimed to have found a great revolutionary force in the medley of races and classes.[39] Substituting reformist phrases for left-wing slogans, Hardy guided the party into making a great turn to the right.

Some enthusiasts went so far as to suggest a separation of forces along racial lines, and an all-white people's front against fascism. Eddie Roux objected to what he thought was a revival of the discredited notion that only whites could make a revolution. No united front was worthy that failed to defend the living standards and rights of all workers. Solly Sachs retorted that Roux suffered from an 'infantile revolutionary exuberance'. A united front between black and white might 'satisfy the revolutionary conscience of our honest but impracticable comrades'. He, Sachs, was a realist who wanted to free the hundreds of thousands of poor whites from imperialism and fascist influences.[40]

Hardy agreed with Roux that there could be only one united front. Any attempt to split it would strengthen the segregation camp. Specialization was called for, however, and the party should give a hand in making the All African Convention the permanent organization of Africans, Coloured and Indians. When linked to the anti-imperialist front, the Convention would strengthen the fight against fascism and 'assist in maintaining the higher standards of the white workers' while obtaining better wages for Africans. Older members of the movement might have heard in these pontifical sentences an echo of Crawford's theories of thirty years before.

Bunting's death on 25 May 1936 was a painful reminder of the casualties suffered in past ideological battles. The 'black republic' slogan, for which he had been sacrificed only five years before, now seemed far removed from current urgencies. The party made amends in an obituary notice that praised his honesty and devotion to the cause. Though expelled for a 'persistent disagreement on fundamental principles', he would always have a place in the history of the revolutionary movement. It was he who had recognized the great importance of Africans in the struggle against imperialism. Under his leadership, the party had begun to organize them for their emancipation. 'Thousands of exploited and oppressed South Africans will remember Comrade Bunting as a staunch fighter.'[41]

Conditions had changed since 1931, the political bureau pointed out in June, and the party must change its policy accordingly. Though it had not given up the aim of overthrowing Anglo-Boer imperialism, the first objective now was to ward off fascism and war. Communists would therefore loyally support a united front and refrain from public criticism of their allies. Roux welcomed the break with the old sectarian approach, yet doubted if its mistakes could so lightly be swept away. The internal struggle had left deep wounds which would heal only if those responsible invited all expelled members to return and get on with the work.

The mistakes, explained the bureau, arose from academic discussions which took the place of mass work, caused inner conflicts, and isolated the party. As a result, it was unable to get on with the urgent business of forming a united front. Kalk and Wolfson were deputed to interview Roux, point out the error of his ways, and bring him back to the fold. He countered by calling them yes-men of the Comintern; and did his stint as a rank-and-file member until he left for Cape Town in 1937. Here he and Kotane wrote, printed and published the *African Defender*, a monthly journal issued in the name of Ikaka Labasebenzi.

Issy Wolfson, the party treasurer, belonged to the new generation of home-born white communists. Born in 1906 at Luipaardsvlei near Krugersdorp, Transvaal, he formed and led the textile workers' and tailors' unions, joined the party in 1934, and rose to the top leadership after Bach's departure. A powerful speaker, he was in demand at outdoor meetings and prominent in the labour movement. He and Kalk carried the main burden of party work among whites on the Rand, attended to their unions, served on the national executive of the Trades and Labour Council, and were active on peace or united front committees. Though devoted to the party, they could not administer it with the single-minded care given to it by former leaders whose interests had been less diffused.

Under Hardy's guidance, the party became less intensively militant and more broadly respectable. Its paper was renamed the *South African Worker* in June 1936 and made a severe cut in the space given to news or comment in Bantu languages. Instead of going to jail for defying the state, communists appealed for world peace and assisted in forming the peace committees that multiplied after the outbreak of civil war in Spain. Wolfson spoke at a Johannesburg peace rally in September alongside a bishop, a rabbi, Mrs Ballinger and Archie Moore. Representatives of the CP, LP, TLC, FSU, League of

Nations Unions, St John's Ambulance and the university senate sat on the platform. With unbounded enthusiasm for the united front, the party offered to back Labour candidates for the provincial council. It was a pity that they stood for complete segregation, said the CP. This apart, Labour was sincere in its endeavours to improve the lot of the poor.

Capitalists drew their profits out of poor blacks and not poor whites, remarked Kalk, while Roux warned that the party might neglect the African's struggle by turning its face to the whites. All faces, white, black and brown, 'should be directed towards the enemy front of Anglo-Boer imperialism', said Hardy, while he led the party into a struggle against greyshirts at home and fascism abroad. Knowing little about South Africa, and unmindful of the great gulf between white and black, he made the mistake of supposing that white workers could be induced to support the liberation movement. 'This is the Communist approach,' he declared. 'Only thus shall we develop a real United Front that will lead to a movement against war and fascism.'[42]

Eighteen white and twenty-two other delegates at the party's national conference in September approved of Hardy's thesis and agreed that the fight for African rights would best be carried on through the All African Convention. Having agreed in principle to a separation of forces, the party joined in forming an all-white People's Front at a conference called in October by the Trades and Labour Council. Communist delegates nearly wrecked the meeting by suggesting that the programme should call for the removal of pass laws, the recognition of African trade unions, and free primary education for all races. Unity was preserved by deleting all references to a separate 'native policy'. 'Let us not discuss details and reforms in face of the great danger,' advised Bill Andrews, the president; 'smash fascism and all other things will follow.'[43]

He took the short-range view that a non-racial organization would alienate white workers and drive them into the arms of greyshirts and blackshirts. A people's front open to all democrats regardless of race was the proper thing for Europe, explained Moore in a presidential address to the TLC's annual conference, but not in South Africa, where racialism dominated politics. The 'bulk of the proletariat, the black man, is in a state of feudal bondage and what is more important voteless'. The united front must therefore 'rely more on right wing elements who believe in and support the democratic principle'.[44]

The united front would split along colour lines, said the communists, unless Africans, Coloured and whites pulled together in double harness on the issue of local, immediate demands. Anti-fascists, Kotane pointed out, were defending the existing state of affairs, which was rotten in the eyes of Africans and Coloured. These would enter the united front only if it helped them to gain democratic rights and higher wages.[45] The proposed strategy never took shape. White men who answered a call to drive greyshirts off the streets refused to assist Africans when struggling against pass laws, police raids and pick-up vans. With the right wing in control, the People's Front never went further than an attempt to combat the spread of fascist propaganda among the whites.

Even so timid and narrow an approach seemed too advanced for the Labour party. It boycotted the inaugural conference and refused to join the People's Front. They should have nothing to do with any movement in which communists appeared, Charles Henderson told delegates at the annual conference in January 1937. They agreed; and also rejected a proposal to change the party's segregation policy. This was little short of fascism, said Duncan Burnside, the Labour MP for Umbilo, and he resigned from the party in order to found a rival Socialist party. Born in Glasgow in 1899, he joined the ILP and served as secretary of the local tailors' union before settling in South Africa in 1922, where he became a member of the Labour party and secretary of the garment workers' union in Durban.

The communists took him to task for splitting the movement. He ought to join their ranks or remain in the Labour party to change its programme; though he was more likely, they said, to follow in its muddy wake by adopting a programme suited to the white voters' prejudices. Three months later, in June 1937, Wolfson suggested a 'working arrangement' between Labour and Communist parties in municipal elections on a platform of slum clearance, reduced bus fares, improved health facilities, and a minimum wage of 10s. a day for white and 5s. for African labourers in municipal employ. Henderson politely replied that his party's constitution ruled out any electoral agreement with another party. In spite of the rebuff, the communists announced that they would urge electors to vote for Labour candidates.[46]

The party put up its own candidates in elections held at that time under the Representation of Natives Act. Mofutsanyana failed to secure a nomination to the Transvaal urban seat in the Native Representative Council. H. Basner, the communist candidate for the senate, lost heavily to J. D. Rheinallt Jones under a system of block voting that enabled chiefs and rural electoral committees to decide the outcome. The party made the mistake of hiding its face behind the All African Convention, said Mofutsanyana, who stood as a communist. 'Even Basner could not get on my platform and speak on my behalf because he thought he might prejudice himself.'[47] Other symptoms of election strain appeared. Marks, having been expelled from the party in June 1937 for 'failing to carry out even the most elementary duties of a disciplined member', helped R. G. Baloyi, the owner of a flourishing bus company, to win a seat on the NRC.[48]

The CP's political bureau reported optimistically in January 1937 that conditions had never been so favourable as they then were for a revolutionary movement. Since it had moved away 'from the domain of sectarianism', the party could hardly keep pace with the rush of new members. The next year's balance sheet was full of gloom. All that stood in the way of fascist reaction were a weak Labour party, incredibly tied to a foolish segregation policy, an African Convention without either a following or a militant programme, a stillborn People's Front, and a small Communist party, the most hated by the exploiting class. The remedy was to form a democratic front by supporting the Labour party, trade unions, and the Convention.[49]

The central leadership lost its bearings and self-confidence. Some members complained in 1938 that the party had disintegrated. The *South African Worker* collapsed in March after nearly twenty-three years of unbroken publication since its first appearance as the *International*. The Trades and Labour Council, having withdrawn from the People's Front, formed a League for the Maintenance of Democracy which excluded the party. Solly Sachs of the garment workers' union took the TLC to court after a bitter quarrel in which Wolfson and Kalk sided with the conservatives on the Council against other communist trade unionists. The political bureau met irregularly, often at intervals of two or three months, ignored letters and rarely issued directives. Party groups and individual members throughout the country received no guidance or assistance from the centre.

The communists seemed to have taken root and to grow only in Cape Town, hunting ground of tourists, artists and leisurely liberals. Kotane, Roux and Andrews, who rejoined the party in May 1938, settled there. The *Guardian*, a radical weekly which first appeared in February 1937, found a wide circle of readers in all racial groups by means of lively journalism, progressive policies and an able analysis of international events. Trade unionism flourished in the hands of energetic, efficient party members and supporters, who systematically organized Coloured, African and white workers in shops and factories. A National Liberation League, founded in 1935, was taking the place of Abdurahman's African People's Organization among Coloured in the western Cape.

The only communists to stand for parliament in the 1938 elections were two members of the party in Cape Town, and they fought under different banners. Jimmy Emmerich, secretary of the tramway union, represented the Labour party in the Cape Flats; Harry Snitcher, a young advocate, contested the Castle division for the Socialist party. In spite of their imposing list of backers, which included Coloured radicals, white trade unionists and Afrikaner intellectuals, most of the electors preferred the United party. It obtained 111 seats, the Nationalists 27, the Dominion party 8, and Labour 3.[50] The Nationalists whipped up Afrikaner sentiment to a crescendo in centenary celebrations of the Great Trek. The climax took place at Bloemfontein in October when the Ossewabrandwag (Oxwagon

Sentinel) was founded. Before long, it served as the main channel for spreading Nazi propaganda and militarism.[51]

The Voortrekker celebrations had given fascism a great boost, Kalk reported at the Communist party's national conference in December; but a majority of Afrikaner nationalists were sincere republicans. The party should work among them through Afrikaner cultural societies, trade unions and the anti-fascist movement; and also redouble its efforts within the Labour party. He went on to admit that the party made a great blunder by hiding its face behind other organizations. It 'rarely came out as an independent political force', lapsed into inactivity, and failed to carry out the decisions of the 1936 conference. 'The blame for this must be laid at the door of the PB which failed on numerous occasions to give a lead on important questions.'[52]

Mofutsanyana, the general secretary, said much the same thing about the party's role on the liberation front. Some members held high positions in the movement, yet the party had neglected it to such an extent that 'we have to admit a complete betrayal of the African people'. The rank-and-file neither understood nor cared about the Munich swindle and other events in Europe which occupied the minds of white communists. 'Our meetings are no attraction to the Africans who are mainly concerned with oppression under which they live.' He was being driven to the conclusion that the party should divide into an African and non-African section connected by the executive committee. Such a division already existed in fact. The African section, which leaned heavily on the whites, felt that the party was not their own and failed to develop a sense of responsibility.

The conference turned the proposal down without hesitation. How could it fulfil its mission to unite workers of all races if the party were to tolerate a racial schism in its own ranks? Its own members would not rid themselves of colour feelings unless they met and worked together as one. Josie Mpama (Mrs Mofutsanyana) pointed out that a white communist could hardly claim to speak for Africans unless he worked among them and saw how they lived. The Cape Town delegates had a mandate to reject the proposal, said Kotane. It appeared to them that Johannesburg wanted an autonomous black party with its own leadership. 'If we have two sections, I shall walk out of the CPSA and join something else.'

On behalf of his district committee, he moved the temporary transfer of the party's headquarters to Cape Town. The suggestion, he explained, arose out of a report made earlier in the year by Andrews on his return from Johannesburg. It was the natural centre, but the party there needed a breathing space so that it could pull itself together, put its finances in order, and clear away the prevailing 'atmosphere of hate'. All attempts to improve things had failed. 'Had I not left Johannesburg I would have lost all hope and would have left the Party. In Cape Town I found a different atmosphere and as a result I am still in the Party.'

Six delegates voted for the motion, five against, and two abstained. A new political bureau, consisting of Ray Alexander, Bill Andrews, Mrs Z. Gool, Sam Kahn, Moses Kotane and H. J. Simons, was elected. Though the transfer was meant to be temporary, the headquarters remained in Cape Town until 1950, when the party became illegal in terms of the Suppression of Communism Act. Far removed from the big industrial towns and the main areas of African population, the legislative capital had none of the Witwatersrand's explosive qualities that made it the storm centre of radical politics. As against this, the party could avoid sudden or extreme changes in policy and organize a fairly efficient system of administration in the calm, rather sluggish, society of the western Cape, where the large Coloured community formed a bridge between African and white minorities.

21 United Front

University graduates, teachers, students, journalists and a handful of artisans produced a new generation of Coloured radicals in the western Cape during the 1930s. Though attracted to communism, they could not square its class concepts with social realities. Embittered by civilized labour policies and the racial exclusiveness of white workers, they wanted an organization of their own in which they could synthesize Marxism and nationalism. Like Dr Abdurahman thirty years before, they refused to play second fiddle to whites of any description; but they turned their backs on his policies and strategy.

The African People's Organization was by then hardly more than a mutual benefit, burial and building society. Dr Abdurahman, though still pre-eminent in the Coloured community, had discredited himself and his party by clinging to the white liberals when they followed Smuts into Hertzog's camp. The younger generation disputed his authority and made a bid for leadership on their own account. Members of his own family led the revolt: his daughters Dr Waradia Abdurahman and Mrs Z. Gool; their mother Mrs Nellie Abdurahman; his son-in-law Dr A. H. Gool; the latter's brother, Dr Goolam Gool; and their sisters Minnie and Janub Gool. Growing up in a cross-cultural stream of Islamic and western influences, they straddled the ideological gap between Muslims and Christians.

Mrs Zainunissa Gool (1900–1963), affectionately known as Cissie and as rare a beauty as her grandmother, took up the weapons that her father had laid aside on entering the maze of white supremacy politics. He and she spoke at a meeting held in Cape Town on 27 April 1931, to protest against the bill that gave the vote to white women and denied it to Coloured, Indian and African women. 'I am slowly going Red,' she said. 'I fear that I shall be blacklisted as a revolutionary.' Could anybody conceive a greater tragedy, asked a sympathetic liberal, than 'this cultured woman going Red and meditating the casting of her personality and her talents to feed the flames of revolution?'[1] Three years later she, La Guma, Gomas and Ahmed Ismail debated whether they should form a new party in opposition to the APO.

'Clarity on this issue is of tremendous importance for us,' wrote Gomas, 'for we saw Communists farcically and dramatically opposing each other in this debate.' The party cried out for unity in struggle, yet it would be suicidal to wait until white workers, who were 'steeped in stinking social-imperialism and race hatred', opened their ranks. They used the slogan of equal pay for equal work to lay hold on the darker man's job; and aided the ruling class to add to his burden of oppression. Communists ought therefore to organize the people on colour lines for work, land, equality and majority rule.[2]

In 1935 Cape Town celebrated one hundred years of emancipation from slavery and twenty-five years of George V's reign. Gomas was sentenced to six months' hard labour and Minnie Gool to one month's for distributing an anti-imperialist pamphlet which, the court ruled, impaired the monarch's dignity.[3] Gomas issued another pamphlet on behalf of the party, drawing attention to the sham of the centenary. Far from bringing freedom, emancipation made possible a form of servitude many times more subtle and deadly than slavery. The Coloured man knew only the freedom to starve; his women were exploited economically by day and sexually by night; his children, reared in slums, grew old and died before their time. 'Without land, bread and equality of opportunity, there can be no freedom. After a century, the non-European must still fight for that freedom which should rightly have been his since 1834.'

The gist of this appeared in the preamble to a draft programme of the National Liberation League, founded in December 1935 with Cissie Gool as the president and La Guma as secretary.[4] It was probably the most emphatic and detailed claim yet made to complete equality before the law. The twenty-three specified aims included demands for equal voting rights and parliamentary representation; no bars to employment in public services or private enterprise; an end to discrimination in school, games, the army and social services; and the removal of bans on sex or marriage which 'legalise the fiction of race inferiority'. Radical in terms of orthodox liberalism, the programme showed no trace of socialist thinking apart from a homily addressed to white workers on 'wage slavery'.

The League gave voice to the resentment and uncertainties of a depressed minority. As the report by the Cape Coloured Commission of 1934–7 showed, the Coloured were hemmed in by racial barriers and squeezed between the pressures of whites on top and Africans from below. Starved of food and education, wasted by drink and disease, housed in slums and farm hovels, the bulk of the people were being ground down into a state of degrading poverty and despair. Abdurahman, who sat on the commission, had tried to rescue his people by trading votes for concessions. The new radicals looked for salvation to militant mass action; though they, too, knew that the Coloured could not make headway on their own.

Visions of class solidarity had faded since the days when Abdurahman pleaded for unity with the labour movement. The League, however, renewed the plea in the interests of all workers, white and black. Neither could be free under Anglo-Boer imperialism; both should shed their prejudices and realize that they were 'inevitable' allies. White workers must cut themselves loose from the ruling class before it dragged them down 'to the oppressed and degraded position of the non-European'.

The appeal was no more than a pious gesture to Karl Marx's shade as long as white workers continued to exchange class attitudes for racial prejudices. It was to the African that the Coloured radicals looked for mass support, and they drafted the League's programme with him in mind. Their aim was 'national liberation', not socialism. They set out the grievances of 'Non-Europeans', and not of Coloured only; reserved a place on their national convention for the 'kings, chiefs, and princes' of Bantu tribes or clans; and stipulated that the leadership should 'at all times and on all governing bodies be predominantly non-European'. In effect, and no doubt by intent, the League was cast in a mould that would enable it to compete with the African National Congress.

For this reason the League undertook to 'discourage organization on racial and sectarian lines among the oppressed peoples themselves'. The clause should be scrapped, suggested Reginald Bridgeman, international secretary of the League against Imperialism. Such organizations were a consequence and not the cause of colour bars, he argued.[6] The clause remained, however, as a reminder that the ANC closed its doors to Coloured as well as to whites. Since Congress was sluggish and steeped in reformism, the League itself would rally the African masses to the cause of national emancipation. From then on and for the next twenty-five years, Coloured radicals of the western Cape would strive to shape the aims and strategy of African nationalism.

La Guma and Dr G. H. Gool, the League's new president, summoned their 'Fellow Non-Europeans, Businessmen, Professionals, Intellectuals, Workers' in September 1937 to a national convention of 'Bantu, Coloured, Indian, Malay'. It must be obvious to all, they said, 'that our political line since the granting of the franchise to the non-European of the Cape has been tactically and ideologically incorrect'. Because of ignorance or treachery, past leaders had put their trust in imperialist parties – South African, Nationalist, and United – which had encircled their people with a forest of colour bars. Representing an imperialism within an imperialism, Afrikaner nationalists had no intention of freeing the subject races, and found a mass basis in the privileged white working class. 'Our only hope lies in unifying all those forces that feel the weight of oppression as we do, into a cohesive and determined whole in opposition to Imperialism.'[7]

The African National Congress, Dr Seme promised at a special convention in January 1933, would set their people free if only every African took out a membership card. Let us now, he urged, 'extend our feeble hands to our grown up brothers in other parts of Africa and to the emancipated slaves in the United States of America, asking for their help'.[8] He led a deputation in July 1934 to D. L. Smit, the secretary for native affairs, to explain ANC aims. It was not a political party, but a spontaneous national movement for social reform. Its leaders were respected men of distinction in whom the people had full confidence. Congress aspired to become 'the Native Parliament of South Africa' under their chief, the minister of native affairs. 'We all love him and respect his person and his position in the African nation,' said the deputation. The ANC would be honoured if he were to attend their conferences. 'As our great chief he can meet us as his Councillors according to the Native Laws and Customs.'[9] Or so said Seme; and his cant barely hid the bankruptcy of his policy. Imbeciles and unpatriotic folk, he wrote, kept crying 'Congress is dead, Congress is dead', and yet did nothing to revive the national organization.[10]

The APO had no better plan for defeating white labour policies than to recommend support for Coloured businessmen. Africans and Coloured, called together by Abdurahman and Jabavu at Port Elizabeth in January 1934, agreed on a boycott of firms employing only whites. Abdurahman, that 'arch lackey of the white ruling class, sabotaged the decision', complained Gomas a year later. 'This is all that has come of the thirty-four years' record of the APO.' It would never free the Coloured.[11]

Radicals traced this futility to the influence of a 'native bourgeoisie'. It existed, practically and ideologically, as a definite class, said J. B. Marks. Only by understanding the class structure could one distinguish between the revolutionary and counterrevolutionary forces. The bourgeoisie formed the 'social basis of national reformism' and dominated Congress, as was plain from its appeal for funds to set up businesses under African managers, chosen, no doubt, from among the traders in the ANC.[12]

The theory seemed far-fetched to some communists. Eddie Roux, for one, thought that the 'bourgeois elements' scarcely formed an 'organized capitalist class'. Quoting a thesis of the Comintern's sixth congress in support, he argued that Anglo-Boer imperialism had stifled the growth of an African capitalist class. Jameson Coka agreed. He gave figures showing that Africans in Johannesburg owned between them only 230 dilapidated shops, coffee stalls, barber shops and eating-houses, which employed perhaps 450 persons and represented a capital of not more than £3,000. There was a widespread bourgeois ideology but no bourgeois class, he maintained, because the whites would not allow African entrepreneurs to take root.[13]

Coka, himself an aspiring bourgeois, encountered these obstacles in person when he took up journalism as a career. 'The White Press,' he discovered, 'was almost inaccessible to an African writer unless he happened to share anti-Africanism.'[14] After being expelled from the party, he tried to become an entrepreneur by publishing the *African Liberator*, and looked for financial backing to the white liberals whom he had previously berated. He now listed their good works and accused his former comrades of turning African trade unions into pawns. Black and white must cooperate, he pleaded; while every true Christian should do his duty by his black neighbour.[15]

Such trite sentiment revealed the kind of reformism that some radicals detected in an African bourgeois class. Bach, its sternest critic before leaving for Moscow, insisted that there was a bourgeoisie in the form of 'higher traders, the moneylenders, the owners of small shops with hired labour' and others who in one way or another 'exploit the Native toilers and make money out of them'. Having in mind this middle class, he disputed with Kotane in 1934 on the issue of the 'independent native republic'.[16]

Kotane argued that its first and true meaning implied two stages, one leading to a democratic state under majority African rule, the second to a full-blown socialism. Bach followed the hard line taken by Bunting in 1928 and insisted that the two stages were synchronic. One should take a second look at the reasoning, if only because it crops up in present-day discussions of policy for newly independent states. Can the middle class be trusted, radicals ask, to 'complete the African revolution', or should socialists form a party to compete with the bourgeoisie for power?

The bourgeoisie, said Bach, wanted to be free and therefore stood up against discrimination. The freedom that they had in mind included the right to exploit others, however, and this interest caused them to waver. They were afraid that workers when liberated would curb the power to exploit. They accordingly protested against white supremacy yet sided with it when workers took to open struggle, as Kadalie had done. If allowed to obtain control after the revolution, the bourgeoisie were bound to use it in their interests. This must not be allowed.

The alternative was for workers and peasants to seize power, introduce democracy, and move by degrees towards socialism. In that event, the slogans of an 'independent native republic' and a 'workers' and peasants' government' would represent an identical concentration of power. Persons who stressed the differences between the slogans and who wanted the bourgeoisie to control the independent republic were 'consciously or unconsciously the supporters of the Native bourgeoisie – they speak in its name'.

Bach laid too much stress on the middle class and undervalued its radical bent. Then, as now, Africans could not easily obtain or invest capital. Even today, few own factories, shares and real estate. The 16,000 business men, 100 doctors, 50 lawyers, 26,000 teachers, 7,000 nurses who, with clerks, salesmen, pastors and social workers make up the present-day African 'middle class', find no more dignity or security in the segregated ghettoes than do wage workers. These are the reasons, a contemporary African sociologist has noted, for the racial policies of the African National Congress and the Pan African Congress. 'The African middle class has no stake in the country, and sees its salvation in making common cause with the masses with whom it shares common disabilities.' Now, as thirty years ago, Africans of all ranks 'see their struggle as a struggle against white domination'.[17]

This was how Kotane saw the struggle. 'I am first an African and then a Communist,' he told the conference of top party leaders in December 1938. 'I came to the Communist Party because I saw in it the way out and the salvation for the African people.'[18] Born on 9 August 1905 of Tswana stock in the western Transvaal, he belonged to a peasant family, worked as herdsboy, domestic servant, waiter, miner and baker, attended confirmation classes, and taught himself to read and write as he went from job to job. He joined the ANC in 1927, the African Bakers' Union in 1928, and the party in 1929, when his political education really began. After spending a year at the Lenin school in Moscow, he returned in 1933 to become the party secretary and editor. A Marxist fledgling, ready to trade dialectics with the most doctrinaire of members, he was also a fervent patriot who showed no trace of colour consciousness in his dealings with whites. His theory of the class struggle blended harmoniously with a strong feeling of national pride.

Convinced that Africans could hold their own in fair competition, he despised white supremacy and would not tolerate any trace of it either in the party or in its approach to Africans. They were to be emancipated and not to be manipulated in a struggle for power. The Communist party and the African Congress were not competitors, he urged, but the mailed fists of a single political force which would succeed only if both were trained to strike their blows at the same time and in total agreement. Impatient of theory that seemed remote from current needs, he brushed Bach's polemics aside and made it his business to strengthen the two arms of the liberation front.

It was stirred into activity in 1935 by the appearance of the Hertzog-Nicholls bill to disfranchise Africans in the Cape. Seme and Professor Jabavu took the initiative in calling yet another convention to meet the challenge. The communists, having discarded Bach's 'go it alone' policy, also approved. The party, they said, had often suggested united action with the ANC and the ICU, which the leaders always refused. 'The more heartily we greet now the initiative of the African National Congress.' This would be the first convention to represent the vast masses.[19]

The 'mammoth convention', said to be the greatest ever held, met at Bloemfontein on 15 December 1935. It was brought together, said Jabavu, by the *Madimo*, ancestral spirits that guided the children of Makana, Sekhukhuni, Cetshawayo and Moshwe-shwe. The 400 delegates represented all the political clans, left, right and centre; trade unions, farmers, shopkeepers, teachers, churchmen, and a score of local communities. A people's front so widely based was bound to cheer the radicals and follow the moderates.

A cable from Moscow urging delegates to set about their

historic task aroused great enthusiasm. The convention approved Gomas's motion that meetings of protest be organized in every village. No taxes should be paid, said J. B. Marks, until the people had won their rights. Dr G. H. Gool, the brother-in-law of Cissie Gool, wanted delegates to lay the basis of a national liberation movement against all repressive laws. The only effective decisions taken were to make the All African Convention a permanent body and to send another deputation to the prime minister. Clements Kadalie warned from past experience that the deputation would certainly fail.[20]

Its mission was to oppose the bill and ask for a round-table conference. For reasons never explained, Jabavu, Mahabane, Champion, Selby Msimang and the other five delegates agreed, or gave the appearance of agreeing, to the compromise of a separate communal roll for Africans. The rest of the convention's executive, including Edwin Mofutsanyana and the Drs Xuma, Moroka and Molema, hurried to Cape Town. After a week of wrangling, the executive publicly rejected the compromise. But the damage had been done. Hertzog announced at a joint session of the two houses in February that he had accepted the compromise; and introduced an amended bill which was carried on the third reading by 169 votes to eleven.[21]

Six members of the United party and five of the Dominion party, then angling for the Coloured vote, opposed the bill. All Labour members voted for it, as did Malan's Nationalists after being defeated on a motion to treat Coloured and Africans as one group. Dr N. J. van der Merwe, leader of the Free State Nationalists, who seconded the motion, argued that social equality followed political equality and led to 'mixing of blood', which ruined the white race. Hertzog said much the same thing. Whites feared the 'intermingling of blood' and black domination, he explained. These dangers, hanging like a sword over their heads, prevented them from doing justice to Africans.[22]

The vote-catching phrases were familiarly centred round the themes of blood, sex and black power. Behind them lay the alliance of maize growers, sugar planters, mine and factory owners, white workers and the urban bourgeoisie against all Africans, peasant, worker, intellectual and storekeeper. A handful of white liberals objected. J. H. Hofmeyr, the minister of the interior, told parliament that white civilization had no future 'save with the consent and goodwill of the non-European people'. Sir James Rose Innes, a former chief justice, headed a campaign to save the franchise. The bill, he said, brought South Africa nearer to fascism. When the shouting had died away, the role of the liberal was to soothe, to counsel patience, and to persuade Africans to make what use they could of the Representation of Natives Act.

African voters in the Cape were removed from the common rolls on which they had been registered since 1854. Voting on a communal roll, they would elect three whites to the assembly, then consisting of 150 members elected by whites and a sprinkling of Coloured; and two whites to the provincial council. Chiefs, local councils, urban advisory boards and election committees in all provinces were to elect four whites to the senate by a system of block voting. The act also created a Native Representative Council of six white officials, four nominated and twelve elected Africans. The councillors were to receive a stipend of £120 a year, discuss grievances, and tender advice which the government usually ignored. 'We have been asked to cooperate with a toy telephone,' said councillor Paul Mosaka in 1946, on the verge of the council's collapse. 'We have been speaking into an apparatus which cannot transmit sound and at the end of which there is nobody to receive the message.'[23]

A small left-wing group foresaw the futility yet made no headway against the missionary-trained reformist leaders, lured by the meagre stipend or the prestige of sitting in a mock parliament. When the All African Convention met again in June 1936, Jabavu turned down proposals to boycott the elections. Africans could startle the whites, attract wide attention and win their rights 'by using the fear of a bloody revolution'; but to succeed, they must have complete unity and a perfect organization. Without these, a policy of reprisals resting on force might end in disaster. He preferred to use what could be used, fight for the repeal of colour bars, and encourage people to strengthen the African middle class of traders, doctors and lawyers.[24]

'Trotskyists and other opportunists,' said George Hardy, were playing into the government's hands by proposing a boycott. A foundation member of the British CP, Hardy (1884–1965), suspected a Trotskyist in every left-wing critic of communist policy. The son of a Yorkshire farm labourer who raised a family of nine on 18s. a week, he left school at the age of twelve, worked as a farm hand, joined the army, and migrated to Canada and the United States where he served as secretary of the IWW during the First World War. On the strength of his overseas experience, he was deputed to steer the South African party away from its alleged unreal and sectarian outlook. Almost wholly ignorant of the country's social structure, he thought it possible to detach poor whites and small farmers from their allegiance to Afrikaner nationalism.[25]

A boycott, he argued, would fail, drive the militants into a blind alley, and prevent the Convention from becoming what it should be, a mass movement of Africans, Coloured and Indians. The proper thing to do was to elect staunch fighters against imperialism to parliament and the Native Representative Council. If the government expelled their representatives, the people would resist and make the boycott a political reality.[26]

The African National Congress also decided to take part in the elections and to concentrate on strengthening the African's position in the economy. Dube, Mahabane, Msimang, Skota and Thema sat on the executives of both Congress and the Convention. Why then should they compete? asked Seme. He knew that the younger men wanted nothing less than social equality, whereas the ANC had little to do with such dreams. It was 'deeply concerned with the great beauty of our own African society'.[27] The Convention had failed in the purpose for which it was formed, he argued; and should be disbanded so that all patriots could fight from within the ANC under a single command.

Two hundred delegates meeting at Bloemfontein in June 1936 decided otherwise and formed themselves into a permanent Convention, to which 'all African religious, educational, industrial, economic, political, commercial and social organizations shall be affiliated'. Dr Seme, who attended, was elected to the executive committee together with Dr G. H. Gool. The office bearers were Professor Jabavu, president; Dr A. B. Xuma vice-president; H. Selby Msimang, the general secretary; R. H. Godlo, the record secretary; Z. K. Matthews and S. D. Ngcobo, the clerk-draughtsmen; and Dr J. S. Moroka, the treasurer. The 112 societies and communities represented at the conference spanned the whole range of the African and Coloured liberation movement; among them were the ANC, ICU, CP, National Liberation League, APO, and the Cape Voters' Association.[28]

Personal ambitions, regional loyalties, the ANC's failures, and the evergreen hope that a new organization might cure old weaknesses influenced the decision to put the Convention on a permanent footing. Communists and Coloured radicals hoped to find a mass basis in its broad, loosely knit structure. The party's national conference in September undertook to weld it into a powerful movement. This was a major change in outlook. The communists were returning to their earlier concept of a united front with African nationalism.

Applying their faith in a grass-roots organization, they suggested that the Convention should form a network of local committees for immediate, daily needs. Given a broad and active basis all the year round, it could not possibly drift into becoming an annual debating society like the ANC. Moreover, and this was to be an important function, the committees would serve as the Convention's agents in elections under the Representation of Natives Act. They should aim at electing brave and trustworthy fighters under the Convention's banner.[29]

The Convention never hoisted a party banner. Attempts to draw up a list of approved candidates threatened to split the assortment of political, religious, professional, welfare and residential groups. The Convention delegated the function of nominating candidates in the Cape to the Native Voters' Association and made no recommendations in the northern provinces. Former allies opposed one another in the elections of 1937 for the Native Representative Council. Of the ANC's leaders, only Dube in Natal, Mapikela in the Orange Free State and Selope Thema in the Transvaal were elected. Edwin Mofutsanyana, the communist candidate and a member of the Convention's executive in the Transvaal, was knocked out in the first round, which decided the nominations. H. M. Basner, a

Johannesburg lawyer and the communist candidate for the senate in the Transvaal-OFS division, obtained more votes than Ballinger and two other candidates in the nominations, but lost the actual election to Rheinallt Jones by 66,000 votes to 404,000.

Mofutsanyana complained that the electoral colleges were inconsistent. They voted against him and for Basner, though both stood on the same platform. Apart from their lack of funds, the communist candidates failed because of the party's isolation from the rural population, the virtual disfranchisement of urban residents, and the conservative attitude of the electoral colleges. Deluded by a hundred years of missionary and liberal illusions, they disobeyed the mandate of the taxpayers whom they represented. Radicals had blundered, said Mofutsanyana, by allowing the urban advisory boards to become the agents of white municipalities. The proper course was to secure the election of militants who would conduct a struggle against high rents, lodgers' permits, beer brewing and other vexatious regulations.[30]

Africans at Vereeniging, once a communist stronghold, went into battle on their own on Sunday, 19 September 1937. The police, carrying out raids in the township, were set upon by the infuriated residents. Using sticks, stones, iron bars and pocket knives, they drove the police away, killed two of their number and smashed the pick-up van. Reinforcements fired on the Africans, wounded many and arrested 450. Of the fifty-four charged, eleven were convicted and sentenced to imprisonment for periods ranging from three to seven years.

White racists agitated for a ban on communism and 'the liberalist doctrine of equality'. Hertzog said that Africans living in towns were in the 'white man's country' and must obey his laws. Anybody 'so presumptuous as to claim equal authority with the white man in the Union will experience the greatest measure of disappointment and failure'.[31] A commission of inquiry found that ill treatment by police and the municipality had contributed to the outbreak. The Communist party traced it to a brutal system of exploitation promoted by repressive laws and daily assaults on the African's rights and dignities. 'The aim of these laws is to thrust Natives in huge numbers on to the labour market: to over-supply it, so that the Native is robbed of his fair chance of getting a competitive wage; and constantly to force him to sell his labour under threat of immediate arrest.'[32]

'African leaders are lagging behind the masses,' said the communists in a comment on the Vereeniging outbreak. 'Unless a new leadership is created and spontaneous fights are transformed into an organized struggle, the fight of the masses against oppression, the struggle for the liberation of the African people will be without success.'[33] The advice might be sound; but it could not be pursued until the movement had put its house in order.

Neither the communists nor the ANC were able to organize effective opposition against pass laws and other racial statutes that led to the conviction of one African in every fourteen. The party called for a mass defiance of the census held under the Native Laws Amendment Act of 1937. The most ferocious of the measures adopted to curb the movement of work-seekers from farms and reserves, the act was so framed as to limit the size of the African urban population to the bare number needed for 'reasonable labour requirements'. No other law caused so much alarm as this, for it exposed the great majority of Africans to a constant danger of being endorsed out of any town by hard-faced white bureaucrats. Appeals for a boycott of the census were moderately successful on the Rand and attracted a good number of the best fighters to the party. 'However this is not sufficient,' reported Mofutsanyana. 'Our independent work as a party has suffered a considerable setback in the last few years.'[34]

The liberation movement, he pointed out, was almost confined to the industrial centres, 'while the bulk of the African people living in the reserves, protectorates and kraals remain isolated'. Little or no work was being done among them by the Convention, Congress or the Communist party. The movement had no press to speak of and hardly did more than hold occasional meetings in the towns. Since many leaders were badly trained in consequence and drifted into self-seeking careers, political organizations came and went like paper fires. The chiefs were another stumbling block. Their people respected them, though they were agents of the government. The government itself refused to let chiefs sit in conference with other members of the ANC and used them against the movement. Yet Basutoland's Lekhotla la Bafo (League of the Poor) had shown that peasants when properly led would oppose both chiefs and the colonial administration.

'Basutoland has now become the battlefield, where the exploited and oppressed peasants and workers fight against the imperialist forces,' claimed H. M. Tsoene, president of the Lekhotla. Facing a charge of criminal defamation that arose from an article in the *Worker*, he appealed to the communists for aid. L. C. Joffe, who represented the paper, was subpoenaed to give evidence for the prosecution and to produce the original article. He attended the court at Teyateyanang near Maseru in November 1937, refused to testify, and when threatened with committal for contempt of court, declared that communists would never betray the common people's struggle for freedom. His defiance caused so much excitement that the magistrate adjourned the case and released Tsoene on his own bond.[35]

Transkeian and other peasants would follow the Sotho example, said Mofutsanyana, if the All African Convention would only provide them with a practical programme of struggle. The Convention would go the way of the ICU and ANC, to become an empty shell, noisy and without substance, unless it obtained mass support through live and active affiliated units. He and Marks took the initiative in forming a coordinating committee to revive the ANC in the Transvaal. With the Rev. S. S. Tema as chairman and Marks as secretary, the committee made steady progress in a series of meetings on the Rand and refused to be turned aside by the familiar charge that communists were attempting to capture the leadership. That was not their purpose, they said. Like others on the committee, they wanted to put new life into Congress for the sake of unity.[36]

Both Convention and Congress met at Bloemfontein in December. The Convention ratified an amended draft constitution, which gave all chiefs a seat on the executive committee, and adopted a programme. It called for opposition to segregation and colour bars; franchise rights and direct representation in parliament; the removal of restrictions on the right of Africans to buy land; equal pay for equal work; the formation of cooperative societies; and measures 'to stimulate African latent gifts in trading and business capacity'. Pious resolutions were not sufficient, said Mofutsanyana in an address on labour and wages. The Convention must encourage trade unions and local committees to deal with immediate burning demands. Only in this way would it become the active representative of the whole nation.[37]

The Congress celebrated its twenty-fifth anniversary with speeches on past glories and drew a veil over the reasons for its fallen state. With the Convention to spur them on, however, the active members voted Seme out of office. His place was taken by the Rev. Mahabane, then also vice-president of the Convention. Another cleric, the Rev. James Calata, an Anglican minister from Cradock in the eastern Cape, took on the post of secretary general. Mofutsanyana and Champion, who sat on the executives of both bodies, failed in their efforts to secure the affiliation of Congress to the Convention. Unable to develop a mass basis, the Convention lapsed into inactivity until the early forties, when Coloured and African radicals in the western Cape revived it with the aim of putting themselves at the head of the liberation movement.

The Coloured formed a bridge between white and black, explained La Guma in 1937. Their existence made nonsense of pure race myth and of the agitation to put a ban on sex between members of different colour groups. He urged the darker races to rid themselves of their inferiority complex, and to combine in struggle for complete equality.[38] Having this in mind, the National Liberation League held a conference of trade unions, cultural societies and political parties at Cape Town in March 1938. The delegates agreed to form a Non-European United Front of Africans, Coloured and Indians against all colour bars; voiced their faith in the principle of working-class solidarity; and hoped that white labour would support their efforts to secure equality in political, social and economic life.

White supremacy politicians were then preparing for battle in the pending general election by pouring out a flood of poisonous propaganda. Afrikaner nationalists set the pace. They thundered forth against aliens, communists, Jews and men of colour; and

issued an election manifesto that was to form the basis of their
legislative programme after 1948. It promised to do away with
African representation in parliament; stop the buying of land
for Africans; remove 'surplus' Africans from the towns; segregate Africans, Coloured and Indians in separate areas, trade unions
and places of work; reserve preferred jobs for whites; prohibit
their employment by persons not of their own skin colour; and
ban marriage or sex between whites and any darker man or
woman.

Having lost the election, the Nationalists made ready for the
next by circulating their racial programme throughout the
country in the form of a petition, which so alarmed the government that it hastened to get in first. The Cape provincial council
passed an ordinance giving municipal councils the power to
enforce segregation in public places, buses and residential areas.
Richard Stuttaford, the minister of interior, who had resigned
office a year before because of an alleged insult to 'God save the
King', gave notice of a scheme for 'complete and parallel'
segregation. For the first time in a hundred years, the Coloured
of the Cape were faced with the prospect of being herded into
ghettoes.

'Race and colour discrimination is a weapon used by the rich
to protect their interests,' said the communists, and they urged
Africans, Coloured and Indians to unite against the colour bar.[39]
The Non-European United Front circulated a counter-petition
demanding the repeal of racial laws, and organized a great
demonstration in Cape Town on 27 March 1939. 'Our weapons
will be the strike, the boycott and peaceful demonstrations,'
declared Mrs Gool, president of the NEUF and the Liberation
League, in a powerful agitational speech. The demonstration
that followed the meeting ended in a race riot. The police attacked
the demonstrators outside the houses of parliament and continued
to assault the residents of District Six, the Coloured quarter,
until the early hours of the morning.[40]

The government vetoed the ordinance and dropped its own
segregation proposals. For once the militants could claim that
they had blocked the way to racial totalitarianism. Instead of
combining their forces for a further advance, however, they fell

out with one another in a series of clashes. Abdurahman said that he preferred peaceful negotiation to forceful threats; and refused to join the NEUF or admit it to the APO's annual conference in April 1939.[41] Yet he had backed Mrs Gool when she stood for election and won a seat on the Cape Town municipal council in September 1938. His appearance on her platform gave rise to a dispute in the Liberation League between communists and Nationalists.

La Guma wished to debar whites from holding office in the League. The Coloured, he argued, should lead their own organizations and encourage young people to take their place in the van. Dr Gool said that he objected not to the presence of whites in the leadership but to 'the present reactionary and reformist policy' of the communists, who sacrificed the League's principles to the aim of winning elections.[42] La Guma's motion was defeated at the League's third annual conference. He and others withdrew, took possession of the books, and claimed to represent the League. This then expelled La Guma, Gool, A. Brown and Miss Hawa Ahmed for 'unauthorized activities', and took them to court, which ordered them to return the books and to refrain from collecting money in the name of the League.[43]

Adding to the confusion, a group of white Trotskyists, calling themselves the Workers' Party, gave their blessing to the Goolam Gool faction and denounced the League's general council in scurrilous language through the medium of their duplicated paper the *Spark*. Two members of the group, Miss C. R. Goodlatte, a former nun turned Marxist, and Paul Koston, the owner of a bookshop, published an apology for the defamation. Their intervention gave rise to the notion that the League or the Coloured intellectuals who opposed it were followers of Trotsky.[44] The Coloured were actually radical nationalists who drew heavily on Trotsky's writings for their polemics with the communists; and who insisted that unity between Coloured, Africans and Indians should come before unity with whites.

Communists, Trotskyists and members of every racial group sat together at a Non-European United Front Conference in Cape Town on 8 April 1939. C. van Gelderen represented the Fourth International; B. Kies, the New Era Fellowship, a students' society allegedly under Trotskyist influence; G. R. Baloyi and his secretary J. B. Marks, the Transvaal United Front. The conference unanimously passed resolutions, moved by Sam Kahn, a young Cape Town lawyer, denouncing segregation and calling for complete equality. Boycotts, active and passive resistance, strikes and demonstrations, it was agreed, would be employed to free the people. Among those elected to the national council were Mrs Gool, the president; Baloyi, senior vice-president; M. Kotane, the secretary; W. H. Andrews, the treasurer; Dr Dadoo of Johannesburg and H. A. Naidoo of Durban.[45] The seed of a grand non-racial alliance had been planted; but seventeen years were to pass before it bore fruit.

All genuine opponents of class distinction or racial discrimination belonged together, said the communists. To exclude whites because of their colour would amount to an inverted racialism and a denial of class solidarity. All sections of the liberation movement, though divided by race and social conditions, were working along parallel lines and must converge in the course of struggle into one great army. Speaking at Pretoria, Josie Mpama urged Africans to forget that Coloured and Indians had failed to help them in the past, and to take the lead in the campaign for unity. The Transvaal ANC turned down a proposal to join the Non-European United Front.[46] Indians, rather than Africans, responded to its appeal in the north.

Tortuous negotiations between South Africa and British India had produced the Cape Town agreements of 1927 and 1932. Each was followed by anti-Asian legislation and bitter wrangling among the spokesmen of South Africa's 200,000 Indians.[47] The leaders tried to defend their position by taking part in white man's politics; but, unlike Abdurahman, had no votes to offer as a bargaining counter. Advised by India's agents-general to cooperate with the government, the S.A. Indian Congress lost its sense of direction and floundered in a series of intrigues, deputations, dignified protests and abject surrenders. A section of the Natal community revolted in 1933, when the SAIC nominated S. R. Naidoo to represent it on a commission appointed to explore ways and means of inducing Indians to settle in distant lands. The victims would be Hindu workers and not the merchants who controlled the Congress, said Albert Christopher, a Durban lawyer, and he formed the Colonial-born Settlers' Indian Association.

The feud between the Association and the Natal Congress dragged on for seven years, while the SAIC itself fell apart in a struggle between Hindu and Muslim leaders. Steeped in religious and caste prejudice, they turned the marriage of the agent-general Sir Raza Ali, a Muslim, to Miss P. V. Sammy, a Hindu of Kimberley, in 1936 into an occasion for a political brawl. The president, secretary, treasurer and four other members of the S.A. Indian Congress, with twenty-two members of the Natal Congress, resigned their positions and demanded Ali's recall because, they said, his marriage was an insult to Hindu women and a threat to Indian unity.[48] The indignation was largely spurious and contrived with a view to sweeping the Hindus into one camp behind Sorabjee Rustomjee, a prominent Parsee merchant and the political rival of A. I. Kajee. As a result of the split, Muslims obtained control of the SAIC, and Kajee became its undisputed leader.[49]

The growth of trade unionism at that time added a new dimension to Indian politics in Natal. Among the organizers were communists, such as Mannie Peltz, H. A. Naidoo and George Poonen, whom Eddie Roux recruited to the party in 1934–5. Its African membership had almost disappeared under the police terror; but it was making steady gains among young Indian dissidents. They were South Africans, not expatriates, and they turned their backs on the narrow communal ways of their elders. Much of the friction among Indian leaders resulted from a new cultural trend that Naidoo and others of his group personified.

Born at Durban in 1915 of Hindu parentage, Naidoo and the rest of his family followed his grandmother into the Christian faith. The conversion encouraged his radical bent, which was to find full expression in the working-class movement, where he finally rejected all racial and caste taboos. Indeed, like Poonen later, he overcame the obstacles that stood in the way of an inter-racial marriage, and found a wife among his white party comrades. Emancipated Indians of Naidoo's generation came to despise the opportunism of the SAIC and the futility of its appeals to India, Britain and courts of law. The younger men wanted to break down the isolation of the Indian minority. Its only hope to putting an end to the stream of anti-Asian laws, they said, was to make common cause with Africans, Coloured and radical whites in a united front.

Kajee, on the other hand, wanted Indians to accept voluntary, self-imposed segregation – not to buy land from whites, employ them or marry them – in every area where segregation by statute threatened. The government regularly accepted the compromise, allowed the opposition to simmer down, and then passed the very law that Indians had tried to avert by surrendering their principles. This sequence of events preceded and followed the Transvaal Asiatic Land Tenure Amendment Act of 1936 and the Asiatics (Land and Trading) Act of 1939. They spelt ruin to the great bulk of Asians throughout the province; yet Congress acquiesced because the leaders hoped that a handful of property owners would benefit by obtaining title to land. A group of militants, calling themselves the nationalists, objected to any compromise. 'Passive resistance is the only way to defend our interests,' said Dr Y. M. Dadoo, and he formed a Transvaal section of the Non-European United Front.

Appeals for united resistance made little impact on the Muslim traders and property owners who claimed to speak for the 25,000 Indian inhabitants of the Transvaal. Years of reliance on court actions, negotiations with governments, compromise and the bribery of white officials or politicians had dampened the spirit that once inspired Gandhi's satyagrahis. The idea of a political alliance with poverty-stricken, voteless Africans seemed no less dangerous than absurd to the conservative leaders. Even Gandhi disapproved.[50] Indians were 'different', he told the Rev. S. S. Tema at a world missionary conference in India; while Sir Raza Ali said in Johannesburg at a farewell ceremony that the way to avoid a Non-European front was to give Indians and Coloured the same rights as whites. 'We are thus led to ask,' remarked *Imvo*, 'whether Indians, strangers to Africa, have a stronger claim than the indigenous Africans in the Union to the equal franchise.'[51]

Indians, said Dadoo, had no more and no less of a claim than Africans. Neither would achieve equality without a long and hard struggle. Born at Krugersdorp in 1909, he was one of the few Transvaal Indians of his generation who refused to make commerce their career. After matriculating in India, he took a medical degree in 1936 at Edinburgh, where he joined the ILP and served as secretary to the local branch of the All India National Congress. Returning to Johannesburg to practise medicine, he made politics his chief occupation, and organized the nationalist group in the Transvaal Indian Congress.

Militants and conservatives clashed at a conference held at Johannesburg in June 1939 to decide the issue of passive resistance. Bottles, clubs, knuckledusters and knives were used on the nationalists, who scorned to defend themselves. Five were seriously wounded and one, Dahyabhai Govindji, died of his injuries. 'Better to die fighting for a righteous cause than live as helots' was Dadoo's message to a meeting held in Durban to mourn the death. Indian radicals in all provinces began to rally round him as the true leader of their people.[52]

Mrs Gool's propaganda tour on behalf of the Non-European United Front in June and July brought valuable aid to militants in Natal and the Transvaal. They gained the support of Christopher and Rustomjee, both seeking to weaken Kajee's grip on the S.A. Indian Congress. Six thousand Indians, meeting in Johannesburg on 9 July, pledged themselves to take part in passive resistance on 1 August. The Indian community seemed willing and prepared to resume the struggle that Gandhi had initiated thirty years before. Then he, of all people, intervened to dampen their ardour. War threatened; the time was not ripe for satyagraha; and he had high hopes that India and Britain would act in order to bring about an 'honourable settlement'.[53] Dadoo acquiesced and called off the campaign. The impact of external events had once again turned the national liberation movement away from the path of mass struggle.

22 The Battle for the Unions

Men and women of all races streamed into factories as the depression lifted. The number employed in manufacturing rose by fifty-eight per cent from 192,420 in 1932–3 to 303,557 in 1935–6. The labour force in the latter period consisted of approximately 103,000 white males; 26,000 white females; 165,000 other males; and 10,000 other females. The respective percentage increases from the figures for 1932–3 were 47; 52; 68; and 35.[1]

Most of the newcomers were Africans and Afrikaners with a rural background, alien and unacceptable to the English-speaking artisans who dominated the trade unions. Jimmy Briggs and A. A. Moore, founder and secretary of the mining unions' joint committee, returned with a dismal report from the national conference held at Kimberley in 1934 to discuss the 'poor white problem'. Attempts were being made, they told the TLC, to eliminate unemployment among rural whites by relaxing apprenticeship rules and other safeguards against labour dilution. Skilled urban workers were in danger of being ousted by 'the less skilled lower paid rural migrant'.[2]

Blinkered by craft jealousy, male arrogance, cultural and colour prejudice, the labour aristocracy ignored the effects of industrialism on the composition of the working population. Ironmoulders struck in protest against the replacement of apprentices by semi-skilled whites in railway workshops. Engineers and boiler-makers refused to organize unskilled whites in foundries, steel mills and motor assembly plants. In 1935 the TLC's annual conference rejected a motion urging the unions to admit Africans in open or parallel branches. Objections were raised to the sharp rise in the number of women employed in factories and shops. Years of racial propaganda and collaboration with the employing class had blunted the artisan's feelings for social justice and class solidarity. He had neither political ambition nor compassion that might move him to assist any group of workers, white or black, whom he regarded as inferior because of their sex, race or lack of skill.

'The trend of trade union development,' observed the Industrial Legislation Commission of 1935, 'is definitely, and we consider rightly, along industrial lines.' Though craft unionism had certain advantages to offer the skilled worker, its influence would necessarily decline 'owing to the continuous changes which are taking place in industrial techniques'.[3] Communists and other radicals who did not share the artisan's prejudices recognized the trend and made it their business to form industrial unions for workers of all races and both sexes who performed much the same kind of work in the new secondary industries. Largely as a result of these efforts, the number of unions, including the unregistered, increased from 129 in 1934 to 166 in 1939, and their membership from 126,000 to 264,000.

In so far as the new unions supplemented rather than competed with the craft unions, conservative and radical leaders could work together without much friction, the more so because both were threatened by the divisive effects of an aggressive Afrikaner nationalism. Industrial unions laid a firmer basis than any yet provided for a non-racial class movement. The organizers, who came from all racial groups and both sections of the white population, introduced a new spirit of radicalism, which spread across the colour line.

The TLC became more representative and militant than at any time since 1925. Instead of confining its activities to the affairs of craft unions, it took up the grievances also of lower-paid workers, raised funds for strikers, assisted in negotiations with employers and the labour department, and agitated for improvements in the industrial laws. The battle for recognition had to be fought again in some industries, as hostile employers victimized trade unionists and refused to negotiate with the union. Backing from the TLC might make all the difference between success and failure in such cases. The minister accused the council and its secretary A. G. Forsyth in 1935 of 'aiding and abetting illegal strikes'. Its annual conference replied by unanimously demanding the 'deletion of the anti-strike provisions, in the Industrial Conciliation Act'.[4]

The number of strikes increased from twelve in 1934 to thirty-four in 1937; and of the 5,900 strikers in the latter period, 4,800 were Africans, Coloured and Indians. Though small and short-lived, the strikes indicated that conditions were relatively favourable to the organization of the lower-paid workers. Africans remained outside the scope of industrial conciliation procedures; but organizers applied more often than in the experimental period, and with greater success, for wage determinations. These ceased to be regarded primarily as a means of creating employment for unskilled whites, and gave the urban worker some protection against unscrupulous employers and undercutting migrants. An employer could be prosecuted for paying less than the prescribed wage. Offenders were therefore open to pressure from trade unions, which succeeded in recovering through the labour department underpayments amounting to £9,370 in 1935 and £25,485 in 1938.[5]

None of these gains could compensate, however, for the effects of the Africans' continued isolation. They combined with Indians or Coloured on occasion, as in the strike at Durban's Falkirk iron works in 1937; but white unions hardly ever tried to enlist their support. Strikes were usually partial and therefore unsuccessful, Coka pointed out in a review of recent disputes on the mines and in the furniture, clothing and laundry trades. White workers, being the more class conscious, should take the lead, he urged, in removing the causes of the movement's chronic weakness.[6]

Would workers who themselves employed Africans in their homes assist them to obtain higher wages? Inequalities of status and bargaining power were both the cause and effect of racial antagonism. The African factory worker was a packer, cleaner or general labourer, and seldom a craftsman or machine operator. Though excluded from any industrial council, he could be fined or jailed if he went on strike. Thus handicapped, he had little to contribute, or so it seemed, to the success of a campaign for higher wages by the privileged white workers.

Appeals to class solidarity carried little weight without the backing of strong African unions. The radicals knew this and persisted in their attempts to organize the unskilled. All the old obstacles remained: the instability of the urban African population, a high turnover of migrant workers, legal discrimination, police repression, and opposition from employers and the administration. Max Gordon and D. R. Koza outlined some of the difficulties at the annual conference of the Trades and Labour Council in 1940. The labour department, they said, refused to recognize African unions or deal with their officials. Wage determinations, remarked A. A. Moore in his presidential address, were being judged almost entirely by their effects on white workers, who ignored the African's claims except when their own position was affected.[7]

Not more than six African unions joined the Council in any one year. Discouraged from using their own language at its conferences, cold-shouldered by racists and pushed into the background, African organizers on the Rand preferred to be on their own. The African Federation of Trade Unions decided in 1936 to widen its base and attract former colleagues back into the fold. Two years later, on 7 August 1938, the Non-European Trades Union Coordinating Committee was formed in Johannesburg with Gana Makabeni as chairman. The delegates agreed unanimously to bar all whites from office though not from the executive. Gordon, then the secretary of four African unions, subsequently objected to the racial barrier and withdrew to set up a rival joint committee.

White men governed the country, supervised all establishments, owned the factories and commercial enterprises, said Makabeni in his presidential address at the second annual conference of the NETUC in November 1939.[8] 'Must we have European leaders even in our own association?' he asked. Like all average whites, Gordon did not want to serve under the Africans whose friend he claimed to be. They valued his services, yet could not accept him as their leader. 'It is our lot and duty to shape the future of the non-European workers in this country.'

Gordon was a leather worker from Cape Town who moved to Johannesburg in 1934. He revived some unions that had dropped out of the African Federation and formed new ones, notably of distributive workers and general labourers. Though reputed to be a 'Trotskyist', he steered clear of politics and confined his criticism of communists to what he said was their 'reckless policy of calling workers out on strike with little hope of success'. His own practice of keeping a tight grip on the unions under his supervision antagonized some of the officials, who broke away from his leadership after he had been interned in 1940 under war emergency regulations. The joint committee subsequently merged with the coordinating committee into the Council of Non-European Trade Unions at a conference presided over by Kotane in November 1941. Makabeni was the president, Daniel Tloome the vice-president, David Gosani the secretary, and James Phillips a trustee of the new body. One of its priorities was to strengthen the African mine workers' union.[9]

The communists had kept alive the nucleus formed by Bunting and Thibedi in 1931. Leaflets issued in 1933 and 1935 advised the men to set up a complaints' committee in every compound; and listed a number of specific demands drafted after a careful, first-hand study of conditions in the gold mines. African wages had been pegged for thirty years at the basic rate of 1s. 8d. for surface and 2s. for underground workers. Men were made to refund the cost of train fare to and from the mines out of their wages. They bought their own mining boots, received no protective clothing, and drew no pay during sickness or when disabled on duty. The union demanded a minimum of 4s. for an eight-hour day from bank to bank; three hot meals and meat twice a day; a free issue of a mattress, blankets and boots; free transport; full pay during sickness; a lump sum of £250 as compensation for death; the equivalent of three years' wages for total disablement; protection against assaults by overseers; the abolition of compounds; the right to form trade unions and the right to strike.[10]

The owners ignored the demands, refused to negotiate with the union, and prosecuted organizers found in the compounds. Small, sporadic strikes broke out every year in different compounds, for higher wages, better food or sleeping quarters, and against brutal treatment by officials. On almost every occasion the police were brought in to arrest the leaders, intimidate the men and drive them back to work by force. Little more could be done in the circumstances than to keep up a propaganda campaign and maintain contact with a fraction of the 250,000 Africans employed on mines along the Reef.

White miners could do much to foster trade unionism among the men working under them. Thibedi, secretary of the African union, pointed this out to the S.A. Mine Workers' Union in 1936 and suggested joint action. He was told that constitutional difficulties stood in the way.[11] The whites had finally declared against inter-racial unity by re-inserting a colour bar in their membership clause. They looked on the African miner as a servant, and not a fellow worker; called him 'boy' or 'kaffir', and feared his potential rivalry. 'We regard as a miner a white underground worker,' the SAMWU's secretary said in 1931 before a parliamentary committee on the phthisis laws.

The unions of white workers employed on the mines formed a joint committee and negotiated a rise in the basic rate from 17s. 6d. to 19s. a shift in 1933. African claims were ignored. The persistence of old antagonisms came to light when East Rand miners struck work because a workmate was dismissed for refusing to supervise more than the customary number of Africans. Madeley told the strikers that the owners, given a free hand, would 'do away with the lot of you and bring about a position where you will have all natives in underground employment'.[12]

By attempting to become a labour aristocrat, the higher-paid worker was pricing himself out of the labour market and thereby assisting the capitalist to level wages downwards. Or so George Hardy, the Communist party's adviser from Britain, maintained in an appeal for working class solidarity. White workers, he said, could best defend their position by organizing unskilled whites and Africans.[13] Working-class cooperation, declared the party, was 'an essential for the preservation of the European worker as much as any'. He had won a privileged position by industrial struggle and because employers could be forced to make concessions out of the surplus profit made on African labour. Circumstances had changed as a result of mechanization, new industrial techniques, competition, and a fall in the rate of profit. It was more profitable 'to skin the native at his relatively lower semi-skilled wage than to employ the privileged European worker'. To save himself, he must help the African to organize and must lead in the fight for equal pay for equal work.[14]

The early socialists argued in the same way and with more convincing reasons. In their day white workers fought, at times with loss of life, for trade union and political recognition. That battle had been won. Surrounded by colour bars, the artisan no longer feared the African and therefore tolerated his presence. If trade union leaders sensed a danger, it came not from that quarter, but from the divisive effects of an aggressive Afrikaner nationalism. The communists mistook the symptoms of insecurity in the labour movement for a revival of militancy; and based their case on an identity of interests with the African which skilled workers refused to acknowledge.

Appeals for social justice met with a more generous response. In 1934 the Trades and Labour Council proposed a minimum wage of 10s. a day for all labourers. This was a 'fantastic suggestion', remarked the industrial legislation commission; it revealed an 'outstanding optimism' and was 'probably beyond the country's capacity for very many years to come'.[15] A government bill introduced at this time specified a minimum of 1s. an hour in selected industries, trades and occupations, to the exclusion of agriculture, railways and public services. Its purpose, explained A. P. J. Fourie, the minister for labour, was to encourage the employment of unskilled whites at a 'civilized' wage.

That meant displacing Africans, said the trades council; yet hundreds of thousands of Africans would 'benefit enormously', as there were not nearly enough whites to take their place. Employers killed the scheme by objecting that any large and general increase in unskilled wages would raise working costs, restrict output, reduce the volume of employment, and lead to the displacement of Africans. The Communist party, influenced by Hardy's reformist ideas and the argument that displacements might outweigh the benefits of equality, proposed 'as an immediate practical measure', a differential minimum rate of 10s. for whites and 5s. for Africans.[16]

Kalk introduced a motion to this effect at the TLC's annual conference in 1937. Andrews and Wolfson agreed to the discrimination in principle, and suggested a minimum wage of 7s. 6d. for Africans. The only objection came from H. W. October, secretary of the Cape Town stevedoring and dockers' union. His members then earned 8s. or 9s. a day, he pointed out, and were asking for 12s. 'It did not matter whether a worker was black or white, he should get that to which he was entitled.' The conference adopted Kalk's motion as the more expedient.[17]

While approving of wage discrimination at the bottom of the ladder, white trade unionists insisted on the rate for the job at a higher level. The new Wage Act and Industrial Conciliation Act of 1937 applied the rule of equal pay for equal work at all levels. No wage-fixing agency was allowed to discriminate on grounds of race and colour. What seemed to be a rare instance of generosity actually amounted to gross discrimination. For it prevented Africans and Coloured from undercutting, and this was the only way by which they could offset prejudice and lack of skill.

Equal pay without equal opportunity gave whites a near monopoly of skilled work.[18] This misuse of socialist doctrine, said Kotane, made unity between black and white impossible. 'Personally I feel that if the only way for us to acquire skill is to undercut the European workers' standards, let us do it, and then we would have power to demand and win something for ourselves.'[19] Hardy, however, argued that communists should defend the position of the skilled worker, though not at the expense of Africans and poor whites.[20] To reconcile these aims, radicals in the labour movement rejected undercutting and demanded equal bargaining rights for Africans under the industrial laws.[21]

The trades council had made this its official policy at the inaugural conference in 1925, and reiterated the demand in January 1929 and October 1930. Hofmeyr, the then minister for labour, rejected it when introducing the Industrial Conciliation Bill in 1937. The time was 'not yet ripe', he said; Africans could not 'at this stage' be fitted into the system of collective bargaining.[22] Instead, he inserted a clause allowing the minister to apply the terms of any wage agreement to Africans, even though they had had no part in the negotiations. In some cases the white trade unionists deliberately sacrificed the African's interests to gain benefits for themselves; in other cases employers arbitrarily fixed a wage rate for the occupations in which he was employed.[23]

African trade unionism expanded in spite of the disabilities. Makabeni reported in November 1939 that eleven of the eighteen unions on the Rand, with memberships ranging from 100 to 1,400, were affiliated to the coordinating committee. Alarmed at the growth, the government decided to 'control' the unions through the native affairs department. Draft regulations were submitted to white trade unionists and members of parliament in August 1939; but the African unions rejected anything less than full recognition and the right to deal direct with the department of labour. The mine owners then intervened. Any form of recognition, they said, would encourage African miners to organize. Faced with this opposition, the government dropped its proposed scheme.[24]

Government, employers and artisans rode on the African's back in splendid harmony, and believed that they had found the ideal basis for industrial peace. The only disturbing element was the unskilled white, a constant and irritating flaw in the dogma of racial superiority. Unwilling or unable to compete with the African, he lived on charity, subsidized jobs, and less reputable enterprises such as the illicit liquor trade. Afrikaner nationalists, who claimed to speak for their weaker brethren, toyed at one time with the notion of a minimum national wage, and hastily put it aside on realizing that it would benefit Africans and inconvenience farmers. The Nationalist party then fell back on its favourite stand-by, and called for white solidarity.

J. G. Strydom, the Transvaal Nationalist leader and a future prime minister, put his party's programme for industrial relations before the House in 1937. No wage legislation, he moved, would be acceptable unless it discriminated on the basis of colour. He proposed to guarantee whites a specified quota of jobs, a monopoly of certain trades, and separate spheres of work. J. H. Hayward, the member for Bloemfontein, added compulsory trade union segregation to the list.[25] Defeated on the motion by sixty-five votes to nineteen, the Nationalists took their policy to the country in a sustained bid for the working-class vote, were returned to office in 1948, and gave effect to their programme in the Industrial Conciliation Act of 1956.[26]

Afrikaner nationalism rested on a triad of language, religion and race. The language identified the group as a separate entity, distinct from the English-speaking. Calvinism provided an ideology, a 'false consciousness' in the Marxist sense, which sanctioned the belief that Afrikaners were born to rule. The racial factor served to divide people into pigmented and dispigmented biological estates of unequal social status. To establish their hegemony, Afrikaner nationalists concentrated on two aims. One was to exclude all black and brown persons, forming eighty per cent of the population, from the centres of power; the other, to consolidate all Afrikaners, forming sixty per cent of the whites, into a single power bloc. As long as these conditions were fulfilled, Afrikaners would dominate the white minority and therefore the whole society.

The key to success was Afrikaner solidarity in the towns. Urban conditions developed close relations between humans of different types, assimilated them into social classes, promoted the growth of sub-cultures, and broke down barriers between ethnic groups. To prevent assimilation, Afrikaner leaders made racial segregation compulsory and formed a wide range of separate voluntary associations. Afrikaner schools, universities, churches, press, political parties, occupational and cultural societies – chambers of industry and commerce, clubs, boy scouts, and the like – insulated Afrikaners from British or radical influences and cultivated a colour consciousness that inhibited the growth of class consciousness.

Colour, not class, had marked the great divide in Afrikaner agrarian societies before the days of industrialism. The Afrikaner's traditional ethos rejected both marked inequalities among whites and liberal or socialist concepts of equality between races. All politicians, *predikants*, teachers, writers, journalists and shopkeepers who made a living out of the Afrikaner community wished to preserve its cohesion. Inter-racial or international class organizations that attracted Afrikaner workers exposed them to a liberating stream of new ideas and experiences which tended to detach them from the Afrikaner bourgeoisie. The Afrikaner bourgeoisie reacted with a vigorous onslaught on free trade unionism and radical socialism.

Predikants and politicians who made it their business to rescue Afrikaners from militant trade unionism had never been obliged to fight for a living wage. Without experience of industrial relations or the determination needed to break new ground, they employed agents to form rank-and-file movements, and tried to capture or split existing unions. The first and most successful of these efforts was the Spoorbond, a union of railworkers organized in 1934 with the backing of the Afrikaner Broederbond.

Both bodies originated with H. J. Klopper, a railway official who joined the service in 1911 and the Nationalist party in 1912. His political activity paralleled his rise from clerk to system manager until he resigned in 1942 to enter parliament. A foundation member of the influential Federasie van Afrikaanse Kultuurverenigings, he formed its first railway branch in 1930 and led the great oxwagon trek during the centenary celebrations of 1938 from which emerged the nazified Ossewabrandwag. In 1939 he took part in promoting the Reddingsdaadbond*, ostensibly created to collect money for budding Afrikaner capitalists, rescue poor whites, and prevent Afrikaner workers from developing into a separate class outside the mainstream of their national culture.[27]

Klopper and his associates made the railways their chief recruiting ground in the Broederbond's formative years. Hungry for promotion and resentful of the English-speaking officials who dominated the service, clerks in the lower grades welcomed a secret society linking them to 'nationally minded' Afrikaners in key positions. Covert pressures could be applied to the administration and government for a redress of Afrikaner grievances. The Spoorbond gave the leaders a mass following and enabled them to compete successfully with the older railway unions.

* Society for active rehabilitation.

One of these, the National Union of Railway and Harbour Servants, was formed in 1910 with the aim of absorbing the dozen railway unions in existence at that time. Led by English-speaking officials and open to members of all colour groups, NURAHS failed to attract the bulk of Afrikaner labourers in the service. Only twenty-five per cent of white employees were organized in 1933, and this minority was divided into eight unions. The Spoorbond, in contrast, enforced a colour bar, agitated for the replacement of Africans or Coloured by whites, conducted its affairs in Afrikaans, and insisted on equal language rights in the administration. It was a spectacularly successful policy. Within three years the Spoorbond claimed to have 16,000 members and forced NURAHS to dissolve. Announcing this decision, the president F. Phillips urged the English section 'to realize that Afrikaners had thrown off their former feeling of inferiority and were now the dominant force in the service'.[28]

The Spoorbond's leaders struck a note new in trade unionism. They repudiated class war and strikes, relied on peaceful negotiations, and called on their followers to render 'loyal service' in keeping with the union's motto: *Verower deur Diens.*[29] 'The Bond was more than a trade union; it was a people's movement – a *volksbeweging* – born out of a spontaneous process of nation building.' Guided by the principles of Christian nationalism, it would promote the welfare of its members, raise the service to the status of a calling, integrate it with Afrikaner national life, and cultivate the use of Afrikaans in order to achieve equal language rights.

The clerks, teachers and *predikants* who dominated the Broederbond and through it the Spoorbond appealed for Afrikaner solidarity, not class solidarity; relied on political pressure, not industrial action; and clamoured for a rise in status and not of wages. The scale of priorities reflected their petty bourgeois aspirations and their desire to combat influences that alienated the working man from a national consciousness. Artisans and clerks who mixed with English-speaking colleagues; labourers, gangers and porters who had nothing except a sense of racial superiority to separate them from African and Coloured

*Conquer through Service.

railwaymen: such would be lost to Afrikanerdom unless they were isolated and welded together behind barriers of language, religion and race. With this composition and programme, the Spoorbond was a potential danger both to craft unions and to men of colour.

The craft unions consolidated their forces in 1936 behind a federal council and challenged the Spoorbond's claim to represent white workers of all grades. After much wrangling, the administration decided on a system of group representation which, the Spoorbond complained, would confine it to the lowest paid.[30] The Nationalist opposition took the dispute into parliament and were told by Pirow, the minister, that he would not allow them to drag the union into the political mire in which they had already plunged many Afrikaner societies. The union accused him of sacrificing the largest Afrikaner union to political ends and 'the antiquated, essentially British-Jewish view that group representation of workers was necessary'.[31]

Both craft and industrial unions, whether led by British or Afrikaner officials, shut their doors on African, Coloured and Indian railwaymen and forced them to organize on their own. The initiative came from Cape Town, where the local dockers' union, formed by the ICU in 1919, provided a stable base for the undertaking. 'Thanks to the initiative and indefatigable activities of H. October, Secretary of the Stevedore Workers' Union, and W. Driver of the railway workers, supported by many earnest and loyal workers, among whom Comrade Ray Alexander deserves special mention,' reported the *Negro Worker* in October 1936, 'it was possible to organize this first successful National Conference of Railway and Harbour Workers.'[32]

The conference, representing some 1,300 members, formed itself into the S.A. Railway and Harbour Workers' Union and adopted a programme of demands: a minimum wage of 1s. an hour; one week's annual leave on full pay; equal opportunities to become skilled; an increase in the number of African and Coloured railworkers; and an end to the policy of displacing them with whites. White employees had by April 1933 recovered the wage cuts made during the depression. In the next five years they received increases and benefits to the combined value of £11 million. The wages of African employees, in contrast, had not been restored by 1938 to the pre-depression period. They ranged from 2s. 6d. to 4s. 6d. a day, and fell far short of the minimum standards fixed for general labourers by wage determinations and agreements.[33] Without political influence, denied representation on negotiating boards and welfare committees, ignored and persecuted by the administration, the union's officials and members were committed to a bitter struggle for social justice and a living wage.[34]

The Spoorbond's main achievement was to isolate white railworkers from Africans and Coloured. It never managed to break down the fences erected by artisans and the salaried staff, who defeated all attempts to merge their craft unions in one large industrial union. Enough progress was made, however, to satisfy the men behind the Broederbond that they could detach Afrikaners from the mainstream of the labour movement. The Federasie van Afrikaanse Kultuurverenigings announced in 1936 that it proposed to sponsor a purely Afrikaans trade union organization. Its aim, said Albert Hertzog, was to 'weld the Afrikaner workers and the Afrikaner nation into a mighty unity'.[35] The son of the prime minister, member of the bar, and a graduate of Stellenbosch, Amsterdam, Leyden and Oxford, he led a crusade to rescue 'poor young Afrikaners' from 'wrong and bad movements'.[36]

His confederates included the Rev. du Toit; Professor N. Diederichs; F. J. Zeeman, the United party MP for Brakpan; and H. Bosman, a director of Volkskas.* Their resources came from the Nasionale Raad van Trustees, created in 1936 with an endowment of £10,000 from Mrs Jannie Marais, the widow of a former MP for Stellenbosch who made a fortune out of Kimberley diamonds. This coterie of intellectuals related their vision of Afrikanerdom to the conflict between German Nazism, British imperialism and world communism; declared that Afrikaner workers were being lost to 'internationalism' in all its forms; and steadily kept before them the aim of capturing the workers' vote for the Nationalist party.

* A bank which has since become one of the most important in the country.

That was the burden of the trade unions' complaint against the FAK's subversive tactics. Their sole purpose, said the trades council in 1936, was to divide the unions for party gain and turn them into Nazi organizations. It was a plot of capitalists and employers, said Johanna Cornelius, president of the garment workers' union, to keep workers backward by fomenting race hatred. Charles Harris, secretary of the miners' union, pointed out that it and the garment workers' union were being singled out for attack. Though more than ninety per cent of his members were Afrikaners, they would have nothing to do with Hertzog's agents. 'The time had arrived to fight. It was a political move to take control of the trade union movement.'[37]

The Federasie fired the first shot by instituting the Afrikaanse Bond van Mynwerkers in 1936, with the stated aim of improving the mining industry 'from the Afrikaner's point of view'. An innocent observer might suppose that this referred to the miner's working conditions; but the Bond's management committee, on which not a single miner sat, had no intention of engaging in battle against the mine owners. The target was trade unionism and not the capitalist. Under the pretence of soliciting support for the Afrikaner's language, tradition and commercial enterprises, the FAK launched a propaganda assault on the miners' union and urged men to resign from membership. A separate organization was necessary, declared Dr N. J. van der Merwe, a prominent Broederbonder, because Afrikaners had little experience of trade unionism and were unable to reform the unions from within.[38]

The SAMWU hit back by reviving the demand for a closed shop and instructed its members to come out on strike against the employment of non-members at the Randfontein mine in October 1936 and the Simmer and Jack in March 1937. The mine owners were no less anxious to check the spread of Nationalist party influence among the men. Reversing the policy adopted in 1922, the Chamber undertook to recognize only one registered union for each class of employees as from 1 June 1937. All whites other than officials and apprentices were required as a condition of employment to join one of the registered unions. In return for this concession, the unions agreed to keep out of politics and to withdraw from activities or organizations not solely concerned with trade unionism.[39]

'We have to do here with trade unions which are out to create a class-consciousness in the Afrikaner ranks,' complained Dr van der Merwe, and he took exception to the closed shop for that reason.[40] The united front of mine owners and unions balked the attempts of the Nationalists to form a rival union. They changed their tactics, dissolved the Bond in 1938, and organized a 'reform' movement within the SAMWU. The Raad van Trustees appointed, financed and controlled the Reformers' general council under an elaborate set of rules. Among other things, the council undertook to capture existing unions; guide them along the lines of Christian-nationalism; cleanse them of 'foreign and wrong' influences; free them from 'the international and communistic' trades council; and 'strive for the maintenance of the colour bar' in all industries.[41]

The programme of the Reformers matched the findings of an Afrikaner church commission appointed in 1937 to examine the effects of communism on the trade unions. Its report appeared in a scurrilous brochure which enabled Solly Sachs to recover damages for libel from the author Dr Wolmarans and the Voortrekkerpers. Communism, the arch enemy of Christianity, said the commission, threatened civilization by preaching class struggle and equality between black and white. Communists such as Sachs and Wolfson misused their position and exploited the unions for propaganda purposes. The Trades and Labour Council, added Wolmarans, was controlled by Jewish and English-speaking communists and their allies. Exploited Afrikaner workers, whom the church had neglected, fell into the hands of unscrupulous communists like Sachs. He had done much no doubt to improve their wages and conditions, but at the cost of their spiritual well-being.[42]

The communists' long record of organizing factory workers of all races was a convincing rebuttal of the malicious gossip and deliberate distortions out of which the case against them was compounded. The outsiders were their accusers, the theologians and academics, who practised precisely what they attributed to the militants: dogmatism, intolerance, subversion, and an unscrupulous disregard of Christian ethics and democratic procedures. An election year lay ahead, however, and the Nationalists were preparing for battle along a wide front of incitement to race hatred.

Eric Louw, resigning his ambassadorial post in France to take part in the 1938 elections, told country audiences that Jews, communists, capitalists and trade unions menaced the great middle class. F. C. Erasmus accused the government of buying farms and tractors for Africans, and of spending £88,000 a year on their education as compared with the £46,000 spent by the Nationalists when in power.[43] The Nationalist election manifesto demanded strict segregation, the reservation of jobs for whites, a ban on mixed marriages, the removal of African representatives from parliament and of Coloured voters from the common roll. The word 'aparte', meaning separate and unequal, appeared three times in this preview of totalitarian apartheid.[44]

Polling 247,765 votes, the Nationalists won twenty-seven seats in a House of 153. This was an 'all-time low', explained the minister of labour, Senator Jan de Klerk, in 1956. 'The struggle could not be waged on this front. In the political sphere the Nationalist party was practically paralysed, and we had this wild flow of Communism engulfing the workers on the Rand. Then the Afrikaner people, in its broad mass, got up in arms and stepped in with all the organizational power at its disposal.' The three Afrikaans churches, the Reddingsdaadbond, the Federasie van Afrikaanse Kultuurverenigings, and the Blankewerkersbeskermingsbond* combined their forces to rescue Afrikaner workers from communism, liberalism and non-racial trade unions.[45]

Apart from its rhetoric, de Klerk's statement gave an accurate account of the reason why his party publicly adopted Albert Hertzog's policy at an inter-provincial congress in November 1938. Regarded as a landmark in the Nationalist party's history, the congress undertook to save white civilization for all time and to submit its apartheid programme in a petition to parliament. D. F. Malan, the party leader, fulminated against com-

* Society for the protection of white workers. Cp. Chapter 24, pp. 562 ff.

munism, liberalism and organized Jewry, the evil genius, he maintained, behind the doctrine of equality. The towns had become the new battle ground against the rising forces of colour. Protected by wage determinations and trade unions, Africans and Coloured were competing with Afrikaner workers. South Africa was becoming blacker and the white race poorer.[46]

Church and party took the message to audiences throughout the country. Albert Hertzog told farmers that their future would be decided at the Blood Rivers and Amajubas of the towns. To win, the Nationalists must conquer the trade unions, more than a hundred of which were controlled by foreign enemies of the Boers or by communists who used them to spread their doctrine of hate against the Volk, the white man, the family and Christianity.[47] Communism, declared the Cape synod of the Dutch Reformed Church, had spread its tentacles over Africans and the unions in a bid for revolution, atheism, equality and the abolition of private property. The church must fight the menace by means of sermons and pamphlets; and would call on government to suppress all communist organizations.[48]

Jacob Hugo, a young working miner, reacted by killing Charles Harris outside Johannesburg Trades Hall on 15 June 1939. Harris, the secretary of the miners' union, was a miner by trade and a Jew by religion. The evidence at Hugo's trial revealed that he hated Jews, belonged to a 'reform' group, and relied on its leader Albert Hertzog 'to get him out of trouble'. Sentenced to life imprisonment, Hugo was given his freedom in 1948, soon after the Nationalist party had taken office. Dr T. E. Dönges, who defended him at the trial, was appointed minister of interior in the new cabinet and was president elect of South Africa at the time of his death in 1967.

Who was to blame for the murder of Harris: Hugo who fired the shot, the Reformers who egged him on, or the *predikants* and politicians whose propaganda moved him to an act of homicidal violence? 'The Reformers and the powers behind them, of which they are the puppets,' reported a government commission, 'constitute a subversive movement, which is detrimental to the interests of the mineworkers.'[49] Subversion and assassination were employed after attempts to capture the union by democratic procedures had failed. Only four of the eighteen seats on the general council went to the reform group on a ballot held in April.[50] Undaunted by the setback, the Reformers kept up their agitation and forced the union to secede from the Trades and Labour Council in November. It was evident, warned the *Guardian*, that the Nationalist party wanted to split the movement by forming a rival trade union centre.[51]

Other fissures and alliances were to develop, however, as a result of South Africa's participation in the Second World War. 'For us it will always be a struggle against capitalism,' declared J. H. van den Bergh, president of the miners' union. 'We in South Africa do not want Fascism, Nazism, or Communism. We know only Afrikanerism.'[52] Yet 3,000 whites employed on the mines enlisted in 1940 for active service in a patriotic wave that pushed the Reformers into the background. In August the union's executive offered to rejoin the trades council if it would change its constitution so as to admit only white delegates and white unions.[53] The council refused under pressure from the radicals, and the union reaffiliated unconditionally. Plunged into internal turbulence by the effects of war, the Nationalists abated their disruptive work in the unions until 1944, when prospects of victory for the Axis powers began to fade.

23 War and the Workers

Parliament decided for war by eighty votes to sixty-seven on 4 September 1939. Hertzog resigned as premier, and Smuts formed a coalition ministry which included Madeley of the Labour party and Stallard of the Dominion party. The anti-war parties, led by Hertzog and Malan, fused in the 'Herenigde Nasionale of Volksparty'. This was scarcely more than a façade behind which factions struggled for leadership. The merger came to an end in November 1940, when the party's Free State congress rejected Hertzog's draft programme guaranteeing full equality to the English. He resigned from the party and parliament, leaving Malan in possession. Three parliamentary groups emerged from the wreckage: a reconstituted Nationalist party, the Afrikaner party led by Havenga, and Pirow's New Order; and all were harassed by the extra-parliamentary Ossewabrandwag under a professed Nazi, Kommandant-Generaal Dr J. F. J. van Rensburg.

All the factions refused to fight in Britain's war, set their hearts on a German victory, and aimed at the goal of a white man's republic; but they disputed bitterly about its content and their methods of struggle. Pirow preached the essence of Hitler's national socialism; Van Rensburg's storm troopers practised it by blowing up railways, power lines, telephones and post offices. Hertzog and Malan put their faith in the white man's parliament which had served them so well, and held divergent views on the relation between Afrikaners and English. The republic, Hertzog argued, should come into being with the consent of both, on the basis of complete equality, and through their assimilation into a common nationhood. Malan stood out for a modernized version of Kruger's republic, established if necessary by a bare majority in parliament and firmly seized by united Afrikanerdom.[1]

The strength and strategy of the rivals, their policies and attitudes to one another, fluctuated with the fate of Hitler's armies. Pirow and Van Rensburg relied wholly on a German victory; Malan, the more wily, kept his escape lines open for the possibility of a German defeat. They wrangled over seats in parliament – always a major obstacle to Afrikaner unity – and fixed their eyes on the central issue: who was to be South Africa's Gauleiter under a Hitler peace?

Perspectives changed as the Red Army gained the upper hand. The Afrikaner tide of Nazi support passed its flood in 1943 after the surrender of 300,000 German troops at Stalingrad. Malan's party, securing forty-three seats at the general election in July, emerged as the only opposition in parliament. From then on the New Order disintegrated, the Ossewabrandwag lost ground, and the Nationalists, turning to their tribal drums, beat out the familiar battle cry of white solidarity against communism and the darker man.

Communists were the most uncompromising critics in the labour movement of the government's war policy. The Munich agreement, signed on 30 September 1938, by Britain, France, Germany and Italy, had convinced them that war could not be avoided, and that those who spoke for the western democracies could not be trusted. This view was elaborated in *The Munich Swindle*, a *Guardian* pamphlet issued soon after the event. Chamberlain, Daladier and the classes they represented, it declared, were not concerned to stem the tide of Nazi aggression; their chief aim was to turn it against the Soviet Union. Such doubts multiplied in the anxious months that followed, and were decisive in shaping the Communist party's attitude to the war up to the German invasion of the Soviet Union in June 1941.

Unlike communists in English-speaking countries, and without any prompting or instructions from outside, the party's central committee went into opposition immediately on the outbreak of war. It was an 'imperialist war' for 'raw materials, markets, capitalist domination, and the power to exploit colonial peoples in Africa and Asia'.[2] The War-on-Warites of 1914 had arrived at a similar conclusion, though with a different emphasis.

The communists spent little time on denunciations of war in general and of capitalism. Their main endeavour was to rally the people against a government that claimed to defend democracy abroad yet enforced a vicious system of racial discrimination at home.

'The fight against Fascism must start in our own country,' the central committee argued in June 1939. 'It must be fought against the present system of poverty, cultural backwardness and race discrimination, which are the breeding grounds of the Fascist mind.'[3] That was the keynote of communist policies throughout the war. Every worker had a duty to fight for a 'free and equal South Africa', and not to defend gross inequalities and colour bars. Africans, Coloured and Indians, the party declared, would gladly join the army if they were given full rights of citizenship. They could not be expected to fight, however, as long as the army segregated them, limited them to manual labour, denied them the right to carry arms, and paid them half or less than half the white soldier's pay.[4]

Like their predecessors in 1914, the Labour party's leaders brushed aside all doubts and undertook to back the war effort. Though bound by conference resolutions to reject any coalition, the national executive approved of Madeley's decision to enter the cabinet where, he explained, he could best encourage workers to defend democracy against fascism.[5] Trade union leaders, taking note of anti-war sentiments in their own ranks, adopted a more cautious approach. The Trades and Labour Council asked for safeguards against labour dilution and inflation; and demanded adequate representation on war emergency committees. Smuts assured them that he had a better understanding of their claims than in 1914, and promised to protect trade union rights.[6]

The unions were divided on questions of principle. The first big clash took place at the TLC's annual conference in 1940 on a motion introduced by E. S. Sachs which denounced the 'selfish imperialist ends' of the belligerent states and urged conference 'to demand an immediate cessation of hostilities'. Afrikaner delegates refused to fight for the British who had deprived them of their independence. The communists maintained that the first duty of workers in all countries was to stop the war before it engulfed the Soviet Union and to intensify the struggle for socialism. Accused of having turned a complete somersault on instructions from Moscow, the anti-war group replied that not they but world conditions had changed. Sachs's motion was defeated, and conference decided by thirty votes to twenty-three that it would carry on the struggle 'until aggression had been eliminated'.[7]

The divergence of theory never came close to an open schism. Facing the more immediate aggression of Afrikaner nationalism, the two factions presented a common front in defence of the worker's rights. The 'pro-Nazi, anti-trade union, anti-colour Nationalists' were the main enemy, declared the Communist party's central committee in 1940. It acknowledged that this approach 'weakened the line of struggle against the war, since it meant a passive acceptance of the Smuts Government and its war policy'. The only way to avoid the dilemma caused by the split in the ruling class was to oppose the war and to resist the Nationalists.[8]

If communists were to emphasize their anti-imperial aims, they would drift into a dialogue with Afrikaner republicans who practised their own local brand of imperialism and were determined to maintain the existing class structure and system of colour oppression. It was not in South Africa's interests that this kind of republic should be established. The party's national conference of April 1941 came to this conclusion after a lengthy debate on a new constitution and programme.[9] Some delegates from Pretoria suggested that it might be necessary to support the Afrikaner movement for separation from Britain; but the majority felt that they could have no truck at any time with the most fanatical adherents of white supremacy.

Questions that had perplexed communists between 1927 and 1935 cropped up again. Would there be two stages or only one stage in the advance to socialism? Was it conceivable for South Africa to develop into a democracy under capitalism? Or would the struggle for democracy unleash such great forces as to make a socialist revolution inevitable? The conference agreed that it was impossible to trace the course of events with certainty. The 'national struggle' for inter-racial equality was bound to over-shadow the class struggle. Workers were not the only ones who suffered oppression, and it was the party's mission to liberate all oppressed classes. With this perspective, the conference adopted a draft constitution that kept all options open. The party would prepare the way to a socialist republic by striving for the abolition of imperial rule, the introduction of universal adult franchise, and the removal of all colour bars that held up the progress of any national group or that divided the working class.[10]

As in 1914, radical socialists parted company on the war issue with the African National Congress. A number of its affiliated bodies urged the leaders to refuse cooperation unless Africans were given full military training and the right to bear arms. The ANC's annual conference at Durban in December 1939 approved, however, of parliament's declaration of war, asked the government to 'consider the expediency' of admitting all peoples to citizenship, and called for the inclusion of all sections in the defence system on equal terms.[11] The government ignored the plea and proceeded to recruit thousands of Africans to dig, fetch and carry for the white troops.

Coloured opinion was deeply divided. Dr Abdurahman, ailing and resentful of the United party's attempts to segregate his people, kept aloof. The APO was little more than a shell and gave no lead. Coloured ex-servicemen, proud of their record in the First World War and stirred by victorian loyalties to Britain, promised Smuts their unqualified support. Pale-faced Coloured enlisted as whites in the Cape Scottish Highlanders, while darker men joined a non-combatant essential services corps.

Militants in the National Liberation League and the Non-European United Front, led by Mrs Gool and Moses Kotane, agreed with the communists that their first duty was to struggle for democratic rights on the home front. Unless all South Africans were treated as citizens without discrimination, said the League, no government could expect to receive their loyal support.[12]

Some of the leaders found the call to arms irresistible. Lance Morley-Turner, the League's assistant secretary and once an officer of the Black and Tans in Ireland, joined up, to become the 'Red Sergeant' whose jeep flaunted a red flag in the East African campaign. Booker Lakey, the League's general secretary, followed him into the army. With a characteristic independence of mind, James la Guma stood out for a united front with bourgeois democracy against the Nazis. Twice defeated in municipal elections, once by Abdurahman in 1939 and after his death in 1940 by Ahmed Ismail, the forty-six-year-old La Guma enlisted in September. Promoted to the rank of staff sergeant in the Indian-Malay corps, he went north with his regiment to Abyssinia, and was demobilized only in 1947.

Of all those in the liberation movement, the Indian radicals put up the strongest resistance to the government's war policy. In British India, where Congress had demanded the right of self-determination and independence, Pandit Nehru declared that his people would not fight to defend imperial rule.[13] Fired by this example, the militants, organized in a 'nationalist bloc', responded eagerly to the communist appeal for combined action against racial discrimination. They called for a boycott of the Broome 'penetration' commission, which had been set up in 1940 to investigate the extent of Indian occupation in so-called white areas; and attacked the conciliatory policy of the bourgeois leaders who controlled the Transvaal Indian Congress, the Natal Indian Association and the Natal Indian Congress.[14]

The conservatives, while praising the spirit of Gandhi's satyagrahis, discouraged all forms of mass struggle and sought relief from further discrimination by offering the services of Indian workers in the war. 'If the restrictions that bind us today are removed,' replied the nationalist bloc, 'we shall be the first to defend democracy.' Defeated on their war policy, the conservatives in the Association expelled seven committee members, including Dr G. M. Naicker and the communists C. I. Amra, H. A. Naidoo and D. A. Seedat. The militants then launched a campaign against the war and for citizenship rights that changed the political outlook of Indians in Natal. Members of the bloc were prosecuted under the War Measures Act, and Seedat went to jail in April 1941 on a charge of subversion.

Dr Dadoo, leader of the nationalist group in the Transvaal

Indian Congress, served a sentence of four months' hard labour for similar offences arising out of protests against attempts to recruit men for the Indian labour corps. 'If we were as free as Europeans we would probably give our services as freely,' he said at a recruiting meeting in Pretoria; and he issued a miniature charter of rights in the name of the Non-European United Front. 'Don't support this war, where the rich get richer and the poor get killed,' he appealed. When standing trial on a charge of incitement under war emergency regulations, he told the court that the war would be just only if full democratic rights, freedom and independence were extended to the oppressed peoples of South Africa, India and the colonies.[15]

Internment camps were reserved for whites, either German and Italian nationals or South Africans who opposed the war. An overwhelming majority of the latter were members of the Ossewabrandwag, among whom a small group of left-wing internees maintained a lonely and unhappy existence. They included the communists Arnold Latti, Dr Max Joffe and his brother Louis; the trade unionists Max Gordon and Fritz Fellner, husband of Johanna Cornelius; the veteran socialist J. E. Brown and E. J. Burford of the Labour party, both interned because they agitated against Madeley's presence in the cabinet.

The Joffe brothers and Gordon were accused of spreading communism and forming trade unions among Africans.[16] Their crime, the Johannesburg district party committee protested, was to resist efforts of employers, aided by many trade union leaders, to lengthen hours, dilute labour and keep down wages. This was a 'scurrilous attack', the Trades and Labour Council said, and it decided to abandon interned communists to their fate. They were the supreme quislings, maintained A. A. Moore in his presidential address to the Council's annual conference in April 1941. They exploited genuine grievances and democracy for their own aim of frustrating the war effort.[17] Archie Crawford had sold the workers in 1915, Bill Andrews commented sadly, whereas Archie Moore went further: he was giving them away.

The immediate cause of Moore's splenetic outburst was a dispute over Madeley's Factories Act of 1941. In the original draft, the minister was authorized to prohibit the employment of any class of workers in a specified occupation. A number of industrial unions protested in a memorandum drawn up by Solly Sachs that the purpose of this 'Nuremberg clause' was to introduce racial segregation such as the Nationalist party had proposed. Madeley told a trade union deputation that 'it was frequently desirable in some instances to separate European females from Africans' and invited the TLC's assistance.[18] Sachs, acting in 'a purely technical capacity', thereupon submitted a draft clause that would allow a factory inspector to prevent 'objectionable contact' between white women and employees of any other class.

This was acceptable to the right-wing leaders, who welcomed any measure likely to discourage the employment of Africans; but the radicals renewed their pressure and forced the minister to withdraw the clause. Accused by the Nationalist opposition of yielding to communist agitation, Madeley assured them that he would introduce healthy racial separation through the medium of regulations under the act. When these appeared, it was found that the minister, purporting to safeguard the physical, social or moral welfare of workers, could require an employer to segregate them by race or sex on the factory floor, in rest rooms and toilets.[19] Madeley had given way to the Nationalist party and racists in the trade union movement.

In matters not involving a racial taboo or direct conflict with white workers' interests, the trades council could be persuaded to recommend an identical treatment, as when it asked the minister to avoid racial differentiation in benefits under the Workmen's Compensation Act of 1941. This was no more than a sop to the radicals, since all parties knew that neither parliament nor the mine owners would agree to a departure from the principle of discrimination embodied in the original act of 1934. In terms of the statute of 1941, a non-African, if totally disabled, received a lifelong pension equal to seventy-five per cent of his monthly earnings. An African, similarly incapacitated, was entitled to no more than a lump sum of £150 – the equivalent of a pension for only three and a third years in the case of a worker earning £60 a year.[20]

Inferior in status and segregated by law, the African was

isolated from the mainstream of the labour movement. White workers with few exceptions accepted discrimination as a normal and desirable condition. Solly Sachs claimed to have no colour prejudice; yet he, too, compromised under the pressure of inciters to race hatred. In 1940 his garment workers' union in Johannesburg established a separate branch for its Coloured members, ostensibly 'to educate them in the spirit of militant trade unionism and to train leaders in the factories'.[21] Once introduced, segregation gradually spread, until it included separate entrances, lifts and offices for Coloured and African garment workers. They resented segregation, and Sachs maintained that it was the only way by which he could appease the 'violent prejudices' of his white members.[22]

Obsessed with protecting and promoting white privileges, the country failed to use all its available resources at a time of urgent need. Imports fell drastically, the supply of goods to civilians was regulated and reduced, a serious scarcity of material required for the military developed, and the number of skilled workers fell far short of the demand. Yet white supremacists in every walk of life refused to release the productive capacity of black and brown South Africans; and excluded them from the centres opened in 1940 to train skilled and semi-skilled workers for the engineering, electrical and motor trades. White women were trained in factories to produce armoured cars, guns and shells; but only unskilled labour was made available to Africans and Coloured in the whole field of industrial war work.

Only a society deeply divided and despotically ruled could tolerate so glaring a contradiction between its war aims and its war effort. Smuts never agreed to arm Africans, not even in the darkest period of the war; nor would the craft unions ever relent in their determination to keep them out of the skilled trades. It was 'no good training 40,000 mechanics for 1,000 jobs', delegates at the Trades and Labour Council conference told Ray Alexander in April 1942, when she moved that the facilities of the Central Organization for Technical Training should be extended to Africans and Coloured; and the Council rejected her proposal. She returned to the attack in the following year, and persuaded a majority to recommend free compulsory education for children of all races; but, said J. Calder of the electrical workers' association, 'we will never agree at the present stage that the trades should be thrown open to everybody'.[23]

On 22 June 1941, when German troops crossed the Soviet frontier, the Communist party's central committee called for the defence of the home of socialism. Its defeat would be capitalism's greatest triumph; its victory would bring about the destruction of fascism, the liberation of oppressed nations, and a rapid transition to world socialism. Consequently, all workers, democrats and oppressed peoples should redouble their efforts in the struggle for liberty and social justice.[24] The central committee complained in August that the war effort was hampered by the refusal to arm Africans, Coloured and Indians, or to employ them on skilled work. Churchill and Roosevelt had declared their intention of allowing all peoples to choose their own form of government. 'The Communist policy is to press for these rights to be granted not only in Europe after the war, but here and now within the British Empire itself.' Only by granting full rights to the peoples of Africa, India and the colonies could the fight for democracy become a reality.

Afrikaner nationalists accused the communists of turning Africans against the whites. Critics of another kind said that the party had changed sides on instructions from Moscow. According to Eddie Roux, the party as ever subordinated 'the South African struggle to the needs of the world situation' after the invasion of the Soviet Union.[25] The communists claimed to be consistent in principle, and saw no conflict of interests such as Roux implied. A complete mobilization of resources would lead to complete liberation from national oppression. If Africans were trained for skilled work and to use arms, they could no longer be treated as inferior. Communists drove the point home by condemning discrimination in the pay of soldiers: 12s. 3d. a day for a white private with wife and child, 7s. for a Coloured or Indian, and 2s. 3d. for an African. The scales, remarked *Inkululeko* (Freedom), the party's fortnightly in Johannesburg, revealed the government's stubborn insistence on fighting the war on a colour bar basis. Yet discrimination undermined morale in the army, discouraged civilians and harmed the whole war effort.[26]

Japan's attack on Pearl Harbor in December and the sensational advances made by her troops brought the danger of war nearer home. A communist party statement issued in January 1942 called for complete mobilization, the rapid training of Africans, Coloured and Indians for skilled work, and the creation of a national army in which men of all races would bear arms and receive the same treatment. In February, after the fall of Singapore, the party warned that South Africa under existing policies was as powerless as Malaya to resist an invasion. When the Cape provincial council urged the government to prohibit 'subversive Communist activities', the central committee replied in May that many of its members were on active service or otherwise engaged in promoting the war effort. Proposals to arm Africans, train them for skilled work, and raise their living standards to the white man's level were of primary importance to the country's future.[27]

'Before the Japanese take this country,' Smuts promised parliament on 11 March 1942, 'I will see to it that every Coloured and every Native that can be armed will be armed.' This must be done now, urged the communists, and they warned people not to put their trust in the Japanese, whose victories in the Pacific fired the imagination of many Africans and Coloured with the hope that they, too, might be liberated by an invasion. Such wishful thinking, said Dadoo, resulted from the oppressive nature of the regime. 'Free us to defend our homes and our country before it is too late.'[28] Kotane, the party's general secretary, echoed the appeal in a widely distributed pamphlet. 'South Africa is what we Non-Europeans allowed her to be,' he declared; and 'in the future she will be what we ourselves make of her.' If Africans, Coloured and Indians were organized and stood together, there would never have been industrial and social colour bars.[29]

The party broadcast its message at meetings, in a steady output of leaflets and pamphlets, and through the medium of its press: *Inkululeko*, a fortnightly published at Johannesburg in African languages; the *Ware Republiken* (True Republican), addressed to Afrikaner workers; the *Call*, a duplicated journal published in Durban; and the *Guardian*, whose circulation rose from 12,000 in 1940 to 42,000 in June 1943. A Defend South Africa campaign, launched in 1942, attracted large audiences and many recruits to the party. Its membership increased from 400 to 1,500 between April 1941 and December 1943. These figures represented a stable body of politically educated activists, who were expected to fill a leading role in trade unions, national movements, local communities, factories and radical organizations.

Edwin Mofutsanyana, Alpheus Maliba and John Lekgotha represented the party in elections to the Native Representative Council in 1942. Though defeated, they received wide backing in the rural areas of the Free State and Transvaal, where Maliba (1901–67) had founded the Zoutpansberg Cultural Association, an organization of Venda peasants.[30] He came to Johannesburg in 1935, learnt to read and write in the party's night school, and was elected to the local district committee. A leader of the Venda and the African National Congress, he was banned from political work in the 1950s and imprisoned under the 'terrorist' act in 1967. He died in his cell, allegedly after hanging himself, on 9 September 1967.

Nine white communists entered the field in the parliamentary elections of 1943: four on the Rand, three in Cape Town, one in Durban, and one in East London.[31] All were South African born; four were Afrikaners; six were trade unionists with a working-class background. They suffered defeat, polling only 6,800 votes between them, or one-tenth of those cast in the nine constituencies, but they claimed to have brought home to voters the need for unity against poverty, disease and oppression. The Labour party won nine seats with the support of the United party and the Trades Council. Solly Sachs and Johanna Cornelius, backed by the Transvaal garment workers' union, stood and lost in the name of the Independent Labour party on a platform of 'progressive capitalism'.

Criticized for having ignored African and Coloured claims in his electioneering campaign, Sachs replied that the communists were wrong in 'preaching pure doctrinaire Socialism'. He was more successful with the policy of forming parallel racial unions and concentrating on the struggle for higher wages. The

'Bourgeois Bolsheviks' who led the party, he said, had committed 'terrible blunders' which 'brought the greatest disaster to the Working-class Movement'. It was because of them that hundreds of thousands of white workers had turned to the camp of reaction.[32]

Reproaches of this kind had been levelled against radical socialists since Crawford's time; and the communists, unabashed, continued to fight elections on a platform of democratic rights for all. Their first successes came towards the end of 1943, when Sam Kahn and Betty Radford, the talented editor of the *Guardian*, were elected to Cape Town's city council. She and her husband George Sacks, a leading surgeon, had joined the party in 1941 after serving a long apprenticeship in radical politics. Assisted by a small unpaid editorial staff and without financial backing, she started the paper in 1937, edited it for eleven years without any monetary reward, raised its circulation to 50,000 by the end of the war, and made it a model of left-wing journalism.

Twenty-five years of work against hostile propaganda, said Bill Andrews, the Communist party's chairman, had been rewarded by the election of the first communists to an official body. Reporting on progress at the end of 1943, the central committee claimed full justification for its policy of appealing to white voters to reject all colour bars, which kept four-fifths of the population in servitude and strengthened capitalism. By adopting it, the party had achieved the impossible. 'We have brought together in our organization men and women of all racial groups in South Africa, working together in comradeship for common ends on a basis of complete equality. We have done this in the teeth of bitter opposition and in the face of the dominant prejudices of society.'[33]

Others on the left shared this optimism. 'Congress is looking up,' said the veteran James Gumede at the ANC's annual conference in December 1943. 'I see in the enthusiasm and youthfulness of the delegates a new hope.'[34] The conference adopted a Charter of Rights modelled on the Atlantic Charter drawn up by Churchill and Roosevelt in August 1941; and undertook to support an anti-pass campaign launched by the Johannesburg Communist party in November. 'We must demand full adult franchise,' declared Dr Xuma in his presidential address. 'If you talk of action,' said Kotane, 'we are all behind you.'

The battles of Britain, Stalingrad and Alamein turned the tide against the Axis. Enthusiasm for the Red Army mounted as it drove Hitler's armies westward from the Volga to the Dnieper and beyond. The Soviet Union, that 'Colossus of Europe' in Smuts's phrase, had confounded its critics and vindicated the faith of its most ardent admirers. Its first consular representatives in South Africa arrived in 1942; the Friends of the Soviet Union, with Colin Steyn, the minister of justice, as a patron, flourished; and collections by Medical Aid for Russia topped the £100,000 mark in 1943. The Dutch Reformed Church asked Steyn to ban the Communist party. He refused, saying that it had neither broken the law nor threatened the state with subversive activity.[35]

The army, a body of volunteers without any conscripts, showed that white South Africans could be more tolerant of darker men and women when abroad than at home. The Army Education Service opened the minds of front line troops to progressive ideas, while the Springbok Legion organized them for political action on a liberal programme. Formed in September 1941, the League grew out of a Union of Soldiers initiated by Morley-Turner in Libya and a parallel movement started in a South African army camp by Vic Clapham, the *Guardian*'s cartoonist. Its six-point programme undertook to secure a fair deal for soldiers, ex-servicemen and their dependants; preserve unity between the races; defend democracy and promote Liberty, Equality, Fraternity. *Fighting Talk*, a lively journal published in English and Afrikaans, carried on a vigorous campaign for soldiers' rights, condemned racial discrimination, and alerted the League's 40,000 members to the disruptive work of nazified nationalists.

Victories on the battle front and high profits at home engendered a mood of euphoria in the pro-war parties. Amid much talk in 1943–4 of social security for all, the government extended school feeding schemes, old age pensions and invalidity grants on discriminatory scales to black and brown South Africans. Optimists thought that the time was ripe for a reversal of apartheid policies. 'Isolation has gone and I am afraid segregation has fallen on evil days too,' Smuts had philosophized at the height of the war danger.[36] Yet he would not introduce reforms liable to weaken the structure of white supremacy. Shortly before the general election of 1943, he decided to disarm the Nationalists and placate the Coloured by introducing administrative segregation. Coloured affairs were to be dealt with by a special section in the department of interior and by a permanent commission of Coloured notables.

Communists and Coloured radicals made an immediate and emphatic protest. Separation, they predicted, would lead to segregation along the lines of the detested native affairs department. The New Era Fellowship, a leftist debating society, took the initiative in forming the Anti-CAD on 28 February 1943. Its mission was to obstruct the proposed Coloured Affairs Department and to 'canalize all non-European sentiment and endeavour – economic, political and social – in one mighty stream that will expunge from the statute book all discriminatory legislation'.[37] Apart from I. B. Tabata, the leading members were Coloured intellectuals: Dr Goolam Gool, the chairman; his wife, Miss H. Ahmed; his sister, Janub Gool (Mrs Tabata); B. Kies, R. E. Viljoen, A. Fataar and the Rev. D. M. Wessels.

Dr F. H. Gow, president of the APO and leader of the African Methodist Episcopal Church, advised the community to accept the government's 'gesture of goodwill', but a large number of his members turned against him. Some 200 delegates attended the first National Anti-CAD conference in Cape Town on 29 May 1943. They represented 109 societies and groups, including branches of the APO, Communist party, National Liberation League, Non-European United Front, trade unions, teachers' and students' organizations. The conference decided to institute a political and social boycott of the Coloured Advisory Council, and to promote a united front against all forms of discrimination.[38]

The Anti-CAD would remain Coloured and 'eventually founder on the rock of isolation', Kotane pointed out, unless it broadened its scope to include the demands of Indians and Africans.[39] Aware of this weakness, Gool and his colleagues attended a conference convened by the All African Convention at Bloemfontein in December. An assortment of political bodies, trade unions, ratepayers' societies, church and welfare organizations agreed to form a Non-European Unity Movement on the basis of a Ten Point programme, and with an executive of sixteen members: eight from the Convention, four from the Anti-CAD, and four from the S.A. Indian Congress; with Jabavu as the chairman, Gool and A. I. Kajee as vice-chairmen.[40] Kajee and his fellow Indians declined.

Kajee was then negotiating the Pretoria Agreement with Smuts, who undertook in 1944 to suspend the 'Pegging' Act on condition that a licensing board be appointed to control the occupation by Indians of houses formerly occupied by whites in Durban. When this was made known, another storm of protest divided the Indian community. Voluntary segregation, said Dadoo, will lead to 'national suicide'; Dr G. M. Naicker and twelve other members of the Natal Indian Congress executive repudiated the agreement; and an Anti-Segregation Council was formed to agitate for adult suffrage on a common roll.[41]

Representatives of the S.A. Indian Congress, the All African Convention and the Anti-CAD met in the midst of this uproar at Johannesburg in July to resume negotiations on the proposed unity movement. The Indians suggested cooperation on specific issues, such as passes, the Pegging Act, and the Coloured Advisory Council; and were told that the Ten Point programme constituted an absolute minimum for unity. That was quite unreal, Dadoo argued, and unacceptable to the reactionary leaders of Congress. Moreover, neither the Convention nor the Anti-CAD was a representative body, since they relegated the APO to a subordinate position and virtually ignored the African National Congress, which 'most certainly has roots among the African people as their premier national body'.[42]

Dadoo maintained that the leaders of the Anti-CAD wished to 'isolate the African National Congress and to revive the defunct All-African Convention'. He thought that the better approach was to strengthen 'existing national liberatory organizations, by making them live and active bodies'. The executives of the ANC, APO, SAIC and Anti-CAD should lay a basis for unity through cooperation in common struggle. The Anti-CAD insisted, however, that agreement on principle must come first; and undertook to appeal to the Indians over the heads of the 'merchant class'.[43]

Though open to all societies 'genuinely willing to fight segregation' and prepared to accept its programme, the Non-European Unity Movement attracted few Indians or whites, and consisted mainly of Coloured and African intellectuals in the Cape. The programme itself was not a stumbling block. Less comprehensive and specific than the National Liberation League's charter, it contained nothing that would displease a radical. Its objectives were similar to demands put forward by opponents of discrimination since 1910: equality of franchise rights, civil liberties and personal security; freedom of education, movement and occupation; and a 'revision' of the 'land question', the legal code, taxation and labour laws in accordance with the principle of equality. The wording was meant to be restrained, vague and ambiguous, so that the programme might appeal to the wide range of political opinions represented in the Convention and the Anti-CAD.[44]

The Non-European Unity Movement made the programme its chief battle ground. No meeting, demonstration, strike or passive resistance met with approval unless it was 'principled' in terms of the programme, and directed by the NEUM. Making non-collaboration its major principle of struggle, and the boycott its great weapon, the NEUM called for withdrawal from the Coloured Advisory Council and the Native Representative Council. 'There must be a parting of the ways,' announced the All African Convention's executive committee in July 1944: 'Either *with* the people *against* the Government, against the oppressors, or *with* the government *against* the people. The appeal, the demand of the Convention should go out to all the elected members of the NRC to resign collectively and immediately. Should a few refuse to serve the interests of the people, the rest must expose them.'[45]

By the end of 1944 the Anti-CAD claimed to have penetrated every type of Coloured institution, gained control of the APO and the Teachers' League of S.A., isolated the Coloured Advisory Council and discredited its members. Reviewing its record three years later, Brian Bunting, son of S. P. Bunting and later a member of the Communist party's central committee, wrote that Anti-CAD had 'brought some of the most militant figures in the Coloured community to the fore'.[46] The spirit of nationalism kindled by La Guma, Gomas and Gool in 1935 when they founded the National Liberation League was spreading slowly through the community.

One cannot tell how far the spirit spread. From all accounts it made small progress among artisans, other workers or businessmen. Though deeply resentful of colour bars, they shared the white man's language and culture, enmeshed with him at many levels and regarded themselves as an integral part of his society. The great bulk of Coloured were indifferent or hostile to the idea of unity with Africans which the Anti-CAD put in the forefront of its campaign. New fissures consequently developed. Conservatives, led by Dr Gow, chairman of the CAC, and his successor George Golding formed rival organizations: the Coloured People's National Union and the Teachers' Educational and Professional Association. Without popular support, the boycott movement failed to achieve its aim of breaking 'the chain of collaboration' that bound the people 'through their leaders to their oppressors'.[47]

The Anti-CAD intended, Tabata explained in January 1945, to form local coordinating unity committees which would 'draw the community into the struggle, prepare the masses for a concerted onslaught against oppression and rally them in the fight for liberation'. The phrases struck a familiar note, as did his warning that group prejudices would not disappear overnight. 'If we try to ignore historical processes we shall break our necks.' People must be taught to forget their racial groups and think only of their common oppression. They would reach that stage by taking part in actual struggle on the basis of the Ten Point programme.[48]

Apart from racial animosities between Coloured and Africans – which the government and conservative Coloured leaders exploited to the full – the teachers who controlled the Non-European Unity Movement had to cope with grave personal problems. Employed in government and mission schools under a strict disciplinary code, they risked their careers if they joined in direct, physical and potentially unlawful forms of protest. Even the most courageous might hesitate to jeopardize a hard-won status and means of livelihood in a society that offered few openings of equal worth to an educated Coloured or African. Partly for this reason, the NEUM held its followers back from joining in demonstrations, strikes and defiance campaigns organized by the African National Congress and its allies; concentrated instead on propaganda; and called for a boycott of segregated institutions.

The boycott was a strategy of withdrawal, useful in so far as it developed a group resistance to segregated institutions, though without an appreciable effect on the administration, which could readily dispense with African and Coloured advisory boards or councils. Teachers could therefore demand a boycott with immunity; and at the same time give vent to resentments by denouncing as 'quislings' and 'collaborators' those who took part in elections to the 'dummy councils'. Among them, said B. M. Kies, a prominent teacher and leader of Anti-CAD, were 'dozens and dozens of so-called Radicals and Socialists and Communists who paid lip-service to the emancipation of the Non-European, while they rode into the Council or Parliament on his back, or grew rich at his expense by organizing trade unions'.[49] This was an inaccurate statement. There were then three communists on the Cape Town municipal council and none in parliament. No communist trade union official earned more than the workers whom he organized.

The Anti-CAD, like the APO in its salad days, initially followed the Marxist line. 'We, the Non-European oppressed,' said Kies, 'must never confuse the European worker, aristocrat of labour though he may be today, with the European ruling class.' Economic exploitation, national or colour oppression, sprang from the same root; and the white worker must willy-nilly find his way to the Coloured and African worker, his real ally, on the basis of the Ten Point programme. The door would be kept open to him, for the Anti-CAD had no desire to replace the White Herrenvolk by a Black Herrenvolk.

Colour dichotomy soon took the place of class dichotomy in the polemics of the Anti-CAD. It lumped all whites together –

worker and employer, liberal and racist, communist and capital-ist – under the 'herrenvolk' label. This approach seemed to correspond more closely to the outward appearance of things, appealed to the heightened colour consciousness of a sorely stricken minority, and served to discredit the communists, whom the Anti-CAD regarded as its greatest rival. By abusing them, it warded off the danger of being persecuted as a subversive organization, and discouraged its members from being attracted to a non-racial radicalism. The main achievement of the Anti-CAD was to immobilize a generation of Coloured intellectuals, immunize them against Marxist theory, and isolate them from the rest of the liberation movement.

Confident of their theoretical and technical competence, the Coloured nationalists of the Anti-CAD rejected white leadership in every sphere. It was their destiny, they said, to lead the masses to freedom, not through irresponsible and opportunist minor skirmishes, but in one great battle that would sweep all colour bars aside. This holistic concept of 'principled struggle' against the 'whole machinery of oppression' was never put to the test. Tabata, Kies and Gool dissipated their energies on denunciations of militants outside their ranks and turned 'non-collaboration' into a synonym for inactivity. The diatribes bred a mood of angry defiance in many Coloured and African teachers in the Cape, and alienated African and Indian congressmen.

Young intellectuals in the ANC, no less confident of their own ability to lead, formed the African Youth League in 1943. Some, like Oliver Tambo, Nelson Mandela and Govan Mbeki, had studied at Fort Hare; Anton Lembede, the League's president, was a lawyer from Seme's office; Walter Sisulu, another foun-dation member, had come up the hard way through the gold mines and factories.[50] The League, too, called for non-collabora-tion, boycotts and a programme of positive action; and related its demand for equality and freedom to a vision based on traditional African values adjusted to the conditions of an industrial society. Much of the ANC's history for the next five years centred round a conflict between Xuma's old guard, on the one hand, and the young militants or communists on the other.

Further signs of a resurgent militancy appeared: an epidemic of African strikes, the Alexandra bus boycotts, and a great campaign against the pass laws in 1944. Between 40,000 and 60,000 Africans and Coloured lived in Alexandra township about nine miles from the centre of Johannesburg. In August 1943 thousands walked eighteen miles a day to and from work rather than submit to an increase in bus fares from 4d. to 5d. Having won the first round after protesting with their feet for nine days, they resumed the struggle in November 1944 against another attempt to raise the fare. The Alexandra branch of the Communist party, led by Gauer Radebe and David Bopape, secretary of the Transvaal ANC, called on the residents to walk. For seven weeks they trudged to Johannesburg and back again before they could claim a victory. They 'have displayed the courage, unity and determination', said the communists, 'which is necessary for all of us if we are to win the kind of South Africa we want'.[51]

Thousands of homeless African families took possession of vacant land adjoining the big township of Orlando in Johannesburg; built shelters out of split poles, packing cases, hessian, canvas, paraffin tins or corrugated iron; adopted the slogan '*Sofazonke*' – we die together – coined by their leader James Mpanza; and defended Shanty Town against the government, police and municipality. Prohibited from buying land, Africans were condemned, wrote Hilda Watts (Mrs Bernstein), the only communist on Johannesburg's city council, 'to breeze-block slums, to sub-tenancies, to sharing rooms, to living with their families in corridors, shacks and yards, without any immediate hope of relief'.[52] Squatters' camps sprang up in peri-urban areas throughout the country as Africans, hamstrung by law and neglected by the housing authorities, found their own solution to the problems caused by overcrowding in segregated ghettoes.

Shanty towns, Dr Xuma told an anti-pass rally at Cape Town in April 1944, grew out of conditions created by repressive laws that were 'calculated to deliver the African worker to the European employer as the cheapest form of labour'.[53] Land hunger forced peasants into the towns, only to be harassed under pass laws which he described as 'an instrument of oppression, a stigma of inferiority, an economic barrier to progress and self-respect'.[54] Under his leadership, the African National Congress threw itself into the campaign initiated by Johannesburg communists against the pass system and urged its branches to take part in forming a network of local anti-pass committees.

African nationalists were breaking away from the reliance on verbal protests, respectable conformism and red-baiting that had demoralized Congress under Seme's rule. The decision to embark on mass action, galvanize Congress branches and enter into an open alliance with communists began a process that was to result in the Congress Alliance of 1955. The National Anti-Pass Council elected in May at a conference attended by 540 delegates included Xuma as chairman and the communists Dadoo as vice-chairman, Bopape as secretary, Josie Mpama as a trustee, Mofutsanyana, Marks, Maliba and Kotane.[55] Never before had militants in the liberation movement established so broad a basis for active struggle.

The campaign produced a whirlwind of propaganda but failed to reach the target of a million signatures to a petition. When a deputation headed by Dadoo and Selope Thema took it to Cape Town in June 1945, the acting premier J. H. Hofmeyr refused to meet them. Six years of war had made no change in the essential elements of the social structure. Uniformed members of the Ossewabrandwag, meeting in Johannesburg on the eve of Labour Day, heard Führer van Rensburg accuse communists of plotting to set up a black republic. A week later nearly 2,000 African miners assembled to discuss a report on their union by its chairman J. B. Marks. In September Springbok Legionaires routed a Nationalist party conference in Johannesburg and suffered 160 casualties in clashes with Nationalists and the police. The country was back to normal.

The Communist party's central committee met in July to chart a course for the immediate future and found small reason for optimism. The united front phase of defensive action, it concluded, had come to an end. The war boom would give way to economic depression and an attack on the worker's standards. White supremacists would resume the offensive against African, Coloured and Indian rights. A period of bitter class and national struggle lay ahead. The Malans, Pirows and van Rensburgs would attempt to impose the kind of fascist dictatorship that had been defeated in Europe. 'The ultimate result of failure to raise the living standards of the poorest section and to extend democracy will be wage cuts and loss of democracy for all.'[56]

The Labour party was more hopeful. Encouraged by postwar discontent and Labour's victory in Britain, the national executive decided that Madeley should withdraw from the cabinet and issued a statement to this effect shortly before Johannesburg's municipal elections in October. The party's electoral manifesto denounced the communist policy of equal rights for all. Right-wing Labour leaders appeared on public platforms with Nationalists in a campaign for stern measures to cope with the crime wave. 'One or two public lynchings would do a lot of good,' suggested R. Knevitt, the Labour candidate in Braamfontein, and his party agitated for stricter pass laws, including a 9 p.m. curfew for all Africans.[57] The Communist party's four candidates were defeated, and Labour won five seats, giving it 18 in all and an uneasy control of the council against the divided opposition of 16 United party and 7 Nationalist councillors.

An emergency committee, chaired by Colin Legum, editor of the *Illustrated Labour Bulletin* and author of the manifesto, urged the government to deport Mpanza and expel squatters from Orlando township. His motion was carried by twenty-seven votes to two after an angry debate in which Hilda Watts, the solitary communist on the council, accused Labour of betraying its principles and disregarding its tradition of struggle against undemocratic deportations. Would the council have dared to call in the police against homeless whites? she asked.[58] The Labour right wing, however, persisted in its efforts to woo a reactionary electorate by demanding repressive action in defence of white supremacy.

Madeley tendered his resignation from the cabinet on 3 October 1945, in deference, he said, to his party's wishes and in order to free himself for winning the peace. That could not be done, he explained, under the system of private enterprise for profit to which the government adhered. In March he claimed that he had resigned because of the government's failure to implement promises made during the war. In September he resigned from the party over the issue of franchise rights for Indians, and declared that a faction in his own ranks had forced him to leave the cabinet in retaliation for the United party's refusal to conclude an electoral pact with Labour in the municipal elections.[59]

Smuts's Asiatic Land Tenure and Indian Representation Bill of 1946 prohibited land transfers between Indians and non-Indians in Transvaal and Natal, except in 'exempted areas' or with the minister's consent. To sugar the pill, Smuts proposed to give Indians two white representatives in the senate, three whites in the assembly, and two, who might be Indians, in the Natal provincial council. Nationalists and Dominionites protested angrily that Indians had no claim to any political rights. The Labour party caucus agreed to the principle of residential segregation, but not on the franchise clauses, and decided that members should vote according to their conscience. Madeley and M. J. van den Berg voted with the opposition; Christie, Latimer, Payne, Sullivan and Wanless, for the bill.[60]

Repudiated by their national council, Madeley and van den Berg resigned from the party, the latter to join the Nationalists. Other resignations followed from Labour's slender parliamentary ranks: senator Henderson, the party's general secretary, Duncan Burnside, Miles-Cadman and Sullivan, who took refuge in the United party. Thirty-seven years after Union, the Labour party had five seats in a parliament of 153 members. Madeley announced that he would form a new party on an anti-Indian platform. He was not a 'copybook maxim socialist', he declared. Labour had fallen into the hands of communists, 'chancers' and intriguers; but 'one could not achieve socialism by handing over the franchise to a body of Indian capitalists'. If capitalism was bad, Indian capitalism was ten times worse.[61] He died in May 1947, rejected by and rejecting the party in which he had spent his entire political life.

Successive electoral pacts had limited the party to a handful of constituencies and undermined the morale of its branches. For the sake of seats in the white supremacy parliament, Labour consistently betrayed its socialist principles. Its appeals to colour prejudice and racial passions encouraged white workers to look for security to the big battalions of the ruling class. Facing political bankruptcy, collapse or absorption by its rivals, the party tried to retrieve its fortunes. A special conference held in November 1946 adopted a new programme for the 'Non-European'.[62] South Africa's racial policies, it declared, met with much criticism abroad, gave 'unrealistic advisers' an opportunity 'to mislead the Non-European', and should be 'lifted above the cockpit of party-political fights'.

It was a sentimental appeal without political substance. Only the communists accepted an invitation to attend an all-party conference to discuss the policy. The programme itself revealed much muddled thinking, a mild liberalism, and tenacious adherence to the essentials of white supremacy. Among other things, the Labour party wished to do away with the exploitation of 'cheap and docile' labour, include Africans in the definition of employee under industrial laws, provide industrial training for Africans with safeguards for white workers, and give Coloured and Asians the right to elect persons of their own race to parliament. Africans would continue to be represented by whites, but on a bigger scale. Radical only in terms of Labour's traditional attitudes, the programme reflected the militant mood aroused by the Indians' passive resistance campaign and the African miners' strike of 1946.

Thousands of workers had joined the Natal Indian Congress. With this reinforcement, the Anti-Segregation Council routed the Kajee-Pather leadership in October 1945 and took control of Congress. 'Our programme,' announced Dr Naicker, the new president, 'is to enable Indians to live as free citizens in a free society.'[63] Some months later, Dr Dadoo became the president of the Transvaal Indian Congress. A conference of the S.A. Indian Congress held at Cape Town in February 1946 called on Indians to prepare for 'a concerted and prolonged resistance' against Smuts's ghetto bill.[64] Passive resistance councils were set up in Natal and the Transvaal. Segregation, declared Dadoo in April, led to political and economic serfdom, inculcated a feeling of inferiority and subservience to the ruling class, crushed the spirit of freedom, and assisted the growth of fascism based on racial hatred and white domination.[65] A joint passive resistance council appealed in June for 'a day of Hartal' (mourning) as soon as the governor general assented to the bill.[66]

Indians showed once again that they were the most cohesive and politically mature community in the subjugated population. More than 2,000 resisters – among whom were 300 women, as well as factory workers, peasants, doctors, lawyers, teachers and shop assistants – went to jail in the next two years. Some followed the example of Gandhi's satyagrahis by illegally crossing the Natal-Transvaal border; most were convicted on a charge of occupying land reserved for whites. Dr Dadoo and Dr Naicker were among the first batch of prisoners. Convicted for a second time and sentenced to six months' hard labour, the two leaders were among the last of the resisters to be released in July 1948. The Nationalists were then in power, and the passive resistance council suspended the campaign. Before long the new government repealed the franchise provisions but retained the ban on transfers of land to Indians.[67]

The resisters could console themselves with the knowledge that they had left a permanent mark on African and world opinion. The African National Congress, Dr Xuma said in April 1946, stood four square behind the campaign. Bogged down in the struggle against pass laws and shaken by the effects of the miners' strike in August, African leaders could hardly offer more than moral backing. But they drew the correct conclusions. In March 1947 Xuma, Dadoo and Naicker signed a declaration of unity in which they undertook to work together for full franchise rights and equality with whites. A basis was being laid for closer cooperation between Africans and Indians than any achieved elsewhere in Africa.

Natal Indians decided in March 1946 to press for immediate economic sanctions, the withdrawal of India's high commissioner, and an appeal to the United Nations.[68] Thus persuaded, the Delhi government under Nehru recalled the high commissioner, cut off trade relations with South Africa and indicted its racial policies before the general assembly of the United Nations in November. Smuts pleaded that the position of

Indians was a purely domestic affair; but his critics, led by Mrs Pandit and Alexei Vyshinsky, carried the day. An overwhelming majority of the assembly demanded that the treatment of Indians should conform to agreements between India and South Africa and to the relevant clauses of the Charter. Smuts fared no better with his proposal to annex South West Africa. That, said Mrs Pandit, would mean 'permanent helotry' for Africans. The assembly recommended instead that the territory be placed under United Nations trusteeship. White South Africa had suffered a serious moral defeat. National liberation could claim its first significant victory in the long struggle to arouse world opinion against white supremacy.

24 Resistance and Reaction

Trade unionism flourished under conditions of full employment and inflation during the war. Organizers began gathering the results of their stubborn efforts in the preceding decade. Union membership rose from 264,000 in 1939 to 410,000 in 1945, and the number of registered unions from 139 to 203. At the end of 1945 the Non-European Trade Union Council claimed to represent 119 unions and 158,000 organized workers. The movement spread into country districts in the wake of industrial expansion. A food and canning workers' union, organized by Ray Alexander in 1941, spread through small towns and fishing hamlets of the western and eastern Cape. 'Five years ago it was very difficult to form trade unions,' reported H. A. Naidoo, secretary of the Natal sugar workers' union in 1942. 'But today we find workers organizing spontaneously to improve their conditions.'[1]

Africans provided nearly two-thirds of the increase in the labour force during the war. Without them, industry could not have satisfied the demand for goods that were strategically important or vital to the economy: foodstuffs, footwear, clothing, cement, coal, iron, gold, chemicals, explosives and munitions. The number of Africans employed in manufacturing rose by 57 per cent, from 156,500 in 1939 to 245,500 in 1945; and their share of the total so employed rose from 48·6 to 54·6 per cent. At the end of 1948 they accounted for 80·8 per cent of unskilled employees, 34·2 per cent of the semi-skilled, and 5·8 per cent of the skilled in occupations regulated by wage determinations.[2]

A medium-sized African family could not provide for its basic needs with less than £6 10s. to £7 12s. 6d. a month in the big towns; yet government and municipal departments, following the standards set on the mines, paid their labourers from £3 to

£4. The Non-European Trade Union Council campaigned in 1942 for a minimum wage of 40s. a week, but obtained no more than 25s. rising to 27s. on a sliding scale recommended by the wage board for unskilled labourers in some thirty occupations in the Transvaal.

Organized and unorganized workers responded with a series of strikes on docks, railways, coal mines and sugar estates; in municipal services, dairies, laundries and factories. A record number of 304 strikes, involving 58,000 Africans, Coloured and Indians and 6,000 whites, were reported in 1939–45, as compared with 197 strikes in the fifteen years from 1924 to 1938.[3]

Africans had no statutory right to collective bargaining and were prosecuted if they withheld their labour. This was a major reason for their poverty and discontent, said Dr Xuma, when leading a deputation to the government in March 1942. David Gosani, secretary of the Non-European TUC and a member of the delegation, described in detail how employers and the administration ignored or harassed the unions. He contrasted their position with that of white trade unions before and during the First World War. Like them, he said, Africans were fighting, but under far greater handicaps, for trade union recognition and a living wage.[4]

The African lost on both counts. His poverty was a function of white domination, a contrived inequality that limited his average share of the national income to one tenth of the white man's. Skilled wage rates were from four to five times the unskilled rate in most trades, and from eight to ten times on the mines. Nothing short of a social upheaval could change these proportions. In the exceptionally favourable circumstances of war production, the African's average earnings in private manufacturing rose from 19·8 per cent of white earnings in 1937–8 to 26·6 per cent. This was an interlude. The gap widened again after the war; and the proportion fell to 18·5 per cent by 1957.[5]

Sporadic local strikes might secure small gains; but they canalized the workers' resentments in well-worn grooves and made no lasting impression on wage patterns or opportunities of employment. Committed to a policy of maximizing output during the war, trade union leaders called for restraint. The Communist party pointed out that workers went on strike because they had no other means of obtaining relief from crushing burdens; yet urged them to apply all other forms of pressure 'to obtain a satisfactory settlement, while avoiding any stoppage of work'.[6] The high incidence of strikes indicated a tendency to emphasize immediate demands. There was no intention of turning the strike wave into a revolutionary assault on the bastions of white supremacy.

Police repression and statutory penalties were by far the most effective deterrents. War measure 6 of 1941, published in February with the approval of the trades council, authorized Ivan Walker, the secretary for labour, to fix wages and settle disputes in controlled industries. When African dockers at Durban struck work in August for a wage increase from 4s. to 8s. a day, he made stevedoring a controlled industry, banned the strike and granted an increase of 1s. War measure 9 of 1942 prohibited strikes in industries declared to be essential, and provided for compulsory arbitration. Both measures applied to workers of all races and were especially obnoxious to Africans who, being excluded from industrial councils and conciliation boards, had the least prospect of reaching an agreement with employers.

'Let us realize that we are oppressed, firstly as a race and secondly as workers,' Makabeni told delegates to the Non-European TUC conference in November 1942. 'If this were not the case we would not have to put up so bitter a struggle for recognition of our Trade Unions.' Hopes of finding a liberal solution were then running high. Madeley said he had convinced the cabinet that the level of organization among Africans warranted their inclusion in the system of collective bargaining.[7] Defying racial taboos, he took the unprecedented step of opening the NETUC's conference. 'Don't be too explosive on the question,' he cautioned. 'Recognition of your unions will come about; but you must rely on me.'

Three weeks later he betrayed the confidence for which he had appealed. Unable or unwilling to defy the established order, he set the seal on the African's subordinate status by enacting war measure 145 of 1942. It outlawed strikes by Africans, exposed strikers to the savage maximum penalty of a £500 fine or three years' imprisonment, and imposed compulsory arbitration at his discretion. Repressive action which enabled employers to pay starvation wages would not stop strikes, the Communist party warned, and it called for the repeal of the measure, the recognition of African unions and the extension of collective bargaining.[8] The trades council's annual conference withheld its protest in the interests of national unity.[9] The measure was renewed from time to time long after the war, until the Native Labour (Settlement of Disputes) Act came into force in 1953, when strikes by Africans were made illegal in all circumstances.

No mercy was shown to those who resisted, as on the Northfield colliery near Dundee, Natal, where 400 miners set fire to the company's buildings in September 1942. After making repeated and fruitless complaints to the management, the men had decided on direct action. Some would go to jail, they had said, but the rest might receive better treatment. Their grievances were genuine, Judge Brokensha of the Native High Court acknowledged: assaults by mine policemen and white overseers; overcharging in the company's stores; inadequate rations; bare concrete slabs for beds; and twelve hours underground without food. Yet he sentenced thirty-five miners to terms of imprisonment varying from one year to five years for public violence.[10]

The Johannesburg city council persuaded Madeley to exempt it from a wage determination prescribing a minimum of 24s. a week for unskilled workers, but agreed to pay the new wage after 2,000 African employees struck work in December. Three weeks later, when employees of the Pretoria municipality demonstrated against the council's failure to implement the determination, soldiers were summoned. They fired, killing fourteen Africans and wounding 111. Smuts expressed his deep sorrow and appointed a commission of inquiry. It blamed Madeley, who had illegally exempted the council from the determination; the council, which housed its employees in a slum and fed them badly; and the soldiers who had fired without justification. The recognition of African unions, the commission added, would facilitate the amicable settlement of disputes and avoid strikes more effectively than war measure 145.[11]

British and Afrikaner racists sent up a chorus of protest. It would be very dangerous, said Marwick, leader of Natal's Dominion party, to confer the privileges of trade unionism on 'undisciplined Natives' who were 'devoid of a sense of responsibility and almost barbarian in their outlook'.[12] Heaton Nicholls, chairman of the native affairs commission, denied the validity of the class theory in South Africa, and warned that people 'just emerging from barbarism' would inevitably succumb to the dangerous promptings of 'some unbalanced semi-educated native' or 'disreputable European' battening on 'Native ignorance and cupidity'.[13]

Reactionary trade unionists said much the same thing at a conference called by Madeley in October 1943. Those present included twenty Africans and thirteen whites representing trade unions, the ANC, the Native Representative Council and the S.A. Institute of Race Relations. They agreed that the Industrial Conciliation Act should be so amended as to give Africans the same rights and responsibilities as other workers. The only dissenting note came from three representatives of the Trades and Labour Council: A. J. Downes, the president; W. J. de Vries, the general secretary; and T. C. Rutherford, secretary of the typographical union.

They took the view that though annual conferences of the TLC had repeatedly asked for the full recognition of African unions, few delegates understood all the implications. Race prejudice could not be stamped out by acts of parliament, Rutherford argued. White trade unionists would refuse to admit Africans as members or sit with them on industrial councils. Africans, said de Vries, 'have not yet reached a stage of mental and cultural development in which they can be entrusted with the rights and duties involved in recognition of their unions'.[14]

His plea for discrimination was transparently false. A significant number of viable African unions had emerged after twenty-five years of painful endeavour. Capable organizers like Makabeni, Koza, Tloome and Marks had proved their ability to cope with police repression, hostile employers and opposition from right wing labour leaders. The immaturity of the rank-and-file was also a myth. Africans were accustomed in their traditional peasant society to democratic procedures and the discipline of majority rule which, the Industrial Legislation Commission of 1951 observed, formed 'an admirable background to their participation in trade unionism'.[15]

The right wing of the labour movement would have it that Africans were unfit to manage their own affairs. The Labour party's parliamentary caucus said as much in February 1944, when it turned down a request from the Cape Federation of Labour Unions to press for the recognition of African unions. The Trades and Labour Council rejected a motion to that effect in April on a card vote, and thereby reversed the stand it had taken on the issue since 1925.[16] The council unanimously agreed, however, to a Workers' Charter, a statement of high ideals in the best traditions of social democracy. The charter proclaimed the virtues of socialism, called for planned production, and listed a series of universal rights, including free trade unionism and collective bargaining. All crucial questions relating to class solidarity, such as the colour bar and the status of African unions, were ignored or submerged in clichés. This rejection of the African's claims proved to be decisive. A conference of 142 delegates from seventy-five unions convened by the Non-European TUC in August 1945 resolved to continue the campaign, but it had lost momentum and never again came so close to victory as in 1943–4.

A number of consequences followed to which employers and the administration took exception. Some left-wing unions evaded the law by admitting Africans to membership and were threatened with deregistration. The Supreme Court uncovered loopholes in the Industrial Conciliation Act by holding that the definition of employee included all African women and some men such as parliamentary voters in the Cape.[17] Uncontrolled unions, said employers, were likely to fall into the hands of communists, extremists and subversive elements.[18] A strike of African miners in August 1946 provoked alarm and spurred the government into action. Smuts told parliament that 100 African unions were functioning and would 'fall under the influence of the wrong people' unless they were recognized 'on a basis of apartheid so that unnecessary difficulties will not arise'.[19]

A bill embodying these ideas appeared in May 1947.[20] It sought to make trade unionism illegal and a criminal offence for Africans in mining, farming, railways, government and domestic service; outlaw all strikes by Africans; isolate them in segregated registered unions; prohibit them from forming unregistered unions; and prevent any non-African or African alien from holding office without the minister's consent. Disputes would be referred to local conciliation committees of employers' and workers' representatives. Failing agreement, a mediation board of government officials and nominees might make an award under compulsory arbitration.

Trade unions, the African National Congress, Native Representative Council and Communist party protested vigorously. The bill threatened the rights of all workers, they said; violated the principles of the TLC's Charter and the International Labour Charter of Philadelphia; and was meant to give government officials the power 'to dictate wages and conditions of employment to African workers, whether they like them or not'.[21] On the other hand five Afrikaner unions withdrew from the Trades and Labour Council because it refused to bar the affiliation of African unions. In view of these cross currents, the government decided to refer the bill to an industrial legislation commission. It was actually appointed by the Nationalist government which took office in May 1948. The commission recommended a system of racial segregation for trade unions, and some of its findings were incorporated in the Natives (Settlement of Disputes) Act of 1953. The Act reproduced the worst features of Smuts's bill and deprived African unions of any recognized role. He would leave them to die a natural death, said B. J. Schoeman, the minister of labour.[22]

With a candour characteristic of the regime, the industrial legislation commission of 1948–51 refused to conceal its motives behind false assertions of racial inferiority, and frankly acknowledged that Africans were feared for their vigour and capability. If allowed to secure parity of bargaining power, they 'could not be restricted indefinitely to unskilled or even semi-skilled work, but would get an increasing hold on skilled occupations'. Nothing less than white supremacy was at stake, or so the commission argued. For, it said, the 'logical result' of the proposal to include them in the definition of employee was 'solidarity of labour irrespective of race' and in the long run the 'complete social and political equality of all races'.[23]

White workers fought tenaciously to protect their privileges against all pressure to expand production. The acute housing shortage that developed during the war underlined the inflexibility of the colour bar. Some 130,000 new houses were needed by 1945 for whites and a far greater number for other groups. The scarcity became a national scandal, and the government reacted by passing the Housing (Emergency Powers) Act of 1945. It authorized public authorities to expropriate land and materials, build houses and conscript workers. Artisans registered under the act were guaranteed full employment or eighty per cent of their basic wage for ten years. The building unions reciprocated by undertaking to absorb 5,000 discharged soldiers; and turned down a government proposal to train Africans to build houses for their own people.[24]

The government went ahead, however, and authorized COTT, the Central Organization for Technical Training, to train African ex-servicemen at Milner Park, Johannesburg, as bricklayers, plasterers, painters and carpenters. Building unions blacklisted the scheme, placed pickets outside the centre, and ordered the instructors to withdraw under the threat of losing their union membership.[25] Danie du Plessis, secretary of the Johannesburg branch of the building workers' union and a leading communist, was expelled for publishing a resolution urging that training facilities be made available to men of all races. According to the general secretary, W. Blake, his union was 'inflexibly opposed to the training of Natives as building artisans'.[26]

Building labourers did all the heavy, dirty work for a basic wage of 9½d. an hour as compared with the artisan's wage of 4s. 5d. In 1947, during an eight weeks' strike of white building workers on the Rand, the labourers were left to starve while the strikers drew £3 a week in strike pay out of funds subscribed by trade unions and the general public. The strikers refused to assist their co-workers or support their demand for a wage of 1s. 5d. an hour. When the strike was settled, the whites received an increase of 10½d., and the labourers went back to work at the old rate of 9½d.

After a year of wrangling during which some 200 Africans completed the course of training, the government closed the Milner Park centre in November 1947 and decided to train building artisans at Kingwilliamstown in the eastern Cape. They would be employed at Zwelitsha (New Era), an adjoining African township for employees of a textile factory built with public funds and conducted jointly by state and private enterprise. It was the first 'border' industry established to absorb landless peasants and keep them out of the cities. Here they could be employed as operatives and artisans without the restraint of colour bars, trade unionism or the rule of equal pay for equal work.

All this was grist to the Nationalist party's electoral mill on the eve of the 1948 general election. The government was said to have played into the hands of communists who had abandoned their earlier slogan of a 'white South Africa' for a programme of racial equality.[27] 'Here we have the thin edge of the wedge,' declared J. G. Strydom, a future prime minister. 'Therefore with all the strength that in me lies, I protest against their policy, because it will mean another nail in the coffin of the White man and of European civilization.' Africans, he warned, would compete for skilled work and drive white men out of the trades.[28] Within a fortnight of being installed as minister for labour in the new cabinet, B. J. Schoeman announced that the training of Africans as artisans would be suspended until legislation had been passed to protect the white worker. The safeguards were introduced by the Native Building Workers Act of 1951, which prohibits Africans from performing skilled work on buildings in urban areas except in the segregated townships.[29]

The involvement of Nationalists in trade union politics intensified after 1944, when they formed the Blankewerkers-beskermingsbond (society for the protection of white workers). Any white Christian protestant willing to fight for white civilization was invited to join. The Bond's membership in June 1946 consisted of 1,058 workers drawn from seventy-two occupations; and 1,308 others, listed as professional men, farmers, housewives, pensioners and persons of no stated occupation. Seldom has a reputed labour organization had so variegated and dormant a body or so distinguished a head. Besides four *predikants* and the ex-teacher D. E. Ellis, later the general secretary of the miners' union, the Bond's executive committee included seven men who were to sit in parliament. Five would hold cabinet rank: Dr Verwoerd as prime minister; Dr Diederichs as minister of commerce; B. J. Schoeman as minister of labour and then of transport; J. de Klerk, also as minister of labour and later of interior; and F. E. Mentz as a deputy minister.

The calibre of the leadership denoted the importance attached to the work of the Bond. Its professed aim was to propagate christian nationalism, combat communism, agitate for segregation and generally to promote workers' interests. Functionally it served to detach Afrikaners from the labour movement and secure their allegiance to the Nationalist party. Through the medium of their monthly journal *Die Blanke Werker* (The White Worker), Diederichs and his fellow crusaders preached the doctrine of organic solidarity between Afrikaner employer, worker and consumer. In an earlier, happier age South Africa, it was said, knew no class divisions except between white and black. The humble share-cropper ate at the table of the farmer's family; men were judged by birth, deeds and character, and not by education, wealth or rank. It was the foreigner, capitalist and trade unionist, who disrupted the idyllic order. Working in collusion, they grew fat on the blood and sweat of the simple-minded Afrikaner, implanted unnational ideas, and divided the Volk into antagonistic classes. The Bond's mission was to restore harmony between members of the Volk who felt as one and belonged together.[30]

The naivety of this ideological folk tale revealed the single-mindedness of the Bond and the narrow range of its design to foster a fervent nationalism which would dispel all traces of class consciousness in the Afrikaner worker. A compact, highly organized community linked by language, religion and race would resist assimilation into the dominant English culture or the internationalism of the labour movement. Taking their cue from Holland's Christian nationalists, the pedagogic Calvinists who forged the intellectual armoury of the Afrikaner bourgeosie produced a local brand of totalitarianism suited to their hegemonic aspirations. Liberal concepts of free competition, individual liberty and equality before the law were as obnoxious as the communist doctrine of economic determinism, class struggle and socialist equality. Communism and free trade unionism, which alienated Afrikaner workers from the Nationalist party and church, were the greater menace and the Bond's chief target of attack.

The Bond, said its chairman Ben Schoeman, would purify the unions of unnational influences and eradicate the communist leaders who preached atheism and stirred up class war. His party, he told parliament, proposed to introduce 'a new economic order' in which the state would regulate wages and confine the unions to the role of looking after domestic matters and the workers' spiritual welfare.[31] The theme was elaborated in the Nationalist social and economic programme of 1946. It rejected the one-sided aims of capitalism and communism, acknowledged the virtues of private property, and declared that labour was no less necessary than capital to economic welfare, though neither should be applied to selfish ends. The state ought to control key industries; ensure a fair distribution of profits between workers, shareholders and the community; and maintain 'the proper and necessary equilibrium between the respective sectional interests'. In return for these benefits, labour would have to accept state control. The Afrikaner nation was a moral and economic entity in which human values took precedence over financial considerations.[32]

As greedy for profits as their British counterpart, Afrikaner capitalists flourished in later years under the Nationalist regime and ignored banal phrases culled from fascist doctrines of the corporate state. Mussolini at least claimed to speak for Italians of all classes; whereas the Nationalists excluded four-fifths of the population from their vision of the ideal society. Black and brown South Africans appeared in the programme as 'an important and valuable economic factor' whose welfare would be considered only after effective steps had been taken to segregate them. Their destiny was to remain wards under trusteeship, that essential instrument for the protection of the white man's status and civilization. Or so the programme declared.

Its appeal was limited to Afrikaners. They were promised protection and privilege within the warm, familiar embrace of the Volk and under the mantle of bourgeois politicians, *predikants*, teachers and lawyers whom they had learned to honour and obey. Exposed to a massive propaganda campaign while still in a state of transition from the rural community, many workers found the appeal almost irresistible, the more so because of the alien character of the capitalist class. English-speaking for the most part, unsympathetic to the Afrikaner's language, tradition and religion, employers as a body recognizably conformed to the stereotype of the Bond's propaganda.

The flabby clique that controlled the Labour party never offered a real alternative. Predominantly English, deeply divided and discredited by its long association with Smuts, the party failed to secure the backing of even the right wing in the Trades and Labour Council. 'Labour will not win for many years,' said L. J. van den Berg, secretary of the iron and steel trades association, an Afrikaner union centred in Pretoria, when addressing the council's annual conference in 1946. 'We know that we cannot get our own members to agree on supporting any one party, but they are sick and tired of these divisions.' He moved that the council 'immediately take steps to get direct representation as strong as possible in the House of Parliament'.[33] Conservative and radical delegates rejected his motion, and thereby wrecked any prospect of detaching a significant number of Afrikaners from their allegiance to the Nationalist party.

In the following year van den Berg and George McCormick, secretary of the engine drivers' and firemen's union, moved an amendment to the council's constitution which would bar African unions from membership. Conference defeated the motion by 115 votes to thirty, and the delegates of five Pretoria unions withdrew. The slogan of racial equality, they said, emanated from the communists, resulted in the exploitation of the African, and undermined the position of the white worker.[34]

The dissident unions formed Die Ko-ordinerende Raad van Suid-Afrikaanse Vakverenigings in 1948. Its constitution denied affiliation to any union in which Africans, Coloured and Indians had full rights of membership. Afrikaner nationalism had achieved its first major success in the long struggle to penetrate the trade union movement.

The Nationalists made little headway in unions under militant leaders who gave their members political education in addition to material benefits. E. S. Sachs survived twenty years of vilification, physical violence and hooliganism by defending the garment workers' union with skill and courage; and by obtaining substantial benefits: a rise in weekly wages from £1 to £7 for women and from £3 to £15 for men; a reduction in the working week from fifty hours to forty; and an increase in the number of paid holidays from two to twenty-eight a year.[35] The national union of distributive workers and the food workers' union in the western Cape were equally successful in beating back attacks by the Blankewerkersfederasie, an organization formed in 1944 as a parallel movement to the Beskermingsbond.

J. W. van Staden, the moving spirit behind the federation, was a former organizer of the Nationalist party who resigned the position so that he could devote himself, he said, to the mission of rescuing Afrikaners from foreign communists, Jewish trade unionists, class war and racial intermingling. The practical advantages of trade unionism, he argued, did not compensate for the spiritual injury it inflicted on Afrikaners, whose true home was the Nationalist party.[36] Not surprisingly, van Staden never produced a viable union. He was allowed to register five unions for white workers only, and they disintegrated after the manoeuvre had served its purpose. 'The necessity for such an organization [as the Federasie] disappeared when the National party came to power,' the latter's official historian recorded, 'and Mr van Staden was taken into the party's administration.'[37] He became its assistant secretary and was elected to the provincial council in 1949 and to parliament in 1958.

The disruptive strategy of the Nationalists scored its only success in the mine workers' union, largely because of the executive's bad management and compromising relations with the mine owners. Starting with a wage demand in 1943 and the rejection of strike action by a majority of members in a ballot, the executive followed the precedent set by Crawford and Forrester Brown in the First World War and agreed in September 1944 to waive all claims to a general increase of wages 'until existing conditions underwent a very material change'. In return, the Chamber would pay £100,000 a year for five years into a fund, to be used for housing loans to miners, the financing of cooperative stores, and the purchase of farms managed by the union. The scheme led to the undoing of the general secretary, B. B. Brodrick, and his committee. Without experience or ability in commercial enterprise, they incurred heavy losses, made improper loans to officials and organizers, falsified the minutes and exposed themselves to a charge of corruption.[38]

The Blankewerkersbeskermingsbond exploited these failings to its great advantage. Ellis and Hertzog revived the rank-and-file opposition movement under the name of the action committee, later styled the united mine workers' committee; urged miners to withhold their subscriptions to the union; and in 1946 called a strike in protest against the dismissal of one Hattingh who, having refused to pay membership fees, was expelled from the union and consequently lost his job. Dr Malan moved the adjournment of the House on a matter of urgent public importance in order to discuss the strike; the union's general council terminated Brodrick's employment in April; and Smuts appointed a commission to inquire into the union's affairs. 'The strikers,' jubilated the Nationalists, 'had won with the help of the Nationalist party and our great national newspaper *Die Transvaler*.'[39]

The commission made a scapegoat of Brodrick and his committee but concealed the role of the Nationalists and their disruptive agencies. They organized another strike in January 1947 which received financial aid from Nationalist party members of parliament, branches, trade unions and churches.[40] 'The mine workers of the Reef,' said Dr Albert Hertzog, 'refused to work as long as the existing management of the Mine Workers' union remained in office.'[41] Three successful court actions brought by the united mine workers' committee between August 1946 and

May 1948 led to the annulment of elections in which the committee's nominees had suffered defeat. Success came to them in November 1948, five months after the Nationalists had taken office and in elections supervised by the government. Ellis was appointed general secretary of the union in the same month. Like his predecessor, he enforced a closed shop and told the miners to 'pay up or get out'; but sugared the threat by claiming that they had gained a million pounds in higher wages and other benefits under his leadership.[42]

Yet another commission, proposed by Smuts and actually appointed by Schoeman, reported in September 1949 that miners were worse off than in 1938, both absolutely and in comparison with workers in secondary industry.[43] Three days later, the government devalued the £ by thirty per cent in terms of dollars. The price of gold rose from 172s. 6d. an ounce to 248s. 3d.; the mining of low-grade ores became profitable; and the Chamber agreed to an increase of twelve or fifteen per cent in wages with improvements in pensions and other benefits.[44] The change of government, the capture of the union by Ellis's faction, the commission's report and devaluation had averted a deadlock such as the one that resulted in the great miners' strike of 1922.

Ellis claimed the credit for the increases; and continued his predecessor's bad habits. Ruling the union with a firm hand, 'he was very much in the position of a dictator'.[45] Under his guidance and using the money contributed by the Chamber in terms of the 1944 agreement, the union paid £176,000 for a building constructed at a cost of £108,000 and which the owners were willing to sell for £140,000. At the same time the owners offered Ellis a one-third interest in a liquor store valued at £6,100. Other members of his executive might have been negligent, reported a government commission; only Ellis was corrupt.[46] He was sentenced to eighteen months' hard labour for falsitas in a private prosecution instituted by P. J. Visser, the union's president, but the Supreme Court set the conviction aside on the ground that Visser had no title to prosecute.[47] Ellis was reinstated as secretary of the union and retained the position until his death in 1963.

Untainted by corruption and doomed to failure under the combined onslaught of government, owners and white miners, the struggle of the African miners for a living wage had the epic quality of a mass movement of industrial serfs who risked life and liberty for elementary justice. The basic cash wage per shift of an underground worker was 2s. in 1942, as compared with 1s. 8d. in 1936 and 2s. 6d. in 1890. Yet the government specifically excluded mine labourers from the compulsory cost of living allowance paid by employers in terms of war measure 28 of 1941.

The excuse given was that men housed in compounds received free quarters and food as part of their wage. Yet, as the African Mine Workers' Union told Smuts by letter on 12 September 1941, miners were paying inflated prices for boots, blankets, cigarettes and food purchased to supplement the compound rations. Moreover, and this was a major complaint, the rise in prices had seriously affected the peasant families of migrant workers. By removing the discrimination against African miners, the union argued, the government would give the people some reason to believe its claim that the war was being fought 'for a better world, for democracy, for a secure and better living for every human being'.

The union was then being revitalized by an organizing committee appointed at a conference held on 3 August 1941 in Johannesburg on the initiative of the Transvaal African National Congress, and attended by eighty-one delegates from thirty-nine trade unions, Communist party branches, the Non-European United Front and the S.A. Institute of Race Relations.[48] The moving spirits were S. P. Matseke, the Transvaal chairman of the ANC; Gauer Radebe, a member of the congress executive and of the Communist party; and James Majoro, a clerk on the Nourse mines and leading member of the African Mine Clerks' Association. The Chamber had refused to pay the statutory cost of living allowance to the clerks and other employees who were not housed in compounds. Bitterly aggrieved, many clerks supported the union and influenced the 'boss boys', and through them the working miners, to follow its lead; but the organization had to be built slowly and under great difficulties by means of direct individual contacts.

The formation in 1942 of the African Gas and Power Workers' Union, representing men employed by the Victoria Falls Power Company which supplied electricity to mines along the Reef, introduced an important factor. Excluded from a wage determination in November for unskilled labourers, the union's members submitted a demand for £1 15s. a week and, when this was refused, struck work in December at the Rouxville power station. The company then agreed to negotiate but would not make any concession, allegedly because it would spark off similar demands by the miners. Both unions thereupon urged Madeley to refer the dispute to an arbitrator or the wage board.

In response to this pressure, the government announced in February 1943 that it had appointed the Witwatersrand Mine Natives' Wages Commission under the chairmanship of Justice Lansdowne to investigate wages and conditions of Africans employed on gold mines. Its terms of reference were extended in July to include employees of the V.F.P. company. The commission began its inquiries in May and reported to the government in December. J. B. Marks, who had taken over the presidency of the miners' union early in the year, launched a vigorous recruiting drive with the assistance of Majoro, the union's secretary. Organizers were appointed and meetings were held along the Reef. In 1944 the union claimed to have more than 25,000 registered members, each paying 1s. enrolment fee and a monthly subscription of 6d.

A strike of 2,600 power station employees in January revealed their mood of resentful impatience. They had tried for twelve months to reach a peaceful settlement, the union declared, and were not prepared to wait any longer. 'Our strike is now the responsibility of the Company and the government. The V.F.P. Company made £1,250,000 profit last year. We are expected to live on 16s. a week!' Members of the Native Military Corps were used to break the strike; and the strikers went back to work with a promise that improvements resulting from the Lansdowne commission would be made retrospective to 1 January.[49]

The commission rejected the company's argument that its African employees should receive the same wage as the miners because the mines were its largest customers. The V.F.P.

workers, the commission recommended, should be brought under the wage determination for unskilled labourers and receive 25s. a week and two weeks' annual leave on full pay. As for the miners, the commission proposed an increase of 5d. a shift, a cost of living allowance of 3d. a shift, a boot allowance of 3s. per thirty completed shifts, and overtime pay at the rate of time and a half. Permanent employees should receive a cost of living allowance of 5d. a shift and two weeks' paid leave a year. The cost of these improvements to the mine owners was estimated at £2,642,000 a year.[50]

The government and Chamber of Mines accepted the commission's recommendation on overtime pay; rejected the proposed cost of living allowance, boot allowance and paid annual leave; and granted increases of 4d. and 5d. per shift for surface and underground workers respectively. This would mean an increase of £1,850,000, or 7d. per ton milled in working costs. The commission had pointed out that the industry, which distributed £17,000,000 a year to its shareholders and contributed £27,500,000 in direct payment to the state, could well afford an additional £2,600,000 in wages to its lowest paid employees. Smuts disagreed, and told parliament that the government would assist the mines by refunding the proceeds of the gold realization charge of 32s. per ounce of fine gold.[51] Taxpayers and not mine owners were to bear the cost of the wage increase.

Employees of the Victoria Falls Power Company would receive no more than the increase of 4d. a day awarded to surface workers on the mines. That, said the union, meant a miserable weekly wage of 14s. plus 4s. cost of living allowance. The union threatened strike action. Smuts told the Trades and Labour Council that any further increase would 'create uncontrollable consequences and lead to great dissatisfaction among the mine workers'.[52] The African miners' union called a conference in August 1944 which was attended by 700 delegates and 1,300 members from every mine along the Reef. Marks told them that 'the whole system of colour discrimination, segregation and oppression directed against the African people was powerfully supported by the Chamber of Mines'. Backed by Dr Xuma, the

ANC president. Victor Poto, paramount chief of Pondoland Lekhotla la Bafo and other leaders, the conference declared that the government's proposals were 'hopelessly inadequate'; demanded a wage board inquiry; and undertook to continue the struggle for the union's recognition.[53]

Though generally in favour of African unions, the Lansdowne commission deplored the influence of communists and considered that miners 'had not yet reached the stage of development which would enable them safely and usefully to employ trade unionism'.[54] This, the union told the commission, was a 'complete misconception' and contrary to its own experiences. Whereas the Chamber maintained that compound managers dealt adequately with individual grievances, the union cited cases of 'barbaric treatment' meted out to workers by managers or their subordinates; and asked for the abolition of the compound system. It tended to cause overcrowding, unbalanced diets, the neglect of sick and injured workers, and ill treatment by the mine police.[55] The *Guardian* published extracts from the union's memorandum and was sued for libel by four companies. They claimed £10,000 damages each and were awarded £750 with costs, which the paper paid out of donations from readers and supporters at home and abroad.

The Chamber refused to negotiate with the union, instructed officials to ignore its letters, planted a spy in its council and victimized its members. The government struck a more serious blow in August, soon after the conference, by enacting war measure 1425 which prohibited gatherings of more than twenty persons on proclaimed mining ground. Forced back into a state of doubtful legality, the union held clandestine meetings at night under mine dumps. The ban, observed Marks, was 'the beginning of the undoing of the union'. The collection of subs and the registration of new members became almost a physical impossibility. Arrests and assaults of organizers and union leaders were the order of the day. An all-out attempt was made to drive the union out of existence.[56] A deputation from the ANC, Labour party and Non-European TUC interviewed Colin Steyn, the minister of justice, in November 1945 and asked him to withdraw the measure. He was sympathetic, he said, and assured them that the position would be reviewed; yet the ban was renewed, and expired only on 30 June 1956, more than ten years after the end of the war.[57]

Added to these troubles was a food shortage in 1945 that led to the reduction of rations in the compound and the substitution of limited quantities of canned beef for fresh meat. The Chamber of Mines paid a tribute to the men for 'their reasonable and peaceful acceptance' of the cuts; but patience wore thin towards the end of the year as peasant families, sorely stricken by famine, appealed to husbands and sons for an increased remittance. Miners complained of not being able to supplement their reduced rations, and went on deputations to compound managers. Police attacked a group of protesting miners outside the compound kitchen of Modderfontein East mine in March 1946, killed one man and injured forty. More than 2,000 delegates from shafts and compounds attended a conference called by the miners' union in April and resolved to demand a minimum wage of 10s. a day, adequate food and the withdrawal of war measure 1425.[58]

One-day protest strikes broke out when miners presenting these demands met with a blank refusal. Commenting on the disturbances, the native affairs department issued a denial in May of rumours that the government intended to ask the Chamber to grant an increase of pay. As in 1922, Smuts decided to 'let things develop' and ignored all warnings and appeals for his intervention. The climax came in August. On Sunday the 4th, some 1,000 delegates from the Rand mines attended an open air conference and decided to call a strike on the 12th. The proceedings were widely publicized, but mine owners and government refused to credit Africans with the capacity to organize concerted action on a large scale in defiance of the elaborate system of surveillance, intimidation and espionage that operated in the compounds.

The Chamber took precautions. On 10 August it agreed with representatives of the white mining unions and the Trades and Labour Council on measures to prevent flooding and a breakdown of power in the event of a strike.[59] Encouraged by the willingness of white workers to scab, the Chamber refused to negotiate with the African miners' union. Migratory, tribal, peasant miners, the gold producers' committee argued in November, were 'not yet sufficiently advanced for trade union-ism'. They did not want a trade union, 'had fallen an easy prey to control by alien interests', and showed 'a serious element of irresponsibility' in demanding 10s. a day.[60]

In reality, the mine owners crushed every attempt by the men to think for themselves, follow leaders of their own choosing, and act collectively for the achievement of aims freely adopted. The Chamber, said the committee, pursued the national policy of European trusteeship and the preservation of tribal society. 'Conflict between the allegiance demanded by a trade union and those owed to the tribe would tend to disrupt tribal life, a result diametrically opposed to the basic principle of national policy.' This was an astounding and impudent distortion of the actual policy adopted by a gigantic organization that over the years had sucked millions of men, at the height of their manhood, into the degrading life of compounds situated in the midst of the most urbanized, sophisticated and depraved society in Africa.

The Chamber devoted six lines of print in its annual report to the strike which, it said, had led to a stoppage of work by 76,000 men for a wage of 10s. a day. 'There were instances of violence on the part of some of the strikers which necessitated police intervention. The strike was spasmodic and within four days all the Natives had returned to work. The mines involved suffered serious loss owing to the full or partial cessation of mining operations.'[61] The austerity of the comment masked the fact that this was the biggest strike and one of the most shameful episodes in South Africa's long record of repression.

A huge army of peasant workers had sacrificed health and life in the bowels of the earth for sixty years. On the owners' own showing, the miner's wage was not sufficient to keep himself and his family alive. The mines were being subsidized by peasant families throughout the sub-continent, who produced from forty-five to sixty per cent of their household income and depended for the rest on money earned by the working miner. The owners, shareholders, industrialists, merchants and farmers of South Africa owed much of their wealth to this gross exploitation. For it was a proud claim of the mining interests that gold made a major contribution to the country's economic growth and prosperity.

The African miners had not shared in the prosperity. When they struck for a wage that fell far short of the value of their contribution to the national income and the shareholders' dividends, they were forced back to work by police and compound officials who drove them out of their rooms, beat them with clubs and rifles, and fired on them when they gathered outside the compounds or marched in procession to claim their passes with a view to returning home. Their leaders were arrested and charged with breach of contract, or public violence, or violation of the Riotous Assemblies Act or war measure 145.

Clinging obstinately to the stand taken up during the years of organization and pressure for a peaceful settlement, mine owners and government used force to break the strike. It demonstrated the miners' will and capacity to organize and the importance of their role in the industry. In 1922, when all white miners stopped work, the mines maintained a measure of production. The Africans' strike in contrast brought twelve mines, where the stoppage was complete, to a standstill and partially paralysed nine others.

Most of the stoppages began on Monday the 12th; the last of the strikers to return to work did so on Saturday the 17th; and the strike was broken on the 15th, when the police went into action with rifles and clubs. Nine Africans were reported to have died and 1,248 injured in the clashes, but the actual number of casualties was never made known. No policeman or civilian was attacked, and no property was damaged. All the violence came from the police. The government refused to appoint a commission of inquiry, the Chamber never reported fully on the strike, and the African miners' union was nearly destroyed by the arrests and prosecutions that followed.

Our account of the actual course of the strike must be confined to a few of the significant events described in the press and by the prosecution's witnesses at trials of members of the Communist party's central committee.[62] The police arrived at Sub Nigel mine on 12 August at 8 a.m. to find 1,500 strikers sitting in their dormitories in the compound. The manager called for the arrest of five ringleaders, but the police advised against the action and sent for reinforcements. When these came, the native commissioner was addressing the men, who shouted him down and returned to their rooms where they remained until the next day. The police were called in again, arrived at 8.30 a.m., and found the strikers sitting, standing, talking, dancing or waving sticks on an embankment outside the compound. The police began to encircle them, whereupon they advanced and threw sticks. Unarmed police recruits and African constables took to their heels, while the police with arms fired on the strikers. They turned and fled to the compound in such panic that many were jammed in the gates. Four Africans died from being trampled on, one man was shot dead, and ten or twelve were wounded by bullets.

The men went down the Nigel mine on the 15th; while 1,000 staged a sit-down strike in the stopes. Favoured by the cramped space, policemen attacked the strikers, broke them up into small groups, and drove them up stope by stope, level by level, until they reached the surface, where they were confronted by a large reinforcement of police. A similar sit-down strike took place on the same day in the City Deep mine after the men had been shepherded to the shaft heads. Once underground they refused to work. The police then drove them back to the compound, using their batons freely in a general stampede and injuring some fifty strikers.[63]

Police armed with fixed bayonets attacked groups of demonstrators and hunted strikers who fled into the veld rather than go down the mine. A large body of some 4,000 men set out from West Springs towards Johannesburg on Tuesday the 13th. The police intercepted them, fired on them and, fanning out, herded them back to the compounds. The incident figured prominently in the trials as alleged evidence of a plot to attack the city, though the prosecution could establish no motive other than an intention to recover passes from the Witwatersrand Native Labour Association and for a return home to the villages.

There were many reasons for the failure of the strike: insufficient preparation, tactical weaknesses, the early arrest of the union's leaders, poor communications between the union and the strikers, their virtual isolation in the compounds which were turned into armed fortresses, and the violence of the police. It was no small achievement, however, for the men to have lifted a corner of the veil of professed benevolence and parental care that the Chamber had drawn over conditions on the mines. The attacks on unarmed men, the employment of some 2,000 policemen to drive strikers back to work, and the refusal to allow men to return to their villages – all this went to show that the mines employed forced labour on a vast scale. Neither the Chamber nor the government could afford to let it be known that the miners had real and substantial grievances. It was necessary to find a scapegoat.

Smuts 'was not unduly concerned', he told the Transvaal head committee of the United party on the third day of the strike, because, he said, it 'was not caused by legitimate grievances but by agitators' who were 'trying to lead the natives and the country to destruction'. Africans had to be 'protected from these people'; and he would 'take steps to see that these matters were put right'.[64] He had in mind the usual dreary round of police harassment, raids, arrests and prosecutions. Marks, the chairman of the miners' union, was arrested on the second day, together with other union officials, distributors of leaflets, and strikers. The arrest of James Philips, chairman of a general strike committee, and members of the Non-European Trade Union Council, followed. By Friday the 16th, eighty-eight persons had appeared in the Johannesburg magistrate's court for alleged breaches of the Riotous Assemblies Act or of the Native Labour Regulation Act.

The decision to call a general strike was taken on the 13th at a meeting over which Marks was presiding when the police burst in and arrested him. The strike committee issued leaflets which the police confiscated; called meetings which the magistrate banned; and met with a positive response only from Coloured workers at two tobacco factories, who were beaten up and dispersed by the police.[65] Miners were told that the general strike was coming to their aid; but 'the courage was ebbing out', a participant noted, and with it the confidence that had inspired the moving spirits.[66] Daniel Koza and Gana Makabeni urged the committee to dissolve when it met at Orlando on the 17th; and withdrew after it had rejected their proposal. The rump adjourned in a mood of despondency and could not be brought together again.

The parallels with the 1922 strike come irresistibly to mind.[67] On both occasions communists were in the vanguard, directing operations, writing, printing and distributing leaflets, exhorting the masses to stand fast and to extend the strike. In 1946, as in 1922, a proposed general strike fizzled out, and the miners were left to battle on their own. The white miners fought harder, with greater violence and more skill, but they, too, went down to defeat before the state's armed force, in spite of material and moral backing from the whole labour movement and the Nationalist party. In 1946 the Labour party's national council, local committees of the Trades and Labour Council, and a group of prominent white liberals denounced the police terror and called for negotiations between miners and mine owners.[68] The national executive of the TLC, or those who spoke in its name, responded to a request for information from the World Federation of Trade Unions with a cable reading: 'Appears natives were misled by irresponsible people. Police methods controlling strike drastic but warranted. Such action was necessary to maintain law and order and prevent chaos.'[69]

Both strikes had repercussions that tended to deflect currents of class struggle into channels of nationalism. The strike of 1922 led to an alliance between white labour and Afrikaner nationalism; that of 1946 to an alliance between communists and African nationalism. By means of political power, the white miners achieved their aim of sheltered employment behind statutory colour bars under the Nationalist-Labour pact government. African miners suffered a lasting defeat. Their strike was followed by the dissolution of the Native Representative Council; the prosecution of communists and the suppression of their party by statute; the formation of the Congress Alliance; and the emergence under a Nationalist party government of a police state using fascist techniques to entrench white supremacy and extend a colonial empire.

25 The Police State

'You can do what you like, you can shoot us, arrest us, imprison us, but you are not going to break our spirit,' said Paul Mosaka in the Native Representative Council, when it met in August 1946 at the height of the miners' strike. 'We shall continue fighting for our rights until the day dawns when we shall have the right to live like human beings in the land of our birth, in the land that is ours.'[1] An energetic businessman in Johannesburg and co-founder with senator H. Basner of the African Democratic party, Mosaka voiced the feelings of all the elected councillors. He condemned the 'wanton shooting by the police' and blamed the strike on the government's refusal to recognize African trade unions. On a motion introduced by Dr Moroka, the council unanimously deprecated 'the Government's postwar continuation of a policy of Fascism which is the antithesis and negation of the letter and spirit of the Atlantic Charter and the United Nations Charter'; called for the abolition of all discriminatory legislation affecting non-Europeans; and decided to adjourn the council in protest.[2]

This defiant mood was also evident in the African National Congress. Meeting in October, it dismissed an appeal by Kadalie and Msimang to organize yet another petition to parliament. An overwhelming majority of the 500 delegates voted instead for a motion introduced by Moses Kotane, general secretary of the Communist party, and Anton Lembede, leader of the ANC Youth League. Their resolution urged Africans to struggle for full citizen rights, and to boycott elections to the NRC and to parliament.[3] It appeared to be a drastic reversal of policy; yet as events would show, the African elite were not prepared to cut themselves off from the 'toy telephone' of the

Native Representative Council, or to surrender the prospect of office, salary and a political platform.

The council reassembled on 20 November to hear the acting prime minister, J. H. Hofmeyr, deliver the government's reply. He rebuked councillors for making 'violent and exaggerated statements' and refused to entertain the idea of repealing discriminatory laws. Legislation to recognize African trade unions was being drafted, he said, but they would not be permitted on the mines. The rebuff caused much resentment, which councillors expressed during a week of fruitless argument. Unable to extract 'a more reassuring' statement of the government's intention to bring its policy 'into line with the changing conditions of African life', the councillors abandoned the session, in order, they said, to consult with the people.[4]

The people, speaking through delegates to the ANC's annual conference in December, called for a boycott. So also did the Communist party's conference in January 1947, though with an implied reservation. Doubting both the tactical value of a boycott and the ANC's determination to see it through, the party agreed only to 'participate in any active campaign to make this decision effective'. Communists on their own could not conduct a boycott campaign, Kotane explained. 'The initiative came from and will in future have to come from African organizations.'[5] Edwin Mofutsanyana was more explicit. Boycotts, he argued, were a method of struggle and not a principle of policy. They might be an effective weapon if and when 'there exists a situation in which the masses are organizing and mobilizing for a new upsurge against the existing order of society, and from which can emerge a real – not verbal, but active – struggle for State power'.[6]

Apart from any differences of theory, communists had a practical objection to a rigorous boycott policy. Being a non-racial party, they could take part in elections at many levels. African communists sat on advisory boards and contested elections to the NRC. Coloured communists stood for election to municipal councils in the Cape. White communists fought in municipal, provincial and parliamentary elections. The party had a long electioneering tradition and was intent on putting its policy of racial equality under socialism before all sections of the population. It was a class party, argued H. A. Naidoo, a member of the central committee, and should not tail behind the national organizations or become so closely identified with them as to lose its independence. Its purpose was to lead persons of all races and nations towards a united socialist South Africa.[7]

The communists loyally refrained from contesting a Transkeian by-election in June 1947. Douglas Buchanan, a prominent white liberal, was returned unopposed in the teeth of a strong boycott movement.[8] It was apparent that no boycott could be complete; and to succeed in raising the level of political understanding, the campaign should be conducted by a resolute and single-minded body of activists. The communists drew this conclusion and noted with misgiving that members of the Native Representative Council had discussed their future with Smuts in May. He would make no promises, he emphasized, and was merely throwing out 'a bone for the Council to chew on'; but he suggested an enlarged and wholly elective council with subordinate legislative powers. Six months later the caucus of elected councillors issued a statement spurning the bone; though they did not call for the dissolution of the council. They proposed instead that it be given wider powers; and that Africans in the north be allowed to elect white representatives to parliament and provincial councils. The only acceptable policy, said the councillors, was one that would give their people a sense of security and recognize them as 'citizens of this country and not things apart'.[9]

Hofmeyr was prepared to concede that claim in principle. Africans, he told parliament, were integrated as wage earners, consumers and taxpayers into a single society with whites and shared some of their interests. By standards of elementary justice and for the sake of the white man's own security, Africans were entitled to a measure of political representation according to their state of development.[10] It was a logical, eloquent and futile appeal. The Nationalist opposition declared that the Native Representative Council was 'a breeding ground of agitators'; and demanded racial segregation – 'politically, residentially and as far as practicable, also industrially'. The

Nationalist view prevailed. Smuts had thrown away such opportunities as the war presented to broaden the basis of the franchise, strengthen his party and move towards an open society.

African leaders persisted in their efforts to open the door by appealing for inter-racial collaboration on the basis of justice, goodwill and social realism. Their reluctance to force the issue to breaking point came to the surface at the ANC's thirty-fifth annual conference in December. Delegates were in two minds about the boycott but agreed that Congress had failed to mobilize people behind its policy. Oliver Tambo of the Youth League and Gana Makabeni suspected that some leaders had deliberately sabotaged the decision; Xuma doubted its wisdom; and Mofutsanyana complained that there was no discipline in Congress. 'A positive boycott,' he said, 'must be one in which the leaders go to the people in town and country.'[11]

A compromise resolution was adopted by sixty-seven votes to seven. It affirmed the boycott in principle and nullified it in practice. To advise the electorate to abstain from voting, conference agreed, would cause great confusion, divide their ranks and leave the field clear for collaborators to undermine the campaign. Congress would intensify the boycott campaign, and the most effective way of attaining this objective was to work for the return of sitting councillors as far as possible and to secure the election of others on a boycott ticket. The resolution left the field wide open to all candidates for office under the Representation of Natives Act.

The act was a vicious piece of racial discrimination which cloaked the country's undemocratic social order, declared the Communist party at its annual conference in January 1948. Parliament would continue to perpetuate backwardness and oppression as long as the vote was denied to Africans, Coloured and Indians. The primary aim of communists in the forthcoming general election would be to bring about the defeat of the pro-fascist Nationalist party, advance the struggle for a universal franchise, and rally the people for socialist democracy. The party would put up its own candidates for parliament and support those candidates in elections to the Native Representative Council who pledged themselves to work for the abolition of the council, the repeal of the act, and the introduction of universal franchise. Edwin Mofutsanyana, Alpheus Maliba and A. S. Damana would represent the party in the NRC elections.[12]

The conference also demanded the withdrawal of criminal charges then pending against members of the central executive as a direct consequence of the strike by African miners in 1946. Detectives had raided the party's offices in Cape Town and Johannesburg on 16 August during the strike. Ten days later a preparatory examination was opened in Johannesburg against forty-seven men and five women, who were charged under the Riotous Assemblies Act and war measure 145. It was the biggest political trial since 1922 and the most representative in the country's history. The accused included 31 Africans, 11 whites, 6 Indians, 3 Coloured and 1 Chinese. At least twenty-nine were communists, among them Moses Kotane, the party's general secretary, Danie du Plessis, secretary of the Johannesburg district committee, and the other ten whites on trial. One was advocate Bram Fischer, grandson of the first prime minister of the Orange Free State. The Africans included J. B. Marks and J. J. Majoro of the African miners' union; Gilbert Coka and sixteen other members of the African National Congress. Dr Yusuf Dadoo, chairman of Johannesburg's district committee and president of the Transvaal Indian Congress, had been brought under escort from Newcastle, Natal, where he was serving a sentence of imprisonment for his part in the passive resistance campaign against the ghetto act.

The trial ended in an anti-climax on 16 September. Kotane and five other accused were discharged. The remaining forty-six, having pleaded guilty to aiding an illegal strike, were fined £15 or £50, half of which was suspended. It was evident that the government had made up its mind to go after bigger game. On the 21st, police officials acting on instructions from Harry Lawrence, the minister for justice, swooped down on radicals in the six largest towns and removed papers, letters, pamphlets and books. It was the biggest police raid to date and extended to many private homes as well as to the offices of left trade unions, the Springbok Legion, the *Guardian*, the central and district committees of the Communist party.

The party's executive committee accused the government of pursuing a political vendetta. 'With an eye on the impending by-elections and the future General Election, the Government is trying to steal the thunder of the Nationalists, who for years have been creating the bogey of a "communist menace".' Then too, the government was subservient to the gold mining interests, those die-hard opponents of progress, who objected both to trade unions for low-paid workers and to democratic rights for all sections of the population. Worst of all was the dangerous trend revealed by the raid towards administrative lawlessness. 'It is a trend paralleled by the developments in Italy, Germany and other countries that resulted in Fascism. Unless checked by the united forces of democracy, the Government's policy must similarly result in Fascism here.'[13]

After two months spent in working through the huge mass of documents, the police arrested eight members of the central executive committee in Cape Town: W. H. Andrews, the national chairman; Moses Kotane, the general secretary; Fred Carneson, secretary of the Cape district committee; I. O. Horvitch, who succeeded Andrews as chairman in 1949; Lucas Phillips, an African trade union secretary; Betty Radford, editor of the *Guardian*; H. J. Simons and Harry Snitcher. They appeared in the magistrate's court on 16 November and were remanded for a preparatory examination, which opened on 20 January with a dramatic and misleading propaganda statement by the public prosecutor, Dr Percy Yutar.[14]

The crown, he said, would bring a charge of sedition as a result of the miners' strike during August 1946; and perhaps an even more serious charge relating to the securing of classified military information. Evidence would be led to show that the party had 'secret police' and a 'military bureau'; and that there was talk of building a 'proletarian army'. Because of financial difficulties and a decline in membership, he suggested, the party had made a desperate bid for the support of Africans. It became more militant and attempted to gain control of trade unions, particularly the African miners' union, whose secretary, J. B. Marks, sat on the Johannesburg district committee. In the event, Dr Yutar maintained, the party had engineered the strike as part of a plot to overthrow the government and substitute a communist regime by means of 'revolutionary upheavals for the seizure of political power by the workers'.

The supposed breach of the Official Secrets Act turned out to be a legal technicality relating to appeals for a boycott of boats carrying cargo to troops in Indonesia. What the prosecution called 'secret police' were in fact the Springbok Legion, which had no organizational ties with the party. The number of party members in good standing fell from 2,000 to 1,800 between January and November 1946, but the decline could not be regarded as serious or permanent. As for the sedition charge, it became evident during the twenty-four days of the preliminary trial that the prosecution relied mainly on obscure passages in letters exchanged between the Johannesburg district committee and the central executive on the likelihood of a strike by African miners.

As far back as May, the district committee had drawn up a plan of campaign involving the formation of five broad non-party committees to assist in the event of a strike. On receiving the report, the central executive hastily instructed its Johannesburg office to postpone further action pending discussions with the general secretary. Any decision to strike had to be taken by the miners' union and not by the party. A subsequent letter suggested, in somewhat cryptic language for security reasons, that the entire trade union movement on the Rand should be mobilized to induce the mine owners to negotiate. If all else failed, and a strike appeared to be unavoidable, it should be conducted by trade union leaders in cooperation with the miners' union and other sympathetic parties.[15]

The accused elected to give evidence at the preliminary hearing and were subjected to an exhaustive inquiry about their policy, the role of communists in trade unions, and their attitude to strikes. The party stood for unity of workers regardless of colour, Dr Simons told the court, and had made 'a singular contribution to the labour movement in the promotion of racial harmony'. Communists were required to be active in the unions for which they were eligible and had done much to organize unskilled and semi-skilled Africans, Coloured and Indians. 'A good Communist must win the confidence of the workers by proving that he is a good trade unionist, honest and reliable.' But it was not the party's function or intention to decide policy for the unions, control them, call workers out on strike or for that matter tell them not to strike. 'This would be construed as interference, and the Party policy was not to interfere with trade unions.'

The strike, said witnesses for the defence, was a genuine and justifiable protest against exploitation and bad treatment. Senator Basner, the parliamentary representative of Africans in the Transvaal and Orange Free State, told the court that the authorities were well aware of the miners' discontent. Marks and Majoro had reported to him in May 1946 that the men were threatening to strike whether or not the union agreed. He then tried to persuade Dr Steyn, the minister of justice, to set up a board of arbitration, but without success. The strike would have been avoided at that stage, the senator thought, if any small increase had been offered. To receive a living wage, the miner required four times his existing rates of pay, or something like the 10s. a day demanded by the union. To make that possible, the government would have to reorganize the industry, in which it was a major partner.

Dr Yutar rejected the defence's explanation. 'The African mine workers,' he argued, 'constituted a very fruitful and ripe field for the Communist Party. There were 400,000 of them in one bloc, and it would be possible for the Communist Party to make and win demands for them, win their support and so strengthen the union and the party.' He inferred that J. B. Marks, the union's president, 'received his instructions from the Johannesburg District Committee with the approval of the Central Executive Committee'. The magistrate thereupon committed the accused for trial on charges of sedition arising from the strike and of contravening the Official Secrets Act in the 'Hands Off Java' campaign of October 1945.

Seven of the original accused and two others appeared before a special court in Johannesburg on 16 October.[16] They objected to irregularities in the proceedings; the court upheld the exceptions; the prosecutor withdrew the charges; and the police re-arrested the accused in open court. After a fresh preparatory examination had taken place in December, the accused were again committed on a charge of sedition and stood trial in Johannesburg on 3 May 1948.[17] The seditious element, said the attorney general, flowed largely from the basic principles of communism. The African miners' union, he contended, was a concealed wing of the party; the strike had been engineered by the Johannesburg district committee; and the central executive had conspired to initiate the strike, which resulted in the use of violence against the state authority.

There was no doubt of the party's strong and continuing interest in the miners' union since the pioneering work carried out by Bunting and Thibedi in 1930. A fresh start was made in 1940 by the party's national conference, which gave the Johannesburg district 'a particular duty' to organize the miners. Reporting on progress a year later, Michael Harmel, the district secretary, explained that the party could not manage on its own. 'The African miners are cut off from the rest of the people, are constantly changing and going back to the countryside.' Moreover, the Chamber of Mines behaved as though trade unionism on the mines was illegal. That attitude should be challenged, he urged, by means of a broad and public campaign. The issue concerned all sections of the working class because the organized strength of 300,000 miners would benefit national liberation and the trade union movement. 'It is our duty to bring the realization of these facts to every worker and particularly to every Non-European.'[18]

As a result, the Transvaal African Congress called a conference in June 1941 for the purpose of electing a committee to organize the miners. This was done. The union soon developed a momentum of its own, and became an autonomous body, paying its way and making its decisions without external control. To support his contention that the union was no more than a concealed wing of the Communist party, the prosecutor relied on mere inference and the fact that Marks belonged to the party. He omitted to point out that Marks was also a member of the ANC's national council.

The prosecution never could trace a causal link between the

central executive committee and the strike, or establish the element of unlawful violence and political revolt that constitutes the crime of sedition. For these reasons the attorney-general failed to present a valid indictment. It was quashed in the final trial in May because, the judges said, the accused 'are entitled to know in what way they are alleged to have taken part in the gatherings where sedition is alleged to have been committed'.[19] So ended the abortive trial. The Nationalist government took office later in the month and withdrew the charges in October, two years after the first arrests of the communists.

The after-effects of the long legal battle made a greater impact than the trial itself. Unable to convict the communists by judicial process, the government outlawed them by statute and ministerial decrees. The trial created an atmosphere favourable to the enactment of the Suppression of Communism Act of 1950. That in turn led directly to an alliance between the Communist party, the African National Congress and the Indian National Congress. From the mass of documents seized during the raids, the police extracted information for the listing, banning and persecution of communists and their supporters. By and large, the miners' strike and the witch hunt conducted by the Smuts government prepared the way for a further development of the police state under the Nationalist regime.

It was a miracle, some Nationalists said when they won 'the most dramatic and astounding' election in the country's history.[20] *Die Transvaler*, then edited by Dr Verwoerd, gave praise in its leading columns to divine providence. 'That which seemed humanly impossible was possible to God who has always watched over Afrikanerdom. It behoves each and all of us who contributed to the victory to thank Him in prayer for what He has brought to pass.'[21] Believing that they had supplanted Jews as the chosen people, Afrikaners gave credit to the god of the Old Testament, the god of wrath, vengeance and jealousy against the idolators. Brandishing the sword of white supremacy, they marched under the banner of Christian nationalism to their Jerusalem of Afrikaner domination.

Malan's Nationalists and Havenga's Afrikaner party had joined forces in an electoral pact. Profiting from the bias in favour of rural constituencies and an advantageous delimitation, they obtained seventy-nine seats with a minority vote of 443,700. Opposition candidates polled 623,500 votes and won 71 seats, of which 65 went to the United party and 6 to Labour.[22] The Nationalists scored their biggest gains in country districts of the Transvaal and Cape; and took eight seats on the Witwatersrand and five in Pretoria.[23] 'The Nationalist party is no longer on its way to the city,' they exulted. 'It has arrived.'[24] A large proportion of voters in the party's urban constituencies were Afrikaner miners, railwaymen, transport, factory and steel workers. The Labour party retained four seats on the Rand and two in Natal with the backing of the United party; but the Nationalists were becoming the political representatives of the white working class.

That was a major theme in the Nationalists' pre-election propaganda. The worker, they said, was the 'nerve-centre and driving-force' in economic life, no less necessary than capital, and entitled to the special care of the state. A Nationalist government would discourage class war; defend the national interest against organized money power; guarantee the worker a proper wage; insure him against unemployment, accidents and illness; protect him from communist domination in trade unions; enforce racial segregation in the unions; and exclude Africans who were 'obviously not fit for trade unionism'. The Nationalists claimed that they had for years championed the cause of labourers in the civil service, railways, factories, mines. 'And now that the last remains of the Labour Party has fallen into the lap of the capitalistic United Party, the National Party has become absolutely indispensable to the worker.'[25]

The Nationalist party was no less indispensable to the pale skins of the ruling race, said Malan when he announced his election platform on 20 April.[26] 'Will the European race in the future be able and also want to maintain its rule, its purity, its civilization; or will it float until it vanishes for ever, without honour, in the black sea of South Africa's Non-European population?' Only a Nationalist victory, he warned, could save the whites from coloured blood, the black peril and the red menace. Communism was their greatest enemy and the Smuts-Hofmeyr government its best agent. Communist agitators and foreign influences had raised the demand for the removal of apartheid measures to a dangerous level of intensity. If they took office, the Nationalists would dissolve the Communist party; deport Indians; segregate the Coloured, with privileges over the African; do away with the Native Representative Council and with parliamentary representation of Africans, bar them from white universities and exclude those who were 'redundant' from the towns.

The communists proclaimed that their message of workers' unity, racial equality and socialism had made a deep impression. Future historians, wrote Kotane on the occasion of the party's twenty-sixth anniversary, would no doubt pay tribute to its work in educating and organizing Africans, Coloured and Indians. 'When people talk of the struggle of Non-Europeans for democracy, equality of opportunities and for full citizenship rights, they never think of this as being the result of the political education by communists.' But the Chamber of Mines, the big farmers and Afrikaner churches understood the party's role and what it meant to the people. That was why the reactionaries were calling for its suppression.[27]

Communists held leading positions in the African and Indian congresses, the Non-European TUC and the Trades and Labour Council. Active party branches functioned in country towns of the western and eastern Cape, the main centres of Natal and many towns in the Transvaal. Progress was being made also in rural areas, said Kotane, reporting on a conference – called by the Pretoria district committee in November 1947 – of delegates from Lydenburg, Middelburg, Nelspruit, Pietersburg, Pienaarsrivier and Makapanstad.[28] They complained of low wages and bad treatment on farms, evictions from reserves and municipal land, unpaid forced labour for tribal authorities, and of tribalists who compelled Christian boys to undergo circumcision rites. The problems were so diverse that the conference was unable to suggest a general solution, though it worked out a remedy in each instance. 'The important thing about the Conference,' Kotane added, 'is that some start has been made.'

Three communists – Fred Carneson in Cape Town, Danie du Plessis and Michael Harmel in Johannesburg – contested seats in the general election and were heavily defeated on a platform of votes for all. 'We have only one aim,' the party declared in its election manifesto: 'to advance the struggle of the workers of all races and religions against the capitalist class, and to build a free and equal socialist republic.' The capitalist parties sought to divide the workers by fomenting race hatred and appealing to colour prejudice. Only under socialism would it be possible to eliminate the root causes of racial conflict: poverty, ignorance, the fear of unemployment, competition for jobs and insecurity.[29]

The party blamed Smuts for the Nationalists' victory and warned that it had placed supreme power in the hands of men who were determined to stamp out the last vestiges of political freedom. Smuts, said the central committee, had prepared the way by failing to deal with fundamental issues. He had appeased the parties of reaction and resisted all attempts to broaden the basis of democracy. 'So long as the franchise is restricted largely to the European population, it will be impossible to prevent the growth of reactionary forces in our political life, based on the exploitation of the voteless Non-European majority.' The party urged trade unions and the national liberation movement to close their ranks and continue the struggle for full political and citizenship rights for all South Africans. There was no other way of guaranteeing that 'freedom will survive and flourish'.[30]

The communist cause continued to flourish in spite of the sedition trial, police harassment and the government's threats. In November 1948 Sam Kahn, one of the party's representatives on the Cape Town city council, was returned to parliament by an overwhelming majority of African voters in the western Cape.[31] His victory, wrote Stanley Silwana, a member of the YCL in 1923, 'clearly shows that the African rank and file is swinging to the Left – a warning to African leaders that they must move with the times'.[32] Kahn's election, said Kotane, enabled the party and the African people 'to have a voice, if only a lonely one, in a Parliament dominated by an arrogant, reactionary and racialistic capitalist ruling class'.[33]

The sword of Damocles was hanging over him, Kahn told the House in his maiden speech on 27 January. He was threatened with 'dual-medium liquidation', both as a communist and as a representative of Africans. Let no man imagine, he urged, that the government's real or only aim was to abolish the Communist party. 'Democracy itself is in jeopardy.' Parliament would never be able to solve the country's problems until it included the representatives and spokesmen of Africans, Coloured and Indians. They would yet break the Lilliputian knots of pass laws and apartheid. South Africa had no future unless it released the enormous productive forces that lay dormant in the people.

In March he visited the Rand and Pretoria to address a series of meetings on the theme of 'Apartheid and Equality – the Communist Party's Answer'. C. R. Swart, the minister of justice, ordered the meetings to be banned under the Riotous Assemblies Act. Members of the special branch trailed Kahn everywhere, even to the Zoo, where he guided them, he explained, because he 'had a certain nostalgia for this House'. If the government persisted in regarding the ideal of equal human rights as a danger to public peace, said Kahn, the time would come when magistrates and jack-booted policemen might read the Riot Act from pulpits where priests were preaching the doctrine of human brotherhood. Towards the end of the session, Swart banned him from attending any public gathering on the Rand for a period of one year. 'It adds insult to grievous injury,' Kahn told the House, 'that it should be done to one who is a member of Parliament.' In reply to a member who said that Johannesburg was not his constituency, Kahn retorted: 'Where there is an injustice in South Africa, there is my constituency.'

His sarcasm goaded the Nationalists beyond endurance, while his cool and systematic reasoning exposed their myths and taboos, as in the debate on the 'mixed marriages' bill, which would prohibit marriage between a 'white' and a 'not white' person. He called the bill 'the immoral offspring of an illicit union between racial superstition and biological ignorance'. Its author, Dr Dönges, minister of the interior, was the country's 'leading political misanthropologist', who had discovered a new germ, the 'bacillus blanc supremacoccus', and was now elevating melanin to the rank of a deity. Apart from the million registered Coloured, at least half a million of the officially registered whites were actually of Coloured descent. That surely was 'no mean miscegenatory feat'.

Sir de Villiers Graaff, later Smuts's successor as leader of the United party, and member for Hottentots Holland – 'a very aptly-named constituency' quipped Kahn – dealt with the bill's legal implications. Even more significant and shameful, Kahn argued, were the 'so-called master race theories' of the pigmentocrats, who would expose every marriage to the hazard that some nosey-parker might reveal a skeleton in the ancestral cupboard. There was nothing biologically disharmonious, inferior or evil about the offspring of mixed marriages. The evil lay in the social pattern that doomed them to an inferior status and deprived them of privileges which should be the inherent right of every citizen. 'Would you marry a Coloured woman?' interjected a member. 'Are you a marriage broker? Have you a client you are seeking to marry?' Kahn replied. He concluded by saying that the remarks coming from the government benches could have been lifted bodily out of the speeches of Goebbels, Streicher, Rosenberg and Hitler. They, too, were once regarded as cranks; but from their theories of racial superiority came the concentration camps, crematoria, and the conflagration that led to the slaughter of many millions.

Never before had parliament listened to so pungent and uncompromising a condemnation as Kahn's of the racial taboos, discrimination and oppression that made up the substance of apartheid policies. This was more than the Nationalists were prepared to tolerate. Using procedures laid down by the Suppression of Communism Act, the government unseated him in May 1952, together with Fred Carneson, the communist representative of Africans in the Cape provincial council. Swart simultaneously banned the *Guardian*, which promptly reappeared as the *Clarion*, and ordered leading party members – among them Kotane, Dadoo, Marks, Bopape and J. N. Ngwevela – to resign from their organizations and not to address political meetings for two years. 'What has brought me into conflict with this government,' Kahn told the House in his last parliamentary speech, 'has not been my belief in socialism or my belief in a republic, but it has been my advocacy of complete equal rights for black and white in this country. That is what I am being tried for, and they wish to make that the modern blasphemy, the twentieth-century heinous crime in politics.'[34]

African voters demonstrated their contempt for these methods by electing Brian Bunting, editor of *Advance* (the *Clarion*'s successor) to the vacant parliamentary seat in November with a record majority.[35] He was expelled in turn in October 1953 on a motion supported by the United party opposition, which had voted against Kahn's expulsion. 'It has been suggested,' said Bunting in the House, 'that I should abjure my past opinions and announce myself to be a reformed character. I am not prepared to do so. If the price I have to pay for being true to my opinions is expulsion from this House. I am prepared to pay it.' In his last speech he warned the House that when government degenerated into a tyranny, the people were historically justified in using force to overthrow it and to bring about a better social order.[36]

Africans in the Cape western division went to the polls once again in April 1954 to elect a successor to Kahn and Bunting. Ray Alexander (Mrs H. J. Simons), the banned ex-secretary of the food and canning union, contested the seat. 'If I had my way,' she told the electorate, 'an African – one of you – would be taking my place.' The campaign was in full swing when parliament hastily amended the Suppression of Communism Act so as to exclude her and any other listed communist. In spite of the discouragement, she was returned by an over-whelming majority.[37] On her attempting to enter the House, the police forcibly removed her from its precincts and then served a notice informing her that she was 'incapable' of being elected. She recovered damages for the assault but never took her seat. The voters had sacrificed their privilege of being represented, but their victory, she assured them, 'once again taught the oppressors that the people cannot be bullied into slavish sub-mission'.[38]

As much could not be said of the white labour movement. It buckled and broke under the pressures produced by the Nationalist victory of 1948. The disintegration involved three trends, each marked by bitter wrangling over the status of

African unions and the role of communists. First in order of time came the secession of Afrikaner unions centred in Pretoria. This was followed by the departure of conservative unions led by English officials, many of them foundation members of the Trades and Labour Council. The third stage resulted from action taken by the government under the Suppression of Communism Act.

Nine Pretoria unions formed the Ko-ordinerende Raad van S.A. Vakverenigings (Coordinating Council of S.A. Trade Unions) in 1948, allegedly because of the TLC's refusal to exclude Africans, and were joined a year later by the miners' union, then under the control of Afrikaner nationalists. Representing only 28,000 workers, the Raad was a small, sectarian body, yet it received preferential treatment from the government and strengthened the influence of racists in the white trade unions. The activities of the Trades and Labour Council 'have been marked by timidity, hesitation and compromise', the Communist party's central committee reported to its national conference in January 1950.[39] Instead of taking a resolute stand against the Nationalists, the council was scheming to appease them by isolating the African. He, too, was at fault and, like the white worker, should learn to place his class interests above 'national' interests. By remaining outside the TLC, the African unions had deprived it of a valuable ally against the fascists. The communists would resist the pressure of 'nationalism' from every quarter; and 'strive to bridge the gap that is widening with the impact of racialism in the trade unions'.

Intimidated and divided, the right wing had no heart to resist attacks on the low-paid workers. The new government was no more successful than its predecessor in preventing inflation. Retail price indices showed an average annual increase of eight points between 1948 and 1954 as compared with an annual increase of four points in 1937–46. An amended scale of cost of living allowances grossly favoured the higher-paid and predominantly white wage earners.[40] The government stopped the payment of family allowances to Indians in December 1948; excluded rural Africans from school feeding schemes in 1949; and reduced the food grant for African pupils in the towns from

2d. to 1½d. a day, as compared with the 6d. allowed for every white pupil, on the pretext that Africans should support themselves. An amendment in 1949 to the Unemployment Insurance Act deprived Africans earning less than £182 a year of benefits and excluded seasonal workers because, the minister of labour alleged, they would rather live on benefits than work for farmers and mine owners.[41]

The second wave of secessions from the Trades and Labour Council took place in 1949–51. Printers, engine drivers, municipal employees and Natal furniture workers left because of, they said, the TLC's 'African policy', the refusal of radicals to compromise, and more specifically 'the disharmony created by the Communistic element'.[42] To appease them, the right wing proposed to exclude politics and Africans from the council's proceedings; but the rupture became final when parliament passed the Suppression of Communism Act. Intimidated by the penalties prescribed for listed communists and fearing the effects of guilt by association, thirteen unions disaffiliated in the next six months, among them the boiler makers, iron moulders, woodworkers, electricians and bank officials.[43] In October 1951 most of the breakaway unions formed the S.A. Federation of Trade Unions. It represented sixteen unions with 80,000 members, opened its doors to all registered unions, including those with Coloured and Indian members, and barred affiliation by African unions.

Relatively strengthened by the defection of the conservatives, the militants in the TLC were able to elect Issy Wolfson as its representative to the conference of the International Labour Organization and the World Federation of Trade Unions in 1949; but the council moved sharply to the right when the Suppression of Communism Bill appeared in 1950. Though the TLC denounced the bill as a threat to trade unionism and civil liberties, the Amalgamated Union of Engineers undertook to support legislation outlawing organizations that aimed at 'a totalitarian form of government'; and Jerry Calder, the TLC's president, four members of its executive, and six other trade union leaders assured the minister of justice that they supported the bill. The council subsequently decided to assist any of its members who were unjustifiably accused of being a communist, and to show no sympathy to an avowed communist or supporter of communism.[44]

The first banning orders issued against trade unionists under the act were served in May 1952 on Wolfson and Sachs, both members of the TLC's national executive. It was then stirred into calling a conference of registered trade unions to discuss the effects of the act on the trade union movement. Africans were excluded from the conference, and this set the tone for the betrayal that followed. Some fifty delegates from the Koordinerende Raad walked out when they realized that the conference would not pass their motion of confidence in the government. Another batch, headed by the bank officials and engine drivers, followed after conference had rejected their motion of cooperation with the government. To avert more withdrawals, the militants agreed to a mild resolution urging the government to give banned trade unionists a right of appeal to the courts. George McCormick, president of the S.A. Federation of Trade Unions, congratulated the delegates for not defending communism. It was their 'bounden duty', he said, to rid themselves of the communists in their ranks, and that, he added, meant anyone who preached equality of rights for all persons irrespective of colour.[45]

A few unions, notably those of the garment, canning and laundry workers, struck work and demonstrated in protest against the removal of their banned leaders. The general body of trade unionists made no attempt to defend either their colleagues or the principle of trade union autonomy from arbitrary interference by the state authority. The Suppression of Communism Act authorized the minister of justice to prohibit any listed communist from holding office or taking part in the activities of a union. What the Nationalists had failed to do by means of slander, intrigue and subversion, they accomplished by act of parliament. By the end of 1955, the minister had driven fifty-six officials out of the unions.[46] Among them were 28 whites, 17 Africans, 7 Coloured and 4 Indians; and 9 out of 26 members of the Trades and Labour Council's national executive.

They were expelled because they championed the cause of racial equality and liberty for all South Africans. Anyone who held similar views ran the same risk, the prime minister indicated in 1952. 'All six members of the Labour Party in the House of Assembly were "Liberalistic". Some of them came very close to communism. The Native Representatives wanted equal rights for Natives in all ways and they were also not far from communism.'[47] The banned leaders 'were probably among the most competent trade union organizers in the country', and had done 'a great deal for their members', said Schoeman, the minister of labour, 'but he was determined that they should not gain control of Unions'.[48]

By eliminating the communists, the government removed the main obstacle in the trades council to the adoption of a colour bar for which racists had hankered since 1947. They wanted it more eagerly than ever to restore their numerical strength and prestige. In 1952 the council had fifty-one affiliated unions representing 82,600 workers, as compared with 111 unions and 184,000 members in 1947.[49] Snubbed and ignored by the government, the council had no representative on a committee appointed by the minister of labour in 1953 to assist him in drafting legislation for compulsory apartheid in trade unions.[50] To retrieve its fortunes and obtain official recognition, the council dissolved itself in October 1954, regrouped under the name of the S.A. Trade Union Council, and adopted a constitution that limited its members to unions 'other than those of African workers or those which include Africans'. Some of the breakaway unions – including the printers, boiler makers, woodworkers and electricians – returned to the purified fold; while the handful of unions that rejected colour bars merged with the Non-European TUC to form the S.A. Congress of Trade Unions.

'South Africa is entering a period of bitter *national* conflict,' the Communist party's central executive warned in its report to the annual conference of 1950.[51] Racial oppression and an aggressive Afrikanerdom were provoking a corresponding national consciousness in other population groups. 'On all sides the national and racial differences are being emphasized, and the realities of the *class* divisions are being obscured.' The party itself could not escape the effects of compulsory segregation and language differences. Its African membership was increasing by leaps and bounds, and tended to be concentrated in unilateral branches in the townships. A similar process of ethnic grouping could be observed among non-African party members, particularly outside the main urban centres. This was an old problem, and the party would continue as before to preserve its international class character by means of political education, general members' meetings, social functions and joint activities.

Communists were the only ones able to 'transcend racial feelings', Kotane noted in a report on violent clashes between Africans and Indians at Durban in January 1949.[52] Africans had rioted, stabbed and clubbed Indians, raped women, burnt houses, looted stores; and in turn were fired on by Indians, police and soldiers. The estimated casualties were 142 deaths – 87 of them African – and 1,087 wounded; 300 buildings were destroyed and 1,700 were damaged. The inevitable commission of inquiry put the blame on the indiscipline of urban Africans, their resentment of Indian traders and landlords, the example of lawlessness set by Indian passive resisters, and the unsettling effects of agitation by British liberals at home and abroad against racial policies.[53] Durban communists accused white racists of spreading 'poisonous anti-Indian propaganda'; while Indian and African Congress leaders traced the ultimate causes to the system of racial discrimination and 'the preaching in high places of racial hatred and intolerance'.[54]

Xuma, Naicker, Kotane and other leaders set an example of tolerance and goodwill by appealing for closer cooperation between the two communities, mutual understanding and unity in struggle for national liberation. Kotane drew attention to the effect of social inequalities. Indian businessmen, he regretted, practised segregation against Africans in tearooms and cinemas, charged exorbitant rents for shacks, grew rich in trading with Africans and yet refused to employ them as salesmen, clerks, bus drivers or conductors. High-sounding political statements meant little unless backed by the people. Africans, Indians and Coloured would achieve real unity only when they met 'as equal partners in the common struggle'.

Africans and Indians might agree on united action, but Coloured leaders of the Non-European Unity Movement held back, vented their rage on the communists, broke up their meetings in Cape Town, and charged them with 'using the liberatory struggle only to bargain with the ruling class in their essential role of collaboration and deception of the people'. It was an odd kind of collaborator who bore the main brunt of persecution by the ruling class, said the communists, and they urged the NEUM to emerge from its boycott laager for battle against the enemy.[55] The gap between the two organizations could not, however, be bridged after the collapse of the campaign in 1948 against racial segregation in Cape Town's suburban trains.

Both took part in setting up a train apartheid resistance committee to organize a civil disobedience movement. Big meetings were held, volunteers were recruited, and ten of the organizers, including Dr and Mrs Gool, B. M. Kies, and the communists Fred Carneson and H. A. Naidoo were acquitted in the magistrate's court on charges of incitement to public violence, creating racial hostility and instigating a breach of railway regulations. The communists proposed to send batches of defiers into the coaches reserved for whites, while Gool and Kies argued that only 'principled mass resistance would succeed'. It was suicidal adventurism to act before the people had been fully organized. Delay would be fatal to the campaign, said the communists, and they resigned from the committee because the majority had 'rejected our repeated requests that action be taken to defy the regulations'.[56] The Coloured had been betrayed by the 'false organizational and political concepts of the Unity Movement' and should look elsewhere for a new leadership.[57]

The Coloured teachers of the Anti-CAD and the NEUM had no taste for humiliating encounters with policemen, courts and overcrowded prison cells; and deplored the 'vulgar exhibitionism' of Indian passive resisters. Far from being 'heroes', Naicker, Dadoo and M. D. Naidoo had deserted the people in their hour of need and were contaminating them with the poison of Gandhi. The Anti-CAD was more responsible and disdained to seek 'the sanctuary of jail'.[58] Such political polemics appealed also to members of the Cape African Teachers Association. Led by A. C. Jordan, C. M. Kobus and I. Tabata in the western

Cape and by N. I. Honono and W. M. Tsotsi in the Transkei, CATA acceded to the NEUM and strengthened its resolve to gain the allegiance of Africans through the medium of the All African Convention.

Twelve African leaders issued a declaration of intent in October 1948. Alarmed at the government's 'callous disregard of the fundamental rights of Africans', they would convene an all-African conference with a view to pooling their forces on a common programme of action for liberation. The signatories included Dr Xuma, president of the African National Congress; Professor Jabavu, president of the Convention; Dr J. S. Moroka, a senior member of the Convention's executive; and the Rev. Mahabane, president of the NEUM. Dismayed by the prospect of being ousted by the proposed merger, the Coloured intellectuals denounced it as an insincere manoeuvre of liberals and reactionaries in the ANC. The only basis for principled struggle was the Ten Point programme, said the Cape western committee of the Convention, and it repudiated Jabavu's agreement to unite with Congress.[59]

A joint conference presided over by Xuma and Jabavu at Bloemfontein in December agreed to merge the two organizations in spite of strong protests by a group of NEUM delegates. I. B. Tabata proposed that the ANC should affiliate to the Convention and accept its federal structure, the Ten Point programme and a policy of 'non-collaboration with the oppressor'. That, objected Professor Matthews, meant that one mouthpiece wanted to swallow the other mouthpiece. A federation, Kotane pointed out, would perpetuate differences. 'We want to eliminate conflicting directions, interests and ideologies. We want one political organization.' The conference agreed and adopted Mahabane's motions endorsing the October statement and instructing the executives to work out the details of a unity programme.[60]

Meeting at about the same time in Bloemfontein, the Convention accepted Jabavu's resignation and installed a new president, the Fort Hare graduate, former teacher and budding lawyer, W. M. Tsotsi, who could be relied on to maintain the NEUM's role in a federation. He and other members of his executive met the ANC's leaders in April 1949 and failed to agree

on the crucial issue. The Convention wanted a federal organization embracing a wide range of African, Coloured and Indian
associations – political, religious, economic and social; while
Congress, unwilling to risk being swamped by so heterogeneous
an assortment, insisted on a national All-African organization.
This was tribalism masquerading under the banner of nationalism, said Tsotsi at the Convention's conference in December,
and he accused Congress leaders of being hostile to Coloured and
Indians as well as to whites.[61]

This was untrue, said Dr Moroka, the ANC's new president
at a meeting in Newclare, Johannesburg, in February 1950, a
week after police raids on the township had resulted in violent
clashes with the residents and the arrest of more than 600 men
and women. 'I want to assure the Coloured and Indian communities that they need have no fear of African nationalism. We
are fighting for their freedom as well as for our own, and will join
hands with those Europeans who are prepared to fight with us.'[62]
Past presidents had said as much, but his words were the more
significant because of a spate of apartheid laws and the emergence
of a hard core of militants in the African Youth League, to whom
Moroka owed his election and Dr Xuma his defeat at the annual
conference of Congress in December 1949.

The League's programme of action appeared in July over the
signatures of James Calata, A. P. Mda, G. Pitje, Robert Sobukwe
and M. Secenywa.[63] It repeated old slogans; rejected segregation, apartheid, trusteeship and white leadership; reaffirmed
Lembede's scheme of commercial and financial cooperative
enterprises; undertook to consolidate trade unions into an
industrial wing; and struck a new note by claiming the 'right of
self-determination'. The League's aim was to achieve 'national
freedom from White domination and the attainment of political
independence'.

There were obvious ambiguities in the formulation, as communists were quick to point out.[64] Self-determination and independence implied a right to secede, and that was hardly possible
unless the country were partitioned into a 'black' and a 'white'
state, which would amount to apartheid. Or did the League have
in mind the expulsion of the white population? The wording

was less important than the intention. The young militants of the ANC were feeling their way to the concept of 'black power' such as the Communist party had projected in its slogan of 'an independent native republic' in 1928.

Three leaders of the Youth League, Nelson Mandela, Walter Sisulu and Oliver Tambo, urged Xuma in December to accept their principles of African nationalism, Africa for the Africans, and a boycott of segregated institutions. The first two, he replied, were consistent with the policy of Congress since its inception, but he objected to a boycott because it would split their ranks.[65] The League thereupon threw its weight behind Moroka and secured his election on a boycott platform at the annual conference of Congress later in the month. Sisulu became the secretary general, and the programme of action was adopted as the official policy of Congress. It had taken a new turn, as events would show. The boycott decision had little effect, however, for reasons set out by the Communist party's central committee in a report to its annual conference of January 1950.

Boycotts, the party explained, might extract concessions from the ruling class when it needed cooperation, as in war or to forestall a revolutionary situation. That clearly was not the position. On the contrary, the government itself proposed to abolish the native representative council, advisory boards and the African franchise. This being so, the boycott movement tended to turn in on itself, isolate people from active struggle, and produce a negative acceptance of segregation as a despairing alternative to equality. 'For apartheid (the humiliating substitute for "the right of self-determination") does afford a protected field for a small number of Non-Europeans (traders in locations, teachers, ministers of religion, politicians, even trade union organizers) who will use national sentiment as a weapon against European competition.'

Misgivings on the efficacy of boycotts received confirmation in January 1949 when Gordon Mears, the secretary of native affairs, told councillors that the government had decided to do away with the Native Representative Council. It was merely advisory, created a sense of frustration and served no useful purpose.[66] Dr Verwoerd, the Hollander who made it his mission to rescue Afrikanerdom from British imperialism, pronounced the death sentence two years later at the council's last session. The government, he said, 'deemed it essential' to abolish the council, which would accept nothing less than equality with whites in parliament. So impotent a body was bound to produce 'irresponsible criticisms' and 'must necessarily fail'. He proposed to substitute a 'natural Native democracy' by reviving tribalism and chiefly rule in the reserves under a Bantu Authorities Act.[67]

The government had contemptuously rejected every claim advanced by the liberation movement in half a century of struggle for social justice, national unity, and equality of treatment. Arrogating to itself all the pride and power of nationhood, Afrikanerdom denied to Africans the right and opportunity to evolve from tribe to nation. Parliament was set to work, laying the statutory foundations of the ghettoes foreshadowed in the Nationalist party's election appeal for 'total apartheid as the ultimate goal of a natural process of separate development'.

There was nothing natural in the Unemployment Insurance Amendment Act of 1949, which excluded the great bulk of Africans from benefits; the Railways and Harbours Amendment Act of 1949, which enforced racial segregation in trains; the Prohibition of Mixed Marriages Act of 1949 and the Immorality Amendment Act of 1950, which outlawed sex in all its forms between pigmented and non-pigmented persons; the Population Registration Act of 1950, which classified people in racial groups according to skin colour and descent; or the Group Areas Act of 1950, which imposed compulsory residential segregation on whites, Coloured, Malays, Asians and Africans. There was nothing natural about the Suppression of Communism Act of 1950, the political cornerstone of this racial totalitarianism, which outlawed the Communist party and gave ministers dictatorial powers to ban organizations, newspapers, periodicals, gatherings and persons deemed to promote the spread of statutory communism.

'Those who are keeping us down do so not because we are Communists,' Dr Moroka told 528 delegates to a Defend Free Speech Convention at Johannesburg in March 1950, 'but because they want to exploit us, they want to eat the fat of the land alone.'[68] Called together by the Transvaal ANC, Indian Congress, APO and Communist party, the delegates demanded the removal of bans on Sam Kahn and Yusuf Dadoo, protested against the threatened pass law for women, and declared Freedom Day on I May, when people of all races would stay away from work so as to demonstrate for freedom, land and the repeal of colour bars.

The appeal went out from Moroka; from J. B. Marks, president of the African miners' union; from Gana Makabeni, president of the Non-European Trade Union Council; from Indian and communist leaders throughout the country. 'Force will be met with force,' the police commissioner threatened. And the joint secretaries of the convention, David Bopape, Yusuf Cachalia and Dan Tloome, replied that no violence was or ever had been advocated or contemplated. But violence came to the Rand on I May, as the police broke up gatherings in the evening, attacked groups of Africans who defended themselves, and fired, killing eighteen Africans and wounding more than thirty.[69]

James Moroka, a graduate of Edinburgh university, physician, landowner, businessman, and great-grandson of the Rolong chief Moroka who had sheltered the Voortrekker leader Andries Hendrik Potgieter in 1836, summoned the ANC's executive to an emergency meeting on his estate at Thaba 'Nchu in the Orange Free State. The committee decided on a national day of protest, a general strike of all freedom lovers, both to commemorate 'Africans who have lost their lives in the struggle for liberation', and to demonstrate against the Unlawful Organizations Bill, the forerunner of the Suppression of Communism Act. Though appearing to be directed against communists, declared Sisulu, the bill was designed to suppress the struggles of all oppressed peoples. The whites were determined to keep Africans in a state of permanent subordination; and the African National Congress would resist by all the means at its disposal.[70]

Dr Malan, the premier and former *predikant*, insisted that South Africa outlaw communism. He sent the bill to a select committee which returned it with stiffer penalties and more draconian powers. United party members on the committee proposed to make communism a treasonable offence punishable with death; John Christie, the Labour leader, and Mrs Ballinger, who represented Africans of the eastern Cape, voted against the measure. Its immediate purpose was to liquidate the Communist party, place its members and supporters under police surveillance, hound them out of political life and the trade unions, and reduce them in terms of civic rights to the African's status. The long-range aim was to destroy the liberation movement and entrench white supremacy behind despotic ministerial powers.

In addition to the doctrine of Marxian socialism as expounded by Lenin, Trotsky and the Third International, communism was defined as any doctrine or scheme which aimed at the establishment of a one-party state, or at changing the social order by unlawful acts, or at bringing about any change under the direction of a foreign government, or at the encouragement of hostility between whites and other races 'the consequences of which are calculated to further the achievement' of a one-party state or of social change by unlawful acts. The definition had far less significance in practice than the arbitrary discretionary powers vested in the government to ban, prohibit and deport without a right of appeal by the victim to courts of law.

'Remembering the path which has been blazed by our members for over thirty years and inspired by the example of such fighters for freedom as Nkosi, and many others, who died for their opinions, let us face boldly the renewed and perhaps more ruthless attacks which are threatened,' said Bill Andrews, then just turned eighty, in a message to the party. Its central committee lodged a firm and sombre protest with the select committee. 'Threatened with forcible disbandment, facing the prospect of endless persecution of our members, we have every right to expect from the instigators of this measure a precise statement of the charges levelled against us, the evidence on which they are based, and an opportunity to make our reply before an impartial tribunal. Instead, we have received nothing but abusive and uncorroborated statements, and a *fait accompli* in the form of a Bill.'[72]

After surveying the party's record, its policies and its relations with trade unions and the national movements, the central committee examined the long range effects of the bill. Its main aim was to stifle the demand so vigorously advocated by the party for democratic rights and equal opportunities for all. Punitive action would be taken against any organization with similar objectives. 'There can be little doubt that once the Communist Party of South Africa is outlawed, all those individuals, organizations, churches and institutions who raise the demand for an end to racial discrimination in South Africa will be branded in terms of this Bill and declared illegal.' No law could 'crush the desire of the overwhelming majority of the people in South Africa of all races for a society based on justice and equality'. No government could 'deprive those who are fighting for socialism of their passionate desire for peace and security for all, which we believe is only possible under the socialist order'.

The central committee met at Cape Town in June with the knowledge that no amount of protest would stay the enactment of the suppression law. There were seventeen members, all of whom have appeared in these chronicles: Andrews, Bunting, Carneson, Dadoo, du Plessis, Fischer, Harmel, Horvitch, Kahn, Kotane, La Guma, Marks, Mofutsanyana, Naidoo, Poonen, Simons and Wolfson. They had to decide on how best to continue the struggle. Deep-seated loyalties, communist tradition and fierce contempt for the oppressor urged them to defy. On the other hand, could the party make the transition to illegality without being annihilated? The police were in possession of its membership lists, seized during the raids of 1946; attempts to create the skeleton of an underground organization had failed. After years of activity in the full glare of publicity members could not be expected to adopt illegal methods overnight. Having joined a legal party, was it proper to expect them to incur the severe penalties prescribed by the bill without long discussion and preparation which were not possible in the circumstances. Moreover, and this weighed heavily, the experience of the German Communist party under Nazi rule had shown the difficulty involved in passing from legal to illegal work without a pause.

Except for Andrews and Harmel, who voted against the resolution, the committee decided on dissolution. Kotane and

I. O. Horvitch, the national chairman, visited each party district in turn and explained the decision. It was accepted without dissent. Sam Kahn read the declaration of dissolution in the house of assembly on 20 June.[73] 'Recognizing that on the day the Suppression of Communism Bill becomes law, every one of our members, merely by virtue of their membership, may be liable to be imprisoned, without the option of a fine, for a maximum period of ten years, the Central Committee of the Communist Party has decided to dissolve the Party as from today.'

The decision was forced on the party by a government with a majority of seven in the assembly and one in the senate – where sat the former Communist party member S. M. Pettersen, now a Nationalist senator. Voted into office by a minority of the electorate, representing at most one and a quarter million people in a population of eleven million, the government had adopted the fascist technique of destroying the democracy that it professed to defend. 'Such vestiges of democratic rights as have been left in South Africa, are being extinguished in the present Parliament by a clique in its efforts to impose a dictatorship, suppress all opposition, and remove every obstacle to a fascist republic.'

'Communism and Socialism have stood the test of time. For more than a hundred years, in one country after another, the enemies of the people have ruthlessly, inhumanly, sought to crush the movement for social justice and economic liberation, for the end of class war, for peace and socialism.' In spite of all these attempts, communism lived on, gaining in strength and stature. 'Rooted in the history of the working class, expressing their deepest aspirations and needs, Communism cannot be destroyed as long as society is divided into two worlds: rich and poor, oppressor and oppressed.' Fascism could not kill the will for the good life. 'Nothing can stop the people of South Africa in their struggle for full democracy, for removal of colour bars, for justice and for socialism.'

June 26 was declared the national day of protest and mourning. 'If ever there was a time when the African people were required to put their eight-million force behind the principles of democracy, in alliance with other freedom-loving members of the

South African community, that time has come,' urged Dr Moroka. Leaders of the Indian Congress, APO, and Communist party pledged their support and joined the ANC on a coordinating committee with Sisulu and Cachalia as joint secretaries. The Congress Alliance was taking shape. 'Never before in the history of South Africa,' Dr Dadoo noted, 'have the national leaders acted so swiftly and with complete oneness of purpose to beat back the fascist attack of the Government on the lives and liberties of the people.' They were rewriting the country's history, declared Sisulu, in a new era of liberation.[74]

The call for a general strike met with wide response on 26 June. Renamed Freedom Day, it became a focal point for resistance in later years. It was on 26 June 1952 that the African National Congress launched a campaign for the defiance of unjust laws which resulted in the imprisonment of more than 8,000 and the enactment of more repressive laws. In terms of the Criminal Laws Amendment Act of 1953, a person convicted of breaking any law by way of protest against any law could be sentenced to a maximum of £300 fine, three years' imprisonment, and ten lashes, while leaders who incited others to commit such an offence were liable to a fine of £500, five years' imprisonment and fifteen lashes. The Public Safety Act of that year authorized the government to proclaim a state of emergency amounting to martial law for a period of twelve months.

In the hour of dissolution as a legal party, the communists could claim the achievement of an objective that had been central to their purpose since 1928. The class struggle had merged with the struggle for national liberation. In its report to the last national conference before the dissolution, the central committee charted the course of struggle for the coming years.[75] It will be appropriate to present the thesis in the present tense and to examine its implications in terms of the existing society.

26 Class Struggle and National Liberation

South Africa's malaise stems from the impact of an advanced industrialism on an obsolete, degenerate colonial order. Stress and conflict are symptoms of an inner disharmony. Contradictions or antagonisms occur between the society's structure and superstructure, between the dynamic potential of a multi-racial labour force and the strait-jacket of racially segregated institutions; between the dominant collective role of Africans in the economy and their exclusion from the centres of power. Material conditions are favourable to the emergence of an open society. If productive forces were allowed free play and harmonized with social relations, skin colour would be irrelevant to status and function. A rigid racial hierarchy obstructs the birth of a free society. Some four million whites combine the privileges of a colonial autocracy with the technology and amenities of the machine age and employ coercive measures to keep fifteen million Africans, Coloured and Indians in permanent subordination.

The imperial-colonial qualities of the society, which may not be evident at first sight, become visible by comparison with the typical colony. In its normal form, the colony is a distinct territorial entity, spatially detached from its imperial metropolis, and allowed to retain as much cultural autonomy as is compatible with the interests of its absentee owners. These invest capital in the colony, promote trade and economic growth, introduce skills, create the rudiments of a modern administration, and generate social change. They also perpetuate archaic social forms among the colonial population, inhibit its spontaneous development, and impose autocratic methods of government. White settlers and officials monopolize the sources of power, all key positions and preferred occupations; appropriate far more than their fair share of educational, health and other social services;

and maintain a wide cultural gap between themselves and the darker people.

The model fits in broad outline. White South Africans do behave as though they were imperial masters of a distant colony. Yet they delude themselves. The country has in fact advanced well beyond the limits of a primitive colonialism. Nowhere else in Africa has so large a part of the population been dispossessed of land or absorbed in the capitalist economy. Africans are allowed to acquire a permanent domicile and landed property in barely more than one-tenth of the surface area. They depend wholly or largely on what they earn in the remaining nine-tenths which have been declared 'the white man's country'. This is the developed sector, containing virtually all the mines, farms, factories, towns, ports, railways and strategic centres, and could be equated with an imperial state. But it is 'white' only in terms of proprietary rights and political authority. Black and brown people outnumber the whites in almost every town and rural district.

Africans, Whites, Coloured and Asians interact on many planes and cooperate in a wide range of activities. Interdependence is not confined to the market place or to the production of goods. Behaviour patterns, institutions and ideas cut across the colour line. Significant numbers of black, brown and white South Africans hold the same religious beliefs, belong to the same kind of family organization, play the same games and pursue common political objectives. The degree of cultural uniformity is high, and would be higher but for the elaborate system of colour discrimination and compulsory segregation. The discrimination is total, and the totalitarianism reveals the extent to which South Africans have merged into a single, indivisible society.

Previous governments actively promoted integration, and used catchwords like 'guardianship' and 'trusteeship' to account for white domination. The present government turns to the vocabulary of decolonization, rejects integration and insists that it can be reversed. The ideal way to resolve racial conflict, the government argues, is to impose maximum segregation, develop autonomous ethnic communities, and concede their right to self-determination, perhaps even secession. Rather than share power with Africans, apartheiders would partition the country into small, independent states. Or so they say.

The vision has no substance. It is out of line with the historical record, unbending realities, and the aspirations of most South Africans. Apartheid dogmas are to be regarded not as a blueprint for decolonization but as a formula for freezing the society in an archaic colonial mould. They provide a pretext for total discrimination and for denying the African's claim to majority rule. Apartheid is also a party slogan, a battle cry to rally voters behind the platform of Afrikaner nationalism.

Antagonisms between Afrikaners and British dominated party politics for most of our period. The British had many initial advantages. Backed by the imperial state and representing a world-wide culture, they behaved with the arrogant assurance of conquerors. They dominated mining, industry and commerce, controlled banks and finance houses, and supplied most technical skills. Their urban culture engulfed the Afrikaner, left a permanent imprint on his style of life, fostered class divisions, introduced a liberal and a socialist radicalism, and undermined the values of his traditional agrarian society. Resisting absorption, Afrikaners acquired a national consciousness in their fight for political independence, language rights, religious cohesion and white supremacy.

They were exhorted to support *ons eie mense* – our own people; to buy from Afrikaner shopkeepers, invest in Afrikaner firms, read Afrikaans, attend Afrikaner churches, join Afrikaner societies, and participate in Afrikaner cultural activities. They were spurred into making a great national effort to catch up with the British in the business of making money, by contributing to funds established to assist Afrikaner entrepreneurs. A few of the latter were spectacularly successful, but the gap remained. Like other underdeveloped communities, Afrikaners found that national sentiment and party loyalties were not enough for a successful assault on an entrenched capitalism. Collectively and individually, they made little headway against the accumulated weight of British capital, technology, managerial experience and imperial connexions. In the event, political power proved to be more effective than private enterprise.

The Afrikaner made his great leap forward on the political front. Here he had the advantage of numerical superiority over the British, a greater cultural cohesion, a score to settle and a demonic will to rule. The British created the conditions for his success by introducing parliamentary government, the two-party system, and an all-white franchise in the northern provinces. With the vote limited to whites, sixty per cent of whom were Afrikaans-speaking, the Nationalist party needed only to consolidate the Afrikaners, or a sufficient majority, in one voting camp. The intelligentsia – politicians, *predikants*, teachers, lawyers, writers and civil servants – prepared the ground. They harped on past injustices under British rule; isolated Afrikaners in separate religious, social and economic institutions; agitated for equal language rights; pressed for total racial segregation; and carried on a remorseless vendetta against Africans, Coloured and Indians.

Afrikaners and British never allowed their antagonisms to disrupt the racial order. They manipulated Africans and Coloured for party gain, and made common cause against them in defence of white supremacy. At the crucial constitutional stages – in 1902–7 after the Anglo-Afrikaner war; in 1909–10, when the terms of unification were being decided; and again in 1936, the year in which Cape Africans were removed from the common roll – the British agreed to the principle of exclusive white power. An extension of the franchise across the colour line would certainly have improved their electoral prospects, and might have tilted the balance in their favour. Yet they chose to remain a political minority within the white elite. The powers of government passed to Afrikaner nationalism. The British had the satisfaction of continuing to possess the bulk of the country's industrial and commercial wealth.

Economic conflicts between Afrikaans- and English-speaking whites are likewise settled where possible by introducing some kind of racial discrimination from which both stand to gain. Competing shopkeepers or estate agents will unite in pressing for measures to limit the business activities of Asians, prevent Africans from trading in the main shopping areas, or give whites an exclusive right to own land in selected suburbs. Competition for African workers, to take another example, has been a chronic cause of dissension between farmers and industrialists. The farmers have clamoured for and obtained stringent pass laws to direct the flow of peasants away from industrial areas to the farms. Industrialists and mine owners have found another solution, more satisfactory to themselves. They recruit foreign Africans from territories in southern and central Africa, thereby obviating labour scarcities from which the home-born African would benefit.

Farmers avoid that other thorny labour problem, the competition between white and black workers, by simply employing Africans and Coloured on all sorts of manual work, both skilled and unskilled. This was the colonial pattern, which left little room for white farm hands; and it persists in spite of considerable mechanization in agriculture. The practice of reserving preferred jobs for whites is an essentially urban phenomenon, which might not have developed into a rigid system if industrialists had been allowed a free hand. They have never ceased to complain (less vigorously now than in the early days of industrialism) that a division of labour by race insulates white workers against competition, deprives Africans of the opportunity to acquire and apply skills, and makes for inefficiency in both groups. Because of this, it is said, outputs are low, costs are high, and manufacturers cannot hold their own in competition with foreign producers.

White liberals concluded that the industrial colour bar was incompatible with economic expansion, that Africans and industrialists had a common interest against defenders of the colonial order, and that substantial industrialization would erode racial rigidities. The absorption of a large and growing number of peasants into the permanently urbanized population would, it was hoped, narrow the cultural gap between whites and Africans, and promote cooperation between them. Then, too, labour scarcities resulting from economic growth were expected to unlock doors through which Africans could enter the skilled trades, to the greater good of all concerned: employers, benefiting from lower unit costs; Africans from higher wages; the domestic market from increased purchasing capacity; and white workers from wider opportunities for technicians and supervisors. As in western Europe in the nineteenth century, manufacturers would press for the removal of impediments to a rationalized capitalism which, acting as a solvent of social rigidities, would prepare the way for a multi-racial parliamentary democracy.

Contrary to such expectations, however, industrialism has not visibly eroded colour bars. Racial discrimination is more pervasive, onerous and humiliating than it was twenty years ago. The urban African population is six times greater than in 1900, yet it has never been so hemmed in and insecure as now. Low unskilled wage rates and a growing disparity between average white and African incomes have not prevented the growth of a large internal market or a considerable export of primary and secondary products. Statutory colour bars have been extended from mining to manufacturing industries despite scarcities of skilled workers. Rather than admit Africans to the skilled trades, the government subsidizes the immigration of whites. Any preference that industrialists have for a free, competitive labour market is discounted by the benefits they derive from a regimented labour force.

Mine managements employ indentured, migrant peasants; pay them less than a living wage; house them in compounds; repatriate the diseased, crippled and enfeebled to their villages; and renew the supply of able-bodied men by drawing on rural communities throughout the sub-continent. Low African wage rates offset the cost of recruiting and training peasants under expensive white instructors and supervisors. By tapping human resources in the outer regions of South Africa's economic empire, mine owners can freeze the African's wage and keep him out of skilled work. The gap between the wages of white and African miners is wider than it was thirty years ago; the number of Africans working on the gold mines is greater (370,000 as compared with 297,000); and the proportion of home-born Africans to the total African labour force on the mines has dropped from fifty-two to thirty-four per cent.

Not all African miners are temporary migrant workers. Many renew their labour contracts for cumulative periods of up to twenty or thirty years; some have wives and children in adjacent municipal townships. But the structure of the mining industry, the compound system and state policy discourage any tendency for men to settle and live with their families near the place of work. It is government policy to impose a similar pattern of instability on Africans employed in factories, workshops, commerce and transport. Pass laws, officially called influx controls, limit the size of the urban African population to the number required for labour purposes. Only persons who were born in a town or have lived there continuously for at least ten years may rent a family house and have their families with them. Men not so qualified may remain in a town only if hired to work for a stated employer. They cannot bring their wives and dependants with them, and must depart if unemployed. Entry is denied to women from rural areas. Africans who are surplus to labour needs and those unable to work because of old age and illness must return to the reserves.

Prosecutions under the pass laws amount to close on half a million cases a year and form twenty-three per cent of all cases tried in the criminal courts. Africans pay a high price in fines, imprisonment and loss of wages for their individual defiance of the detested laws; but the social costs are higher. Migrant labour and influx controls disrupt family life, waste manpower, breed inefficiency and cause instabilities in both rural and urban communities. The system is rational only as a device to fortify the white minority's defences against the emerging African proletariat. The perpetual rotation of Africans under intensive police surveillance has a crippling effect on African labour and political organizations. The fear of being 'endorsed out' of towns has been a major deterrent to mass action against apartheid.

Labour migration accordingly delays the process of consolidating Africans into a class-conscious proletariat. At the same time, racial discrimination obscures any interests they have in common with white workers. Africans and whites may not intermarry, live in the same neighbourhood, or travel, eat, drink and play together. They mingle only at the place of work and never as social equals. White workers are trained for a position of authority; they belong to the racial elite, and share its powers and privileges. Buttressed by laws and conventions against competition, they derive great advantage from an artificially induced scarcity of skills. The average wage of a white worker is more than five times that of the African in manufacturing industries (£119 a month as against £22), and more than fifteen times that of the African in the gold mines (£5 17s. a shift as against 7s. 5d.). The difference in status and living standards instils a sense of superiority in the white and dispels any notion of unity or cohesion with the black worker.

Radical socialists in the early part of the century took the Marxist view that capitalists and workers belonged to mutually antagonistic classes. A social class in Marxist theory comes into existence when persons who perform the same function in the production process become aware of their common interests and unite to promote them against the opposing class. Marxists recognized the competitive element in relations between workers, but believed that it was less important than their identity of interests as wage earners. Racial conflict and colour prejudice were considered by-products of capitalism, which provoked such antagonisms in order to divide the workers. On the other hand, capitalism created conditions that forced workers to recognize their common interests. The productive system had an inherent tendency to reduce the worker's living standards to the lowest level at which he could produce and reproduce. That tendency was being manifested in the substitution of low-paid Africans for more costly white labour. Since it was futile to expect protection from a capitalist government, white workers would be obliged in the long run to organize Africans and combine with them against the capitalist class.

It is arguable on the historical facts that inter-racial class solidarity in the Marxist sense exists as a potential in South Africa; that the specified conditions can be realized if workers of different colour groups are allowed freedom of association. White workers actually acquired a class consciousness, combined in trade unions, formed political parties with a socialist objective, came out on strike, and occasionally, as in 1913–14 and 1922, clashed violently with the forces of government. There was also evidence of inter-racial cooperation. Whites, Coloured and Indians belonged to the same unions in some occupations; whites and Africans joined together in some situations to press for higher wages or trade union rights. Members of the International Socialist League and later of the Communist party filled a leading role in these struggles; and found ample evidence to support their thesis of eventual solidarity among workers of all races against capitalism. On the model of social democracy in advanced industrial countries, the radicals envisaged the development of a non-racial labour movement in which white workers, by reason of their experience, status and social awareness, would take the lead and strive towards a social revolution.

The radical vision failed to materialize. South Africa uniquely demonstrates that a dominant racial minority can perpetuate social rigidities and feudalistic traits on an advanced and expanding industrial base. To recapitulate: civic status is determined at birth and for life by colour rather than class, by genealogy rather than function; a person can move up or down the social scale within his primary colour group, but he cannot transfer to another such group; functional categories cut across the colour line, but members of one race cannot combine freely with co-functionaries of another race. There is, indeed, less working-class solidarity than existed thirty years ago; trade unionism has been fragmented by national and racial cleavages; and African trade unions are mere shadows of their former selves. Racial alienation in the working class is undoubtedly the consequence of contrived factors, and not of innate antipathies or any biological bias.

White Labourism has been a primary cause of policies that incite racial hostility, isolate colour groups, and dissolve class consciousness in colour consciousness. The British immigrants who founded the Transvaal labour movement early in the century aspired to mastery over the African. Starting with the elementary trade union plea for protection against labour dilution and unfair competition, they absorbed the colour prejudices of the colonial order and identified themselves with every attempt to keep Africans and Asians in subjection. By means of trade union combination, political pressure, strikes and physical violence, they secured for white miners and artisans sheltered employment which cut them off from their fellow African worker and filled them with overweening racial pride and arrogance. The Labour party pandered to this sentiment, agitated for an all-white franchise, and fought elections on a platform of white supremacy. It was the party's proud boast that it had been the first to propose total racial segregation. And indeed, by entering into a coalition with Afrikaner nationalism in 1924, Labour enabled the Nationalist party to take office and lay the foundations of apartheid.

Labour's left wing stood out against this trend, refusing to abandon socialist principles for a share of white power. This rejection of racial chauvinism was the more remarkable because it emanated from the heart of the movement, from founders and leaders of trade unions and of the Labour party itself. At first they too, like their conservative colleagues, appealed mainly to white workers, but with a difference. Whereas the conservatives made socialism serve as a pretext for discrimination, the radicals clung to the concept of class solidarity; and insisted that racial antagonisms were actually a variant or sub-species of class conflict. It was an ideology for a mature working class, but made its biggest impact on the new African and Coloured proletariat, and that only after the radicals had renounced white Labourism.

Three events in particular – the First World War, the Russian Revolution, and the Pact Government of 1924 – externalized the radical element and freed it from Labourism's obsession with white parliamentary politics. The war precipitated a split in the Labour party and led to the formation of the International Socialist League. In opposing the war, the League moved from a general denunciation of imperialism to a specific examination of its effects on South Africa's social structure. Radicals gained new insights into the relation between class and colour divisions; they began to claim that Africans were not finally competitors of the white worker, but his potential allies, without whom he could not achieve his own emancipation.

The October Revolution added the new dimension of Marxist-Leninist theory and inspired the formation of the Communist party. During its incubation, the socialists took the decisive step of crossing the colour line. They formed tenuous links with African nationalism, and laid the basis of African trade unionism. Later, when joined to the world revolutionary movement through the Communist International, the party acquired the ideological equipment it needed to cope with the complexities of a society divided into antagonistic classes, races and nationalities. An important determinant of party policy was the International's formula for bringing about a synthesis between working-class and national liberation movements in the colonies. New vistas were opened. The communists completed their transition to a genuinely non-racial party – the first in Africa – and orientated themselves in theory and practice to the struggle for racial equality.

The change took place gradually and with much internal strain. Communists who had spent their working lives in the labour movement could not easily detach themselves from the white worker. Their theory and some experience, notably in the Rand revolt of 1922, convinced them that he was potentially the most revolutionary force in the country. Africans, in contrast, seemed to be unorganized, politically backward, and more responsive to nationalism than to socialism. It appeared obvious to some communists that white workers were the natural instrument for welding Africans into a class-conscious proletariat; and that it was the party's role to make both aware of their historical mission. The Nationalist-Labour government of 1924–8 shattered that belief. Labourism underwent a permanent change, became wholly absorbed in the white power structure, and ceased to operate as an independent political force. The communists continued to proclaim their faith in the eventual triumph of working-class unity. But in 1928 they adopted the dramatic perspective of a Black Republic, which placed them squarely on the side of national liberation.

For the next two decades communists cooperated or competed with the liberation movement in varying phases of protest and struggle. Their primary task was to dissolve racial, tribal and national antagonisms in a common class consciousness, and develop a strategy of mass action against white domination. This was a formidable undertaking which called for much personal devotion and the patient, laborious organization of people in the first stages of industrialization. To be an African and a communist was to run the risk of being victimized on both counts; and only those with a firm ideological conviction would meet the challenge. There was another and more serious hindrance to the reception of Marxist concepts. White labour's persistent pressure for industrial colour bars, its segregation programme and rabid racialism had alienated African and Coloured leaders. Unable to reconcile class theories with the white worker's behaviour, these doubted the authenticity of the socialist vision or thought it too remote to be a sound guide to action. They preferred radical liberalism to radical socialism.

Some commentators traced the preference to the influence of an African bourgeoisie. If that was a factor, its effects were hardly more than negligible. The 'middle class' consisted of small traders, building contractors, owners of bus companies or other minor enterprises in segregated townships. Pinned down in the poorest quarters, starved of capital, unable to buy land or to compete against whites in the open market, African entrepreneurs were virtually obliged to evade the restraints of discriminatory laws by resorting to subterfuge and illegality. Their conditions made them highly vulnerable to official pressures and averse from active participation in politics. In fact, few businessmen played a leading role in the African National Congress.

The leaders of Congress were intellectuals and trade unionists, but trade unionism was too weak to set the pace. The clergymen, lawyers, writers, doctors, teachers, clerks and chiefs who founded Congress or who decided its policies were constitutionalists. Predisposed by education, social position and expediency to a concept of gradual change, they aspired to political equality within the framework of parliamentary government. African nationalism originated in a defence of the Cape's non-racial franchise or in demands for its extension to the northern provinces. The antecedents left a mark. Elsewhere in Africa, national liberation meant the transfer of political authority from an external imperial government; in South Africa it was construed as a sharing of power with the white minority. 'We, the

African people,' declared Congress in its Bill of Rights of December 1945, 'urgently demand the granting of full citizenship rights such as are enjoyed by all Europeans in South Africa.' It was a demand based on doctrines of popular sovereignty: universal adult suffrage, direct representation in parliament, and equality before the law. Congress was a radical liberal movement which never envisaged anything so far-reaching as the socialization of the land, mines, factories and banks.

Radical liberalism emanated from British institutions and values, and received a measure of support from sections of the English-speaking middle class; but it was no more acceptable than was radical socialism to white supremacists. The African elite included men and women who would have risen to eminence in any open society; yet all were relegated by reason of race to a civic status lower than that of the meanest white. Whether wage-worker or peasant, businessman or professional, intellectual or chief, no African was admitted to parliament, municipal councils, the army, civil service, mining and financial houses, or managerial and technical posts. All Africans endured the humiliation and restrictive effects of pass laws, racial classification, residential segregation, and discrimination in public life. None could escape the state's coercive sanctions. The African National Congress spoke for the entire African population when it presented a claim to full citizenship.

The achievements of Congress were considerable. It exposed the myths of white superiority and prevented them from hardening into sacred taboos. It kept the spirit of resistance alive and prevented Africans from sinking into a condition of submissiveness, of apathetic acquiescence in white power. It awakened a national consciousness that transcended language, tribal, provincial and class barriers. It gave the people dignity, pride in their cultural heritage, and a determination to regain their land and liberty. By refusing to compromise, or to accept less than total integration into the entire range of political and economic institutions, Congress stripped white South Africa of its humanitarian pretensions and revealed the true face of apartheid for all the world to see.

Congress was less successful in dealing with the problem of

ways and means. A clear strategic perspective never emerged from the recurring discussion of grievances and goals. Fiery speeches, strong resolutions, deputations and petitions had an educative value, yet brought no relief. Nearly half a century of protest and appeals produced only more repression, greater discrimination. Communists and its own left wing urged Congress to adopt a grass-roots organization based on local branches and cells; and to mobilize the people for civil disobedience, political strikes, passive resistance and defiance of unjust laws. The main core of the Congress leadership remained addicted, however, to politics of a kind that, appropriate to a party competing for votes, acted as a mischievous anodyne on a people who, being voteless, were always the victims and never the makers of policy.

Parliamentary government in a racially stratified society made white interests paramount. If universal suffrage produces a welfare state under capitalism, white suffrage gives rise under colonialism to a colour-bar state. A political party that appeals to white voters alone invariably makes their claims the touchstone of policy, plays on their collective fears of black power, excites and reinforces their racial antagonisms, and consolidates them into a hegemonic bloc in opposition to the voteless majority. As long as Africans and Coloured retained a toehold in the Cape's parliamentary system, they might hope to secure the backing of one or other candidate in search of votes. The removal of Africans from the common roll in 1936, however, virtually eliminated the possibility that any big party would attempt to create a consensus of white and black. The resulting polarization called for a new approach by Congress: an emphasis on strategy rather than on goals. In keeping with this demand for a reappraisal, questions of strategy dominated discussions and became the main cause of dissension in all sections of the liberation movement during the next decade.

For a while, at the time of the attack on the Cape franchise, it seemed as though Africans would move out of the parliamentary orbit and adopt a strategy of mass resistance to white domination. The prospect receded as leaders involved themselves in the election of white 'native representatives' to parliament and of

Africans to the Native Representative Council. A few years later, when the Coloured community faced the first threats of political segregation, a group of intellectuals reacted by launching a campaign for the boycott of segregated institutions. Though tactically unsuccessful, the campaign stimulated young radicals to look for bolder and more imaginative methods of struggle than speeches and deputations. The issue came sharply to the fore again in 1946, when Natal and Transvaal Indians, reviving Gandhi's satyagraha, launched a passive resistance campaign against compulsory residential segregation. At the same time, the great strike of African miners on the Witwatersrand, followed by prosecution of Communist party leaders and the refusal of Native Representative Council members to cooperate with the government, gave another big impetus to the demand for mass action. A process of cross-fertilization set in that held the promise of unity among Africans, Coloured and Indians.

The parliamentary victory of Afrikaner nationalism in 1948 signified a reversal of the post-war trend towards decolonization in Asia and Africa. The new government merged the old colonial autocracy with industrial capitalism in a programme of racial totalitarianism. A series of discriminatory laws completed the segregation of Africans, Coloured and Indians; reduced them to the same level of subordination; and consolidated the whites into one power bloc. Starting with the Suppression of Communism Act of 1950, which outlawed all expression of fundamental dissent as well as the Communist party, the government has used the coercive techniques of colonial rule to silence and suppress its radical opponents. Excluded from the safeguards of judicial process, they have been listed as communists; banned from trade unions and political organizations; exiled to remote, desolate regions; placed under house arrest; or imprisoned for long periods without trial.

Total oppression evoked total resistance. Flushed with success, confident of its ability to muster the great majority of whites behind its policy of apartheid, and contemptuous of the African's will or capacity to fight back, the government mounted a ruthless attack on the champions of an open, non-racial society. They took up the challenge by resorting to mass struggle.

Radical nationalists and radical socialists on both sides of the colour line joined forces in an alliance of the African Congress, the Indian Congress, the Coloured Congress and the Communist party. Defiance campaigns and national strikes led to the Sharpeville massacre of 1960. It marked another turning point. Parliament outlawed the African National Congress and the Pan African Congress, drove the liberation movement underground, and committed it to a strategy of insurrection, guerrilla warfare and armed invasion.

List of Abbreviations

AAC	All African Convention
AEU	Amalgamated Engineering Union
AFL	Anti-Fascist League
AFTU	African Federation of Trade Unions
ALC	African Labour Congress
AMWU	African Mine Workers' Union
ANC	African National Congress
APO	African Political Organization
ASE	Amalgamated Society of Engineers
BWIU	Building Workers' Industrial Union
CAC	Coloured Advisory Council
CAD	Coloured Affairs Department
CATA	Cape African Teachers' Association
CC	Central Committee
CEC	Central Executive Committee
CI	Communist International
CNETU	Council of Non-European Trade Unions
COTT	Central Organization for Technical Training
CPNU	Coloured Peoples' National Union
CPSA	Communist Party of South Africa
CSL	Constitutional Socialist League
ECCI	Executive Committee of the Communist International
FAK	Federasie van Afrikaanse Kultuurverenigings
FNETU	Federation of Non-European Trade Unions
FSU	Friends of the Soviet Union
ICU	Industrial and Commercial Union
ICWU	Industrial and Commercial Workers' Union
IFTU	International Federation of Trade Unions

ILO	International Labour Organization
ILP	Independent Labour Party
ISL	Industrial Socialist League
ISL	International Socialist League (S.A.)
IWA	Industrial Workers (Union) of Africa
IWU	Industrial Workers' Union
IWW	Industrial Workers of the World
LP	Labour Party
LRC	Labour Representative Committee
MWU	Mine Workers' Union
NEC	National Executive Committee
NECMA	Non-European Christian Ministers Association
NETUC	Non-European Trade Union Council
NEUF	Non-European United Front
NEUM	Non-European Unity Movement
NLL	National Liberation League
NP	National Party
NRC	Native Representative Council
NURAHS	National Union of Railway and Harbour Servants
OFS	Orange Free State
ORC	Orange River Colony
PB	Political Bureau
PLL	Political Labour League
RILU	Red International of Labour Unions
SAAEO	South African Association of Employees' Organizations
SACTU	South African Council of Trade Unions
SAIC	South African Indian Congress
SAIF	South African Industrial Federation
SAIRR	South African Institute of Race Relations
SALP	South African Labour Party
SAMWU	South African Mine Workers' Union
SAP	South African Party
SAR	South African Republic
SATLC	South African Trades and Labour Council
SATUC	South African Trade Union Congress

SDP	Social Democratic Party
SDF	Social Democratic Federation
SLP	Socialist Labour Party
SP	Socialist Party
TANC	Transvaal African National Congress
TIC	Transvaal Indian Congress
TLC	Trades and Labour Council
TNA	Transvaal Nationalist Assembly
TNC	Transvaal Native Congress
UAL	United Afrikaner League
UF	United Front
UP	United Party
USANP	United South African National Party
USP	United Socialist Party
VFP	Victoria Falls Power Company
WMEMU	Witwatersrand Mine Employees' and Mechanics' Union
WTLC	Witwatersrand Trades and Labour Council
YCL	Young Communist League

References

Chapter 1

1. Marais, 1957, p. 114.
2. Walker, 1957, p. 135.
3. Marais, 1957, p. 134.
4. ibid., pp. 185, 198.
5. ibid., p. 201.
6. This and the following three paragraphs owe a great deal to S. Trapido, 'The Origins of the Cape Franchise Qualifications of 1853' (unpublished).
7. P.P.1853, Cd.1581, pp. 218–20.
8. *Capetown Weekly Magazine*, 8/4/59; Cape, 1861, cc.2–3, Return of the Rates of Wages, etc.; Cape, 1863, S.C.6, pp. 7–8.
9. Rochlin, S.A. in *Saamtrek*, 20/2/53, and the *Commercial Traveller*, March 1961; W. L. Speight in *Forward*, 1/5/53.
10. Printers and Bookbinders Mutual Benefit Society, *Rules and Byelaws*, C.T.1857.
11. *Cape Mercury & Weekly Magazine*, 8/4/1859, 6/5/1859, 7/10/1859.
12. ibid., 20/5/1859, 17/6/1859.
13. For the occupations of immigrants see the *South African Commercial Advertiser*, 1845–8; and Hattersley, 1951, pp. 35, 43.
14. Pringle, 1824, p. 47.
15. Schnell, 1954, p. 213.
16. Cape, 1879, S.C.26.
17. Noble, 1875, p. 292.
18. Cape, 1865, A27, Annexure, pp. 32–4, 148–50.
19. Mentzel, 1785–7, part 1, p. 49; part 3, pp. 44–5.
20. Marais, 1957, p. 270.
21. Cape, 1859, A.26.
22. Cape, 1871, A.23, Appendix B.
23. Daphne Simon, 1954, in *Democracy and the Labour Movement* (ed. R. L. Meek).
24. Solomon, 1948, p. 205.

Chapter 2

1. P.P.1873, C.732, p. 130.
2. P.P.1871, C.459, p. 46.
3. ibid., p. 65.
4. P.P.1873, C.732, p. 130.
5. Williams, 1902, p. 219
6. Payton, 1872, p. 30.
7. Wilmot, 1904, p. 241.
8. Doughty, 1963, p. 27.
9. P.P.1874, C.882, p. 144.
10. Cohen, 1911, pp. 141–8.
11. Beet, 1931, p. 141.
12. Gross, 1956, p. 28.
13. Ransome, 1903, p. 64.
14. Payton, 1872, p. 138.
15. Cape, 1882, G.86, p. 4
16. P.P.1873, C.732, pp. 100–101, 107; Wilmot, 1904, p. 238
17. P.P.1873, C.732 pp. 102 f.
18. P.P.1876, C.1342, pp. 109 f.
19. ibid., p. 222; P.P.1876, C.1401, p. 10.
20. P.P.1876, C.1342, pp. 106 f.; Matthews, 1887, p. 107.
21. Cape, 1899, G.31, pp. 32–4.
22. Cape, 1882, G.86, p. 20.
23. de Kock, 1924, p. 258 f.; Lockhart & Woodhouse, pp. 78, 108, 118.
24. *Diamond Fields Advertiser*, 17/10/1882, 6/5/1884. Angove, 1910, pp. 181–5.
25. Cape, 1883, G.8., Appdx. pp. 3–4.
26. Ransome, 1903, pp. 64 f.; Angove, 1910, p. 181.
27. Hobson, 1900, p. 237.
28. S.A. Native Races Committee, 1901, p. 141.
29. Chilvers, 1939, pp. 64, 101, 122. Millin, 1933, p. 88. Lockhart & Woodhouse, 1963, pp. 109, 121.
30. Frankel, 1938, p. 64.
31. Knights of Labour of South Africa, 1892, *Manifesto and First Report*.
32. Thomson, 1901, pp. 14 f.
33. Hobson, 1900, p. 239.
34. Cape, 1895, G.25, pp. 4, 9; S.A. Native Races Committee, 1901, p. 141. P.P.1914, Cd.7707, par. 316.

35. S.A.1914, U.G.34, par. 271, 292, 316.
36. *Imvo Zabantsundu*, 5/6/06.
37. ibid., 31/7/1906.
38. Theal, 1919, ii, p. 202.
39. Skota, 1932, pp. 91–4.
40. Simons, 1968, part I.
41. Forman, 1959, p. 9.
42. Rose Innes, 1949, p. 53.
43. *Imvo Zabantsundu*, 23/3/87, 30/3/87, 13/4/87.
44. Rose Innes, 1949, p. 100.
45. *Imvo Zabantsundu*, 25/3/03.
46. *South African Review*, 22/9/99.
47. Walker, 1957, pp. 466, 483, 493.

Chapter 3

1 Flora Shaw in the *Star*, 10/9/92.
2. S.A.R., 1897. p. 449.
3. *Star*, 20/8/92.
4. ibid., 12/9/92, 1/10/92.
5. ibid. 3/9/92.
6. Rose 1902, pp. 31–2, 113–15; Hobson, 1900, p. 67.
7. *Star*, 3/9/92.
8. *Critic*, 3 and 17 February 1893.
9. *Standard & Diggers' News*, 16/11/93; S.A. Rochlin in *Saamtrek*, 29/5/53.
10. *Critic*. 10/2/93; S.A. Rochlin in *Saamtrek*, 22/5/53.
11. Rose. 1902, p. 29.
12. Section 65, Law 3 of 1893.
13. S.A.R., 1893. Tweeden Volksraad, Notulen, 18/5/93, Art.117.
14. Law 12 of 1896, Section 89.
15. ibid., sections 39 (m) and 106.
16. Rose. 1902, pp. 30–31.
17. Chamber of Mines Annual Report for 1896, pp. 61–3.
18. Law 11 of 1897. Section 38 (m); Law 12 of 1898, sections 39 (m) and 104.
19. *Star*, 4/1/93. 10/4/93; *Critic*. 3/2/93.
20. Walker & Weinbren. 1961, p. 286.
21. *Star*. 20/8/92.
22. Chamber of Mines, Annual Reports; Department of Public Health Report, 1905, p. B.31.

23. P.P.1904, Cd.1897, p. 84.
24. S.A.R., 1897, pp. 22, 31.
25. ibid., p. 449.
26. Chamber of Mines, 1897, Annual Report for 1896, p. 161.
27. ibid., p. 155.
28. *Guardian*, 2/7/37.
29. Van der Poel, 1951; Pakenham, 1960.
30. P.P.1904, Cd.1789, 1790, 1791, 1792; *Amery*, 1909; Halperin, 1952, p. 123.
31. P.P.1903, Cd.1551, p. 148; de Wet, C. R., 1902, pp. 403–33.
32. Chamber of Mines, Annual Report for 1901, p. 121.
33. Sik, 1966, i, p. 380.
34. Stewart, 1921, pp. 143–4.
35. Shaw, 1925; Elton, 1939, pp. 90–93; Pease, 1925, p. 128.
36. Luxemburg, 1951, pp. 411–16.
37. Hobson, 1900, pp. 230–31, 240.
38. Marais, 1961, pp. 322–31; Le May, 1965, pp. 26–30.
39. P.P.1901, Cd.547, p. 34.
40. P.P.1901, Cd.528, p. 2.
41. ibid., pp. 4–6.
42. P.P.1902, Cd.1096, p. 12.
43. P.P.1902, Cd.1284, p. 7.
44. Pyrah, 1955, p. 78.
45. *Imvo Zabantsundu*, 8/10/02.
46. ibid., 29/4/03.
47. P.P.1904, Cd.2104, p. 17.
48. P.P.1902, Cd.903, p. 195; P.P.1902, Cd.1365, p. 15; P.P.1903, Cd.1551, pp. 148, 183–5; P.P.1903, Cd.1553.
49. P.P.1904, Cd.2025, pp. 24 f.
50. P.P.1905, Cd.2400, p. 4; 1906, Cd.3250, p. 39.
51. House of Commons, 7/12/1900, c.262; P.P.1901, Cd.547, p. 11; P.P.1905, Cd.2400, p. 7.
52. Pyrah, 1955, p. 92.
53. *Imvo Zabantsundu*, 18/4/05.
54. P.P.1905, Cd.2479, pp. 82–3, 106.
55. *Imvo Zabantsundu*, 7/2/05.
56. ibid., 24/7/06.
57. P.P.1905, Cd.2400, p. 4; 1906, Cd.3250, p. 39; Mansergh, 1962, p. 77.
58. P.P.1905, Cd.2482, p. 78.
59. P.P.1904, Cd.2104, p. 15.
60. Le May, 1965, p. 179.

61. P.P.1895, Cd.7911; P.P.1904, Cd.2239, p. 40.
62. P.P.1903, Cd.1684; P.P.1904, Cd.1895, pp. 39–40; P.P.1904, Cd.2239, p. 41.
63. P.P.1904, Cd.2239, pp. 28–34.
64. P.P.1907, Cd.3308, pp. 2–4.
65. Gandhi, 1928, p. 143.
66. Stuart, 1913.
67. Gandhi, 1928, pp. 153–5.
68. P.P.1907, Cd.3308, p. 44.
69. P.P.1908. Cd.3887, p. 9.
70. Immigrants Restrictions Act, 1907, Township Amendment Act, 1908, Precious and Base Metals Act, 1908.
71. Gandhi, 1928, pp. 302–3.

Chapter 4

1. *South African News* 18/4/04, 2/5/04.
2. *South African Spectator*, 23/3/01. 20/4/01.
3. Minutes of Bespoke Tailoring Arbitration Board, 1906 (Holograph).
4. *South African News*, 28/10/05, 2/12/05.
5. Minutes of the Social Democratic Federation, 1906–8 (Holograph).
6. *South African News*, 23/9/06.
7. ibid., 17/10/05.
8. *Cape Argus*, 12/8/07, 16/9/07, 23/9/07.
9. Minutes of the Social Democratic Federation (*supra*).
10. Government Notice 826 of 1903.
11. Government Notice 173, 196 and 1232 of 1906.
12. Transvaal 1908, T.G.2 p. 1129.
13. P.P.1904, Cd.1895, pp. 194–6, 249, 256–7.
14. ibid., pp. 193–4.
15. ibid., pp. 112, 116, 128, 166.
16. P.P.1903, Cd.1640. p. 13.
17. P.P.1904. Cd.2239 p. 17.
18. P.P.1904 Cd.1896, par. 33.
19. P.P.1903, Cd.1552, p. 5.
20. P.P.1904, Cd.1895, p. 197.
21. ibid., p. 23.
22. P.P.1904, Cd.1896, Minority Report, p. 65.
23. P.P.1904, Cd.1895, p. 337, Appendix I.

24. *Imvo Zabantsundu,* 29/4/03.
25. ibid., 8/12/03.
26. ibid., 8/8/05.
27. *South African News,* 29/2/04.
28. P.P.1904, Cd.1895, p. 177.
29. *Rand Daily Mail,* 1/4/03.
30. Coloured Labourers' Health Regulation Ordinance, 1905; Government Notice 569, 1906.
31. P.P.1904, Cd.2026, p. 38.
32. Chamber of Mines, pp. 132–3, Annual Report for 1899.
33. ibid., p. 53, Annual Report for 1910.
34. ibid., pp. 396–411, Annual Report for 1904.
35. ibid., 1907, pp. 17, 85; Transvaal, 1910, p. 70; S.A.1914, U.G.37, p. 16.
36. South African Medical Record, 1914, vol. xii, pp. 1–3; S.A.1914, U.G.37, p. 102; House of Assembly Debates, 1912, 15 May; 1913, 28 January, 8, 14, 20 May; S.A.1911, Proc. of Meeting between Minister of Native Affairs and Transvaal Chamber of Mines etc. (S.A. Public Library; Typescript).
37. Chamber of Mines, Annual Report for 1896, p. 22.
38. Gorgas, 1914, pp. 5–6.
39. S.A. 1947, p. 2907. Native Law Commission, Minutes of Evidence (unpublished).
40. *Imvo Zabantsundu,* 27/10/08.
41. ibid., 2/7/07, 26/1/09.
42. ibid., 13/10/08, 15/12/08.
43. Walker & Weinbren, 1961. p. 24.
44. *Imvo Zabantsundu,* 11/6/07.
45. Transvaal, 1908, T.G.2, p. 1085.
46. ibid., Report.
47. Transvaal, 1908, T.G.13, Report, par. 84
48. Transvaal, 1908, T.G.2, vol. 1. pt. 2, pp. 380, 480, 503.
49. ibid., pp. 480–81.
50. ibid., pp. 386, 441, 444.
51. ibid., pt. iii, pp. 702–12.
52. Transvaal, 1910, Mining Regulations Commission, Evidence (unpublished) 13/7/07, p. 49.
53. ibid., August 1907, p. 12.
54. ibid., 19/7/07, p. 2; 31/7/07, p. 32; 10/8/07, pp. 7–23, 41.
55. ibid., 13/7/07, pp. 1–22; 14/8/07, pp. 2–34.
56. ibid., Report, p. 249.
57. Chamber of Mines, Annual Report for 1910, p. 43.

58. P.P.1914, Cd.7707, pp. 41, 44, 48.
59. *A.P.O.*, 7/2/14.
60. S.A.1912, U.G.49, pp. 110–11.
61. Transvaal, 1908, T.G.13, p. 346.
62. *Star*, 22/11/07; Transvaal Legislative Assembly Debates, 1907 p. 22, 1908, p. 311, 1909, p. 243.
63. Natal Legislative Assembly Debates, 7/12/09, pp. 1–5.
64. Transvaal, 1908 T.G.2, p. 1426.
65. P.P.1914, Cd.7707, pp. 70–74.
66. Transvaal Legislative Assembly Debates, 7/6/09, C.92–4; 22/6/09, C.645.
67. Natal Legislative Assembly Debates, 28/7/03, p. 362; 19/10/09, p. 74; 25/10/09, p. 202.
68. ibid., 1/11/09, pp. 223–37.

Chapter 5

1. Constitution and Rules of the Witwatersrand Trades & Labour Council (Revised January 1904).
2. P.P.1903, Cd.1552, pp. 23–8.
3. *South African News*, 23/4/04.
4. ibid., 16/4/04.
5. ibid., 16/1/04, 20/1/04, 25/2/04.
6. Minutes of the Social Democratic Federation, 1906–8 (Holograph).
7. *South African News*, 29/7/05.
8. *Transvaal Leader*, 8/2/05.
9. *Star*, 18/2/05.
10. *Rand Daily Mail*, 20/2/05.
11. *South African News*, 13/6/05.
12. *Transvaal Leader*, 8/2/05; *Star*, 11/2/05.
13. *South African News*, 23/5/05, 9/6/05.
14. ibid., 30/1/07.
15. Cope, 1943, p. 82.
16. *Star*, 4/10/07.
17. Walker & Weinbren, 1961, pp. 294–5.
18. *Voice of Labour*, 18/12/09.
19. *Star*, 14/10/07.
20. ibid., 22/1/09.
21. Thompson, 1960.
22. *Imvo Zabantsundu*, 27/3/06, 2/11/09.

23. ibid., 6/10/08, 13/10/08, 3/11/08.
24. ibid., 11/5/09, 18/5/09.
25. ibid., 20/7/09.
26. ibid., 7/11/02, 20/11/02, 27/1/03, 10/2/03.
27. *South African Review*, 24/2/04, 9/9/04.
28. *Imvo Zabantsundu*, 3/2/03, 24/6/03, 20/10/03, 17/11/03, 15/12/03.
29. *A.P.O.*, 23/10/09.
30. *Imvo Zabantsundu*, 17/12/07, 24/12/07.
31. ibid., 21/1/08.
32. ibid., 3/3/08.
33. ibid., 20/7/09.
34. Thompson 1960, pp. 325–6.
35. *A.P.O.*, 6/5/11.
36. ibid., 19/6/09.
37. ibid., 9/3/12.
38. ibid., 5/6/09.
39. ibid., 24/5/09.
40. ibid., 24/5/09.
41. *Manchester Guardian*, 28/7/09.
42. Hobson, 1909, pp. 233, 247.
43. *Labour Leader*, 16/7/09.
44. *A.P.O.*, 11/9/09.
45. Thompson, 1960, pp. 430–31.
46. *A.P.O.*, 25/9/09.
47. ibid., 28/8/09.

Chapter 6

1. Gordon, 1927, p. 155.
2. *Owl*, 16/9/04.
3. *A.P.O.*, 24/7/20.
4. *South African Spectator*, 8/11/02.
5. *Owl*, 7/10/04.
6. *Imvo Zabantsundu*, 9/5/05, 23/5/05.
7. ibid., 24/1/06; *Owl*, 5/1/05.
8. *South African Review*, 5/1/06, 30/3/06.
9. S.A., 1937. U.G.54, p. 224.
10. J. H. Raynard, in the *Sun*, 29/3/40.
11. Thompson, 1960, pp. 190, 211, 225.
12. *A.P.O.*, 12/8/11.
13. ibid., 23/4/10.

14. ibid., 13/1/12.
15. ibid., 30/12/19.
16. ibid., 28/8/09.
17. ibid., 11/9/09.
18. ibid., 30/7/10.
19. ibid., 13/8/10.
20. ibid., 4/12/09.
21. ibid., 26/2/10, 21/5/10.
22. ibid., 7/11/19.
23. ibid., 30/10/20.
24. *Imvo Zabantsundu*, 20/12/10.
25. *A.P.O.*, 10/9/10.
26. ibid., 6/5/11.
27. ibid., 8/10/10.
28. ibid., 27/8/10.
29. *Sun*, 5/4/40.
30. *Imvo Zabantsundu*, 6/9/10.
31. *Voice of Labour*, 12/8/10.
32. *A.P.O.*, 28/8/09.
33. ibid., 27/8/10.
34. ibid., 28/8/09.
35. ibid., 11/9/09.
36. ibid., 21/8/09.
37. ibid., 25/9/09.
38. ibid., 6/11/09.
39. ibid., 7/5/10, 3/12/10, 18/5/12, 15/6/12.
40. ibid., 7/10/11, 4/11/11.
41. ibid., 13/1/12, 27/1/12.
42. ibid., 4/11/11.
43. ibid., 3/12/10, 4/11/11.
44. House of Assembly Debates, 7/2/11, C.1030–1.
45. *A.P.O.*, 30/10/15.
46. House of Assembly Debates, 10/2/11, C.1132.
47. ibid., 13/3/11, C.1754–5.
48. ibid., 18/3/13, C.949; 14/3/12, C.1100.
49. ibid., 7/2/11, C.1021.
50. *A.P.O.*, 25/2/11.
51. ibid., 8/4/11.
52. House of Assembly Debates, 9/3/11, C.1670; 17/4/11, C.2649–50;
    14/3/11, C.1784–5.
53. *Cape Times*, 4/1/12.
54. *A.P.O.* 8/4/11, 15/6/12, 27/6/14.

55. ibid., 8/3/13.
56. House of Assembly Debates, 9/5/13, C.2294–6; 15/5/13, C.2458–60.
57. Representation of Natives Act, No. 12 of 1936; Native Trust and Land Act, No. 18 of 1936.
58. *A.P.O.*, 17/5/13.
59. Plaatje, 1916, p. 17.
60. *A.P.O.*, 7/2/14.
61. *Imvo Zabantsundu*, 23/8/10, 30/8/10.
62. ibid., 15/8/11.
63. Congress adopted the title of the South African National Congress in 1925 and will be referred to in the rest of this book as the African National Congress or ANC.
64. *Tsala ea Becoana*, 9/7/10, 17/12/10.
65. ibid., 28/10/11.
66. ibid., 30/12/11. The 'Native Senators' were four white men appointed by the government in terms of the South Africa Act 'on the grounds mainly of their thorough acquaintance' with 'the reasonable wants and wishes of the Coloured races'.
67. ibid., 10/2/12, 26/4/13; The *Cape Argus*, 17/1/12.
68. Potekhin, 1955, pp. 224–7.
69. *Tsala ea Becoana*, 10/2/12.
70. *A.P.O.*, 10/9/10.
71. *Tsala ea Becoana*, 17/2/12.
72. ibid., 10/5/13, 26/7/13, 9/8/13, 15/11/13, 13/12/13.
73. *A.P.O.*, 18/4/14.
74. ibid., 22/8/14.
75. ibid., 5/9/14.

Chapter 7

1. Harrison, 1947, p. 105.
2. Abdurahman to Gordon, 22/6/05.
3. *Voice of Labour*, 25/9/09, 6/11/09.
4. Gitsham and Trembath, 1926, p. 28.
5. *Voice of Labour*, 16/10/09, 21/1/10.
6. ibid., 25/12/09.
7. ibid., 3/6/10.
8. ibid., 31/7/09.
9. ibid., 22/7/10, 23/12/10.

10. ibid., 9/9/10, 23/9/10.

11. ibid., 9/9/10.

12. ibid., 16/9/10.

13. *A.P.O.*, 10/9/10, 24/9/10.

14. *Voice of Labour*, 23/9/10.

15. ibid., 22/4/10, 29/4/10.

16. ibid., 8/7/10.

17. *Round Table*, 1910, pp. 93–4.

18. *Voice of Labour*, 23/9/10.

19. ibid., 6/1/11, 27/10/11.

20. ibid., 4/8/11.

21. ibid., 25/2/10, 4/3/10, 11/3/10, 25/3/10, 29/4/10.

22. ibid., 22/7/10.

23. Gitsham and Trembath, p. 33–4; Cope, 1943, pp. 117–19; Walker and Weinbren, 1961, pp. 28–30.

24. *Voice of Labour*, 26/5/11.

25. ibid., 30/6/11, 7/7/11. For details see Downes, *Printers' Saga*.

26. *Voice of Labour*, 8/9/11.

27. ibid., 22/4/10, 21/4/11, 22/12/11, 26/1/12.

28. ibid., 11/8/11, 6/10/11, 17/11/11.

29. ibid., 3/11/11.

30. ibid., 16/2/12.

31. ibid., 6/10/11, 20/10/11, 3/11/11, 10/11/11, 6/2/12.

32. ibid., 19/1/12, 8/3/12, 22/3/12, 3/5/12.

33. ibid., 24/5/12.

34. ibid., 24/12/12.

35. *Social and Industrial Review*, January 1926, p. 45.

36. *Voice of Labour*, 19/1/12.

37. ibid., 1/12/11, 12/1/12, 22/3/12.

38. ibid, 8/9/11.

39. ibid., 11/3/10, 18/3/10, 19/8/10, 21/7/11.

40. ibid., 18/3/10.

41. ibid., 25/12/09.

42. ibid., 24/3/11.

43. ibid., 3/3/11.

44. ibid., 14/8/09.

45. ibid., 8/4/10, 3/2/11, 1/3/12.

46. ibid., 10/5/12.

47. Campbell and Munro, 1913, p. 5.

48. *Voice of Labour*, 15/3/12.

49. House of Assembly Debates, 30/1/14, C.75.

50. ibid., C.72.

51. Campbell and Munro, 1913, p. 9.
52. *Round Table*, 1912–13, pp. 750 f.
53. *Worker*, 3/7/13.
54. *News*, 7/7/13 (Issued by the Typographical Union).
55. Smuts, J.C., 1952, pp. 130–31.
56. Walker and Weinbren, 1961, Ch. 5; Cope, 1943, Ch. iv.
57. *Worker*, 28/8/13.
58. *Strike Herald*, 28/6/13, 2/8/13.
59. Jones, 1921, *Communism in South Africa*.
60. cf. *Strike Herald*, 25/6/13.
61. Cope, 1943, pp. 142–3.
62. *Tsala la Becoana*, 9/8/13.
63. Hancock, 1962, pp. 341–3.
64. Calpin, 1949, p. 36.
65. Fatima Meer, 'Satyagraha in South Africa', *Africa South*, vol. 3, no. 2, 1959, pp. 24–5.
66. *A.P.O.*, 11/7/14.
67. *Star*, 1/1/14.
68. *Cape Times*, 5/1/12.
69. House of Assembly Debates, 9/5/13, C.2294–6.
70. *Worker*, 25/9/13.
71. *Cape Times*, 3/1/13.
72. *A.P.O.*, 4/9/15.
73. *Star*, 31/12/13.
74. *A.P.O.*, 4/9/15.
75. Cope, 1943, pp. 170–73.

Chapter 8

1. *Round Table*, 1912–13, p. 375; *Official Year Book*, No. 6, 1910–22, p. 330.
2. *South African Review*, 13/9/12, p. 12.
3. *South African Quarterly*, June–August 1914, vol. 1, No. 1, p. 7.
4. The Industrial Disputes Prevention Bill, Trades Union Bill, Factories Bill, Workmen's Wages Protection Bill and the Public Meetings and Disturbances Bill.
5. *Star*, 7/1/14.
6. ibid., 8/1/14.
7. Smuts, 1952, p. 131.
8. *Star*, 9/1/14, 10/1/14.

9. ibid., 10/1/14, 21/1/14; Cope, 1943, pp. 160–61.
10. House of Assembly Debates, 4/2/14, C.63.
11. Federation of Trades, Acting Executive Manifesto Nos. 1–5. 15, 17, 19, 20 and 22 January 1914 (Johannesburg Public Library),
12. *Worker*, 15/1/14.
13. *Star*, 17/1/14.
14. ibid., 19/1/14.
15. House of Assembly Debates, 2/2/14, C.23–32.
16. Everard, 1914.
17. Slesser, 1941, pp. 61–2.
18. House of Assembly Debates, 27/4/14, C.1973.
19. For biographical details see Roux, 1944.
20. *A.P.O.*, 11/7/14.
21. ibid, 7/8/15.
22. Government Notice No. 1922 of 17 November, 1911.
23. House of Assembly, Annexures, vol. IV, A–5, 1914.
24. *A.P.O.*, 13/6/14.
25. ibid., 22/8/14.
26. ibid., 5/9/14.
27. ibid., 14/11/14.
28. ibid., 20/3/15.
29. ibid., 12/6/15.
30. ibid., 7/8/15.
31. ibid., 24/7/15.
32. ibid., 18/9/15.
33. *Cape Times*, 4/1/13.
34. Roux, 1944, p. 24.
35. Ex. Com. rep. to An. Conf., *Star*, 6/10/15.
36. *Star*, 2/1/15.
37. *War on War Gazette*, 19/9/14.
38. *Worker*, 28/8/13.
39. House of Assembly Debates, 29/4/14, C.2071–2.
40. D. Ticktin, *The Afrikaner and the South African Labour Party*, 1965, p. 5 (unpublished).
41. ibid., pp. 7–8.
42. *International*, 10/9/15, 1/10/15.
43. *A.P.O.*, 2/10/15.
44. ibid., 18/9/15.
45. ibid., 16/10/15.
46. *Star*, 8/10/15.
47. *A.P.O.*, 30/10/15.
48. Walker and Weinbren, 1961, p. 320.

Chapter 9

1. Cope, 1943, p. 185.
2. S.A.1923, Sc.5, p. 74.
3. *International*, 26/11/15, 3/12/15, 15/9/16.
4. *Rand Daily Mail*, 21/12/15.
5. *International*, 22/10/15.
6. ibid., 3/12/15.
7. ibid., 6/10/16.
8. *Eastern Record* 13/3/15.
9. *International*, 27/10/16, 10/11/16.
10. ibid., 19/1/17.
11. ibid., 1/6/17.
12. ibid., 1/6/17, 29/6/17.
13. ibid., 1/6/17, E. H. Becker on 'Revolutionary Industrial Unionism'.
14. ibid., 10/11/16.
15. ibid., 5/10/17.
16. ibid., 7/1/16.
17. ibid., 2/2/17.
18. ibid., 1/10/15.
19. ibid., 19/11/15.
20. ibid., 18/2/16.
21. ibid., 12/5/16, 16/3/17.
22. ibid., 7/4/16.
23. ibid., 19/5/16, 16/6/16, 7/7/16, 25/8/16.
24. ibid., 9/6/16.
25. ibid., 1/12/16, 15/12/16.
26. ibid., 19/10/17.
27. ibid., 15/12/16, 9/3/17, 20/4/17.
28. *Cape Times*, 13/3/17.
29. The Bill was withdrawn: See Simons, 1968, ch. IV.
30. *Diamond Fields Advertiser*, 5/6/17; *Christian Express*, 2/7/17.
31. *International*, 4/5/17, 18/5/17, 29/6/17, 20/7/17.
32. ibid., 6/7/17, 20/7/17.

Chapter 10

1. *International*, 23/3/17.
2. ibid., 1/6/17, 8/6/17, 30/11/17.
3. Andrews' Papers.

4. Report from the International Socialist League (South Africa) to the International Socialist Bureau and the Conveners of the Stockholm Congress, 11/8/17 (Typed).

5. *International*, 3/8/17, 26/10/17.

6. ibid., 5/10/17, 4/1/18.

7. ibid., 3/8/17.

8. *Umsebenzi*, 7/9/35.

9. *International*, 5/7/18.

10. R. Talbot Williams, 1918, *White Trade Unionism or a Call to the Non-European Workers of South Africa*, APO.

11. *International*, 9/11/17.

12. ibid., 30/11/17, 7/12/17, 8/2/18, 26/4/18.

13. *Cape Times*, 13/3/18, 14/3/18.

14. *International*, 15/2/18, 1/3/18. *Rand Daily Mail*, 13 and 14 February 1918.

15. *International*, 21/6/18.

16. ibid., 28/6/18.

17. ibid., 6/9/18.

18. Government Gazette No. 915 of 6/9/18. Report of Commissioner J. B. Moffat.

19. Skota, 1932, p. 171.

20. *International*, 6/9/18.

21. *The African Workers' Struggles and the Communist Party*, 1946 (Andrews' Papers).

22. *International*, 7/12/17, 22/2/18.

23. ibid., 23/6/16, 7/12/17, 15/3/18, 6/12/18.

24. ibid., 16/2/17.

25. ibid., 5/7/18.

26. ibid., 19/10/17, 2/11/17.

27. ibid., 15/2/18, 10/12/20.

28. ibid., 13/4/17, 5/10/17, 18/1/18, 17/12/20.

29. ibid., 5/4/18, 10/5/18, 13/12/18, 21/12/18, 31/10/19.

30. *Abantu Batho*, 16/5/18.

31. *A.P.O.*, 1/8/19.

32. ibid., 15/11/18.

33. ibid., 6/12/18.

34. Interview with Manuel Lopes, 29/1/63.

35. *International*, 26/11/15.

36. ibid., 3/1/19, 10/1/19.

37. ibid., 11/4/19, 25/4/19.

38. ibid., 16/5/19, 29/8/19.

39. *Imvo Zabantsundu*, 24/12/18, 31/12/18, 14/1/19, 20/5/19.

40. *Queenstown Daily Representative & Free Press*, 8/2/19.
41. Van Rooyen, 1956, ch. V.
42. *A.P.O.*, 17/1/20.

Chapter II

1. *International*, 7/3/19.
2. S. Mapogo Makgatho, *Presidential Address*, 1919 (Printed).
3. *Star*, 31/3/19.
4. *International*, 4/4/19.
5. Andrews' Papers.
6. *International*, 11/4/19.
7. Official Year Book, No. 4, 1910–20, pp. 316–19.
8. *Queenstown Daily Representative & Free Press*, 9/5/19.
9. H. S. Msimang, private communication, 24/11/66.
10. Kadalie, 1954, p. 10.
11. *A.P.O.*, 15/8/19.
12. ibid., 29/8/19, 26/9/19, 22/11/19.
13. ibid., 29/8/19, 12/9/19, 17/1/20, 4/9/20.
14. *International*, 28/11/19.
15. *Labour World*, 7/6/18.
16. *A.P.O.*, 1/5/20, 10/7/20, 4/9/20.
17. *International*, 21/11/19.
18. *Labour World*, 21/6/18.
19. *International*, 19/12/19, 9/1/20.
20. Kadalie, 1954, p. 16.
21. *International*, 2/1/20, 9/1/20.
22. *A.P.O.*, 30/12/19, 17/1/20.
23. *International*, 15/10/20.
24. Walker and Weinbren, 1961, pp. 65–74.
25. *International*, 16/1/20.
26. ibid., 23/1/20, 13/2/20.
27. ibid., 20/2/20.
28. ibid., 27/2/20.
29. *Diamond Field Advertiser*, 18/2/20, 21/2/20, 26/2/20.
30. ibid., 24/2/20, 25/2/20.
31. *International*, 27/2/20.
32. Transvaal Chamber of Mines, Annual Report for 1919, p. 69.
33. *Diamond Field Advertiser*, 25/2/20.
34. S.A.1922, U.G.8, p. 110: Annual Departmental Reports, 1920–21.
35. Cope, 1943, p. 215; *International*, 12/3/20, 26/3/20, 2/4/20.

36. *Star*, 20/7/20.
37. *International*, 10/12/20.
38. Transvaal, 1908, T.G.2, p. 1085, 1442.
39. S.A.1914, U.G.37, pp. 38–9.
40. E. J. Way, 1914, *The Economic Use of Workmen on the Witwatersrand.*
41. Government Gazette No. 915, of 6/9/18, par. 22(1): Report of Commissioner J. B. Moffat.
42. S.A.1920, U.G.34, p. 27.
43. *Labour World*, 8/11/18, 29/11/18.
44. ibid., 7/6/19, 28/6/19, 5/7/19, 9/8/19, 16/8/19.
45. *International*, 12/9/19.
46. ibid., 12/9/19.
47. ibid., 13/2/20.
48. *A.P.O.*, 29/8/19.
49. *Labour World*, 27/9/19.
50. ibid., 29/5/20.
51. ibid., 30/8/19, 6/9/19, 27/9/19.
52. *A.P.O.*, 17/4/20.
53. ibid., 17/1/20.
54. *International*, 16/4/20.
55. ibid., 5/11/20, 12/11/20.
56. *Queenstown Daily Representative & Free Press*, 27/5/20; *Friend*, 14/7/20; *Diamond Fields Advertiser*, 15/7/20; *A.P.O.*, 10/7/20; *International*, 6/8/20.
57. S.A.1921.
58. S.A.1921, S.C.12A.
59. *A.P.O.*, 21/4/23.
60. *International*, 29/10/20.
61. *Labour World*, 22/5/20, 30/10/20.
62. *A.P.O.*, 26/2/21, 16/4/21.
63. S.A.1923, U.G.14, pp. 93–5: Annual Departmental Reports, no. 2.
64. *International*, 3/12/20.
65. Kadalie, 1954, pp. 16–18.

Chapter 12

1. *Labour World*, 19/7/18, 16/8/18, 20/9/18, 2/8/19, 30/8/19.
2. *International*, 21/11/19, 28/11/19.
3. Lenin, 1920, ch. 7.
4. *International*, 5/12/19, 12/12/19, 9/1/20, 16/1/20.

5. ibid., 16/1/20; S.A.1922, U.G.35, par. 138.
6. *International*, 20/2/20, 12/3/20.
7. South African Labour Party Platform, March 1920.
8. *Labour World*, 21/2/20, 6/3/20, 20/3/20.
9. ibid., 7/8/20.
10. ibid., 7/6/18.
11. ibid., 19/6/20, 24/6/20.
12. *A.P.O.*, 17/1/20.
13. ibid., 21/8/20.
14. ibid., 23/12/20.
15. Nationalist Party (Cape Province) 1920, *Africa for the Africanders*.
16. *A.P.O.*, 12/9/19, 6/12/19, 14/2/20, 20/3/20.
17. ibid., 22/11/19.
18. ibid., 31/1/20.
19. *International*, 26/3/20, 30/4/20, 7/5/20, 2/7/20.
20. Van Rooyen, 1956, ch. IV.
21. *Labour World*, 13/11/20, 20/11/20, 4/12/20.
22. *International*, 26/11/20.
23. *A.P.O.*, 24/7/20, 7/8/20, 21/8/20, 4/9/20.
24. *Cape Times*, 26/5/20.
25. *East London Daily Despatch*, 1922, 'The Bulhoek Tragedy'.
26. *International*, 17/12/20.
27. S.A.1921, A.4., vol. III. Votes and Proceedings, House of Assembly.
28. *Cape Argus*, 25/5/21.
29. ibid., 26/5/21.
30. *Cape Times*, 26/5/21.
31. *Imvo Zabantsundu*, 21/6/21.
32. *Cape Argus*, 26/5/21.
33. House of Assembly Debates, *Cape Argus*, 15, 23 and 24 June 1921.
34. S.A.1925, U.G.39.
35. *Cape Argus*, 27/6/21, 21/10/21.
36. M. Lopes, 1963, Interview.
37. Degras, 1956, pp. 166–72, vol. I.
38. *International*, 31/12/20.
39. ibid., 22/10/20.
40. ibid., 26/11/20.
41. ibid., 31/12/20.
42. ibid., 18/2/21.
43. ibid., 17/12/20, 25/3/21.
44. *Bolshevik*, January and October 1920.
45. Formed by A. Hitchcock who kept a tailor's shop and published

a book with pictures showing what life would be like under socialism.

46. *International*, 25/2/21, 11/3/21, 1/4/21.
47. Lenin, 1920, *Collected Works*, vol. 30, pp. 146–9; Institut für Marxismus–Leninismus, 1966, vol. 3, p. 300; Degras, 1956, pp. 141–3, Vol. 1; Nollau, 1961, pp. 59–60.
48. *Labour World*, 24/1/20.
49. *International*, 31/12/20; *The Role of a Socialist Party in S.A.*
50. ibid., 10/12/20.
51. ibid., 22/10/20.
52. The ISL, SDP and Marxian Club of Durban; the United CP of Cape Town and the Jewish Socialist Society.
53. *International*, 13/5/21.
54. W. H. Andrews, M. Barlin, S. P. Bunting, A. Goldman, J. J. Hornstein, R. Rabb, F. Robertson, C. Traub, M. Youngelson.
55. D. L. Dryburgh, C. F. Glass, W. Green, W. Harrison, J. Pick.
56. G. Arnold, Mrs. R. Bunting, T. Chapman, J. Den Bakker, R. Geldblum, A. Goldman, H. Lee, E. M. Pincus, R. Rabb.
57. *International*, 12/8/21.
58. ibid., 26/8/21.
59. ibid., 3/12/20.
60. Andrews' Papers; *International*, 6/6/24.
61. ISL Press, Johannesburg, 1921.
62. *Cape Argus*, 22/7/21.
63. H. S. Msimang, 1966, Communication.
64. *Cape Times*, 29/10/21.
65. La Guma, 1963, Ch. 1.
66. Jabavu, 1920.
67. *International*, 21/12/18.
68. ibid., 22/7/21, 16/9/21.
69. ibid., 19/8/21, 2/9/21.
70. *A.P.O.*, 11/6/21.
71. ibid., 18/9/15.
72. ibid., 25/11/21.

Chapter 13

1. Gitsham & Trembath, 1926, p. 66.
2. *International*, 2/1/20.
3. *A.P.O.*, 16/4/21.
4. Walker & Weinbren, 1961, p. 94.

5. *A.P.O.*, 9/7/21.
6. *International*, 18/2/21, 4/11/21.
7. ibid., 18/2/21, 22/7/21; S.A.1922, U.G.35, par. 128.
8. S.A.1922, U.G.35, par. 128; *International*, 10/2/22.
9. *Forward*, 19/6/25.
10. *International*, 28/1/21.
11. ibid., 22/7/21, 9/9/21, 11/11/21, 27/1/22.
12. ibid., 6/2/20, 18/2/21, 25/3/21.
13. Transvaal Chamber of Mines, Annual Report for 1921, p. 133.
14. S.A.1922, U.G.39, par. 107–9.
15. *International*, 18/11/21.
16. ibid., 18/11/21, 25/11/21.
17. 2,159 miners were employed under contract and 1,279 at daily rates of pay in 1921.
18. S.A.1917, U.G.38, p. 14.
19. The occupations specified were those of handyman, fireman, jumperman, drill carrier, cleaner, greaser, compound clerk, attendant of a boiler, pump, meter or change house; and of men employed on sanitary services, transport, haulage, tramming, track and drain cleaning, drill sharpening and simple screwing machines, stone walling and rough pipe fitting, timbering and painting operations. (Transvaal Chamber of Mines, Annual Report for 1921, p. 48.)
20. *Cape Times*, 7, 10 and 30 January 1922.
21. ibid., 26/1/22, 25/2/22.
22. S.A.1922, U.G.35, par. 97.
23. *Cape Times*, 25/1/22.
24. ibid., 21 and 24 January 1922.
25. Defence Committee, 1924, pp. 5, 6, 18.
26. ibid., p. 7.
27. S.A.1922, U.G.35, par. 19.
28. E. Shaw, 1935, 'The Truth about the Council of Action 1922' *Forward*, 29/11/35.
29. *International*, 13/1/22.
30. S.A.1922, U.G.35, par. 152.
31. *International*, 13/1/22.
32. ibid., 3/2/22.
33. ibid., 18/11/21.
34. ibid., 2/6/22.
35. *A.P.O.*, 11/2/22.
36. ibid., 14/1/22, 11/3/22.
37. *International*, 20/1/22, 27/1/22.

38. ibid., 20/1/22.
39. ibid., 27/1/22, 3/2/22.
40. S.A.1922, U.G.35, par. 112.
41. ibid., par. 117.
42. *A.P.O.*, 28/1/22.
43. *International*, 27/1/22.
44. Roux (1949, p. 156) claims that 'Marxist socialists' had converted an old May Day banner by adding words to the original 'Workers of the World, Unite.'
45. *International*, 10/2/22.
46. *Cape Times*, 9/1/22; *A.P.O.*, 14/1/22; *International*, 27/1/22.
47. Defence Committee, 1924, p. 24; Walker & Weinbren, 1961, p. 115.
48. S.A.1922, U.G.35, par. 27, 31.
49. *International*, 10/2/22.
50. ibid., 10/2/22.
51. *A.P.O.*, 14/1/22, 25/2/22, 11/3/22.
52. House of Assembly Debates, *Cape Times*, 22/2/22.
53. Transvaal Nationalist Party Executive Resolution, *Cape Times*, 2/2/22.
54. *Cape Times*, 28/1/22.
55. ibid., 22/2/22.
56. House of Assembly Debates, February 4, 1926, C.256.
57. *International*, 3/2/22, 17/2/22, 24/2/22.
58. ibid., 10/2/22.
59. *A.P.O.*, 25/3/22.
60. *International*, 17/2/22.
61. S.A.1922, U.G.35, par. 68.
62. Walker & Weinbren, 1963, p. 114.
63. Cope, 1943, p. 250.
64. S.A.1922, U.G.35, par. 42, 43, 53, 126.
65. *International*, 3/3/22.
66. Transvaal Chamber of Mines, Annual Report for 1922, p. 163.
67. Cope, 1943, p. 263.
68. W. H. Andrews, 1937, 'The Great Rand Strike', *Guardian*, 25/3/37.
69. ibid., 1941, p. 34.
70. *International*, 3/3/22.
71. *International*, 10/2/22; Walker & Weinbren, 1961, pp. 119–20.
72. S.A.1922, U.G.35, par. 283; ICU of Africa Third Annual Conference; *A.P.O.*, 25/3/22; *International*, 16/2/23.
73. Bunting, S. P., 1922, *Red Revolt*, p. 23.
74. S.A.1922, U.G.35, par. 34.

75. Cope, 1943, p. 272.
76. Bunting, 1922, p. 24.
77. Herd, 1966, gives details of the actual revolt and suggests that Fisher was its 'top strategist'.
78. The Martial Law Commission found that 153 persons were killed or died of wounds in the fighting: 72 members of the government's forces, 39 strikers, 18 white and 24 other civilians. (S.A.1922, U.G.35, par. 71.)
79. Glanville, 1922.
80. *I.C.U.*, Third Annual Conference, January 1923, p. 26.
81. *A.P.O.*, 25/3/22.
82. *International*, 4/8/22, 16/3/23.
83. ibid., 18/8/22.
84. ibid., 16/2/23, 23/11/23.
85. *Bolshevik*, March 1920.

Chapter 14

1. S.A.1922, U.G.39, pp. 15–22.
2. Katzen, 1964, p. 22.
3. Defence Committee, 1924, pp. 20–21.
4. *Rex v.* Hildick-Smith, 1924, TPD at p. 90.
5. S.A.1920, U.G.34, p. 27.
6. S.A.1922, U.G.39, p. 6.
7. House of Assembly Debates, April 6, 1925, C.1920.
8. *International*, 14/9/23.
9. *A.P.O.*, 4/11/22.
10. *International*, 28/12/23.
11. ibid., 28/7/22.
12. ibid., 9/6/22, 30/6/22, 7/7/22.
13. Freislich, 1964, p. 63.
14. *A.P.O.*, 3/6/22, 1/7/22, 5/8/22.
15. *Forward*, 9/12/27.
16. Barlow, 1952, pp. 174–5.
17. Van Rooyen, 1956, pp. 102–5.
18. Van den Heever, 1946, pp. 453–4.
19. *International*, 5/1/23.
20. *Round Table*, vol. xiii, 1923, pp. 862–3.
21. *Cape Times*, 19/1/24, 25/1/24.
22. ibid., 25/2/24.
23. Creswell, 1956, p. 91.

24. House of Assembly Debates, *Cape Times*, 6/2/24.

25. ibid.

26. ICU 1923: Official Report of Proceedings of Third Annual Conference.

27. *International*, 18/5/23.

28. *Cape Times*, 26/1/24.

29. *International*, 21/9/23, 5/10/23, 12/10/23.

30. ibid., 2/11/23.

31. ibid., 10/11/22, 1/6/23, 22/6/23, 13/7/23, 27/7/23, 28/9/23, 12/10/23.

32. ibid., 4/5/23.

33. ibid., 5/1/23.

34. The party's central executive, elected in April 1923, consisted of Julius First, chairman; Sam Barlin, vice-chairman; S. P. Bunting, secretary-editor, C. F. Glass, organizer; S Ward, treasurer, and the committee members R. Gelblum, A. Goldman, H. Lee, R. Rabb, E. Roux, S. Rubin, W. Ward.

35. Jones to Andrews, 13/4/24.

36. *International*, 7/7/22, 5/1/23.

37. ibid., 19/1/23.

38. ibid.

39. Jones to Andrews, 13/4/24.

40. *International*, 30/3/23.

41. ibid., 21/9/23.

42. ibid., 28/12/23.

43. ibid., 30/6/22.

44. ibid., 29/6/23.

45. ibid., 29/6/23, 3/8/23.

46. ibid., 20/7/23, 3/8/23.

47. ibid., 10/8/23.

48. ibid., 1/6/23; *A.P.O.*, 21/7/23.

49. *A.P.O.*, 4/11/22.

50. ibid., 3/2/23, 2/5/24.

51. *International*, 16/11/23.

52. *A.P.O.*, 22/9/23, 26/1/24.

53. ibid., 19/5/23.

54. ibid., 21/4/23, 19/5/23.

55. Kadalie, 1954, ch. iv.

56. See above, p. 305.

57. *A.P.O.*, 5/7/24.

58. Kadalie, 1954, ch. iv.

59. *A.P.O.*, 25/8/23.

60. Tobias, M., 1929, *Social and Industrial Review*, vol. vii, pp. 65–6.
61. Andrews, 1940, *Class Struggles in South Africa*, pp. 37–8.
62. *International*, 28/12/23.
63. S.A.1923, S.C.5, pp. 1–2; *Cape Times*, 14/2/24.
64. *Cape Times*, 31/1/24.
65. Smuts, 1952, pp. 257–8.
66. *Burger*, 3/6/24, 14/6/24.
67. *Cape Times*, 26/1/24; Gold Producers' Committee, 1924, *Party Programmes and the Mines*, 1924.
68. *International*, 23/11/23; *A.P.O.*, 26/1/24, 6/6/24, 5/7/24; *Burger*, 31/5/24, 2, 4 and 5 June 1924.
69. Communist Party of South Africa, 1924, *A Vital Issue. Shall Labour Enter the Cabinet?*
70. Creswell, 1956, pp. 99–101.
71. Described as a 'Labour Journal', it was the successor to the 'Pact Bulletin', and was owned by G. Weinstock.
72. House of Assembly Debates, 25/2/25, col. 286.
73. *Forward*, 24/12/24, 8/1/25, 13/3/25.
74. S.A. Labour Party, 1925, Minutes of Annual Conference.
75. *Forward*, 13/5/25, 21/8/25; Kentridge, 1959, pp. 150–52.
76. *Forward*, 23/11/24.
77. *Voice of Labour*, 19/8/10, 11/11/10.
78. Roux, 1944, ch. 9.
79. Cope, 1943, p. 295.
80. *Forward*, 15/5/25, 12/6/25, 4/9/25.
81. ibid., 2/10/25, 9/10/25, 24/12/25.

Chapter 15

1. *Forward*, 13/11/25.
2. *Official Labour Gazette*, April 1925, p. 24.
3. *Forward*, 15/1/25.
4. ibid., 26/2/25.
5. ibid., 27/3/25.
6. *Official Labour Gazette*, May 1925, pp. 46–7.
7. S.A. Trade Union Congress, circular letter of 30/6/26.
8. See above p. 88.
9. S.A.1926, U.G.14, p. 357.
10. Andrews, W. H., 1926, pp. 47–51: 'African Labour Problems' in *Alberta Labour Annual*, 4 September 1926.
11. Cousins, C. W., 1929, p. 207: *Social and Industrial Review*, March 1929, vol. vii, No. 39.

12. Section 14, Act 11 of 1924.

13. *Social and Industrial Review*, January 1929, vol. vii, No. 37, pp. 56–7.

14. S.A.1935, U.G.37, par. 447.

15. *Social and Industrial Review*, January 1929, vol. vii, No. 37, p. 56.

16. Government Notice 2281 of 24/12/25.

17. Most of the men were excluded by a new definition in Act 36 of 1937.

18. S.A.1935, U.G.37, par. 441.

19. Government Notice 1514 of 11/9/25.

20. Section 48(4) and (6), Act 36 of 1937.

21. S.A.1951, U.G.62, par. 1456.

22. *Social and Industrial Review*, January 1929, vol. vii, no. 37, pp. 65–6.

23. ibid., August 1926, vol. ii, no. 8, pp. 639–40.

24. S.A.1917, S.C.4.

25. The 'civilized habits' clause was deleted by Act 44 of 1937, which also prohibited racial discrimination in the fixing of wages.

26. *Social and Industrial Review*, March 1926, vol. ii, no. 3, p. 140.

27. House of Assembly Debates, 2/4/25, C.1771.

28. S.A.1932, U.G.22, Addendum by F. A. W. Lucas, par. 318.

29. *Social and Industrial Review*, 1927, vol. iv, p. 370, November, (duplicated).

30. P. K. Rao, 1929, p. 9. *Labour Policy in South Africa.*

31. *Social and Industrial Review*, November 1928, vol. vi, no. 35.

32. Official Year Book No. 9, 1926–7, pp. 202–3.

33. *Cape Times*, 16 April, 1926.

34. S.A.1937, U.G.54, ch. 4.

35. *Official Labour Gazette*, April 1925, p. 23.

36. *Forward*, 24/4/25, 26/6/25, 21/8/25.

37. ibid., 28/8/25, 9/10/25.

38. ibid., 27/11/25, 31/12/25.

39. ibid., 26/2/25.

40. S.A.1925, U.G.36, par. 28.

41. House of Assembly Debates, 25/2/25, C.267.

42. ibid., 25/2/25, C.284.

43. *Forward*, 6/3/25.

44. House of Assembly Debates, 4/5/25, C.2793; 18/6/25, C.4660.

45. *Forward*, 10/7/25.

46. Mines and Works Act (Amendment) Act, 1926; Government Notice 1124 of 1937, par. 285.

47. *Star*, 14/11/25.

48. Joint Sitting of Parliament, 12–15/2/29, C.169.
49. The Coloured Persons' Rights Bill; Representation of Natives in Parliament Bill; Union Native Council Bill; Natives Land Bill (Government Gazette Extraordinary 1570 of 23/7/26).
50. *Forward*, 4/12/25.
51. ibid., 20/11/25, 27/11/25.
52. *Cape Times*, 17/6/26.
53. *Star*, 16/11/25.
54. ibid., 14/11/25.
55. *Workers' Herald*, 15/12/25.
56. *Star*, 4/1/26.
57. ibid., 3/1/27.
58. ibid., 18/4/27.
59. ibid., 16/4/27.
60. *Diamond Field Advertiser*, 24/6/27; *South African Outlook*, 1/9/27.
61. *Star*, 3/6/27.
62. Simons, 1968, ch. V.
63. House of Assembly Debates, 28/4/27, C.2907–8, 2914–19.
64. *Star*, 2/6/27.
65. *South African Worker*, 2/3/28, 16/3/28, 19/9/28.
66. *New Leader*, 30/9/27.
67. House of Assembly Debates, 20/6/27, C.5300–1, 5316–18, 5326.
68. Boydell, 1947, pp. 287–92.
69. House of Assembly Debates, 30/6/25, C.5224–77.
70. Creswell, 1956, pp. 109–10.
71. S.A. Labour Party 1927, Minutes of Annual Conference held at Bloemfontein, 1–3 January 1927.
72. *Star*, 18/6/27, 20/6/27; *Forward*, 28/10/27.
73. *Forward*, 4/11/27.
74. ibid., 23/12/27.
75. The expelled members were Creswell, Boydell, Brown, Fordham, Lomax, McMenamin, Mullineaux, Sampson, Snow and Strachan.
76. Stuart to SALP, 7/3/28 and to Andrews, 23/3/28.
77. *Forward*, 10/8/28
78. ibid., 9/3/28, 23/3/28, 30/3/28.
79. ibid., 16/3/28, 6/7/28.
80. ibid., 16/10/28.
81. ibid., 9/11/28.
82. ibid., 9, 16 and 23 November 1928.
83. ibid., 8/1/25, 10/7/25.
84. SALP, 1929, p. 29: *Our Policy, Platform and Outlook*.
85. *Forward*, 7/6/29, 14/6/29.

86. *Star*, 19/4/29.
87. *Daily Dispatch*, 1/5/29.
88. Joint Sitting of Parliament, 21/2/29, C.241–2; *Burger*, 2/3/29.
89. *Star*, 17/5/29.
90. Oliver, G. R., 1929: *To all Cape Coloured Friends in the Union*, (Central Committee of the African National Bond).
91. Roux, 1949, pp. 225–30.
92. *Forward*, 14/6/29.
93. *Star*, 1/1/29.

Chapter 16

1. Liga gegen Imperialismus, 1927, p. 95 (our translation).
2. ibid., p. 126.
3. *Star*, 24/1/27.
4. *South African Worker*, 8/10/26, 14/1/27, 4/11/27.
5. Kadalie, 1954, pp. 56, 69–72.
6. *South African Worker*, 24/12/26; La Guma, 1964, pp. 24–6.
7. *Star*, 24/1/27.
8. *South African Worker*, 24/12/26, 31/12/26, 14/1/27, 25/2/27, 29/4/27, 6/5/27.
9. E. R. Roux, 1928, *International Press Correspondence*, vol. 8, no. 72, pp. 1316–17.
10. *Umsebenzi*, 6/6/30.
11. *South African Worker*, 7/1/27.
12. Gitsham and Trembath, 1926, p. 125: Interview with J. A. La Guma, May 1957; *Star*, 19/2/29.
13. Skota, 1932, p. 429.
14. *Udibi Lwase Afrika*, September 1927.
15. Kadalie, 1954, p. 67.
16. ICU, 1923. *Third Annual Conference, Official Report of Proceedings*.
17. Kadalie, 1954, p. 52–4.
18. ICU 1925. *Audited Financial Statement of Head Office for 1925*.
19. Kadalie, 1954, p. 124.
20. We are indebted to Miss Sylvia Neame for this summary.
21. Kadalie, 1954, p. 56.
22. ibid., p. 72.
23. *New Leader*, 8/7/27, p. 6.

24. E. R. Roux, 'White and Coloured Workers in South Africa', *Labour Monthly*, vol. 9, no. 10, pp. 632–3; *International Press Correspondence*, op. cit.

25. Kadalie, 1954, pp. 35, 57.

26. *Workers' Herald*, 15/11/26.

27. *Nation and Atheneum*, 10/9/27, pp. 741–2.

28. *South African Worker*, 28/2/29.

29. *New Leader*, 8/7/27, p. 6.

30. F. McGregor, 1929, pp. 56–7: 'Conciliation in South African Industries', *Social and Industrial Review*, vol. vii, no. 37.

31. Kadalie, 1954, ch. iii.

32. ibid., p. 134; E. R. Roux, 1928, pp. 55–6; 'Agrarian Revolt in South Africa', *Labour Monthly*, January 1928.

33. *South African Worker*, 1/7/27, 8/7/27, 15/7/27; *Star*, 16/6/27, 26/6/27, 7/7/27, 8/7/27; *Workers' Life*, 12/8/27; E. R. Roux, 1949, pp. 180–81.

34. *Workers' Herald*, 30/11/28.

35. *Star*, 18, 21, 25, June 1928.

36. *South African Worker*, 17/6/27.

37. Kadalie, 1954, pp. 198–200.

38. House of Assembly Debates, 6/3/28, C.1749–51.

39. *Workers' Herald*, 18/1/28.

40. A. W. G. Champion, 1929, *Mehlomadala: My experiences in the ICU*, pp. 22–3.

41. *Star*, 19/11/27.

42. *Udibi Lwase Afrika*, March 1928.

43. *Friend*, 3/4/28, 5/4/28.

44. *South African Worker*, 16/3/28.

45. *Udibi Lwase Afrika*, March 1928, pp. 6–7.

46. Kadalie, 1954, p. 141.

47. A. W. G. Champion, 1929, op. cit., p. 23.

48. *Workers' Herald*, 30/11/28.

49. *Friend*, 3/4/28.

50. *Star*, 16/11/27.

51. *South African Worker*, 27/8/26.

52. *Forward*, 21/1/44.

53. *Star*, 16/1/28.

54. *Cape Times*, 19/1/28.

55. S.A. Trade Union Coordinating Committee, 1928: *Memorandum on the question of affiliation of the Industrial and Commercial Workers' Union*.

56. Bunting to La Guma (c. September 1927).

57. S.A. Trade Union Congress, 1927; *Report of Conference of National Executive Council with Executives of affiliated Unions*, 11 September 1927.
58. *Star*, 7/1/28, 16/1/28.
59. N. G. Moodley, 1961, 'History of Indian Trade Unions in South Africa', *Graphic*, 30/12/60, 6/1/61.
60. *Cape Times*, 5/1/28; *Social and Industrial Review*, January 1929, vol. vii, no. 37, pp. 56–7.
61. *Forward*, 6, 13, 20 and 27 April 1928.
62. Cope, 1943, pp. 235, 314; *South African Worker*, 15/4/27.
63. loc. cit., p. 315.
64. *Forward*, 12/10/28.
65. Kadalie, 1954, p. 152.
66. C. D. Modiakgotla, *Manifesto of the Clean Administration Group*, 1928 (Duplicated).
67. *Star*, 19/7/28, 3/12/28.
68. ibid., 23/11/28.
69. A. W. G. Champion, 1929, op. cit., pp. 22–7.
70. Leubuscher, 1931, p. 177.
71. *Star*, 23/10/28, 4/2/29, 11/2/29.
72. *Rand Daily Mail*, 11/2/29.
73. *Star*, 9/2/29.
74. Kadalie, 1954, pp. 153–4.
75. Roux, 1949, p. 196.
76. *South African Worker*, 30/3/29, 30/4/29.
77. Wolton to La Guma, 3/2/28.
78. *Star*, 18/2/29.
79. B. Weinbren, 1944, 'The Inside Story of S.A. Labour', *Forward*, 21/1/44, 21/4/44, 12/5/44.
80. *International Press Correspondence*, 17/10/28, vol. 8, no. 72, pp. 1316–17.
81. RILU, 1928, pp. 44–5: *Report of the Fourth Congress*, published by the National Minority Movement, London.
82. *South African Worker*, 19/9/28.
83. *Forward*, 25/5/28; *Star*, 8, 9 and 11 June 1928.
84. *South African Worker*, 31/10/29, 30/11/29; *Umsebenzi*, 1/8/30.
85. *Forward*, 3/8/28; *South African Worker*, 30/9/29.
86. S.A. Trade Union Congress, 1929, *The Industrial Organization of the Non-European Worker* (Duplicated).
87. *Star*, 21/8/28.
88. *Forward*, 14/9/28.
89. ibid., 19/7/29.

90. ibid., 1/2/29.
91. *Star*, 19/2/29.
92. *Indian Views*, 18/10/29.
93. *Forward*, 1/2/29.
94. ibid., 14/9/28.
95. S.A.1955, S.C.3, pp. 208–9.
96. S.A. Trade Union Congress, 1929, *The Industrial Organization of the Non-European Worker*.
97. S.A. Trade Union Congress and Cape Federation of Labour Unions, 1927. *Résumé of Proceedings of Meeting etc.*, *on* 17/4/27.
98. Cape Federation of Labour Unions, 1930, *Reasons for holding an all-in Conference of labour unions, 15/8/30*.
99. S.A. Trade Union Coordinating Committee, *Minutes of meeting held on 29 December 1927*; Stuart to Andrews, 7/12/27.
100. Kadalie, 1954, p. 159.
101. *Umsebenzi*, 25/7/30, 29/8/30, 5/9/30.
102. ibid., 10/10/30.
103. All-In Trades Union Conference, 4–6 October 1930: *Report of Proceedings*.
104. *Umsebenzi*, 10/10/30, 31/10/30.
105. ibid., 14/11/30; *Forward*, 14/11/30.
106. S.A. Trades and Labour Council, *Minutes of Meeting of the N.E.C. with Union executives*, 7/12/30.
107. Botha, 1928, p. 29 (our translation).

Chapter 17

1. S. P. Bunting, 1928, *Imperialism and South Africa*, ch. viii.
2. S.A. Native National Congress: The Constitution, par. 12(9).
3. *Rand Daily Mail*, 2/6/23.
4. *Forward*, 2/11/28.
5. ibid., 22/11/29.
6. S.A. Labour Party: National Organizing Committee, Memorandum of 1/1/30 by J. Allen, L. Karovsky and S. J. Smith (Per D. Ticktin).
7. C. L. Henderson to W. Harrison, 2/2/43.
8. *South African Worker*, 13/8/26.
9. It consisted of J. Shields, chairman; B. Weinbren, vice-chairman; S. P. Bunting, general secretary; A. H. Michaelson, treasurer; and Rebecca Bunting, W. Kalk, E. J. Khaile, Gana Makabeni, E. Mottushek, E. S. Sachs, Violet Shields and T. W. Thibedi.

10. *South African Worker*, 1/4/27.
11. La Guma, 1963, p. 29.
12. Liga gegen Imperialismus, 1927, pp. 95, 129.
13. La Guma, 1963, p. 37.
14. Roux, 1944, pp. 88–9.
15. Liga gegen Imperialismus, 1927, p. 225.
16. Bunting to La Guma, *circa* June 1927.
17. Bunting to Gibarti, *circa* September 1927.
18. Bunting to La Guma, *circa* June 1927.
19. *South African Worker*, 1/7/27, 5/8/27.
20. ibid., 15/4/27, 22/4/27, 29/4/27.
21. ibid., 15/7/27.
22. ibid., 5/8/27.
23. *Udibi Lwase Afrika*, September 1927.
24. *Workers' Herald*, 18/1/28.
25. Bunting to La Guma, 27/9/27.
26. Bunting to Gibarti, *circa* September 1927.
27. J. A. La Guma, *Report on the South African Situation in the Party*, 2/12/27.
28. S. P. Bunting, 1928, *An Independent Native Republic for South Africa* (typed).
29. *South African Worker*, 11/5/28.
30. ibid., 27/4/28.
31. J. A. La Guma, 1928, *A National Revolutionary Movement of Black South Africa* (duplicated).
32. Wolton to La Guma, 17/2/28.
33. Interview with Wolton, 9/4/67, 3/6/67.
34. *South African Worker*, 17/2/28.
35. ibid., 11/5/28, 27/7/28.
36. ibid., 30/3/28, 25/5/28, 27/7/28.
37. ibid., 30/3/28, 27/7/28, 22/8/28.
38. ibid., 22/6/28.
39. ibid., 2/3/28, 30/3/28.
40. ibid., 2/3/28.
41. Wolton, 1947, pp. 70–71.
42. *Friend*, 7/4/28.
43. ibid., 10/4/28.
44. ibid., 11/4/28.
45. *South African Worker*, 13/4/28, 27/4/28.
46. ibid., 25/5/28.
47. Roux, 1944, pp. 88–9.
48. ibid., 1949, p. 264.

49. cf. Walker, 1957, p. 624.
50. S.A. Communist Party, *The Cape District Party Organizer*, May 1944.
51. Sik, 1966, vol. ii, p. 153.
52. *International Press Correspondence*, 3/8/28, vol. 8, no. 44, pp. 780–82; 13/8/28, no. 49, p. 872; 23/8/28, no. 53, p. 943; 19/9/28, no. 64, p. 1156.
53. ibid., 8/11/28, no. 78, pp. 1451–3.
54. Roux, 1944, p. 98.
55. *Forward*, 30/3/28, 16/11/28, 21/11/28.
56. J. A. La Guma, 1928, *Who's for the Third International Thesis on S.A.* (holograph).
57. Roux, 1944, pp. 102–3.
58. *South African Worker*, 30/11/28, 31/1/29. The executive consisted of S. P. Bunting, chairman and treasurer; E. S. Sachs, vice-chairman; D. G. Wolton, general secretary and editor; A. Nzula, organizer and assistant secretary; S. Malkinson, book-keeper; T. W. Thibedi, Rebecca Bunting, Molly Wolton and J. Nkosi.
59. *South African Worker*, 30/9/29.
60. ibid., 15/3/29, 30/9/29, 31/10/29, 31/12/29.
61. Wolton, 1947, pp. 60, 68; Interview with Wolton, 9/4/67.
62. *South African Worker*, 24/10/28.

Chapter 18

1. *Indian Opinion*, 21/6/29, 9/8/29.
2. *Cape Times*, 6/8/29.
3. House of Assembly Debates, 8/8/29, C.584, 587.
4. *South African Worker*, 31/8/29.
5. ibid., 30/9/29, 31/10/29.
6. *Forward*, 16/8/29, 15/11/29.
7. *Rand Daily Mail*, 20/7/29.
8. *South African Worker*, 30/9/29, 31/10/29.
9. *Star*, 11/11/29.
10. *Star*, 14/11/29; *Cape Times*, 15/11/29.
11. *Rand Daily Mail*, 14/11/29.
12. *South African Worker*, 30/11/29.
13. *Rand Daily Mail*, 20/11/29.
14. Roux, 1944, p. 114; 1949, p. 235; House of Assembly Debates, vol. 14, 1930, C.732–77.
15. *Star*, 6/12/29, 7/12/29.

16. *South African Worker*, 31/12/29.
17. *Star*, 9/12/29.
18. *South African Worker*, 31/12/29.
19. *Umsebenzi*, 20/6/30, 4/7/30, 18/7/30.
20. *South African Worker*, 30/11/29.
21. ibid., 30/11/29, 31/12/29, 31/1/30.
22. Olive Budden, 1929, pp. 1446–7: 'Revolutionary Developments in South Africa', *International Press Correspondence*, vol. 9, no. 68, 6/12/29.
23. *Star*, 15/1/30.
24. ibid., 27/1/30; *South African Worker*, 31/1/30.
25. *South African Worker*, 28/2/30.
26. *Umsebenzi*, 18/4/30.
27. *Friend*, 22/4/30.
28. *Abantu Batho*, 27/4/30.
29. *Umsebenzi*, 25/4/30.
30. The Women's Enfranchisement Act of 1930 and the Franchise Laws Amendment Act of 1931.
31. The number of white voters rose from 410,728 in 1929 to 850,182 in 1931, while the number of African, Coloured and Indian voters fell from 41,744 to 38,991 and decreased relatively from 9·3% to 4·4% of the total electorate. (Tatz, 1962, p. 64.)
32. *Cape Times*, 1/5/30.
33. ibid., 2/5/30; *Umsebenzi*, 25/4/30, 5/5/30, 9/5/30, 16/5/30.
34. *Umsebenzi*, 4/7/30.
35. *Umsebenzi*, 23/5/30, 13/6/30.
36. ibid., 5/9/30.
37. ibid., 31/10/30.
38. ibid., 12/9/30, 19/9/30, 21/11/30.
39. S.A.1932, U.G.22, par. 69.
40. Section 12(1)(d), Act 21 of 1923, as inserted by Section 7, Act 25 of 1930.
41. *Dispatch*, 12/12/30; *Star*, 12/12/30.
42. *Natal Advertiser*, 10/2/31.
43. *Umsebenzi*, 23/1/31, 30/1/31.
44. ibid., 19/12/30.
45. ibid., 6/2/31, 27/3/31.
46. Roux, 1949, pp. 257–63.
47. ibid., pp. 262–3; Benson, 1966, p. 59.
48. *Friend*, 6, 7, 8 and 9 January 1931.
49. *Umsebenzi*, 16/1/31.

Chapter 19

1. *Praesidium of the ECCI to the Communist Party of South Africa*, 7/5/30 (duplicated).
2. *Abantu Batho*, 3/7/30, 4/12/30.
3. *Umsebenzi*, 16/5/30.
4. ibid., 12/9/30, 26/9/30. Lopes joined the Nationalist Party in July 1937.
5. Wolton to Simons, 4/5/67.
6. *Umsebenzi*, 5/12/30.
7. ibid., 9/1/31; D. Wolton, 1931, 'Fighting the Right Danger in South Africa', *International Press Correspondence*. vol. 11, no. 9, 26/2/31, p. 183.
8. R. Alexander, 25/2/31, circular letter (duplicated).
9. Wolton, 1947, p. 73.
10. *Umsebenzi*, 15/5/31, 12/6/31.
11. ibid., 10/7/31. The unions represented garment, furniture, leather and sweetworkers in Johannesburg.
12. ibid., 10/7/31.
13. ibid., 24/7/31.
14. ibid., 5/2/30, 28/11/30, 27/3/31.
15. W. H. Andrews, *Memorandum of May 30th, 1931 to Political Bureau, CPSA* (typed).
16. *Umsebenzi*, 4/9/31.
17. *Star*, 8/9/31.
18. *Umsebenzi*, 2/10/31, 30/10/31.
19. La Guma to District Party Committee, Cape Town, 30/9/31.
20. S. P. Bunting, 1931. Circular letter to members of the Communist Party, October 1931.
21. Roux, 1944, Ch. 17.
22. *Umsebenzi*, 22/10/32.
23. Roux, 1944, p. 125.
24. Wolton explains that he wanted to credit African comrades with the work he had done in South Africa (Wolton to Simons, 23/8/67).
25. *Umsebenzi*, 25/12/31, 8/1/32, 22/1/32.
26. *Umteteli wa Bantu*, 9/1/32.
27. *Friend*, 19/4/33.
28. *Umsebenzi*, 7/4/34, 21/4/34.
29. ibid., 5/11/32.
30. *Worker* (USA), 5/2/61, 28/1/62.
31. House of Assembly Debates, 9/2/32, C.777; Official Year Book No. 14, p. 169; no. 16, p. 191.

32. *Star*, 1/5/30.
33. House of Assembly Debates, 3/2/31, C.50.
34. Official Year Book, No. 17, p. 113.
35. *Star*, 1/8/31.
36. ibid., 11/8/32.
37. *Labour Gazette*, September 1930, p. 1.
38. The Carnegie Commission 1932, *The Poor White Problem in South Africa*, part 1, par. 110.
39. S.A.1932, U.G.30, par. 9, 90.
40. *Umsebenzi*, 27/5/32.
41. ibid., 1/5/33, 27/5/33.
42. *African Leader*, 12/3/32.
43. *Friend*, 5/1/31; *Forward*, 6/11/31, 31/12/31.
44. *Umsebenzi*, 4/3/32, 18/3/32, 1/4/32.
45. O. Huiswood, 1932, *The Tasks of the Revolutionary Trade Union Movement in South Africa*.
46. *Umsebenzi*, 17/3/34.
47. ibid., 15/4/32.
48. ibid., 17/3/34, 24/3/34, 31/3/34, 5/5/34.
49. *Rand Daily Mail*, 7/9/32.

Chapter 20

1. van den Heever, 1946, p. 594.
2. *Umsebenzi*, 10/3/33.
3. S.A. Labour Party 1933, Report of the National Executive Committee, etc., 25 March 1933 (duplicated).
4. *Star*, 3/8/31, 4/8/31.
5. S.A. Labour Party, 1933, 'Memorandum on Native Policy'; *Forward*, 6/1/33.
6. Election Manifesto of the Communist Party of South Africa, May 1933.
7. Roux, 1944, p. 148.
8. Act 8 of 1930.
9. *Star*, 28/12/31.
10. *Umsebenzi*, 1/7/33.
11. *Umteteli Wa Bantu*, 21/10/33.
12. *Umsebenzi*, 16/6/34, 21/7/34, 25/8/34, 1/9/34.
13. ibid., 27/1/34.
14. *Cape Times*, 6/6/34.
15. *Umsebenzi*, 24/2/34, 16/6/34, 23/3/35.
16. Scholtz, 1943, p. 226.

17. Quoted by Hertzog in his speech at Smithfield, *Star*, 7/11/35.
18. Nicholls, 1961, pp. 286-7.
19. S.A. 1935, Report of the Joint Committee, No. 1, 1935.
20. *Umsebenzi*, 7/7/34, 11/8/34, 8/9/34, 17/11/34, 5/1/35.
21. S.A. Trades and Labour Council, 1935, pp. 60–61, *Minutes of Fifth Annual Conference*.
22. *Forward*, 19/7/35.
23. Andrews to Harrison, 23/1/34.
24. Communist Party of South Africa, 1934, *What is the Native Independent Republic?* (duplicated).
25. *Umsebenzi*, 27/4/35.
26. ibid., 20/8/32, 10/9/32, 22/10/32, 7/10/33, 21/7/34.
27. ibid., 5/5/34.
28. J. C. Smuts, 1930, *Africa and Some World Problems*, p. 68.
29. *Rand Daily Mail*, 16/12/33, 13/11/34, 24/11/34.
30. *Star*, 14/12/35.
31. D. D. T. Jabavu, 1935, *The Findings of the All African Convention*, p. 3.
32. Institut für Marxismus-Leninismus Deutschlands, 1966, vol. 5, pp. 105–12.
33. *Umsebenzi*, 21/9/35, 11/1/36, 18/1/36.
34. ibid., 19/5/34.
35. *Umsebenzi*, 27/7/35, 26/9/35. A. Kagan, B. Levenberg, H. Sacks and A. Spilkin were expelled; I. Diamond was suspended.
36. Coka, 1936.
37. Roux, 1944, pp. 154–5.
38. *South African Worker*, 19/6/37; *Sunday Express*, 18/7/37.
39. CPSA, 1936, *Organize a People's Front in South Africa*.
40. *Forward*, 3/4/36, 17/4/36.
41. *Umsebenzi*, 6/6/36.
42. CPSA, 1936, loc. cit., p. 19.
43. *Forward*, 9/10/36.
44. SATLC, 1938, *Report of Eighth Annual Conference*, p. 13.
45. CPSA, 1939, *Minutes of Meeting*, Johannesburg, 29 December 1938 to 1 January 1939 (typed), p. 36.
46. *South African Worker*, 20/3/37, 12/6/37, 17/7/37.
47. CPSA, 1939, op. cit., p. 5.
48. *South African Worker*, 26/6/37.
49. ibid., 9/1/37, 5/2/38.
50. The Labour members were Madeley, Burnside who rejoined the Party after standing as a Socialist and the Rev. Miles Cadman, a cleric from Durban.

51. Roberts and Trollip, 1947, ch. iv.
52. This and the following discussion is based on the reports and minutes of the December–January meeting, op. cit.

Chapter 21

1. Empire Group of South Africa, 1931, *Franchise Rights and Wrongs*.
2. *Umsebenzi*, 21/7/34, 28/7/34, 11/8/34.
3. Roux was sentenced to four months' and Josiah Ngedlane to one month's hard labour in Durban for the same offence. All convictions were set aside on appeal.
4. *For Equality, Land and Freedom* (duplicated).
5. S.A. 1937, U.G.54.
6. Bridgeman to the National Liberation League, 25/3/36.
7. *Liberator*, vol. 1, no. 5, 1937, pp. 8–11.
8. *Umteteli Wa Bantu*, 4/2/33.
9. ibid., 28/7/34.
10. ibid., 19/3/35, 23/5/35.
11. *Umsebenzi*, 26/1/35.
12. ibid., 16/2/35.
13. ibid., 9/2/35, 20/4/35, 27/4/35.
14. Coka, 1936.
15. Coka (no date) *Friends or Foes?*.
16. CPSA, 1934, *What is the Native Independent Republic?*
17. N. Mkele, 'The Emergent African Middle Class', *Optima*, vol. 10, no. 4, 1960, pp. 217–26; 'The African Middle Class', *The Inst. for the Study of Man in Africa*, 1961, pp. 1–18.
18. CPSA, 1939, *Minutes of Meeting*, Johannesburg, 29 December 1938 to 1 January 1939, p. 19 (typed).
19. *Umsebenzi*, 26/10/35.
20. D. D. T. Jabavu, 1936, *The Findings of the All African Convention.*
21. *Umteteli Wa Bantu*, 8/2/36, 15/2/36, 22/2/36, 11/4/36.
22. S.A. 1936, J.S.1–36, J.S.2–36, *Joint Sitting of Both Houses of Parliament, Representation of Native Bills*, C.59, 147–54, 522–9.
23. S.A. 1946. Native Representative Council: *Verbatim Report*, 14–15 August, 1946, pp. 36–41.
24. D. D. T. Jabavu (ed.), 1936, *Minutes of the All African Convention*, pp. 42–5.
25. Hardy, 1956, p. 229.
26. CPSA, 1936, *Organize a People's Front in South Africa*, pp. 16–17.
27. *Umteteli Wa Bantu*, 27/6/36.

28. D. D. T. Jabavu (ed.), op. cit.
29. *South African Worker*, 27/6/36, 8/8/36, 5/9/36, 19/9/36, 3/10/36, 10/10/36, 17/10/36.
30. ibid., 13/3/37, 3/7/37, 10/7/37.
31. Cit. by Roux, 1949, p. 293.
32. CPSA, 1938, *Vereeniging: Who is to Blame?*
33 *South African Worker*, 6/11/37.
34. CPSA, 1939; *Minutes of Meeting*, Johannesburg, 29 December 1938 to 1 January 1939: 'Report on the Struggle of Africans' (typed).
35. *South African Worker*, 6/11/37, 20/11/37.
36. ibid., 1/8/37, 4/9/37, 6/11/37.
37. *Minutes of the All African Convention*, December 1937.
38. J. A. La Guma, 1937, 'We demand social equality', *Liberator*, vol. I, no. 1, March 1937, p. 9.
39. CPSA, February 1939, *Back to Slavery!*
40. *Guardian*, 31/3/39.
41. ibid., 14/4/39.
42. *Sun*, 28/4/39, 12/5/39, 2/6/39, 9/6/39.
43. *Guardian*, 23/6/39.
44. cf. Walker, 1959, p. 652.
45. NEUF, 1939, *Minutes of Conference*, 8 April 1939. Issued by M. M. Kotane (duplicated).
46. *South African Worker*, 12/2/38; *Guardian*, 5/5/39.
47. See Joshi, 1942.
48. *South African Indian Review*, February 1936.
49. Calpin (no date) p. 39.
50. *Sun*, 9/6/39.
51. *Imvo Zabantsundu*, 2/4/38.
52. *Guardian*, 9/6/39, 23/6/39, 30/6/39.
53. Joshi, 1942, p. 260; G. H. Calpin (no date) p. 117.

Chapter 22

1. Industrial Census
2. *Forward*, 2/11/34.
3. S.A.1935, U.G.37, par. 368.
4. SATLC, *Annual Report for 1935*, pp. 44–5; *Minutes of Sixth Annual Conference*, 1936, p. 74.
5. S.A.1937, U.G.4, p. 70; 1939, U.G.51, p. 60. Department of Labour Reports.

6. *Umsebenzi*, 24/11/34.
7. SATLC, 1940, *Report of Tenth Annual Conference*, pp. 9, 24–6.
8. NETC, C.C. 1939, Presidential Address (Typed).
9. D. Tloome, 1956, *Memorandum on Council of Non-European Trade Unions* (holograph).
10. *Umsebenzi*, 14/4/33; 8/6/35.
11. *South African Worker*, 21/11/36.
12. *Forward*, 1/12/33.
13. CPSA, 1936, *Organize a People's Front in South Africa*.
14. ibid., 1937, *Communism and the Native Question*.
15. SATLC, 1935, pp. 57–8, *Report of Fifth Annual Conference, 1935*; S.A. 1935, U.G.37, par. 127–8.
16. 'Programme of Immediate Economic and Political Demands', *Umsebenzi*, 11/7/36.
17. SATLC, 1937, *Report of Seventh Annual Conference, 1937*, pp. 44–50.
18. S.A.1951, U.G.62, p. 159.
19. CPSA, *Minutes of Meeting*, Johannesburg, 1938–9 (typed), pp. 19–20.
20. ibid., 1936, *Organize a People's Front*, p. 13.
21. SATLC, 1938, *Report of Eighth Annual Conference*, pp. 72–3.
22. House of Assembly Debates, 23/3/37, C.3687–8.
23. S.A.1951, U.G.62, p. 196.
24. SATLC, 1940, *Report of Tenth Annual Conference*, pp. 61–6.
25. House of Assembly Debates, 20/4/37, C.5120–1; 26/4/37, C.5420.
26. See Alexander and Simons, 1959.
27. N. Diederichs, 1939, *Die Reddingsdaad-Strewe*.
28. *Skakel*, May 1936.
29. 'Conquer through Service'.
30. J. A. Adam, 1952, ch. 8.
31. House of Assembly Debates, 18/2/38, C.262; 4/3/38, C.1003–5.
32. *Negro Worker*, vol. 6, no. 8, 1936, p. 7.
33. House of Assembly Debates, 30/5/33, C.30; 23/9/38, C.3535–8.
34. *We Want to Live: The Case of the Non-European Railway and Harbour Workers, 1938*.
35. *Forward*, 22/9/39.
36. House of Assembly Debates, 8/4/37, C.4435.
37. SATLC, 1937, *Report of the Seventh Annual Conference*, pp. 32–6.
38. House of Assembly Debates, 23/4/37, C.5366.
39. *Mynwerker*, April 1937.
40. House of Assembly Debates, 26/4/37, C.5456–7.
41. S.A.1941, pp. 6–7.

42. H. P. Wolmarans (no date) *Kommunisme en die Suid-Afrikaanse Vakunies.*

43. *Cape Times*, 28/3/38, 31/3/38.

44. *National Party Election Manifesto*, 1938; House of Assembly Debates, 1/3/38, C.754.

45. House of Assembly Debates, 6/2/56, C.1076.

46. Federale Raad van die Nasionale Party, 1938, *Die Groot Beslissing.*

47. *Die Burger*, 10/3/39. Afrikaners won a battle at Blood River against the Zulu in 1838 and at Majuba against the British in 1881.

48. *Cape Argus*, 13/11/40.

49. S.A.1941, p. 7.

50. *Forward*, 6/4/39, 28/4/39.

51. *Guardian*, 24/11/39.

52. *Forward*, 29/9/39.

53. *Guardian*, 19/9/40, 3/10/40.

Chapter 23

1. cf. Roberts and Trollip, 1947, chapters ii, vii.

2. *Guardian*, 8/9/39.

3. CPSA, 1939, *Must we Fight?*

4. ibid., Cape District Committee, December 1939.

5. *Forward*, 22/9/39.

6. SATLC, 1940, *Annual Report for 1939*, pp. 17–21.

7. ibid., *Report for Tenth Annual Conference*, 1940, pp. 67–88.

8. CPSA, 1940, *The War and South Africa* (duplicated).

9. ibid., 1941, *Minutes of the National Conference*, Johannesburg, 26–7 April, pp. 19–28 (typed).

10. The final constitution adopted in 1944 omitted the reference to imperialism but retained the substance of the other aims here specified.

11. *Umteteli Wa Bantu*, 23/15/39; *Guardian*, 26/1/40.

12. *Guardian*, 29/9/39, 22/12/39.

13. *Indian Opinion*, 13/10/39.

14. The Association was formed in October 1939 by merger between the Colonial Born Association and the Natal Indian Congress, but a section of the latter, led by A. I. Kajee, broke away and regrouped in the NIC.

15. *Guardian*, 29/8/40, 6/2/41.

16. ibid., 30/1/41.

17. SATLC, *Annual Report for 1940*, p. 27; *Report of Eleventh Annual Conference*, 1941, pp. 11 f.

18. ibid., *Minutes of National Executive Committee*, 4/2/41.

19. Section 51 (3), Act 22 of 1941; chapter ii, Regulations published under Government Notice 1227 of 4 September 1941.

20. Benefits are correspondingly disproportionate for lesser degrees of disablement. See chapters v and ix, Act 30 of 1941.

21. *Guardian*, 26/9/40; Ray Adler, 'The Garment Workers', *Liberation* no. 27, September 1957, pp. 24–6.

22. Sachs, 1957, p. 119.

23. SATLC, *Report of Annual Conference*, 1942, pp. 43–4; 1943, p. 64.

24. CPSA, Political Bureau Statement of 23 June 1941 (duplicated).

25. Roux, 1949, p. 317.

26. *Inkululeko*, 11/4/42.

27. CPSA, 1943, *Communists Plan for Victory*.

28. *Guardian*, 12/3/42.

29. M. M. Kotane, 1942, *Japan – Friend or Foe?*

30. A. M. Maliba, 1939, *The Conditions of the Venda People* (duplicated).

31. F. Boshoff, D. J. de Plessis, R. Fleet, I. Wolfson (Rand), Miss Joey Fourie, G. Sacks, H. Snitcher (Cape Town), E. Shanley (Durban), A. Muller (East London).

32. *Garment Worker*, November/December 1943, pp. 8–10.

33. CPSA, 1944, 'Report of the Central Committee' *Freedom*, vol. 2, no. 5, January, pp. 6–13.

34. *Inkululeko*, 15/1/44.

35. *Guardian*, 9/9/43.

36. J. C. Smuts, 1942, *The Basis of Trusteeship in African Native Policy* (S.A. Institute of Race Relations pamphlet).

37. *Sun*, 19/2/43; *Cape Standard*, 2/3/43.

38. National Anti-CAD Conference, 29–30 May 1943, *Report of Proceedings*.

39. M. Kotane, 1943, 'CAC – a Politicial Retrogression', *Freedom*, vol. 2, no. 3, August, pp. 3–5.

40. *Cape Standard*, 11/1/44.

41. *Guardian*, 11/5/44.

42. Y. M. Dadoo, 1945, 'The Non-European Unity Movement', *Freedom*, vol. 4, no. 1, February, pp. 7–10.

43. *Cape Standard*, 25/7/44.

44. Second National Anti-CAD Conference, 4–5 January 1944. *Report of Delegation* (duplicated).

45. All African Convention, 7 July 1944, *Along the New Road*.
46. B. P. Bunting, 1947, 'What has the CAC achieved?', *Freedom*, vol. 6, no. 6, December, pp. 19–21.
47. I. B. Tabata, 1952, *The Boycott as Weapon of Struggle*, p. 26.
48. NEUM, 1945, *Third Unity Conference*, 4–5 January, pp. 14–15.
49. ibid., pp. 8–9.
50. Biographical details from Benson, 1966, ch. 7.
51. CPSA, 1945, *They Marched to Victory!*, p. 22.
52. Hilda Watts, 1946, 'Shanty-Towns', *Freedom*, vol. 5, no. 6, December, pp. 8–12.
53. *Guardian*, 6/4/44.
54. A. B. Xuma, 1944, 'The Pass Laws', *Freedom*, vol. 2, no. 5, January 1944, pp. 3–5.
55. *Inkululeko*, 29/5/44.
56. *Guardian*, 12/7/45.
57. ibid., 22/11/45; *Inkululeko*, 3/12/45.
58. *Inkululeko*, 18/2/46, 11/3/46; *Forward*, 22/3/46.
59. *Cape Argus*, 30/10/45; *Cape Times*, 21/3/46, 7/9/46.
60. House of Assembly Debates, 15/4/46, C.5570.
61. SALP 1946, *Minutes of 36th Annual Conference*, 28–9 December (duplicated); *Cape Times*, 30/10/46, 11/12/46, 16/1/47.
62. SALP, 1946, *Declaration of Non-European Policy* (duplicated).
63. *Guardian*, 1/11/45.
64. ibid., 14/2/46.
65. Transvaal Indian Congress 1946, *Passive Resistance Council*.
66. *The Passive Resister*, 1946, vol. 1, no. 1, June.
67. Asiatic Laws Amendment Act of 1948.
68. *Guardian*, 4/4/46.

Chapter 24

1. *Guardian*, 6/8/42; Rex Close, 1950, *New Life*.
2. Alexander and Simons, 1959, p. 10.
3. Clack, 1962, Appendix C.
4. Council of Non-European Trade Unions, 1942, *Minutes of the First Annual Conference*, 28–9 November 1942, Johannesburg (duplicated).
5. Nancy Dick, 1957, 1961, 'Wage Inequalities', *Fighting Talk*, vol. 11, no. 2, February 1957; vol. 11, no. 3, March 1957; vol. 15, no. 8, September 1961.
6. *Guardian*, 22/10/42.

7. SATLC, 1943, *Annual Report for 1942*, p. 7; *Forward*, 5/6/42.

8. CPSA, 1942, 'The Strike of African Workers and Compulsory Arbitration', 31/12/42 (duplicated).

9. SATLC, 1943, *Report of Thirteenth Annual Conference*, pp. 53–4.

10. *Natal Mercury*, 19/12/42, 2/3/43.

11. *Guardian*, 7/1/43, 27/5/43.

12. House of Assembly Debates, 16/2/43, C.1672.

13. S.A.1937, U.G.48; S.A.1941, U.G.42, p. 8.

14. Julius Lewin, 1943, 'Report on Conference with Minister of Labour on 27/10/43', S.A. Institute of Race Relations, R.R. 141/43 (duplicated).

15. S.A.1951, U.G.62, par. 1628.

16. SATLC, 1944, *Report of the Fourteenth Annual Conference*, pp. 45–7.

17. Baloyi and Okolo *v.* Industrial Council for the Clothing Industry (Tvl) TPD, December 1944; Sweet Workers' Union *v.* the Minister of Labour, CPD, December 1945.

18. *S.A. Industry and Trade*, December 1945, p. 133; *Inkululeko*, May 1946.

19. House of Assembly Debates, 14/4/47, C.2664.

20. The Industrial Conciliation (Natives') Bill, *Government Gazette Extraordinary*, 16/5/47.

21. Ray Alexander, 1947, *Defend Your Trade Unions* (C.P. pamphlet).

22. House of Assembly Debates, 4/8/53, C.872.

23. S.A.1951, U.G.62, par 1593.

24. Western Province Building, Electrical and Allied Trades Union, 1945, *Memorandum of June 23rd, 1945* (duplicated). 2,740 white and 296 coloured trainees had been placed in employment by the end of 1948.

25. *Forward*, 15/11/46, 3/1/47.

26. *Star*, 16/6/48.

27. *Blanke Werker*, October 1946.

28. House of Assembly Debates, 8/3/48, C.2839–40.

29. Alexander and Simons, 1959, p. 14.

30. *Blanke Werker*, November 1946, February 1947, July 1947.

31. House of Assembly Debates, 19/3/42, C.4190; 19/1/43, C.87–8.

32. *Kruithoring*, 7/8/46.

33. SATLC, 1946, *Report of Sixteenth Annual Conference*, pp. 49–50.

34. ibid., 1947, *Report of the Seventeenth Annual Conference*, pp. 26–31.

35. Sachs, 1952.

36. *Burger*, 14/3/45; *Kruithoring*, 7/8/46, 12/2/47, 23/4/47.

37. van Rooyen, 1956, p. 234.

38. *Mynwerker*, April 1943; Transvaal Chamber of Mines, 1944, *55th Annual Report*, p. 32; S.A.1946, U.G.36, par. 53.
39. *Kruithoring*, 3/4/46; House of Assembly Debates, 19/3/46, C.3799.
40. *Labour Bulletin*, 26/2/47.
41. *Mynwerker*, July 1947.
42. ibid., November 1949.
43. S.A.1950, U.G.28, par. 261.
44. Transvaal Chamber of Mines, *Annual Report for 1949*, p. 28.
45. S.A.1951, U.G.52, par. 5.
46. ibid., par. 33.
47. *Rand Daily Mail*, 27/1/53, 20/3/53, 11/4/53.
48. *Guardian*, 5/6/41, 7/8/41, 14/8/41.
49. ibid., 27/1/44.
50. S.A.1944, U.G.21.
51. House of Assembly Debates, 24/3/44, C.3817–19.
52. SATLC, 1945, *Annual Report for 1944*, p. 20.
53. *Inkululeko*, 26/8/44.
54. S.A.1944, U.G.21, par. 459–74.
55. African Mine Workers' Union, 1943, *Memorandum to the Commission* (duplicated).
56. Marks to Simons, November 1958.
57. Section 1, Act 51 of 1954 as amended by Act 58 of 1956.
58. *South African Outlook*, 1/5/45; *Inkululeko*, 28/1/46, 11/3/46; *Guardian*, 25/4/46.
59. SATLC, 1947, *Report of Seventeenth Annual Conference*, p. 51.
60. *Star*, 30/11/46.
61. Transvaal Chamber of Mines 1947, *Annual Report for 1946*, p. 26.
62. *Guardian*, 15/8/46, 22/8/46, 29/8/46.
63. *Rand Daily Mail*, 16/8/46.
64. *Star*, 14/8/46.
65. African Mine Workers' Union Strike Committee, 1946, *Strike Bulletin*, Nos. 1–5 (duplicated).
66. L. Bernstein, October 1946, *Notes on the African Miners' Strike*, p. 18 (typed).
67. See W. H. Andrews, 1946, for a contemporary comparison: 'Aftermath of the Strike' *Freedom*, vol. 5, no. 5, October–November 1946, pp. 9–11.
68. *Labour Bulletin*, 21/8/46.
69, The Annual Conference repudiated the cable in 1947 by sixty-nine votes to twenty-three: SATLC, 1947, *Report of Seventeenth Annual Conference*, p. 54

Chapter 25

1. Natives Representative Council, *Verbatim Report*, 14–15 August 1946, pp. 22–3, 29–30.
2. ibid., p. 31.
3. M. Kotane, 1947, 'The Boycott of Elections', *Freedom*, vol. 6, no. 5, September–October, pp. 14–17.
4. Native Representative Council, *Verbatim Report*, 20–26 November 1946, p. 40.
5. M. Kotane, 1947, loc. cit.
6. E. Mofutsanyana, 'Some Aspects of the Boycott Question', *Freedom*, November–December, 1947, vol. 6, pp. 22–3.
7. H. A. Naidoo, 'The Party and the National Organizations', *Freedom*, vol. 7, no. 1, Summer 1948, pp. 16–18.
8. *Guardian*, 3/7/47.
9. C. M. Tatz, 1962, pp. 117–19.
10. House of Assembly Debates, 23/1/47, C.11092–5.
11. *Guardian*, 25/12/47.
12. ibid., 8/1/48.
13. ibid., 26/9/46.
14. A summary of the proceedings is contained in *Freedom*, vol. 6, nos. 1 & 2, April 1947, pp. 8–39.
15. *Guardian*, 13/2/47, 20/2/47.
16. L. C. Joffe and H. A. Naidoo were joined as co-accused; and proceedings were dropped against Betty Radford.
17. W. J. Roberts was joined while charges against Andrews and Jaffe were withdrawn.
18. CPSA, 1941, *Minutes of the National Conference*, Johannesburg, 26–7 April, 1941, p. 9 (typed).
19. *Guardian*, 13/5/48.
20. J. J. Van Rooyen, 1956, p. 151.
21. *Transvaler*, 28/5/48.
22. *Star*, 28/5/48.
23. Germiston, Kempton Park, Krugersdorp, Maraisburg, Mayfair, North East Rand, Randfontein and Westdene; Gezina, Koedoespoort, Pretoria Central, Pretoria West and Wonderboom.
24. *Burger*, 29/5/48.
25. HNP, 1948, *The Road to a New South Africa*, pp. 4, 18; *Apartheid and Guardianship*.
26. *Burger*, 21/4/48.
27. M. M. Kotane, 'Greetings on the 26th Anniversary', *Freedom*, vol. 6, no. 4, July/August, 1947, pp. 2–3.

28. M. M. Kotane, 'We do not know their difficulties', *Freedom*, vol. 6, no. 6, November–December 1947, pp. 13–15.
29. *Guardian*, 20/5/48.
30. ibid., 3/6/48.
31. A.P. v.d. Merwe (Nat.) 194.
32. *Guardian*, 2/12/48.
33. CPSA, 1949, *Sam Kahn Speaks*, p. 2.
34. *Clarion*, 29/5/52.
35. He polled 4,123 votes, A. G. Long 495, C. C. Johnson 387 and H. M. Joynt 58.
36. *Advance*, 1/10/53, 8/10/53.
37. She polled 3,525 votes, J. Gibson (Lib.) 998 and Mrs J. Jonker Fiske (Indep.) 656.
38. *Advance*, 6/5/54.
39. *Freedom*, (new series), vol. i, nos. 27–28; December 1949, p. 12.
40. The allowances were increased in 1948 by amounts ranging from 1s. a week at the bottom of the scale to 90s. and more at the top.
41. House of Assembly Debates, 25/5/49, C.6514–9.
42. *Cape Times*, 3/9/49.
43. SATLC (1949) *Annual Reports* for 1949, p. 4; for 1950, p. 3.
44. SATLC (1949) *Minutes of the National Executive Committee*, 11/5/50, 22/5/50, 7/9/50; *Cape Times*, 15/6/50, 16/6/50.
45. SATLC (1949), *Annual Report for 1952*, pp. 13–17, 37–9; *Clarion*, 19/6/52.
46. House of Assembly Debates, 20/1/56, C.182.
47. *Cape Argus*, 15/3/52.
48. House of Assembly Debates, 9/9/53, C.3150–51; S.A. Federation of Trade Unions, *Report of Third Annual Meeting*, 1954, p. 2.
49. SATLC (1949) *Annual Reports* for 1947, p. 6; for 1952, Annexure 3A.
50. Alexander and Simons, 1959, p. 28.
51. *Freedom*, (new series), vol. 1, nos. 27–8, December 1949, pp. 4–6.
52. M. M. Kotane, 'My Visit to Durban', *Freedom*, (new series), vol. 1, no. 10, March 1949, pp. 1–2.
53. S.A. 1949, U.G.36.
54. *Guardian*, 27/1/49, 10/2/49.
55. 'Non-European Chauvinists', *Freedom*, (new series), vol. 1, no. 13, May 1949.
56. *Torch*, 23/8/48, 25/10/48, 10/2/49.
57. 'Short History of Betrayal', *Freedom*, (new series), vol. 1, no. 5, 1 November 1948.
58. *Torch*, 22/7/46.

59. ibid., 11/10/48, 1/11/48, 15/11/48.
60. *Guardian*, 23/12/48.
61. *Torch*, 25/4/49, 9/5/49, 29/12/49.
62. *Guardian*, 9/2/50.
63. *Inkundla Ya Bantu*, 30/7/48.
64. *Freedom*, (new series), vol. 1, nos. 27–8, December 1949, p. 9.
65. *Guardian*, 23/3/50.
66. Native Representative Council, *Report of Proceedings*, 4–5 January 1949, pp. 2–6.
67. ibid., 5–7 December 1950.
68. *Guardian*, 30/3/50.
69. ibid., 4/5/50.
70. ibid., 25/5/50.
71. ibid., 11/5/50.
72. ibid., 1/6/50.
73. ibid., 22/6/50.
74. ibid., 15/6/50.
75. *Freedom*, (new series), vol. 1, nos. 27–8, December 1949.

Parliamentary Papers

Great Britain (PP)

1853. Cd.1581. *Representative Assembly at the Cape.*
1871. C.459. *Affairs of the Cape.*
1873. C.732. *Affairs of the Cape.*
1874. C.882. *H.M.'s Colonial Possessions.*
1876. C.1342. *Griqualand West and the Diamond Fields.*
1876. C.1401. *South Africa.*
1895. C.7911. *Indians in the S.A.R.*
1901. C.528. *Negotiations between Botha and Kitchener.*
1901. Cd.547. *Affairs in South Africa.*
1902. C.903. *Affairs in South Africa.*
1902. Cd.1096. *Terms of Surrender of Boer Forces.*
1902. Cd.1284. *Interview between the Secretary of State and the Generals.*
1902. Cd.1365. *Transvaal and O.R.C.*
1903. Cd.1551. *Administration of the Transvaal and O.R.C.*
1903. Cd.1552. *Finances of the Transvaal and O.R.C.*
1903. Cd.1553. *Administration in the Transvaal and O.R.C.*
1903. Cd.1640. *Customs Union Convention.*
1903. Cd.1684. *British Indians in the Transvaal.*
1904. Cd.1789, 1790, 1791, 1792. *Commissioners on the War in South Africa. Reports and Evidence.*
1904. Cd.1895. *Affairs of the Transvaal and O.R.C.*
1904. Cd.1896, 1897. *Transvaal Labour Commission, Report and Evidence.*
1904. Cd.2025. *Conditions of Native Labour in Transvaal Mines.*
1904. Cd.2026. *Transvaal Labour Importation Ordinance.*
1904. Cd.2104. *Affairs in the Transvaal and O.R.C.*
1904. Cd.2239. *British Indians in the Transvaal.*
1905. Cd.2400. *Constitutional Changes in the Transvaal.*
1905. Cd.2479. *Constitutional Changes in the Transvaal.*
1905. Cd.2482. *Transvaal and O.R.C.*
1906. Cd.3250. *Transvaal Constitution, 1906.*
1907. Cd.3308. *Asiatics in the Transvaal.*

1908. Cd.3887. *Asiatics in the Transvaal.*
1914. Cd.7707. *Dominions (Royal Commission) Report and Evidence.*

Cape of Good Hope (Cape)

1859. A.26. *Votes and Proceedings, Vol. II, Appendix I.*
1863. A.6. *Select Committee on Railway Labourers.*
1865. A.27. *Report on the Railway Bill.*
1871. A.23. *Select Committee on Masters and Servants Act.*
1879. A.26. *Select Committee on Labour Market.*
1882. G.86. *Diamond Mining Commission.*
1883. G.8. *Blue Book on Native Affairs.*
1895. G.25. *Report of Inspector of Mines.*
1899. G.31. *Blue Book on Native Affairs.*

South Africa (SA)

1912. U.G.49. *Mines Department, Annual Report for 1911.*
1914. U.G.34. *Tuberculosis Commission.*
1914. U.G.37. *Native Grievances Commission.*
1917. U.G.38. *Departmental Committee on Underground Mining Contracts.*
1917. S.C.4. *Regulation of Wages (Specified Trades) Bill.*
1920. U.G.34. *Low Grade Ore Mines Commission.*
1921. *Report of Commissioners re Native Disturbances at Port Elizabeth. House of Assembly, Vol. III.*
1921. U.G.44. *Native Affairs Commission re Israelites at Bullhoek.*
1921. S.C.12A. *Native Affairs.*
1922. U.G.35. *Martial Law Inquiry Judicial Commission.*
1922. U.G.39. *Mining Industry Board.*
1923. S.C.5. *Industrial Conciliation Bill.*
1925. U.G.36. *Mining Regulations Commission.*
1925. U.G.39. *Native Churches Commission.*
1926. U.G.14. *Economic and Wage Commission.*
1932. U.G.22. *Native Economic Commission, 1930–32.*
1932. U.G.30. *Unemployment Investigation Committee.*
1935. U.G.37. *Industrial Legislation Commission.*
1937. U.G.48. *Native Affairs Commission for 1936.*
1937. U.G.54. *Cape Coloured Commission.*
1941. U.G.42. *Native Affairs Commission for 1939–40.*
1941. *Mine Workers' Union Commission.*

1944. U.G.21. *Witwatersrand Mine Natives' Wages Commission.*
1946. U.G.36. *Mineworkers' Union Commission.*
1949. U.G.36. *Commission of Inquiry on Riots in Durban.*
1950. U.G.28. *Commission on Employment in Gold Mines.*
1951. U.G.52. *Mineworkers' Union Commission.*
1951. U.G.62. *Industrial Legislation Commission.*
1955. S.C.3. *Industrial Conciliation Bill.*

South African Republic (SAR)

1897. *Industrial Commission.* Published by the Witwatersrand Chamber of Mines.

Transvaal

1908. T.G.2. *Mining Industry Commission.*
1908. T.G.13. *Transvaal Indigency Commission.*
1910. *Mining Regulations Commission,* Vol.1.

Bibliography

Adam, J. A., *Wheels within Wheels*, published by the author, Johannesburg 1952.

Alexander, Ray, and Simons, H. J., *Job Reservation*, Enterprise, Cape, 1959.

Amery, L. S., ed., *The Times History of the War in South Africa 1899–1902*, Vol. VII, Sampson, Law, Marston & Co. Ltd, 1909.

Andrews, W. H., *Class Struggles in South Africa*, Stewart, Cape Town, 1941.

Angove, John, *In the Early Days: The Reminiscences of Pioneer Life on the South African Diamond Fields*, Handel House, Kimberley, 1910.

Barlow, Arthur G., *Almost in Confidence*, Juta, Cape Town, 1952.

Beet, George, *The Grand Old Days of the Diamond Fields*, Maskew Miller, Cape Town, 1931.

Benson, Mary, *The Struggle for a Birthright*, Penguin African Library, 1966.

Botha, J. H., *Die Arbeidsvraagstuk van Suid-Afrika*, H. J. Paris, Amsterdam, 1928.

Boydell, Thomas, *My Luck Was In*, Stewart, Cape Town, 1947.

Bunting, S. P., *Red Revolt and the Rand Strike*, ISL Press, Johannesburg, 1922.

Calpin, G. H., *Indians in South Africa*, Shooter and Shuter, Pietermaritzburg, 1949.

—, *A. I. Kajee*, no date.

Campbell, J., and Munro, J. R., *The Great Rand Strike*, Aldington, Johannesburg, 1913.

Chilvers, Hedley, *The Story of De Beers*, Cassell, 1939.

Clack, G., *The Changing Structure of Industrial Relation in South Africa*, unpublished Ph.D. thesis, University of London, 1962.

Cohen, Louis, *Reminiscences of Kimberley*, Bennett & Co., 1911.

Coka, Gilbert, 'The Story of Gilbert Coka', in ed. Margery Perham, *Ten Africans*, Faber & Faber, second edition, 1936.

Cope, R. K., *Comrade Bill*, Stewart, Cape Town, 1943.

Creswell, Margaret, *An Epoch of the Political History of South Africa*, Balkema, Cape Town, 1956.

Defence Committee, *The Story of a Crime*, Johannesburg, 1924.

Degras, Jane, *The Third Communist International 1919–1943*, Oxford University Press, 1956.

Bibliography

De Kock, M. H., *Selected Subjects in the Economic History of South Africa*, Juta, Cape Town, 1924.

De Wet, C. R., *De Strijd tusschen Boer en Brit*, Houeker en Wormser, Amsterdam, 1902.

Doughty, Oswald, *Early Diamond Days*, Longmans, 1963.

Downes, Albert James, *Printer's Saga*, South African Typographical Workers' Union, Johannesburg, 1952.

Elton, Lord, *The Life of James Ramsay MacDonald*, Collins, 1939.

Everard, C. C., *Botha and Labour: The Iron Heel at Work*, 'Daily Herald' 1914.

Forman, Lionel, *Chapters in the History of the March to Freedom*, New Age, Cape Town, 1959.

Frankel, S. H., *Capital Investment in South Africa*, Oxford University Press, 1938.

Freislich, Richard, *The Last Tribal War*, Struik, Cape Town, 1964.

Gandhi, M. K., *Satyagraha in South Africa*, S. Ganeson, Madras, 1928.

Gitsham, E., and Trembath, J. F., *A First Account of Labour Organization in South Africa*, Commercial Printing Co., Durban, 1926.

Glanville, E., *Through the Red Revolt on the Rand: A Pictorial Review*, 'Star' Johannesburg, 1922.

Gordon, Lady Duff, *Letters from the Cape*, Oxford University Press, 1927, (first published 1864).

Gorgas, W. C., *Recommendations as to Sanitation concerning Employees of the Mines on the Rand*, Argus, 1914.

Gross, Felix, *Rhodes of Africa*, Cassell, 1956.

Halperin, Vladimir, *Lord Milner and the Empire*, Odhams, 1952.

Hancock, W. K., *Smuts: The Sanguine Years*, Cambridge University Press, 1962.

Hardy, G., *Those Stormy Years*, Lawrence & Wishart, 1956.

Harrison, W. H., *Memoirs of a Socialist in South Africa*, published by the author, Cape Town, 1948.

Hattersley, Alan, F., *Portrait of a City*, Shooter and Shuter, Pietermaritzburg, 1951.

Herd, N., *1922: The Revolt on the Rand*, Blue Crane, Johannesburg, 1966.

Hobson, J. A., *The War in South Africa*, Nisbet, 1900.

—, *The Crisis of Liberalism: New Issues of Democracy*, P. S. King, 1909.

Institut für Marxismus-Leninismus, *Geschichte der deutschen Arbeiterbewegung*, Institut für Marxismus-Leninismus, East Berlin, 1966.

Jabavu, Davidson Don (Tengo), 'Native Unrest in South Africa', *Int. Rev. Misc.* Vol. II, 1962.

Jones, D. I., *Communism in South Africa*, International Socialist League, Johannesburg, 1921.

Joshi, P. S., *The Tyranny of Colour*, E. P. & Commercial Printing Co., Durban, 1942.

Kadalie, Clements Musa, *Autobiography* (ed. E. R. Roux), unpublished, 1954.

Katzen, L., *Gold and the South African Economy*, Balkema, Cape Town, 1964.

Kentridge, Morris, *Memoirs of 'I Recall'*, Free Press, Johannesburg, 1959.

La Guma, Alex, *Jimmy la Guma: A Biography*, unpublished, 1963.

Le May, G. H. L., *British Supremacy in South Africa 1899–1907*, Clarendon Press, 1965.

Lenin, Nikolai, *'Left-wing' Communism – an Infantile Disorder*, Communist Party of Great Britain, 1920.

Lenin, V. I., *Collected Works*, 39 vols., Moscow, 1963–8.

Leubuscher, Charlotte, *Der südafrikanische Eingeborene als Industriearbeiter und als Stadtbewohner*, Jena, 1931.

Liga gegen Imperialismus, *Das Flammenzeichen von Palais Egmont*, Berlin, 1927.

Lockhart, J. G., and Woodhouse, C. M., *Rhodes*, Hodder & Stoughton, 1963.

Luxemburg, Rosa, *The Accumulation of Capital*, Routledge & Kegan Paul, 1951.

Mansergh, Nicholas, *South Africa 1906–1961*, Frederick A. Praeger, New York, 1962.

Marais, J. S., *The Cape Coloured People 1652–1937*, Witwatersrand University Press, Johannesburg, 1957.

—, *The Fall of Kruger's Republic*, Clarendon Press, 1961.

Matthews, J. B., *Incwadi Yami*, Sampson, 1887.

Mentzel, O. F., *A Geographical and Topographical Description of the Cape of Good Hope*, Part I, Van Riebeeck Society, 1785.

Mentzel, O. F., *A Complete and Authentic Geographical and Topographical Description of the Famous and (all things considered) Remarkable African Cape of Good Hope*, Part III, Van Riebeeck Society, 1787.

Millin, S. G., *Rhodes*, Chatto & Windus, 1933.

Nicholls, G. Heaton, *South Africa in My Time*, Allen & Unwin, 1961

Noble, John, *Descriptive Handbook of the Cape Colony – Its Condition and Resources*, Juta, Cape Town, 1875.

Nollau, Günther, *International Communism and World Revolution*, Hollis & Carter, 1961.

Pakenham, Countess of, (Elizabeth Longford), *Jameson's Raid*, Weidenfeld & Nicolson, 1960.

Payton, Charles A., *The Diamond Diggings of South Africa*, Horace Cox, 1872.

Bibliography

Pease, Edward R., *The History of the Fabian Society*, Allen & Unwin, 1925.

Plaatje, Sol T., *Native Life in South Africa*, P. S. King, 1916.

Potekhin, I. J., *Formirovanie Natsionalnoi Obshchnosti Yuzhnoi Afrikanskich Bantu*, Akademia Nauk, Moscow, 1955.

Pringle, Thomas, *Some Account of the Present State of the English Settlers in Albany, South Africa*, T. & G. Underwood, 1824.

Pyrah, G. B., *Imperial Policy and South Africa, 1902–10*, Clarendon Press, 1955.

Ransome, Stafford, *The Engineer in South Africa*, Constable, 1903.

Roberts, M., and Trollip, A. E. G., *The South African Opposition, 1939–1945* Longmans, 1947.

Rose, E. B., *The Truth about the Transvaal*, 'Morning Leader' Publication Department, 1902.

Rose Innes, James, *An Autobiography*, ed. B. A. Tindall, Oxford University Press, Cape Town, 1949.

Roux, E. R., *S. P. Bunting*, published by the author, 1944.

—, *Time Longer Than Rope*, Gollancz, 1948.

Sachs, E. S., *The Choice Before South Africa*, Turnstile Press, 1952.

—, *Rebel Daughters*, MacGibbon & Kee, 1957.

Schnell, E. L. G., *For Men Must Work*, Maskew Miller, Cape Town, 1954.

Scholtz, G. D., *Dr N. J. van der Merwe*, Voortrekkerpers, Johannesburg, 1943.

Shaw, Bernard, *Fabianism and the Empire*, Grant Richards, 1900.

Sik, Endre, *The History of Black Africa*, 2 Vols., Akademiai Kiado, Budapest. 1966.

Simons, H. J., *African Women: Their Legal Status in South Africa*, C. Hurst & Co., 1968.

Skota, T. D. M., *African Yearly Register*, Orange Press, 1932.

Slesser, Sir Henry, *Judgment Reserved*, Hutchinson, 1941.

Smuts, J. C., *Jan Christian Smuts*, Cassell, 1952.

Solomon, Gladstone, W. E., *Saul Solomon, 'The Member for Cape Town'*, Oxford University Press, Cape Town, 1948.

South African Native Races Committee, ed., *The Natives of South Africa*, John Murray, 1901.

Stewart, William, *J. Keir Hardie: A Biography*, Cassell, 1921.

Stuart, J., *A History of the Zulu Rebellion 1906*, Macmillan, 1913.

Taft, P., *Organized Labour in American History*, Harper, 1964.

Tatz, C. M., *Shadow and Substance*, Natal University Press, Pietermaritzburg 1962.

Theal, George McCall, *History of South Africa from 1873 to 1884*, Allen & Unwin, 1919.

Thompson, L. M., *The Unification of South Africa, 1902–10*, Clarendon Press 1960.

Thomson, H. C., *The Supreme Problem in South Africa: Capital and Labour* 1901.

van der Heever, C. M., *General J. M. B. Hertzog*, A. P. B., Johannesburg, 1946.

van der Poel, Jean, *The Jameson Raid*, Oxford University Press, 1951.

Van Rooyen, J. J., *Die Nasionale Party*, Kaaplandse Nasionale Party, Cape Town, 1956.

Walker, Eric A., *A History of Southern Africa*, Longmans, 1957.

Walker, Ivan, and Weinbren, B., *2,000 Casualties*, Natal Witness, 1961.

Williams, Gardner, F., *The Diamond Mines of South Africa*, Macmillan, 1902.

Wilmot, Alex, *The Life and Times of Sir Richard Southey*, Maskew Miller, Cape Town, 1904.

Wolton, D. G., *Whither South Africa?*, Lawrence & Wishart, 1947.

Index of Legislative Measures

Index of Organizations and Newspapers

Index of Selected Names

More about Penguins

Penguinews, which appears every month, contains details of all the new books issued by Penguins as they are published. From time to time it is supplemented by *Penguins in Print* – a complete list of all our available titles. (There are well over three thousand of these.)

A specimen copy of *Penguinews* will be sent to you free on request, and you can become a subscriber for the price of the postage – 4s. for a year's issues (including the complete lists). Just write to Dept EP, Penguin Books Ltd, Harmondsworth, Middlesex, enclosing a cheque or postal order, and your name will be added to the mailing list.

Some other books published by Penguins are described on the following pages.

Note: *Penguinews* and *Penguins in Print* are not available in the U.S.A. or Canada

The Struggle for Mozambique

Eduardo Mondlane

Despite the ignorance of the rest of the world (connived at by the Portuguese authorities) the war of liberation in Mozambique is now being fought with increasing success on several fronts. Its importance transcends Mozambique's national boundaries: its success could revolutionize sanctions against the white supremacists in neighbouring Rhodesia; and it is also a paradigm case for the unshackling of 'Portuguese' Africa.

The author of this book was, until his assassination early in 1969, the President of FRELIMO, the Mozambique Liberation Front, which has already freed large areas of the country. As a Negro intellectual he himself experienced the racial discrimination which is the foundation of Portuguese institutions in Africa. In this book he analyses the origins of the war in the economics of exploitation, in education for submission, and in general cultural deprivation; and he shows how his people's liberation struggle implies a radical transformation of society at all levels – social and cultural, as well as economic, administrative, and political.

The Penguin African Library

'Penguins . . . breaking new ground in politics on a scale unmatched since their spate of Penguin Specials on the eve of the last war' – *Financial Times*

Titles already published in the series include:

★NOT FOR SALE IN THE U.S.A.

Published by Penguin Books